# A HISTORY OF EUROPE

*by the same author*

MOHAMMED AND CHARLEMAGNE

*The book which contains Pirenne's celebrated theories of the close of the ancient world and the rise of the Middle Ages. Also translated by Bernard Miall*

# A HISTORY OF EUROPE

## *from the Invasions to the XVI Century*

*by*

HENRI PIRENNE

*Sometime Member of the Académie Royale de Belgique, Associate of the Académie des Inscriptions de France, Sometime Professor Emeritus of the University of Gand*



*London*

GEORGE ALLEN & UNWIN LTD

RUSKIN HOUSE · MUSEUM STREET

FIRST PUBLISHED IN GREAT BRITAIN 1939
SECOND IMPRESSION 1940
THIRD IMPRESSION 1948
FOURTH IMPRESSION 1949
FIFTH IMPRESSION 1952
SIXTH IMPRESSION 1955
SEVENTH IMPRESSION 1958
EIGHTH IMPRESSION 1961
NINTH IMPRESSION 1967



SBN 04 940019 3

TRANSLATED BY BERNARD MIALL

*from the French of the 8th Edition*
*Librarie Félix Alcan, Paris,*
*and Nouvelle Société*
*d'Editions, Brussels,*
*1936*



PRINTED IN GREAT BRITAIN
BY PHOTOLITHOGRAPHY
UNWIN BROTHERS LIMITED
WOKING AND LONDON

# CONTENTS

## Book Three

# FEUDAL EUROPE



## Book Four

# THE WAR OF INVESTITURES AND THE CRUSADE



## Book Five

# THE FORMATION OF THE BOURGEOISIE

CONTENTS

*Book Six*

## THE BEGINNINGS OF THE WESTERN STATES



*Book Seven*

## THE HEGEMONY OF THE PAPACY AND OF FRANCE IN THE THIRTEENTH CENTURY



*Book Eight*

## THE EUROPEAN CRISIS (1300–1450)

### The Avignon Papacy, the Great Schism and the Hundred Years' War

## *Book Nine*

## THE RENAISSANCE AND THE REFORMATION

# PREFACE

On March 18th, 1916, about nine o'clock in the morning, a German officer of the Army of Occupation called at the house in which my father, M. Henri Pirenne, was then living (in the Rue Neuve Saint-Pierre, in Gand) and requested him to follow him to the "Kommandantur." There he was received by a major, who informed him that he was to leave for Germany immediately. When my father asked him why he had been arrested, the officer confined himself to replying: "I don't know; it's an order."

My mother was allowed to come and bid her husband farewell in the presence of an officer; but his son Robert, who was then in school, was not able to come and kiss his father good-bye, for an hour after his arrest M. Pirenne was already on his way to the Crefeld Camp.

Suddenly torn from his family and friends, and obliged to leave my mother alone in a country occupied by the enemy (her health had already been shaken by the death of her son Pierre, killed on the Yser on November 3rd, 1914), my father, on his arrival at the officers' camp at Crefeld, having resolved that he would not give way to dejection, immediately set to work. As a number of Russian officers were interned in the camp, he began, with the help of one of them, to study the Russian language.

My father's internment at Crefeld was provisional only, as was that of his friend and colleague Paul Fredericq at Gütersloh, whither he had been deported on the day of my father's arrest. The German authorities had hoped, by thus arresting them, to intimidate the professors of the University of Gand, and to induce them to resume their lectures, as they had been requested. The result disappointed their expectations. The University refused to re-open its doors during the alien occupation. The consequence of this resistance was not long delayed. On May 12th, 1916, the order reached Crefeld to transfer my father to the camp at Holzminden. His internment there influenced him profoundly.

The camp, as he describes it in his *Souvenirs de captivité*, "contained at this time from eight thousand to ten thousand prisoners, divided among eighty-four great wooden barracks, arranged in rows in a space of some ten acres. The central avenue, 'Avenue Joffre,' as the prisoners called it, was thronged from morning to evening by a heterogeneous crowd in which all national types and all social classes were represented, and in which every language was spoken, excepting English, for there was not a single Englishman at Holzminden.

"In the centre of the camp ten barracks enclosed by a wire trellis sheltered the women and children. Every day, between noon and three o'clock, the women were allowed to leave this enclosure. As for the children, of whom there were a certain number in the camp, one could see them, of a morning, going to the schools which certain good people had somehow managed to provide for them.

"Naturally, the bulk of this heterogeneous population consisted of men of the people. Holzminden was the receptacle into which Germany poured, pell-mell, undesirable or inconvenient persons from all the occupied countries. A barrack near that which I occupied sheltered the inmates of the prison of Loos, near Lille, among whom were a certain number of convicted murderers. With a few exceptions, all these men endured their fate with a resignation that was truly admirable. Many, in the long run, were physically debilitated; there were sick men, and neurasthenics, and a few cases of insanity; but in nearly all the mental and moral faculties remained intact. Yet many of them had already been there for two years. For that matter, these were the most resolute. They had known the miseries of the first months of the war, suffered the brutality of the sentries, endured the cold of winter in unheated barracks, and witnessed the agony of the unhappy citizens of Louvain who were thrown into the camp in September 1914. Little by little they had organized themselves. Thanks to the consignments of food from the committees in all parts of Europe which watched over the welfare of the prisoners, and to the parcels received from friends and relatives, the alimentary conditions had become tolerable. Clothing had been received, medicines, and books. Private initiative had got to work in a thousand ways. Some French students had had a small barrack built at their own expense, 'the University,' in which professors and engineers gave lectures, and which contained a library, whose volumes were bound by a bookbinder from Brussels. Benevolent societies were organized, and schools established for the children. Cafés and even restaurants were opened. Some Catholic priests had installed a chapel in the barracks. Some Belgians had fitted up an empty space for ball games: there was a skittle alley too, and a bowling green, much frequented by players from the North of France. Not many, however, indulged in athletic sports; there was too little room, and all were weakened by captivity and lack of exercise.

"We seldom came into contact with the Germans. The General in command of the camp was hardly ever visible; he left things to his subordinate, a harsh and brutal reserve officer. The organization of the camp, which was under his supervision, was simple enough, the officials being recruited from among the prisoners themselves. There was a *chef de camp*, a *chef de district* and a *chef de baraque*, who were responsible for the discipline of the camp; and it was with them that the prisoners came into contact. Every evening a bulletin appeared, containing the orders and regulations for the following day. Only police duties were left to the soldiers and the non-commissioned officers; and they performed these duties without amenity. The barracks were constantly searched; letters were seized, and the 'guilty' persons were sent to the cells for one or more days' solitary confinement. Such punishments were an everyday matter; one would often see a notice affixed to the door of 'the University': 'Professor X—— will not lecture to-day, as he is in prison.' "[1]

My father found his place immediately in this strange environ-

[1] Henri Pirenne, *Souvenirs de Captivité en Allemagne*, 1921, pp. 31–35. These reminiscences appeared also in the *Revue des Deux Mondes*, February 1st and 15th, 1920.

ment. As director of the benevolent society he came into contact with the most unfortunate of the prisoners, whose miseries he endeavoured to alleviate. But he devoted himself above all to the work of sustaining the morale of his companions in misfortune, by organizing two courses of lectures. "For my own part," he writes, "I delivered two courses of lectures, one on economic history for two or three hundred Russian students who were captured at Liége in August 1914, and another in which I related to my fellow-countrymen the history of their native country. I never had more attentive pupils, nor did I ever teach with such pleasure. The lectures on the history of Belgium presented a really striking spectacle. The listeners were jammed together, some perched on the palliasses which were piled up in one corner of the barrack that served as lecture-hall, others crowded together on the benches, or standing up against the boarded partitions. Some were gathered outside under the open window. Inside a suffocating heat was radiated from the tarred paper roof. Thousands of fleas were jumping all over the place, leaping in the sunlight like the drops of a very fine spray. Sometimes I fancied I could hear them, so profound was the silence of all these men, who listened while a fellow-Belgian spoke to them of their native country, recalling all the catastrophes which it had suffered and overcome. No doubt the size of my audience made the 'Kommandantur' uneasy. One day I received an order to the effect that I must discontinue my lectures. I naturally protested against a measure which was directed against myself alone among all the teachers in the camp. I sent the General a note which he promised to forward to Berlin, and this was the beginning of an interminable correspondence. For a whole fortnight I had to furnish notes and reports and explanations of every kind. At last I received permission to resume my lectures. But I had to pledge myself to deliver every night, at the *bureau du camp*, a summary of the next day's lecture, and I had to put up with the presence, among my audience, of two or three soldiers who understood French."[1]

And while he was devoting himself to teaching others, my

[1] Henri Pirenne, *Souvenirs de Capitivité en Allemagne*, 1921, pp. 38–39.

father continued, under the guidance of a student, the study of the Russian language which he had begun at Crefeld.

The course of lectures on economic history which he was delivering to an audience of students led him to consider a plan which he had already been cherishing for some years: that of writing a general history of Europe; and by degrees, even in the depressing atmosphere of the camp, deprived of all comfort, and all possibility of research, he elaborated in his mind the plan of the vast synthesis of which he dreamed. He managed to obtain some of the works of certain Russian historians, the study of which was to open new horizons, and to enable him to produce a work that no historian had ever attempted to undertake unaided—a general history of Europe, expounded on the lines followed in his *Histoire de Belgique*.

My father's arrest and internment had called forth many attempts at intervention; the Academy of Amsterdam proposed that he should be interned in Holland; American professors begged that he might be sent to the University of Princeton; President Wilson, King Alfonso XIII, and the Pope had endeavoured to persuade the German Government to release him.

Eleven months before his arrest—on April 6th, 1915—the Swedish Academy had conferred upon him the title of Associate Member, though it was only in the Holzminden camp that he received the official notification of his nomination; and finally a pamphlet published by Professor Christian Nyrop of Copenhagen, on *L'Arrestation des professeurs belges et l'Université de Gand*, had moved the scholars and scientists of all the neutral countries. The German Government wished to respond to these manifestations by an act of clemency. In June 1916, it made my father an offer: he could choose, as his place of residence, one of the University cities of Germany. As he refused to leave the camp, he was transferred to Jena on August 24th, 1916.

There he found his friend Paul Fredericq, and for some months he was able to make use of the University library, and to devote himself methodically to the study of the Russian historians. But the German "clemency" proved to be ephemeral indeed. On

January 24th, 1917, the rooms of the exiles were suddenly searched, and their letters and papers seized. Brought before a colonel, the burgomaster, and the *Bezirksdirektor*, they were reproached with having abused the "hospitality of Germany." A few days later, while M. Fredericq was sent to Burgel, my father was deported to Kreuzburg on the Werra, a little Thuringian town of two thousand inhabitants, a few miles from Eisenach.

Described as "extremely dangerous," he was refused a room in the best hotel. He was installed in the "Gasthof zum Stern," where they consented to give him lodging. "It was a large house in the market-place, opposite the church and the Rathaus, with a big tiled roof, a wide *porte cochère*, and, at the back, a courtyard enclosed by a stable, a barn and a dairy."[1]

My father was able to go about as he pleased, but once every day he had to present himself before the burgomaster and give in his correspondence, which had to be censored at the *Bezirksdirektion* of Eisenach.

It was then that the work took shape of which he had elaborated the plan in the barracks of Holzminden. My father has himself described the circumstances under which it was written: "I decided immediately that I could never hold out against the monotony of my detention unless I forced myself to undertake some definite occupation, with every hour of the day reserved for its special task. I continued the study of the Russian language. . . . Every afternoon, from two o'clock to five, I went for a walk. At five o'clock I set to work on the draft of a book of which I had often thought before the war, and of which I carried the plan in my head. This occupied me until supper-time. I read the newspaper, and the day was done, and on the following day I observed the same time-table. I never departed from this regimen, whatever the weather or season. It offered me the inestimable advantage of knowing, in the morning, what I had to do until the evening. It set a barrier to my vagrant imaginings, calmed my anxieties and banished boredom. In the end I became really interested in my work. I thought about it during my solitary walks in the fields and woods. There was

[1] Henri Pirenne, *Souvenirs de Captivité en Allemagne,* 1921, p. 64.

nothing there to recall the war, and I forced myself to forget it. I used to talk to myself. Having no duties to perform, no work to do, and being free from all mundane or social obligations in my solitude, I tasted the charms of meditation, of the slow and progressive elaboration of the ideas that one carries in one's mind, the ideas with which one lives, and in which one finally becomes absorbed.

"In short, I understand, or at least I think I did understand, the voluntary seclusion of Descartes in his 'room with a Dutch stove.' I too was living in 'a room with a stove,' and if I was living there despite myself, there were moments when I managed to forget this. . . . Every morning, about ten o'clock, I interrupted my work to call on the burgomaster, whom I found on the first floor of the Rathaus. This was the most exciting moment of the day. Should I find there some of those letters which were the sole distraction and the only solace of my exile? . . .

"One by one I made the acquaintance of the aristocracy of the village, the *Honoratioren*, to employ the consecrated term. The most important and also the most cultivated of these gentlemen was the Superintendant.[1] We used to exchange a few words whenever we met, and at times I was able to get him to speak of the war. He was a good talker, and he was fond of talking. He certainly had no idea of the pleasure I felt on hearing him expatiate on a subject with which I had long been familiar, thanks to my talks at Jena. Race and its historic influence was constantly recurring in his conversation. Romanism, Germanism! For him, these were everything. Romanism was the Catholic Church, where form had precedence over content, convention and tradition over liberty of thought and the individual conscience. Apart from this he ascribed the history of the world to Protestantism and Protestantism to Germanism.—'But, after all, Calvin!' I protested, one day.—'Calvin!' he said, 'is Luther adapted to the Roman spirit . . .'

"On another occasion we spoke of political freedom. This too was the appanage of the Germans. Luther had announced the true formula—a formula, of course, not to be understood by foreigners.

[1] Crefeld is the seat of a Lutheran "superintendance."

—'After all,' I suggested, 'the truth is, very probably, that this notion of liberty is characteristic of a people whose own liberty is of recent date. With us, serfdom was abolished in the 13th century; but it still existed in Germany at the beginning of the 19th century. For people who have been accustomed to liberty for the last six hundred years, and for those whose grandfather perhaps was liable to render "ban service" to his lord, and was *adscriptus glebae,* words have not the same meaning, and they find it hard to agree.'—The Superintendant gazed at me in astonishment. He was doubtless asking himself if I was really in earnest. . . . The more I learned of Germany the more obvious it seemed to me that her discipline, her spirit of obedience, her militarism, and her lack of political ability and understanding, were largely explained by the renaissance of serfdom that occurred in the 16th century. In these respects there is a profound and radical difference between Germany and the Occidental countries. But for the almost universal serfdom of the rural populations to the east of the Elbe, could Lutheranism ever have spread as it did, and could the organization of the Prussian State have been conceivable?"

It was in this solitude, a solitude occupied with meditation, and interrupted by conversations which often opened wide horizons, that my father wrote his *History of Europe.*

When he first set to work, a few days after he was installed in the Thuringian inn, he had no books at his disposal other than a little historical manual which was used in the local school. To begin with, he reduced to writing, in small school exercise-books, the plan which he "carried in his head." On March 23rd, 1917, he began the first draft. The dates which he noted every day in the margin of his manuscript enable us to follow the progress of the work. Written without interruption and almost without erasure, consisting of short chapters, themselves divided into paragraphs, we feel that we have here the expression of a mind which had indeed reached the zenith of its development. In the midst of the most dramatic episodes the author's self-restraint was such that he preserved the most perfect objectivity. Yet he was not living in a hermetic cell, and the proof of this is in his work. If I have recalled certain conversations to which he draws attention in his *Souvenirs*, it was simply because one feels that they were clearly related to the pages which he was then writing; the eagerness of the official German scholarship to explain everything by race inspired several observations which show us the utter falsity of this historical theory, which is born of political necessity, and the character of the population in whose midst he was living evidently inspired certain social explanations which are among the most striking passages in the book. Deprived of any access to sources, unable to refer to details or to verify dates, my father was obliged to confine himself to the study of historical aspects; social history, economic evolution, and the great religious and political movements absorbed his attention, the historical data serving, after all, merely as the supporting basis of the great fresco which he painted with broad strokes, embracing East and West in a single perspective.

The reader may perhaps be surprised to find that so many dates are cited in brackets. In the manuscript they were nearly all absent; the brackets were there to be filled in later, and I thought it best, in publishing this history, to add the dates as my father would have done.

The *History of Europe* ends abruptly about 1550. Yet the plan which the manuscript follows, page by page, is continued down to 1914. Events interrupted the full elaboration of the plan. The arrival at Kreuzberg on August 8th, 1918, of my mother and my younger brother Robert, who, after more than two years, had at last obtained permission to share my father's exile, caused only a few days' interruption. It was the armistice that set a term to the work.

Returning to Belgium, my father was chiefly preoccupied with the continuation of his *Histoire de Belgique*, and the *History of Europe* was laid aside. Yet *Les Villes des Moyen Age*, *La Civilisation occidental en moyen age*, and his last work, which my father completed only a few months before his death, *Mahomet et Charlemagne*, are merely partial developments of the *History of Europe*.

How often we have spoken of this work, which I for my part consider to be his masterpiece! It was his intention to complete it one day. But I must publish it—he told me—if he did not live to finish it. In offering it now to the public I am performing a pious duty.

Yet on reading the *History of Europe* one must not forget that the author was unable to give it its definitive form. It is published as it came from his pen; he did not even re-read it; so that it may seem, here and there, a little unpolished as to its style, but all the more attractive in the vigour and boldness of its thought, still untarnished by careful considerations of form. My father wrote the *History of Europe* for himself. The book that he would have given to the public, had he lived, would doubtless have been illustrated by a greater number of data and references and quotations, and its style would have been more chiselled. It could not have been more vital, more compressed, more pregnant with thought. The author has poured himself into the mould of his book. At the time of writing it he had already built up the great synthesis of which the books which he published after the war were merely the development.

The *History of Europe* is the outcome of all the research which my father had undertaken during the thirty-five years which he had devoted to history before 1914; it is the synthesis of all his knowledge, ripened in meditation at a time when, being deprived of access to books, he could confront that knowledge only with his own thought.

It is this thought, in which the whole man lives again, that my mother and I have felt we must offer, in all its spontaneity, to those who seek in history the fundamental explanation of the great historical movements which have given birth to our own age.

JACQUES PIRENNE

# AUTHOR'S PREFACE

I AM alone here with my thoughts, and if I cannot succeed in controlling them, they will end by allowing themselves to be controlled by my sorrow,[1] my ennui, and my anxieties for my dear ones, and will drive me into neurasthenia and despair. I absolutely must react against my fate. "There are people," my dear wife writes to me, "who allow themselves to be prostrated by misfortune, and others who are tempered by it. One must resolve to be of these latter." I shall try, for her sake and my own.

At Holzminden the Russian students for whom I improvised a course of economic history expressed the desire, and I could see that it was sincere, that I should publish my lectures. Why should I not attempt to sketch here, in its broad outlines, what might be a *History of Europe*? The lack of books cannot prove a great handicap, since this is a question of a broad sketch only. I had already thought of it at Jena, and I made some notes for it. It seems to me that I saw certain relations unravelling themselves. In any case, this would be an occupation. It seems to me that I am no longer thinking very clearly, and my memory has certainly deteriorated. But perhaps the effort will do me some good. The essential thing is to kill time and not allow oneself to be killed by it.

I dedicate my work to the memory of my beloved Pierre, to my dear wife, and to my dear sons.

H. PIRENNE

KREUZBURG A.D. WERRA

GASTHOF ZUM STERN

*January 31st*, 1917

[1] The writer had lost his son Pierre, who had enlisted as a volunteer in the Belgian Army, and was killed at the age of nineteen, on November 3rd, 1914, in the course of the Battle of the Yser.

*Book One*

# THE END OF THE ROMAN WORLD IN THE WEST

(To the Musulman Invasions)

## CHAPTER I

# THE BARBARIAN KINGDOMS IN THE ROMAN EMPIRE

### 1. *The Occupation of the Empire*

It would be a great error to imagine that the Germans who established themselves in the Empire in the 5th century were like those whom Tacitus has described. Their contact with Rome had taught them many things. The Empire, too, which appeared less formidable once they had crossed the frontier, was becoming more familiar to them; they were growing accustomed to it now that it was no longer inaccessible to them. And the Empire, in its turn, since it could no longer treat them with arrogance, was beginning to be more accommodating. Julian, in 358, allowed the Franks to settle in Taxandria, in return for military service, and through these Franks how much Roman influence must have crossed the Rhine!

At the other extremity of the Empire, on the banks of the Danube, the contact was still closer. The Goth Ulfila had brought Christianity from Byzantium, and had spread it among his compatriots. To be exact, this Christianity was that of the Arians, who were then predominant in the East. But the consequences of this fact would not appear until a later period. The essential thing was that even before they entered the Roman world, the Goths, the most powerful of the Germanic peoples, had abandoned their paganism, and with it had lost the great safeguard of their national individuality.

The Empire itself was swarming with Barbarians who had come to take service in the legions, and on whom fortune had smiled. Stilicho was a Barbarian; and Aetius; the two last great warriors of Western antiquity. And we can imagine how many of their compatriots would find their way, under the protection of such men, into the civil as well as the military administration. Even in Rome, or at the Imperial court, the sons of northern kings were found, who had gone thither to learn the Latin tongue, or to be initiated into the Latin civilization. So, little by little, the Empire was becoming accustomed to the Barbarians. They were no longer strangers. The danger still existed, but it was less urgent.

But with the invasion of Europe by the Huns (372) the peril recurred in all its gravity. The Goths, who were established on both banks of the Dniester—the Ostrogoths, as their name indicates, to the east of the river, the Visigoths to the west—did not attempt to resist the Mongol horsemen, the very aspect of whom filled them with terror. Before them the Ostrogoths retreated in disorder; the Visigoths, pressed by this retreat, found themselves driven against the Danube frontier. They demanded the right to cross it. The danger had come so suddenly that they had not been able to take measures to cope with it. Nothing of the kind had been foreseen. The very terror of the Visigoths made it clear that they would not hesitate to use force if their request were refused. They were given permission to pass, and they continued to pass for many days before the wondering gaze of the Roman outposts: men, women, children and cattle, on rafts and in canoes, some clinging to planks, and others to inflated skins or barrels. An entire people was migrating, led by its king.

And it was in this very fact that the peril of the situation lay. What was to be done with these newcomers? It was impossible to disperse them among the provinces. The Romans had to deal with a whole nation, which had left its own territory in order to occupy another country. And they would have to find a country for it within the Empire. A people which would retain its own institutions and its own king would have to be admitted to the Empire, and allowed to live under the Roman suzerainty. It was the first time that such a problem had presented itself. The Romans tried to circumvent the problem by a subtle manœuvre. The king of the Visigoths was proclaimed a Roman general, so that without ceasing to be the national leader of his people he had his place in the Imperial administration; a fantastic and equivocal solution of a contingency no less equivocal and fantastic.

The first consequence of this solution was to give the revolt of the Visigoths, which broke out a little later (A.D. 378),[1] a very disconcerting character. It was actually the insurrection of an alien people, which was asking for territory and the right of permanent settlement in the very heart of the Empire. But it could also be regarded as a military mutiny, and this made it possible to negotiate with the enemy. In order to prevent the pillage of Thrace, the Emperor Arcadius, reigning in the East, ordered the Visigoths to occupy Illyria, which he claimed his brother Honorius, reigning in the West, was holding in defiance of his rights. The rebels asked nothing better than to profit by this "order." They conscientiously occupied Illyria. But this rugged country was not what they were looking for. Italy was close at hand. The Germanic peril, which had hitherto menaced both halves of the Empire at once, now definitely turned away from the East and concentrated itself upon the West. The Greek world was to have no further contact with the Germans.[2]

To save Italy from this menace the West mustered all its forces in one supreme effort. Stilicho recalled from Gaul and Noricum and Rhaetia the legions which were defending the passage of the Rhine and the Danube. He defied the Barbarians in two great battles, at Pollanzo and Verona, and drove them back into Friuli. Flatterers were not lacking to compare him with Marius. A poem in his honour which has come down to us fills the reader with melancholy surprise; it still expresses such enthusiasm for the majesty of Rome, and is so convinced of the immortality of the Empire.

But the Empire, alas, was ruined. Its exhausted finances no

[1] On August 9th, 379, Valens was defeated at Andrinople. The peace of Theodosius enabled the Goths to establish themselves in Mesia. There was a fresh revolt under Alaric in 395.

[2] Three-quarters of a century later Byzantium was once more to feel the pressure of the two Theodorics, and of the Ostrogoths, but once again she contrived to divert their attention to Italy.

longer enabled it to maintain on its frontiers the compact armies which might have contained at any point the thrust of the Germans driven back by Attila, whose hordes were still triumphantly advancing towards the West, overthrowing, as they came, people after people. Stilicho saved Italy only by leaving undefended all the Transalpine provinces. The result could not be long delayed.

The Vandals crossed the Rhine with bands of Suevi, passed downwards through Gaul, pillaging as they went, crossed the Pyrenees, and halted only by the shores of the Mediterranean, where they installed themselves in the south of Spain and on the coast of Africa. The Burgundi followed the course of the Rhone and spread through its basin as far as the Gulf of Lyons. Less adventuresome, the Alamanni contented themselves with colonizing Alsace, the Ripuarian Franks the neighbourhood of Cologne as far as the Meuse, and the Salic Franks the plains of the Scheldt and the Lys.

At the same time a second attack was made upon Italy. Some bands of Germans crossing from Noricum and Rhaetia crossed the Alps under the leadership of Radagaisus, ravaging the Cisalpine territories and marching upon Rome, demanding land. A second time Stilicho stayed the flood. The invaders were cut to pieces and massacred under the walls of Florence (405). Then the victor himself perished (408). Thereupon the Visigoths took it upon themselves to avenge him. Under the pretext of punishing his assassins they resumed their march upon Rome. Stilicho's army was still in being; but as might have been expected of an army of mercenaries, it did not care to oppose the avengers of its leader. There was no resistance. Honorius shut himself up in Ravenna while Alaric entered Rome. This was the first time Barbarians had entered the gates of the Eternal City since the invasion of the Gauls in 390 B.C. True Barbarians as they were, they contented themselves with wrenching off the ornaments of gold and silver that glittered in the Forum and on the pediments of the public buildings. They had no hatred of Rome and they did not maltreat the population. What they wanted was land, and the charm of the country growing upon them as they marched southwards, they continued on their way through the enchanting landscape of Campania.

Alaric would have led them into Sicily, but he died suddenly not far from Cosenza (410). His companions gave him a funeral of epic majesty. They dug the warrior's grave in the bed of the Busento, whose stream was diverted from its course. Then the river was allowed to return to its bed, and to flow above his last resting-place. The slaves who had dammed the river and dug the grave were slain, that the position of the grave, which is still inviolate, might for ever remain a secret.

The Visigoths acknowledged Athaulf, the brother of Alaric, as his successor. We may judge of the progressive Romanization of the Barbarians from the fact that he was passionately desirous of alliance with the Imperial family. In order to get rid of him, Honorius resigned himself to giving him in marriage his sister Galla Placidia. The nuptials were celebrated with great pomp, to the accompaniment of the inevitable epithalamium inviting Venus and Cupid to shower their gifts upon the spouses. Athaulf was evidently anxious that the Romans, and his wife, should pardon his origin. He asked nothing better, he said, than to place the forces of his Barbarians at the service of the Empire. He was asked to employ them in expelling the Vandals who were still infesting the south of Gaul. He led them into Aquitaine, and there they settled, and also in the north of Spain.

But was the Empire to become the property of the Germans? Or would Germans and Romans share the same fate and fall beneath the Tartar yoke? Soon, for the first time, the Yellow Peril was menacing the whole of Europe. Attila made his appearance, conquering the Germanic populations, or driving them before him. Already he was crossing the Rhine, and his hordes, veering towards the south-west, were invading the north of Gaul. It was there, near Chalons-sur-Marne, that the last warrior of antiquity, Aetius, came forward to offer him the decisive battle. The Franks, the Burgundi and the Visigoths had sent him reinforcements, and the army which he commanded was really a microcosm of that Empire which, though submerged by the Germans, refused to disappear. Before it perished it did humanity a supreme service in repulsing the Hun invasion. The superior tactics which Aetius owed to the civilization for which he was fighting saved that civilization from inundation by the Barbarians. After two days of battle Attila decamped, and turned back to Germany. This retreat was not yet a rout, and in the following year the "Scourge of God" ravaged upper Italy. But once again he withdrew, and in the year 453 he died, suddenly, in the midst of an orgy.

The Empire of this predecessor of Jenghiz Khan crumbled as rapidly as that of his follower eight hundred years later, leaving nothing to mark its existence but ruins, and a lasting memory of terror in popular tradition.

Aetius, the conqueror of Attila, was assassinated by order of the Emperor Valentinian III. With him vanished, says a contemporary chronicler, "the salvation of the Western State." Rome was taken and pillaged by the Vandals in 455; and the noble Majorian was unable to avenge the insult. But more and more the power was passing into the hands of the German chieftains: Ricimer, Orestes and Odoacer placed themselves, in succession, at the head of the German soldiers and adventurers who had been pouring into Italy since the Hunnish catastrophe, and who were eager to obtain land.

The last Emperors were deposed; the last of all, Romulus Augustulus, the son of Orestes, was banished to Campania, and the Barbarian Odoacer, not venturing to call himself Emperor, conferred upon himself the only title at the disposal of the Germans: that of king.

It was in the midst of this lamentable disorder that another king, Theodoric, followed by a whole people, descended on Italy from the Alps. The Ostrogoths who followed him, and who had been driven back from the Dniester toward the Upper Danube by Attila, and then subjected by him, profited by their release to claim their share of Italy. Between them and the disorganized horde that recognized Odoacer fortune was not long in the balance. The Herulian adventurer, defeated in open battle (488), took refuge in Ravenna. Unable to reduce the city by siege, Theodoric invited him, under a sworn safe-conduct, to an interview, and slew him with his own hand (493). Henceforth Italy was his.

This was the last war of the widespread invasion. In the West, the whole Empire was now submerged by it. A medley of kingdoms covered all its provinces: Anglo-Saxon kingdoms in Britain, a Frank kingdom in the north of Gaul, a Burgundian kingdom in Provence, a Visigoth kingdom in Aquitaine and in Spain, a Vandal kingdom in Africa and the islands of the Mediterranean, and lastly, an Ostrogoth kingdom in Italy. As a matter of fact, this Empire, whose territory was thus dismembered, had not ceded an inch of soil to its invaders. In law, they were only occupiers of the soil, and their royal titles meant nothing save to the peoples they had brought with them. This is so true that, even though each of them reigned over a far greater number of Romans than of Germans, they did not call themselves King of Gaul, or King of Italy, but King of the Franks, King of the Ostrogoths, etc. But what followed? There was no longer an Emperor. And the Empire, one may say, disappeared in virtue of this adage of Roman law, that "in the matter of possession, occupation is equivalent to title."

## 2. *The New States*

If we compare a map of the Roman Empire in the West with a linguistic chart of modern Europe, we see that the domain of the Germanic languages has undergone very little expansion, although the whole Empire was in the hands of the Germans. There are only five frontier provinces in the whole or part of which a Germanic language is spoken, apart from the British Isles: the second Belgium, in which Flemish is spoken, and the two Germanies (the Rhenish province, Alsace), Rhaetia, and Noricum (Switzerland, Basle, Württemberg, Southern Bavaria, Austria), which are German by language. Everywhere else the Latin tongue has survived into our own days, in the form which it has assumed in the various Romance languages: French, Provençal, Spanish, Portuguese, Romansh, Italian. It was only on the extreme frontier of the Empire that the Germans descended *en masse*, submerging the Latinized population, which, of course, in these constantly threatened regions, must have been extremely sparse. Everywhere else the contrary phenomenon was observed. The Germans who penetrated farther into the Empire, being there in the minority, were absorbed by the provincials. After two or three generations their language had disappeared; and inter-marriage did the rest. The number of French or Provençal words of Germanic origin hardly exceeds five hundred. We should seek in vain to-day among the populations of Provence, Spain and Italy for the fair hair and the blue eyes of the invaders of the 5th century—and if we did find them, should we not attribute them to the Gauls? The Germanic manners and customs resisted no better. For example, the monumemts of Visigothic law that have been preserved show how superficial the Germanization of the Empire was in actual fact. It is not correct to say that the Roman world became Germanized. It became "barbarized," which is not at all the same thing.

With the exception of the Anglo-Saxons of Britain, the Germanic peoples did not import their political institutions into the Empire. The exception confirms the rule: for in Britain the provincials retreated before the invaders, and the latter, finding themselves alone, naturally continued to govern themselves as they had done in their old home. But everywhere else the Roman population not only remained in its place, but continued to live under almost the same conditions as before the conquest. There was, of course, a great deal of pillage and massacre, and there were individual acts of violence, but there was no systematic spoliation; still less was there any enslavement of the people. Nor was any rational resistance offered by the provincials (with honourable exceptions in Gaul and Britain), nor were the Germans hostile to them. Perhaps there was a little contempt on the one side, a little respect on the other. For that matter, the people could not be quite sure that the Germans were not soldiers of the Empire.

Moreover, the Germans, like the Romans, were Christians; and while they entered the Empire as conquerors, they submitted themselves to the Church, which, under her authority, merged the Germans with the Romans.

The Christianity which they professed was certainly one of the essential causes of their immediate rapprochement to the populations of the conquered countries, and there seems to be no doubt that the readiness with which the Barbarians abandoned their national tongues was explained by the fact that the language of the Church was Latin.

The Germans, for that matter, did not attempt to superimpose themselves upon the Roman populations; they settled down beside them. In the South of Gaul the Visigoths established themselves on the principles in force for the billeting of the Roman armies (the *tertia*), according to which one-third of the inhabitant's dwelling had to be placed at the disposal of the soldiers. The measure was extended to the land, the German occupation being now permanent, and a sort of peaceful penetration took place, concerning which, however, we have very little information. In the north of Gaul the newcomers were settled on the domains of the treasury or on unoccupied land. As for the juridical status of the person, this remained, on either side, what it had been. Germans and Romans continued to live in conformity with their national laws, each retaining their special customs in respect of property and the family and inheritance. The "territoriality" of the law was replaced by its "personality," and this "territoriality" made its reappearance only during the 9th century, when the fusion of the two peoples had become complete.

This intermingling of two distinct but equal nationalities obviously excluded the possibility of applying to the more numerous and more civilized people the political institutions of the other. Moreover, these institutions, applicable to Barbarian life, were no longer so to the new conditions to which the Germans had just been introduced. They fell into desuetude of themselves, and no one thought of reviving them.

Nothing illustrates more clearly the transformation which had occurred in this respect in the 5th and 6th centuries than a glance at the situation of royalty.

The Germans, we know, had kings. But with them the royal power was completely subordinated to the assembly of the people, who conferred it on whom they pleased, since it was elective. But there was nothing of this after the conquest. Set high above his fellows by the power which conquest had conferred upon him, the king was henceforth possessed of absolute authority. There was now only one power in the State—the king's; the constitution was reduced to the simple exercise of personal government. The king had shed all vestiges of his primitive origin. He no longer bore any resemblance to his Germanic ancestors; but only to the Roman Emperor. At all events, the irresponsibility and the autocratic power of the Emperor were his.

However, he willingly proclaimed himself the lieutenant of the Emperor. While for his Germanic subjects he was a national king, for the Romans he was merely a general of the Empire, and the titles which he assumed or demanded of the Emperor enabled the latter to regard him as the representative of the Imperial authority.

Installed in Ravenna after the Goths had established themselves in the north of Italy, Theodoric continued the Roman traditions and was recognized by the population, and by the Church, as the representative of legality. Genseric himself, after he and his Vandals had conquered Africa, the richest and most prosperous of the Western provinces, had all the appearance, despite his rupture with Rome, of a Romanized king, whose absolutism was manifested in the bloody repression of any leanings toward independence on the part of the Germanic aristocracy, and found expression within the framework of Roman institutions. The court of the Visigoths —first at Toulouse, then at Toledo—was also completely Roman. The population of the old, conquered provinces retained its Roman institutions and officials, adopted by the new rulers, and its Roman judges, and continued to pay its taxes. The Germanic army, installed in the midst of the conquered population in accordance with principles of "hospitality," had blended with it so completely in less than a century that it had lost all its old national institutions, its language, and even its military organization.

The ephemeral Burgundian kingdom, which from 534 onwards was to become merged in the Merovingian Francia, effected, with the greatest ease, the fusion of the victors and the vanquished, under the absolute rule of a Barbarian king who had the greatest respect for the Roman Empire in whose name he ruled, and whose municipal institutions he left intact, both in Lyons and in Vienne.

Only the Franks, in the north of Gaul, were to retain their customs, their language and their institutions. But being far removed from the capital of their kings, who had suddenly become the masters of the immense Gallo-Roman kingdom, they exercised no influence over the destinies of Francia before the Carolingian epoch. Of all the Barbarian kings, the Frankish were the most remote from the Roman conception of power. They regarded the kingdom as their patrimonial estate, and they applied to the succession to the throne the principles which regulated the succession to real estate, under the Salic law: that is, on the death of the king his sons divided the kingdom into equal shares. Here we find a crude ideal of despotic royalty, departing no less completely from the Germanic customs than from the absolutism of the Empire. Yet the king, like the Emperor, was the supreme military commander, and the sovereign justiciary of the kingdom; and it was incumbent on him to ensure that peace reigned within his frontiers.

However, the Frankish kings were quickly becoming Romanized. As a matter of fact, from the time of their installation in the Empire they had to assume a definitely defensive attitude in respect of Germania—so much so that they tended to forget those of their people who were segregated in the extreme north, and even allowed them to retain their pagan religion until far into the 7th century. On the other hand, the old Imperial administration which they found in Gaul was bound to impress upon them the Roman conception of the State.

It is true that the Frankish king employed the officers of his court to administer his property and his kingdom. The court was composed of various dignitaries whose titles show that they were once borne by slaves, as was the case with all dignitaries of Germanic origin: the marshal (the horse-slave), the seneschal (the senior slave), the majordomo (the chief domestic servant), the butler (the cellar slave). But these servants, these household officers, shared in their master's fortunes, and naturally enough, since what was royal was public, they became his ministers. In addition to these ministers there was an official of the Roman type, the referendary, at the head of the scribes taken over from the Imperial bureaucracy, who despatched the royal precepts or diplomas.

While the administration of the country was falling into a state of decadence in so far as it was separated from Rome—that is, from the central government, on which the whole administrative machinery was dependent—it continued to work after a fashion.

The king confided the government of the provinces, which coincided almost everywhere with the old Roman "cities," to paid officers—counts (*comites*), dukes (*duces*) and prefects (*praefecti*)—the great majority of whom were Gallo-Roman; but they were commonly favourites of the king, and sometimes of the lowest origin. They were subject to no supervision, no control. All that was required of them was that they should furnish certain sums of money to the treasury every year: for the rest, they could oppress the people unchecked, and they did not fail to do so. One must read Gregory of Tours to realize the brutality and cruelty of the Merovingian counts. In their demoralization and their arbitrary use of power they merely followed the example of the court.

Perhaps there has never been a more depressing spectacle than that which was offered by the Western world during the two centuries that followed the Germanic invasions. Brought too suddenly into contact with civilization, the Barbarians, in their haste to enjoy its advantages, adopted its vices, and the Romans, no longer restrained by the strong hand of the State, acquired the brutality of the Barbarians. There was a general unleashing of the crudest passions and the basest appetites, with their inevitable accompaniment of perfidy and cruelty.

But decadent and semi-barbaric though it was, the administration was none the less Roman. Only in the north shall we find royal officers with Germanic names: *grafio, tunginus, rachimburgi.*

The financial system too was still Roman. The king's private fortune was clearly separated from the public treasury. The monetary system and the impost were still the foundation of the royal power. The gold solidus was still current everywhere. Moreover, gold was still being coined. The State, it is true, was no longer able to regulate the minting of money, nor to guarantee a standard. The Frankish king even left the minting of money to private enterprise, without troubling himself about the debasement of the currency which was the natural consequence.

Thus all the Barbarian kingdoms which divided the Western Empire between them presented a number of common characteristics, by virtue of which they were not barbaric States, but "barbarized" Roman kingdoms. All had abandoned their national tongue and their pagan religion. Being Christian, they had by that very fact become the faithful subjects of the Church, which was completely imbued with the Roman civilization. And yet, like the Empire, these kingdoms were essentially secular. The bishops, in theory appointed by the clergy, were actually nominated by the king; their influence, however great, was confined to the religious domain; no bishop filled a public office before the advent of the Carolingians. The king, moreover, held his power in his own right, without the intervention of the Church. Like the Emperor, he was an absolute sovereign, free from all popular tutelage; for although the Germanic armies were occasionally assembled in *conventus*, this did not in any way resemble the ancient Assembly of the people.

Lastly, the new States—and this is an essential point—had preserved a fiscal organization and a considerable treasury. The public fisc or treasury had immense resources: the Imperial domain with its villas, its forests, its mines, its ports, and its highways, its treasure in minted gold, and the revenue from taxes, which, although it was dwindling from day to day, was still, for a long time to come, considerable.

The financial administration, with its offices and its books, was still staffed by scholars, and was still able—though with increasing difficulty—to recruit its personnel from laymen who had been educated on Roman lines.

Down to the time of the Merovingian decadence the financial resources of the Barbarian kings were very much greater than those of any other Western State would be until the close of the 13th century.

These kingdoms were not Roman merely because the Roman civilization had furnished them with the framework within which, and thanks to which, they had succeeded in organizing themselves, but also because they *wished* to be Roman. The king spoke of his *palatium*, of his *fiscus*, gave his officials titles which were borrowed from the Constantinian hierarchy, and made his chancellery imitate the formula and the style of the Imperial edicts. Theodoric, in Italy, took Cassidorus for his prime minister, was for a time the patron of Boetius, rebuilt the aqueducts of the Roman Campagna, organized games in the circus, and at Ravenna built, in a purely Byzantine style, Sant' Apollinare and San Vitale. The Vandal and Visigoth kings did their best to follow his example, and there was not one of them, even to the sons of Clovis, who was not proud to confer his patronage on the poor poet Venantius Fortunatus, when he came to seek his fortune at his court.

On the other hand, there was a cultivated class, and they were Roman jurists who codified, for the Barbarian kings, the Germanic and Roman laws of their subjects. Of course, the standard of the lay schools sank to a very low level; indeed, except in Italy, only a few lingered on. They were replaced, to some extent, by the religious schools which sprang up beside the churches, and, before long, in conjunction with the monasteries.

However this may be, and however deplorable the decadence of culture and learning under the Merovingian kings, the latter always had literate officials at their service.

The aspect of the civilized world, as it existed after the invasions, presented the spectacle, not of youth, but of the decadence of the Imperial civilization; and Gregory of Tours, who lived in this world, and was horrified by it, sorrowfully summed up his impression of it in these discouraged words: *Mundus senescit* (the world grows old).

CHAPTER II

# JUSTINIAN—THE LOMBARDS

## 1. *Justinian*

The Visigoth peril once averted, the eastern provinces of the Empire had nothing further to fear from the Germans. Attila, in pushing the latter westward, had, at least for the moment, driven them away from the frontiers of the Empire. But in the 6th century other Barbarians—the Slavs—began to appear on the left bank of the Danube. Being much nearer to Constantinople than the Germans to Rome, they were conscious at once of the attractive power of the great city. They flocked thither in ever-increasing numbers, taking service there as labourers or as soldiers, and more than one achieved a position of wealth and influence.

It is usual to date the latter period of the history of the Roman Empire, which is quite properly known as the Byzantine period, from the reign of Justinian. Yet it was Constantine, in imitation of Diocletian, whose residence was in Nicomedia, who made Byzantium the capital of the Imperial government of the East. Henceforth, while Rome was abandoned for Milan or Ravenna by the successors of Theodosius, Byzantium was always, until in 1453 it fell into the hands of the Turks, the residence of the Emperors, the city of the Tsars, the *Tarsagrad* of the Russians. Favoured from the first by its incomparable geographical situation, the privilege of sheltering the court, and with it the central government, soon had the result of making it the chief city of the East. We may even say that from the time of the Moslem conquests it was to become the one great city of the Christian world. While after the Moslem invasions all the urban centres of the West became depopulated and fell into ruin, Byzantium retained a population of several hundreds of thousands, whose alimentary needs placed under requisition all the territories bordering on the Black Sea, the Aegean, and the Adriatic. It was Byzantium that promoted the trade and the navigation of the Empire, and the attractive force which it exerted on the whole of the Empire was the surest guarantee of its unity. Thanks to this force, the Byzantine Empire presented, so to speak, an urban character, in a much greater degree than the old Roman Empire. For Rome had merely attracted to herself the exports of the provinces, but had given them nothing in return; she restricted herself to the rôle of consumer. Byzantium, on the contrary, both consumed and produced. The city was not only an Imperial residence; it was a trading centre of the first order, into which were poured the products of Europe and Asia, and it was also a very active industrial city.

By language it remained a Greek city, but a Greek city more than half Orientalized. Incomparably richer, more thriving, and more populous than Thrace or Greece proper, the provinces of Asia Minor exercised an irresistible ascendancy. Syria, the most active of the provinces, exerted a preponderant influence on the capital. Byzantine art is really a Hellenic art transformed through the medium of the art of Syria.

But of Greek thought and Greek science only as much survived as Christianity had seen fit to spare; and this was little enough. Justinian, as we know, closed the school of Athens, where a faint echo of the ancient philosophers might still be heard. But the dogmas and mysteries of religion provided an abundance of material for the passionate love of dialectic which had for so many centuries characterized Hellenic thought. No sooner did Christianity appear than the East began to teem with heresies: there were pitched battles in the great cities, Council attacked Council, and the three Patriarchs of Byzantium, Antioch and Alexandria engaged in conflict. Naturally, all these heresies had their repercussions in the capital, and in every conflict the Emperor had to take sides, for the old conception that made him the religious leader, as well as the head of the State, had been perpetuated in Constantinople. In the capital every theological debate became a governmental affair. The parties pulled what wires they could at court, each seeking to obtain the all-powerful support of the sovereign. Turn and turn about, orthodoxy or heresy, according to the choice he made between them, became the religion of the State.

With all this the Empire, though confined to the East, was, nevertheless, the Roman Empire. From the 9th century onwards the title of *Βασιλεὺς τῶν Ρωμαίων* was actually the official title of the Byzantine Emperor. From the reign of Diocletian the government of the Empire was often divided between two Emperors, but this division of power did not destroy the unity of the Empire.

To speak, as we do for convenience' sake, of the Empire of the West and the Empire of the East, is to employ an inaccurate description. In actual fact, although for administrative purposes it was divided into an eastern and a western portion, the Empire was nevertheless a single organism. If the ruler of one of these two halves disappeared, it passed, by this very fact, under the power of the other ruler. And this is precisely what happened at the time of the invasions. The Emperor of the West having disappeared, the Emperor of the East found himself henceforth the sole Emperor. And as we have seen, he did not cede any portion of the Empire; his right to the possession of the whole remained intact. Even after the conquest the memory of his supremacy lingered. The Germanic kings recognized that he exercised a sort of primacy over them; it was not clearly defined, but they betrayed their feeling by the respect which they paid to the Emperor. For the Pope, he remained the legitimate sovereign, and the pontifical chancellery continued to date its Bulls from the year of the Consulate—that is, from the accession of the Byzantine Emperor. Moreover, in the Church the tradition persisted that the Empire was both necessary and eternal. Did not Tertullian and Saint Augustine proclaim its providential nature?

The Romans had yet another reason to regret the Empire. Their new masters, the Germanic kings, were not orthodox. Apart from the King of the Franks, who was converted to Catholicism at the beginning of the conquest of Gaul by Clovis, the others—Visigoths, Ostrogoths and Vandals—were Arians by profession.

To the Arian heresy, which had been so formidable in the 4th century, and which had caused so much bloodshed in the East, the Germans obstinately adhered. In actual fact it was not very dangerous. The Arian Church was making no proselytes in the heart of the Roman population, and there is reason to believe that as the Barbarians became absorbed by the latter the number of its adherents was progressively decreasing. But enraged by its very impotence, and confident of the favour of the kings, it was aggressive and intolerant in its treatment of the Catholic clergy. And the quarrels of the priests embittered and exasperated the orthodox population. In Italy the conflict became so acute that the Pope, in his despair, having invoked the intervention of the Emperor, Theodoric flung him into prison, to the great scandal of the faithful.

All this was known in Byzantium; it was known also that the strength of the new kingdoms was not very alarming. In all of them the dynasty was destroying itself by intestine quarrels and domestic murder. In the Visigoth and Ostrogoth kingdoms the various competitors for the crown begged the Emperor to come to their assistance. In the Ostrogoth kingdom, after the death of Theodoric, Theodatus had his consort Amalasontha, the daughter of the late king, assassinated, in order that he might reign alone. What with religious persecution and political scandals, there were plenty of pretexts for intervention!

Justinian (527–565) did not fail to profit by them. He had restored peace in his States, reorganized the finances, and renovated the army and the fleet; he now employed them to reconstitute the Roman Empire. The first blow was struck at the Vandals. In the year 533, five hundred ships landed in Africa 15,000 men, led by Belisarius. The campaign was as brief as it was brilliant. Within a few months the Vandal kingdom was completely conquered, and its king sent to Byzantium to figure in the Emperor's triumph. The Visigoths, who had stood aside indifferently while their neighbours were being defeated, now suffered the same fate. The whole maritime region was occupied and subdued without difficulty; the Byzantines did not trouble to pursue the king, who had fled to the mountains. The Ostrogoth kingdom held out longer.

Only after eighteen years of warfare was its fate decided by the bloody defeat of its last forces on the slopes of Vesuvius (553).

The Mediterranean had once more become a Roman, or should we say, was becoming a Byzantine lake. On every side the Byzantine dukes and exarchs were organizing the administration of the reconquered provinces. Rome was once again part of the Empire, and, as in the good old days, the Emperor's orders ran as far as the Pillars of Hercules.

It might well have seemed that the Byzantine civilization, after performing such brilliant services, would become the European civilization, and that Constantinople, where Justinian was building the basilica of Saint Sophia in lieu of a triumphal arch, was destined to draw the entire West into its orbit.

## 2. *The Lombards*

But these successes were brilliant rather than lasting. When he died, in the year 565, Justinian left the Empire oppressed by crushing taxation and incapable of further effort. And yet the task was not completed. Even now, if the Empire wished to assure itself of the mastery of the Mediterranean, it must fight the one independent State that bordered its shores—the Frankish kingdom. For the coast of Provence had been spared by Justinian's armies. To complete and consolidate the task which had been begun, this omission must be made good. But once Provence was subdued it would evidently be necessary to go further, and, in order to assure its conquest, to revive the policy of Caesar, and annex Gaul. Then, defended once more by the Alps and by the Rhine, the Roman world, centred on the Mediterranean, would be, as of old, protected against all invasion. But in the Franks the Empire had to deal with an enemy far more formidable than any it had yet encountered.

How could Justinian's successor, his nephew Justin II (565–578), have dreamed of such an enterprise? Not only were his finances in confusion, but new enemies had just appeared on the Danube. Advancing in the East, coming from the Russian steppes, whence they had driven the Slavs toward the Carpathians and southwards, were the furious Avars; and in the West two Germanic peoples, the Gepidae and the Lombards, were occupying the middle course of the river. At the other extremity of the Empire, in Asia Minor, the Persians were assuming a menacing attitude on the frontier. Far from making preparations for distant enterprises, the Empire had to apply itself to the task of defence.

Justin thought he had struck a masterly blow by inciting the Lombards and the Avars against the Gepidae. This unhappy people was annihilated, but the Avars immediately occupied its territory, and the Lombards, feeling that they were the weaker, made way for them. Like the Ostrogoths a hundred years earlier, they marched upon Italy, and invaded Cisalpine Gaul, which thenceforth bore their name (568). The Lombard conquests continued until the reign of Rotharis (636–652), who conquered Genoa and the Ligurian coast.

The Byzantines, surprised by the attack, did not attempt to resist, but took refuge in the cities, which fell one after another. They succeeded in retaining only the coast of Istria, the country about Ravenna, Pentapolis, the region surrounding Rome, and that part of the peninsula that lies to the south of Spoleto and Benevento.

This epilogue to the Germanic invasions—the descent of the Lombards into Italy—was of great significance.

The newcomers, by interposing themselves between the Byzantine Empire and the Frankish kingdom, rendered impossible the conflict which must have occurred had the two States remained in contact. On the other hand, their arrival on the south of the Alps was to determine the fate of Italy even down to the 19th century. This was the end of the unity of that country which had created the unity of the civilized world. The struggle of the Lombards and the Byzantines for its possession was only the first chapter of its tragic history, in the course of which the land was invaded, occupied, and dismembered by the Germans, the Normans, the Spaniards, the French, and the Austrians, until the day when it at length shook off the alien yoke, realized the secular longing of its patriots, and accomplished its *risorgimento*. The Italian question which in different forms intruded itself into every chapter of European history had its beginning in the Lombard invasion. At the moment which we are now considering, the solution provided by the success of the invaders must still have seemed extremely precarious. Byzantium had retreated, but had not renounced the struggle, and might still hope for the success of a counter-offensive. In spite of all that had happened, her position in the West, where she possessed a good part of Italy, Sicily, Africa, and the coasts of Spain, permitted her to reckon on the future. But a new upheaval, the most profound and the most violent that Europe had ever experienced, was about to decide otherwise.

## CHAPTER III

# THE MUSULMAN INVASION

### 1. *The Invasion*

In the whole history of the world there has been nothing comparable, in the universal and immediate nature of its consequences, with the expansion of Islam in the 7th century.

The overwhelming rapidity of its propagation was no less surprising than the immensity of its conquests. It took only seventy years from the death of Mohammed (632) to spread from the Indian Ocean to the Atlantic. Nothing could stand before it. At the first blow it overthrew the Persian Empire (637–644); then it deprived the Byzantine Empire, one by one, of each of the provinces which it attacked: Syria (634–636), Egypt (640–642), Africa (698), and Spain (711). The Visigoths had retaken Spain from the Byzantines, and their last king, Roderick, fell in the battle of Cadiz (711).

The onward march of the invaders was checked only at the beginning of the 8th century, when the great movement by which they were threatening Europe from both sides at once was halted beneath the walls of Constantinople (717) and by the soldiers of Charles Martel on the plain of Poitiers (732). It was checked; its first expansive energy was exhausted; but it had sufficed to change the face of the globe. Wherever it had passed the ancient States, which were deeply rooted in the centuries, were overturned as by a cyclone; the traditional order of history was overthrown. This was the end of the old Persian Empire, the heir of Assyria and Babylon; of the Hellenized regions of Asia which had constituted the Empire of Alexander the Great, and had thereafter continued to gravitate in the orbit of Europe; of the ancient Egypt, whose past was still living beneath the Greek veneer that had covered it since the days of the Ptolemies; and of the African provinces which Rome had won from Carthage. Henceforth all these regions were subject, in religion and political obedience, to the most powerful potentate who had ever existed, the Caliph of Baghdad.

And all this was the work of a nomadic people which had hitherto lived almost unknown in its rock-strewn deserts, which were disdained by all the conquerors, and numbered infinitely fewer inhabitants than Germany. But this people had just been converted by a prophet who had issued from its womb. It had shattered all its old idols, and had suddenly adopted the purest monotheism, and its conception of its duty to God had a formidable simplicity: it was, to obey Allah and compel the infidels to obey Him. The Holy War became a moral obligation, and its own reward. Warriors who fell with their weapons in their hands enjoyed the beatitudes of Paradise. For the rest, the booty of the rich traders who surrounded poverty-stricken Arabia on every side would be the lawful prize of the military apostolate.

There can be no doubt that it was fanaticism—or if you will, religious enthusiasm—that launched the Musulmans on the world. Between the invasions of these sectaries, who surged onward invoking Allah, and those of the Germans, who left their country only to acquire more fertile soil, the moral difference is impressive. Yet the social constitution of the Arabs fitted them admirably for their rôle. Nomads and poor, they were fully prepared to obey the command of God. They had only to saddle their horses and set off. They were not, as the Germans were, emigrants dragging behind them women and children, slaves and cattle; they were horsemen, accustomed from childhood to cattle-raids, and now Allah had laid upon them the duty of raiding the world in His name.

It must be admitted, however, that the weakness of their adversaries very greatly facilitated their task. Neither the Byzantine nor the Persian Empire, surprised by the unexpectedness of the attack, was in a condition to resist it. After Justin II the government of Constantinople had grown continually weaker, and nowhere, from Syria to Spain, did the invaders find armies before them. Their fiery onset encountered only disorder. Of the conquests of Justinian nothing was left, after 698, but Italy. Christianity, which had reigned on all the shores of the Mediterranean, now held only the northern shore. Three-fourths of the littoral of this sea, hitherto the common centre of European civilization, now belonged to Islam.

And they belonged to it not only by occupation, but also by virtue of religious and political absorption. The Arabs did not, like the Germans, respect the *status quo* in the conquered territories. They could not. While the Germans, on abandoning their religion for Christianity, immediately fraternized with the Romans, the Musulmans appeared as the propagandists of a new faith, an exclusive and intolerant faith to which all had to submit. Religion, wherever they ruled, was the basis of political society; or rather, the religious organization and the political organization were for them identical; Church and State forming a single unity. The infidels could continue the practice of their cult only as simple subjects, deprived of all rights whatsoever. Everything was transformed, from top to bottom, in accordance with the principles of the Koran. Of the entire administration—justice, finance, the army—nothing was left. Kadis and emirs replaced the exarchs of the country. The Musulman law replaced the Roman law, and the Greek and Latin languages, before which the old national idioms of the coasts of Syria, Africa and Spain had long ago disappeared, were ousted in their turn by the Arabic tongue.

These two elements—religion and language—constitute the Arab's contribution to the Musulman civilization. This civilization, despite its brilliant achievements during the first few centuries of Islam, can boast of little that is original. The conquered peoples were all more refined than their nomad conquerors, and the latter borrowed from them in a wholesale fashion. The Arabs translated the works of their scholars and philosophers, drew inspiration from their art, and adopted their agricultural, commercial and industrial methods. The extent and diversity of the countries and the nations upon which they imposed their rule subjected them to a quantity of influences, which blended together, giving the Musulman civilization an aspect of great variety, but little depth, Of these influences, that of Hellenism rivalled that of Persia. This should not surprise us, when we reflect that the Arabs occupied the richest and most populous sections of the contemporary Greek world—Egypt and Syria.

Their architecture gives us a fairly precise idea of the variety and the relative importance of their borrowings. We see in its decoration characteristics which are evidently of Persian or Indian origin, but the general conception, and the essential members of the buildings, reveal an obvious relationship with Byzantine architecture. The predominance of Greek thought is even more plainly evident. Aristotle was the master of the Arab philosophers, who added nothing essential to his philosophy. On the whole, in the intellectual domain, the Musulman civilization did not greatly influence the European peoples. The explanation is simple: there was much in it that was artificial, and the sources upon which it drew most freely were, for the most part, European sources.

But the case is different in respect of the economic domain. Here, thanks to their contact with the West and the far East, the Arabs were valuable intermediaries. From India they imported sugar-cane into Sicily and Africa, rice into Sicily and Spain (whence the Spaniards took it to Italy in the 15th and 16th centuries), and cotton into Sicily and Africa; they acclimatized in Asia the manufacture of silk, which they learned from the Chinese; and from the Chinese also they learned the use and manufacture of paper, without which the invention of printing would have been valueless, or would not have been made; and from China they imported the magnetic compass. But it was a long while before these innovations—with many more—became the property of the European peoples. At first they only helped to make Islam a more formidable enemy to its European neighbours, as being both richer and more perfectly equipped. From the 7th to the 11th century Islam was incontestably the master of the Mediterranean. The ports which the Arabs constructed—Cairo, which succeeded to Alexandria, Tunis, and Kairouan—were the *étapes* of a commerce which circulated from the Straits of Gibraltar to the Indian Ocean, through the Egyptian ports, which were in communication with the Red Sea, and the Syrian ports, which gave access to the caravan route to Baghdad and the Persian Gulf. The navigation of the Christian peoples was restricted to a timid coastwise trade along the shores of the Adriatic and southern Italy, and among the islands of the Archipelago.

## 2. *The Consequences of the Invasion*

An unforeseen event is always followed by a catastrophe in proportion to its importance. It flings itself, so to speak, across the current of historic life, interrupting the series of causes and effects of which this current is constituted, damming them up in some sort, and by their unexpected repercussions overturning the natural order of things. This was what happened at the time of the Musulman invasion. For centuries Europe had gravitated about the Mediterranean. It was by means of the Mediterranean that civilization had extended itself; by means of the Mediterranean the various parts of the civilized world had communicated one with another. On all its shores social life was the same in its fundamental characteristics; religion was the same; manners and customs and ideas were the same, or very nearly so. The Germanic invasion had not changed the situation in any essential respect. In spite of all that had happened, we may say that in the middle of the 7th century Europe still constituted, as in the time of the Roman Empire, a Mediterranean unity.

Now, under the sudden impact of Islam, this unity was abruptly shattered. The greater portion of this familiar sea—which the Romans had called "our sea," *mare nostrum*—became alien and hostile. The intercourse between the West and the East, which had hitherto been carried on by means of this sea, was interrupted. The East and the West were suddenly separated. The community in which they had lived so long was destroyed for centuries to come, and even to-day Europe is still suffering from the consequences of its destruction.

Obliged to meet the menace from the East, the Empire could no longer stand firm on the Danube. The Bulgars, Serbs and Croats spread through the Balkans, and only the cities remained

Greek. The invaders did not mingle with the population, as the Germans had done. The Byzantine Empire ceased to be universal; it became a Greek State.

The Bulgars, in 677, subdued the Slav tribes, and became merged with them in Mesia. In the middle of the 9th century their prince, Boris, was converted by Methodius and took the name of Michael.

The Byzantine Empire, henceforth confined between the coast of Illyria and the Upper Euphrates, devoted the bulk of its forces to withstanding the pressure of Islam. In its long history, down to the day when it finally succumbed, in the middle of the 15th century, under the blows of the Turks, it was still to know some moments of splendour, and was to witness the development of a civilization whose originality consisted in the blending of ancient traditions with orthodox Christianity and an increasing Orientalization. But this history, most of the time, was alien to that of Western Europe. Venice alone kept in touch with Byzantium, and found, in her rôle of intermediary between East and West, the beginning of her future greatness. For the rest, although Byzantium had ceased to intervene in the West, she none the less continued to exercise an influence which was to outlive her by many centuries. It was Byzantium that Christianized the Slavs of the South and East—the Serbs, Bulgars and Russians—and it was the people of the Empire who, after bearing the Turkish yoke for 400 years, reconstituted the Greek nationality in the 20th century.

As for the West, its separation from Byzantium confronted it with a completely novel situation. This separation seemed to exclude it from civilization, since from the beginning of the ages all the forms of civilized life and all social progress had come to it from the East. True, with the Arabs established in Spain and on the coast of Africa the East was at its door. But in spite of material contact, the difference of religious faith prevented any moral contact between its Christian population and this Musulman Orient. For the first time since the formation of the Roman Empire Western Europe was isolated from the rest of the world. The Mediterranean by which it had hitherto kept in touch with civilization was closed to it. This, perhaps, was the most important result, as regards the history of the world, of the expansion of Islam.[1] For the Christianity of the West, when its traditional lines of communication were cut, became a world apart, able to count only on itself, and in respect of its further development it was thrown upon its own resources. Driven off the Mediterranean, it turned to the still barbarous regions beyond the Rhine and the shores of the North Sea. European society, continuously expanding crossed the ancient frontiers of the Roman Empire. A new Europe was created with the rise of the Frankish Empire, in which was elaborated the Western civilization which was one day to become that of the whole world.

[1] See Henri Pirenne, *Mohammed and Charlemagne* (in preparation).

*Book Two*

# THE CAROLINGIAN EPOCH

CHAPTER I

# THE CHURCH

## 1. *The Atony of the Fifth to the Seventh Century*

During the vicissitudes of the 5th, 6th and 7th centuries, while Europe was torn by the conflicts of the Germans, the Empire, and Islam, what became of the Catholic Church, the great force of the near future? It contented itself with continuing to exist, or rather to vegetate. Its influence upon the course of events was negligible; its moral influence over society was imperceptible. And yet, amidst the ruins of the Empire, it remained intact. It had saved its organization, its hierarchy, its incalculable wealth in land. And it had no enemies. The Germans no less than the Romans were its dutiful children. The Arian heresy, as we have seen, was only ephemeral, and never gave it real anxiety.

The apathy of the Church, however, is very simply explained. Something had happened to it which had happened, though in a greater degree, to the whole of society after the invasions: it had become barbarized. The Latin literature of Christendom, which was still so vigorous in the 4th century, the century of Saint Augustine, had nothing to show in the 5th century but epigoni of the type of Salvian. After this the life of the mind became dormant; the vein opened by the Fathers of the Church was exhausted. A few clerks continued to write biographical or historical narratives, but the world had to wait for Gregory the Great before the study of theology and religious and moral philosophy was revived, though in quite a new spirit. More striking still was the inertia of the Church in the face of the pagan or grossly heretical Barbarians who had lately made their way into the Empire, and were living within reach of it. When they did become converted they merely followed the example of their kings, who, for reasons of political interest, or in imitation of Roman manners, had adopted Christianity: as the Franks were converted after the baptism of Clovis. As for the Germans, who in the north of Gaul and beyond the Rhine had preserved their old national cult, the Church made no attempt to bring them into the fold. The apostles to the Salic Franks, St. Amand and St. Remaculus, were inspired by personal enthusiasm. The kings supported their efforts, but we do not find that they received any backing from the ecclesiastical authorities. The latter, indeed, were so far from taking any interest in the apostolate that they left the work which was incumbent upon themselves to foreigners. Introduced into Ireland in the 4th century, Christianity had rapidly spread through the country. In this remote isle, which had no communication with the Continent, it created for itself an original organization, in which the great monastic colonies were the centres of a most ardent religious life. In these centres there were large numbers of ascetics and proselytes, who, from the 6th century onwards, began to leave their native country, some to seek, in distant lands, inaccessible solitudes, and others, souls to be converted. When the Norsemen discovered Iceland in the 9th century they were astonished to find that the only inhabitants of its misty shores were monks who had come from Ireland. They were Irishmen, too, who devoted themselves with such enthusiasm to the conversion of Northern Gaul and Germany. The hagiography of the Merovingian period is teeming with saints to whom are attributed the foundations of a host of monasteries in Northern France and Belgium. St. Columban and St. Gall are the most celebrated representatives of this tribe of missionaries, whose intellectual culture, disinterestedness and enthusiasm found a sad contrast in the boorishness of the Merovingian clergy. They could not, however, rouse the clerics from their apathy. The bishops, nominated by the clergy of the diocese, but really appointed by the kings, rarely owed their sees to anything but the favour of the sovereign. One must have read the portraits which Gregory of Tours has traced of some of his colleagues to form any idea of the state of their knowledge and their morals. Many of them could hardly read, and indulged without concealment in drunkenness and debauchery. The honest Gregory is indignant with such behaviour, yet it is evident, from what he says, that his indignation was but faintly echoed. And what an example he furnishes in his own person—greatly superior though he certainly was to the majority of his colleagues—of the decadence of the Church! The Latin which he writes—as he is well aware—is a barbarous idiom, taking strange liberties with grammar, syntax and the vocabulary; and his morality—but this, unhappily, he does not realize—is capable of very irregular indulgences and very surprising judgements. And after his time things were even worse. At the close of the 7th century and the beginning of the 8th not only the language but the very thought was like that of a paralytic. The so-called Chronicle of Fredegarius, and certain Lives of Saints of this period, are incomparable examples of the inability to express the simplest notions.

Nevertheless, decadent though it was, the Church was the great civilizing force of the period; indeed, we may say the only civilizing force. It was through the Church that the Roman tradition was perpetuated; it was the Church that prevented Europe from relapsing into barbarism. The lay power, left to its own devices, would have been incapable of preserving this precious heritage. Despite the good intentions of the kings, their crude and clumsy administration was quite unequal to the task which they wished to perform. Now, the Church possessed the personnel which the State lacked. As it was formed and developed under the Empire, so it continued after the invasions. The hierarchy was still intact, and, moulded as it was on the pattern of the administrative organization of Rome, it retained its firm and simple structure in the midst of the growing disorder. The metropolitan sees established at the capital of each province, the episcopal sees instituted at the capital of each "city," disappeared, for a time, only in the northern regions. Everywhere else they were spared or respected by the conquerors. While the civil administration lapsed into decadence, the ecclesiastical administration remained unshaken, with the same structure, the same dignitaries, the same principles, the same law, the same language as in the days of the Empire. In the midst of the surrounding anarchy, the Church remained intact, in spite of its temporary decadence; the clergy were protected by the mighty edifice that sheltered them, and by the discipline imposed upon them. Ignorant, negligent and immoral though some of the bishops may have been, they could not absolve themselves from the essential duties of their functions. They were obliged to maintain, in connection with their Cathedral, a school for the education of young scholars. While lay education disappeared, and the State was reduced to employing illiterate servants, the Church continued, by a necessity inherent in its very existence, to train a body of pupils of whom each member was at all events able to read and write Latin. By this very fact it exercised a preponderant influence over secular society; it possessed, without having sought or desired it, the monopoly of knowledge. Its schools, but for rare exceptions, were the only schools, its books the only books. Writing, without which no civilization is possible, appertained so exclusively to the Church from the end of the Merovingian period that even to this day the word that describes the ecclesiastic also describes the scribe: *clerc* in French, *clerk* in English, *klerk* in Flemish and Old German, *diaca* in Old Russian. During the 8th century intellectual culture was confined to a sacerdotal class; so that the Catholic clergy acquired a position which had never been allotted to any other clergy before them. Not only were the clergy venerated because of their religious character; not only did they possess, in the eyes of laymen, the prestige which knowledge enjoys in an ignorant community, but they were also an indispensable auxiliary to civil society. The State could not dispense with their services. In the Carolingian period, when the last traces of lay education had disappeared, it was from the clergy that the State was obliged to borrow its staff of scribes, the heads of its chancellery, and all those agents or counsellors in whom a certain degree of intellectual culture was essential. The State became clericalized, because it could not do otherwise, under penalty of relapsing into barbarism; because it could not find elsewhere than in the Church men capable of understanding and accomplishing the political tasks which were incumbent upon it. And if it could find them only in the Church, this was not because their character as the apostles of Christ made them peculiarly fit to serve it. The servants of Him who has said that His kingdom is not of this world had not learned from Him the conduct of secular affairs. If they had the requisite knowledge it was because they had acquired it from Rome; because the Church to which they belonged had survived the ruin of the ancient world, and because this world was perpetuated in it for the education of the new world. In short, it was not because it was Christian, but because it was Roman that the Church acquired and maintained for centuries its control over society; or, if you will, it exercised a preponderant influence over modern society for so long merely because it was the depositary of a more ancient and more advanced civilization. It goes without saying that the Church profited by this situation to realize its religious ideal, and to bend to its will the State which had called upon its services as auxiliary. The inevitable collaboration between Church and State, which was presently established, bore within it the germ of formidable conflicts, which no one could have foreseen in the beginning.

On entering the service of the State, the Church did not submit itself to its employer. Whatever the concessions which it may have made, at certain moments, of its own free will, or under compulsion, it still remained, with regard to the State, an independent power. It claimed and enjoyed, in Western Europe, a liberty which it did not enjoy in the Roman or the Byzantine Empire. This was not so much because the Western sovereigns never exerted a power comparable to that of the Emperors, as because the Church was from the first in an economic situation which enabled it to live and develop itself on its own resources. And here again we see in the Church the heir of Rome. The immense fortune in real estate which lay at its disposal it owed to Constantine and his successors, who transferred to it the wealth of the pagan temples. They not only made the Church the greatest landed proprietor in the world; they also made it a privileged proprietor, by exempting its members from the poll-tax and its property from the land tax. Both property and privileges were respected by the Barbarian kings, so that at the time when the history of the modern peoples begins the Church was in possession of incomparable wealth. This explains how it was able to pass through the crises of the invasions without becoming enfeebled; how it could safeguard its organization and recruit and maintain its clergy in a time of political and social turmoil.

Thus, from whatever angle we examine it, we see that the Church, despite its decadence in the 5th, 6th and 7th centuries, was still powerful and capable of future development. The cause of its decline was not in itself but in the circumstances of the moment. Moreover, when we speak of its decadence we are thinking only of the official Church, of the secular clergy, the only clergy visible as yet; in addition to whom, in a state of gradual development, were the clergy whom we do not yet perceive, but who were gradually making a place for themselves, and obscurely rehearsing the part which they would presently play: the regular clergy, the monks.

## 2. *The Monks and the Papacy*

The asceticism which necessarily springs from an exclusive conception of Christianity had undergone rapid development, from the 2nd century onwards, in the Eastern provinces of the Roman Empire. For a long while its adepts were simply laymen who renounced the activities and the goods of this world in order to devote themselves in solitude to the salvation of their souls. These solitaries were the first monks (*μοναχος, μονος*). St. Pachomius (348) conceived the notion of imposing a rule upon them, and, for this purpose, of organizing them in a community. The monks who adopted this new kind of life grouped themselves in enclosures formed by cells built around a central chapel. To distinguish them from the solitaries the inhabitants of these pious colonies were given the name of cenobites. To this cenobitic institution belonged the Western monasteries, of which the first was founded in the 6th century, on Monte Cassino, near Naples, by St. Benedict. The originality and also the importance of Benedict's achievement (*c.* 543) was that he withdrew the monk from secular life, making of him a religious bound to his vocation by the three perpetual vows of obedience, poverty and chastity, and imposing upon him the obligation of priesthood. Side by side with the secular clergy, whose origins go back to the constitution of the primitive Church, a new clergy makes its appearance, emerging from asceticism, and unfolding to those who wish to realize it in this world the ideal of the Christian life. Its rule—to which it owes its name of *regular*—is not merely a rule of prayer and of pious exercises: it also requires the monk to honour God by labour—whether by manual work or by study.

The diffusion of the monasteries proceeded rather slowly at the outset. They gradually spread through Italy, and reached the south of Gaul, and then, thanks to the apostolate of the Irish, they established themselves in considerable numbers in the north of the Frankish kingdom during the 7th and 8th centuries.[1] But so far they had no mutual relations, and no influence over the outer world, and it seems that they were by no means favourably regarded by the diocesan bishops, who hardly knew what to do with these newcomers.

It was reserved for the Papacy to utilize this great force, unconscious of its own strength, and to make it serve the State, constituting—so to speak—a permanent reserve army at the disposal of the State. It was the first of the great Popes, Gregory the Great (590–604), who was responsible for this stroke of genius.

Until the reign of Gregory the pre-eminence of the Papacy was ill-defined; it had little basis beyond the twofold quality of the Pope as the successor of St. Peter and the Bishop of Rome. It was manifested rather by the respect which was paid to him than by the authority which he exercised. In the various kingdoms the bishops appointed by the kings paid him deference at the most: their relations with the Papacy went no farther. The Pope himself was regarded by the Patriarchs of Alexandria, Antioch, Jerusalem and Constantinople as an equal merely. The Emperor of Byzantium, indeed, reserved to himself the right to ratify the nomination of

[1] The monasteries of Ireland were very different from the Benedictine monasteries. But the monasteries which the Irish missionaries founded on the Continent were organized in conformity with the Benedictine communities.

the Pope, no less than the nomination of the Patriarchs, or, after Justinian, to have it ratified in his name by the Exarch of Ravenna. The situation of Italy, and especially the position of Rome, since the turmoil of the invasions, restricted the activity of the Popes, or directed it to tasks which had nothing to do with the government of the Church. Since the Emperor no longer resided in the "city," the Pope had actually become its most important personage. It was incumbent on him—in the absence of lay authorities—to negotiate with the invaders, and to supervise the administration, the revictualling and the fortification of the city: and this, as Rome became depopulated and impoverished, rendered more and more arduous the task of keeping its enormous area and its monuments in some sort of order and repair. After the invasion of the Lombards in particular the Popes had to contend against difficulties and dangers with which they could cope only by forcible measures; for the Emperor, engrossed in the defence of the Syrian and Danubian frontiers, left it to the Popes to resist the new enemies, who were obstinately bent on the conquest of Rome. At the most he sent the Popes, from time to time, a few troops, and a few subsidies, both equally inadequate. The Exarch of Ravenna, who was himself threatened, was in no position to furnish effective collaboration. At the moment when Gregory the Great, in 590, ascended the throne of St. Peter, he evidently despaired of the future, comparing Rome to a ship battered by the tempest and on the point of foundering.

Gregory the Great may be regarded as the first interpreter of religious thought after the Fathers of the Church. But he did not continue the work of the Fathers. He was not interested in questions of dogma: for him they had been finally answered. He was concerned rather with drawing the moral consequences from the dogmas, with organizing the Christian life in respect of its aim—in respect of "last things" which were summed up in the terrifying dilemma of Heaven and Hell. His vision, so to speak, was fixed upon the Beyond, and the pictures which he drew of the life to come were enormously effective in helping to give mediaeval religiosity that gloomy and agonized cast, that preoccupation with terror, that obsession with eternal torments, which found their immortal expression in the "Divine Comedy." The Church being the instrument of eternal salvation, its power over men's souls must be augmented in order that they might be saved from the abyss. And here, in Gregory, as in other great mystics—in St. Bernard, for example, and Loyola—that practical genius revealed itself, which, in order to attain the supraterrestrial end that it had proposed to itself, excelled in organizing the affairs of the pressing world which it held in disdain. Perhaps his origin—he came of an ancient family of Roman patricians who had by tradition played their part in the administration of the city—was not without its influence on this side of his character. One can hardly believe on reading his letters, that they were written by the author of the *Moralia* and the *Dialogus*. They show him at work restoring the patrimony of St. Peter—that is, the enormous domains of the Roman Church—scattered all over Italy and the coasts of Illyria and Sicily, which the disorders of the invasions had dismembered, ruined, and disorganized. We see him laying claim to lands that had been alienated or invaded, appointing intendants, laying down the rules which they were to follow, and enforcing the measures necessary for the collection and centralization of the revenues. He therefore merits the twofold and singular honour of being regarded as at once the earliest mystic and the earliest economist of the Middle Ages. For the rest, his economic activity was entirely impregnated with Roman practices, and he did much toward preserving and diffusing, by the intermediary of the Church, the domainal institutions of the Empire. In a few years the task upon which he had embarked was completed. The Papacy found itself in possession of a regular income and abundant resources. It had become the first financial power of its time.

To this first source of strength Gregory added a second, by associating the monks with the Papacy. He was impelled to take this step no less by his leanings to asceticism than by his lucid grasp of realities. He perceived very clearly what an ascendancy the Papacy would acquire from those monasteries which were scattered all over Europe by constituting itself their protector. He did not confine himself to founding new monasteries in the Eternal City; he also conferred upon a number of them privileges of exemption which placed them under the direct authority of the Holy See. Since the days of St. Benedict the monks had formed part of the Church; and from the days of Gregory the Great we may say that they were associated in its activities.

It was, in fact, to the monks directed and organized by him that Gregory confided the great achievement of his pontificate, the evangelization of the Anglo-Saxons.[1] But this would have been impossible if he had not had at his disposal the funds required for its realization; so that the two great reforms of his reign—the reconstitution of the patrimony of St. Peter and the alliance with monasticism—contributed harmoniously to an enterprise which was itself in perfect harmony with the religious ideal and the practical abilities of its initiator.

The conversion of England was a masterpiece of tact, reason and method. After long preparation for their task by the Pope, St. Augustine of Canterbury and his companions went to work in accordance with instructions which were the fruit of ripe meditation, and inspired throughout by charity, indulgence, toleration and common sense. Nothing could be more unlike the rash and enthusiastic attitude of the Celtic missionaries than the patient and prudent behaviour of the missionaries of Gregory. They arrived in England only after they had studied its language, customs and religion. They were careful not to offend the prejudices of the English: they did not try to obtain premature results, and they even renounced their ambition to achieve martyrdom. They won men's confidence before they won their souls: and so they won them completely. Sixty years later the Anglo-Saxons were not only Christians, but were already on the point of furnishing the Church with missionaries worthy of those who had converted them. One hundred and twenty years after the landing of St. Augustine on Hastings beach (596) St. Boniface embarked upon the evangelization of pagan trans-Rhenian Germany (716).

[1] Saint Augustine landed in England in 596: the work of Christianization was practically completed by 655.

The conversion of England marks a decisive stage in the history of the Papacy. The direct foundation of the Pope, the Anglo-Saxon Church, was subject from the beginning to the immediate control and direction of Rome. It was in no sense a national Church; it was apostolic in the full meaning of the term. And the trans-Rhenian Church which it proceeded to organize was given the same character. It is easy to understand what additional strength and glory the prestige and authority of the Papacy won thereby. While in Rome itself the Popes were still regarded by the Emperor of Byzantium and the Exarchs of Ravenna as Patriarchs of the Empire, and were still obliged to apply to them for the ratification of their election, the new Christians of the North revered in the Popes the Vicars of Christ, the representatives of God on earth. Thus the Papacy had made a position for itself which was henceforth incompatible with the state of subordination to the Emperor in which it had hitherto existed. Sooner or later it would break the traditional tie between itself and the Emperor, which, now that there was no longer an Empire in the West, was merely a burden, a humiliation and an embarrassment. If only the Emperor had still been an effective protector, or if he had at least given evidence of his good will! But he not only dissociated himself from Rome, leaving her defenceless against the advance of the Lombards: he even became her adversary.[1]

In the Byzantine *milieu*, torn by theological passions, a new heresy had just emerged: Iconoclasm. The Emperor Leo III not only proposed it (726), but attempted to force it on Rome. This was too much: the Pope refused to submit himself to the will of a master who expected to find him as complaisant as the Patriarchs of Constantinople or Antioch. Gregory II (715–731) confined himself to threats: if the rupture was not effected then and there, it was only because the Imperial tradition was still so potent that he hesitated to take a decisive step. Moreover, to abandon the Emperor was to launch oneself into the unknown, and to risk reprisals which might expose the Church to the gravest perils.

[1] In 653 Constans II sent Martin I into exile. In 692 Justinian II would have done the same to Sergius I if Rome had not rebelled.

Before the Pope could do anything so decisive—before he could assume, in respect of the Emperor, the attitude not of an equal merely, but of a superior—before he could break with the heretic East and establish in the West the bases of a universal Christianity—before he could cease to be Roman in the old sense of the world, and become Catholic—before he could free the spiritual power from the fetters imposed upon it by Caesarism, he must find a powerful and loyal protector. And who, in the Europe of that day, could play such a part? There was only one such man, and he himself was seeking an ally capable of legitimately conveying the crown to him: the Mayor of the Palace of the Merovingian kings.

CHAPTER II

# THE FRANKISH KINGDOM

## 1. *The Dislocation of the State*

Of all the kingdoms founded by the Barbarians on the soil of the Roman Empire, that of the Franks was the only one whose frontiers enclosed a compact block of Germanic population. Even before the conquests of Clovis in Gaul the Salic Franks, the Ripuarian Franks, and the Alamans had colonized, *en masse*, the whole of the left bank of the Rhine, and had pushed forward some considerable distance into the valleys of the Moselle, the Meuse and the Scheldt. Clovis himself, in the beginning, was merely one of the numerous petty kings among whom the government of the Salic Franks was divided. His kingdom, which must have corresponded very nearly with the area of the ancient Roman "city" of Tournai, did not provide him with sufficient force to ensure the success of the attack which he was meditating upon Syagrius, the Roman officer to whom the region between the Loire and the Seine, in the heart of invaded Gaul, still owed obedience. He therefore obtained the collaboration of his kinsmen, the kings of Térouanne and Cambrai. But he alone profited by the victory. Syagrius defeated, he appropriated his territory, and took advantage of his now crushing superiority over his former equals to get rid of them. By violence or by cunning he overthrew or destroyed them, and was acknowledged by their peoples, and in a few years he had extended his power to the whole of the region encircled by the Rhine, from Cologne to the sea. The Alamans, established in Alsace and Eifel, who threatened the new kingdom with a flank attack, were defeated and annexed. Having thus assured himself of the possession of the whole of Northern Gaul, from the Rhine to the Loire, the King of the Franks was able to apply himself to the conquest of wealthy Aquitaine. It was then the country of the Visigoths. Converted to Catholicism since the year 496, Clovis found in their heresy a pretext for making war upon them, defeated them at Vouillé (507) and advanced the frontier to the Pyrenees. Provence still divided him from the Mediterranean. But Theodoric did not intend to allow the Frankish kingdom to extend itself to the gates of Italy; and Clovis had to renounce Provence (which Theodoric, for greater safety, annexed to his own States). His sons, however, completed the task so well begun, seized upon the kingdom which the Burgundi had set up in the valley of the Rhone (532), and took possession of Provence from the Gulf of Lyons to the Rhone. Henceforth the whole of ancient Gaul was subject to the Merovingian dynasty.

Conformably with the Mediterranean character which Western Europe retained until the end of the 7th century, it endeavoured, to begin with, to expand in a southerly direction. For a time Frankish armies disputed Northern Italy with the Lombards. But the Musulman invasion, as we have already seen, was to call a sudden halt to the traditional southward orientation of the Northern countries. The last of the Merovingian conquerors, Dagobert I, directed his efforts towards Germany, and even advanced as far as the Danube. Then the expansion ceased, and decadence set in.

The closing of the Mediterranean by the Musulmans marked not only a new political orientation of Europe, but also, one may say, the end of the ancient world.

For until the reign of Dagobert I the Merovingian State had not broken away from the Roman tradition. The social state of the country, after the profound disorder inflicted upon it by the invasions, reassumed its old Roman character. The lands of the Imperial fisc, it is true, passed to the king, but the great Gallo-Roman landowners, with rare exceptions, had retained their domains, organized as they had been under the Empire. In this connection it is impressive to note that Pope Gregory the Great, in order to restore the administration of the enormous territorial properties of the Church, merely reconstructed the Roman domainal system.

Commerce, once peace was re-established, resumed its activity. Marseilles, the centre for the great maritime trade with the East, became the resort of those Syrian merchants who were also to be found in the more important cities of the south of Gaul, and who, with the Jews, were the principal traders in the country. In the towns of the interior there was still a middle class of traders, some of whom, in the middle of the 6th century, are known to us as wealthy and influential notables.

And thanks to this regular trade, which maintained a considerable circulation of merchandise and money among the population, the king's treasury, fed by the market dues, had always important resources at its disposal: as great as, if not greater than, those which it derived from the revenue of the royal domains and the booty of war.

It is true that the surviving civilization of the Empire had fallen into a state of extreme decadence, but it had retained its essential characteristics.

It is evident that the important officials, who were chosen from among the magnates, were singularly independent in their attitude to the supreme power, and there is no doubt that the impost was often collected by the count for his own benefit; which explains why it was beginning to be described, in the language of the day, as an "exaction."

The enfeeblement of the old Roman administration, which had now lost touch with Rome, and of which the king, with some difficulty, was preserving the last vestiges, allowed the aristocracy of great landowners to assume a position of increasing strength with regard to the king and to society. In the north, especially in Austrasia, where the Roman influence was almost entirely effaced, it assumed, from the 7th century, an almost absolute preponderance.

This aristocracy, whose influence was continually increasing, was not in any real sense a nobility. It was distinguished from the rest of the nation, not by its juridical status, but only by its social position. Its members, in the language of their contemporaries, were grandees (*majores*), magnates (*magnates*) and potentates (*potentes*), and their power was derived from their fortune. All were great landed proprietors; some were descended from rich Gallo-Roman families, who were wealthy before the Frankish conquest; others were favourites, whom the kings had generously endowed with estates, or counts who had profited by their position to create spacious domains for themselves. For that matter, whether they were of Roman or Germanic birth, the members of this aristocracy formed a group which was held together by community of interests, and in which differences of origin soon disappeared and were merged in an identity of manners. In proportion as the State which they provided with its most important agents became more incapable of fulfilling its essential and primordial task—that is, of safeguarding the persons and the property of its subjects—their preponderance grew more marked. Their personal situation profited by the progress of the general anarchy, and the public insecurity augmented their private influence. As officers of the king the counts persecuted and fleeced the poor people whom they should have protected; but from the moment when these same poor people, having no alternative, had surrendered their property and their persons, and had been annexed to the domains of the counts, the latter, in their rôle of great landowners, granted them their powerful protection. Thus the very officers of the State worked against the State, and by continually extending their patronage over the inhabitants, and their private property over the land, they deprived the king, with surprising rapidity, of both his immediate subjects and his taxpayers.

For the relation which was established between the powerful and the weak was not the mere economic relation which exists between a landowner and his tenant. Born of the need of effective protection in a society given over to anarchy, it created between them a peculiar bond, as between superior and subordinate, which extended to the whole person, recalling in its intimacy and its closeness the family tie. The "contract of recommendation" which made its appearance from the 6th century onwards gave the protected man the name of vassal (*vassus*) or servitor, and the protector the name of ancient or seigneur (*senior*). The seigneur was pledged not only to provide for the subsistence of his vassal, but also at all times to grant him his succour and aid, and to represent him before the law. The freeman who sought protection might preserve the appearance of liberty, but in actual fact he had become a client, a *sperans*, of the *senior*.

The protectorate which the seigneur exercised over freemen in virtue of the "contract of recommendation" was naturally exercised with greater strictness over the individuals belonging to his domain—old Roman colonists, attached to the soil (*adscripti glebae*), or serfs, the descendants of Roman or Germanic slaves, whose very persons, by virtue of their birth, were the lord's private property. Over all this dependent population the seigneur exerted an authority which was at once patriarchal and patrimonial, like that of a magistrate and judge combined. In the beginning this was merely the factual position. But nothing more clearly illustrates the impotence of the State than the way in which it was forced to recognize the situation. From the 6th century onwards the king granted privileges of immunity in ever-increasing numbers. There were privileges granting a great landowner exemption from the right of the public functionaries to intervene in his domain. Thus the privileged landowner took the place of the officers of the State on his own territory. His competence, purely private in origin, received its legal consecration. In short, the State capitulated to him. And as this immunity became more widely diffused, the kingdom was covered with an increasing number of domains in which the king could not intervene, so that in the end there was nothing under his immediate control save the few inconsiderable regions which the great landowners had not yet absorbed.

The situation was the more serious in that of the properties of the king himself, which had originally comprised all the territorial possessions of the Roman State, there was nothing left, at the close of the Merovingian period, but insignificant fragments. Morsel by morsel, they had been ceded to the aristocracy with a view to purchasing its loyalty. The continual divisions of the monarchy among the descendants of Clovis, the alternate division and reunion of the kingdoms of Austrasia and Burgundy, the constant re-tracing of frontiers, and the civil wars that resulted therefrom, offered the magnates an excellent opportunity of bargaining for the price of their devotion to the princes whom the chances of inheritance had called to reign over them, and who, to assure themselves of the crown, were quite ready to sacrifice the patrimony of the dynasty.

For the first time there was a growing opposition which was to manifest itself between the Romanized aristocracy of Neustria and the magnates of Austrasia, who had remained more faithful to Germanic manners and institutions. The advent of the aristocracy very naturally provoked a manifestation of local influence; and so diversity took the place of monarchical unity.

The conquest of the Mediterranean by the Musulmans was fated to precipitate the political and social evolution which was already commencing. Hitherto, in the midst of a society that was tending to become a régime of seigneurial landowners, the towns, and with them a free bourgeoisie, had been kept alive by commerce.

In the second half of the 7th century all trade ceased on the shores of the Western Mediterranean. Marseilles, deprived of her ships, was dying of asphyxia, and in less than half a century all the cities in the south of France had lapsed into a state of utter decadence. Trade, no longer fed by sea-borne traffic, came to a standstill throughout the country: the middle class disappeared: there were no longer merchants by profession; there was no circulation of goods, and as a natural result the market dues no longer fed the royal treasury, which was henceforth unable to defray the expenses of government.

Henceforth the landed aristocracy represented the only social force. The king was ruined, but the aristocracy, with its land, possessed wealth and authority. It only remained for it to seize political power.

## 2. *The Mayors of the Palace*

The last of the Merovingians have been described by tradition as "idle kings," *rois fainéants*: but they could more truly be described as impotent kings, for their inaction was explained, not by their idleness or their apathy, but by their weakness and lack of power. After the middle of the 7th century, although they still reigned, it was the magnates who governed, established on the ruins of the monarchy which they had defeated, whose subjects they had divided among themselves, and whose functions they performed. In each of the three portions into which the monarchy was divided —Neustria, Austrasia and Burgundy—as king succeeded to king, the mayor of the palace became metamorphosed into the minister of the king, the representative, at his court, of the aristocracy. In actual fact it was henceforth the mayor of the palace, supported by the aristocracy, who governed the country. Of the mayors of the palace one—the Burgundian—disappeared before long, and the other two came into conflict. The landed aristocracy of Austrasia, more powerful than the great landowners of Neustria, being farther removed from the king and the old Roman administration, inevitably won the upper hand in a State exclusively based on territorial wealth.

The struggle was just as unequal between the mayor of Austrasia, Pippin, who represented the magnates, and the mayor of Neustria, Ebroin, who had remained loyal to the old conception of royalty: Pippin was victorious. Thereafter there was only one mayor of the palace for the whole of the monarchy, and it was the Carolingian family that provided him.

For a long while this family had held in the north of the kingdom a position which it owed to its territorial possessions. Its domains were many, above all in that semi-Roman, semi-Germanic region of which Liége, then a mere village, was the centre, and were distributed on either side of the linguistic frontier, in Hesbaye, Condroz and Ardenne; Andenne and Herstal were its favourite residences. Wealthy marriages increased its ascendancy. Of the union between the daughter of Pippin of Landen and the son of Ansegisel of Metz was born Pippin of Herstal, the first of the race to play a part of whom history has any record. We know that he fought with success against the pagan Frisians, who were troubling the northern parts of the kingdom by their incursions, and that he thereby won a popularity for himself and his family which lifted them out of obscurity. Sending his natural son Charles Martel to continue the struggle against the Barbarians, he himself led his vassals and his loyal supporters, inured to the hardships of frontier fighting, against Ebroin, whom he conquered, and thenceforth he governed the whole kingdom as regent. It was well for the kingdom that the government was in the hands of this robust warrior at the moment when the Arabs of Abderrahman crossed the Pyrenees and invaded Aquitaine. Charles Martel offered them battle on the plains of Poitiers, and the charge of the Musulman cavalry was broken against the ranks of his heavy footsoldiers. The literary decadence of this period was so complete that we have no account of this decisive battle. That, however, is of little importance; its result was enough to immortalize it. The invasion was checked: the invaders retreated, and the Musulmans retained no possessions in Gaul apart from the environs of Narbonne, from which Pippin expelled them in 759.

The victory of Poitiers made Charles Martel the master of the kingdom; and he took advantage of this to give it a strong military organization. Hitherto the army had consisted only of freemen, levied in the counties in time of war. It was a mere militia of footsoldiers, equipped at their own cost; difficult to mobilize and slow in its movements. After Poitiers Charles decided to create a cavalry—following the example of the Arabs—which could rapidly confront the enemy and replace the advantage of numbers by that of mobility. Such a novelty called for a radical transformation of traditional usages. It was out of the question to expect freemen to maintain a warhorse and acquire the costly equipment of the horse-soldier, or to undergo the long and difficult apprenticeship that would qualify them to fight on horseback.

To attain his object, Martel had to create a class of warriors with resources to correspond with the part they were expected to play.[1] A generous distribution of land was made to the strongest vassals of the mayor of the palace, who did not hesitate, for this purpose,

[1] It is interesting to note that in Russia, in the 15th century, Ivan III created a cavalry arm in the same fashion. He even gave land to serfs. (Milioukov, *Histoire de Russie*, vol. i, p. 117.)

to secularize a good number of ecclesiastical holdings. Each man-at-arms thus provided with a tenure—or, to employ the technical term, a benefice—was required to rear a warhorse and to do military service whenever required. An oath of fidelity confirmed his obligations. The vassal, who originally was only a servant, thus became a soldier whose livelihood was assured by the possession of landed property. This institution was soon introduced throughout the kingdom. The immense domains of the aristocracy enabled each of its members to form a troop of horse, and they did not fail to do so. The original name of the benefice was presently replaced by that of fief. But the feudal organization itself, in all its essential features, was comprised in the measures taken by Charles Martel. This was the greatest military reform that Europe was to experience before the appearance of permanent armies; but, as we shall presently see, its repercussions on society and the State were even more profound than those of permanent armies. Fundamentally it was merely an adaptation of the army to a period when the whole economic life of the country was dominated by the great domain, and it resulted in giving the landed aristocracy both military and political power. The old army of freemen did not disappear, but it was now merely a reserve to which less and less recourse was made.

The monarchy allowed this transformation to be effected, which placed the army beyond its control, leaving it only the vain appearance of power. Henceforth the kings were so completely effaced in the shadow of their powerful mayor of the palace that we can hardly distinguish one from another, so that the historical experts disagree as to their names. Einhard is doubtless only echoing the opinion current in the entourage of the Carolingians when he amuses himself by caricaturing the monarchs as stupid and rustic persons, with unkempt beards and worn garments, like those of the peasants of their lost domains, and travelling, like the peasants, in an ordinary ox-cart. He has neither pity nor respect for them; there is nothing about them that he does not make fun of, down to their long hair, an old Germanic symbol of the royal power.

### 3. *The New Royalty*

Despite the service which Charles Martel rendered to Christianity under the walls of Poitiers, the Church preserved no sympathetic memory of him. It resented his policy of secularization; and it did not forget his refusal to come to the help of the Papacy, hard pressed by the Lombards, even when Gregory III paid him the honour of sending him a special embassy in order to make the solemn presentation of the keys of the tomb of the Apostles. Less absorbed in warfare, his son Pippin the Short, on the contrary, who succeeded him in 741 as mayor of the palace and ruler of the kingdom, was almost from the first in constant touch with Rome.

At the moment of his accession to power the Anglo-Saxon missions to the pagan Germans beyond the Rhine had recently begun their task under the direction of St. Boniface (719, 755 in Friesland). Pippin's treatment of St. Boniface was marked by a degree of zeal and benevolence to which the apostles of Christianity were little accustomed. His conduct, however, was inspired by political interest. He understood that the most effectual means of mitigating the barbarism of the Frisians, the Thuringians, the Bavarians and the Saxons, thus making them less dangerous neighbours and paving the way for future annexation, was to begin by converting them. Hence his interest in the plans of Boniface, and the support which he gave him, and the favours which he bestowed upon the see of Mayence, which, being created the metropolis of the new Germanic Church, allied the latter, from its birth, to the Frankish Church.

Boniface, however, being as an Anglo-Saxon the obedient son of the Papacy, did not set to work until he had asked and obtained the consent and the instructions of Rome. He thus became, thanks to his intimate relations with the mayor of the palace, the natural intermediary between him and the Pope. And by the very force of circumstances, each of them, having need of the other, asked nothing better than to be brought into closer touch with him. Pippin, already king *de facto*, aspired to the status of king *de jure*. But he hesitated to wrest the crown from its lawful possessor, the incarnation of a long dynastic tradition. In order to accomplish without scruple the *coup d'état* which had become inevitable, he must be able to shelter himself behind the highest possible moral authority, by obtaining the public approval of the Roman pontiff. As for the Pope, his position was equally untenable, and clamouring for a solution. The moment had arrived for him to break with the Emperor, whose heretical Caesarism was becoming more and more arrogant, and who, either through impotence, or in a spirit of malevolence, was allowing the Lombards to advance to the very walls of Rome. (Some time after 744 the Lombard king Aistulf had seized the Exarchate.) Here too a *coup d'état* was imminent, and in order to accomplish it the help which Charles Martel had refused some years earlier was required of his son.

With the ground prepared, the alliance established itself automatically. In 751 Pippin's deputies sent to the Pope and solemnly asked him whether it was not fitting that the royal title should appertain rather to him who exercised the supreme authority than to him who enjoyed only the appearance of authority. No less solemnly, the Pope corroborated their opinion on this point of political morality. A few weeks later Pippin had himself proclaimed king by an assembly of magnates. The last descendant of Clovis —Childeric—was sent to end his days in a monastery. We do not know the date of his death. Never was the disappearance of a dynasty attended by such indifference; never was a *coup d'état* so easy and so necessary.

Mounted upon the throne by the help of the Pope, the first of the Carolingian kings was not slow to repay the debt thus contracted. Stephanus II came in person, in the following year, to claim his assistance against the Lombards. This was the first time in the history of the Church that a Pope had been seen to the north of the Alps. With this the die was cast; Rome broke with Constantinople and associated her destiny with that of the dynasty she had lately consecrated.

Pippin solemnly promised to march against the Lombards, and, having conquered them, to give to the Roman Church the territory surrounding the Eternal City. Neither Pippin nor Stephanus was deterred for a moment by the notion that they were thus disposing of a region whose legitimate possessor was the Emperor. The campaign which was fought in 754 gave the victory to the Franks.[1] The Pope[2] received the promised territory: the State of the Church was founded. The capital of the ancient world, now the capital of the Christian world, was amenable henceforth only to the successor of St. Peter. At the same time, this question of the temporal sovereignty of the Pope gave rise to serious complications and conflicts. The Papal State was small and feeble; it was bound before long to succumb to the assaults of the Lombards unless it could count on the protection of the conqueror who had just bestowed it upon the Church. How could the independency of the Papacy be reconciled with the urgent need of military tutelage? While waiting for a more satisfactory solution, Stephanus adopted the emergency measure of bestowing upon Pippin a title which could be interpreted in any sense, according to circumstances, but which established a permanent bond between the Frankish king and Rome: the title of *patricius Romanorum*, Roman patrician.

The first war of the new dynasty was thus undertaken in the interest of the Church; and this was quite consistent with the character which had been impressed upon the dynasty at the outset. The royal power of the Merovingians had been purely secular: but that of the Carolingians reveals a profoundly religious imprint. The ceremony of consecration, which appeared for the first time at the coronation of Pippin, made the sovereign in some sort a sacerdotal figure. The king affirmed his submission to the commands of God and his desire to serve Him, not merely by including the Cross among his emblems, but by entitling himself, in Christian humility, "King by the grace of God." From this time forward—and here the Carolingian monarchy was inaugurating the tradition which was to outlive it by many centuries—the ideal of the king was not to be Caesar, a potentate deriving his power and authority only from earthly sources; but to ensure that the divine precepts prevailed on earth, and to govern in accordance with Christian morality: that is, in accordance with the Church. This, of course,

[1] Aistulf presently renewed the campaign, and Pippin returned in 756.
[2] Stephanus III; Stephanus II having died in 752. (*Tr.*)

was the ideal which St. Boniface and Stephanus II were bound to set before Pippin, and this ideal he bequeathed to Charlemagne.[1] We find it expressed in all the treatises of the 9th century on the sovereign power; in the *Via Regia* of Smaragdus as in the *De rectoribus christianis* of Sedulius. Actually, it made religion an affair of State. Only those who belonged to the Christian society could belong to the public society, and excommunication was equivalent to outlawry.

[1] The ancient or Roman ideal of monarchical power was replaced by the Christian ideal until its reappearance in the 12th century.

## CHAPTER III

# THE RESTORATION OF THE EMPIRE IN THE WEST

### I. *Charlemagne* (768–814)

Charlemagne conferred the title of Great upon himself, and posterity has ratified this title so completely that it has, by a unique phenomenon, combined it with his name (Charlemagne, *Carolus magnus*). Caesar and Napoleon alone enjoy a fame universal as his. Just as in the Germanic languages "Caesar" (Kaiser) became the synonym for "Emperor," so in the Slav tongues, and in Hungarian, Charles (*Carol*, *Kiral*, *Kral*) has acquired the significance of "king." In the Middle Ages the Carolingian legend was one of the most prolific sources of literature in the vulgar tongue. From this legend proceeded the oldest French epic poem: the *Chanson de Roland*. And again, during the Renaissance, it inspired Tasso and Ariosto.

If we examine it more closely, however, we soon perceive that the reign of Charlemagne, from whatever point of view we regard it, was only the continuation, and, as it were, the prolongation of his father's reign. It exhibits no originality: the alliance with the Church, the struggle against the pagans—the Lombards and Musulmans—the transformations in the methods of government, the endeavour to rouse scholarship from its torpor—the germ of all these things is visible under Pippin. Like all those who have changed history, Charles did no more than accelerate the evolution which social and political needs had imposed upon his time. The part he played was so completely adapted to the new tendencies of his epoch that it is very difficult to distinguish how much of his work was personal to himself and how much it owed to the force of circumstances.

At the moment when he succeeded to his father (768) the religious question, or, if you will, the ecclesiastical question (which at this period was one and the same thing) was predominant above all others, and its solution was imperative. The conversion of Germany was still incomplete, and no definite *modus vivendi* had been found between the King of the Franks and the Papacy, which was still threatened by the Lombards. We may say that Charles's utmost efforts during the first part of his reign were directed to the accomplishment of this twofold task.

Beyond the Rhine was a powerful nation which still retained its independence and was loyal to its ancient national cult: the Saxons, established between the Ems and the Elbe, from the shores of the North Sea to the Hartz Mountains. Of all the Germans, they alone, in the great upheaval of the invasions, had put to sea in search of new territories. During the whole of the 5th century their ships had harried the coasts of Gaul and Britain. There were Saxon settlements—which have left their traces to this day in the formation of place-names—at the mouths of the Canche and the Loire. But it was only in Britain that the Saxons and the Angles—a people from the south of Jutland, closely akin to them—had established themselves permanently. They drove the Celtic population of the island into the hilly or mountainous regions of the west—into Wales and Cornwall—whence, finding themselves too closely packed, they migrated, in the 6th century, to Armorica, which thenceforth took the name of Brittany, just as Britain[1] itself was called Angle-land, England, after its invaders. Seven small Anglo-Saxon kingdoms, whose names survive to this day in those of as many English counties, were established on the territory abandoned by its old inhabitants. But these insular Saxons did not remain in touch with their fellows on the Continent. They had so far forgotten them that when, after their conversion by the missionaries of Gregory the Great, they themselves undertook to convert the Germans, their missionaries went not to the Saxons, but to Upper Germany.

Even as late as the middle of the 8th century the continental

[1] Bretagne = Britanny *or* Britain. (*Tr.*)

Saxons, by a singular chance, had never been subjected to Roman or Christian influence. While their neighbours were becoming Romanized or were converted to Christianity, they remained purely German, and during the long centuries of their isolation their primitive institutions, like their national cult, had developed and become firmly established. The Frankish kingdom, their immediate neighbour, was incapable of influencing them by its prestige and its power of attraction, as the Roman Empire had formerly influenced the Barbarians. They had preserved their independence, and they clung to this all the more tenaciously in that it permitted them, under the pretext of war, to pillage the frontier provinces. They held fast to their religion as the token and guarantee of their independence.

Charles's Saxon campaigns of 780 and 804 may be regarded as the first of the European wars of religion. Hitherto Christianity had been peacefully diffused among the Germans. On the Saxons it was imposed by force. They were compelled to accept baptism, and the death penalty was decreed against those who should continue to sacrifice to "idols." This new policy was the consequence of the ecclesiastical character which the monarchy had recently assumed. Holding his power from God, the king could not permit dissent in the matter of faith or worship among his subjects. To refuse baptism, or, having received it, to violate the baptismal promises, was to leave the community of the Church, and thereby to outlaw oneself: it was to commit a twofold act of infidelity towards the Church and the State. Hence the violence and the massacres in the wars against the Saxons, and hence too the obstinacy with which they defended their gods, the guardians of their liberty. For the first time Christianity encountered, among the pagans, a national resistance; because for the first time it was forced upon them by conquest. The Anglo-Saxons were converted by the words of a few monks. The Saxons of the Continent fought desperately to preserve their cult, and this struggle was the first of the series of bloody conflicts which the doctrine of the State religion was to provoke in the course of the ages.

It must be recognized, however, that the security of the Frankish kingdom necessitated the conquest of this people, who represented a continual menace on the northern frontier. The annexation and conversion of Saxony brought the whole of the ancient Germany into the community of European civilization. When they were completed the eastern frontier of the Carolingian Empire extended to the Elbe and the Saale. Thence it ran to the head of the Adriatic, across the mountains of Bohemia and the Danube, including the land of the Bavarians, whose duke, Tassilo, was deposed in 787. Beyond this was the region of barbarism: Slavs on the east, Avars in the south.

And the Avars had to be fought immediately. This nation of horsemen, of Finnish origin, who in the 6th century had annihilated the Gepidae in conjunction with the Lombards, had since then established themselves in the valley of the Danube, whence they harried both the Byzantine Empire and Bavaria. Several expeditions were needed to effect their purpose. These were campaigns of extermination. The Avars were massacred to the point of disappearing as a people, and even in our days the Russian proverb: "He has vanished like the Avars," recalls the impression that must have been produced in Eastern Europe by the annihilation of these cruel and savage raiders, who for a century had subjected the Slavs of the Carpathians to an insupportable tyranny. The operation completed, Charles, to guard against further aggression, threw a *march* or *mark* across the valley of the Danube: that is, a defensive territory under military administration. This was the Eastern March (*marca orientalis*), the point of departure of modern Austria, which has retained the name.

Before the end of the 7th century the Slavs had advanced into Central Europe. They had taken possession of the country abandoned by the Germans between the Vistula and the Elbe, and by the Lombards and the Gepidae in Bohemia and Moravia. Thence they had crossed the Danube, and had penetrated into Thrace, where they scattered through the country until they reached the shores of the Adriatic.

On this side also it was necessary to assure the security of the Empire. From 807 onwards other marches or marks were established along the Elbe and the Saale, barring the further progress of the Slav tribes of the Wends, Sorabi (Sorbs) and Obodrites.

This frontier was at the same time—as the Rhine had been in the 4th and 5th centuries—the frontier between Christian Europe and the pagan world. It is interesting, as illustrating the religious ideas of the time, to note that on the frontier there was a temporary revival of slavery. The Slavs, as pagans, were beyond the pale of humanity, and those who were taken prisoner were sold like cattle; and the word for slave in all Western languages (*esclave*, *sklave*, *slaaf*), is merely the name of the Slav people. For the people of the 9th and 10th century the "slave" was what the "black" was for the people of the 17th, 18th and 19th centuries. The economic constitution of the epoch, as we shall presently see, had no need of slave labour, and this, no doubt, explains the fact that there was no great development of the slave trade or of slavery.

At the other side of Europe, along the Pyrenees, the kingdom was in contact not with the pagan Barbarians, but with the Musulmans. Since their defeat at Poitiers they had not again threatened Gaul. The rearguard which they had left in Narbonne had been driven back by Pippin the Short. Spain, where the Caliphate of Cordova had lately been established, no longer looked toward the north, and the activities of the brilliant civilization which unfolded itself under the first Omayyads were directed towards the Islamic settlements on the shores of the Mediterranean. The rapidity of the progress made by Islam in the sciences, arts, industry, and commerce, and all the refinements of civilized life, is almost as amazing as the rapidity of its conquests. But the natural consequence of this progress was to divert its energies from the great enterprises of proselytism and to concentrate them upon itself. While science progressed and art flourished, religious and political quarrels broke out. Spain had her share of these, like the rest of the Musulman world. It was one of these quarrels that gave rise to Charlemagne's expedition beyond the Pyrenees. Three Arab emirs, at war with the Caliph of Cordova, had applied to him for assistance. He came in person, in 778, at the head of an army, and drove the Musulmans back across the Ebro, but he was unsuccessful at the siege of Saragossa,[1] and recrossed the Pyrenees after a somewhat inglorious campaign, the only result of which was the erection of the Spanish March between the Ebro and the Pyrenees. This afterwards served the petty Christian kingdoms which had established themselves in the mountains of Asturias as an advance-post against the Arabs in the long struggle which was to terminate, in the 15th century, in the liberation of the Peninsula.[2] Charlemagne's contemporaries were hardly aware of this expedition. The memory of Count Roland, killed in a skirmish with the Basques, who fell upon the baggage-train of the army in the pass of Roncesvalles, was perpetuated, at first, only among the people of his province in the neighbourhood of Coutances. It took the religious and warlike enthusiasm that seized upon Europe at the time of the first Crusade to make Roland the most heroic of the paladins of the French and Christian epic, and to transform the campaign in which he fell into a gigantic attack upon Islam by "Carles li reis nostre emperere magne."

Of all the wars of Charlemagne the campaigns against the Lombards were the most important in respect of their political results, and they also very plainly reveal the intimate connection between Charles's policy and that of his father. The alliance with the Papacy compelled them to fight the Lombards, not only in the interests of the country, but also in the interest of the King of the Franks. Pippin, towards the end of his reign, had hoped to conclude a pacific agreement with the Lombards. Charles, accordingly, married the daughter of their king, Didier. But this marriage was like all royal matches in which there is no compatibility of thought and interest; it served no purpose. The Lombards continued to threaten Rome, and their king entered into dangerous intrigues against his son-in-law with the Duke of the Bavarians and Charles's own sister-in-law. Charles repudiated his wife and crossed the Alps in 773. The dynasty was dethroned, and Charles proclaimed

[1] This city, however, had declared itself independent of the Omayyad Caliphate.

[2] Barcelona was taken in 801 by Louis, ruling in Aquitaine, and the March was then established.

himself King of the Lombards. Didier, after prolonged resistance in Pavia, was sent to a monastery.

Thus the Lombard State, whose birth had destroyed the political unity of Italy, brought upon the country, as it perished, a foreign conqueror. Henceforth it was merely an appendage of the Frankish monarchy, and it broke away from the Franks at the end of the 9th century only to fall, before long, into the hands of the Germans. By a complete reversal of the course of history, the Lombard power, which had formerly annexed the north of Europe, was now annexed by it; and in a certain sense this destiny was merely a consequence of the political upheavals which had shifted the centre of gravity of the Western world from the Mediterranean to the north of Gaul. And yet its fate was decided by Rome—but by the Rome of the Popes. One does not see what interest could have induced the Carolingians to attack and conquer the Lombard kingdom if their alliance with the Papacy had not constrained them to do so. Here for the first time the influence is plainly manifested which the Church, once rid of the Byzantine tutelage, was henceforth to exercise over European politics. Henceforth the State could not dispense with the Church; between the two an association of mutual service was established, which, by constantly bringing the two powers into co-operation, led also to the continual amalgamation of spiritual and political questions, making religion an essential factor of the political order. The reconstitution of the Roman Empire in the year 800 was the definitive manifestation of this new situation, and the pledge of its future duration.

## 2. *The Empire*

Enlarged by conquest until it extended to the Elbe and the Danube in the east, and to Benevento and the Ebro in the south, the Frankish monarchy, at the close of the 8th century, comprised nearly the whole of the Christian Occident. The small Anglo-Saxon and Spanish kingdoms, which it had not absorbed, were a negligible quantity; moreover, they paid the monarchy a deference which practically amounted to the recognition of its protectorate. And in actual fact, the power of Charlemagne extended to all countries and all peoples that recognized in the Pope of Rome the Vicar of Christ and the head of the Church. Outside this area was the barbaric world of paganism, the hostile world of Islam, and the old Byzantine Empire: Christian, indeed, but marked by a highly capricious orthodoxy, which was centring itself more and more upon the Patriarch of Constantinople, and ignoring the Pope. Further, the sovereign of this immense monarchy was at once the debtor and protector of the Church. Its faith was as firmly founded as its zeal for religion was ardent. Is it surprising that under these circumstances the idea presented itself to the Papacy of profiting by so favourable a conjunction to reconstitute the Roman Empire? —but a Roman Empire whose head, crowned by the Pope in the name of God, would owe his power only to the Church, and would exist only to aid the Church in its mission: an Empire which, not being of secular origin, would owe nothing to men, and would not, properly speaking, be a State, but would be conterminous with the community of the faithful, whose temporal organization it would be, directed and inspired by the spiritual authority of the successor of St. Peter. In this way Christian society would be given its definitive form. The authority of the Pope and that of the Emperor, while remaining distinct one from the other, would nevertheless be as closely associated as the soul with the flesh in the human body. What St. Augustine had desired would be accomplished. The terrestrial State would be but the preparation for the journey to the Celestial City. A grandiose but purely ecclesiastical conception; Charlemagne seems never to have realized exactly its whole scope and all its consequences. His simple and positive genius could not have understood that the part which was assigned to him went far beyond that of a mere protector of the Pope and of religion. It may be, however, that he had some suspicion of the fact, and that before crossing the Rubicon in support of the Church he may have shown some hesitation and asked for further light on the matter. To make short work of the affair, the Pope, sure of his man, ventured on a sudden *coup*.

In the year 800, in the basilica of the Lateran at the termination of the Christmas mass, Leo III went up to the King of the Franks, and amidst the acclamation of the people placed the crown upon his head, and having saluted him with the name of Emperor, prostrated himself before him and "adored" him in accordance with the Byzantine ritual. The decisive step was taken; the Roman Empire was reconstituted, and by the hands of the successor of St. Peter.

Charles manifested some displeasure. He must have thought it strange that he, who had come to Rome merely to quell a revolt, and who a few days earlier had sat as judge between the Pope and the magnates of the city, should now receive the Imperial crown from one whom he regarded as his protégé. In 813 he had the offending ceremonial altered for the benefit of his son Louis, whom he appointed his successor; the crown was laid upon the altar, and Louis set it on his head with his own hands, without the intervention of the Pope. This innovation, which was subsequently abandoned, did not in any way affect the character of the Empire. Willy-nilly, it remained a creation of the Church; something external to and above the monarch and the dynasty. Its origin was in Rome, and the Pope alone could dispose of the Imperial crown.

This he did, of course, not as prince of Rome, but as the successor and representative of St. Peter. Just as he received his authority from the Apostle, it was in the name of the Apostle that he conferred the Imperial power. That power, and his own authority, proceeded directly from the same divine source, and the mosaic of St. John Lateran, which represents Leo III and Charlemagne kneeling at the feet of St. Peter, and receiving from him, one the keys, and the other the banner, symbolizes very exactly the nature of their powers, combined in their origin but distinct in their exercise.[1]

But in order that practice should correspond with theory, in order that the spiritual and the temporal power should not encroach upon each other, or rather, in order that their inevitable mutual encroachments should not lead to conflicts, and shake the majestic edifice that rested upon them, it was necessary that they should

[1] In his official title Charles styles himself *Deo coronatus*, which perfectly corresponds with the conception which we are endeavouring to explain.

be associated, and that they should, as it were, keep step in a spirit of intimate and absolute confidence. But charged, as they were, the one with the government of men's souls, and the other with the government of their bodies, who was to indicate the exact limits of their competence? It is all the more impossible to trace them, inasmuch as the Pope's authority over the Catholic hierarchy was still undefined. The Emperor appointed bishops, convoked synods, and legislated in respect of matters of ecclesiastical discipline and religious instruction. In the case of a Charlemagne, this presented no inconvenience. But after him? How safeguard the Pope against the intentions of his successors? And how, on the other hand, were his successors to be safeguarded against the intentions of the Pope? For if the Imperial idea brought the State into the Church, it also brought the Church into the State. And what would happen when the successor of St. Peter felt it incumbent upon him to intervene in the civil government, to correct or guide it?

Until such time as the future should propose and debate these formidable problems, the restoration of the Empire was evidently to the common advantage of religious and civil society. Thanks to the zeal and vigilance of the Emperor, the Church enjoyed a tranquillity, an authority, an influence and a prestige which it had not known since the days of Constantine. Charles extended his solicitude to the material needs of the clergy, their moral condition, and their apostolate. He showered donations upon sees and monasteries, and placed them under the protection of "advocates," appointed by himself; and he made the tithe compulsory throughout the Empire. He was careful to appoint as bishops only men as noted for the purity of their morals as for their piety; he encouraged the conversion of the Slavs on the frontier; above all, he urged the bishops to improve the education of the clergy, and, faithfully seconded by Alcuin, he required the cathedral and monastery schools to observe the exact rules of the chant, and imposed upon them the graphological reform which gave rise to the Caroline "minuscule," so clearly formed that the Italian printers of the Renaissance borrowed from it the characters of modern typography.

The study of the Holy Scriptures was revived, and also of classic literature, and in the schools a generation of clerks was trained who professed the same disdain for the barbarity of Merovingian Latin as the humanists were to nourish, seven hundred years later, for the scholastic jargon of *magistri nostri*. There were even those who studied the most varied rhythms of prosody, so that modern scholars have been able to compile an anthology of 9th century poems, some of which are not lacking in charm. But this poetry was merely the recreation of workers whose inspirations and tendencies were essentially religious. The so-called Carolingian Renaissance was as the poles removed from the Renaissance properly so-called. There was nothing in common between the two, apart from a renewal of intellectual activity. The true Renaissance, purely secular, steeped itself in the ideas of the classic authors. The Carolingian Renaissance, exclusively ecclesiastical and Christian, regarded the classic authors merely as models of style. For them, study was justified only by its religious aims. The three fingers that held the pen were, so they told themselves, the symbol of the three Persons of the Holy Trinity. Like the Jesuits of the 16th century, the Carolingian clerks wrote only to the glory of God, and while we must not carry the comparison too far, their attitude toward antiquity was not dissimilar to that adopted by the Company of Jesus.

It was not only for the sake of the Church that Charlemagne founded and endowed schools. Since lay education had disappeared the State had perforce to recruit the élite of its officials from among the clergy, or else relapse into barbarism. Under Pippin the Short the chancellery was staffed exclusively with ecclesiastics, and we may conclude that Charlemagne, when he required that the teaching of grammar should be perfected, and that handwriting should be improved, was as much concerned with the linguistic and calligraphic accuracy of the diplomas issued in his name, and the capitularies which he promulgated, as with that of the missals and antiphonaries of the Church. But he had more than this in mind. He had evidently conceived the notion of educating lay officials by sending them to school with the Church, or rather, by having them reared in the Church schools. Just as the Merovingians had sought to graft their administration on to the Roman administration, so, in creating a body of State functionaries, he sought to imitate, as far as possible, the methods employed by the Church for the training of the clergy. His ideal, without a doubt, was to organize the Empire on the pattern of the Church: that is, to provide it with a personnel taught and trained in the same fashion, speaking among themselves and addressing the sovereign in the Latin tongue, which, from the Elbe to the Pyrenees, was to serve as the administrative language, as it was already the language of religion. His practical mind must inevitably have realized the impossibility of maintaining the administrative unity of his vast Empire, in which so many dialects were spoken, by means of illiterate functionaries, each of whom would know only the tongue of his own province. This difficulty would not have existed in a national State, where the vernacular might have become the State language, as it had in the little Anglo-Saxon kingdoms. But in this medley of peoples that was the Empire the political organization had to assume the same universal character as the religious organization, and to superpose itself on all the subjects of the Empire, just as the religious organization embraced all believers. The intimate alliance of Church and State was yet another reason why Latin should become the language of the lay administration. From whatever standpoint we consider the question, it is evident that without the use of Latin administration by the written word would have been impossible. The requirements of the State necessitated the use of Latin; it became, and it was destined to remain for centuries, the language of politics and of business, and also the language of science.

Charlemagne, however, fell very far short of success in creating the educated and Latinized officialdom which he had hoped to bequeath to his successors. The task was too difficult and too enormous. But he gave proof of a touching sincerity and goodwill. He himself learned to write in his old age, and nothing, perhaps, could give us a better idea of the energy and perseverance of this great man than the passage in which Einhard describes him as employing the hours of his wakeful nights in tracing letters on a slate. At his Court a sort of little academy, directed by Alcuin, provided a literary education for sons of some of the greatest families of the Empire, who were destined for a career in the Church, as bishops, or in the administration, as counts, advocates or *missi*. All his children received the training in grammar and rhetoric which constituted the literary education, and there is no doubt that the Imperial example found many imitators among the aristocracy.[1] The few laymen and laywomen who produced Latin works during the reign of Louis the Pious and his sons—for example, Nithard and Duodha—or who, like Count Eberhard of Friuli and Count Robert of Namur, took some interest in men of letters, show that all these efforts were not wasted. However, this attempt to extend the ecclesiastical education to the upper classes, born of the desire to perfect the organization of the Empire, was not destined to outlive the latter.

The institutions of the Church furnished Charlemagne with the inspiration of many other reforms. His capitularies, drawn up after the model of the decisions promulgated by the synods and councils of the Church, reveal innumerable attempts at reform, or improvement, or innovation, in every department of civil life and administration. He introduced, in the palace tribunal, in place of the barbarous and formalistic process of Germanic law, the procedure by inquest which he borrowed from the ecclesiastical courts. The ideal of administrative control which was realized by the creation of the *missi dominici*—itinerant commissaries whose duty it was to supervise the conduct of the functionaries—was very probably borrowed from the Church and adapted to the needs of the State.

The passion for amelioration and reform that marked the whole of Charlemagne's legislative achievements was only the continuation, or, to be more exact, the efflorescence of the attempts at improvement to be noted in Pippin the Short. Pippin had tried to remedy the chaos into which the monetary system had lapsed. Charles accomplished the task which Pippin had begun. He finally abandoned the coining of gold, which had become too rare in the

[1] The daughters of Charles the Bald were educated by Hugbald, of the Abbey of Saint-Amand.

West to keep the mints at work. Henceforth only silver monies were minted; and the ratio which he fixed between them continued in use all over Europe until the adoption of the metric system, and is still current in the British Empire. The unit was the livre or pound, divided into 20 sous, each consisting of 12 deniers. Only the deniers were real money; the sou and the livre were nominal values; and so they continued until the great monetary reforms of the 13th century.

It is, of course, impossible to give in these pages even an approximate idea of the content of the capitularies. The majority of them indicate a programme rather than effective reforms, and it would be a great mistake to suppose that their innumerable decisions can ever have been carried into effect. Those that were actually realized—as, for example, the institution of the courts of aldermen—were far from penetrating to every portion of the Empire. Such as they are, the capitularies remain the finest surviving monument of the Carolingian Empire. But it is obvious that the power of the monarchy was not commensurate with its intentions. The personnel at its disposal was insufficient, and, above all, the power of the aristocracy constituted a limit which it could neither surmount nor suppress. The realization of the politico-religious ideal of Charlemagne would have necessitated resources and a degree of power and authority which the social and economic constitution of the period were unable to place at his disposal.

## CHAPTER IV

# ECONOMIC AND SOCIAL ORGANIZATION

### 1. *The Disappearance of the Cities and of Commerce*

The most important fact, from the social point of view, of the period extending from the Musulman invasions to the Carolingian epoch, was the rapid reduction, and, in the end, the all but complete disappearance, of the urban population.

In the Roman Empire the cities constituted, from the first, the very basis of the State. The political organization was essentially municipal. The country was merely the territory attaching to the city; it had no independent existence; it produced only for the city and was ruled by the city. Wherever the Roman State was established it founded cities and set them up as administrative centres. In the Roman Empire the provinces were so intimately related to the cities on which they were dependent that the same word, *civitas*, was employed to denote the city and the province. And this state of affairs continued until the end of the Byzantine Empire.

The constitution of States whose administrative and social organization no longer corresponded with the urban type of the Roman State was therefore a most surprising novelty, and one hitherto quite unknown in the Western world. It was explained—at all events, as far as the administrative function of the towns was concerned—by the fact that the conquerors of the Empire found it impossible to preserve unaltered all the institutions of the Empire. And it was these institutions of the Empire which had assured the existence of the cities in the provinces occupied by the invaders—Gaul, Spain, Italy, Africa and Britain. Some of them, of course, beside the shores of the Mediterranean—Marseilles, Narbonne,

Naples, Carthagena—carried on a more or less important maritime trade, and almost all the towns in the interior of the country depended on their regular commercial activities; so that the majority of their population consisted of a middle class of shopkeepers and artisans. But none of these cities were comparable with the great ports or industrial centres of the East: Alexandria, Constantinople or Antioch. They existed less by virtue of their own energies than by the general operation of the political and economic activity of the Roman world. Their importance was due to the place which they occupied in the State, to their function as administrative centres, to the presence in them of a numerous staff of officials, and to the relations which the population of the provinces necessarily maintained with them. In short, their situation was fairly analogous to that of those modern cities whose only distinction is that they are royal residences, or have the advantage of possessing some important State institution. Rome herself differed from the provincial cities in this respect only by reason of the glory and importance which she derived from the presence of the Emperor and the central government. The history of her decadence, from the moment when Constantine deprived her of the rank and the advantages of the capital of the world, was repeated, on a smaller scale, in all the cities of the West, as the officials abandoned them amidst the turmoil of invasion, and later, under the rule of the Germanic kings; so that the offices, law-courts and schools were closed, the postal service no longer operated, the inertia and incapacity of the administration allowed the bridges and aqueducts to fall into ruin, and the police and the revictualling services disappeared.

The sea-borne trade, until the period of the Musulman conquests, had maintained, in the coastal towns, a commercial activity by which the adjacent regions of the interior profited. It is true that this trade had lost its principal export market now that an impoverished and depopulated Rome no longer required the grain of the provinces for her subsistence. Nevertheless, until the middle of the 7th century the Western ports of the Mediterranean were still assiduously frequented by Syrian and Jewish merchants. In the time of Gregory of Tours a Jewish colony of some importance existed at Clermont-Ferrand. The papyrus employed in the Merovingian chancellery was imported from Sicily, which shows that navigation was still providing articles of current consumption. But these relations with the Byzantine world came to an end once the preponderance of Islam made it impracticable for Christian traders to risk themselves beyond the waters of Greece and Southern Italy. From this time forward the sea no longer excited the spirit of enterprise in the Western countries. Now, when men looked out seawards, there was dread in their hearts, lest enemy sails should appear on the horizon. And just as the Mediterranean was in the power of the Musulmans, so the North Sea was traversed only by the ships of the Scandinavians. Washed by the waves on the south, north and west, the Carolingian Empire no longer showed the slightest trace of maritime activity. Its only ports—Quentovic, at the mouth of the Canche, and Duurstede—still maintained a certain degree of commercial activity until the 9th century, when they were devastated by the Normans, after which they lapsed into complete decadence. From the 8th century onwards Europe existed for three hundred years without any intercourse with the countries overseas.

The inevitable consequence was an almost complete cessation of trade, and apart from a few local industries, such as the weaving of cloth, which still survived in Flanders, there was an almost total failure of industrial activity, and money no longer circulated.

Henceforth, in the depopulated cities, the deserted quarters fell into ruin, serving as quarries to the few inhabitants who, gathered together in some corner of the old city area, found means to defend and shelter themselves by utilizing the materials furnished by the deserted buildings. At Nîmes the walls of the Roman circus served as the ramparts of the little town that nestled amidst the ruins. At Treves a window of the ancient palace, adapted as well as might be for purposes of defence, became one of the gates of the city, and the *porta nigra*, whose blocks of stone were too heavy to be carried away, was deprived, for the benefit of the local smithy, of the iron cramps which bound them together. Even in Italy, where the decadence was less profound, it was none the less lamentable. Rome seemed lost within the vast circuit which the wall of Aurelian described about what was left of the city. In 848 Pope Leo, to guard against a sudden attack, caused the inhabited portions on the left bank of the Tiber to be enclosed (the "Leonine city"), and turned the tomb of the Emperor Hadrian into a fortress.

In Gaul, urban life was so completely extinct that the kings no longer dwelt in the towns, where they were unable, owing to the complete lack of transport, to obtain the necessary victuals for their retinue. Henceforth they lived all the year round on their domains, passing from one to the other as they emptied the barns and granaries. And like the kings, the provincial officers lived in the country, on their own estates, or on those of the persons under their jurisdiction, on whom they imposed the *droit de gîte*. By a curious phenomenon of regression, the administration, on losing its urban character, became nomadic instead of sedentary.

Ruined and depopulated though they were, the cities had not lost all their significance. Abandoned by the civil administration, they remained the centres of the religious organization. The episcopal see established under the Empire in the capital of each "city" was still extant, and the strong Roman scaffolding of the Church still rose from the ruins of the State. And so, in the heart of a purely agricultural society, something of the municipal character of the ancient State was preserved by the Church. It was owing to the Church that the cities did not disappear altogether, but waited for the still distant day when they would become the cradles of the new middle class.

Just as the Pope, after the Emperors had deserted Rome, took it upon himself to protect the Eternal City, so in each "city" the bishop extended his authority over the few inhabitants who grouped themselves about the Cathedral and provided for the needs of the clergy. Thus the religious life and the religious organization maintained, amidst the ruins of the ancient cities, a small assemblage of laymen who continued as best they could to carry on the Roman trades and practise the Roman technique, but who had no longer anything in common, whether in the spirit that inspired them or in the administration that governed them, with the municipal populations of old.

## 2. *The Great Domains*

The disappearance of the towns led to a profound transformation of rural economy. The products of the soil, which had flowed into the urban markets, gradually lost their purchasers. Once the division of social labour came to an end, which in all advanced societies places the town and the countryside in the mutual relation of consumer and producer, the agricultural population began to produce only for its own needs; or in other words, as it now constituted the nation, it was henceforth both the producer and the consumer of the products of the soil. There was now only one kind of wealth—landed property—and only one kind of worker—the tiller of the soil—and the only economic relations which existed between man and man were conditioned by their quality of landowner or tenant.

Since no dates are available, we cannot form a very exact idea of the agricultural crisis which must have been provoked by the restriction, and then the complete disappearance, of the urban markets. Very probably it finally ruined such small landowners as still survived. As for the great domains, it would certainly have increased their area and modified their organization. It increased their area by forcing the small farmers, deprived of their outlet, and therefore of their resources, to attach themselves to the neighbouring domain, adding their land to it in return for tenant rights. It modified their organization by forcing them to adapt themselves to a system in which there was no such thing as production for sale. The transformation must have begun some time in the 5th century; by the end of the 8th century it was complete. Its final stage was the great domain of the Carolingian epoch, an exact description of which may be found in the polyptych of Abbot Irminon and the *Capitulare de villis*.

The pattern followed was that of the great ecclesiastical domain, better organized than others because the Church had not abandoned the use of writing; and we may be confident that beyond the

Rhine the domains of the Church were the earliest types of domainal organization.

The domain, as an economic phenomenon, was entirely original; there was nothing of the kind at any period of Graeco-Roman antiquity. It was doubtless related, by direct filiation, to the great estate of the late Roman Empire; it preserved, in its essential features, the organization of the Roman *villa*, whose name is retained, and the institution of the *colonatus* appears to have been the preponderating influence in the condition of its tenants. But its actual operation, both in principle and in effect, was something quite new. One may define it by saying that the idea of profit was completely unknown to it. This will be readily understood if we consider that since it could not regulate production with a view to export and sale outside the domain, it was forced to regulate it with a view to its distribution and consumption within the domain. Its aim was to ensure that the domain should be self-sufficing, living on its own resources, without selling and without purchasing. This system is commonly described as "closed economy"; it would be more exactly described as "economy without outlets." For it was the absence of outlets that produced this self-sufficiency of the domainal constitution. And from this many very important consequences followed, which dominated the entire economic life of the Middle Ages down to the 12th century. With them, indeed, the economic life of the Middle Ages originated. To begin with, the regression of agricultural methods is obvious. It was useless to make the soil yield more than was required to satisfy the needs of the cultivator, for since the surplus could not be exported it would neither improve the condition of the tiller of the soil nor increase the rental value of the land. The farmer was therefore satisfied with a minimum of care and effort, and agronomic science was allowed to fall into oblivion, until the possibility of selling the crops should once more encourage the owners of the soil to adopt improved and therefore more lucrative methods. But then the land would begin to be regarded as a value, and not as a mere means of subsistence.

Another characteristic of domainal exploitation was the almost complete substitution of payments in kind for payments in money. It goes without saying that this was a natural and necessary consequence of the absence of sale outside the domain. The landowner, whose livelihood depended on his domain, fixed in natural products, and sometimes even in raw material worked up by the peasant, the quota of each tenure in what might be called its alimentary revenue. At stated periods, in conformity with a permanent assessment, the various tenures would have to deliver to him grain, eggs, cheese, smoked meats and ells of cloth.

It would be a great mistake to suppose that we are confronted here with a return to an age preceding the invention of money, and the rather unfortunate description of "natural economy" so often applied to this system is a very imperfect definition of its character. As a matter of fact, money did not cease to exist as an instrument of exchange and a measure of values. We do not find that natural products of any kind took the place of money from the 9th to the 12th century, or fulfilled its function. All that we can truthfully say is that inside the domain it was very naturally replaced by the practice, imposed by necessity, of supplying consumer's goods. Outside the domain it was in normal use, and the few commodities—eggs, poultry, and the like—which the peasants took each week to the little local markets with which no society can dispense entirely, were paid for in deniers and oboli.

We must consider, too, that the prestation[1] of each tenure was invariable, and that for so long as he furnished it the tenant enjoyed a hereditary right to the land which he occupied. And this too was the inevitable consequence of the economic system from which the idea of profit was absent. What mattered to the landowner was the annual regularity of his income in kind, and the best way of guaranteeing this was to give it the character of a permanent tax. Between the lord of the domain and his peasants there was no relation comparable to that which subordinates the workers to a capitalist. The domain was not in any sense an exploitation, whether of the soil or of human beings. It was a social institution, not an economic enterprise. The obligations of its inhabitants were not

[1] Payment in kind. (*Tr.*)

based on personal contracts, but depended on right and custom. Each domain had its own law, established by traditional usage. The seigneur was at once more and less than a landed proprietor in the Roman or modern meaning of the term; less, because his property right was limited by the hereditary rights of his tenants to their tenures; more, because his power over these tenants was far in excess of that of a mere landowner.

In fact, he was their lord and they were his men. Many of them, the descendants of enfranchised slaves or body-serfs, constituted part of his patrimony. Others, the heirs of colonists of the Roman epoch, were *adscripti glebae*. Others, again, bound to the seigneur by "recommendation," lived under his protection. Over all of them, in various degrees, he exercised a patriarchal authority, and all were subject to his private jurisdiction. It was by virtue of this family group, which he protected, and ruled, that he was powerful. For at this period of sparse population men were far more important than land; there was more than enough land, but men were rare, and the great thing was to keep carefully as many as the seigneur possessed. There were consequently many provisions for preventing a man from leaving the domain. Over his serfs the seigneur possessed the right of pursuit; they could not, without his consent, marry wives outside the domainal community. Adscription to the soil, originally confined to the descendants of slaves and colonists, was gradually extended to freemen living under the seigneur's jurisdiction. This gradual extension of servitude to the whole agricultural population was the most notable phenomenon of the 9th century and the two following centuries. As a general rule, the peasant of this epoch was not free; he was so far from being free that in contemporary documents the words denoting the peasant (*villanus, rusticus*) became synonymous with serf (*servus*).

It must not be supposed that those who were subject to this servitude felt it as a burden. On the contrary, it was so completely adapted to their condition of hereditary tenants under the protection of a powerful lord that they regarded it as their natural state and submitted to it of their own free will. It was a necessary result of the domainal organization: the inevitable juridical consequence. How could liberty be valued by men whose very existence was guaranteed only by the place they occupied on the land, and under the jurisdiction of their seigneur, and whose security was therefore all the greater in proportion as they were more intimately incorporated in the domain?

Whether lay or ecclesiastical, the great domain of the first few centuries of the Middle Ages (before the 13th century) had nothing in common with the great exploitation. By the end of the Roman Empire the *latifundia* with their slaves had already disappeared, and it seems that the landed proprietors were progressively abandoning agriculture on the grand scale and dividing their estates into tenures. The complete cessation of the trade in agricultural products naturally favoured this tendency, and in the great domain of the Carolingian epoch and the following centuries we see its almost complete triumph. The domain was divided into two very unequal parts: the seigneurial land (*terra indominicata*) and the mansionary land (*mansionaria*). The first, by far the less extensive, was exploited directly and wholly to the profit of the seigneur. The work on this land was performed by domestic serfs who did not possess tenures, much like our agricultural labourers, or by tenants who were subject to corvées. The mansionary land was reserved for such tenants. It was divided into units, of variable extent according to the quality of the soil and the region; but each was large enough to support a family. These were the manses (*mansus*), and their possession was hereditary, subject, as we have seen, to prestations in kind and in labour. The whole constituted a rural *villa*. The common centre was the seigneurial court (*hof, curtis*), in which lived the seigneur's intendant or bailiff, the mayor (*meyer, major, villicus*) entrusted with the supervision of and jurisdiction over the villeins (*villani*). The court, surrounded by a moat and a palisade, served as the master's residence when he resided on his estate, and included the barns and granaries where the crops and other revenues were stored. It was here too that the domainal tribunal assembled, composed of tenants and presided over by the mayor or the seigneur. Here and there, even in the 9th century, and more and more frequently as time went on, a chapel, built by the seigneur, and served by a priest whom he chose and appointed, provided for the needs of religion. Many rural parishes owe their origin to these domainal chapels; and these, too, explain the right of presentation which many local seigneurs retained until the end of the *ancien régime*, and of which traces still linger in certain countries.

Surrounding the cultivable land, the woods, meadows and marshes were apportioned to the use of the seigneur and the villeins, in proportion to the share of the soil which they exploited. Often, if a stream crossed the domain, the seigneur built a mill upon it, for his own use and that of the inhabitants. A portion of flour was deducted from each sack by the miller, to provide for his maintenance: and this was the origin of the customary dues which survived until the French Revolution.

Despite local differences, the general features of the organization just described were to be found everywhere; but this organization was more perfect on the ecclesiastical properties than on those of the lay aristocracy. It exercised such a profound influence on society that in all Western European languages it has left its traces on the geographical and onomatological vocabulary. One has only to consider the number of French place-names ending in *ville* or *court*, or in the Germanic languages in *hof*, and the frequency of such family names as Lemaire, Mayer, De Meyer, Le Mayeur, etc.

Ordinarily a large domain consisted of several *villae*. That of Saint-Germain des Prés, in Charlemagne's day, comprised a whole series, scattered about from Brittany to the banks of the Moselle. The monasteries of the northern regions almost always endeavoured to acquire, in the wine country on the banks of the Rhine, the Moselle or the Seine, a *villa* which would furnish them with the wine that could no longer be obtained through the channel of trade.[1]

This last feature adds the final touch to the rural economy without outlets, of which the domain of the early years of the Middle Ages was the organ, just as the trade guild would subsequently be

[1] The Abbey of Saint-Trond, for example, had vineyards at Briedel and Pommeren on the Moselle.

the organ of the urban industrial economy. Despite their profoundly different character, both were alike in one respect. Both economies were based on petty exploitation, with the result that they preserved intact, through the centuries, in the one case the bourgeois artisan, in the other the small farmer. Paradoxical though it may seem, it may truthfully be said that the great domains of the Middle Ages safeguarded the class of peasants. For them servitude was a benefit. At a time when the State was powerless, and when the earth alone supplied men's wants, it assured them of a protector and guaranteed them the possession of a share of the soil. Since it was not organized with a view to profit, the domainal constitution imposed only small prestations in return for considerable advantages. As the peasants were part of the seigneur's property, he was interested in their preservation: he defended them in the event of war and fed them from his stores in time of famine. War and famine were the two plagues that afflicted them in turn; war being a consequence of the increasing weakness of the State, and famine the inevitable result of commercial stagnation. A bad harvest was an irremediable disaster at a time when a country could not make good the deficit from the surplus of a neighbouring country. The period extending from the 9th to the 12th century is *par excellence*, in the economic history of Europe, the age of alimentary crises. They recurred every few years with the regularity of a natural phenomenon.

But while they were much more numerous than those of the following centuries, these famines were also less cruel. This is explained by the absence of an urban population and the very low numerical strength of the rural population. The domainal organization which we have described, with its small productive power and its peasant class consisting almost entirely of tenants, evidently presupposed an extremely restricted number of inhabitants. There were, of course, landless folk, "poor men," as the contemporary texts describe them; men of a wandering habit, begging their way from monastery to monastery, hiring themselves to the villeins at harvest-time. But these disinherited children of a social order which was based on the possession of the soil were neither a responsibility nor a danger, which is proof of their small number.

It is impossible to estimate, with any approach to accuracy, the density of the population, as no reliable data are available. All that we can say is that in the Carolingian epoch the population was very small; undoubtedly smaller than at any previous epoch, owing to the extinction of the urban population. And it seems to have remained almost stationary until the beginning of the 11th century, for the natural excess of births did no more than fill the gaps constantly made by famine, war, and the disturbances and catastrophes of every kind that descended upon the West from the middle of the 9th century.

*Book Three*

# FEUDAL EUROPE

## CHAPTER I

# THE DISSOLUTION OF THE EMPIRE

### 1. *Internal Causes*

Despite the fame of Charlemagne, we must be under no illusion as to the solidity of his political achievement. As a matter of fact, nothing could exceed the fragility of the Empire. The weakness of Louis the Pious, the quarrels of his sons, and the incursions of the Normans, Slavs and Saracens, merely hastened a dissolution whose causes were internal, and so obvious that they force themselves upon our attention.

The immense territory of the Empire, stretching from the marches of the Elbe and the Danube to the march of the Ebro in Spain and the Papal possessions in Italy, had none of the essential characteristics of a State. The Merovingian kingdom did at least endeavour to establish itself on the basis of the Roman institutions. However crude its organization, its administrative absolutism was, after all, a political system. We shall seek in vain for anything of the kind in the Carolingian monarchy. Here all seems incoherent. The power of the sovereign, which should have set the whole mechanism in motion, was not able to impose itself sufficiently. Obliged to reckon with the aristocracy to whom they owed their crown, Pippin the Short and Charlemagne could not refuse it a place in the government. The magnates of the kingdom deliberated with them, assembling at court in a *conventus* at the feasts of Christmas and Easter. But what were the competences and what the attributes of these councillors? They were as vague and unsettled as the very composition of their assemblies; aggregations of ecclesiastics and laymen who, without title or mandate, were considered as representing the people. *Lex fit consensu populi et constitutione regis*, says a capitulary; the law is made by the assent of the people and the king's constitution. A fine formula, but actually devoid of meaning. As a matter of fact, many of the capitularies were never submitted to the assemblies, and in the case of those that were submitted to them we do not know what part the assemblies played in the matter. Nothing could be less deserving of the name of laws than these capitularies, a heterogeneous mass of administrative decisions, regulations, statements of principles, emergency measures, or perpetual edicts; and in most cases we do not know whether they were ever put into force, nor whether they related to the whole Empire or merely to one of its regions. Moreover, they are full of contradictions, and we never know whether the later texts abrogate the earlier ones, or whether we should seek as far as possible to reconcile them. The general impression emerging from this confusion is that of a royal will, ardently desirous of good, eager for progress, order and justice, and endeavouring, without success, to realize them. As manifested and expressed in these documents, the royal power seems that of an absolute sovereign, but of one whose absolutism is doubly limited. It is limited, in the first place, by Christian morality, and it accepts this limitation. It is limited further by the necessity of avoiding anything that will displease the aristocracy, and to this limitation it submits. It is evident that in his heart the Carolingian Emperor felt responsible only to God, and that if he tolerated the intervention of the magnates it was because he could not do otherwise. Between him and the magnates with whom he took counsel there had been from the beginning a lack of confidence, and before long their relations were vitiated by a lack ot good faith. In short, we may say that the Carolingian constitution was based on a disagreement. The two forces that seemed to be in alliance were in reality two adversaries.

The more powerful of the two, under Charlemagne, tricked out in the glamour of his victories, and in the novel dignity of the Emperor, was the sovereign. But the aristocracy was the more vigorous; circumstances and the organization of society were on its side. This aristocracy declared that it was the people, and to a certain extent it was right; for the people had disappeared into the aristocracy. It had absorbed the people into its domains, and for all those who were dependent upon it—that is, for the greater part of the population—it replaced the public power of the State by a private power of protection and jurisdiction. The direct subjects of the sovereign, outside the jurisdiction of the aristocracy, were very few in number, and becoming fewer year by year. Charles saw the danger, and he tried to guard against it. He attempted, by reducing the burdens that military service and the judicial service imposed on freemen, to safeguard those who had preserved their liberty, which was becoming increasingly rare. His measures met with the common fate of all attempts to deter social evolution from gravitating in the direction of interests and necessities; they could not prevent the inevitable. The peasants continued to cede their lands to the magnates and attach themselves to their domains.

And here again we recognize the disagreement at the base of the Carolingian organization. In this matter of the maintenance of freemen the interests of the Emperor and those of the aristocracy were in direct conflict. But it was to this very aristocracy that the Emperor had to entrust the realization of his plans, for it was from their ranks that he recruited his officials. The rest of the aristocracy had to choose between their own advantage and that of the sovereign. They could serve the sovereign only to their own detriment. How could he hope that they would decide in his favour?

And against this inertia or this ill-will there was no remedy whatever. In law, no doubt, the Emperor could dismiss the counts, since he appointed them. In actual fact he could do nothing against them. For they were not the mere instruments of his power, mere agents, independently selected, strangers to the men under their administration, and passing, at their master's orders, from one district to another. On the contrary, each one of them belonged to the region which he governed; there he was the largest landowner, as his family might have been for generations, and the man of the greatest influence; his family estates were scattered all over his county; the inhabitants, from father to son, were his serfs or his tenants; he was born in their midst, and there he would die, unless he fell far from home on the battlefield; and it was the same with his father, to whom he almost always succeeded in the dignity of count. Thus, in the region over which he presided he was regarded as a seigneur rather than a representative of the Emperor. Consequently, if he were sent elsewhere or divested of his charge, his successor would seem, in the eyes of the people, a usurper and an intruder.

This impotence of the State with regard to its agents is explained by the financial situation. What was left of the Roman impost had disappeared at the close of the Merovingian epoch, when it was commuted into fines which were usurped by the magnates. The Imperial treasury was still fed from two sources: one of them—war booty—intermittent and capricious; the other—the revenue of the domains belonging to the dynasty—permanent and regular. Only this latter source was capable of furnishing the necessary resources for current requirements. Charles gave it his careful attention, and the well-known *Capitulare de villis* proves, by the minuteness of its details, the importance which he attached to the good administration of his estates. But their yield consisted of prestations in kind, just enough to revictual the court. Properly speaking, the Carolingian Empire had no public finances, and when this has been said we can appreciate how rudimentary was its organization compared with that of the Byzantine Empire or the Empire of the Caliphs, with their taxes levied in money, their financial control, and their fiscal centralization, which provided for the salaries of officials, public works, and the upkeep of the army and the fleet.

Reduced to the resources of his private domains, the Emperor could not meet the expenses of an administration worthy of the name. Now if the official is to be dependent on the State, the State must not only appoint him, but must also pay him. Here, having no money, the State was obliged to have recourse to the gratuitous services of the aristocracy, which placed it in the paradoxical situation of taking as its collaborators the members of a social class whose power was bound to increase as that of the State diminished. The danger of this arrangement was so evident that attempts were made to guard against it. From the end of the 8th century a special oath of fidelity, like that sworn by the vassal, was required of the counts when they entered upon their duties. But the remedy was worse than the disease. For the bond of vassalage, by attaching the functionary to the person of the sovereign, weakened or even annulled his character as public officer. It made him, moreover, regard his function as a fief; that is, as a possession to be enjoyed, and not as a power delegated by the crown and exercised in its name. Further, this system, at each succession to the throne, gave rise to a crisis of the most dangerous character. The new sovereign found himself confronted with the alternative of retaining in office the confidants of his predecessor, or replacing them by confidants of his own. In the first case he was reduced to governing with a staff whose members were unknown to him; in the second he was bound to provoke, from the very first, a formidable sense of resentment.

However we look at it, the administrative organization of the Empire was lacking in the features which are essential to any State administration: subordination and discipline. Compared with that of the Church, where the hierarchy allotted to every man his rôle and his responsibility, it seemed to be plunged into the crudest anarchy. The institution of the *missi dominici* was evidently designed to improve the system by the exercise of control. Here Charlemagne's personal initiative is clearly manifested, and his tendency to ameliorate lay institutions by following the example of the Church. Just as the Church was divided into archiepiscopal sees, each of which comprised a certain number of dioceses, so he divided the Empire into vast circumscriptions (*missatica*), each of which included several counties. In each of these circumscriptions two Imperial envoys (*missi dominici*), an ecclesiastic and a layman, were entrusted with the supervision of the officials, the noting of abuses, the interrogation of the people, and the annual production of a report on their mission. Nothing could have been better, nothing more useful and salutary than such an institution—so long as there was any sanction behind it. But in actual fact there was no such sanction, since the so-called functionaries, as we have seen, were practically irremovable. We cannot find that the *missi dominici* were anywhere successful in curing the defects of which they must have noted many in all directions: the reality was more powerful than the good intentions of the Emperor.

The creation of the *missi* is enough to prove that Charlemagne —doubtless under the influence of his ecclesiastical counsellors— had acquired a very clear notion of the imperfection of his means of government. His ideal—but he had not the power to realize it—was to reform them in accordance with the example furnished by the administration of the Church. The spirit by which he was actuated was, we may say, entirely Roman. It is a complete illusion to see in him, as so many have done, the adept of some sort of indefinable Germanism, of which we shall vainly seek for any traces in his achievements. Here legend has seen more clearly than many of the historians. In the popular memory of the Germans Charles has remained the legislator *par excellence*, the conqueror of barbarism, the founder of the social order. For the pagan or semi-pagan peoples he was actually all these things, but it was by virtue of his ecclesiastical government. The definitive establishment of the Church in Germany and the subordination of the people to its dogmas and its moral laws was so far his personal achievement that he appears in tradition as a quasi-sacred personality. It was doubtless this tradition that inspired the imagination of Albrecht Dürer, when he gave him the strange and majestic appearance that makes us think of a lay Pope rather than an Emperor. The close alliance of State and Church, the identification of political unity with Christian unity, and its necessary consequence of a State religion—this is the essential Carolingian achievement; it was this that survived the dynasty, and determined, for centuries to come, the development of European society.

### 2. *The Pope and the Emperor*

The death of Charlemagne (January 28th, 814) did not provoke the slightest crisis. In 813 he had caused five provincial synods to frame a series of dispositions regarding the organization of the Empire. They were ratified the same year by a General Assembly convoked at Aix-la-Chapelle, in the course of which he took the precaution of setting the crown, with his own hands, on the head of Louis, his only surviving son.

Louis succeeded to the throne in an atmosphere of general approval. The Empire was rejoicing in the profoundest peace; nothing in the outer world gave warning of the imminent outbreak of the disorders which would presently overwhelm it. The essentially ecclesiastical ideal of the Imperial power which Charles had cherished was revealed in the education to which his son had been subjected. It was wholly Latin and clerical, and it was for good reason that the second Carolingian Emperor was known to tradition as "the Pious." But his piety, if we may say so, was pre-eminently a political piety. It was blended with a conception of the secular power which regarded the maintenance and protection of the Church as its *raison d'être*. Charles, who had become Emperor late in life, had retained something of his independence as a sovereign, something of his original character as king of the Franks; but with his son this independence disappeared. Louis, on his accession, abandoned the title of King of the Franks and Lombards; the only title which he bore was that of Emperor: signifying that his authority was as universal as that of the Pope, extending, like the latter, to all Christians. And this, of course, had been the tendency of the Carolingian policy since the coronation of the year 800. There was no opposition of tendencies between Charles and Louis, despite the enormous difference of personal genius and power. The Imperial power, as Louis understood it, was only the complete and logical development of the idea that had dominated Charlemagne throughout the latter part of his career, and the great Emperor himself had willed and prepared the spirit in which his weak successor was to reign.

Louis found himself at once confronted by a question which his father had been spared, and which would presently enable him to test the solidity of the Empire. He had three sons: Lothair, Louis, (the German) and Pippin. How should he order his succession? The idea of equal partition among the sons of the sovereign had always been applied from the beginning of the Frankish monarchy.

On the other hand, the Imperial power was by its very nature as indivisible as the power of the Pope. Should he then regard the Empire as so indissolubly merged in the State that the succession to the State must be ruled by the same principle as succession to the Empire? Or, distinguishing the one from the other, should he proceed to partition the State, while reserving the Imperial authority to one of the heirs? Louis decided on a measure which, without breaking altogether with the custom of partition, nevertheless sacrificed it to the principle of unity. In 817 he associated with himself, as co-regent of the Empire, his eldest son, Lothair, and appointed him his heir. At the same time the two younger sons received each a sort of appanage with the title of king: Pippin being King of Aquitaine and Louis of Bavaria. In so doing Louis decided against the old conception of the secular monarchy as it had been held and put into practice by the Merovingians, and in favour of the new ecclesiastical conception of the Empire; and we can hardly doubt that he made these arrangements by agreement with the Pope. But the younger sons considered that they had been unjustly treated, and only waited for the opportunity of taking their revenge. The opportunity came to them: they had no need to provoke it. A widower, in 819 Louis had married, for her beauty, Judith, the daughter of the Duke of the Alamans. Amorous and sensual by temperament, as were nearly all the early Carolingians, he soon fell under the domination of his wife, and when in 823 she made him the father of a fourth son, Charles (the Bald), he had not the energy to check the intrigues into which she entered in order to assure this child of the largest possible share of the paternal heritage. Judith had no difficulty in persuading Louis and Pippin to see things as she did, and to incite them against Lothair, and it was an easier matter still, by means of promises, to assure herself of the help of the aristocracy. Two parties, or rather two factions, were thus formed within the Empire: one adopting as it programme the sharing of the succession among all the sons of the Emperor, and the other remaining faithful to the idea of unity.[1]

[1] These are, as it were, party labels. Actually only the ecclesiastics can have had a programme; the laymen grouped themselves according to their sympathies and interests.

The first of these parties had the best of it at the outset: Lothair, deprived of his title of regent, went to Italy to submit his quarrel to the Pope, while Louis, in obedience to Judith, proceeded to a fresh partition of the monarchy between his four sons. The advantages which he lavished upon Charles resulted in a quarrel with Louis the German and Pippin, who made it up with Lothair. In 833 the latter crossed the Alps at the head of an army, accompanied by Pope Gregory IV, joined his brothers, and marched with them against his father. They met in the Rhenish plain, near Colmar. The victory was apparently Lothair's, but actually the Pope's. In the name of the peace of the Church, of which the Empire was only the temporal power, he claimed the right to intervene, restored Lothair to his original dignity, and imposed on the old Emperor, as guilty of troubling the peace of Christendom, a humilitating penance. The first consequence of the intimate conjunction of Pope and Emperor followed with pitiless logic: the Emperor gave way, the Pope increased his influence, and the original alliance of the two powers was replaced by the subordination of the Emperor to the Pope.

But this was not what Louis the German and Pippin had wanted. They took up arms again, and the struggle continued, with a sort of muddled obstinacy, between rival ambitions and personal interests. Neither the death of Pippin (838) nor that of the Emperor interrupted it. Not until 843 did it finally terminate—thanks to the exhaustion of all parties—in the Treaty of Verdun.

This was a compromise, but one that strangely diminished the scope of the Imperial idea. The entire monarchy was divided into three equal parts. The middle portion, cutting across Europe, and extending, without regard for natural frontiers or the character of the peoples, from Friesland to the Papal States, was allotted to Lothair. He retained also the title of Emperor, exercising an ill-defined primacy over his brothers Louis and Charles, who reigned respectively over the regions to the east and west of him. Thus the identity between the Empire and the Frankish State which had existed under Charlemagne and Louis the Pious disappeared. The Imperial unity now existed only in theory; its universality no longer corresponded with the reality of things, as the Emperor actually ruled over merely a third of Western Christendom.

After the death of Lothair (855) matters were even worse. He too had three sons, and they, in their turn, divided his territories between them. The eldest, Louis II, took for his share Italy and the Imperial title. Under Lothair the Emperor had still been at least as powerful as the two kings his brothers. Under Louis II he was no more than a secondary sovereign, infinitely less influential than his uncles Louis the German and Charles the Bald. The contrast between the Emperor as he was and the Emperor as he ought to have been was steadily increasing. One may say, indeed, that even though there was still an Emperor, he had no longer an Empire.

This continual decline of the Imperial power was accompanied by the correlative and simultaneous increase of the power of the Pope. Once the equilibrium between the two forces set over Christendom was broken, one of them was bound to profit by the losses of the other. Already circumstances had led Gregory IV to judge between Louis the Pious and his sons. Under Louis II, Nicholas I (858–867) claimed and enforced the superiority of the pontifical over the Imperial power. With him the political alliance which had been concluded under Charlemagne came to an end. The head of the Church, in virtue of the divine origin of his power, regarded himself henceforth as the judge and the director of the depositories of the temporal powers, whether kings or emperors. Amenable to him as Christians, liable to his moral jurisdiction as sinners, it was essential that they should be subject to a sanction which would guarantee their obedience. Henceforth the Pope could and must, if he judged it necessary to the service of God and the Church, intervene in the affairs of the princes, and Nicholas unhesitatingly entered upon the path which was afterwards to be followed by Gregory VII and Alexander II, and which led Innocent III and Innocent IV to the theocratic hegemony which was ended by the catastrophe of Boniface VIII. He had no occasion, however, to intervene in matters of high policy. The excommunication which he thundered against the King of Lotharingia, Lothair II, on the occasion of his divorce, and which ended in the humiliation of the culprit, was no more than a moral manifestation, but its repercussions were felt throughout Europe.

The "false decretals" which were published in the middle of the 9th century in Northern France, and whose apocryphal texts, cleverly forged, gave the Pope a power over the whole body of the episcopate which he had never yet actually exercised, helped to confirm the primacy of Rome. Nicholas even sought to compel the Eastern Church to recognize this primacy, and launched his excommunication against the patriarch Photius: the only result being still further to aggravate the conflict which was poisoning the relations between the Greek and Latin halves of Christendom.

The death of Louis II (875) furnished the Papacy with a fresh opportunity of affirming its superiority over the Empire, and of showing that the Empire was dependent on the Papacy and not on the dynasty. Louis had no children, and his nearest male relation was Carloman, the son of Louis the German, whom he had appointed his heir. John VIII (872–882) decided otherwise, summoned Charles the Bald to Rome, and crowned him.

Since the middle of the 9th century the ascendancy of the Pope over the Emperor had continued to increase. But if it was possible to exercise this ascendancy, it was only because the Emperors consented. By himself the Pope, reduced to the possession of his little Roman State, would have been absolutely incapable of resisting the least aggression. Further, in the last resort he owed the authority which he enjoyed, and of which he had given such striking proof, to the Carolingians whom he had crowned, and who, in return, granted him their protection. A paradoxical situation, which permitted the Pope to dominate the Emperor for so long as the Emperor guaranteed his liberty; which allowed the spiritual power precedence over the secular only by virtue of the support which it received from the latter! And now the political anarchy into which Europe was falling, with increasing rapidity, at the close of the 9th century, suddenly deprived the Pope of this indispensable protector. Charles the Bald was the last Emperor to enjoy any real prestige, to exercise any real power. After him, under the irresistible pressure of feudality, under the blows of the Normans, the Saracens, the Slavs and the Hungarians, under the influence of regional particularism, and of personal ambitions and intrigues and rivalries, what was left of the Carolingian order foundered, and the princes, whether they called themselves kings or emperors, were equally powerless. Henceforth Rome was abandoned to her fate, and the Papacy suddenly found itself confronted with dangers far greater than those which had menaced it of old, in the days of the Lombards. For while the Lombards persisted in their attempt to conquer Rome, they wished no harm to the Pope. Now, on the contrary, the very liberty of the Papacy was threatened. Since the Pope had the disposal of the Imperial crown, it would be possible henceforth to obtain it by subjecting him to violence and compelling him by threats to exercise his power. Already, after the death of Charles the Bald, Charles the Fat, marching upon Rome at the head of an army, had forced John VIII to crown him (881). Then, not long afterwards, the world witnessed the sorry spectacle of the simultaneous debasement of Pope and Emperor. After the deposition of Charles the Fat and the final rupture of the Carolingian unity two Italian magnates, the Marquis of Friuli, Berenger, and the Duke of Spoleto, Gui, disputed for the ancient Lombard crown, and each had himself crowned king in Pavia. The Imperial dignity was vacant: Gui resolved to seize it. He had only to enter Rome with his soldiers in order to obtain it from the Pope, Stephanus VI (891), and some time later he compelled Stephanus' successor, Formosus, to confer it also on his son, Lambert.

To what a depth had the Empire and the Papacy fallen in the course of a few years! Formosus felt that the only means of restoring them was to appeal to force. Arnold, Duke of Carinthia, had just won a brilliant victory over the Normans, and seemed to hold forth the promise of a glorious reign. The Pope solicited his assistance against the odious tyranny to which he was subjected. Arnold crossed the Alps, took Rome—defended by the Spoletans—by assault, received the Imperial crown (896), and returned to Germany. Lambert could take his revenge. It was tragic and repulsive, as were the political and religious customs of the time. Formosus being dead, Lambert proceeded, in the presence of the corpse, to a simulacrum of judgement, after which the Pope's body was delivered to the populace, who proceeded to fling it into the Tiber. Arnold did not cross the Alps again, and the Papacy was more than ever the plaything of ambitious intriguers, who disputed for the Empire as others quarrelled elsewhere for a fief or a province, and the world took little more heed of them. Lambert dead, Berenger of Friuli was once more supreme in Italy. Louis, King of Burgundy, made war upon him, defeated him, and took the opportunity of having himself crowned Emperor by Benedict IV (900). Five years later Berenger took him prisoner at Verona, had him blinded, and drove him out of the peninsula. Then, in 919, he in turn had himself consecrated Emperor by John X. It was difficult to do anything further to degrade the title inaugurated by Charlemagne; and as a matter of fact it was not further disgraced. After the assassination of Berenger of Friuli (924) there was not another Emperor until the coronation of Otto I (962).

### 3. *The Enemies Without*

The enemies from which the Empire suffered so cruelly in the course of the 9th century—the Normans and the Arabs—did not attack it merely because of its weakness: nor were their attacks deliberately directed against the Empire. The Normans' sphere of action was the northern seas; the Arabs', the shores of the Mediterranean; in each case the regions affected went far beyond the coasts of the Carolingian State. The aggressions of which the latter was the victim were no more than an episode in the history of the maritime incursions which it could not hope to escape, but of which it was never the only, nor even—at any rate, in the beginning—the principal object.

The advance of the Arabs in the Western Mediterranean at the beginning of the 9th century was no longer related to the great movement of religious expansion which had followed the death of Mohammed. The political unity of Islam was broken, since the Caliph of Baghdad was not recognized by all believers. In Spain, at the close of the 8th century, a new Caliphate was erected under the Omayyads. In Africa the Berbers of Morocco, Algeria and Tunis were really independent. Finally established in their new conquests, these Musulmans of Spain and Africa turned to the sea. Tunis, founded beside the ruins of Carthage, looked, as Carthage had done, towards Sicily; and before long the Tunisians, like the Carthaginians of old, sought to conquer the beautiful island, always, throughout history, a bone of contention between Europe and Africa. The Byzantines were unable effectually to defend this remote province. Between 827 and 878 they were gradually driven toward the Straits of Messina, and at last they were obliged to fall back on the Italian coast. Already in possession of the Balearics, Corsica, and Sardinia, the Musulmans now held all the islands of the Mediterranean, which served as naval stations, and as bases of attack upon the continental coasts. From Sicily expeditions were despatched against Calabria, which ended in the conquest of Bari and Tarento. Other fleets harried the coasts of Central Italy. Pope Leo IV was obliged to put what was left of Rome in a state of defence against the pirates, who landed, having nothing to fear, at the mouth of the Tiber. The mouths of the Rhone, which were equally unprotected, were even more exposed. The Arabs established military posts along the Corniche, the ruins of which may still be seen. However, they made no attempt to establish themselves in the interior. The possession of the coasts was all that mattered to the new masters of the Mediterranean, and as there was no Christian trade no serious efforts were made to dislodge the Arabs, and the littoral was left in their hands. The Christian population withdrew farther inland, and the derelict towns in the region of Nîmes fortified themselves as best they could.[1]

The Norman invasions were more devastating, and their results were much more important. These were the sudden incursions of a people of whom so little was known that they had not even been given a name, and for want of a better description the inhabi-

[1] In 916 Pope John X, with King Berenger and Byzantine reinforcements, captured the fortfied camp of the Musulmans in the Garigliano. Henceforth Central Italy was free of the enemy.

tants of the northern coasts, who were the first to come into contact with them, gave them the name of the region from which they came: they were Noord-mannen, Northmen, Normans.

The maritime raids of the Scandinavians can be explained only by hypotheses—though these are plausible enough. The first condition of such raids was obviously the need experienced by part of the population to seek abroad the means of subsistence which the poor and thankless soil of their native country did not provide in sufficient abundance to satisfy a hardy and vigorous people. If to this economic distress we add intestine quarrels between local chiefs, and allow for the pride of the vanquished, who would refuse to submit to the conqueror, but would rather put to sea with their comrades in arms, hoping to return in triumph after profitable adventures, we shall have some idea of the motives which from the close of the 8th century impelled the Danes, Norwegians and Swedes to set sail across the North Sea, the Baltic, the blue wastes of the North Atlantic, and even the sunny waters of the Mediterranean. The Swedes, moreover, were actuated by a motive unknown to the Scandinavians of the West. The influence of the two great Empires of the South—the Byzantine Empire and the Empire of the Caliphs—was felt, like a gleam of golden light, even in the frozen ends of the earth. From the latter part of the 7th century trade routes had been coming into existence, on the one hand between the Baltic and the Caspian, from the Gulf of Finland, the Neva, Lake Ladoga, Lake Onega, to the course of the Volga, and on the other hand between the Baltic and the Black Sea.

More than 200,000 Arabic and Byzantine coins have been exhumed from the soil of Sweden, the oldest dating from 698. The Swedes began at an early date to adventure on the paths that led to the lands of the sun and fortune. The Slavs called these strangers by the name of *Rus*, which their mutual neighbours the Finns had given them. These Scandinavian Russians soon established themselves in large numbers in the *pogostes* (markets) which the Arab or Khazar merchants visited at fixed intervals in order to buy their honey and their furs. There they quickly replaced the other foreigners; to such an extent that along the course of the Dnieper the rapids have retained throughout the years the names which the Swedes bestowed upon them. Towards the middle of the 9th century they imposed themselves as masters on the population in the neighbourhood of the *pogostes*. According to tradition, Rurik founded Novgorod, and two of his companions, Askod and Dir, took possession of Kiev, the most important commercial centre of the whole of the southern plain. In 892 Olaf, Rurik's successor, established himself in Kiev, which was then beginning to extend its political domination over all the surrounding regions. From this moment may be dated the birth of a Russian—that is, a Swedish—State in the basin of the Dnieper. The princes, and their comrades in arms and in trade, who continued, until the beginning of the 11th century, to receive reinforcements from their country of origin, preserved almost until this period their Scandinavian tongue and customs.[1] But in the end they were absorbed by the population whom they governed and exploited, and thus the name of these hardy adventurers of the 9th century, by an extraordinary trick of fortune, has been borne, through the vicissitudes of history, by the greatest of the Slav peoples and the most far-flung Empire in the world.

Owing to the situation of their country, the Danes and the Norwegians looked to the West. The lands which tempted them to adventure were not, like the Byzantine Empire or the Arab Empire, flourishing States, full of cities, and promising great commercial profits, but purely agricultural regions, having nothing to buy or sell. Thus, while the Swedes, on finding themselves in touch with societies which were, economically speaking, highly developed, were anxious above all to trade with them, the Danes and Norwegians made their appearance as pirates and pillagers or sea-rovers.[2]

And while they assailed the coasts to the south and the west, their vessels explored the northern waters. Norwegians installed themselves in the Faroes at an early date; and in 874 they discovered Iceland, which they colonized, and a century later they sailed

[1] These newcomers were known, in Russian, by an old Swedish word meaning "foreigners" (*vaering*). Hence the Varangians, βαραγγοι, of the Constantinople guard, which was at first composed mainly of Scandinavians.

[2] The Russians, however, attacked Constantinople in 865, 907, 941, 944 and 1043.

westward to the shores of Greenland. But the European countries naturally offered them the greatest hopes of booty. England was the first to suffer their attacks. As early as 793 a landing was effected in Northumberland, where the monasteries of Lindisfarne and Jarrow were pillaged and burned. After this raid followed on raid, the incursions becoming more frequent and more devastating. The Anglo-Saxon kings were unable to repulse the invaders. By the middle of the 9th century the greater part of Eastern England belonged to them, and in 878 Alfred the Great was obliged by treaty to abandon to them all the country lying to the east of a line drawn from London to Chester, which for long afterwards was known by the name of the Danelaw.

Nor did Ireland escape the Scandinavian invasion. Dublin, from the middle of the 9th century to the beginning of the 11th, was a sort of Norman colony. From the insular outposts the hardy adventurers boldly set sail for the south. They infested the coasts of Portugal and Spain, where they attacked Lisbon and Seville (884), passed the Straits of Gibraltar, pillaging Algeciras and the Balearics, reached the mouths of the Rhone, and at times—as far-travelled rivals of the Moslem pirates—they landed on Italian soil.

The Frankish Empire, owing to its nearness, the extent of its littoral, and the great number of deep rivers debouching into the sea, was bound to be—and was in fact—the greatest sufferer at the hands of the Northmen. From the reign of Louis the Pious to the beginning of the 10th century their incursions were incessant. At the outset they appeared now at one point, now at another, baffling the defenders by the sudden and unexpected nature of their attacks. They ascended, in succession, as far as their waters were navigable, the Rhine, the Scheldt, the Meuse, the Seine and the Loire, completely devastating their banks. Then, as they became familiar with the country, they set to work in a more methodical fashion, concentrating on the region extending from the north of the Seine to Friesland. The port of Duurstede, pillaged four times in rapid succession (834–837), was left a heap of ruins: Utrecht was destroyed in 857. It seems that a pagan, Scandinavian State was on the point of being founded in Friesland, for in 890 the Emperor Lothair, unable to repulse the viking Rurik, granted him in fief the banks of the Waal, and in 882 Charles the Fat renewed this concession in favour of Godefroid, another Barbarian. The year 879 marked the apogee of the crisis. A veritable army landed on the banks of the Rhine and the Scheldt, and basing its operations on a series of fortified camps—at Gand and Courtrai, then at Elsloo, near Maestricht, and finally at Louvain—for several years it systematically exploited the country. In 884 Charles the Fat succeeded in turning it aside from Rhenish Germany only at the price of a humiliating treaty. It then marched upon the Seine, and for a year it besieged Paris, but did not succeed in taking the city (885). Having wasted all the north of France, it returned to Louvain in 891. There it was attacked and at last annihilated by Arnold of Carinthia. After this the Northmen risked only a few raids on the Low Countries. But the Seine was long their objective. At last, in 911, Charles the Simple, unable to repulse them, ceded in fief to their chieftain Rollo the regions lying between the Seine and the Epte, which thereafter constituted the Duchy of Normandy. This was the end of the invasions. Scandinavia, exhausted by its effort, and sated with conquest, ceased to discharge its surplus population upon the Continent.

The success of these aggressions is to be explained only by the weakness of the Carolingian State and its increasing decomposition. To resist the Barbarians a fleet would have been necessary. But how could a fleet be built without financial resources? And how could fortresses be built to defend the coasts? While the kings were fighting among themselves, and the monarchy was decaying, how could the State concentrate its efforts and send its armies against the enemy? As a matter of fact, the kings abandoned the attempt, leaving it to the aristocracy to check the invaders as best they could, by local and uncoördinated efforts. The chroniclers of the period have recorded the heroism of many of the feudal seigneurs, who, like the Counts of Paris, Robert the Strong and Eudes (the future king), made their reputations in these conflicts. But others beheld in them only an opportunity of blackmail—of obtaining still greater wealth, inasmuch as they alarmed the feeble kings by threatening to ally themselves with the Barbarians. Even without the Norman invasions the great Carolingian scaffolding must have collapsed. The shocks to which it was subjected only hastened its fall.

The cession of Normandy to Rollo took place only a few years later than the conquest of Kiev by Oleg.[1] The comparison between the two States is interesting. In Russia the Northmen were and remained the masters of the country, and they instituted a government in accordance with their national customs, treating the Slavs as their subjects. In France, where they were in contact with a superior civilization, their attitude was very different. Rollo and his followers went over to Christianity, and the process of assimilation began immediately. It proceeded with astonishing rapidity. Twenty-five years after their arrival the Scandinavian tongue was no longer spoken save at Bayeux, and doubtless along the coast, where the place-names ending in *beuf* remind us of the presence of a people speaking a Germanic tongue. The process of Gallicization was so complete that there is not a single Scandinavian word in the Norman dialect. Nor was there anything Scandinavian in the institutions of the Duchy. These were immediately adapted to the environment, and did not in any essential feature differ from those of the other great fiefs. Fifty years after Rollo's time Normandy was as French a province as Burgundy or Champagne. It must not be forgotten that it was here that the *Chanson de Roland* was born, and that it was on Norman soil that some of the finest specimens of Romanic architecture were erected, such as the great churches of Caen and Bayeux. But of Germanism not a trace remained. So little had survived that when the Normans invaded Sicily, and then England (1066), they appeared as French conquerors. What did survive was the spirit of adventure, which, from the beginning of the 11th century, drove masses of them southwards into Italy. There forty Normans, returning from a pilgrimage, had taken service as mercenaries, and spread the news of what was to be gained in that country. But we must doubtless regard this movement, like the Flemish and Brabantine migrations of the period, as to some extent the consequence of over-population.

[1] It was only in the course of the 11th century that the Scandinavians became assimilated to the Slavs. In 1018 Kiev was still wholly Scandinavian.

## CHAPTER II

# THE DIVISION OF EUROPE

### 1. *The Treaty of Verdun*

The Roman unity was replaced, in the epoch of the Invasions, by States which were independent of one another, conquered by different peoples, and governed by dynasties belonging to these peoples. The Europe of that age, in respect of its political division, was much nearer to the Europe of the modern epoch than it would be again for a long time to come. All these States—excepting the Anglo-Saxon kingdoms and the Visigoth kingdoms of Spain—were fused together in the Carolingian conquest, and absorbed into the great politico-religious unity of the Empire. It was upon its ruins that the States of continental Europe established themselves. But the process of their formation was very different from what it had been at the end of the Roman Empire. There was nothing national in the partition of the monarchy under the sons of Louis the Pious. The question of different peoples did not enter into the case. But how should it have done so? Since the government to which they were subjected was of a universal and ecclesiastical character, the political divisions of the monarchy did not have the effect of subordinating them to one of their number. The Carolingians were, so to speak, transferable; they could govern anywhere; their nationality mattered no more than the nationality of the Pope mattered to the Church. The difference between Romans and non-Romans—a very real difference, but one of which the peoples were not conscious—was of no practical consequence. The quarrel between Lothair and his brothers—the one wishing to preserve the unity of the Empire to his own advantage, the others wishing to divide it—ended in the compromise of Verdun (843).

This was the first of the great treaties of European history, and none was to have more lasting consequences. Even to this day we see its traces in Western Europe, where—between France and Germany—Holland, Belgium, Switzerland and Italy represent the share of Lothair.

But we must hasten to observe that it was history that gave the treaty this significance: not those who negotiated it. All they wanted to do was to divide the Empire into three equal parts. The standpoint from which they regarded the matter was imposed upon them by the economic constitution of the period. Society was purely agricultural; there was no commerce; there were no longer any towns. All they could do, therefore, was to give each party to the treaty, as far as possible, a region whose revenue would be approximately equal to the revenue of each of the other shares; and they had not to take into consideration such matters as trade routes and highways and the extent of the coasts, and all the other considerations which would have rendered the partition of Europe on the lines then followed quite impossible at a later period. The whole destiny of Europe depended on the share to be awarded to Lothair, the elder and the holder of the Imperial title, which gave him at least a moral supremacy over his brothers. Evidently he must be given the central portion. It consisted of Italy, plus a region bordered on the east by the course of the Rhine, and on the west by the Rhone, the Saône and the Meuse, a line running from Mézières to Valenciennes, and finally, the course of the Scheldt.

This central portion being thus delimited, the rest went to his brothers: Charles the Bald taking all that lay between the western frontier and the sea, and Louis all that lay to the east, as far as the confines of the marches established against the Slavs. It was due to chance that Louis' share consisted entirely of Germanic peoples, and that of Charles of peoples almost entirely Romanic. But we have only to consider Lothair's share to realize how little attention was paid to national differences. Nothing could have been more contrary to all geographical and ethnographical considerations. Intersected by the Alps and the Jura, it included, counting from north to south, Frisians, Flemings, Walloons, Germans, Provençaux and Italians. Evidently no more regard was paid to the populations than modern States have paid to the negro tribes on partitioning Africa. And this method answered very well: no one had cause for complaint, since the peoples were conscious only of the rule of the aristocracy, and the aristocracy was everywhere local.

There were no nations in the 9th century. There was only Christendom. All Europe could be cut up into States, as into dioceses, and no one would be injured thereby. The division concerned the dynasty; it was made over the heads of the peoples, and no one was inconvenienced. The Treaty of Verdun was therefore perfectly adapted to a Europe in which the only policy was universal, and the domainal economy had no outlets. Without these two essential conditions it would have been impossible in the form which it actually assumed.

Thus, the first step on the path which was to lead Europe, at the cost of so much bloodshed, to its division into national States, was taken without any regard for the various nationalities, and was even—as a matter of fact—directly opposed to national considerations. The same spirit was manifested throughout the Carolingian decadence.

On the death of Lothair (855) his three sons divided his Empire. The eldest, Louis, took Italy, with the Imperial dignity; the second, Charles, the territory extending from the Jura to the Mediterranean; the third, Lothair, the territory to the north of the Jura. This time the partition seems to have been determined by geographical considerations, but the nationalities were once more completely disregarded. The kingdom of Lothair II was heterogeneous in character; it was impossible to give it a national name, so it was called by the name of its king—Lotharingia. When Charles died childless (863) his two brothers naturally divided his share between them, Louis taking the South and Lothair the North. But the procedure was less regular when Lothair II died in his turn—also without lawful heirs (869). If the previous rule had been followed, Louis II should have inherited his kingdom. But as the unfortunate man was too feeble, his uncles, Louis and Charles, each hoped to secure the succession. They met at Meersen, and instead of fighting they negotiated. Lotharingia was divided into two parts, and on this occasion more or less along the linguistic frontier; not on principle, but because it was thus divided into two approximately equal shares. Charles the Bald, on the death of his brother Louis (876), attempted to seize his States. He was defeated by his nephew Louis III, then King of Germany, at Andernach. This was the first battle in which a French and a German army fought for the prize of Lotharingia, although there was as yet no talk of France or Germany. Contemporaries, indeed, gave the same name of France to the kingdom of the East and to that of the West, merely adding the adjective, Eastern or Western. Charles died (October 6th, 877) before he could repeat his attempt. His son, Louis the Stammerer, who succeeded him, died not long afterwards (August 10th, 879) and Louis III adroitly took advantage of the disturbances which broke out at this moment among his vassals in order to obtain the cession of all the territory which Charles the Bald had acquired. This time the whole of Lotharingia was annexed to the Eastern kingdom.

While this northern portion of the territory of Lothair I was thus disputed, another fragment, in this same year of 879, set itself up as a kingdom. Count Boson of Vienne, son-in-law of the Emperor Louis II (875), had himself elected, by a few bishops and magnates, king of Lower Burgundy or Provence. The power of the aristocracy was growing greater and greater. However, this was still no more than a local manifestation. In 885, the Carolingian family being almost extinct,[1] the whole Empire, with the exception of Burgundy, adopted Charles the Fat as the sovereign. And this again shows how little influence national questions exercised over all these events. For Charles was the youngest son of Louis the German: yet the whole of France recognized him.

But his incapacity, and the shameful treaties which he concluded with the Normans, exhausted the patience of the aristocracy. Arnold, who was governing Carinthia, rebelled against him. He was deposed by the Easterners in 887, and went to end his days in

[1] There were left only Charles, son of Louis the German, and a younger son of Louis the Stammerer.

a monastery, while the magnates bestowed the crown upon Arnold of Carinthia. Arnold himself was a scion of the Carolingian stock, but he was only the bastard son of Carloman, the son of Louis the German. The legitimate heir of the Carolingians was the little Charles the Simple, but he was still a child, and no one recognized him as king. The magnates of the Western kingdom followed the example of the Burgundians: they gave themselves a king, and they chose Eudes, Count of Paris, who had defended the city against the Normans in 886, and whose father, Robert of Paris, had been slain while fighting them. At last, in 888, a new kingdom, once more the creation of the aristocracy, made its appearance in Upper Burgundy (from the Jura to the Pennine Alps), Count Raoul being chosen king. As for Lotharingia, which had acknowledged Arnold, he now (in 895) constituted it a kingdom for the benefit of his son Zwentibold. Probably the magnates of the country had insisted on this step.

However, when Eudes died in 898, Charles the Simple, who had come of age, was proclaimed King of France: so the dynastic idea was not yet extinct. Arnold died in the following year (899), and Zwentibold was killed by the magnates in 900. As Charles the Fat had done formerly, Charles the Simple might have restored the Carolingian unity. But he did nothing of the kind. The magnates of Francia Orientalis recognized as their king the son of Arnold, Louis the Child, who was barely seven years of age, and who, once more, was related to the Carolingians.

Was there in these happenings the beginning of national division? The French did not recognize Arnold in 887; the Germans refused to acknowledge Charles the Simple in 899. But it is impossible to regard these facts as due to a national division. The French, in 883, recognized Charles the Fat because he had been Emperor since 881. Charles the Simple was not Emperor, and Louis the Child was a Carolingian. Here the partition of the monarchy was continued within the dynasty. But the dynasty was badly shaken, and the Italian princelings were contending for the Empire. It was plain that the European unity was breaking down. The aristocracy were disposing of its crowns as they chose. On the other hand, those who dwelt on the periphery of the Empire had lost all interest in what was happening in the centre, in the old historic region between the Seine and the Rhine, as is proved by the separation of Burgundy and Italy. Now, the princes who acknowledged Louis the Child were mainly Trans-Rhenian. The national ideal found so little support among the aristocracy that after the death of Louis the Child in 911 the magnates of Franconia, Swabia, Bavaria and Saxony, the four German duchies, appointed Duke Conrad of Franconia king, while the magnates of Lotharingia, both German and Roman, breaking away from Francia Orientalis, to which they had been attached since the reign of Arnold of Carinthia, acknowledged as their sovereign, after the death of their king Zwentibold, the King of Francia Orientalis, Charles the Simple, who left them their autonomy under Regnier Longneck. The Trans-Rhenians, by appointing Conrad, had definitely broken with the Carolingian dynasty; henceforth this was merely a local dynasty; it had lost its universal character. We may date the final dissolution of the Carolingian unity from the election of Conrad; it was inevitable from the moment when the dynasty ceased to wear the Imperial crown. The greater Francia no longer existed. Henceforth, it is interesting to note, its name was restricted to the territory over which a Carolingian was still reigning. But it was now merely a special name. Henceforth one has to speak of the kingdom of France and the kingdom of Germany. They were separate kingdoms, and they would follow their own destinies, although the distinct nationalities did nothing to cause the separation, and were not even conscious of it. Of the vanished Carolingian unity they both, however, preserved the common heritage, which survived everything, even the Empire: namely, the indissoluble union of the royal power with the Church; as much on account of the intellectual superiority of the Church as by virtue of the still subsisting conception of the duties of royalty.

## 2. *The New States*

Between the two distinct States which had now emerged from the Carolingian unity—France and Germany—there was no necessary and inherent motive of hostility. The nationalities of the two States were different, but not more different, each from the other, than were the peoples within each State: for example, the Bavarians and the Saxons, or the Flemings and the Provençaux. There was no tradition of antagonism. On the contrary: the two countries had lived together side by side and under the same institutions. Their economic constitution did not urge them to encroach upon each other. And yet there arose between them, immediately, that "Belgian question" which one might really call *the* Western question, and which ever since, under various forms, has made periodic reappearances in the course of European history. On this occasion it appeared as a Lotharingian question.

The Lotharingian aristocracy remembered that Lotharingia had been a kingdom. It did not matter that this kingdom had contained nationalities whose languages were different; it nevertheless formed a single social group. On this frontier, when the Carolingians were born, in this extreme north of the Roman world, where Roman and Germanic influences mingled, a sense of autonomy had sprung up among the magnates. They had had kings of their own—Lothair II and Zwentibold—and they wished to continue the tradition. They had not acknowledged Conrad of Franconia, elected by the German Duchies; they had placed themselves under the sceptre of Charles the Simple, who left them under the authority of their Duke Regnier; and he assumed an attitude of such independence that his son Gislebert had already hopes of obtaining the royal title. Conrad could do nothing to prevent him. But as soon as Germany possessed a strong monarch, in the person of Henry the Fowler, the king intervened.

For the Carolingians, Lotharingia had been part of France since the reign of Charles the Simple. For the kings of Germany, it was necessarily part of the German kingdom. It was bound to belong to the stronger country, and the stronger country was Germany. Henceforth there was no intermediate State, in the north, between the two great Western kingdoms. The Franco-German frontier was the Lotharingian frontier (the Scheldt–Meuse frontier). So it was to remain for centuries. The new situation, which came about against the will of the country, was a ferment of discord for the future. The discontented aristocracy had a power at their back to support them. Their manners and customs drew them toward the West rather than the East. Here was the seed of future danger. The oscillations of political preponderance in this Lotharingian territory were to have their repercussions in European history.

Lotharingia became a German duchy against her will, because Germany was stronger than France.

Why was she stronger? Not because she was wealthier or more populous. She was stronger because her king was stronger. And why was he stronger? For two reasons: firstly, because the social evolution of the country was less advanced; secondly, because the Eastern frontier was attacked by the Barbarians.

The social evolution of the country was less advanced in the sense that the local aristocracy comprised fewer powerful families; the further one went from the Rhine, the less developed was the domainal organization. The inhabitants, who were still very much nearer to their old tribal system, lived under the provincial protectorate of a local dynasty. In Saxony and Bavaria especially, far from the administrative centres, the old tribal feeling persisted. The hereditary dukes were recognized as true national chieftains. Nearer the Rhine, in Swabia and Franconia, the social organization was more complex and more advanced, so that there the power of the dukes was less national in character. And across the Rhine, in Lotharingia, matters were very different. There the duke was merely the head of the aristocracy; the dukedom had no national roots, for there was not, properly speaking, a Lotharingian nation.

In Germany, then, the situation was simple. In the place of a multitude of magnates, four dukes, or five at most, held the power in their hands. If they recognized the necessity of allying themselves with the prince whom they accepted as king, they could group the whole country about him.

And this they very soon realized. For the situation of Germany was extremely perilous: not in the West, where the Lotharingian question was mainly dynastic, but in the East, where it was national. It was in the East that Germany was in contact with barbarism, and the Carolingian decadence had given the Barbarians their chance. The Wends, along the Elbe and the Saale, and the Czechs further to the south, had begun to assail the frontiers; and presently a more terrible enemy appeared, the last comer among the European peoples: the Magyars or Hungarians.

They were the last wave of that Finnish inundation which since the days of Attila had never ceased to beat upon the frontiers of Europe: bringing first the Avars, and finally these Magyars, who, like the rest, having traversed the Russian Steppe, made their way into the Danube corridor, driven onward by the Petchenegs. Their earliest raids occurred at the close of the 9th century, when Arnold of Carinthia fought against them. Their arrival in Europe was of the greatest importance to the Western Slavs, whom they cut in two. They destroyed the kingdom of Moravia, founded by the Czechs of Bohemia. The latter were henceforth separated from the Croats and the Serbs, and also from the Poles; so that they were isolated from the Byzantine influence which had recently manifested itself in Bohemia by the despatch of the evangelists Methodius and Cyril, for whom Ratislav, the Prince of Moravia, had sent in order to escape the Frankish influence. From the Danube the Hungarians flung themselves upon Germany and Italy: as terrible as the Normans, and equally adventurous. One of their raids penetrated as far as the Rhine, and as they retired they ravaged Burgundy.

Against these perils Conrad could do nothing. But the case was altered after the election of the Saxon Henry the Fowler (Henry I) in 919. It might have seemed that the royal power was still declining, since after a Carolingian, and after Conrad, a Saxon king was elected.[1] But this Saxon was the most powerful of the German dukes, and his purely military rule did much to enhance the importance of royalty. With his Saxons, Henry repulsed the Slavs, enforced an oath upon the Duke of the Bohemians, and defeated the Hungarians, who had penetrated as far as Merseburg (933).

[1] Conrad was a Franconian, and therefore a native of a comparatively advanced and highly developed country. Henry, a Saxon, was more backward, and a stronger ruler. Here we see the same contrast that was to appear again, later, when Prussia took precedence of the three German States.

He consolidated the royal power to such effect that the princes acknowledged his son Otto as his successor during Henry's lifetime.

Henry had based his power mainly on his duchy of Saxony. Otto entered upon the stage as King of Germany. At his inauguration the dukes served him at table. Despite their revolt, he succeeded in associating them with his military achievements. These continued those of his father. Like his father, he consolidated the German rule in Lotharingia. But his most important work was done in the East. The Hungarians were finally defeated at Augsburg (955). Henceforth they settled down and became Christians, and in so doing, despite their Finnish origin, they entered once and for all into the European community; which proves that racial differences are of no significance—that the historical environment is everything. In the Slav country bishoprics were founded at Meissen, Merseburg, Zeitz, Brandenburg, Havelberg and Oldenburg, which were attached to the archbishopric of Magdeburg, founded in 968. An expedition was despatched to Poland, where Duke Mesko I took the oath, paid tribute, and became a Christian (966), a fact of considerable importance, in so far as it attached Poland to Rome. In the same way, Harold Bluetooth, King of Denmark, was compelled to found bishoprics and to become a convert.

Germany was thus able to turn her attention to the East. She began by reconquering from the Slavs the territory on the right bank of the Elbe, which the Germans had abandoned at the time of the great invasions. So far, however, there was no German colonization of the country, for Germany had no surplus population. What Otto wanted was to settle the Barbarians on the land, and convert them to Christianity. He himself effected a rapprochement with the Church, as the Carolingians had done, but in a somewhat different manner. With the Carolingians the head of the State was closely related to the head of the Church. For Otto such a state of affairs was impossible, both because in his day the Papacy was completely degraded, and because he was not Emperor. It was to the bishops—and not to the Pope—that he looked for support. Through them he was able to oppose a personal policy to that of the secular magnates, and it was from among the prelates that he recruited his counsellors. His brother Bruno was Archbishop of Cologne, and Otto created him Duke of Lotharingia. This is a characteristic example: the bishops were about to become rulers. Otto considered them rather in their secular aspect than from the spiritual standpoint. One might say that what distinguished his policy from that of the Carolingians was that the latter clericalized the State, while he secularized the Church. But if the Church was to furnish him with reliable support it must be powerful. Hence the wholesale gifts to the bishops, the donations of estates and counties. The King of Germany could make such gifts, though the King of France could not, because many of the counties were still dependencies of his own, and because he confiscated the estates of those magnates who ventured to resist him. It was because the evolution of Germany was less advanced, in a feudal sense, that his royal policy was practicable, and it was for this reason that he was able to make his bishops princes of the Empire. The whole of Germany and Lotharingia became covered with episcopal principalities: a feudal system of a special type, which the monarch could extend at will. The prince-bishops were trained in his chapel, like a species of ecclesiastical page. They owed him everything, and wherever they were found, under Otto and his successors, they were distinguished from laymen by their conception of the king's sovereign rights. Their skilful training, and their spiritual education, nurtured in them the idea of discipline. In their eyes the king, not the State, was the stronger, since they themselves were given a portion of the State. Bishop Gerard of Cambrai (1012–1031) refused to introduce the "peace of God" in his diocese because it was the sole prerogative of the sovereign to maintain the public peace. From the bishops, from the 10th century onwards, the Lotharingians learned to admire the discipline of the Germans. The more scholarly they were, the better they served the king. Many of them maintained very notable schools: the schools of Liége were especially celebrated. Here again the Carolingian tradition was revived. For the rest, neither Otto nor his successors meddled in questions of dogma. It was enough for them that they had the Church well in hand. Their *Reichskirche* had something in common with the *Landenkirchen* of a later day.

The Pope, absolutely powerless, did nothing to obstruct the great episcopal policy of the King of Germany. Far from attempting to assert his primacy over the king, he found in him a protector; John XII called on him for assistance, and on February 2nd, 962 restored the Imperial dignity for his benefit. This merely placed the Church more than ever in Otto's hands, until the day when it brought upon Germany the War of Investitures.

The acquisition of the Empire by Otto was simply a consequence of his personal power. Already the Marquis of Ivrea, Berenger, fleeing before King Ugo of Italy, had declared himself Otto's vassal, and in 951 Otto crossed the Alps and assumed the title of King of Italy. The peninsula having been left to its devices for a moment, had taken the opportunity of rending itself to pieces, with the result that for centuries it was tied to Germany.

Otto's intervention was not to be explained, like that of the Carolingians, by his interest in the Papacy. For him, intervention was a dynastic affair, which was quite unrelated to the interests of Germany. There was nothing to draw Germany to the south of the Alps. Her intervention in Italy was actually inconsistent with her movement of expansion towards the East. Was Otto already thinking of the Empire when he undertook this first expedition? In any event, having undertaken it, he was bound to go to Rome and there become Emperor. Whatever strong power appeared in Europe, it must needs gravitate toward Rome.

The Empire having been restored for Otto's benefit, Rome and Italy filled an increasingly important place in the policy of the German sovereigns. Would they be able to support the burden? Already, when Otto was dead (973), Otto II had to march against the Saracens of the South, was defeated by them in Calabria, and died shortly afterwards in Rome (983). Otto III, his son, lost in Imperial dreams, had to establish himself in Italy, forgetting Germany, and there he died in 1002. In Poland, meanwhile, Boleslas Chrobry had asserted his independence, while the Polish and

Hungarian Churches, under the Archbishops of Gnesen and Gratz, had detached themselves from the German Church; the Wends, under Otto II, had revolted and shaken off the yoke, and under Svend Forkbeard paganism had reappeared in Denmark. Henry II, the last of the Saxons, neglected the task of re-establishing his authority on the confines of his kingdom, occupying himself only with Italy, where the Marquis Ardoin of Ivrea (1014) was proclaimed king. It was evident that the Imperial ideal was getting the better of the ideal of kingship. As a matter of fact, there was no King of Germany; the king was presently known as *Rex Romanorum*, and the Emperor as *Imperator Romanorum*. There were no words to describe Germany; she was merged in the Empire. Her kings exhausted their strength in maintaining the Empire. They were all Germans, but they had no German policy. All their strength lay to the north of the Alps, yet they were continually drawn to Italy. They were destined to wear themselves out in pursuit of their policy. Germany has been the victim of the Empire, but her history is confounded with that of the Empire.

The Kings of Germany had evidently undertaken a task beyond their strength. One may ask what would have been the destiny of Europe if instead of squandering their strength to the south of the Alps they had persistently pushed eastwards.

As for the German people, we cannot say that their kings had abandoned them. The people wanted nothing. No necessity, save that of defence, drew them eastwards. The Italian expeditions, thanks to the economic system of the period, did not exhaust their resources. The sovereigns of the 11th century could not conceive of their mission as other than a religious, or shall we say, an ecclesiastical mission. The Carolingian tradition was all-powerful. We can very well understand that Otto could not escape from its influence. So far no such thing as a national policy was possible. The only conception that a powerful monarch could entertain of his power was the conception of Christian universality. In the absence of a national consciousness, the more primitive the economic constitution of the State, the more permissible was it for governments to indulge in universalist idealism; or, in other words, since policy could not be inspired by interests it had its being in the sphere of ideas.

Having died out in Germany with Louis the Child in 911, the Carolingian dynasty survived in France until 987. On the death of Eudes of Paris (878) the magnates of the kingdom had returned to the royal family of tradition, and had acknowledged Charles the Simple as their king, and they turned away from him on the death of Charles the Fat only because he was a minor. However, Charles the Simple and his successors had little of the Carolingian but their names: Charles, Lothair, Louis. None of them bore the Imperial title, none even thought of claiming it. The grandson of Charles the Simple, Lothair, uttered no protest when Otto was crowned in Rome. The only ideal in respect of which they were still faithful to their family traditions was the tenacity with which they endeavoured to recover Lotharingia. Lothair had the satisfaction of advancing as far as Aix-la-Chapelle, where he came near to taking Otto II unawares, and of turning the eagle that surmounted the palace roof to face the east. But his forces were not in proportion to his enterprise. In that same year, 975, Otto II, by way of reprisals, led an army up to the very walls of Paris. Lotharingia, conquered for a moment, was lost to France; only the bishopric of Verdun still remained a French possession.

Lothair's son, Louis V, reigned but a year. At his death only one Carolingian was left—his uncle, Charles, the brother of Lothair, whom Otto II had made Duke of Lotharingia. He tried in vain to conquer the crown, supported by some of the magnates of his duchy, but he was taken prisoner by Hugh Capet in 991. His son Otto, whose name proves that he had become an alien to his race, succeeded him as Duke of Lotharingia. With him the glorious Carolingian dynasty ended in obscurity. We do not even know the exact date of his death (1005 to 1012).

The impotence of its last representatives, which contrasts so strongly with the success and enterprise of the German kings, is not by any means to be explained by their incapacity. Louis, the son of Charles the Simple, and Lothair were both energetic and enterprising princes. But the ground crumbled away from under their feet. The aristocracy had finally acquired an irresistible ascendancy in the countries over which they reigned. The king had only as much power as the aristocracy chose to allow him; and it chose to allow him as little as possible, the better to absorb the counties, and to constitute, by their agglomeration, its feudal principalities. If there had been a question of resisting an invasion it would perhaps have grouped itself about the crown. But since the Normans had established themselves on the coast in 911, France had no external enemies. The magnates were wholly indifferent to the fate of Lotharingia; its possession was merely a dynastic question. The king wanted Lotharingia mainly because it would give him increased power; for he really had no power save in his last domains, and over his last vassals in the Laon country. He could do nothing independently in the interior. If he wanted to take action against one of his vassals he had, for that purpose, to ally himself with another.[1] Lothair endeavoured in vain to prevent the Count of Flanders, Arnold, from advancing to the south of the Lys. The loyalty of his vassals was becoming more and more doubtful. In 922 a party was formed among them which abandoned Charles the Simple and declared Robert of Paris king. Robert was killed in the following year. He was replaced by Duke Raoul of Burgundy, and Charles the Simple died in captivity. Under Louis V Hugh the Great, son of Robert, was all-powerful. It was to him that the king owed his election, and he attempted to exercise tutelage over the monarch. Before long he openly rebelled against his authority, and Otto I of Germany had to come to the assistance of the lawful king and save his crown for him (946). Naturally enough, the King of France had to do what he could to restore his power by directing his efforts toward the outer world. If he contrived to maintain himself within his frontiers, this was not because he was strong like the King of Germany, but because he was weak. His vassals were loyal to him because he was not dangerous, and the most powerful among them found it in his interest to seek his support in order to prevent others from attempting to dispute his authority.

[1] For example: with Flanders against the Normans.

On the death of Louis V, and in the absence of a possible Carolingian heir—for Charles, Duke of Lotharingia, the last representative of the dynasty, was not accepted by the aristocracy of France—the election of Hugh Capet (June 1st, 987) followed, in accordance with the traditions of his family: two of his ancestors had been kings, and the Archbishop of Reims, Adalbéron, supported him. With his accession to the throne a new dynasty began, which was to endure for eight centuries, and achieve hegemony in Europe.

There was nothing to suggest this. The date of the election of Hugh Capet is a date of great significance: but the fact of his election was not important. Nothing was changed; or hardly anything. There had already been Capetian kings: so his election was not a novelty. The conception of royalty was not in any way modified by it.

To suppose that Hugh and his successors had a different conception of royalty from the last of the Carolingians would be completely erroneous. Nothing was changed: neither the title, nor the emblems of royalty, nor the organization of the court. The king was still anointed by the Church; he still considered himself the temporal guardian of order and the protector of the Church. The Carolingian ideal was the royal ideal: there was no other. What is more, the royal power had only *de facto* limits. No one, save the Church, could say where this power should stop. All depended on the strength of the king and of the aristocracy. It was a delicate matter to say just how far the royal power should extend.

The Capetians accepted the situation. They were not by any means feudal kings in the sense of considering that their power was legally restricted by that of the aristocracy. They were simply opportunists, who knew how far they could go. They knew this better than the Carolingians, and for two reasons. Firstly, with their accession the kingship had become purely elective. True, it had become elective in the case of the Carolingians; but they, none the less, constituted a dynasty. The Capetians, on the contrary, had to create a dynasty. It was this necessity that dictated their policy: they were careful to give the magnates no cause of discontent which might excite their mistrust. They kept out of difficulties at home and abroad. This explains why the Capetians allowed the question of Lotharingia to drop. They were content to live, and to leave behind them—as it was their good fortune to leave—an heir whom they had elected in their own lifetime. For them, as for the first Ottos, the hereditary principle was thus established as a fact; but while in Germany it was imposed by the prestige of strength, in France it insinuated itself by virtue of weakness.

The first Capetians dug themselves in, without any undue amour-propre. Philip I, defeated by the Count of Flanders, Robert the Frisian (1071), was reconciled with him and married his step-daughter. The kings were sustained only by their own domains of Paris, Amiens, Orléans and Bourges. They could not create prince-bishops, like the Ottos: the great lay nobles had absorbed all the territory. The kings let them go their way; and it was the Church, not the king, that organized the "peace of God." They contented themselves with taking part in the feasts and assemblies of the magnates and giving diplomas to the abbeys. They were so modest that they have no history. They married mere princesses. They did not leave their own territories, or show themselves abroad: they neither despatched embassies nor received them. Robert the Pious, the son of Hugh (946–1031), refused the crown of Italy, which he was offered by the *grandi* of Lombardy. Henry I (1031–1060) allowed the Emperor Conrad to take possession of the kingdom of Burgundy. Philip I (1060–1108) did nothing to make his reign remarkable. But the Capets endured, and they struck roots in the soil. At the same time their residence, Paris, which they rarely left, was gradually becoming a capital. It was the first capital that Europe had known. Hitherto the kings had moved about: the Capets, territorial princes, settled down and provided the country with a centre. There was no reason why Paris should become the capital of France. It became the capital because it was the residence of the Capets.

So, while the German kings, fortified by the vigour of a primitive society, spent and exhausted their strength in grandiose enterprises, filling Christendom with the sound of their names, but without attaching themselves to the soil, the kings of France, living humbly and modestly amidst a more advanced society, which restricted their power, were quietly and obscurely building up the future. Compared with their immoderate and poetical German contemporaries, they were prosaic and practical. They were sensible folk, who knew their strength, and imperceptibly increased it. And when, under Philip I, an age of peril began with the conquest of England by William the Conqueror (1066), the monarchy showed that it was already sufficiently established to enter upon the conflict which was henceforth to shape the history of France.

## CHAPTER III

# THE FEUDALITY

### 1. *The Disintegration of the State*

We are accustomed to give the name of "feudal" to the political system which prevailed in Europe after the disappearance of the Carolingian dynasty. This habit of ours goes back to the French Revolution, which indiscriminately attributed to the feudal system all the rights, privileges, usages and traditions which were inconsistent with the constitution of the modern State and modern society.. Yet if we accept the words in their exact sense, we ought to understand, by the terms "feudal" and "feudal system," only the juridical relations arising from the fief or the bond of vassalage,[1] and it is an abuse of language to stretch the sense of these terms to include a whole political order, in which the feudal element was, after all, only of secondary importance, and, if we may say so, formal rather than substantial. We shall follow the common usage, but we shall also call attention to the fact that the most significant feature of the so-called feudal system was the disintegration of the State.

Everything tended to accomplish this disintegration, once it had proved to be materially impossible, after the kingdoms founded by the Germanic invasions were established, to continue the Roman State. Disintegration was already on the way at the close of the Merovingian period, when the monarchy, on which everything depended, recovered its influence for the time being, through its great conquests and its alliance with the Papacy. But these con-

[1] The old feudal seigneurs, down to the close of the 18th century, were under no illusion in this respect. It was generally admitted by all that "fief and justice have nothing in common." In reality, feudal law was a special kind of law, like commercial law.

quests, and this influence, retarded only for a moment the process of disintegration, for the causes of the latter were inherent in the social order itself. The king alone could maintain the political organization of the State. Theoretically the State was monarchical and administrative; but we have seen how weak it was, even under Charlemagne. It was weak because its political constitution did not match its economic nature. Since commerce and the towns had disappeared the State had entered upon a period when the great domains absorbed both the land and the inhabitants, placing the revenue of the former and the arms of the latter at the disposal of a class of magnates. These were rendered the more independent by the fact that their economic life was subject to no perturbations; the whole produce of the domain was applied to the maintenance of the domain itself. There was therefore nothing to be feared or expected from the State. This decided the fate of the monarchy. Sooner or later, accordingly as the evolution of society was more or less advanced, it was doomed to allow its rights and prerogatives to pass to the magnates who were now almost its only subjects, since they had interposed themselves between it and the people, and it was obliged to govern through them. To an ever-increasing extent, its only effective power was that which it derived from its own domains. Where it was reduced to the exercise of a purely political sovereignty its rule soon became purely formal. Deprived of taxes, deprived of the possibility of paying its functionaries, how was it to maintain itself? By throwing itself upon the Church, as it had done in Germany? But this had been possible only because in the time of the Ottos the lay aristocracy was still in an undeveloped condition. And again, the episcopal principalities were themselves destroying the State. Thanks to them the monarch alone was strong from the military point of view. But his governmental efficacy was not enhanced by them, and the State was destroyed notwithstanding his military power. Thus, in the economic circumstances of the age the power of the king was inevitably bound to decline, until it depended entirely on his military activity and his personal prestige. And in fact, since the days of Charlemagne the decadence of the monarchy had progressed very rapidly. The king's position, in respect of the magnates, was growing steadily weaker. Matters had gone so far by the close of the 9th century that the monarchy had become purely elective.

It might have disappeared. It did not disappear, and this was characteristic of the age.[1] It did not occur to the magnates that they could dispense with the king. They still had a lingering sense of the unity of the State. Here, above all, the Church had to intervene, for it did not acknowledge the magnates; for the Church the king was the guardian of the providential order of the world. And he, for his part, protected the Church and guaranteed its property. And the magnates themselves needed a king as judge and arbiter: just as in the law-courts there must be a judge or magistrate who presides over the proceedings and pronounces sentence. The king was indispensable to the social order, to the "public peace." But it was clearly understood that the king reigned and did not govern.

And yet, in law, there was no limit to his power. He took no oath of capitulation. He renounced no prerogative. Theoretically he was absolute. But he was paralysed. The members no longer obeyed the head. As far as appearance went, nothing was changed. The kings continued to employ all the old formulae, to receive, in the official language, all the marks of respect. But they had allowed the reality of power to pass into the hands of the aristocracy. The modern jurists have constructed the prettiest theories of the State of the early Middle Ages, and of the rights of the monarch: but they are only theories. The reality was very different. The State was disintegrating, falling to pieces, and from its ruins it reconstructed itself in another form. After Charles the Bald there were no more capitularies, and not until the 12th century do we find the king acting again in a legislative capacity.

What had happened was simply this: the power had spontaneously declined from the hands of the king into those of the aristocracy, which included his officials. We may therefore say, with perfect truth, that the official usurped the functions which he performed.

[1] The election of the king was a mark of progress in the sense that it assured the unity of the monarchy: there would be no more partitions of kingdoms.

The thing happened quite naturally, without deliberate intention, without any violent disturbances, because the official was the seigneur of many of the persons under his administration, and the proprietor of a good portion of his circumscription.

It should be noted, however, that there was a very clear distinction between his private powers over his estates and his men, and the public power, the crown rights which he exercised in the king's name, but henceforth for his own benefit. He possessed the first in his own name as a part of his patrimony. The second he held only by delegation from the crown. If the count, in his county, was supreme justiciary, military commander, collector of what remained of the old Roman *census*, beneficiary of the *droit de gîte* and collector of market tolls, this was because he was a functionary. But all these powers, which he exercised in the king's name, he exercised for his own benefit, and the king could not prevent him from doing so.

Further, the power of the aristocracy broke up and reconstituted for its own benefit the circumscriptions of the State. The State, since the Merovingian epoch, had been divided into counties. These counties were very small, so small that the count-officials were able easily to cover their counties in the course of a day. But from the 8th century onwards the more powerful of these counts had begun to usurp the power in a number of counties adjacent to their own. Fortunate marriages, friendly arrangements, violence, the king's favour, or the fear which they inspired in him, soon enabled them to amalgamate, in a single territory, a greater or smaller number of the old circumscriptions. The new county established by these encroachments became a principality, just as the count became a prince. The name borrowed from the Roman bureaucracy still adhered to him, but this sometime agent of the central power, having absorbed the power which was delegated to him, and enlarged the circumscription in which he exercised that power, was now, and would remain for centuries, a petty local sovereign.

All this was accomplished in the midst of unspeakable violence and treachery. The 10th century, like the 15th, was an epoch of political assassination. The territorial power of the feudal princes was no more scrupulous in the choice of means than that of the absolutist monarchs or the tyrants of the Renaissance; it was merely more brutal. Each sought to increase his power to the detriment of his neighbour, and any weapon was permissible. The passion for land ruled the actions of all these feudal magnates, and as there was no one to stop them, they struck at each other with all the brutality of their instincts. The king was powerless, and when on occasion he attempted to intervene his functionary made war upon him. It was thus that Charles the Simple died in the prison of the Count of Vermandois.

Nevertheless—and here the feudal element appears—the princes were bound to the king by the oath of fealty. The old subordination of the functionary had been transformed into the oath. The feudal seigneurs were the king's men, his faithful servants. In theory, the king was still the supreme possessor of the powers which had been usurped from him, and this the feudal oath acknowledged. We must not say, therefore, that the feudal system broke down the State, for the truth is the reverse of this. It still maintained a bond—or at least a formal bond—between the king and those parcels of the kingdom of which the great functionaries who had become princes had possessed themselves, and whose feudal oath made them vassals. Here was a principle which the jurists would exploit at a later period, when the king was strong once more. For the time being the king gave way to the seigneurs, and recognized the usurpations which he could not prevent. The hereditary principle was in force among the feudal magnates. The son succeeded to the father, and from the 11th century onwards the hereditary principle was extended to women.

The king, who still regarded himself as the possessor of all the power of the State, was now envisaged by the princes, his great vassals, only from the feudal standpoint. For them he was no more than a magnate to whom they were allied by a contractual bond. They owed him aid and counsel, and the king owed them protection: if he attacked them, taking his king's point of view, they considered themselves justified in marching against him. The princes envisaged the monarchy otherwise than the king himself. But the consequences of this difference of conception were not felt until a later date; and until the 12th century the kings, with rare exceptions, allowed matters to go their way.

Thus, from the end of the 9th and the beginning of the 10th century the State was reduced to an empty form. The provinces had become principalities, and the functionaries princes. The king, except on his own territory, was merely the "enfeoffed sovereign" of his kingdom. A multiplicity of local sovereignties had replaced the old administrative unity derived from the Roman Empire. But it must be recognized that this was the normal and sensible situation, which was in correspondence with the social condition, and therefore with the needs, of the community. The agrarian and domainal constitution of the epoch made it impossible to maintain the administrative unity that even a Charlemagne could not transform into a living reality. How could the political power have remained centralized in the hands of the king at a time when the people were entering *en masse* into the cadres of the great estates, into dependency on the seigneurs? Political power was bound to follow effective power, and to crystallize itself, so to speak, around those who really possessed that power. The protection of human beings is not merely the primordial function of the State: it is also the origin of the State. Now, the king no longer protected his subjects; the magnates protected them. It was therefore necessary and beneficial that they should dismember the State to their own advantage. They certainly had public opinion—or shall we say, the sentiment of the peoples—on their side. Nowhere do we see that the "little man" attempted to save the monarchy. He no longer knew what monarchy was.

It was in the restricted centres of the territorial principalities that a system of government and administration was first organized that actively influenced those who were subject to it. The kingdom was too extensive. It had inevitably to restrict itself to an administration which could not be adequately supervised, and which did not reach the masses. It was otherwise with the new system. The territorial princes were in touch with reality; their private function enabled them to govern effectively a territory of moderate extent: the number of their dependants and vassals was in proportion to its area, and provided them with a staff. Each of these princes set to work in his own way; their methods varied in detail, but were broadly the same. It was this obscure task that was the most important feature of the period, as regards the formation of society, and where it was first undertaken—in the Low Countries and in France—society was more advanced than elsewhere. The kings were in the front of the stage; the emperors occupied themselves with high policy. But it was the princes who created the first original type of political organization that Europe had known since the Roman Empire.

They had, of course, no theory, no conscious conception. Practice automatically fitted itself to the reality.

The foundation of the territorial organization was the landed property of the prince, since it was from this that he derived his power. The principal "counts" of his domain, or the most favourably situated, were provided with defensive works, and became castles (*bourgs*), the centres of the military, financial and judicial organization. They were usually great walled enclosures, with dwelling-houses, store-houses, and lodgings for the garrison of knights. A châtelain, whom the prince chose from among his men acted as his substitute in the circumscription, which bore the name of *châtellenie*. It was the châtelain who commanded the fortress, watched over the countryside, and presided in the local court of justice. In order to support the châtelain and the knights of the castle prestations in kind were levied on the population: and here the principle of the salary made its appearance, a principle unknown to the kings: of payment in the form of fixed dues to be made to the public authority. Moreover, as early as the 11th century we find traces of a county impost (*petitio*, *bede*), and this was a fresh sign of progress, despite the still primitive form of assessment and collection. Thus, at a time when the king had no financial resources outside his domains, the prince was organizing them. Moreover, the prince minted money, for he usurped the right of coining money with the other crown rights, and he made a handsome profit by debasing the coinage. He had also the market tolls, and, of course, he continued to take his share of the fines.

From every point of view, then, his power was greater than that of the king. For while the king was now elective, the principality was hereditary, and at an early period—as early as the 10th century—the right of sole succession was established, so that the principalities were not divided. It is interesting to note how unchanged they continued until the end of the *ancien régime*, which preserved them as provinces. The prince, from the 10th century, had a historiography. He had a court, modelled on that of the king: chancellor, marshal, seneschal, cup-bearer. He had his vassals, who were more loyal to him than he was to the king, by reason of their proximity, and the greater disproportion of their powers. He was the advowee of all the monasteries within his territory, and he exacted dues or services from them. The documents call him *princeps, monarcha, advocatus patriae, post Deum princeps.*

He was in actual sense the territorial chieftain, the head of the *patria*, and we should note that in the Latin of the Middle Ages people were beginning to apply this beautiful word to these little local "counties." In them was formed, for the first time, the patriotism which in modern society has replaced the civic sentiment of antiquity. There was something in it of the sense of family, and it was embodied in the man who from father to son was the chief and protector of the group. His armorial bearings became those of the people, and their common loyalty to him was a bond of service. Nothing like this had existed under the Merovingians or Carolingians, and in later periods men had this feeling only for their kings. Modern patriotism, born of the dynastic sentiment, was in the first place nurtured in the principalities.

The prince was really the protector of his men. He discharged his duty in person: his life, and his social function, were active in the extreme. Not only did he lead his men to the wars, and with them fling himself upon the enemy: he also presided in his courts of justice, supervised the work of his tax-collectors, and gave his personal decision in all important questions; and above all, he watched over the "public peace." He assured the safety of the roads, and extended his protection to the poor, and to orphans, widows, and pilgrims; and he fell upon highway robbers and hanged them. He was the supreme justiciary on his own territory, the guardian and guarantor of public order, and in this respect his function was essentially social in character. When one speaks of the "bloodthirsty" feudal magnates one should make reservations. The feudal seigneur was bloodthirsty when abroad, in his enemy's country, but not in his own; and one thing is certain—that society began to receive its political education within the *cadre* of the feudal principalities. The great State of which the principalities were the dismembered parts did not really influence people; its activities were carried on over their heads. The monarchy had designed the framework of political life, introduced Christianity, allied itself with the Church, and created an ideal of royalty which still survived, and would be a force in the future. But it had no actual hold upon men and women. To reach them, to govern them, the immediate, firm and active power of the local princes was needed. And these princely men-at-arms with the fantastic names, these rough soldiers, despite their pillaging of their neighbours' territories, must be given their place among the civilizers of Europe. In the political and social life of the continent, they were the first instructors.

## 2. *Nobility and Chivalry*

In the 10th century a new juridical class had sprung up in the European States: the nobility. Its importance is sufficiently shown by the fact that in lay society the nobles alone had political rights. Later on the bourgeoisie would take its place beside the nobility. This place would become more and more considerable, but down to the end of the *ancien régime* it would still be regarded as a secondary place. In the history of Europe the nobles have played—though under very different conditions—almost the same part as the patricians in Roman history, while the bourgeoisie may be compared with the plebeians. It is only in the modern State that they have become merged in the mass of the citizens, much as in the

Empire the general bestowal of civic rights effaced the old difference between the patriciate and the plebs.

The noblesse exercised so great and so general an influence over the history of Europe that it is not easy to realize that it constituted an original phenomenon, and one peculiar to the Christian society of Western Europe. Neither the Roman nor the Byzantine Empire, nor the Musulman world, had ever known a similar institution. Doubtless all primitive societies have comprised a nobility of mythological origin. But these nobilities disappeared on the advent of civilization: like the old Germanic nobility, which did not outlive the invasions. The nobility of the Middle Ages, five centuries later, was quite a novel creation, and very different in character.

It was preceded by the powerful aristocracy, partly Roman, and in part consisting of the parvenus and functionaries who had been making their appearance, and playing a more and more important part, since the formation of the new kingdoms. But this aristocracy was not a nobility, in the sense of being a juridical class to which a man belonged by birth. It was merely a social class, which consisted of a group of powerful individuals. Moreover, whatever its actual power, it possessed no privilege in law. The greatest landowner of Charlemagne's day was in the same position, in a court of justice, as the simple freeman.

Two causes contributed to the formation of the nobility: the constant diminution of the number of freeman, and the feudal form of military service: and of these two causes the second was far more important than the first, and could even have dispensed with its action.

The domainal system, as it expanded, resulted in the juridical degradation of the rural population, reducing it to a more or less complete servitude. Those who had retained their liberty were in a privileged situation, and from the 10th century the word *liber* took on the meaning of *nobilis*. The old juridical usages relating to the family and inheritance now applied only to these privileged persons. The common law of freemen was modified into a special law. The *connubium* was enlarged in Roman law: at the beginning of the Middle Ages it was reduced. Family right was finally the apanage only of the few; and the same was true of free hereditary property (*allodium*).

These freemen, whose numbers it is impossible to estimate, naturally retained the right to bear arms. Their estate enabled them to maintain a war horse. They were above all warriors.

But beside them, and far more numerous—at any rate, in France—was another class of freeman: the vassals. Their means of livelihood was provided not by their personal property, their *allodium*, but by the fief which, in this agricultural age, served as their salary. Like the others, and even more than the others, they were warriors. But unlike the first class, they were not hereditary warriors; for the fief did not pass from father to son unless the son was a good soldier. If the father left only daughters, or sons incapable of bearing arms, the fief lapsed to the seigneur. But such a case was rare. In France, from the time of Charles the Bald, the fiefs were hereditary, and while in Germany their hereditary character was not formally recognized until the reign of Conrad, they were certainly handed down from father to son before that date.

In addition to these free soldiers—some the proprietors of *allodia*, others the holders of fiefs—there were also soldiers who were not free. These were loyal and sturdy serfs whom the seigneurs took with them as bodyguards when they went to the wars, and employed, in times of peace, in confidential posts, as *ministeriales* or *Dienstmannen*; in Germany, more especially, they were numerous, and they constituted the aristocracy of servitude.

All, whether free or not, were united by the sense of professional community, and were regarded with special consideration by the rest of the population; for since all the intellectual functions were allotted to the clergy, only the trade of arms could give the laymen a privileged position in society.

The warrior entered the military class only on coming of age. A special ceremony was necessary before he could be admitted; at this his arms were conferred upon him by the seigneur or by one of his companions. By this ceremony he was consecrated knight, *chevalier*, which meant simply horse-soldier. It gave the recipient of the honour the advantages and the prestige of his position. At first, unless the son of a knight was himself dubbed knight, he was a villein merely, and his daughters, since they could not be knighted, enjoyed no special consideration. But this was evidently a transitory phase; and fact was followed by law. As a general rule, the son of a knight would himself become a knight. He was therefore counted, from birth, as belonging to the military caste; and the daughters of a knight would be regarded as belonging to the same social class. And as soon as this state of affairs was reached—which in France, at all events, was by the close of the 10th century—the nobility was born: that is, a hereditary class, conferring a particular rank in the State, independently of social position. All those who belonged to the *milicia*, or whose ancestors had belonged to it, were *nobiles*. It was not absolutely essential that the "noble" should be free; for in the end the *ministeriales* came to be regarded as nobles.[1]

Thus the class of vassals was practically merged in the nobility. However, nobility did not depend upon the possession of a fief. After all, a man could be knighted who did not possess a fief; and it was not for some time—not until the 13th century—that the plebeian was debarred from the possession of a fief. It was therefore the social function that made the noble; but it was a social function that presupposed economic independence, based upon the noble's personal property (his *allodium*) or his feudal property (his fief). The nobility was really the army. Hence its privileges. They were explained by the nature of the service rendered, and conferred as consideration for that service. The noble did not pay the count an impost on account of his land, because he furnished him with military service. This was the sole privilege, so-called, of the nobility: it had no others. His special juridical situation, his special status in respect of his family, and the special procedure by which he benefited in the law-courts, were merely the survival of the common law of freemen, which had been modified for villeins.

The importance of the nobility resided in its social rôle. Uplifted

[1] But this was not definitely the case until the 14th century.

by its military functions above the rest of the population, in constant touch with the princes, it was the nobility and the nobility alone that furnished the administrative personnel, just as it was the nobility alone that constituted the army. It was from the nobility that the châtelains were chosen, the mayors, and all the other agents of the territorial administration. It was therefore regarded not only as a military but also as a political caste. Beside the nobility was the clergy. Below the nobility and the clergy was the mass of plebeians, by whose labour they lived; in return for which service the clergy directed their souls while the nobility protected their bodies. This is not a theoretical *a posteriori* view. The writers of the period were perfectly well aware of this mutual relation, and recorded it in plain language.

This nobility was extremely numerous; especially when the domainal system was well developed, so that the number of fiefs could be readily increased. One may say that the evolution of society was in proportion to the numbers, or rather to the density of the chivalry, which decreased as one proceeded from the French frontier in the direction of the Elbe. In France and the Low Countries one could count on finding a number of knights in every country town, and we certainly shall not be far out if we estimate that in these countries they represented at least one tenth of the population.

We must not imagine that their mode of life was especially refined. Their fiefs and their little domains just enabled them to live. Their military equipment consisted of a lance, an iron casque, a buckler, and a suit of buckram. Only the wealthiest knights possessed a coat of mail. They were formidable soldiers, however, and when war left them any leisure they kept themselves in training by means of tourneys that were like veritable battles. They attended them in their hundreds, grouped according to regions, and charged one another heavily until more than one was left on the ground. Further, they were the most turbulent of men, furiously destroying one another in the private wars and family vendettas in which they were continually involved. In vain did the Church, from the close of the 10th century—first of all in France, and later in Germany—restrict the days of battle by the "peace of God"; custom proved to be too strong for it. At the end of the 11th century the chronicler Lambert of Waterloo related that ten of his father's brothers were slain by their enemies on the same day, in an encounter near Tournai; and about the same time the Count of Flanders, Robert the Frisian, drawing up the list of murders committed in the neighbourhood of Bruges, stated that it would take more than 10,000 marks of silver to pay the "compositions" in respect of these murders.

Naturally, in such an environment there was no intellectual culture. Only in the wealthiest families would a clerk teach the daughters to read. As for the sons, who were in the saddle as soon as they could mount a horse, they had no knowledge of anything but fighting. Their literature consisted of soldiers' songs, such as the song that Taillefer sang at the Battle of Hastings. They were violent, gross, and superstitious, but excellent soldiers. Consider the exploits of the Normans in Sicily, the conquest of England, the Flemish knights who so amazed the Emperor Alexis as they passed through Constantinople, and above all the extraordinary enterprise of the Crusades. The qualities that made the knights of France and the Low Countries the finest warriors of their time had nothing to do with race; they were the fruit of training. This training was better in the West because there the chivalry was more numerous, and it was so because of the greater extension of the domainal system.

At the close of the 11th century chivalry was extremely widespread. But "chivalrous" manners—by which I mean the code of courtesy and loyalty which distinguished the gentlemen after the age of the Crusades—had as yet no existence. To produce them greater refinement was necessary. Still, the two sentiments on which they were based were already widely diffused among the knights: namely, devotion and honour. Nothing could exceed the piety of these soldiers, despite their superstitions and their brutality. They were scrupulous in their respect for the right of sanctuary: they would halt in their pursuit of an enemy as soon as they saw the towers of a monastery upon the horizon. They followed with exemplary piety the relics which the monks carried in procession through the countryside. They went on distant pilgrimages, to Rome and to Jerusalem; and it would even seem that the songs of the feudal epoch were evolved on the pilgrim routes. As for honour, the sentiment which the modern world has inherited from them, this was wholly a military virtue. It was not precisely the honour of our day, which is more refined. It was, before all, the sentiment of fidelity and loyalty. These knights were ready enough for treachery, but they did not break their given word. Homage (*homagium*)—a word which has gradually lost its full meaning in our language—meant for them the complete offering of their person to their seigneur. Felony was in their eyes the worst of crimes.[1] They regarded everything from the personal point of view, as between man and man. The sentiment of obedience and discipline was entirely foreign to them. The moment that they considered they had been injured they rebelled, and their habit of plain speaking was quite extraordinary. Their economic independence naturally generalized among them certain mental and moral attitudes, which persisted under different conditions, though they assumed more refined forms. It was then that the normal foundation on which the nobility was to build in later times was laid. It was easily comprehensible, and entirely dissimilar to the foundation from which the bourgeoisie rose to a position of influence. To the very last the great majority of the nobility would retain the traces of their descent from a class of men to whom all notions of profit and productive labour were alien. To a certain extent the ancient idea that labour is unworthy of the freeman was revived by the chivalry of Europe. But the freeman of antiquity devoted his leisure, which he owed to the labour of his slaves, to public affairs: the knight of the Middle Ages profited by the gift of land which he received to devote himself to the calling of arms and the service of his lord. When centuries had passed, and when the nobility had gradually been ousted from the rank which it held of old, the expression "to live like a nobleman" finally came to mean, "to live without doing anything."

[1] See Ganelon in the *Chanson de Roland.*

*Book Four*

# THE WAR OF INVESTITURES AND THE CRUSADE

F

CHAPTER I

# THE CHURCH

## 1. *The Papacy*

As the Empire declined the Papacy, as we have seen, profited by its rival's loss of vitality and prestige. But it could not of its own strength maintain itself at the height to which it had climbed. It had leant on the Empire: it had, so to speak, climbed upon its back. When the Empire collapsed the Papacy was involved in its fall. To begin with, assailed by the self-made kings who fought one another for the possession of Italy and the Imperial crown, it became the prey—at the beginning of the 10th century—of the Roman feudality. The lords of the Roman Campagna fought among themselves to obtain the Papacy for their own family. True, the Pope was still appointed by the clergy and the people of the city, but it was only too easy to impose him on the electors by force, or to overthrow the pontiff elect who did not suit the book of the more powerful party. The election of the Pope by the community of the clergy and the faithful took place regularly as long as there was a strong power at the side of the Papacy. At first it was supervised by the exarch, then by the *missi*. But since the Empire had fallen into decadence the Pope was appointed under pressure from the feudal signori. The Popes of this period appeared and disappeared at the will of the feudal factions: some were assassinated, others died in prison. In this Roman environment, whose immorality was equalled only by its brutality, the intrigues of the women more than once disposed of the tiara. Marozia and Theodora, working through their successive husbands or lovers, had it conferred upon their sons; the legend of Pope Joan is merely an exaggeration, to the point of caricature, of the only too actual scandals of the period. One of Marozia's sons, Alberic of Tusculum, finally became the lord of Rome and the maker of Popes. He took the precaution of making the Romans acknowledge his son Octavian as his successor, and the future Pope. When he died Octavian succeeded him as the master of the city, and in 955, at the age of 18, he received the sovereign pontificate as he might have received a fief, under the style of John XII. And yet it was this feudal Pope who was the instrument of the restoration of the Empire. We need hardly say that the sole consideration that moved him to restore it was his own interest, and for him this great action was no more than a mere expedient. When in 962 he summoned Otto I to Rome, and set the Imperial crown upon his head, he did so because at this moment he was soliciting Otto's help against the Marquis Berenger of Ivrea, the so-called King of Italy, his mortal enemy. The traditions of the age of Leo I and Charlemagne were so degraded that John can hardly have supposed that Otto's conception of the Empire was more exalted than his own of the Papacy. No Roman of his day had any understanding of the great words that had once dominated history. When he saw that the new Emperor was taking his position seriously, and that his lordship of Rome was threatened, he made haste to betray him and intrigue against him. Otto returned to Rome, convoked a synod, which deposed John XII, and made the Romans swear an oath to the effect that they would not in future appoint a Pope without his consent, or that of his son. Leo VIII was elected in his presence: then he departed. But the Romans had yielded only to force. Otto had hardly left Rome when they drove Leo from the throne, and recalled John: and after his death, heedless of their oath, they replaced him by Benedict V. Otto had to return and besiege the city. Seizing Benedict, he exiled him to Hamburg, and restored Leo. On the death of Leo, John XIII, appointed under German influence, was soon driven from the throne by a revolt, and in 966 the Emperor had to cross the Alps once more in order to restore him.

We see that in all these conflicts the Pope, as compared with the Emperor, was merely the lord of Rome, and almost like a disobedient vassal. The contrast is obvious between the majestic memories evoked by his name and the local rôle to which he was restricted. Thanks to its remoteness from Germany, the Roman feudality always recovered its position after it had yielded. Under Otto II the Crescenzi were as powerful in Rome as Alberic had been before them, and the defeat of Rossano did nothing to diminish their influence.

Otto III had a vague dream of establishing the alliance of Pope and Emperor, in accordance with the Carolingian theory, but not the Carolingian reality. He dreamed of making Rome the centre of the twofold power, the indissoluble union, which from that centre would govern Christendom. At the age of twenty-five he entered the city, caused his cousin Bruno to be elected Pope, under the name of Gregory V (996), and received from him the Imperial crown. At Gregory's death Otto chose, as the occupant of St. Peter's throne, the most learned man of his time: Gerbert, Archbishop of Reims, then of Ravenna, who took the name of Sylvester II, thus recalling that Sylvester I of whom legend relates that he baptized Constantine. The Emperor installed himself beside the Pope on the Aventine, in a palace whose pomp recalled that of Byzantium, and whose etiquette borrowed its austerity from the rules of the monastic orders. Losing himself in the idealistic day-dreams that betrayed the influence of his mother Theophano, and of the bishops who had educated him, he seems to have believed in the possibility of making Rome once more the centre of the world—but a Rome in which the Pope would share in the Imperial power. Neither he nor Gerbert, lost in their dreams, could perceive the reality. And this reality avenged itself cruelly: a revolt of the Romans forced him to flee, and on January 23rd, 1002, he died at Paterno, at the foot of Monte Soracte: died of the shattering of his dream.

Once more the factions fought for the mastery of the city: the Crescenzi on the one hand, the Counts of Tusculum on the other. Benedict VIII, the creature of the Counts, maintained himself in power by appealing for aid to Henry II, just as John XII had appealed to Otto. He was succeeded by his brother, John XIX (1024–1033), a layman, who received all the degrees of the ecclesiastical hierarchy on one and the same day. He crowned Conrad II. After him a third member of the Tusculum family was elected: Benedict IX. The Crescenzi drove him from the throne, replacing him by Sylvester III, who a little later was expelled in his turn by his adversary, returning at the head of his party. Sylvester then sold his title to Gregory VI, so that there were three Popes at the same time.

We see, then, that the restoration of the Empire had not the effect of strengthening the Papacy. With the exception of Otto III the new Emperors did not continue the Carolingian tradition. They governed with the Church—that is, with the bishops—but not with the Pope. He was useful only because he crowned them.

For the rest, they did not succeed in restoring order in Rome; but this did not concern them greatly. The Pope, moreover, could do little to embarrass them, for he exercised no authority over the Church. And the clergy of Rome, being in the hands of the factions, uttered no protests, and made no effort to restore the throne of St. Peter to its ancient glory, or even to its ancient dignity. The reformation which was to restore it, and which, as a necessary consequence, was to bring it into conflict with the Emperor, came from the outer world.

## 2. *The Clunisian Reformation*

The discipline, the morality, the learning and the wealth of the Church had been restored or increased under the Carolingians. They were dependent upon the support of the Carolingians, and therefore upon their power. The decline of the dynasty subjected them to a crisis which, like the crisis of the political constitution, was the point of departure for a renewal of activity. In Germany, where the Imperial Church, since the reign of Otto, had stood on solid foundations, the crisis was of brief duration, and under the guidance of the bishops the Carolingian tradition was quickly restored, and the intellectual culture of the clergy once again followed the path traced by Charlemagne and by Alcuin. But it was otherwise in the West. The feudal system, in destroying the State as it spread over Western Europe, as a natural consequence undermined the Church. In France, in Lotharingia, and in Italy the position of the bishops was almost the same as that of the Pope in Rome. They had to defend themselves against the feudal authorities of the neighbourhood, or they were imposed upon the clergy by these authorities; they were driven from their sees if they did not please the most powerful party, and were sometimes assassinated if they defied it too openly. The Pope could do nothing for them: in France the king could protect only the bishops of his own domain, whom he appointed. The situation of the monasteries was still more lamentable. The lay seigneurs who forced themselves upon them as advowees, when they did not simply assume the title of abbot, pillaged their estates, created fiefs for their men at the cost of the monastic domains, compelled them to support their servants and their packs of hounds, and, in short, plundered them, and no one could intervene.

As the secular power grew weaker the Church passed through a temporary crisis, from which it emerged more powerful than before, since it was now alone. It was fully capable of maintaining itself, and of applying to its own benefit the forces which had for a time been diverted to the service of the State. This renovation had naturally to come from those of the clergy who were least involved in secular allegiances—namely, from the monks.

The evil afflicting the Church, unlike the malady of the State, was only on the surface. It was feeling the consequences of the feudal expansion, but its constitution, since it stood outside the political community, was not thereby affected. However great the disorder in the Church, it destroyed nothing essential. The episcopal organization survived, just as the monasteries survived; and so did piety, for while learning and discipline declined, piety increased in the sense that it became more widespread. In the 10th century the parishes extended over the whole country. The rural churches became a feature of the landscape. The monastic domains, better organized than those of the lay proprietors, attracted the people *en masse*. Many of the new inhabitants became *cerocensuales* (that is, serfs of the Church); and these, faithful to the saintly patron of the monastery, provided him with a following which spread his cult and lauded his miracles. This, the period of local government, was also the period of local saints: St. Lambert, St. Hubert, St. Bavon, St. Trond. They were, so to speak, the great vassals of God, under whose protection men were glad to place themselves. Their relics exercised a magic influence. The monks bore them in procession about the countryside. They served to dissuade the knights from private warfare. And their miraculous power was reflected upon the monks who guarded them. For the saints, as a rule, dwelt in the monasteries, not in the bishops' palaces. The influence of the abbeys was increased by the fact that many of the rural churches belonged to them, or were dependent upon them; and the monks officiated in them. The contemporary ideal of sanctity was the monastic ideal; the renunciation of worldly joys in order to save one's soul; the withdrawal from social activities, and even from all other virtues than those of renunciation, humility, and chastity. And it was to this ideal that the Church owed its renaissance: not to the bishops, whether they were semi-feudal as in France, or faithful to the Carolingian tradition, as in Germany. Their learning made no impression on this uncultured public. The people wanted saints and workers of miracles.

The feudal nobles, even more than the people, regarded the bishops as their enemies. They pillaged the monasteries, but they respected them, and on their deathbeds the princes who had pillaged them most mercilessly made large donations to them. They all revered holiness, and they deplored the disorder into which the monasteries had fallen, although they were the cause of this disorder.

We can judge of their feelings by the encouragement which they accorded to asceticism whenever this made itself conspicuous. Gérard de Brogne, a knight who had become a religious, and who soon became famous for the discipline that he enforced in the little monastery which he had founded on his estate, was entrusted by the Counts of Hainault and Flanders with the task of reforming the abbeys in their territories. This local movement is significant, and shows how far the ground was prepared for the decisive reformation that proceeded from Cluny. This monastery, founded in

910 by Duke Guillaume d'Auvergne, under the direction of men like Odo († 943) or Odilon de Mercœur († 1099), played a part whose importance might be compared with that of the Jesuits in the 16th century. Here, of course, there was no question of grappling with heresy. The point at issue was the orientation of religious thought and feeling. I think we may say that by the reform of Cluny monasticism set its stamp upon Western Christianity for centuries to come. Of course, the monks had already played an important part: notably in the conversion of England. But the secular clergy were the more important: it was through them that the alliance of Church and State was manifested. The bishops, in the Carolingian epoch, were almost royal officials; in Germany they were made princes. Now, it was precisely this that the Clunisians condemned. For them, the world was the antechamber to Eternity. Everything had to be sacrificed to supra-terrestial ends. The salvation of the soul was everything, and it could be effected only by the Church: and the Church, in order to fulfil its mission, must be absolutely innocent of temporal interests. Here there was no question of the alliance of Church and State, but only of the complete subordination, in the spiritual domain, of man and society to the Church, the intermediary between man and God. Anyone who lent himself to the meddling of the secular power in religious affairs was therefore regarded as guilty of simony. The priest belonged to the Church and the Church alone. He could have no seigneur, just as he could have no family. The marriage of priests, tolerated in practice, was an abomination which must disappear. The complete spiritualization of the Church, the absolute observation of canon law: this, if not the programme properly so-called, was at all events the tendency of Cluny. In the domain of piety it made for asceticism: in the political domain, for the complete liberty of the Church, and the breaking of the ties that bound it to civil society. In this sense, Cluny might be described as anti-Carolingian. But it was Papist; for obviously the Church, in order to be independent, must gather round its head, who was in Rome.

The political consequences implied in this reform were not

immediately manifested. At first there was nothing to be seen but a renaissance of the ascetic life at Cluny, while in all parts of the country princes and bishops called upon the monks to regenerate the abbeys in their territories. From the middle of the 10th century the reform spread through the whole of France, and into Italy, Flanders, and Lotharingia—whence, at the beginning of the 11th century, it overflowed into Germany. And wherever it made its way there was an increase of piety—of the outward piety which consists, above all, in obedience to religion, in respecting the feasts of the Church, in resigning oneself wholly and in all things to the Church, the bride of Christ, His representative on earth, the mystical source of grace and salvation. More knights adopted the religious life,[1] more princes died in the monastic habit,[2] and more than ever new monasteries were founded. There were many new foundations in the 10th and 11th centuries.

The Church was regarded as a purely superhuman institution. Men lived in an atmosphere of wonder; miracles were matters of everyday experience. Every epidemic gave rise to miracles. Every plague, every famine provoked extraordinary manifestations, such as the great procession of Tournai (11th century). At Saint-Trond the annual product of the offerings of the faithful surpassed all the other revenues of the monastery. The building of the new church at Cologne having been decided upon, the people voluntarily carted thither the stones and columns brought down the Rhine. The "peace of God" which interrupted the private wars on the occasion of the great annual feasts was one of the results of the extraordinary influence which the Church exerted over men's thoughts and feelings. But the riots which broke out in the 11th century to mark the popular disapproval of married priests were also the direct result of this influence.

There were plenty of conservative thinkers who were alarmed by the new dispensation. Egbert of Liége and Sigebert of Gembloux considered that the monks were going too far: they were dismayed by the arrogant and absolute nature of their opinions. And such feelings were at first very general among the Imperialist clergy.

[1] Pippin, who became Abbot of Stavelot. [2] Godefroid le Barbu, Duc d'Ardenne.

Gérard of Cambrai refused to introduce the "peace of God" in his diocese. Yet all the noblest minds, all the purest hearts turned to the new movement as to a great ideal. And no one dared to oppose it, for that would have been to make war on God Himself.

The power of the movement has left its traces to this day. It was then that the first great churches were built; it was then that religious art began to make temples too vast for the people, but still too small for the Divine Majesty.[1] The 11th century was an extraordinary period of church-building, the point of departure of the great schools of Western architecture, which hitherto had always been dominated by Byzantium and Ravenna. It also demonstrated the enormous increase of the Church's fortune. As regards the monasteries especially the 10th and 11th centuries were *par excellence* the age of donations. Their wealth naturally enabled them to augment their social influence, to increase their almsgiving, their protection of the poor, etc.

It must once more be noted that while the Church was a sacerdotal caste, and also, more and more, like the nobility, a military caste, it was none the less open to all. A serf could not enter the nobility, but he could enter the Church. He had only to go to school and learn Latin. As soon as he had the tonsure he was *clericus*, and in the prestige that enveloped his class the recollection of his origin was effaced. Every man, however poor, might be said to carry a bishop's crozier in his pack. From above the clergy might seem to be a closed corporation; but nothing could have been more democratic than its recruitment from below. We must not forget that Gregory VII was the son of a peasant. Later on there would be a change. But whenever there was a renewal of faith in the Church, manifesting itself by a reform, it was accompanied by the regeneration of the Church by the people. This was very notable among the Cluniacs; which was one of the causes of their success.

In short, it was in the 10th and 11th centuries that the Church finally conquered the privileged situation that it retained until the

[1] The Abbaye aux Hommes and the Abbaye aux Dames at Caen; the cathedrals of Tournai, Spire, etc.

end of the *ancien régime*. Clerics were then exempted from the civil courts, and the ecclesiastical tribunals extended their competence to all civil matters touching the religious life: whether because, like marriage, they were essentially dominated by the sacrament, or because, like contracts, they were accompanied by an oath which made them religious acts.

We see, then, that as it grew weaker the Carolingian State ceased to go hand in hand with the Church, its ally. The Church suffered for the moment, and the secure position of its upper hierarchy, from the Pope to the bishops, was shaken, except in Germany. But the enfeeblement of the Church which resulted was atoned for by complete liberty, and by an orientation of the religious sentiment which, troubling no more about the things of this world, turned exclusively heavenwards. The monks, and above all the Cluniacs, were the propagators of these new tendencies. They had a twofold result: on the one hand, the Church, being the necessary medium of salvation, on concerning itself exclusively with the eschatological motives, obtained an ascendancy over men's souls which it had never before enjoyed. On the other hand, the new tendencies conferred upon it an extraordinary strength, by causing it to reject all tutelage, all secular meddling in its affairs, as an affront to its purity. Lastly, its prestige brought it enormous wealth, in land, in alms, in privileges.

The whole movement evolved outside Rome and apart from the Papacy. But it was bound to reach Rome, suddenly giving to St. Peter's successor—degraded by feudal intrigues and party conflicts, the impotent protégé of the Emperor—the control over this enormous force, which was working for him and awaiting the moment when it should act in obedience to his command.

## CHAPTER II

# THE WAR OF INVESTITURES

### 1. *The Empire and the Papacy since Henry III* (1039)

By restoring the fallen Empire in 962—the Empire, debased by its last rulers, and since the year 915 without any ruler at all—Otto had undoubtedly intended to revive the Carolingian tradition. On receiving the crown from the hands of John XII, and assuming the title of Emperor of the Romans (*Romanorum imperator*), he conferred upon himself the rôle of the temporal head of Christianity, which was the very essence of the Imperial dignity. The power which he assumed was a universal power, universal as obedience to the Church. But what a contrast between that which was and that which should have been! Under Charlemagne, under Louis the Pious, even under Charles the Fat, the Empire included almost the whole of the West; its actual extent, we may say, coincided with its universality. Otto, on the other hand, reigned only over Germany and Italy. In reality, the Empire as he founded it, and as it continued to be after his day, consisted merely of a constellation of States, to which, from Conrad's reign, was added the kingdom of Burgundy, acquired by cession from its last king, Rudolph III (1033). While it possessed the title, it had no longer the reality of Christian universality.

Nor had it preserved that intimate union with the Papacy, that collaboration of the spiritual and the temporal power in the government of the world, which lay at the basis of the Carolingian conception of empire, and constituted its majesty. Under the new Emperors the Pope was either in open rebellion against the monarch who should have been his ally, or he was his creature, with neither influence nor prestige.

Otto's dream of renewing the mystical marriage of the Papacy and the Empire was cruelly dispelled. The mosaic of St. John Lateran had become a lie. The Pope, in the new order of things, played so subordinate a part that the King of Germany, even before his coronation in Rome, assumed the title of King of the Romans, thus indicating his right to the crown which the Pope, like a sort of master of ceremonies, set upon his head, and which he could not dream of refusing.

Henceforth, in fact, the Imperial dignity was merely an appendage, a consequence of the German monarchy. It was the King of Germany, the king recognized and accepted by the German princes alone—for the princes of Italy and Burgundy never took part in his election—who bore the title of Emperor. But the Empire—and here we find ourselves in the presence of tradition—although it belonged to the King of Germany, was by no means a German Empire. Debased though it was, its universality prevented it from becoming nationalized. Being Roman, it could not become the property of any nation. Just as Charlemagne and his successors were not Emperors of the Franks, so Otto and those who followed him were not Emperors of the Germans. Instead of Germany having nationalized the Empire to her own advantage, her kings, one may say, by the very fact that they knew themselves to be Emperors designate, denationalized themselves to her detriment. Their mission, from the first day of their reign, was out of proportion to their country: exceeding it and reducing it to no more than a part of the whole over which they reigned. In short, the new Emperors were condemned to occupy the unprecedented situation of being neither universal sovereigns nor German sovereigns. In the one case, reality was the obstacle; in the other, tradition.

Down to the end of the 12th century they were incontestably the most powerful of the continental monarchs, and yet, when we come to consider them closely, we quickly perceive that their strength was more apparent than actual. The Imperial territory has the appearance, at first sight, of a vast, imposing mass, containing in itself all the conditions of a formidable expansion. Washed on the north by the North Sea and the Baltic, in the south it extended to the shores of the Adriatic, and it was seemingly destined, by the possession of Italy and the shores of Provence, which it had acquired with the Kingdom of Burgundy, one day to dominate the Mediterranean. Unfortunately, it did not and it could not constitute a State. The power of the Emperors was based, after all, only on the Church, or rather, on the episcopal principalities, whose extent and resources each of the Emperors, after Otto, had taken pains to augment, and whose incumbents they appointed from among their loyal followers. It was from these principalities that they drew the better part of their revenues and their military contingents. As for the lay princes, in proportion as the feudal evolution favoured by the economic causes responsible for propagating the domainal institution made its way into Germany, they became, as in France, more and more independent; but unlike the King of France, the Emperor possessed no dynastic territory, no principality of his own, whose soil and whose inhabitants belonged to him, and where he felt that he was on firm ground. He had no capital; and he wandered about the Empire, an eternal traveller, sometimes beyond the Alps, sometimes in Saxony, Swabia, or Franconia. And naturally, this wandering power had no secular administration. There was and there could be no such thing; for the economic conditions which had ruined the Carolingian administration still existed, and were still producing their inevitable results. Conrad II was obliged formally to recognize the hereditary character of the fief. The parcelling out of the Empire into principalities was more accentuated with each succeeding reign. And the further it was carried, the more truly could it be said that the Emperor could really count on no one but the bishops.

We must not exaggerate the power which he derived from them. Actually it was not very great. It sufficed to make him more powerful than any individual prince; it was not enough to enable him to intervene beyond his frontiers and impose his will upon the foreigner.

Partially subdued by Otto I, under Otto III the Slavs rebelled, and from that time no fresh attempt was made to force Christianity upon them, or subject them to German hegemony. This too, since the end of the 10th century, had been declining in the countries of the north. It was not the Emperors, but the Danish princes of England who introduced Christianity into Denmark (during the reign of Canute the Great, 1018), into Norway (under Olaf the Saint, 1016), and into Sweden (under Olaf the Child, 1006). Bohemia and Hungary had completely shaken off the dependence which Otto I had imposed on them for a time. In the West the situation was equally unpromising. After the death of Otto II there was no longer any question of claiming the least pre-eminence over the Kings of France. The acquisition of Burgundy by Conrad II was a proof of the weakness rather than the strength of the Empire, for it signified only a nominal enlargement. The German sovereigns never attempted to rule over the country; they left it so completely to its own devices that the inhabitants did not even realize that they had passed under the sovereignty of a German dynasty. On the western frontier of the kingdom of Germany, Lotharingia, which had been forcibly annexed in 925, was still turbulent and discontented, and would evidently break its fetters, despite the loyalty of the bishops of Liége, Utrecht, and Cambrai, if only the feudal princes could induce the prudent Capetians to support their rebellion. The misadventures of Henry III, who, after years of conflict, could neither suppress their rebellion against him—for they had rebelled under the leadership of Duke Godfrey the Bearded—nor even force the Count of Flanders, Baldwin V, who had deliberately defied him, to lay down his arms, leave no room for doubt that the Empire would soon have succumbed if its internal troubles had been complicated by the necessity of waging war beyond the frontiers. Fortunately the old enemies of the Empire in the East—the Slavs, Danes, Bohemians and Hungarians—were neighbours no less friendly than the Kings of France. In the 11th century Bohemia and Poland were at war. The Emperors did not meddle in their conflict, apart from endeavouring, by political intrigues, to profit by them.

It was thanks to the security which he enjoyed as far as his neighbours were concerned, a security which he wisely did nothing to compromise, that the Emperor was able to employ such forces as he possessed in his endless Italian enterprises. Every coronation in Rome necessitated a military expedition, and it was only by fighting his way that the Emperor could reach St. Peter's. Once there, he could rely on the bishops of his own appointment; but the lay feudality and the Roman factions did not accept the German yoke, and took advantage of every least occasion to rebel against it. Italy gave the Emperor nothing but fatigue, anxiety and danger, but being Emperor he could not renounce it, although the burden paralysed and exhausted him. In the beginning the conquest of the entire peninsula had appeared indispensable. The Byzantines and the Arabs were then contending for the South. Otto II attempted to subdue them, but his disastrous defeat at Rossano (982) was at all events a salutary lesson for his successors. They no longer risked such perilous adventures: so that Sicily, Apulia and Calabria, which the Emperors would not attempt to conquer, fell, before their eyes, into the hands of the Normans: a paradoxical spectacle.

The story of the foundation of the Norman State in the south of Italy reads like a *chanson de gestes*. This extraordinary episode gave striking proof of the military strength of the Northern chivalry, and was a prelude to those two even more astonishing episodes: the conquest of England and the first Crusade.

In 1016, when the Saracens were besieging Salerno, forty Norman knights, returning from a pious pilgrimage to the Holy Land, passed that way, following the customary route (for the pilgrims used to cross Italy to Bari, where they embarked for Constantinople), took advantage of this opportunity of breaking a lance in the name of Christ. It was a wonderful country, and the state of anarchy in which they found it—attacked by the infidels and rebelling against the Byzantines—held a promise of profitable adventure. Normandy soon had wind of the matter, and little companies of younger sons, or warriors in search of loot, set out to join their compatriots. They took service indiscriminately with all the disputing parties, which bid against one another for the swords of these formidable warriors. It mattered nothing to them whether they fought against Byzantium or for it; since gain was their only motive. About 1030 one of them, Raoul, had already acquired such a position that Prince Pandolfo of Capua gave him, as fief, the county of Arezzo. The Normans had now won a foothold in the country; they were soon to take complete possession of it. In 1042 one of their leaders, Guillaume, was proclaimed Count of Apulia. It was too late to resist these auxiliaries, who had now become conquerors on their own account. Pope Leo IX, to whom the Prince of Benevento had appealed for assistance, marched against them with a body of German troops, who were defeated, leaving the Pope a prisoner in the hands of the Normans (1053). Meanwhile, Robert Guiscard installed himself in Calabria, and in 1057 inherited the county of Apulia.[1]

Between the pontificates of Leo IX and Nicholas II the attitude of Rome toward the Normans underwent a complete transformation. The schism between the Latin and Greek Churches, which had so long been threatening, became definitive in 1054, after which date the Pope was directly interested in the expulsion from Italy of the few Byzantine troops which still remained there.

On the other hand, the nature of the Pope's relations with the Emperor Henry III foreboded a serious conflict in the near future. It was therefore not surprising that he should conclude a close alliance with his enterprising neighbours in the South, and that he should favour their expansion. In 1059—though he was really disposing of territory which did not belong to him—he gave Capua as fief to Richard of Arezzo, and to Robert Guiscard, Apulia, Calabria and Sicily. Two years later Guiscard seized Messina, and thirty years later still the island was completely liberated from the Musulman invasion. The last of the Byzantine outposts in Italy were similarly conquered. Bari and the Lombard duchies were annexed (1071); and then, not content with having expelled the Greeks from the peninsula, Robert attempted to gain a footing on

[1] The story of these Normans offers a convincing proof that the south of Italy was economically more advanced than northern Europe. The princes of the country hired the Normans as mercenaries, and in this anarchical region—for it was divided into a score of petty and hostile States—they went to work much as the great military companies attempted to do in the 14th century. They were pure mercenaries, who carved out principalities for themselves. It was because there was money in the country that they were able to obtain immediate reinforcements from Normandy.

the Adriatic coast, seizing Durazzo and sending expeditions into Thessaly. His death in 1085 interrupted these plans for the time being. Nevertheless, they proved the warlike vitality of the new State, which, thanks to the astonishing energy of its adventurous conquerors, had succeeded in installing itself at this southernmost point of Europe, where for 500 years, despite the Lombards, the Carolingians, the German Emperors and the Musulmans, Byzantium had succeeded in maintaining an outlet toward the West. What none of the successive masters of Italy had been able to do the Normans had accomplished in less than fifty years. The State which they had founded at this meeting-point of three different civilizations was very soon to assume a political importance of the first order, when it would play an unexpected part in the destinies of the Empire.

Nothing could show more clearly how deceptive was the Empire's appearance of strength than the completely passive attitude of Henry III in respect of the young and enterprising power which was growing up upon his frontiers. For him there could be no Italian question; he was not strong enough. It was enough for him that he had arrived at a provisional solution of the question of the Papacy.

The situation of Rome, at the time of his coronation, was more deplorable than ever. While the Cluniac reformation was taking hold on men's souls, and the Church was aspiring, in all its purest and most ardent elements, to assure its spiritual domination by a more fervent piety and a stricter discipline, the see of St. Peter offered the scandalous spectacle of three Popes quarrelling or bargaining for the tiara. Full of zeal for the religious reformation, Henry wished to prevent once and for all the repetition of those incessant conflicts and feudal intrigues which had for so long prevented the Papacy from fulfilling its mission. A synod which he convoked at Sutri deposed the three rival pontiffs, and the Romans were bidden to appoint a candidate chosen by the monarch—the Bishop of Bamberg, Suidger, who assumed the title of Clement II (1046). The other Popes who succeeded him during Henry's reign —Damasius II (1048–1049), Leo IX (1049–1054) and Victor III

(1055–1057)—were, like him, Germans, or at any rate subjects of the Empire, and imposed upon the Romans by the Imperial will. Further, they were all excellent pontiffs, and convinced Clunisians, who restored to the Papacy the prestige and influence which the Church had wished to see it recover. But it recovered them only in violating, by a flagrant contradiction, the very principles by which it was henceforth inspired. True, the tyranny of the counts of Tusculum no longer falsified the pontifical elections for the benefit of unworthy favourites; but was not the intervention of the Emperor, however beneficial its results might be, a direct encroachment upon the domain of canonical law, and, to speak plainly, a flagrant act of simony? Henry had not realized that in restoring the Papacy he would inevitably be provoking a conflict between it and the Empire. It was evident that by choosing his Popes from the ranks of the Clunisian clergy he was hastening the moment when his interference would be regarded, by the very Popes who owed the triple crown to him, as an insupportable and criminal usurpation. Leo IX, having been appointed by Henry, was seized with conscientious scruples, and had himself re-elected by the Romans in accordance with the traditional forms. Sooner or later the dormant conflict was bound to become manifest. The unexpected death of the Emperor in 1056 brought about the crisis.

## 2. *The Conflict*

His successor, Henry IV, was a child of six, under whose reign Germany was for a long time paralysed, in the first place by a stormy regency, and then by a dangerous revolt of the Saxons. Rome took advantage of the circumstances. On the death of Stephen IX (1058) the aristocracy, reverting to tradition, hastened to proclaim one of its faithful supporters, Benedict X. But times were altered; the series of the feudal Popes—and also that of the Imperial Popes—was brought to an end by the election of Nicholas II, who owed the pontificate to the party of reform. The Church had decided to throw off all tutelage—that of Germany no less than that of the Roman barons. The name chosen by the new pontiff recalled the Nicholas who, in the 9th century, had to vigorously proclaimed the superiority of the spiritual weapon. The Church could not more plainly have indicated its intention of effecting a new orientation.

During the fifteen years which had elapsed since the pontificate of Clement II, the Papacy, thanks to the nominations of Henry III, had not only recovered its position at the head of the Church, but was regarded with a veneration and had acquired an influence such as it had never yet enjoyed. The religious renewal which had been accomplished outside the Papacy was now directing the prayers and the devotions of the whole Church, clergy and faithful, toward the successor of St. Peter. The immense moral force which had been evoked by the asceticism of the monks had at last given Rome the head for whom she was waiting, and who was assured beforehand of her enthusiastic obedience. The loyalty to Christ which had inspired men's souls was now confounded with loyalty to His Vicar. When he spoke his words would be heard and revered to the ends of Catholic Christendom. And the Catholic world had not only increased its fervour: it had also extended its area. Since the beginning of the 11th century Christianity had spread into Denmark, Sicily, and Norway, and even remote Iceland, and although the Papacy had taken no part in these new conquests it was towards the Papacy that they now gravitated. Never had Rome possessed so vast a spiritual domain, so potent an authority. Her definitive rupture with the Greek Church in 1054 had shown what confidence she had in her own strength.

How could she continue to tolerate the simoniacal protection of the Emperor? How continue to allow him to dispose of the tiara on behalf of the German bishops, humbling her universal power to benefit the sovereign of a single nation? The minority of Henry IV enabled her to shake off the yoke. In 1059 Nicholas II, in order henceforth to guard the nomination of the Popes from any alien influence, confided it to the College of Cardinals. Thus, at one stroke, he put an end to the tumultuous elections which had caused the long decline of the Papacy, and to the interference of the Emperor. Henceforth the election of the Vicar of Christ would be a matter for the Church alone, which would choose him in peace and liberty. A special clause in the Bull decreed that the election, contrary to the tradition hitherto followed, need not necessarily take place in Rome: the Cardinals were free to assemble where they chose if they thought themselves unsafe in Rome at the moment of the Consistorium.

The conflict between the Papacy and the Empire may be dated from this reform. It was henceforth inevitable, and Nicholas II had no illusions as to the future. It was not due merely to chance that he concluded a treaty of alliance with the Normans in the very year in which the right of electing the Pope was conferred upon the Cardinals.

At the same time the Pope took measures to prohibit the marriage of priests, and in prevention of simony, which showed that he could henceforth count upon the support of the masses. In the north of Italy the people rebelled against the Imperial bishops who attempted to disobey the orders of Rome. However, the insurgence of the *pataria*—the *canaille*—as the princes of the Church and their supporters disdainfully called their enemies—was not exclusively due to religious motives. Under the influence of reviving commerce a new social class, the bourgeoisie, was growing up in the Lombard cities, and it took advantage of the motive provided by piety in order to rebel against the bishops, whose administration took no account of its new requirements.

It was the Bishop of Lucca, the protector of the *patarias*, who in 1061 succeeded to Nicholas II, taking the name of Alexander II. Thus the first election of a pontiff by the Cardinals called to the throne of St. Peter a declared anti-Imperialist. Henry IV was as yet in no position to interfere. His governors were reduced to supporting the Antipope Cadaloüs, whom the feudal party in Rome had set up in opposition to Alexander, and who almost immediately disappeared. In 1073 Gregory VII succeeded to Alexander, and at last the war broke out.

The new Pope, since the advent of Nicholas II, had been the inspirer and the private counsellor of his predecessors. When at last he succeeded them, he was firmly resolved to adopt, in respect of the Empire, an attitude which would either lead to war, or would compel the first sovereign of the West to recognize the supremacy of Rome over the temporal power. In 1075 he solemnly condemned, under penalty of excommunication, the investiture of any ecclesiastical function by the secular authority.

Nothing, of course, could be more consistent with the principles of the Church, but nothing could have been more impossible for the Emperor to concede. Since the reign of Otto I, in proportion as the secular princes became more completely feudalized, the Imperial power depended more and more upon the bishops. Reign after reign, the monarchs had accumulated their donations of territory around the episcopal sees, in order to make the bishops more and more powerful. But they had done so, obviously, on condition that they themselves should appoint the bishops and invest them in their office. By giving them the crozier and the ring, the emblems of their function, the Emperor showed the bishops that they were bishops only by the Imperial will—that it was to the Emperor that they owed the government of their diocese and their principality. To give obedience to the Pope, to return to the canonical prescription, and consequently to allow the chapters to appoint the bishops, and therefore to invest them in their secular fiefs, would have been equivalent to placing in unknown and possibly hostile hands the power which the Empire had conferred upon the prelates—in its own interests, not in theirs. Were they to tell the Emperor that he must renounce the power of investiture? But that would have been to tell him that he must henceforth be a nonentity, since he would have been deprived of the very foundation of his power. Gregory VII was never under any illusion in this respect. But what did the power of the Emperor matter to him? Together with all the most radical partisans of the religious reformation, he regarded the temporal power merely as a source of division. The Church alone was divine, the Church alone could guide man to salvation, and the Church was united in the Pope, "whose name alone could be uttered in the churches and whose feet all kings should kiss."

For these reasons Gregory has been regarded as a sort of mystical revolutionary, an Ultramontane endeavouring to ruin the State.

But this is to introduce modern ideas into a conflict where they are entirely out of place. To begin with, in the case of Gregory there was no trace of Ultramontanism. Ecclesiastical discipline was still very far from being dependent on Rome. He made no claim whatever to nominate the bishops. What he wanted was to ensure that the Church should no longer be defiled by secular meddling. As for his conflict with the State, what does the accusation mean? The Empire was not a State. It was actually governed not by the Emperor but by the princes. As we have seen, there was no administration; nothing in the shape of what we must call, for the want of a better term, a central power, giving it a hold over its inhabitants. If the Emperor's power was diminished what injury was inflicted on society? None, since it regarded him with indifference; since it was not he who defended and protected it. No catastrophe could follow from the victory of the Pope, and the Church was bound to benefit by it. If we are to understand the situation we must regard it from this point of view. We must not forget that this was the heart of the feudal period, and that social and political evolution were on the side of these princes, who, as we have seen, were the real organizers of society. And they were on the side of the Pope. The feudality was working for him, just as he, without intending to do so, was working for it. A little while ago it was the rising bourgeoisie that was taking the part of Rome; now it was the feudal magnates. Here what we call the State is not secular society, but the royal power, subjecting the Church and diverting it from its mission in order to support itself.

In the beginning, this exploitation of the Church by the State goes back to the Carolingian tradition. Otto I did no more than somewhat complicate the ecclesiastical policy of Charlemagne. In reality what Gregory was attacking was the political conception that made the Emperor the equal of the Pope. For the alliance of the two powers he substituted, in the affairs of the Church, the subordination of one to the other. Once more, it must not be said that it attacked the State. It would be more correct to say that he deprived it of its clerical character. After all, by depriving the Emperor of the investiture of the bishops he was accelerating the secularization of the State, and this secularization was intensified after his death. What if the Empire had been triumphant? The theocracy would have held the power; the priests would have governed in the name of the prince. Gregory, on the other hand, withdrew the priests from the government. What he really did was to launch the State on the path of secularization.

He did it without realizing what he was doing; or perhaps we may say that he did it in contempt of the laymen whom he did not wish to meddle in the affairs of the Church. But he knew very well that these laymen were in the Church and wished to remain there. Henry IV himself was a convinced Catholic. And it was precisely this that constituted the strength of the Pope and the weakness of his adversary. Against the Pope the Emperor could employ no means but those of the Church. It did not and could not occur to him to oppose the Pope face to face, in the name of the rights which he held—from whom?—From God. But the Pope was God's representative on earth. He was this so completely that the Emperor could not dispense with the Pope at his coronation. There was only one way of resisting the Pope within the Church, and that was to get the Church to declare that the Pope was unworthy of his office.

And this is what Henry did. He had at last defeated the rebellious Saxons. He was free. There were still enough bishops in Germany who were devoted to the sovereign, and discontented, to make it possible for him to act. He assembled them at Worms, and on January 24th, 1076, he induced them to declare that Gregory was unworthy of the Papacy. Only twenty years earlier Henry III had still appointed the Popes; but what a radical transformation in the situation of the two powers had been effected since then!

Conservators, when they are not men of genius, imagine that it is enough to restore the past without taking account of the present. To attempt the deposition of a Pope by a few German bishops after a Nicholas II and an Alexander II testified to a complete ignorance of the spirit of the age. Nothing could have served the cause of Gregory better than this pretension on the part of the King of Germany to dispose, as the master, of the head of Catholic

Christendom. He replied by excommunicating Henry, and absolving from their oath all who had sworn fidelity to him. It then became evident that the decision of the Synod of Worms was not accepted even by the princes of Germany. For if they had considered it valid they need have paid no attention to the excommunication of the king. But the response of one and all to the sentence of Rome was to abandon Henry. In order to avoid a general revolt the king did not hesitate to repudiate the judgement of his own bishops and to humiliate himself before the Pope whom he had just had declared unworthy. On January 28th, 1077, he appeared before the Pope, in the garb of a penitent, at the fortress of Canossa, and obtained his pardon. But Gregory reserved to himself the right to intervene between the Emperor and the princes. As Henry had resumed the royal title without waiting for their agreement, a number of them had given the crown to Rudolph of Swabia. A civil war broke out. Henry, feeling that he was stronger than his adversary, recovered confidence, and with incorrigible obstinacy treated Gregory with flat defiance, reverting to the means which had already served him so ill. At Brixen a synod convoked in obedience to his orders gave the Papacy to the archbishop Guibert of Ravenna. A second and more solemn excommunication was the reply to this fresh proclamation. But Rudolph had just been killed in battle near Merseburg (Grona), and Henry, taking his Pope with him, marched on Rome. This, before his day, had been a means that had never failed to subdue the feudal and turbulent Popes of the old dispensation. But this time the Germans entered Rome only to suffer a fresh humiliation. Gregory, having withdrawn to Castel Sant'Angelo, was impregnable. All that Henry could do was hastily to consecrate Guibert, who, taking the name of Clement III, placed the Imperial crown upon his head. And then the successor of Charlemagne beat a hasty retreat, for Robert Guiscard and the Normans were approaching the city. Gregory accepted their hospitality and withdrew to Salerno. There he died on May 25th, 1085, uttering the famous words which have since then comforted so many exiles: *Dilexi justiciam et odivi iniquitatem, propterea quod morior in exilio.*

Clement III occupied the Lateran palace. But what did men care for this intruder, who was acknowledged, as a matter of duty, only by a few German bishops? For the Church, Rome was wherever the true Pope was: the elect of the Cardinals, the successor of Gregory. Never was the Papacy so powerful as during these years of exile: powerful not by reason of its acknowledged authority, an authority accepted and feared as under an Innocent III, but in the enthusiastic veneration and devotion of the faithful. It was a wandering Pope, far from his capital—Urban II—who in 1095 sent forth a Europe tremulous with the love of Christ to the conquest of Jerusalem. And while the Pope thus gathered Europe about him, the Emperor, now in Italy, now in Germany, dragged out a reign that was troubled by rebellion, treason, flight, and the vicissitudes of fortune; wearing himself out and destroying what little prestige remained to the Imperial power in the civil war which his son Conrad, and then his son Henry V, waged against him: a war which doomed him also to die in exile, at Liege, in 1106, where Bishop Otbert, one of the last to be faithful to him, watched over the last days of his tragic career. But his death did not settle the question of the investitures which had provoked the conflict. Henry V no longer claimed to dispose of the tiara, and no longer ventured to appoint Antipopes. At last a clear-cut question came up for discussion, and since the Emperor now acknowledged the Pope as head of the Church—and how could he have done otherwise in the time of the Crusades?—it was finally solved by the first of those concordats which the Papacy concluded with the secular power: the Concordat of Worms (1122). The Emperor renounced the right of investiture by crozier and ring, and accepted the liberty of ecclesiastical elections. In Germany the bishop-elect was to receive the investiture of his fiefs (*regales*) from the sceptre before consecration; in other parts of the Empire (Italy and Burgundy) after consecration. There was thus a distinction between the spiritual power, in respect of which the Emperor could no longer interfere, and the temporal power, which he continued to confer, but which he could not refuse without a conflict. As for the election of bishops by the chapters, these would now be influenced not by the Emperor but by the neighbouring princes. In reality, the Imperial Church was in ruins; there remained only a feudal Church. The Empire suffered thereby; the Papacy gained in prestige; but the discipline of the Church was not improved; on the contrary. Every election was bound to be a conflict of influences, and while there was no longer simony on the part of the Emperor there was still pressure and intimidation on the part of the magnates. The true solution would have been that of Pascal II, according to which the bishops would have abandoned their fiefs; but to this the Emperor would not give his consent, for the vast territorial wealth of the Church would have passed into the hands of the princes. In the last resort, the quarrel of the investitures ended in the triumph of the feudality over the Church. There were no more such learned and cultured bishops of the Empire as Notger, Wazon, and Bernhard of Worms. Elected by chapters in which the younger sons of the nobles predominated, they were now entirely feudal, and with them the dominating influence was the temporal. In seeking to liberate the clergy from secular influences the Church had made it more than ever subordinate to them.

CHAPTER III

# THE CRUSADE

## *Causes and Conditions*

The conquest of Sicily in the 9th century, completed in 902 by the capture of Taormina, was the last advance of Islam in the West. From this time forward it made no further conquests. Spain, like the States which had sprung up on the African coast—Morocco, Algiers, Kairouan, Barka, and even Egypt—had lost its primitive power of expansion. The Musulmans no longer attacked the Christians; they dwelt beside them, in a civilization that was more advanced and refined, and had now become less vigorous. They asked only one thing: to be left in peace, and, of course, in possession of the Mediterranean, the whole of whose southern and eastern shores they now occupied.

Unfortunately for them, this was impossible. If they wished to live in security, they should have done what the Romans had done of old: they should have provided themselves with defensible frontiers. Spain was theirs, but they did not hold it up to the Pyrenees. All the islands of the Tyrrhenean Sea were theirs, but neither Provence nor Italy. And how could they retain Sicily without Italy? One might say that they stopped too soon, as though in fatigue. There was something incomplete about the present state of their domain. Nothing could have been more difficult to defend than their advanced positions in Europe. It was inevitable that their neighbours should attack them, being poorer than they, and inspired, since the 10th century, by an ever-increasing religious enthusiasm.

It was in Spain that the counter-attack began. The petty Christian principalities of the North, whose soil was poor and infertile, naturally tended to enlarge their territory in the absence of natural frontiers. The ancient march of Spain had achieved independence during the Carolingian dislocation, as the county of Barcelona, and later, Catalonia. In the mountains various little kingdoms had been constituted: Navarre, the Asturias, Leon, and finally Castile and Aragon. Portugal, a dependency of Castile, established itself as an independent kingdom at the period of the First Crusade, under the rule of the Burgundian prince Henry († 1112). Between these petty states and the Musulmans there were continual frontier wars, in which the Christians were not always victorious. At the end of the 10th century, under the Caliph Hischam II, Barcelona was destroyed (984), and also Santiago, whose Christian inhabitants were forced to remove their bells to Cordova. But after the extinction of the dynasty of the Omayyads (1031) the 11th century was marked by Christian successes. In 1057 Ferdinand of Castile advanced as far as Coimbra and forced several of the Emirs, including even the Emir of Seville, to pay him tribute. His son Alfonso VI (1072–1109) captured Toledo and Valencia and besieged Saragossa. Defeated by the Almoravides of Morocco, whom the Emir of Seville had called to the rescue in 1086, he was checked in his victorious progress, after having advanced with his army as far as the Straits of Gibraltar. But already the progress of the Christians was very appreciable; once it was no longer possible to dislodge them from the mountains they would make their way to Gibraltar.

In Italy events were more decisive. The Byzantines, who had not defended Sicily, were still holding the south of the peninsula when the arrival of the Normans replaced their domination, and that of Islam, by a new, vigorous and warlike State. The conquest of Sicily, and presently that of Malta, meant that the Christians possessed two strongholds in the midst of the Musulman Mediterranean. Moreover, the Pisans had taken part in the war. For some time they had been fighting on the sea against the Moors of Sardinia, whom they expelled in 1016. They played an active part in the conquest of Sicily. The Duomo of Pisa is a sort of *Arc de Triomphe* in honour of the forcing of Palermo Harbour in 1067. Genoa too was beginning to send out expeditions and was harassing the coast of Africa. There was no commerce as yet, but rather privateering, piracy, warfare; the Christian ideal, in the minds of these sailors, being combined with the notion of profit.

Generally speaking, then, from the middle of the 11th century, the Christian Occident was assuming, in a series of detached efforts, the offensive against Islam. But this offensive had nothing in common with a religious war. These wars of conquest would have taken place even between peoples of the same religion if the circumstances and the geographical situation had tended to provoke them. For that matter, the Normans quite impartially attacked both Byzantines and Musulmans.

If we take a general view of the matter, the Crusade, as an episode of world history, was evidently connected with these happenings, being a continuation of the offensive against Islam. But it had only one feature in common with them: the fact that it was directed against Islam. In all other respects—in its origins, its purpose, its tendencies and its organization—it was completely different.

To begin with, it was purely and exclusively religious. In this respect it was intimately related, in respect of the spirit that inspired it, to the great wave of Christian fervour of which the War of Investitures was another manifestation. It was further related to this movement by the fact that the Pope, who had instigated and waged this war, was also the instigator and organizer of the Crusade.

Its objective, to be exact, was not Islam. If the Crusaders had merely wished to repel the Mohammedans they would have had to help the Spaniards and the Normans. Their objective was the Holy Places, and Sepulchre of Christ in Jerusalem. This had been in the hands of the Musulmans ever since the 9th century, but no one had paid much attention to the fact. At this period, under the Arab government, the Christians were not molested, and their piety was not as yet unduly susceptible. But just as it was becoming susceptible, towards the end of the 11th century, Syria was seized by the Seldjukid Turks, and they, in their fanaticism, did molest the pilgrims, who broadcast everywhere their indignation at the insult offered to Christ. Now, among the pilgrims there were many princes: for example, Robert the Frisian. It was not, of course, the tales of the humble pilgrims (and of these not many can have reached Jerusalem) but those of the knights and the princes that roused public opinion.

And while the pilgrims complained, the Emperor of Byzantium made certain proposals. The situation of the Empire, since the Seldjuks had appeared in the Near East, was most precarious. In the 10th century the Macedonian Emperors, Nicephorus Phocas, John Tzimisces and Basil II, had largely repulsed Islam, advancing the frontier to the Tigris. But the Seldjuks, in the 11th century, reconquered Armenia and Asia Minor. When Alexius Comnenus ascended the throne (1081) only the coasts were still Greek. There was no fleet, and the army was inadequate. Alexius thought of the Occident. To whom should he address himself, if not to the Pope? The Pope alone could influence the whole of the Western world. But he could be moved only by a religious motive. In 1095 Alexius sent an embassy to Urban II, and the Council of Piacenza, hinting at the possibility of a return to the Catholic communion. Some months later, on November 27th, 1095, at Clermont, the Crusade was enthusiastically proclaimed by the crowd that had flocked about the sovereign pontiff.

The Crusade was essentially the work of the Papacy; as regards both its universal character and its religious nature. It was undertaken not by the States, nor yet by the people, but by the Papacy; its motive was wholly spiritual, divorced from any temporal preoccupation: the conquest of the Holy Places. Only those who set forth without the spirit of lucre in their hearts could share in the indulgences granted by the Pope. Not until the first wars of the French Revolution did history again show combatants so completely careless of any other consideration than devotion to an ideal.

But religious enthusiasm, and the authority of the Pope, could not of themselves have promoted so vast an undertaking if the social condition of Europe had not rendered it possible. The coincidence of these three factors was necessary: an ardent religious faith, the preponderant power of the Papacy, and favouring social conditions. A century earlier the thing would have been impossible, as it would have been a century later. The ideal realized in the 11th century persisted, as an ideal motive, under very different conditions, becoming less and less effective. It survived even into the Renaissance, for the Popes, in the 16th century, still dreamed of a Crusade against the Turks. But the true Crusade, the parent of all the others, was the First, and this was essentially the child of the age.

To begin with, there were as yet no States. The nations had no governments which could command them. Christianity was not yet politically divided, but could group itself as a whole around the Pope.

Further, there was a military class which was ready to set forth at any moment: the Order of Chivalry. The army was in being; it had only to be mustered. What it could accomplish it had already shown, by the conquests of the Normans in Italy and England. And it was an army that cost nothing, since it was endowed, from father to son, by the fiefs. There was no need to collect money for the Holy War. It was enough to appoint the leaders and lay down the routes to be followed. Regarded from this point of view, the Crusade was essentially the one great feudal war, in which the Western feudality acted in a body, and, so to speak, of its own accord. No king took part in this Crusade. The curious thing is that nobody gave any thought to the kings, to say nothing of the Emperor, who was the enemy of the Pope.

It is therefore not surprising that the Crusade recruited its troops mainly from those countries in which the feudal system was most advanced—from France, England, the Low Countries, and Norman Italy. Considered from this point of view it was above all an expedition, we will not say of the Roman peoples, but of the Roman chivalry.

Without that chivalry the Crusade would have been impossible, for it was above all the enterprise of the knights and the nobles. It must not be envisaged as a sort of migration of the Christian masses to Jerusalem. It was before all things an expedition of warriors, and otherwise it would merely have provided the Turks with victims to massacre. Consequently the Crusaders were by no means as numerous as is generally supposed. At the very most they numbered some tens of thousands: a comparatively enormous figure, but in no way comparable with the numbers of a mass migration.

## 2. *The Conquest of Jerusalem*

The expedition was carefully prepared under the direction of the Pope. Monkish propagandists were sent out in all directions; but the more worldly expedients were not neglected. However great the love of Christ, it was with men that the Papacy had to deal, and it did not hesitate, in order to "excite" them, to appeal to other than the mystical passions. The *excitatoria* who were then despatched throughout Christendom vaunted, in one breath, the quantity of relics to be found in Asia Minor, the charm and luxury of its customs, and the beauty of its women. Measures were taken on behalf of those who were setting forth: their possessions were under the guardianship of the Church; they were certain of finding them intact on their return. As for the plan of campaign, this should not present any great difficulty in view of the large numbers of Western pilgrims who had made the journey to Jerusalem. In the absence of a sufficient fleet they would have to follow the overland route. Only the Normans from Italy and the contingents from the north of the peninsula would cross the Adriatic, to disembark at Durazzo, whence they would march to Constantinople, which was the general rendezvous. There were three armies: the Lotharingians under Godfrey, who marched by way of Germany and Hungary; the Frenchmen of the North, with Robert of Normandy, brother of William II of England, Stephen of Blois and Hugues de Vermandois, brother of Philip I, the King of France, and Robert of Flanders, who went southwards by way of Italy, where they joined the Normans under Bohemund of Tarento, the son of Robert Guiscard, and his nephew Tancred; and lastly, the Frenchmen of the South, under Raymond of Toulouse, accompanied by the legate, Bishop Adhémar of Puy, who passed through northern Italy and along the Adriatic coast. All assembled at Constantinople, where they arrived in successive groups, in the year 1096.

Bands of enthusiasts, excited by the preaching of Peter the Hermit, without leaders, without discipline, had already set forth, at the beginning of 1096, pillaging and massacring the Jews. Those of them who reached Constantinople were hurried across the Bosphorus by the Greeks and cut to pieces by the Turks.

If the Pope had hoped to bring the Greek Church into the Roman fold by means of the Crusade he was assuredly disillusioned. When the Westerners and the Greeks came into contact the antipathy between them was increased, and the gulf widened, but the mystical purpose which had made the Crusaders take up arms was achieved. After battles and fatigues and perils which are comparable to those of the retreat from Moscow, and must have been equally murderous, what was left of the army appeared at last before the walls of Jerusalem on June 7th, 1099. On July 15th the city was taken by assault, and rivers of blood were shed in the name of the God of peace and love whose sepulchre had at last been recaptured.

The result of the conquest was the establishment of petty Christian States: the kingdom of Jerusalem, of which Godfrey of Bouillon was elected sovereign under the name of Advocate of the Holy Sepulchre; the principality of Edessa, whose inhabitants had given the title of count to Baldwin, brother of Godfrey, as he marched through; and the principality of Antioch, of which Bohemund of Tarento made himself the prince after taking the city in 1098. All these were organized in accordance with feudal law, far from Europe as they were, and threatened on every side by an almost undamaged Islam. They were colonies which did not answer to any of the requirements of colonies. There was no need to establish a surplus population so far from home, no need to organize trading-posts. While the spirit of lucre was far from absent from the minds of all those who took part in the Crusade, not a single Crusader had any thought of commerce. They were actuated only by the religious ideal. But the immediate result was a commercial one. The Christians' military base, which had thus been established in the East, had of course to be revictualled. Venice, Pisa and Genoa at once undertook the task. The Crusader principalities became the objective of their fleets. The eastern Mediterranean was now in communication with the West. From this time forward Christian navigation underwent an incessant development. Those who finally derived the greatest profits from the Crusades were the middle classes of the Italian seaports. But their purpose had not been commercial. Their truest manifestation was the alliance of the military with the religious spirit in the Orders of the Templars and the Hospitallers.

As Christian establishments, the possessions of the Crusaders were extremely difficult to defend. Edessa fell no later than 1143, and a new Crusade had to be undertaken—the Second, which failed in its object. In 1187 Saladin, Sultan of Egypt, conquered Jerusalem, and it was not again recaptured.

And so the great movement of the Crusades had hardly any final result, beyond the greater activity and more rapid movement of trade on the Mediterranean. They did nothing, or very little, to make the West better acquainted with the economic and scientific progress of Islam. These became known through the intermediary of Sicily and Spain. The Crusades might at least have opened up the Greek world; but they did nothing of the kind. It was too early for the West to take an interest in the treasures that lay dormant in the Byzantine libraries. The Western world would have to wait for the moment when the refugees of the 15th century brought them to Italy. It was with the East as it was with America, discovered by the Norsemen and then forgotten, because, in the 11th century, the world had as yet no need of it.

On the whole, then, the immense effort of the Crusades had but few direct results. They did not repulse Islam, they did not recover the Greek Church, they could not even retain Jerusalem or Constantinople. On the other hand, they were of considerable importance in a domain which was totally opposed to the spirit which had inspired them: for their true result was the development of Italian maritime commerce, and, from the time of the Fourth Crusade, the establishment of the colonial empire of Venice and Genoa in the Levant. It is highly characteristic that the whole formation of Europe can be explained without a single reference to the Crusades, but for this one exception of Italy.

The Crusades, however, had yet one more consequence of a religious order. From the time of the First Crusade the Holy War was substituted for the evangelization of the non-Christian world. Henceforth it would be employed against heretics also. The heresy of the Albigenses, and later, that of the Hussites, were extirpated by means of the Holy War. As for the pagans, the methods employed against the Wends, the Prussians and the Lithuanians were characteristic of the age: the infidel had no longer to be converted, but exterminated.

*Book Five*

# THE FORMATION OF THE BOURGEOISIE

## CHAPTER I

# THE REVIVAL OF COMMERCE

### 1. *The Trade of the Mediterranean*

The economic organization which imposed itself upon Western Europe in the course of the Carolingian epoch, and which was preserved, in its essential features, until the close of the 11th century, was, as we have seen, purely agricultural. Not only did it know nothing of commerce, but one may say that by regulating production in accordance with the needs of the producers it excluded the very possibility of any professional commercial activity. Profit-seeking, and indeed the very idea of profit, were foreign to it. The cultivation of the soil assured the existence of the family, and no one attempted to make the soil yield him a surplus, for he would not have known what to do with it.

This does not mean that there was not in those days any species of exchange. It was impossible for each domain to produce every imaginable necessity; it was impossible to dispense entirely with any sort of importation. In the northern countries wine had necessarily to be brought from the southern regions. Moreover, local famines were frequent, and in case of dearth the affected province did its best to obtain help from its neighbours. Again, at reasonable intervals there were small weekly markets which provided for the current needs of the surrounding population. But the importance of all these matters was purely accessory. People traded their goods as occasion required; they did not become traders by profession. There was no such thing as a class of merchants, nor was there a class of industrial workers. Industry was restricted to a few indispensable artisans—serfs working at the domainal "court" to supply the needs of the domain, wheelwrights dispersed about the villages.

and weavers of linen or woollen stuffs for family consumption. In certain regions, as on the coast of Flanders, the quality of the wool and the conservation of the old Roman technique gave a higher quality to the products of the peasant weavers, so that there was a demand for them in the neighbouring countries. This was a speciality, just as the production of good building-stone or timber was a speciality. There was consequently a certain amount of traffic on the rivers, and this was a convenience to travellers and pilgrims. Small seaports in northern France and the Low Countries served the needs of the few travellers going to or returning from England. But if all these things had never existed the economic order would have been essentially the same. The rudiments of commercial life in the Carolingian epoch did not respond to any permanent need, or any primordial necessity. The best evidence that this was the case is the history of the unification of weights, measures and currency established by Charlemagne. By the end of the 9th century this unity had been replaced by diversity. Each territory had its own weights and measures and currency. This regression could not have taken place if there had been any appreciable amount of trade. But while these conditions obtained in the Carolingian Empire, matters were very different in the two portions of Western Europe which still belonged to the Byzantine Empire: Venice and Southern Italy. The seaports of Campania, Apulia, Calabria and Sicily continued to maintain regular relations with Constantinople. Even thus far afield the attractive power of the great city still made itself felt. Bari, Tarento, Amalfi—and until Sicily was conquered by the Musulman, Messina, Palermo and Syracuse—were regularly despatching to the Golden Horn their vessels laden with grain and wine, which returned to them with the products of Oriental manufactures. But the volume of their trade was soon exceeded by that of Venice. Founded in the lagoons by fugitives at the time of the Lombard invasion, the refuge of the patriarchs of Aquileia, the city was at first no more than an agglomeration of little islands, divided one from another by arms from the sea, the principal island being the Rialto. The agglomeration was given the name of Venetia, which had hitherto been applied to the coast. The arrival of the relics of St. Mark from Alexandria, in 826, gave it a national patron. Fishing and the refining of sea-salt were at first the principal resources of the inhabitants. For these, of course, the market was not Italy, lying close at hand, for Italy, congealed in the agricultural and domainal organization, had no needs; the market was the remote and voracious city of Byzantium. And nothing more clearly illustrates the contrast between the two civilizations than this orientation of Venice toward the East. The advance of Islam in the Mediterranean, by restricting the number of ports which fed the great city, was advantageous to the sailors of the lagoons. On the shores of the Bosphorus the Venetian traders were soon preeminent over all their competitors. This city without territory, entirely dependent on the sea, was in some ways reminiscent of ancient Tyre. With wealth it gained independence, and without any violent rupture it shook off the Byzantine domination, and constituted itself, under a Doge (Duke), a merchant republic, such as the world had never seen. From the 10th century onwards its policy was directed exclusively by commercial interest. We can get some idea of the wealth of Venice by considering her strength. For the sake of her navigation she was obliged to exercise dominion over the Adriatic, which was troubled by the Dalmatian pirates. In 1000 Doge Pietro II Urseolo (991–1009) conquered the coast from Venice to Ragusa, and assumed the title of Duke of Dalmatia. Venice could not allow the Normans, after the conquest of Southern Italy, to establish themselves on the Greek coast. The Venetian fleet therefore co-operated with the Emperor Alexis to drive Robert Guiscard out of Durazzo. For that matter, Venice contrived to get well paid for her collaboration. In 1082 the Venetians received the privilege of buying and selling throughout the Byzantine Empire without the payment of duties, and they obtained, for residential purposes, a special quarter of Constantinople. Purely commercial, they did not hesitate to enter into relations with their enemies. But already their vessels were encountering new competitors in the eastern Mediterranean. In the course of the 10th century the Pisans and the Genoese had begun to fight the Musulman pirates in the Tyrrhenean Sea. They ended by taking possession of

Corsica and Sardinia, and the Pisans, after giving battle on the Sicilian coast, were making bold, by the middle of the 11th century, to harry the coast of Africa. While the Venetians were merchants from the very beginning, the Pisans and the Genoese remind one rather of the Christians of Spain. Like them, they made war upon the infidel with a passionate religious enthusiasm; a Holy War, but a very profitable one, for the infidel was wealthy and yielded much booty. In them religious passion and the appetite for lucre were merged in a spirit of enterprise which we find expressed in curiously vivid language in their ancient chronicles. Success attending their efforts, they grew bolder, and finally, passing the Straits of Messina, scoured the waters of the Archipelago. But the Venetians took very little interest in the conflict between the Cross and the Crescent. Their object was to reserve for themselves the market of Constantinople and the navigation of the Levant. And their fleets did not hesitate to attack the Pisan vessels engaged in revictualling the Crusaders.

Once the Christians were established in Palestine it was impossible to persist in such an attitude. However unwillingly, the Venetians had to allow the Pisan and Genoese ships to take part in the maritime traffic between the Crusader States of the Syrian coast and the West. The continual transport of pilgrims, of military reinforcements, of foodstuffs and munitions of all sorts, made this navigation such an abundant source of profit that the religious spirit which had at first inspired the seamen of the two cities was snbordinated to the commercial spirit. Before long their ships were sailing not only to Christian ports but also to Musulman harbours. From the 12th century onwards there was a busy trade with Kairouan, Tunis, and Alexandria. The Pisans, in 1111, and the Genoese in 1115, obtained commercial privileges in Constantinople. Venetian, Pisan and Genoese colonies were established in the commercial centres of the Levant, grouped under the jurisdiction of their national consuls. And presently the movement began to spread farther afield. Marseilles and Barcelona got busy in their turn; the Provençaux and the Catalans utilized the routes which had been opened up by the Italians. By the end of the 11th century one may say that the Mediterranean had been reconquered for Christian navigation. While the Musulmans and the Byzantines undertook their own coasting trade, the commerce between distant parts was entirely in the hands of the Westerners. Their ships were to be seen everywhere in the seaports of Asia and Africa, while in the Italian, Catalonian or Provençal harbours only Greek or Musulman vessels were to be found. The Second Crusade, like the First, took the overland route, but the Third, and all the rest, crossed the sea. They were thus the occasion of much profitable traffic. The Fourth Crusade was quite different from all the rest: for Venice contrived to divert it to her own advantage, and to that of the other maritime cities.

The plan of this Crusade was as follows: the Crusaders proposed to attack the Musulmans in Egypt, and thence to march along the coast of Palestine. The Crusaders had made arrangements with the Doge, Enrico Dandolo. The Venetian fleet was to transport the 30,000 men of the crusading army in return for a payment of 85,000 marks of silver. But the Crusaders were unable to pay the agreed sum. Venice then proposed that they should acquit themselves of their debt by taking possession of Zara for her, a Christian port but a rival of Venice. Zara was captured, and the fleet was making ready to set sail for Egypt, when the Greek prince Alexis, whose father, the Emperor Isaac, had been dethroned not long before (1195), proposed that the Crusaders should restore him to the throne of Constantinople. Despite Pope Innocent III, who went to the length of excommunicating the Venetians, the Crusaders accepted the proposal. On July 6th, 1203, the fleet forced the harbour, the Crusaders occupied Constantinople, and Alexis was crowned. Then, disputes with the new Emperor having arisen, the city was captured anew, on April 12th, 1204, and the Latin Empire was founded. Venice received, as her share, everything that could favour her maritime commerce: part of Constantinople, Andrinople, Gallipoli, the Island of Euboea, with a host of other islands, the southern and western shores of the Peloponnesus, and the whole of the coast from the Gulf of Corinth to Durazzo. The Black Sea was opened up to Italian trade, and immediately

Venetian, Genoese and Pisan establishments were founded on its shores.

One cannot say that the Mediterranean had again become what it was in antiquity, a European lake. But it no longer constituted a barrier to Europe. It was once more the great highway between Europe and the East. All its trade routes ran to the Levant. The caravans which came from Baghdad and from China, bringing spices and silk to the Syrian coast, now made for the Christian vessels which awaited them in the Levantine ports.

## 2. *The Northern Trade*

The cause for this vigorous expansion, whose effects upon European civilization were incalculable, was external to Europe, or at all events to Western Europe. Without the attraction exercised by Byzantium, without the necessity of fighting the Musulmans, Europe would doubtless have continued for centuries in a state of purely agricultural civilization. There was no internal necessity which might have compelled her to venture forth into the outer world. Her commerce was not a spontaneous manifestation of the natural development of her economic life. It may be said that owing to stimuli arriving from the outer world it anticipated the moment when it must have come into being as a natural development.

And singular though it may appear at first sight, this was true not only in the Mediterranean, but also in the North Sea and the Baltic. In antiquity the waters of these seas had enclosed the Roman world as definitely as the waters of the Atlantic. Beyond the Channel, across which plied the vessels that maintained a connection between Gaul and Britain, there was no navigation at all, or at all events no commercial navigation, and this situation remained unchanged until the 9th century. Apart from Quentovic (which took the place of Boulogne) and Duurstede, which maintained occasional relations with the Anglo-Saxons of Britain, the entire coast of the Frankish Empire, until the mouth of the Elbe was reached, was lifeless, almost deserted. Beyond the Elbe, in the Baltic, one came to the unknown regions of pagan barbarism. Here the situation was exactly the contrary of that which obtained on the shores of the Mediterranean. Instead of being neighboured by more advanced civilizations, the Christian Occident was in contact with peoples who were still in their infancy. Yet it was under the influence of such peoples that these northern waters were awakened to commercial activity. Strangely enough, the centre of this activity was not, as one might have supposed, on the coasts of Flanders and England, but in the Gulf of Bothnia and the Gulf of Finland. And this is explained by the fact that the attraction of the East, and of Byzantium, made itself felt even in these distant lands, so that the same external stimulus that provoked the rise of Italian navigation was also responsible for the beginnings of the northern trade.

We have already referred to this fact, in the chapter on the Scandinavian invasion; we have seen that the Swedes, half conquerors and half merchants, began to make their appearance, from the middle of the 9th century, on the waters of the Dnieper, and that they established there the first political centres round which crystallized the still amorphous mass of those eastern Slavs who borrowed from the Swedes their name of "Russians." Until the close of the 11th century these establishments remained in touch with the mother-country, and continued to receive reinforcements. They maintained commercial relations—very active relations—with Byzantium and the Musulman countries on the shores of the Caspian; at all events, until the invasion of the Petchenegs.[1] Constantinople was the great commercial centre. There slaves were sold, furs, honey, and wax. Constantine Porphyrogenitus gives a curious description of the Russian trade about the year 950. He tells us how in the month of June the boats from Novgorod, Smolensk, Lubetch, Tchernigov, and Vychegrad assembled at Kiev. Armed, and setting out in a body, the traders descended the river, towing their boats where the stream was interrupted by rapids, and defending themselves against the Petchenegs, and then skirted the coast as far as the mouths of the Danube, and so on to Constantinople. These trading expeditions, armed and directed by the

[1] This explains how it is that 20,000 Arab coins have been found in Sweden, and very many in Russia.

prince, were very like the expeditions of the modern African slave-traders. But even as early as the 10th century merchants, properly so-called, were taking part in these expeditions. At this time the Russians were still pagans. They had as yet no notion of landed property, and already, on account of this trade with Constantinople, they had merchants, and were founding towns. These were palisaded towns (*gorod*) or *pagost*: that is, places inhabited by foreigners (*gostj*).

Kiev, by the beginning of the 11th century, was unrivalled in importance by any other town in the North of Europe. Thietmar of Merseburg describes it as it was in 1018, with its forty churches (the text says 400, but that is doubtless an error) and its eight markets. The population still consisted largely of Scandinavians. They were even more numerous at Novgorod, where the men of Gothland, in the 12th century, had a *Gildhalle*. The movement that had its beginning in these centres naturally spread into the Baltic. The island of Bornholm (Denmark), in the words of Adam of Bremen, was *celeberrimus Daniae portus et fida statia navium, quae a barbaris in Graeciam dirigi solent.* But even in the 10th century the Scandinavians, who had been initiated into commerce by Byzantium, were pushing westward. The Flemish coins of the 10th and 11th centuries found in the country show that they frequented the shores of the North Sea. This navigation must have been intensified by the Danish dominion in England. In the 10th century a new port, Kiel, on the Waal, took the place of Duurstede in Holland, and Bruges began to develop. The conquest of England by the Normans, by attaching this country to the Continent, was a further stimulus to navigation on the North Sea and the Channel.

The impulse, then, came from Byzantium, through the intermediary of the Swedes, but the Scandinavian navigation began to decline in the 11th century: on the one hand, the invasion of the Kumans, in the south of Russia, cut the route to Constantinople, and on the other hand, the competition of the Venetian and Italian trade in the South was too much for it. And just at this time the Germans were beginning to spread along the Baltic. The volume of trade had now become so great that it was beginning to expand northwards.

From Venice, by way of the Brenner Pass, it gradually made its way into Southern Germany; or perhaps we should say that Venice attracted this trade to herself, for the Venetians did not travel overland. But the movement was much more active in the direction of France. Under the stimulus of the coastal trade both commerce and industry were becoming established in the Lombard plain, which from the middle of the 11th century was transformed by their influence. Through the passes of Saint Gothard or Mont Cenis the Lombard merchants ventured northwards. The magnet that drew them northwards was Flanders, the centre of the North Sea trade. From the beginning of the 12th century these Lombard merchants frequented the fairs of Ypres, Lille, Messines, Bruges, and Thourout. Then the centre of commercial exchanges shifted southwards, and the great markets of the 12th and 13th centuries were the famous fairs of Champagne: Troyes, Bar, Provins, Lagny, Bar-sur-Aube.

There, through the intermediary of the Flemings and the Lombards, the two commercial worlds, the northern and the southern, touched and intermingled. Of the two, the southern was the more advanced, the more complete and progressive. And this is not surprising. In constant relations with highly developed civilizations, the Italians were early initiated into their commercial practices, and all the complexities of a trade more intensive and more complicated than that of the North. This explains why the first means of exchange, which made their appearance at the close of the 12th century, were Italian. One may say that the organization of European credit is entirely Romanic. Banks, bills of exchange, the lending of money at interest, and commercial companies were exclusively of Italian origin, and probably became generalized through the medium of the great fairs of Champagne. The most striking result of the renaissance of trade was the revival of money, the return to circulation of currency. The stock of precious metals was not actually increased, but money began to circulate again. As exchange became more general money made its appearance wherever man traded. Things which had never been valued in terms of money were now beginning to be so valued. The notion of wealth was undergoing transformation.

### 3. *The Merchants*

Now we have to consider—and this is an essential question—how the mercantile class which was the instrument of this commerce came into being. The question is very difficult to answer, because of the paucity of documents, and it is probable that it will never be completely elucidated.

To begin with, we note that the merchants (*mercatores*) were "new men." They made their appearance as the creators of a new kind of wealth, side by side with the possessors of the old territorial wealth, and they did not emerge from the class of landowners.

They were so far from originating from the class of landowners that the contrast between the idea of nobility and the mercantile life subsisted for centuries, and has never been completely dissipated. Here were two separate and impermeable worlds. There can be even less question of their ecclesiastical origin. The Church was hostile to commercial life. It saw in commerce a spiritual danger. *Homo mercator nunquam aut vix potest Deo placere*. The clergy were forbidden to engage in trade. The ascetic ideal of the Church was in flagrant opposition to the ideals of commerce. The Church did not condemn wealth, but it condemned the love of riches and striving after wealth. Not the slightest encouragement, therefore, could be expected on the part of the Church.

Did the merchants emerge from the class of villeins, these men who had their definite place in the great domains, living on their *mansus* and leading an assured and sheltered existence? There is no evidence that they did so, and everything seems to point to the contrary.

Strange as it may seem, then, only one solution remains: the ancestors of the merchants must have been the poor men, the landless men, the nomadic folk who wandered about the country, working for hire at harvest time, living from hand to mouth and going on pilgrimages. An exception must be made in the case of the Venetians, since their lagoons made them, from the first, fishers and refiners of salt, which they carried to Byzantium.

Landless men are men who have nothing to lose, and men who have nothing to lose have everything to gain. They are adventurers, relying only on themselves; they have given no hostages to fortune. They are resourceful people, who know their way about; they have seen many countries, can speak many languages, are acquainted with many different customs, and their poverty makes them ingenious. It was from this floating scum, we may be sure, that the crews of the first Pisan and Genoese corsairs were recruited. And in the north of Europe, what were the Scandinavians who set out for Constantinople but men without possessions who were seeking their fortune?

"Seeking their fortune": that is the current expression. How many never found it, but disappeared in battle, or were dogged by poverty? But others succeeded. Starting with nothing but their courage, their intelligence, and their hardihood, they made their fortune. . . .

It seems a simple matter to-day. An intelligent man, with nothing but his wits to rely on, may find capital to back him. But we must consider that the men of whom we are speaking had no hope of capital. They had to make their capital out of nothing. It was the heroic age of commercial origins, and it is worth our while to give a thought to these poor devils, who were the creators of personal property.

Here is a very simple case, which must often have been repeated. A man takes part in a successful privateering expedition; a Musulman fort is pillaged; a tight vessel with a rich cargo is captured. The privateers return to their port of origin, and now they can recruit a few poor fellows on their own account, and begin over again, or they can buy corn cheap somewhere, and carry it to some country where there is a famine, where they can sell it very dear. For this was one of the prime causes of the creation of mercantile wealth. Everything was local. At the distance of a few leagues you would find the contrast of poverty and abundance, and consequently, the most astonishing fluctuations of price. In this way a man with very little wealth can make a great deal.

On the Rhine, the Scheldt or the Rhone a wide-awake boatman could make considerable profits in time of famine. More than one who began by carrying small parcels of goods to the markets, or selling candles to pilgrims, may suddenly have acquired a useful liquid capital which would enable him to put to sea.

And we must not forget that in the beginning there would have been a great deal of dishonesty and a great deal of violence. Commercial honesty is a virtue of very late growth.

Thus, in this agricultural society, whose capital wealth was dormant, a group of outlaws, vagabonds, and poverty-stricken wretches furnished the first artisans of the new wealth, which was detached from the soil. Having gained a little, they wanted to gain more. The spirit of profit-making did not exist in established society; those whom it inspired were outside the social system; they bought and sold, not in order to live, not because they had vital need of their purchases, but for the sake of gain. They did not produce anything; they were merely carriers. They were wanderers, guests, *gostj*, wherever they went. They were also tempters; offering jewellery for the women, ornaments for the altar, cloth of gold for the churches. They were not specialists; they were one and all brokers, carriers, sharpers, chevaliers of industry. They were not yet professional merchants, but they were on the way to becoming merchants.

They became merchants when commerce had definitely become a specific way of life, detached from the hazardous and hand-to-mouth existence of the carrier. And then they settled down. As soon as they had really entered upon the normal exercise of trade they found that a place of residence was necessary. They established themselves at some point which was favourable to their way of life: a landing-place for river-craft, or a favourably-situated episcopal city where they found themselves in the company of their fellows, and as their numbers increased still others arrived. And then, quite naturally, they began to form mutual associations. If they wanted to enjoy any security they had to travel in companies, in caravans. They banded together in guilds, religious associations, confraternities. All the trade of the Middle Ages, until nearly the end of the 12th century, was undertaken by armed caravans (*hanses*). This not only increased the security of trade, but also its efficiency, for while the companions protected one another on the highways and caravan routes they also bought goods in common in the markets. Thanks to the accumulation of their petty capitals, they were able to undertake transactions of considerable importance. From the beginning of the 12th century there were attempts to corner grain. About this period many merchants had already realized fortunes which enabled them to purchase valuable real estate.[1] Moreover, it was the merchants' guilds that attended to the fortification of the town in which they resided.

Of one thing we may be absolutely sure, that these men were inspired by a greedy spirit of profit-seeking. We must not think of them simply as respectable folk doing their best to make both ends meet. Their one object was the accumulation of wealth. In this sense, they were animated by the capitalist spirit, which the rudimentary psychology of our modern economists would have us regard as something highly mysterious, born in penury or Calvinism. They calculated and they speculated; to their contemporaries they appeared so formidable that no one would have been surprised to learn that they had made a pact with the devil. No doubt the majority were unable to read or write. Many great fortunes have been made by illiterates. To deny that they were actuated by a commercial spirit would be as absurd as to deny that the princes who were their contemporaries were actuated by the political spirit. In actual fact, the capitalist spirit made its appearance simultaneously with commerce.

To be brief: the history of European commerce does not present us, as many would like to believe, with the spectacle of a beautiful organic growth of the kind that delights the amateur of evolution.

[1] To understand what great commercial profits could be made in an age when wars and famines were of continual occurrence, we have only to remember what happened in the recent war.

It did not begin with petty local transactions which gradually developed in importance and in range. On the contrary, it began, in conformity with the stimulus which it received from the outer world, with long-range trading and the spirit of big business—big in the relative sense. It was dominated by the capitalist spirit, and this spirit was even more potent in the beginning than later on. Those who initiated and directed and expanded the commerce of Europe were a class of merchant-adventurers.[1] This class was responsible for reviving urban life, and in this sense we must refer to this class the origin of the bourgeoisie, very much as we refer the origin of the modern proletariat to the great industrialists.

[1] I think the description of merchant-adventurers is that which best fits these precursors, who could not as yet be described as great merchants.

CHAPTER II

# THE FORMATION OF THE CITIES

## 1. *The Episcopal "Cities" and Fortresses*

A society in which the population lives by the soil which it exploits, and whose produce it consumes on the spot, cannot give rise to important agglomerations of human beings; each inhabitant being tied, by the necessities of life, to the soil which he cultivates. Commerce, on the other hand, necessarily involves the formation of centres in which it obtains its supplies and from which it sends them forth into the outer world. The natural result of importation and exportation is the formation in the social body of what might be called nodes of transit. In Western Europe, in the 10th and 11th centuries, their appearance was contemporaneous with the renewal of urban life.

Naturally, such factors as geographical conditions, the contours of the soil, the direction and navigability of water-courses, and the configuration of sea-coasts, by the direction which they imposed on the circulation of men and goods, at the same time determined the situation of the first commercial settlements. But almost invariably these sites were already inhabited when the afflux of merchants restored them to renewed activity. Some—and this was the case in Italy, Spain, and Gaul—were already occupied by an episcopal "city"; others—for example, in the Low Countries, and the regions to the east of the Rhine and the north of the Danube—were already the site of a *bourg*—that is, a fortress. The reason for this is easily understood.

In the territory of the ancient Roman Empire the episcopal "cities" were built at the most favourably situated points, since the diocesan centres were established, from the beginning, in the principal towns, and these towns owed their importance to the advantages of their position. As for the *bourgs*, which were constructed in the North and the East in order to shelter the populations in time of war, or to check the incursions of the Barbarians, the majority were situated at points which were indicated by facility of access as places of refuge or defence.[1] But neither the "cities" nor the *bourgs* presented the faintest trace of urban life. Those, for example, which were built, like the castles constructed by the Counts of Flanders to hold back the Normans, or like the fortresses erected by Charlemagne and Henry the Fowler along the Elbe and the Saale to check the Slavs, were essentially military posts, occupied by a garrison of men-at-arms and the people necessary for their upkeep, the whole being under the command and supervision of a châtelain.[1] The "cities," on the contrary, were distinguished by their wholly ecclesiastical character. Besides the Cathedral and the canons' close there were usually several monasteries, and the residences of the principal lay-vassals of the bishop. If to these we add the schoolmasters and the scholars, the pleaders cited to appear before the local tribunal, and the host of worshippers flocking from all directions to take part in the numerous religious festivals, we shall be able to form some idea of the activity that must have prevailed in these small religious capitals. They were incontestably more populous and more lively than the *bourgs*, but like the latter, they contained nothing that resembled a bourgeoisie. In the "city," as in the *bourg*, beyond the priests, knights, and monks, there were practically only the serfs employed in the service of the ruling class, and cultivating, for the benefit of that class, the adjacent soil. "Cities" and *bourgs* were merely the administrative centres of a society which was still wholly agricultural.

It was in the "cities" of Northern Italy and Provence, on the one hand, and on the other in the *bourgs* of the Flemish region, that the first merchant colonies were established. By the very fact that they had outstripped the rest of Europe in the history of commerce, these two territories were those in which the first manifestations of urban life occurred. Here and there, in these "cities" and

[1] There were naturally exceptions: for example, Thérouanne.

*bourgs*, the merchants founded, in the 10th century, settlements concerning which, as a matter of fact, very little is known; in the 11th century these settlements were multiplied, enlarged, and consolidated. Already, in the "city" as in the *bourg*, the merchant colony was beginning to play the leading part. The immigrants dominated the old inhabitants just as the commercial life of the place dominated the old agricultural life, and the opposition of these two interests gave rise to conflicts and necessitated expedients by force of which, amidst innumerable local experiments, a new order of things was elaborated.

If we are to understand this phenomenon of the formation of the middle classes, a development so pregnant with consequences, we must try to realize clearly the full extent of the contrast which existed, from the beginning, between the old population and the new. The old population, consisting of clergy, knights, and serfs, lived by the soil, the lower class working for the upper classes, who, from the economic point of view, were consumers who produced nothing. It is of no real consequence that there existed in most of the "cities" a few artisans who provided for the needs of local customers, and a small weekly market, attended by the peasants of the countryside. These artisans, and this market, had no real importance of themselves; they were strictly subordinated to the needs of the agglomeration which contained them, and it was only for its sake that they existed. They could not possibly undergo development, since this agglomeration itself, whose means of support were limited by the yield of the land which surrounded it, could not by any means increase.

In this tiny, changeless world the arrival of the merchants suddenly disarranged all the habits of life, and produced, in every domain, a veritable revolution. To tell the truth, they were intruders, and the traditional order could find no place for them. In the midst of these people who lived by the soil, and whose families were maintained by labours which were always the same, and revenues that did not vary, they seemed in some way scandalous, being as they were without roots in the soil, and because of the strange and restless nature of their way of life. With them came not only the spirit of gain and of enterprise, but also the free labourer, the man of independent trade, detached alike from the soil and from the authority of the seigneur: and above all, the circulation of money.

It was not only the work of the merchant that was free: by a no less astonishing innovation, his person also was free. But what could anyone really know concerning the legal status of these newcomers, whom no one had ever seen before? Very probably the majority of them were the children of serfs, but no one knew this for certain, and as their condition of servage could not be presumed, they had of necessity to be treated as free men. It was a curious result of their social condition that these forebears of the future bourgeoisie did not have to demand their liberty. It came to them quite naturally; it existed as a fact even before it was recognized as a right.

To these characteristics of the merchant colony, surprising enough in themselves, another must be added: the rapidity of its growth. It presently exercised, upon the surrounding region, an attraction comparable to that which the modern factory exercises over the rural population. By the lure of gain, it awakened the spirit of enterprise and adventure that lay dormant in the hearts of the domainal serfs, and it attracted fresh recruits from all directions. For that matter, the merchant colony was essentially open and extensible. In proportion as its commercial activity developed it provided employment for a host of workers—boatmen, carters, lumpers, etc. At the same time, artisans of every kind came to settle in the town. Some of them—bakers, brewers, shoemakers—found an assured livelihood there, thanks to the constant increase of the population. Others worked up the raw materials imported by the merchants, and the wares which they produced swelled the export trade. In this way industry took its place beside commerce. By the end of the 11th century, in Flanders, the weavers of woollen stuffs were beginning to flock from the country into the towns, and the Flemish cloth trade, being thus centralized under the direction of the merchants, became what it was to remain until the end of the Middle Ages, the most flourishing industry in Europe.

Naturally, neither the ancient "cities" nor the ancient *bourgs* could contain within the narrow circumference of their walls the increasing influx of these newcomers. They were forced to settle outside the gates, and presently their houses surrounded on every side, and submerged by their numbers, the ancient nucleus around which they were assembled. For the rest, the first care of the new town was to surround itself with a moat and a palisade to protect itself from pillagers, and these were replaced later by a stone rampart. Like the original "city" or *bourg*, the new town was itself a fortress: it was called "*nouveau-bourg*" or "*faubourg*"—that is to say, outer fortress; for which reason its inhabitants were known, from the beginning of the 11th century, by the name of *bourgeois*. The bourgeoisie underwent the same development as the nobility in this mediaeval society, which enjoyed, thanks to the abstention of the State, the advantage of complete plasticity. Before long its social function had transformed it into a juridical class. It is obvious that the law and administrative measures then in force, which had come into existence in the heart of a purely agricultural society, could no longer suffice for the needs of a merchant population. The formalistic apparatus of legal procedure, with its primitive means of proof, bailment, and seizure, had to give way to simpler and more expeditious rules. The judicial duel, that *ultima ratio* of the litigants, appeared to the merchants the very negation of justice. To ensure the maintenance of order in their faubourg, which was swarming with adventurers and jailbirds of every kind, such as had hitherto been unknown in the tranquil environment of the ancient *bourg* or "city," they demanded that the ancient system of fines and compositions should be replaced by punishments capable of inspiring a salutary terror: hanging, mutilation of every kind, and the putting out of the eyes. They protested against the prestations in kind which the collectors of tolls demanded before they would pass the merchandise that the merchants were exporting or importing. If it happened that one of their number was recognized as a serf, they would not suffer his seigneur to reclaim him. As for their children, whose mothers were necessarily almost always of servile condition, they refused to admit that such offspring should be regarded as servile. Thus the encounter of these new men with the ancient society resulted in all sorts of clashes and conflicts, due to the opposition of the domainal law and the commercial law, of exchange in kind and exchange for monetary payment, of servitude and liberty.

Naturally, the social authorities did not accept the claims of the nascent bourgeoisie without resistance. As always, they endeavoured first of all to conserve the established order of things: that is to say, to impose it upon these merchants, although it was in absolute opposition to their condition of life; and as always, their conduct was inspired as much by good faith as by personal interest. It is evident that it took the princes a long time to understand the necessity of modifying, for the merchant population, the authoritarian and patriarchial régime which they had hitherto applied to their serfs. The ecclesiastical princes especially displayed, in the beginning, a very marked hostility. To them it seemed that commerce endangered the salvation of the soul, and they regarded with mistrust, as a criminal derogation from obedience, all these innovations whose contagion was spreading from day to day. Their resistance inevitably led to revolts. In Italy and the Low Countries, and on the banks of the Rhine, the War of Investitures provided the bourgeois with an occasion or a pretext for rebelling against their bishops: here in the name of the Pope, and there in that of the Emperor. The first commune of which history makes mention, that of Cambrai, in 1077, was sworn by the people, led by the merchants, against the Imperialist prelate of the city.

## 2. *The Cities*

The princes, by their resistance, were able to impede the movement, but they could not check it. Towards the close of the 11th century it became more precipitate and more widespread and imposed itself upon the authorities. The princes began to realize that they had more to lose than to gain by persisting in their opposition to the movement. For while it undermined their local authority and imperilled certain of their domainal revenues, it more than made up for these drawbacks by the supplementary payments received in the shape of market tolls, and the inestimable advantage of a constant influx of corn and wares of every kind, and of money. By the beginning of the 12th century certain princes had frankly adopted a progressive policy, and were seeking to attract the merchants by the promise of immunities and privileges. In short, whether by agreement or by force, the claims of the bourgeoisie were everywhere triumphant, just as the parliamentary system was everywhere triumphant in the Europe of the 19th century. And great as were the differences between these two transformations in other respects, they offer a really striking similarity in respect of the character of their diffusion. Just as continental parliamentarianism was an adaptation of English and Belgian institutions to the special conditions of each country, so the urban institutions, although they exhibited, from town to town, peculiarities resulting from the nature of the local environment, might none the less be referred, on the whole, to two dominant types: on the one hand, that of the cities of Northern Italy, and on the other hand, that of the cities of the Low Countries and Northern France. Here, as in respect of the domainal régime, the feudal system, the Cluniac reformation, and chivalry, Germany and the other regions of central Europe merely followed the impulse that reached them from the West.

In spite of innumerable differences of detail, the towns of the Middle Ages presented everywhere the same essential features, and the same definition may be applied to one and all. We may formulate this definition by saying that the mediaeval city was a fortified agglomeration inhabited by a free population engaged in trade and industry, possessing a special law, and provided with a more or less highly developed jurisdiction and communal autonomy. The city enjoyed immunities which did not exist in the surrounding country; which amounts to saying that it had a morally privileged personality. It was constituted, indeed, on the basis of privilege. The bourgeois or burgess, like the noble, possessed a special juridical status: bourgeois and noble, in different directions, were equally removed from the villein, the peasant, who until the end of the *ancien régime* remained, in the majority of European countries, outside political society.

However, the privileged condition of the bourgeois was very different in its nature from that of the noble. The noble was, in reality, the old landowning freeman. His privilege, in some sort negative, arose from the fact that the mass of the people had lapsed into servitude under him. He had not ascended; he merely belonged to a minority which had kept its place amidst a general social decline. The privileges of the bourgeois, on the contrary, were very definitely positive. The bourgeois was a *parvenu*, who, of necessity, had made for himself a place in society which was finally recognized and guaranteed by the law. The domainal régime, which set the noble over the head of the peasant, at the same time bound them together by so strong a mutual tie that even to this day, after so many centuries, traces of it survive. The bourgeois, on the other hand, was a stranger both to the noble and to the peasant; both distrusted him and regarded him with hostility, and of this also the traces have not entirely disappeared. The bourgeois moved and had his being in a wholly different sphere. The contrast between him and them was the contrast between the agricultural and the commercial and industrial life. Compared with the noble and the peasant, the direct producers of the indispensable necessities of life, he was a mobile and active element; the traffic of the country was in his hands, and he was an agent of transformation. He was not indispensable to human existence; it was possible to live without him. He was essentially an agent of social progress and civilization.

There was yet another point of difference that divided the bourgeoisie of the Middle Ages from the nobility and the clergy. The nobility and the clergy constituted homogeneous classes, all of whose members participated in the same *esprit de corps*, and were conscious of their mutual solidarity. The case of the bourgeois was very different. Living in segregated groups in the various cities, in them the spirit of class was replaced by the local spirit, or was at all events subordinated to it. Each city was a little separate world in itself; there were no limits to its exclusivism and its protectionism. Each did its utmost to favour its own trade and industry at the expense of the other cities. Each endeavoured to become self-sufficient and to produce all that it needed. Each endeavoured to extend its authority over the surrounding countryside, in order to assure itself of sufficient supplies of food. If it occurred to the cities to act in concert, to conclude temporary or permanent leagues, like the London *Hansa*, and at a later date, the German *Hansa*, they did so in order to take action against a common enemy, or for the sake of a common utility, but within its own walls each had room only for its own burgesses; the foreigner could trade there only through the medium of his brokers, and was always liable to expulsion. In order to live there he had to acquire burgess rights. And all this is readily comprehensible. It was merely a question of local mercantilism. Are not our States, to-day, in the same situation? Do they not raise customs barriers in order to favour within their frontiers the birth of industries which they do not possess? Urban exclusivism came to an end only when the towns were united in the superior unity of the State, just as the exclusivism of the State will perhaps one day disappear in the unity of human society.

The moral result of this exclusivism was an extraordinary solidarity among the burgesses. Body and soul, they belonged to their little local *patrie*, and with them there reappeared, for the first time, since antiquity, in the history of Europe, a civic sentiment. Each burgess was obliged, and knew that he was obliged, to take part in the defence of the city: to take up arms for it, to give his life to it. The knights of Frederick Barbarossa were astounded to find that the shopkeepers and merchants of the Lombard cities were able to hold their own against them. In that campaign there were examples of civic virtue which remind one of ancient Greece. Other burgesses gave their fortune to their city, commuted the market tolls, or founded hospitals. The wealthy gave without stint or reckoning, and no doubt they were inspired by charity as much as by pride.

For the rich men were the rulers. The burgesses of the cities enjoyed civil equality and liberty, but not social equality, not political equality. The bourgeoisie, deriving from commerce, remained under the influence and the leadership of the wealthiest.

Under the name of "*grands*" or "patricians," they kept the administration and jurisdiction of the city in their own hands. The urban government was a plutocratic government, and it actually ended, in the 13th century, by becoming oligarchic, the same families holding power in perpetuity. Yet nothing could have been more remarkable than these governments. They were responsible for the creation of urban administration: that is, the first civil and secular administration known in Europe. It was their work from top to bottom. This has not been sufficiently considered: it should be realized that they had no model, and had to invent everything: financial system, systems of book-keeping, schools, commercial and industrial regulations, the first rudiments of a health service, public works, market-places, canals, posts, urban boundaries, water supply —all this was their work. And it was they too who erected the buildings which even to-day are the glory of so many cities.

Beneath them, the rest of the urban population consisted of artisans, and it was they who formed the majority in every city. As a rule they were foremen or small employers, masters, with one or two journeymen under them, who constituted an active and independent bourgeoisie. While wholesale trade was free, there developed, for the protection of the artisans, a social policy which was a masterpiece no less interesting, in its way, than the Gothic cathedrals; and of which the last traces have only recently disappeared. Its object was the maintenance of all these petty lives which constituted the strength of the city, and to secure its regular revictualling. Each citizen was a producer and a consumer, and regulation intervened in respect of both production and consumption. The municipal authority undertook to protect the consumer. To this end it revived the old municipal regulations of which some traces had perhaps survived in Italy. Nothing could have been more admirable than the precautions taken against "dishonest" products, fraud, and falsification. The consumer was protected in the twofold interest of the local bourgeoisie and of the city's good repute in the outer world.

As for the producer, he protected himself by the trade corporations or guilds which made their appearance as early as the 12th century. Their essential purpose was to prevent competition, and it was this that rendered them so odious to the liberal economy of the 19th century. Every producer had to earn his living; therefore he had to retain his customers. He must accordingly sell his wares at the same price as his comrades, and he must make them in the same way. The trade or handicraft was originally a voluntary association, like our syndicates or trade unions. But it boycotted the "yellow" workers who did not apply for membership, and it was finally recognized by the public authority. Let us note that this organization had nothing in common with the association of workers whose purpose is negotiation with the employer. It was an obligatory syndicate of petty burgesses. It was created essentially for the benefit of the small independent producer. In most of the cities of the Middle Ages there was no proletariat. The craftsmen worked for the local market and reserved it for themselves. Their numbers were maintained in proportion to the number of their customers. They had complete control of the situation. In this sense, they had solved the social problem. But they had solved it only where the city was a "closed State," a situation which was not so general as one might suppose. For there was one industry at least—the cloth industry in Flanders and in Florence—whose products supplied not the local, but the European market. In this industry there could be no limitation of production, nor was it possible for the small employer to acquire his raw material for himself. Here he was in the power of the great merchant, so that in this industry there was a division between capital and labour which we do not find elsewhere. The industrial system was the system of the small workshop. But in the cloth industry the "master" was not an independent producer; he worked for wages, so that here we find something closely resembling the "cottage industry" of our own age. Trade organization existed, but in this case it was far from protecting the artisan efficiently, as it could not affect the conditions of marketing or of capital investment. Hence there were strikes, conflicts of salaried workers, an exodus of the weavers from Ghent, and industrial crises. Hence the uneasy, unruly, turbulent, Utopian spirit that characterized the weavers from the 12th century onwards, and made them the adepts of a naïve communism which was allied with mystical or heretical ideals. It is therefore incorrect to say that the Middle Ages knew only small, independent, and corporative industries. In the more advanced environments there was no lack of labour troubles and social conflicts. The influence of these conflicts was again perceptible in the 14th century.

With the rise of the towns and the constitution of the bourgeoisie the formation of European society was completed; such as it was it remained until the end of the *ancien régime*. Clergy, noblesse, bourgeoisie—these made the trinity that ruled human destinies and played its part in political life. The agricultural people, below the privileged classes, were restricted to their function of food producers until the day when civil equality, and to some extent political equality, should become the common possession of all. For one cannot too strongly insist on the fact that the bourgeoisie was an exclusive and privileged class. It was in this respect that the cities of the Middle Ages differed essentially from the cities of the Roman Empire, whose inhabitants, whatever the standard of their social life, were all in enjoyment of the same rights. The Roman world never knew anything analogous to the European bourgeoisie; nor has the New World seen its like. When the American cities were founded the moment had passed when each social profession had its peculiar law; there were merely free human beings. In our days the word bourgeoisie, which we continue to employ, is completely diverted from its original sense. It denotes a social class of heterogeneous origin which has no common quality except that it is the class which possesses wealth. Of the bourgeoisie of the Middle Ages nothing remains, just as nothing remains of the nobility of the Middle Ages.

## CHAPTER III

# THE GROWTH OF THE CITIES AND ITS CONSEQUENCES

### 1. *The Growth of the Cities*

While in its remotest origins the renaissance of urban life in the West dates back to the first merchant settlements of the 10th century, it was not until the end of the 11th and the beginning of the 12th century that it reached its full development: only then did the first cities, in the full acceptation of the word, make their appearance in history. As we have already seen, the first fully-developed examples came into existence in the two regions whose commercial activity was most intense: in the South of Europe, in Northern Italy; in the North of Europe, in the Low Countries. There were striking parallels in the situation of these two regions. In Italy, as in Flanders, the maritime commerce, and the inland commerce which was its continuation, resulted in the activity of the seaports: Venice, Pisa, and Genoa in the South; Bruges in the North. Then, behind the seaports, the industrial cities developed: on the one hand, the Lombard communes and Florence; on the other, Ghent, Ypres and Lille, Douai, and further inland, Valenciennes and Brussels. It was evidently the proximity of the seaports that gave such an extraordinary impetus to the industry of the cities—an impetus unique in Europe. The Italian and Flemish ports, with their hinterland, acquired an international importance, and in this way they were unique.

For this very reason they necessarily entered into mutual relations. Here the initiative proceeded from the more developed of these two centres: that is, from Italy. The Italian merchants visited Flanders from the beginning of the 12th century. But presently the fairs of Champagne became the point of contact, and, so to speak, the Bourse of Italo-Flemish commerce. Situated on the route which joined the South to the North, running from Lombardy by way of the Gothard Pass, the Lake of Geneva, and the Jura, they kept the merchants of the two countries in touch throughout the year. But these were merely business rendezvous, and no really important cities were founded on the sites of these fairs. Even Troies never developed into a very large city, while Lagny, Provins and Bar-sur-Aube remained places of secondary importance.

The South of France was not far behind Italy. Marseilles, Montpellier, and Aigues-Mortes played their part in Mediterranean commerce. And behind them were Albi, Cahors, and Toulouse, which gravitated toward them, and prospered without interruption until the Albigensian War. In Spain the port of Barcelona likewise acquired great importance, though it did not produce any very active urban centres in the hinterland.

The Rhone is the only Mediterranean river in France, and the only river which by virtue of this fact gave rise at an early date to important cities: Avignon and Lyons. The other rivers flow into the Atlantic and the Channel, and on them there were only coasting and fishing ports, of which the most important is Bayonne, or ports engaged in local traffic with England, such as Rouen and Bordeaux. In the same way, in England navigation was restricted to the opposite coast, and the towns had acquired no importance. Even London did not attain any great importance until the 13th century. One single city in the interior of France developed until it was the peer of the greatest, but this was for political reasons: Paris. It was the only city of the kind in Europe, a true capital, growing larger with every forward movement of the monarchy. With these exceptions there were hardly any but local centres, none of which was comparable with those of Languedoc or Flanders.

Germany had no centre of international trade. She was in touch with Italy through the Rhine and the Danube; on the one river Cologne and Strasbourg made their appearance; on the other, Ratisbon and Vienna. The most important of these centres was Cologne, where the Germany of the West and South came into contact with the Germany of the North, and both were in touch with the Low Countries. The Germany of the North had no other direct communication with the South; it was oriented toward the two inland seas. It had Hamburg and Bremen on the North Sea, and above all, Lubeck, founded by Henry the Lion, on the Baltic. And here we are entering upon colonial territory, and new cities, which had never been subject to the Roman influence. The coastal ports were new settlements, favoured by the princes of the region. They were strung along the coast as far as Lithuanian territory: Danzig, Reval, Memel, Riga, Dorpat. The Baltic had been a German lake since the Russian route had been deserted—on the one hand, because commerce had gravitated to Italy, and on the other hand, because since the middle of the 12th century the advance-guard of the Mongols—the Kumans—made the neighbourhood of Kiev too dangerous. When this happened the Scandinavians lost their commercial significance, which was inherited by the Germans. Visby, in the island of Gothland, was a Teutonic station, and the "Niemetz"[1] made their way as far as Novgorod, where they had a market in the 12th century. Denmark alone attempted to hold her own with them, but was defeated at Bornhöved under Waldemar II (1227), and made way for Germany.

In the interior of Germany, between the Rhine and the Danube, there was no large town. Munster and Magdeburg were places of secondary importance; so were Frankfort and Nuremburg. Berlin was quite insignificant, and so were Munich and Leipzig. As far as urban life was concerned, the country was obviously backward. Frederick Barbarossa had no understanding of the bourgeoisie. Urban life existed only on the periphery, and except on the banks of the Rhine it did not begin to assume any importance until the 13th century. Thus the general picture is that of two great centres, Italy and the Low Countries—that is, Belgium—in which the largest cities existed, and with which all the other important centres were in communication. The commercial movement of the Baltic gravitated toward Bruges, while that of Southern Germany gravitated towards Italy.

[1] The name which the Russians gave to the Germans.

But between the great commercial centres, whether these were of local or of general importance, a host of small secondary towns arose, of the same character as the large cities, and living under the same law. It had now become indispensable that each region should have its little urban centre. The disorganization of the domainal system, and the appearance of free peasants, necessarily called into existence—to replace the "courts" from which the servile population had supplied their needs—little *bourgs*, which offered an asylum to the artisans, and served as commercial centres for the neighbourhood. Their urban life was a spontaneous gift from the great cities. New towns were founded. In Germany the two Fribourgs became important centres. A host of others led a quiet, semi-urban, semi-agricultural existence; Kreuzburg, where I am writing these lines, received its charter in 1213. These were towns of secondary formation, belonging to a period when the bourgeoisie had established itself, and when the princes, impelled by the advantages which they derived from these towns, were establishing them in all directions. Formerly the traveller passed from monastery to monastery; now he journeyed from town to town; there were towns on all the roads, at intervals of a few leagues, constituting a transition between the great cities, like the little beads of a rosary between the *dizaines*.

The rise of the towns provoked an increase of population, relatively comparable to that which occurred in the 19th century. And even more remarkable than the increase of the urban population were the effects of this multiplication of urban centres on the population of the countryside. Compared with the Carolingian population, we may estimate, roughly, that its strength was doubled. The maximum increase was attained at the beginning of the 14th century. From that time, until the 18th century, there was no essential change.

It would be of the greatest importance to obtain some idea of the relative strength of the urban as compared with the rural population. But this is unfortunately impossible. Of this, however, we may be certain, that in all the centres favoured by commerce the bourgeois population continued to increase until about the middle of the 14th century. Everywhere the walled enclosures which had become too restricted had to be enlarged, and faubourgs which had been built outside the gates had to be enclosed by walls. There were now large towns in Europe—relatively speaking, very large towns. But what was a large town at the beginning of the 13th century? The area enclosed by the walls was still—relatively speaking—quite small. The figures provided by contemporaries are of no value, because they are not based on actual enumeration, and the oldest statistics that we have date only from the 15th century. Moreover, they are so contradictory that we cannot admit their validity. At an interval of only ten years, the population of Ypres was estimated respectively at 50,000 and at 200,000 inhabitants. All that we can affirm is that until the end of the Middle Ages no European city attained a population of 100,000. The largest cities—Milan, Paris, Gand—must have contained about 50,000 inhabitants, more or less. The cities of medium size would have contained from 20,000 to 50,000 inhabitants; the small towns from 2,000 to 5,000. But this need not prevent us from speaking of great cities, for size is entirely relative. If we take into account the very low density of the rural population, an agglomeration of 50,000 human beings must appear something very different from what it is to-day.

## 2. *The Consequences for the Rural Population*

Moreover, we must be very careful not to envisage the relation between the cities and the countryside in the Middle Ages as in any way resembling what it is to-day. In our days the town is not sharply divided from the country. There are industries in the villages, and some part of the urban population lives in the country, and returns to it every evening. The case was very different in the Middle Ages. Then the town was absolutely distinct from the open country. It was divided from it even materially, sheltering behind its moat and walls and its gates. Juridically, it was another world. Directly one entered the gates one became subject to a different law, just as one does to-day on passing from one State to another. Economically the contrast was as great. Not only was the city a centre of commerce and industry, but there was no commerce and no industry elsewhere. In the country they were everywhere prohibited. Every city endeavoured to dominate the surrounding countryside, to subjugate it. The country had to provide it with a market, and, at the same time, to guarantee its supplies of foodstuffs. There was not, as there is to-day, constant exchange and interpenetration; there was a contrast, and the subordination of the one element to the other.

This subordination was more or less complete according to the number and the power of the cities. It attained its maximum in Italy, and its minimum in the Scandinavian and Slav countries. The result of this subordination was everywhere a more or less profound disturbance of the rural economic system and a corresponding transformation of the condition of the agricultural classes.

The rise of the towns, in fact, made it impossible to preserve the domainal system. This, as we have seen, may be described as essentially an economy without outlet. Having no market in which to sell its products, the domain restricted its production to the needs of its own consumption, and its whole internal structure—methods of agriculture, forms of tenure, prestations, and relations between the inhabitants and the seigneur—is explained by this special situation. Now, from the moment the towns made their appearance this special situation ceased to exist wherever their influence was felt. For apart from its merchants and artisans, the urban population was a sterile population—to employ a favourite formula of the 18th-century physiocrats. It could live only by sending out of the city for its means of subsistence—that is, by purchasing them from the cultivators of the soil. It therefore provided them with the outlet for their products which they had hitherto lacked. Consequently it awakened in their minds the idea of profit, since henceforth production was remunerative. And so the moral and the economic conditions to which the domainal organization corresponded both disappeared simultaneously. The peasant, whose activity was now solicited by the outer world, no longer regarded his work as a mere burden. Further, as a necessary consequence of the new state of affairs, the seigneur himself was even more conscious of the need of a reformation. For since the prestations of his tenants were fixed by custom, he soon discovered that his resources were dwindling unpleasantly. His revenues were still the same, while his expenses were constantly increasing. The towns, in fact, by their purchases, were putting money into circulation throughout the countryside; and as money became more and more abundant its value diminished in proportion. The cost of living was continually rising, and the landowners, restricted to fixed revenues, found themselves launched on the road to ruin. For the petty military noblesse, who, as a general thing, possessed only small fiefs which just provided them with a living, the crisis was a veritable catastrophe. A large proportion of the chivalry, so numerous in the 11th century, was overwhelmed by poverty at the close of the 12th century.

It is difficult to say whether the increase of the population of the rural districts, which manifested itself at the very time when the conditions of rural life were undergoing such a profound modification, should also be referred to the appearance of the towns. After the devastations of the Normans, the Saracens and the Hungarians, Europe had known a period of relative tranquillity, during which the natural excess of births over deaths must insensibly have increased the numbers of the inhabitants. But it is only in the second half of the 11th century that we perceive, in certain parts of Europe, the traces of a malaise due to the excessive density of the population, and we are almost bound to believe that in affording the peasants new means of livelihood, the towns, by that very fact, had contributed, not, of course, to increase the fecundity of marriages,[1] but to increase their number. However this may be, it is certain that in the Low Countries, for example, the cultivated land, about 1050, was beginning to prove insufficient for the needs of the inhabitants. Moreover, events like the conquest of England in 1066, and the Crusade, evidently justify the supposition that the

[1] The fecundity of marriages was very great, both among the peasants, as may be seen from the Polyptych of Irminion and the monastic charters, and the nobility (on this subject see Gislebert). It is only among the princes that we find any traces of pre-Malthusianism.

population was somewhat excessive, at all events in the North of France.

This excess of population was due also to the rapid increase in the numbers of the inhabitants of the towns, and to the bands of mercenary adventurers which were being formed about this time in Italy—at Genoa, for example—and, under the name of Brabançons and Cotereaux, in France. From the beginning of the 11th century we have something more than presumption to go upon. The peopling of the regions beyond the Elbe by immigrants from the banks of the Rhine, Holland, and Flanders, evidently cannot be explained save by the superabundance of the rural population of these countries.

Thus, at the moment when the ancient domainal system had had its day, and no longer responded to the needs of a more economically advanced society, there were numbers of men who offered themselves to whomsoever would give them land. The great landowners, and above all the territorial princes, did not fail to profit by so favourable a situation. They possessed plenty of uncultivated land, for it seems that to the west of the Rhine and to the south of the Danube, at all events, the great domains had hardly spread beyond the fertile soil already cultivated in the days of the Roman Empire. The rest of the land was untouched forest, heath, and marshland. The time had come to bring this land into cultivation. This great task, which, for the first time since the disappearance of the Roman Empire, increased the territorial wealth of Europe, was begun about the middle of the 11th century, reached its apogee during the course of the 12th century, and was completed, at a gradually relaxing pace, towards the end of the 13th century. From that period until the end of the 18th century the area of cultivable soil was not sensibly increased in the Occident, and this fact alone shows the importance of the progress effected by internal colonization in the Middle Ages. No doubt the intakes would have been less extensive had agriculture been more advanced. The great areas which it occupied, in order to increase its production, were the consequence of the rudimentary methods of an agriculture which was still wholly of the extensive type. The crisis of the domainal organization could have been avoided had it been possible to increase the fertility of the soil by more rational methods.

The system followed in the peopling and cultivation of virgin soil differed greatly, in what might be called its liberal character, from the practices of the preceding epoch. The peasant's relations to the landowner were now merely such as necessarily arose from his quality of tenant. He paid a rent for the land which he occupied, but his person remained free. One of the means most frequently employed by the seigneurs in order to attract colonists, was the foundation of "new towns," which were regular agricultural colonies. The area of the "new town" was divided into a certain number of equal units, and these, on payment of a quit-rent, could be secured under a hereditary title. A charter, usually an imitation of the charter of the neighbouring town, recognized the personal liberty of the inhabitants, and determined the powers and the competence of the mayor and the court who were charged with the affairs of the colony and the administration of justice, and defined the respective rights of the seigneur and the peasants as to forestal usages, etc. Thus a new type of village appeared, the *village à loi*. It no longer had anything in common with the old domainal organization, except for the fact that, like the latter, it presupposed a great property and a small-scale exploitation. For the rest, everything was new. Not only was the peasant a free man, but the prestations which he had to pay the seigneur, instead of consisting of natural products, were usually payable in money. It is not surprising that the demand for land, which became more and more pressing as the population increased, brought the colonists flocking to the new settlements. In all directions they thrust back the frontier of the untamed wilderness, colonizing the great forests, uprooting the heath, and draining the marshes. All over Europe there was a new growth of villages, and the very form of their names, ending in *sart* in the French-speaking countries, and in *kerk*, *kirche*, *rode*, *rath*, in countries where German was spoken, still enable us to distinguish them from their neighbours in the long-settled regions.

The Church played a considerable part in this great cultural task of the 12th century. She entrusted the work to the new orders of Cistercians and Premonstratensians. The extraordinary vitality manifested by the monks at the time of the Clunisian reformation had not survived the triumph of the latter. The object once achieved, the enthusiasm waned. The crisis was succeeded by a decline, and from the close of the 11th century the Benedictine monasteries, whose fortune, by the singular but inevitable irony of things, had been still further increased by the donations of the faithful, which came to them despite their disdain of worldly wealth, were beginning to lapse into a period of lethargy from which they did not emerge until their renaissance in the 17th century. Their religious and social rôle was ended, and they were now little more than great landowners. The Cistercians and the Premonstratensians—the former founded by St. Bernard in 1113,[1] and the latter by Saint Norbert in 1119—resumed the ascetic propaganda which the Benedictines had abandoned. In order that the prescription of manual labour might be applied in all its rigour they established themselves, by preference, in uncultivated regions where there was land to be cleared or drained. The princes made haste to help on the pious work by ceding tracts of moor and marshland to the monks. The two Orders played a great part in draining the Flemish polders and bringing the soil of Eastern Germany into cultivation. The domains which they constituted there were of a completely novel type, in which we see, for the first time in the Middle Ages, the principle of large-scale agricultural exploitation. Instead of being parcelled out in family holdings, the newly-cleared areas were organized into great farms, which were worked by "lay brothers" or free peasants under the direction of a monk. The cultivation of cereals or the breeding of cattle was practised, not as formerly, with a view to immediate consumption by the convent, but for the purpose of sale in the markets. The worker was not burdened with corvées, and the only prestation he had to pay was the tithe. The profits realized enabled the monks to acquire more land, and to continue the work of bringing it into cultivation. The

[1] Citeaux (not far from Dijon) was founded in 1098 by Robert de Molesnes, but it did not become the centre of a movement until Saint Bernard entered it in 1113.

proprietors of the old domains, unable to dispose of their land, on account of the hereditary rights of their tenants, did not find it easy to liberate themselves from tradition. Burdened with debts, and driven to extremities by the uninterrupted dwindling of their revenues, they were obliged, from the end of the 11th century, to take decisive measures. The domainal "courts," formerly cultivated by the serfs, were divided into parcels and ceded in return for a quit-rent, or leased *à metayage*, or transformed into large farms. The peasants were permitted to free themselves, in return for money payments, not only from the corvées, but also from the capital tax, the marriage fee, and mortmain—in short, from all those survivals of a bygone age which had lost their utility. Hardly anywhere, save in regions which were difficult of access, or very remote from the great commercial movements, did serfdom retain its primitive form. Everywhere else, if it did not actually disappear, it was at least mitigated. One may say that from the beginning of the 13th century the rural population, in Western and Central Europe, had become or was in process of becoming a population of free peasants. And this great transformation was accomplished without violence, without the co-operation of principles and theories, as an inevitable consequence of the revival of trade and the appearance of the towns, which, by providing agriculture with the outlets of which it had hitherto been deprived, had compelled it to modify its traditional organization and to adopt freer and more flexible forms of exploitation. Economic progress had destroyed the social patronage which the seigneur had hitherto exercised over his men. In proportion as liberty was substituted for serfdom the landowner put off his old paternal character, and material interest tended to become the sole criterion of his relations with his tenants.

### 3. *Other Consequences*

The appearance of the towns in the course of the 11th century, which so profoundly modified the social condition of Europe, naturally influenced its political and religious life also. By depriving the State of its essentially agricultural character, and subjecting the rural population to the attraction and the influence of the urban centres, the towns restored it to the condition from which the invasions of the Barbarians had deposed it. As in the Roman Empire, although under very different circumstances, the city resumed its position in political society. Thanks to the city, the administration, which had wandered from place to place, was again becoming sedentary. Moreover—and this was the most considerable advance which had been accomplished in civil life since the Carolingian epoch—it was beginning to employ a secular and literate personnel. Hitherto the State had been obliged to borrow from the Church all those of its agents in whom a certain degree of learning was indispensable. Henceforth it was able to borrow them, more and more extensively, from the bourgeoisie. For unlike the noble, whose military profession called for no other apprenticeship than that of arms, the bourgeoisie, in consequence of the needs of commerce, found it necessary to acquire at least a rudimentary education. The ability to read and write was indispensable to the merchant, and from the 12th century onwards there was no city of any importance without its school. At first the education provided was still entirely Latin, and it was in Latin that the most ancient administrative and commercial documents which we possess were written. But this was only an intermediate stage, through which it was necessary to pass, as at first it was impossible to find masters outside the Church. It was obvious that the bourgeois population could not long continue to employ, in its ordinary business affairs, a tongue that was not the language which it spoke. From the beginning of the 12th century the inevitable development took place: the vulgar tongue began to be employed by the urban scribes, and it is characteristic that this innovation made its first appearance in the country whose municipal life was most highly developed: namely, in Flanders. The first document of this kind in our possession is a charter of the corporation (*échevinage*) of Douai, dated 1204, which is written in the Picard dialect. In proportion as the urban administration became more complex, when the magistrates had to undertake a more extensive correspondence, and had to pronounce judgement in more important disputes, while the keeping of the communal accounts demanded more care and greater knowledge, the clerks employed by the city, and the notaries and advocates to whom the private person applied for assistance, had naturally to become more highly educated, and in this way there was formed, in the heart of the bourgeoisie, a class of lay practitioners who were much better qualified, by their knowledge of the world and of business matters, to satisfy the requirements of the civil administration than were the ecclesiastics whom it had hitherto been necessary to employ. From the end of the 12th century an increasing number of such experts entered into the employ of the princes or kings and applied their skill and experience in the service of the State. We may say that the first lay personnel in Europe since the disappearance of the Imperial Roman bureaucracy was furnished by the bourgeoisie.

And even while the cities were thus so effectively secularizing the State, they were influencing its very constitution, and this influence constantly increased in the course of the centuries. Everywhere they began to play a greater and greater part in political life, whether, as in France, they helped the king to oppose the pretensions of the great feudal nobles, or whether, as in England, they united with the barons, in order to wrest the first national liberties from the Crown, or whether, as in Italy or Germany, they constituted themselves independent republics. The absence of the bourgeoisie in the Slav States shows what the West owed to it.

Neither the Church nor civil society could escape its influence. With the renaissance of urban life a period began for the Church in which piety and charity received a fresh stimulus, but at the same time formidable problems presented themselves, and it was an age of bloody conflict. Nothing could have been more ardent or more deep-rooted than the religion of the bourgeoisie. Of this we need no other evidence than the extraordinary number of confraternities and guilds and associations of all kinds, which in every city devoted themselves to prayer, or to the care of the sick, the poor, the aged, and the widows and orphans. From the end of the 12th century the *béguines* and *bégards*, who practised asceticism in secular life, were beginning to spread from city to city. But for the bourgeoisie, the foundation of the new Orders—the Franciscans (1208) and Dominicans (1215)—whose spirit inspired the orthodox mysticism of the 13th century, would have been impossible. With these mendicant monks monasticism, for the first time, deserted the country for an urban environment. They lived on the alms of the bourgeoisie; they recruited their ranks from the bourgeoisie; and it was for the sake of the bourgeoisie that they exercised their apostolate, and the success of this was sufficiently proved by the multitude of brothers of the tertiary order, among both the merchants and the artisans, who were associated with the Franciscans.

Urban piety, as we see, was an active piety. The laymen—and this was still a novel phenomenon—collaborated directly in the religious life, claiming their right to play their part in it beside the clergy. This represented a twofold peril to the Church. The first and the most dangerous of these was the threat to orthodoxy. The greater the interest of the bourgeois in the things of religion, the more liable they were to adopt the Manichaean doctrines which, in the 12th century, were spreading into Europe from the East; or to be impressed by the mystical dreams of the "Apostolics" or the "Brothers of the Free Spirit." It is highly characteristic that the West was not troubled with heresy before the renaissance of the cities. The first and most formidable heresy known to Europe before the advent of Protestantism, that of the Cathars, began to propagate itself in the 11th century, and was therefore precisely contemporaneous with the urban movement. And we must not forget that the sect of the Vaudois (Waldenses) was founded by a merchant of Lyons. Even after the terrible massacres of the Albigenses the urban populations continued, now in this part of Europe, now in that, to harbour their suspect sects, in which the aspirations of the proletariat tended to orientate mysticism toward confused visions of social transformation, and which dreamed of establishing, on the ruins of Church and State, in some sort of communistic society, the rule of the just.

These instances were doubtless exceptions, but one thing was common to all the cities, and it constituted one of the most striking features of the urban spirit: namely, their attitude toward ecclesiastical power. With the rise of the cities the relations between the secular and the spiritual authority entered upon a new phase. Since the Carolingian epoch the conflicts between the two authorities had been due to the efforts of the kings to subjugate the Church and force it to serve their policy. They were merely the consequence of the alliance of the two powers: the question was, which of the two was to be supreme in society. But neither the one nor the other attempted to deprive its rival of its prerogatives or privileges. It was the relation of the two forces, but not their nature, which was at issue. In the cities the case was very different. There the very situation which the Church enjoyed as a privileged corporation was imperilled. The cities openly attacked the tribunals of the Church, its financial exemptions, and the monopoly which it claimed to exercise in respect of education. From the end of the 12th century there were perpetual conflicts between the communal councils and the chapters and monasteries included within the urban precincts, or even between the council and the bishop of the diocese. In vain did the Church blast them with her excommunication or interdict: they still persisted in their attitude. At need, they did not hesitate to compel the priests to sing the mass and administer the sacraments. However religious and orthodox they might be, they claimed the right to prevent the Church from interfering in the domain of temporal interests. Their spirit was purely secular, and for this reason the urban spirit must be regarded as the prime and remote cause of the Renaissance.

We may therefore say that with the appearance of the cities and the formation of the bourgeoisie a new Europe had arisen. Every department of social life was transformed; the population was doubled; liberty was becoming general; trade and industry, the circulation of money, and the achievements of the intellect were becoming more and more important, and were providing new possibilities for the development of the State and of society. Never, until the end of the 17th century, was there such a profound social—I do not say intellectual—revolution. Hitherto men had been mainly restricted to the relations of producer and consumer. Now they were increasingly ruled by their political relations. The only circulation in Europe had been that of the Church toward Rome and the religious centres. Now this was accompanied by a lay circulation. Life began to flow toward the coasts, the great rivers, the natural highways. Civilization was purely continental; but it was now becoming maritime.

We must not, of course, exaggerate. The Church continued to dominate the world of ideas, and the soil was still the foundation which supported the noblesse, and even the State. But the roots of the tree which had recently planted itself upon the wall would inevitably, without intention, by the mere fact of their growth, dislodge the stones. The cities had no desire to destroy what already existed, but only to make a place for themselves. And gradually this place became larger and larger, so large that it presently created a new order of things. In European civilization the cities were essentially elements of progress, not in the sense that everything emerged from them, but in the sense that they furnished the indispensable conditions of all these renewals. Since the appearance of the bourgeoisie civilization seemed to be waking up, to be shaking itself; it was more mobile, more nervous. From the 7th to the 11th century the movement of history was everywhere analogous. But after the 11th century, what variety! The strength of the bourgeoisie differed from country to country, giving to each a national character of its own, a character hitherto unknown. The active centres of the world were the centres in which the urban population was concentrating: Paris, Lombardy, Tuscany, Venice, Flanders, the Rhine.

There is a sort of contradiction in the enthusiasm of the cities of the 13th century for the mendicant orders and their capitalistic activities. They were filled with enthusiasm for the ideal of poverty, but they sought riches.

*Book Six*

# THE BEGINNINGS OF THE WESTERN STATES

## CHAPTER I

# ENGLAND

### 1. *Before the Conquest*

The Barbarian kingdoms erected on the ruins of the Roman Empire, had vainly endeavoured to appropriate, together with the territory, the old system of government. We have seen how and why these efforts were abortive. Pippin the Short and Charlemagne succeeded in restoring the power of the monarchy, with the help of the Church, and they applied themselves, by agreement with the Church, to the institution of a Christian society. The social conditions did not allow them to accomplish their mission. They found it impossible to create a royal administration at a time when the system of great estates subjected men everywhere to the protectorate of the territorial seigneurs. Political unity was replaced by the parcelling out of the State in territorial principalities. The subjects of the king passed under the authority of the feudal princes, and from the end of the 9th century it was really they who acquitted themselves of the onerous task which had proved too heavy for the sovereign's hands. But while the king allowed the princes to govern in his place, he nevertheless continued to reign above their heads, and, faithful to the Carolingian ideal, he awaited the moment when he would be able to exercise the supreme magistrature which he had never renounced. He was therefore the great political force of the future. Without exception, all the European States were the work of royalty, and in all of them the rapidity and the amplitude of their development was in proportion to the royal power.

It was at the end of the 11th century—that is, at the epoch when the appearance of the bourgeoisies was completing the social constitution of Europe—that royalty began to lay the foundations of the first States worthy of the name. Here again progress began in the West: to be exact, in France. Just as feudality and chivalry and the Clunisian reformation spread from France into other countries, it was in France that the forces operated, or it was from France that the forces came which presently created the new States. It was a vassal of the King of France who founded the English State, and the kingdom of France was the earliest of the continental States. For that matter, the vassal preceded the sovereign. So that in this sketch of the political work of the monarchy we must begin with England.

Of all the Roman provinces, Britain was the only one whose inhabitants had refused to accept the domination of the Barbarians at the time of the invasions. After a violent struggle they were driven back into the West, into Cornwall, and Wales—where their Celtic idiom has been preserved to this day—while others emigrated to Armorica, which thereupon took the name of Brittany. The Anglo-Saxons, finding themselves alone in their new country, were able to preserve their national institutions intact. The seven petty kingdoms which they founded there did not reveal the slightest trace of that Romanization which had imposed itself so completely on the Germanic kings on the other side of the Channel. Owing to the restricted area of these kingdoms, they were perfectly adapted to institutions which had been born in the bosom of the tribe, and which would have been unsuitable to a great State. Thus the Germanic States whose conquest by the Franks had checked evolution in Germany continued to develop unhindered in England. The assembly of the freemen, the *Witenagemot*, existed simultaneously with the king, and the popular magistrate, the ælderman, was found side by side with the royal officials, the sheriffs. The Christianization of the country at the end of the 6th century brought no essential modification to this state of affairs. Of course, the Church imported its language, Latin, into its new conquest, but the national development was too alien to the Roman traditions, and the geographical situation rendered permanent contact with the Frankish Church too difficult, for it to be possible that this language should become, as on the Continent, the language of the State. The Latin Church behaved in England as the Greek Church, for the same reasons, behaved in the Slav countries in the 10th century. It accepted the language of its faithful, learned it immediately for the purposes of evangelization, and being forced to recruit its clergy from among its new converts, it taught the latter to read and write their national idiom. There thus developed, beside a scholarly literature in the Latin language, a popular literature in the Anglo-Saxon language, and it was naturally this language that was used in recording laws and regulations, which on the Continent were written exclusively in Latin. Nor did the Church exercise over the political organization the preponderant influence which the Carolingians had given it; the conversion of England did not in any way alter the Germanic character of the country.

The union of all the petty Anglo-Saxon kingdoms under the King of Mercia, Offa († 796), would undoubtedly have opened a new phase in their history had not the Norsemen descended upon their country. From 839 their invasions continued almost without interruption, and their result was the establishment, on the eastern coast of the island, of a numerous population of Danish origin. King Alfred the Great († 901) successfully checked the invaders, to whom he ceded the Danelaw—that is to say, the region situated to the north of a line running from London to Chester. His successors actually ended by reconquering this area. But at the close of the 10th century Svend, King of Denmark († 1014), came to the aid of his compatriots, conquered Mercia, East Anglia, and Wessex, and forced King Ethelred to take refuge in Normandy. England was thus politically attached to Scandinavia, and the bond was tightened under Canute (1035), the son of Svend, who, like his father, was at once a king of England and of Denmark. It was the Anglo-Saxon missionaries who at this period introduced Christianity into Sweden and Norway.

But this state of things could not last. The forces of Scandinavia were never large enough to enable her to impose herself on the outer world. The Danish expansion in the 11th century suffered the same fate as the Swedish expansion of the 17th century under Gustavus Adolphus, and in the 18th century under Charles XII.

The military power on which it depended was quickly exhausted. Under the successors of Canute, Harold and Hardicanute, the Danish dynasty became decadent. An Anglo-Saxon prince, Edward the Confessor, recovered the throne. His death, without issue, in 1066, was the occasion that decided the fate of England, and forced her to enter the European community, in respect of which she had hitherto observed a policy of isolation which could no longer be continued.

For the great island was naturally allied to the Low Countries and Northern France, from which it was divided only by the narrow waters of the Straits of Dover. Civilization had crossed the water with the legions of Caesar, and Christianity with the monks of Gregory the Great. Not until the equilibrium of the world was disturbed by the cataclysm of the Roman Empire could the Anglo-Saxons seize the island and retain possession of it. The economic stagnation of Europe after the period of the invasions, and the almost complete disappearance of commerce, explain very simply why from that time forward their relations with Christian Europe were exclusively religious. Charlemagne never attempted to absorb the Anglo-Saxons into the Empire, and after his death the weakness of his successors was yet another cause of their prolonged isolation. However, at the very time when the Danish invasions were threatening them with the domination of the Scandinavians, the revival of navigation began to re-establish, between them and their neighbours on the adjacent coasts of Flanders and Normandy, the relations that were naturally imposed by their geographical proximity. Bruges and Rouen, from the end of the 10th century, maintained an increasingly active navigation with England. With the return of a more advanced civilization the order of things which had so long been interrupted by the Barbarian invasion once more followed its natural course.

The Norman conquest was merely the consequence and final consecration of what may be called the Europeanization of England. While the incidents that provoked the conquest were due to fortuitous circumstances, and while the orientation of the island toward the Continent might, of course, have been effected in a manner very different from that which we know, this orientation itself responded so profoundly to the natural circumstances that it must have been accomplished sooner or later.

The ducal house of Normandy was closely related to that of Edward the Confessor, whose mother, Emma, was a Norman princess. Being without children, Edward promised the succession to Duke William, thus himself disposing of the royal power, although, in accordance with Anglo-Saxon custom, only the assembly of the people could decide the matter. The assembly paid no attention to the King's resolve. On his death (1066) it elected Harold, the son of Godwin, who, during the lifetime of the feeble Edward, had played the part of a mayor of the palace. War was inevitable, and its issue was not in doubt.

In reality, the Anglo-Saxon kingdom was very weak. The old Germanic constitution, which had survived in its essential features, guaranteed the rights of free men as against the king, but condemned both the king and his subjects to a like condition of impotence. On the Continent the powerful feudal aristocracy had diminished the status of the king only to increase its own; the power had passed from the sovereign into the hands of the territorial princes. In England, on the contrary, no one had any real power. The aristocracy which constituted the National Assembly prevented the birth of the monarchical government, but was itself powerless to govern. Faithful to the old Germanic customs, it was essentially conservative. It consisted of landowners of mediocre importance, who lived by the labour of their serfs and retainers. The feudal system and the order of chivalry were unknown. The Anglo-Saxon earls and thanes, armed with battle-axe and sword, fought on foot.

Both as a political organization and as a military power, Normandy was superior to England in every respect. In all his territory, from the Canche to the Seine, the Duke had no rival. As the protector of peace he governed the people, and as the associate of the clergy, as the suzerain, he ruled the chivalry and the barons who held their fiefs from him. The domains whose comptrollers delivered their accounts every year to his exchequer were a model of good organization. Two great monasteries which he built at Caen, the Abbaye aux Hommes and the Abbaye aux Dames, were evidence not only of the prosperity of his finances: their architectural beauty is sufficient proof of a social progress which appears all the more striking if we reflect on the primitive condition of Anglo-Saxon architecture at this period. While in England literary culture had vanished from the Church amidst the turmoil of the Scandinavian invasions, the Norman clergy were distinguished by such writers as Saint Anselm and Ordericus Vitalis. Lastly, the military power of the Duke was formidable. The Norman chivalry was incontestably the first of the age. To realize its valour, we have only to recall its extraordinary exploits in Italy. It was bound to throw itself with enthusiasm into a conquest which offered it, on the other side of the Channel, prizes and adventures as brilliant as those which Robert Guiscard and his companions had found in Sicily. Moreover, William did not call upon his vassals only. Large numbers of French and Flemish knights and adventurers came to join them. The despatch of a banner by the Pope gave the expedition the semblance of a Holy War, and this tended to increase the ardour of the army.

Without their fleet, the Anglo-Saxons could not oppose its landing. It disembarked at Pevensey on September 28th, 1066, and encountered the enemy on October 14th. Harold had taken up his position on the hill of Senlac, behind a defence of palisades which compelled the Normans to fight on foot. After a violent hand-to-hand encounter their victory was complete. Harold was among the dead; those who had not fallen in the battle understood that further resistance was useless. The day had given England to William. On Christmas Day he had himself crowned in Westminster Abbey, and in order to take possession of the rest of the kingdom he had only to make his progress through it. The Anglo-Saxons, who had so long struggled against the Scandinavian invasion, were subdued in a few years by the Norman conquerors.

### 2. *The Invasion*

The invasion was really the consequence of the conquest; it could not have been otherwise. In order to retain his kingdom, to which he was a complete stranger, and of whose very language he was ignorant, William was obliged to keep a permanent garrison of Normans in the country, and the only means of doing this, under the economic circumstances of the time, was to distribute them amidst the conquered population as so many gendarmes of the Crown. This distribution of the conquerors in the midst of the conquered has a very close resemblance to the colonization of Southern Gaul, Spain, and the Valley of the Rhone by the Visigoths and the Burgundians of the 5th century. But the result was very different. While the Barbarians, brought into contact with a population infinitely more civilized than themselves, became Romanized immediately, it was only with the greatest difficulty that the Normans were absorbed into the mass of the surrounding Anglo-Saxon population. The principal cause of this difficulty was evidently their superior civilization. To this may be added the constant influx of reinforcements, which continued to come, until the end of the 12th century, not only from Normandy, but also, after the advent of the Plantagenet dynasty, from Poitou and Guyenne. The influence of the court, which, until the end of the 15th century, was entirely French in language, if not in manners, must also have been considerable. For the immigrants Anglo-Saxon was merely a barbarous patois which they did not take the trouble to learn. As on the Continent, the native idiom was replaced, as an administrative language, by Latin, and then by French. People left off writing it, and its literature fell into oblivion. But it did not disappear before the language of the conquerors as the idioms of the provinces conquered by Rome had formerly disappeared before Latin, or as in Normandy the Scandinavian tongue itself had given way to the French language. The people continued to make use of it. But nothing could be more erroneous than to explain their fidelity to the national language by their antipathy for the tongue of the conqueror. On the contrary, they borrowed from the latter as freely as they could. Insensibly, Anglo-Saxon became transformed into English; that is to say, into a language whose vocabulary is half Romanic while its grammar and its syntax have remained Germanic.

But at the period which we are considering—the close of the 11th century—the time when this idiom, in the formation of which the conquered collaborated with the conquerors, was to become the language of both, was still far distant. Long centuries were necessary to weld the conquering and the conquered people into a single body, and to make the constitution of England the most national constitution in the world. In the beginning, under William the Conqueror and his more immediate successors, the political system which was installed in England was a system of foreign occupation.

Never was the conquest of the country accompanied by a more complete upheaval of its political institutions, and of the whole organization of the State.[1] Since he held his kingdom only by the sword, since he ruled his new subjects only by force, how could William dream of preserving a system of government which allowed the assembly of the people to reign in conjunction with the king? The indispensable condition of success was to subject everything to the royal power, to make it so strong that nothing could shake it. The constitution had to be, and was in fact, essentially monarchical. It was reserved for a great vassal of the King of France to create the most vigorous monarchy in Europe.

And the first thing to be noted is, that it was precisely because he conceived his monarchy as a feudal prince that he was able to make it so powerful. All the Continental kings were elected by their great vassals, but the great vassals themselves were hereditary. William was the hereditary Duke of Normandy, and he remained a hereditary prince as King of England, so that while the other kings were given their crowns, and could not dispose of them, he was from the first the true possessor of his own crown. At the same time, by virtue of the Conquest, he was the proprietor of his kingdom. The entire territory of England was his property; he exercised over it a right analogous to that which the seigneur of a

[1] Of course, I am speaking only of the conquest of one Christian State by another Christian State. Obviously the Musulman invasion gave rise to far more profound upheavals.

great domain exercises over his estate; in their relation to him, all the private occupiers of land were merely his tenants, so that one of his first cares was to obtain an exact account of these occupiers. It is to him that we owe the Domesday Book, which was compiled between 1080 and 1086, and which may be justly likened to a polyptych, but to a polyptych containing the territorial statistics of the whole State.[1] His enormous territorial wealth enabled him to create a feudal organization, imported from the Continent, but infinitely more systematic, and above all, devoid of alien elements. The feudal system in itself, as we have already seen, was by no means incompatible with the sovereignty of the State. That it rapidly became incompatible with the sovereignty of the State was due to the fact that the great vassals, having usurped the rights of the Crown, attached them to their fiefs, so that they obtained the investiture of these rights simultaneously with that of their land. William took good care to avoid the introduction into England of this confusion of the political and feudal elements. The fiefs which he distributed to his Norman knights gave them no financial or judicial authority. In conformity with the very principle of feudality, they were simply military tenures conferred by the sovereign. The great vassals, who themselves had large numbers of subordinate vassals, constituted the army of the Crown, but to none of them did the Crown surrender the least of its prerogatives. The rights of the monarch were not frittered away into the hands of the great nobles. William, as Duke of Normandy, knew what the establishment of territorial princes all around him must cost a monarch. He took good care to ensure that no one should become, in his kingdom, what he himself was in the kingdom of France, and neither under him, nor at any other time, was the English feudality more than what may be called a purely feudal feudality. It had lands, but no principalities; it had tenants, but no subjects.

Thus, by a unique exception, the power of the King of England was an intact monarchical power; it was not necessary for him, as

[1] In the state in which it has come down to us, the Domesday Book does not contain a complete return of all the occupiers of land in the kingdom. A certain number of counties are missing.

it was for the King of France, to wage a long and difficult war against his vassals in order to reconquer his prerogatives. From the very beginning the State was entirely his property, which explains the different course of political evolution to the north and to the south of the Channel. In France, the king, who was originally very weak, and who had to deal only with individual princes, gradually built up his power from the ruins of theirs, making his own all that he took from them, and adding to his own strength as he restored the unity of the kingdom, so that in proportion as this unity was accomplished the king's government approached the condition of pure monarchy. In England, on the contrary, where from the very first the political unity of the country was as complete as the royal authority was firmly founded, the nation confronted the king as a single body, and when at last it felt the monarchical power pressing upon it too heavily it would find that it was able, by uniting its forces, to insist upon its right to participate in the government, and to wrest guarantees from him.

### 3. *The Great Charter*

Neither under William the Conqueror († 1087) nor under his two successors of the House of Normandy, William II († 1100) and Henry I († 1135), had the nation any grievance to complain of. Faithful to the feudal tradition, the kings took counsel with their great vassals, and were careful to avoid any conflict with them. The first difficulties arose on the death of Henry I, for he left no children. Stephen of Blois, the son of a daughter of the Conqueror, claimed the crown and seized it. His reign was merely the turbulent transition to a new epoch. This opened with the advent, in 1154, of the first Plantagenet, Henry II (1154–1189).

The first kings of England had had no Continental possessions beyond their Duchy of Normandy. Henry Plantagenet added to this the Duchy of Anjou, which he received from his ancestors, and the County of Guyenne, of which he had become possessed, by a stroke of "realistic" policy, through his marriage with the heiress, Eleanor of Aquitaine: whom the King of France, Louis VII, a less complaisant and less practical husband, had just repudiated.

Thus all the coasts of France, with the exception of wild Brittany, belonged to the King of England. The territories which he possessed on the Continent were more extensive than his island kingdom. But his power enabled him to undertake, on the frontier of that kingdom, conquests which the geographical situation made inevitable, sooner or later. In 1171 he took possession of a portion of Ireland. And in 1174 he forced the King of Scotland to swear fealty to him. From his reign the first beginnings of English expansion may be dated. But to his reign also must be referred the origin of that conflict with France which, from then until the beginning of the 19th century, recurred, under many forms and with varying amplitude, throughout the history of Europe. As a matter of fact, even under the Norman dynasty a more or less overt hostility had always characterized the relations between the King of France and his Norman vassal, become a king in his turn. But Philip I and Louis VI, conscious of their weakness, were too prudent to risk open warfare against their neighbour. They confined themselves to wrangling with them, and giving proof, on every possible occasion, of their insuperable malevolence. Louis VII was able to act more vigorously. The Continental domain of Henry II represented too serious a menace: it was inevitable that henceforth the French monarchy should make use of all its resources in its effort to contain an adversary who seemed destined to crush it. The war which presently broke out was the first of the political wars of Europe. Hitherto the kings had fought only to make conquests. Here the origin of the conflict was the necessity of maintaining the rights and the sovereignty of the State against the encroachments of the foreigner. The contest seemed unequal. Neither in power, intelligence or energy was Louis VII comparable to his adversary. Fortunately for him, Henry II's government provided Louis with unexpected auxiliaries in England itself.

With the first Plantagenet the monarchical power, already so strong, tended plainly to absolutism. The feudal forms with which the Norman kings had impregnated their government were disappearing. An excellent administrator, an excellent financier, the new prince made his kingdom a model of organization. But the condition of his reforms, and their result, was the omnipotence of the Crown. He irritated the nobles by subjecting them to a tax which was to provide payment for bands of Brabançon mercenaries. He irritated the Church by forcing upon it the Constitutions of Clarendon, which subordinated the ecclesiastical jurisdiction to the control of royal agents. The Archbishop of Canterbury, Thomas à Becket, who had sought refuge in France, where Louis VII had taken him under his protection, had fomented a spirit of discontent which was all the more formidable in that he justified it by religious motives. And presently the very sons of the King, supported by a party of knights and barons, rebelled against their father, and, reinforced by French auxiliaries, waged war against him in Guyenne and Normandy. Henry was able to hold his own against the rebels and abandoned none of his claims. In order to suppress the discontent which these claims had excited, it was necessary that his successors should be worthy of him. Richard Cœur-de-Lion (1189–1199), by his rash and quarrelsome incapacity, and John Lackland (1200–1216), by his baseness and cowardice, ruined their father's work all the more rapidly in that they had to fight, in Philip Augustus, the first politician of his age and the first great king that France had known. The conflict of the two Western States became more involved, and as it grew more embittered the area of hostilities was extended. Each of the parties sought allies in the outer world. The Kings of England allied themselves with the Guelphs of Germany, while the Kings of France supported the Hohenstaufens. The victory of Bouvines, the first of the great European battles, was as terrible a blow to Otto IV as it was to John Lackland. At the same time, it decided the issue of the political conflict which, since the death of Henry II, had been pending in England.

The feudal opposition which had been excited by the absolutist tendencies of Henry II, and which had been assuaged for a time during the purely military reign of Richard I, broke out more vigorously than ever under John Lackland. In order to carry on the war against Philip Augustus the King had imposed fresh taxes, and had contracted crushing debts. These might have been overlooked had he won overwhelming victories. The confiscation and then the occupation of Normandy and Poitou by France, and the crowning humiliation of Bouvines, finally unchained the rebellion. The barons led the revolt, but the clergy and the burgesses supported the barons' cause, which was one with their own. Equally oppressed by the king's despotism, the three privileged classes, from one end of the country to the other, acted in common accord. The stronger and the more centralized the English monarchy, the more general and the more unanimous was the resistance which it excited. The royal government had made a nation of this people, which spoke two different languages; but to-day this nation, with a common impulse, had turned against the king, and the unity which the government had given it left him isolated as he confronted it. The struggle was brief. Defeated, John capitulated, and submitted to the terms of the Great Charter (1215).

Magna Carta might be called the first Declaration of Rights of the English nation; for it was as truly national as the rebellion from which it emerged. The barons who imposed it upon the king did not forget their allies; they made stipulations not only for themselves, but also for the clergy and the bourgeoisie. At first sight, nothing would appear more incoherent than this charter, which proclaims, without order, entirely at random, the confirmation of feudal usages, clerical franchises, and urban liberties. And it is precisely in this that its strength and its novelty reside. For by wresting pell-mell from the king so many different rights, and by confounding, in a single text, the claims of all the classes, it established between them a solidarity which would endure, and which, of itself, rendered possible the development of the English Constitution. The nobility, the clergy, and the bourgeoisie were not, as on the Continent, separate bodies, acting each on its own account, and pursuing only its own advantage. The common danger, and the common oppression, had here allied and united a solid complex of interests, which were doubtless, at many points, mutually opposed, but which were forced, by the strength of their adversary, to effect a reconciliation and make common cause. Elsewhere the kings had been confronted by different "Estates," deliberating with each separately, and reaching some accommo-

I

dation. In England, the Crown had to deal directly with the nation, had to treat with the whole country.

A remarkable feature of this episode was that the barons of 1215 did not attempt to dismember the royal power. The monarchical State founded by the Conquest remained intact. The victors did not dream of dismembering it, or of depriving it of the rights of sovereignty in order to exercise them in its place. What they wanted, and what they obtained, was not so much a limitation of these rights as the guarantee that they could collaborate in their exercise when it should be necessary, for the welfare of the kingdom, to levy on the wealth of the king's subjects. The principle that taxes should be voted by the nation constituted the essential basis of the Great Charter, and for this reason it was the basis of the first free government that Europe had known. However, this principle was not definitely recognized until the reign of Edward I after the Battle of Falkirk (against Scotland) in 1298.

John understood very well all that the Charter imposed upon him, and he had hardly sworn to observe it when he broke his oath and obtained absolution from Innocent III. The barons took up arms again, and Philip Augustus hastened to send his son Louis to fight beside them. The struggle continued until the death of the king in 1216. The son, Henry III, on ascending the throne, ratified the Charter for the sake of peace. From that time onward it was part of the public law of England.

## CHAPTER II

# FRANCE

### 1. *The King and the Great Vassals*

From Hugh Capet to Philip I, the French monarchy was contented to exist. It was so modest that it was hardly perceptible in the midst of the great vassals. The names of this epoch whose memory posterity has preserved are not those of the kings; they are the names of feudal princes, like the Count of Flanders, Robert the Frisian; the Duke of Normandy, William the Conqueror; or of the heroes of the first Crusade—Godfrey of Bouillon, Robert of Flanders, Robert of Normandy, Raymond of Toulouse. In the midst of the epic of the Crusade, when the princes were covering themselves with glory, the king, who had remained at home, made a very poor show. The *chansons de geste*, which were then becoming the vogue, had barons for their heroes, and often depicted the monarchy as playing a very secondary part.

Towards the end of the 11th century three-fourths of the kingdom were occupied by a few great fiefs which were really principalities, their dependence on their sovereign being merely nominal. In the north, between the Scheldt and the sea, was the county of Flanders; below this, running along the coast as far as Brittany, was the Duchy of Normandy; still further south, on the other side of Brittany, was the County of Anjou, and beyond it, stretching to the Pyrenees, the Duchy of Guyenne (Aquitaine). The County of Toulouse occupied the plain of Languedoc; the Duchy of Burgundy lay in the basin of the Saône, and marched with the County of Champagne, which was watered by the Marne and the upper Seine. In the midst of these territories, and hemmed in by them, was the royal domain, the Île de France, the region surrounding

Paris, which did not at any point touch the sea-coast or reach the external frontiers of the kingdom. Though equal in area to most of the principalities of the great vassals, it was inferior to many of them in point of wealth. The cities of the Midi, and the valley of the Rhone, which were roused to activity by the Mediterranean trade, and the cities of Flanders, which constituted the terminus of the great route that joined the North to Italy, and along which were strung the fairs of Champagne, enjoyed incontestable advantages over the cities of the king's domain. Laon, Orleans and Senlis were engaged only in local trade, and even in Paris the most important merchants were merely wholesale shippers, who obtained their cargoes in the Norman port of Rouen. Thus, neither its geographical position nor its economic resources gave the Île de France a privileged situation. On the other hand, its position was admirably calculated to assist the monarchical policy. Thanks to its central position it was in touch with the different regions of the country, both with the semi-Germanic Flanders in the North and with Languedoc in the South. Interposed between contrasting nationalities and feudal principalities, it enabled the king to keep in touch with the whole of France, and to embark, at the fitting moment, upon his secular task of unification and centralization.

He began this task at the beginning of the 12th century, and it is characteristc that at about the same time the predominance of the dialect of ithe Île de France over the provincial idioms became increasingly perceptible, so that the French language developed harmoniously and contemporaneously with the progress of the royal power, and, by a piece of good fortune unique in history, the formation of the State in France went hand in hand with the formation of the nation. Who knows but that we should look to this fortunate phenomenon for the fundamental explanation of those qualities of lucidity, simplicity and logic which are generally accepted as qualities of the French genius?

Feeble as the monarchy had become, surrounded by its great vassals, and vegetating in their shadow, it none the less harboured within it the principle of its future power. For while in point of fact the feudality had paralysed the royal power, in point of law it had left it intact. The princes who nominated the king, and who, each in his principality, had usurped his authority, had not replaced the old Carolingian monarchical conception by any other. The idea never occurred to them that the king held his power from them, and that his competence was limited by their will. Of the election of the king, as of the election of the Pope and the bishops, it might be said that it merely selected a particular person; it could not confer upon him an authority which it was not within human power to confer, since it came from God. As to this, all the world was agreed. The king was the servant, the minister of God, and the ceremony of consecration, piously retained by the Capets, both attested and confirmed its semi-sacerdotal character. He derived from this ceremony a moral ascendancy which set him beyond all rivalry, which made him a unique personage, whose like was not to be found. Nothing could be more erroneous than to liken the king in the midst of his vassals to a sort of president, *primus inter pares*. Between them and himself there was no common measure. He was above them, out of reach.

It must be admitted that this special situation did not endow him with any clearly defined authority. It inspired in the king the obligation to reign in accordance with Christian morality, although it conferred upon him no formal title, save that of the Defender of the Church. But even this meant a great deal, for the Church helped to maintain his ascendancy throughout the kingdom. In the heart of the great fiefs, even the most distant of them, the monasteries applied to the king for the ratification of their possessions, and it was to him that the bishops appealed in their disputes with their vassals or their baronial neighbours. It mattered little that he was unable to help them; these priests and monks, by invoking him, prevented the world from forgetting him, and reserved a future for him.

Safeguarded by the Carolingian tradition, the king's pre-eminence over the great vassals was preserved. However independent they were in reality, they none the less held their fiefs from the Crown, and they had to swear an oath of fidelity to the Crown, and this involved very definite obligations: military service and counsel.

They were "the king's men," and although they hardly thought of him save when they wanted to meddle in his affairs, and give him, at his court, advice which, often enough, he would have preferred not to receive, they none the less recognized that he exercised over them a right of overlordship, which was one day to become a right of sovereignty.

In order to exploit the advantages of his position, and to proceed from theory to practice, the king must have power, and he secretly applied himself to acquiring it. The first condition of a firmly established monarchy is its hereditary character. It was out of the question that the Capets should impose this condition upon their electors, who were more powerful than they. They contented themselves with appointing their successors during their own lifetime. By good fortune, every one of them had a son, so that from the time of Hugh Capet to that of Philip Augustus the kingdom was spared the dangers of an interregnum. For some two hundred years the kings passed the crown from hand to hand, and by virtue of prolonged possession the State at last became their property. Even by the 12th century the election by the great vassals had become little more than a ceremony. Philip Augustus felt that he was strong enough to do without it. His son Louis VIII succeeded him, and was universally acknowledged without any intervention on the part of the princes. By its persistent patience, the dynasty had achieved the end which it had so obstinately pursued. The French monarchy had become hereditary, without commotion, without a *coup d'état*; hereditary by simple prescription.

At the same time, it had carefully and wisely administered its domain. This domain was neither very wealthy nor very extensive, but thanks to the specific policy of the king it enjoyed, from the reign of Hugh Capet to that of Louis VII, a period of unbroken tranquillity. Paris, where the dynasty led a sedentary existence, which contrasted so strongly with the wandering life of the Emperors, always on the move through Germany and Italy, or that of the kings of England, continually leaving their island for Normandy, was gradually becoming the administrative centre of the Île de France, and preparing for its future rôle as the capital of the kingdom. The Archbishop of Sens came to reside in the city. The provosts of all the king's domains rendered their accounts to Paris. The permanent presence of the court maintained a political and administrative activity whose like was not to be found in Europe. As Rome was the city of the Pope, so Paris was the city of the king, and for that reason its life was more varied and its character less bourgeois than that of other cities. Even in the 12th century the attractive power of the city conferred an ever-increasing importance on the schools attached to its monasteries. Under Philip Augustus the corporation of their masters and scholars gave birth to the first "university" in Europe. It is not surprising that art should have vigorously developed in so active an environment. Abbé Suger de St. Denis, the minister of Louis VII, attracted to his abbey the artisans of the adjacent regions, and Notre-Dame de Paris, begun in 1163, is the first in date of the great Gothic cathedrals. The prestige of Paris contributed greatly to the unity of the kingdom, and from the 12th century onwards, as the one increased, so did the other. The social influence of the capital and the political influence of the monarchy contributed in equal measure to the creation of the nation.

## 2. *The Progress of the Monarchy*

Since the accession of Hugh Capet the monarchy had had no foreign policy. The only neighbour with whom France might have entered into conflict was the Empire, her neighbour along the whole extent of her eastern frontier: on the Scheldt and the Meuse in Lotharingia, and on the Rhone in the kingdom of Burgundy. But on succeeding to the last Carolingians, the new dynasty had abandoned their claims to Lotharingia; and the Emperors having nothing to fear from its weakness and prudence, and being moreover engrossed in their Italian expedition, had given it no cause for uneasiness. The situation was suddenly altered when in 1066 the Duke of Normandy became King of England. A formidable power had now arisen on the western frontier, which, being washed by the sea, had seemed, since the last of the Scandinavian invasions, to be protected from all danger by Nature herself. It was impossible to maintain the same relations of indifference and security with this new power as with the Empire. For being a vassal of the king of France in respect of his Norman duchy, the new king was bound to his sovereign, and his feudal subordination was in too extreme contrast with the power which he wielded on the further side of the Channel to be other than a permanent cause of misunderstanding, suspicion, and hostility. Henceforth the Capets could not persist in the attitude of abstention to which they had hitherto restricted themselves. Anxiety, and the dignity of the Crown, compelled them to confront the external danger, and since they would henceforth find it necessary to pursue a foreign policy, this would give them the opportunity of at last pursuing a monarchical policy in France itself.

This policy was inaugurated by Louis VI (1108-1137), and it naturally began in a very modest fashion. Too weak to act alone, the king sought as an ally the Count of Flanders, an old enemy of Normandy. In connection with his English policy, he conceived the project, in 1127, of profiting by the assassination of Count Charles the Good to invest with the crown of Flanders a Norman prince who was a mortal enemy of the King of England. The project was abortive, but is none the less worth noting: and it was actually the first attempt on the part of the Crown to draw a great fief into the sphere of its influence. The external danger which the king had to face compelled him to exercise his sovereignty over his great vassals in order to absorb their forces into his own.

Louis VII (1137–1180) continued the struggle which his father had begun. His adversary, Henry Plantagenet, was far more formidable than the Norman king. We have seen already how it happened that Louis was able to hold his own against him. The long-drawn war which he fought upon the frontiers of Anjou was merely a succession of small and obscure actions, and meanwhile the great vassals maintained an indifferent neutrality. There was nothing remarkable about Louis, whether as a soldier or as a politician. The manner in which the royal prestige was increased under such a prince is therefore all the more characteristic. It was in his reign that the royal historiographer made his first appearance, and the first minister of the Crown to be remembered in French history: the Abbé of St. Denis, Suger. He was also the last minister whom the monarchy borrowed from the Church. After him, the State felt itself so strong, was so clearly conscious of its task, and was confronted with problems so difficult and so numerous, that it was obliged to require, in its counsellors, a kind of training in direct correspondence with their mission. Its progress compelled it to break with the Carolingian tradition, and it could no longer content itself with collaborators drawn from the clergy. It needed men of affairs, jurists, men of action, whom it would recruit from among the laymen trained in its service, who were drawn from the ranks of those educated bourgeois whose numbers were constantly increasing. Suger appeared at a turning-point of the political evolution of the nation. Before his time the State had been so simple, or rather, so primitive, that a prelate could be entrusted with its direction without previous apprenticeship; after his time its increasing complexity called for specialists, and its personnel would no longer belong to the Church, or would belong to it only in name.[1]

From the reign of Louis VII to that of Philip Augustus the royal power made such progress as cannot be explained merely by the genius of the king. It was due very largely to the economic and social transformations occasioned by the development of the bourgeoisies. During the second half of the 12th century all the cities of Northern France had constituted themselves as sworn communes. Almost everywhere, in the episcopal cities—at Arras, Noyon, Senlis, Laon, Reims, etc.—they had to struggle against the resistance or the ill-will of their bishops, imploring the king to support them, a request which he hastened to grant. In this way an understanding was established between the Crown and the bourgeoisies which assured the royal policy of the co-operation of the youngest, most active, and wealthiest class of society.

[1] This reservation is indispensable, since from Suger to Talleyrand and Fouché the Church constantly furnished the State with ministers and councillors. But these were no longer ecclesiastics in the true and full sense of the word; they were politicians who had retained little of the clerical profession beyond the robe and the benefices.

We may distinguish under Louis VII the first signs of this alliance, the full importance of which was recognized by the clairvoyance of Philip Augustus, who systematically strengthened and extended it. The rapid increase of monetary circulation, a consequence of urban trade, was none the less profitable to the Crown. By permitting the transformation of such prestations and feudal dues as had hitherto been paid in kind into dues payable in money, and by improving the minting of money, and consequently increasing the profits of the mints, it enabled the Crown to procure the indispensable instrument of all political power: financial resources. The royal treasury, hitherto merged in the total private fortune of the king, became a special branch of the administration. The oldest treasury accounts that we possess date from the reign of Philip Augustus. Not only was the king henceforth able to hire bands of mercenaries in time of war, but he was able, above all, to attach to his service men who were true functionaries: that is to say, paid agents who could at need be dismissed. Such were the bailiffs, first mentioned in the year 1173, and presently to be found throughout the royal domain. Capable henceforth of paying his servitors, the prince was no longer obliged to entrust their offices to hereditary incumbents whom he could not dismiss if he chose. The replacement of the old agricultural economy by a monetary economy removed the obstacle which, since the Frankish epoch, had invincibly hindered the development of the State.

The reforms introduced under Philip Augustus in the organization of the royal court adapted it to the necessities of the central government. The assembly of lay magnates and ecclesiastics which, ever since the Carolingian epoch, had assembled at definite intervals round the king, constituting at once a council and a court of justice, without precise attributions, without specified competence—and which more often than not did little more than hamper the activities of the Crown in the interests of the great vassals—was divided into two permanent bodies: the Consel du Roi on the one hand, for political affairs, and the Parlement on the other hand, for judicial business. Both bodies were still composed, for the greater part, of members of the *haute noblesse* and the superior clergy. But already the king was introducing his own men into these bodies, and his influence was steadily increasing, while that of the feudal element was waning. The great officers of the Crown, all chosen from the *grande noblesse* who had hitherto exercised a real tutelage over the king, disappeared, or were reduced to purely honorific functions. The administration of the chancellery broke with the antiquated usages and superfluous phraseology of the Carolingian age, and adopted more practical methods. A record office was established in the Louvre, and in the measures adopted for submitting the annual accounts of the bailiffs we find something like an embryo form of the future *Chambre des comptes.*

Philip Augustus may therefore be regarded as the veritable creator of monarchical power, not only in France, but on the Continent.[1] The surname of Augustus was bestowed upon him by Rigord: *Quia rem publicam augmentabat.*[2]

Before his time the most powerful kings, the Emperors, and even Charlemagne himself, were able to govern only by virtue of the prestige and power which they derived from their victories, or from the support of the Church. Their power depended essentially on themselves, and was merged, so to speak, in their person. Without finances and without functionaries, their activities depended upon the extent to which they were supported by the Church and obeyed by the aristocracy, the latter becoming more and more independent and the former more and more hostile. Henceforth, on the contrary, the king had at his disposal a permanent administration whose activities he himself inspired, and which was independent both of the Church and of the feudality. The rights which tradition recognized as his could now become a reality, and in so becoming real they constituted the State. The young monarchy retained the fundamental principle of the old Carolingian monarchy: the religious character of the royal power. Since the end of the 9th century it had been as though embalmed, preserved intact despite its feebleness, and despite all the feudal usurpations. We have just seen how it acquired a new vigour, and how, as the

[1] Except in Sicily, where the foundations of the State were Byzantine.

[2] Cf. the title of the Emperor: *Mehrer des Reiches.*

neighbour of the English State, it had constituted in France, under very different and much more difficult conditions, a rival State.

The Counts of Flanders, who under Louis VI had fought beside the monarchy against England, under Philip Augustus sided with England against the monarchy. It was very natural that being threatened by the increasing power of their suzerain they should seek support in the great island whose next-door neighbours they were, and on which the industrial cities of their country were dependent for their wool. The cities, which in France supported the Crown, took the side of their prince in Flanders; not, as a superficial view of the case might lead one to suppose, by reason of a pretended sense of racial solidarity, but simply on account of their economic interests. No difference of attitude is perceptible, whether they were Walloon-speaking cities like Lille and Douai, or cities of Germanic language like Bruges and Gand. The policy of the Flemish princes thus assumed, from the beginning of the 13th century, an amplitude which no longer permits us to regard it as a mere policy of feudal resistance. On the one hand, it inaugurated an alliance with England, which, being based on mutual interest, was perpetuated through the centuries, finally becoming one of the most important factors of the future independence of the Low Countries (Holland and Belgium); on the other hand, by relying on the support of the bourgeoisies it assumed the appearance of a national policy, which identified the cause of the bourgeoisies with that of the dynasties,

The protracted war between Philip Augustus and Philip of Alsace (1180–1185) had involved as yet only the king and the Count of Flanders, and was concluded, after alternate victories and defeats, by a treaty to the advantage of the former. But no later than 1196 Baldwin IX formed an alliance with Richard Cœur de Lion, and four years later was able to obtain from the king the restitution of the northern region of Artois, ceded by his predecessor. The Crusade, which periodically interrupted the course of European policy, and in which Philip Augustus, Richard, and Philip of Alsace had taken part together some years earlier, drew Count Baldwin to the East in 1202. In the following year he received in Saint Sophia the crown of the ephemeral Latin Empire of Constantinople, and died mysteriously shortly afterwards (1205), during an expedition against the Bulgars. He left two young daughters, whom their uncle Philip of Namur delivered, at the king's request, to Philip Augustus. The king gave the elder, Jeanne, in marriage to a husband of his own selection, Ferrand of Portugal, having taken the precaution of making him swear a special oath of fidelity, which was ratified by the cities and the barons of Flanders. He counted on being able to take any liberties with this new vassal, who owed him his good fortune. He sent his troops to occupy Aire and Saint Omer, and by the bestowal of fiefs and pensions he secured the connivance of most of the members of the Flemish nobility. Driven to extremities, it was not long before Ferrand gave ear to the advances of the King of England, John Lackland. In 1213 he concluded a treaty of alliance with him.

The conflict in which Flanders was once more involved was this time a European conflict. The policy of Philip Augustus, developed by success and the genius of the king, now embraced the whole Occident, and the war became a general war, which was to decide the fate of the French monarchy.

The war between France and England, interrupted during the last years of Henry II's reign, was resumed as soon as Richard had returned from the captivity in which the Duke of Austria had held him, into whose hands he had fallen on his return from the Third Crusade (1194). It had no decisive result. But no sooner was Richard dead, and his brother John Lackland on the throne, than Philip resolved upon a decisive action. Profiting by the discontent which the new king had provoked, he summoned John to appear before him in his quality of Duke of Normandy, in order to clear himself of the charge of murdering Arthur of Brittany.[1] Since John did not deign to reply, the King of France, acting in the full rigour of his rights as suzerain, confiscated all the fiefs held in France by the Crown of England, and occupied them all, with the exception of Guyenne, thus at a single stroke doubling

[1] Son of Geoffrey, the fourth son of Henry II, who was acknowledged by Brittany in place of John.

the extent of the Crown lands and securing the coast—excepting Brittany—from Bordeaux to Boulogne. The many offences of his rival, already at war with the English barons, which had drawn upon him, in 1209, the excommunication of the Pope, gave gratuitous support to this audacious policy. Philip, having got Innocent III to entrust him with the execution of the sentence pronounced upon John, made active preparations for an expedition against England. These preparations were already completed when John, humiliating himself before the Pope, and acknowledging that his kingdom was a fief of the Holy See, obtained his reconciliation with the Church. Philip employed his army and his fleet against Flanders, advancing as far as Damme, where the English surprised his ships and burned them; he then returned to France, while Ferrand of Portugal resumed possession of his territories.

Meanwhile, the conflict of the Western States had spread to Germany. Of the two parties at war there, Guelfs and Ghibellines, the first had been allied with England since the marriage of Henry the Lion with Matilda, daughter of Henry II. The natural rapprochement followed between the Ghibellines and France. Philip Augustus exploited the situation with brilliant success. The Emperor Otto of Brunswick, the head of the Guelfs, who had been completely won over by John Lackland, was excommunicated in 1210 by Innocent III. The King of France seized this opportunity to exhort young Frederick of Hohenstaufen, then confined in Sicily under the tutelage of the Pope, to take the bold step of entering Germany and placing himself at the head of the partisans of his house. The adventure had a romantic look; in reality nothing could have been more prosaic. The king's treasury had come to the help of his policy, and he had bought the German princes who were necessary to its success. On November 9th, 1212, they elected Frederick King of the Romans.[1] Thus the conflict between France and England divided the whole of Europe into two camps, and its issue was to decide the fate of the West. The enemies of Philip Augustus resolved, in 1214, upon a decisive effort. While John was to attack him through Guyenne, Otto of Brunswick marched upon Paris

[1] On this subject see the following chapter.

through the Low Countries, rallying, as he did so, the troops of Ferrand of Portugal. The army with which Philip went to meet him illustrated, by its composition, the progress of the royal power. Twenty years earlier it would have consisted entirely of the feudal militia. But now, beside the chivalry of the Crown vassals, there were bands of mercenaries and companies of burghers despatched by the cities. The clash took place at Bouvines, near Tournai, on July 27th, and the result was a brilliant triumph for Philip Augustus. This was the first of the great European battles, and if we except Waterloo, where six hundred years later the same adversaries were to confront one another, no other battle had such vast and immediate consequences. In Germany, Otto of Brunswick was replaced by Frederick II. In England John Lackland, humiliated, saw the barons rise against him and enforce his acceptance of the Great Charter. In France the territorial conquests were assured (Treaty of Chinon); the feudality was vanquished in the person of Ferrand of Portugal; and the royal power, which had just proved its strength by defeating the external enemy, was invested in the eyes of the people with a national prestige that endowed it with twofold vigour.

## CHAPTER III

# THE EMPIRE

### 1. *Frederick Barbarossa*

The Concordat of Worms did not end the struggle between the Empire and the Papacy. Under Gregory VII the problem of the relation of the two universal powers had presented itself in all its amplitude, but afterwards, owing to the exhaustion of the two parties, it was restricted to the dispute relating to investitures, and even this had ended in a compromise. By this settlement the Emperor lost as much as the Pope had gained, but neither could be content with a state of affairs that provided no solution of the conflict of principles which had evoked the quarrel.

It was necessary to determine whether the Carolingian conception was to continue in force: that is to say, whether the Church, regarded as the whole body of the faithful, and also as a political society, should continue to have at its head two principals, mutually independent, the first governing men's souls and the second their bodies: or whether, on the contrary, it was the duty of the Pope to dispose of the Imperial crown—whether, in the language of the time, both the spiritual and the temporal sword were his, the Emperor receiving the latter from him as a vassal receives a fief from his sovereign. Only a new war could furnish the reply to this question, for no compromise was possible between the contradictory affirmations of the two adversaries.

This war, which broke out under Frederick Barbarossa, was lost in advance by the Empire. While European society acknowledged the universal authority of the Pope in the Church, it could not concede an authority of equal amplitude to the Emperor. This would have been, in effect, to subordinate all the Western States to the Emperor in the temporal order, reducing them to the status of clients. Since the reign of Otto I the Imperialist theory no longer corresponded with the reality, for the Empire no longer comprised, as in the days of Charlemagne, all the Christians of the Western world. No formal protest had hitherto been made against it, because no prince was powerful enough to break with the German sovereigns. But what likelihood was there that in the middle of the 12th century the young and vigorous monarchies of France and England should amiably accept the Imperial tutelage? Just as the rising feudality had worked for Gregory VII against Henry IV, so the national States in process of formation were to work for Adrian IV and Alexander III against Frederick Barbarossa. It was the misfortune of the Imperial policy that whenever it attempted to impose itself upon the Papacy it merely provoked the opposition of the most active powers in Europe, and oriented them toward Rome.

To this must be added the fact that the Emperor's power within the Empire itself was constantly diminishing. After the Concordat of Worms he no longer appointed the bishops, and the right which he retained of investing them with their principalities was more often than not illusory. In actual fact, the episcopal elections were most frequently determined by the secular princes, who forced the Chapters to accept relatives or allies of their houses. Thus, the Imperial Church on which the German sovereigns had lavished privileges and territories ever since the reign of Otto I was now escaping from their control, and, one might almost say, was becoming feudalized. The great vassals whose power it had hitherto balanced had no longer anything to fear from it, and the ecclesiastical principalities, being no longer at the disposal of the Emperor, were merely fresh elements of political disintegration. At the very moment when in France the king was beginning to get the upper hand over the feudality, in Germany the feudality was getting the upper hand over the Crown. Nothing could be more striking than the comparison of the influence of the princes over the royal power in the two different countries. While in the 12th century the King of France was elective only in theory, and from the reign of Philip

Augustus became the hereditary sovereign, the German princes continued to insist on their right to dispose of the throne. On the death of Henry V they refused the crown to his nearest relative, Duke Frederick of Swabia, and gave it to Lothair of Saxony (1125); then, on the death of Lothair, they reverted to the house of Swabia, and appointed Conrad III (1137). Of course, what determined their selection was the promises and concessions of the candidates, so that the royal power grew weaker in the very act of transmission.

Under such circumstances, how could the Emperor dream of resuming the quarrel with Rome? Instead of treating the Pope as an equal, Lothair obtained the Imperial crown only by a damaging revision of the Concordat of Worms, and by his acquiescence in the Pope's claim to the right of refusing to crown the Emperor if he did not approve of his election. Conrad III was weaker still. His nomination was opposed by the Duke of Bavaria, who took up arms against him, thus inaugurating the quarrel of the Guelfs and the Ghibellines which was so long to trouble Germany and Italy. The struggle was continued after his death by his son Henry the Lion, who in 1142 had to be given the Duchy of Saxony in the place of that of Bavaria, which had become a fief of the house of Babenberg. Poor Conrad had no time to cross the Alps for his coronation; he hoped to increase his prestige by taking part in the Second Crusade, only to suffer the mortification of defeat. He died in 1152, and his nephew Frederick, after previous arrangement with the enemy of his house, Henry the Lion, obtained the suffrage of the princes.

With Frederick Barbarossa a reign began whose brilliance appeared all the greater because of the obscurity of the reigns which had preceded it. The young king, eager and ambitious, had resolved to restore the prestige of the Imperial dignity in the eyes of the world, and with fiery energy he devoted himself to attaining this inaccessible goal, the final result being merely a notorious defeat and the wasting of the remaining forces and the last resources of the German monarchy. At first sight, Frederick's policy seems a continuation of the Carolingian tradition, and the canonization of Charlemagne in 1165 by a German synod appears to confirm this filiation. In reality, there was nothing in common between the Carolingians and the Hohenstaufens but their tendency to universality. As Barbarossa conceived it, the Empire was no longer the Christian Empire which was born in St. Peter's, in the year 800, so intimately allied with the government of the Church, and so closely united to the Papacy, that they were indissoluble. As he conceived it, the Empire was in the full sense of the word the Roman Empire—but the Roman Empire of Augustus, as it was before the invasions. It was from this that he derived his right to govern the world, and since its origin dated back before the birth of Christ, how could it have anything in common with the Papacy? More ancient than the Papacy, it was as independent of the Pope as was the Emperor of Byzantium. The Empire was not contained in the Church, but the Church in the Empire, and notwithstanding his sacred character, the Pope, in the last resort, was merely a subject of the Emperor. The religious mysticism at the root of the Carolingian conception was here replaced by a sort of political mysticism, boldly harking back through the centuries to that eternal Rome who was mistress of the world, and deriving the Imperial claims from her, as the unique source of all temporal power. As early as the 11th century Otto III had flattered himself with the hope of restoring to its pristine magnificence that golden Rome (*aurea Roma*) whose ancient glory still shone in men's minds as the ideal of all terrestrial splendour. But what in Otto were only vague dreams and sentimental aspirations became in Frederick a precise theory. At the beginning of the 12th century the study of Roman law had made considerable strides in Italy, particularly in Bologna, where Irnerius was teaching. For Irnerius and his pupils the Code of Justinian was a sort of Holy Scripture, the revelation of law and civil order. Hence the veneration of these jurists for the Imperial power, which they regarded as the first condition of the maintenance of temporal society. It can hardly be doubted that the doctrines of this school had influenced Barbarossa. According to them, his political conception, unlike that of the Carolingians and their successors, had a secular base; those who were entrusted with its defence were no longer the theologians, but the jurists.

For the first time, in the conflict between the Emperor and the Pope, the opposition between the temporal power and the spiritual power revealed itself.

Many bishops, no doubt, remained faithful to Frederick, and he did his utmost to obtain "good elections" in the Chapters. However, he could no longer lean on the German Church, whose situation, since the Concordat of Worms, had undergone such a profound transformation. He looked for compensation to the lay feudality. Until the reign of Henry V, the Emperors, who could then rely on the bishops, had regarded the feudal nobility with more or less suspicion. Moreover, the nobility had sided with the Pope against the Emperors; since the reign of Lothair the Saxon it had constantly increased its influence by this means, and had even succeeded in imposing its will upon the episcopal principalities.

Frederick frankly accepted this new condition of affairs. In singular contradiction to the unlimited power which he dreamed of possessing as Emperor, as King of Germany he allowed the secular princes to enjoy almost complete independence. Instead of attempting to impose his will upon them as their sovereign, he sought rather to obtain a personal following among them by intervening in their quarrels and flattering their ambitions. To them he seemed rather the leader of a party than a king, and his monarchical policy consisted, at bottom, in creating a Ghibelline faction, which the malcontents and those of contrary views opposed by forming a Guelf faction. However, he did not confine himself to influencing the princes; he endeavoured also to rally the lesser nobility, and to make of it at once a political instrument and a military force. At this period the customs of chivalry were beginning to spread from France and Lotharingia to the right bank of the Rhine. Frederick did his utmost to encourage this diffusion, and to impress the knights with his own prestige, and also to attract them to his court by brilliant feasts and tourneys. He promoted many *ministeriales* to knightly rank, and he utilized what was left of the Imperial domain in creating fiefs for these military retainers. It was under his reign that the mountains of Swabia, Franconia and Thuringia began to bristle with the "feudal castles" of which so many are still to be seen in a state of ruin.

It may thus be said that in Germany Frederick sacrificed the political rights of the monarchy to the necessity of creating a strong feudal army. However, he could not have done otherwise. The social development of the Germanic countries, which were backward as compared with the Western States, did not allow him to create the financial resources which would have enabled him to raise bands of mercenaries. The economic system of Germany, apart from the valley of the Rhine, was still that of the old domainal constitution, and the circulation of money was still extremely restricted. There was hardly any city of real importance, except Cologne, the only commercial centre comparable to those of Flanders; the ports of the Baltic were barely beginning to make themselves felt; and in the south Augsburg, Vienna, and Nuremberg were still only third-rate towns.

Moreover, in Frederick's plans Germany played quite a secondary part; he regarded her merely as an instrument which would enable him to open up the path to Italy and empire. Essentially German as regards his manners, feelings and character, in politics he was as little of a German as it was possible for him to be. His mind was entirely filled with the Imperial ideal. At the very moment when the French and English monarchies were laying the foundations of stable national States he was about to reopen a conflict which was finally to hurl his country into the anarchy of the great interregnum, and leave it for long centuries cut up into feudal subdivisions.

Of the conflict which he was about to provoke he appreciated neither the difficulties nor the extent. It was not the Pope alone whom he would have to fight. Since the end of the 11th century the Lombard plain had become covered with a dense vegetation of urban communes, through which he would have to make his way in order to reach Rome. In all the cities of the Po basin the bourgeoisie, enriched by trade and industry, had wrested the government from the bishops, and had founded municipal republics, which no longer had any regard for the rights of the Empire, and considered themselves to be independent of it. But Frederick, in his ignorance of urban civilization, felt the same disdain for these bourgeois as was felt by the German nobles, and for their republican constitutions he felt the contempt of the successor of Constantine and Justinian. He had made this very clear in 1154, when he crossed the Alps for the first time. Having convoked the princes and the cities of Upper Italy in the Plain of Roncaglia (near Piacenza), he attempted to impose upon them an oath of fealty, and to inform them of their duties toward himself. There was some resistance. Frederick saw fit to crush this by means of terror; he besieged Tortona and razed it to the ground. Then, having crowned himself at Pavia with the crown of the King of the Lombards, he marched upon Rome, where the Imperial crown awaited him.

The city was then in a state of rebellion. However, there was nothing in common between the insurrection of the Roman people, which was supported by the Church, as it had formerly been supported by the Emperors, and the revolts of the active and vigorous Lombard bourgeoisie. The traces which antiquity had left upon Rome were so profound that the inhabitants of the city could not free themselves from the memories and the splendours which surrounded them, and by which they lived. Periodically, the Roman people have lost their heads, intoxicated by the idea that they were still the masters of the world and the descendants of the sovereign people. The only municipal organization that Rome had ever had was that which conquered the world and perished of the conquest. Having become the centre of world politics, and then of the universal Church, the city could not belong to itself: it belonged too completely to Christian Europe. A mere communal council could not take the place of the Senate, yet at every one of these crises of their turbulent history the Romans really believed that they had re-established the Senate, the ancient Senate, the supreme legislator and administrator of human affairs.

Rome was at the height of one of these crises at the moment when Barbarossa approached the Tiber. The Pope had fled; Arnold of Brescia was ruling the city, and dreaming of reforming both the Church and the Empire. In him religious and political mysticism were allied. He wanted to restore the Church to evangelical purity and poverty, while the Emperor, on whom the Roman people had conferred the government of the world, would be the organizer of temporal society and would reduce the Pope to the rank of a simple priest. Thus, by a curious coincidence, antiquity had inspired both the King of Germany and the Italian revolutionary. But how could they have understood each other? The king considered that the Imperial rights were derived from the people, and looked to the people for a renovation of the world. The revolutionary regarded the Imperial power merely as dominion over the world as it was, or rather, as it appeared in the eyes of the feudal warrior. For Frederick, as for the Pope, Arnold was simply a dangerous heretic. Frederick handed him over to Adrian IV, who had him burnt at the stake.

Returning to Rome in the midst of the German knights, the Pope appeared to be under an obligation to Frederick, and Frederick might well have believed, when he received the Imperial crown in St. Peter's (June 18th, 1155), that he would henceforth be safe from the attacks of the Papacy. But Adrian had surrendered none of the claims of the Holy See. Frederick realized this, to his indignation, almost immediately upon his return to Germany. The legate Rolandi went so far as to describe the Empire, in his presence, as a "benefice" (fief) of the Holy Father. At the same time, the Lombard communes asserted their independence, and under the leadership of Milan, were openly preparing for war. This time the Emperor was resolved to strike one great blow, and annihilate his adversaries. In 1158 he was once more in Lombardy; he then and there made the most solemn proclamation of his sovereign rights (*regalia*), condemned the liberty of the cities as a frivolous and criminal rebellion, ordered the demolition of their walls, and subjected them to the jurisdiction of podestàs appointed by himself. The disdainful arrogance of his language and his attitude merely embittered the resistance. The German knights, with surprise as great as their anger, saw that mere townsfolk dared to oppose them in the open country, and were infuriated to discover that they could not carry by assault the ramparts which these vulgar citizens victoriously defended. The contrast of nationalities increased the mutual hatred of the combatants, but the real issue was the opposition of two incompatible forms of society: on the one hand, absolutism supported by a military aristocracy; on the other hand, political autonomy and municipal liberty; and those who proclaimed them were ready to die for them. At a distance of six hundred years, and in a more restricted setting, the resistance of the Lombard bourgeoisies to Frederick Barbarossa resembles the resistance of the French Revolution in 1792 to the armies of Prussia and Austria. Cremona was destroyed by fire after a seven months' siege (1160). Milan defended itself for nine months, and was at last forced to surrender (March 1162) only by famine and pestilence. It could not hope for pardon. Frederick understood nothing of the superior civilization of his enemies. In his naïve brutality he inflicted upon them the punishment which he would have inflicted upon a feudal "bourg" that had dared to hold out against him. He had the city razed to the ground, as though the destruction of a city could prevent its rebirth.

To him this victory must have seemed all the more decisive, as he believed that he had just won another victory over the Papacy. Adrian IV was dead (September 1st, 1159), and the Cardinals being unable to agree on the election of his successor, Alexander III and Victor III each assumed the tiara and excommunicated the other. This was an excellent opportunity for the Emperor to impose his will upon the Church, by deciding, as Henry III had formerly done, between the rivals. He assembled a Synod at Pavia, and the German and Italian bishops who attended it naturally voted for Victor, since Alexander was none other than the insolent Rolandi (February 1160), and the majority of the Conclave, in electing him, had been deliberately affirming its anti-Imperialist policy. But Frederick was immediately forced to realize that Europe was no more inclined than the Lombard cities to surrender to his will. The whole Catholic world ranked itself behind Alexander, and despite the prayers which the Emperor deigned to address to them, the Kings of France and England remained immovable. However, the Emperor persisted. Victor IV being dead, he procured the election of Pascal III (April 20th, 1164), thus prolonging, by his pride, a schism from which he no longer had anything to hope.

He had at least the satisfaction of escorting his Pope to Rome, while Alexander took refuge in France (1167), and of proclaiming the sovereignty of the Empire over the city. He was then obliged to recross the Alps with all possible speed, the plague having broken out in the army.

The state of Italy was more threatening than ever. The terror employed against the Lombard cities had merely fired them to more passionate resistance. They were closely allied with the Pope and had given his name to Alexandria. Milan rose from its ruins and rebuilt its walls. The whole process was beginning over again. A new campaign was opened in 1174, which at first went slowly, a war of sieges, and was suddenly terminated, on May 29th, 1176, by the battle of Legnano, when the Imperial army was cut to pieces and dispersed by the Milanese and their allies. The catastrophe was irremediable, as was the humiliation. At one stroke, Alexander III and the Lombard cities had triumphed over this Emperor, whose arrogance had been so intolerable as long as he had believed in his own strength. From brutality he suddenly passed to deference and humility. He sacrificed the new Pope, Calixtus III, whom he had caused to be elected on the death of Pascal; he acknowledged Alexander, and at Venice, where the reconciliation with the Pope took place, the Emperor dropped the trappings of Augustus, prostrating himself and kissing the Pontiff's feet. The deputies of the Lombard cities, whom the Pope had promised to reconcile with the Emperor, were present at this ceremony. A truce of six years, transformed later, at Constance (June 1183), into a definitive treaty, was concluded: for form's sake, it defined the rights of the Empire to their subsidies and their military contingents, which were never furnished.

Frederick returned to Germany only to find Henry the Lion and his Guelf partisans in open revolt. He succeeded in overcoming the revolt, but his victory did nothing to establish the monarchical power on a stronger basis. Being obliged to conciliate the princes, he found himself compelled to distribute among them what he had taken from Henry. The Duchy of Bavaria was given to Otto of Wittelsbach; the Duchy of Saxony was divided between the Archbishop of Cologne, who was given Westphalia, and Bernard of Anhalt. The fall of Henry the Lion rid the Emperor of a dangerous enemy, but it was a misfortune for Germany. Ruling the country from the Alps to the Baltic, and having conquered and colonized vast Slavish territories beyond the Elbe, Henry wielded a power which, if it had endured, could have imposed its will upon the country as a whole, amalgamating the very different regions into which it was divided. He was overthrown by the coalition of dynastic interests with those of the feudality, and the triumph of his enemies had no other result than still further to increase the feudal subdivision which in Germany was becoming more extreme from reign to reign. It had already gone so far by the end of the 12th century that Frederick realized that if he was to assure the future of his dynasty he would have to find a territorial base outside the country. Hence the marriage of his son Henry, in 1186, with Constance, the heiress to the Kingdom of Sicily. In order to survive, the House of Hohenstaufen was obliged to denationalize itself, turning from Germany to Italy.

This was the only lasting result—but obtained at what a price! —of the turbulent and sterile career of Frederick Barbarossa. Did the Third Crusade seem to offer him some hope of consolation for his misfortunes, and did his chimerical spirit see in it a good opportunity of refurbishing the Imperial majesty, by placing it at the head of a Christendom going forth to reconquer the tomb of Christ? He took the Cross in 1183. On June 10th, 1190, he met his death as the result of a trivial accident, falling from the saddle into the waters of the Cydnus.

### 2. *Before Bouvines*

To his son Henry VI, Frederick Barbarossa bequeathed an ungovernable Germany. Instead of improving the situation of the dynasty the defeat of Henry the Lion had aggravated it. Henry, having retired into England, had directed the attention and the ambition of the Plantagenets to German affairs, and had obtained their support for his partisans. Thus the new reign was greeted by a revolt of the Guelfs, who had to be appeased by concessions and promises. Even more than his father, Henry VI neglected Germany for Italy. Since the universality of the Imperial policy did not ally it to any one nation, it naturally had to make its headquarters wherever it found forces to support it. The heritage of the Kingdom of Sicily, which Henry had received in 1189 on the death of his father-in-law William the Good, anchored him to the south of the peninsula and determined his career.

Raised to the rank of kingdom for the benefit of Roger II by Pope Innocent II, in 1130, the Norman State of Sicily was incontestably the wealthiest, and, in point of economic development, the most advanced of all the Western States. Byzantine as to its continental portion, Musulman as regards the island, favoured by the enormous extent of its coast-line, and by the active navigation which it maintained with the Mohammedans of the coast of Africa, the island Greeks of the Aegean Sea, the Greeks of the Bosphorus, and the Crusader settlements in Syria, it was as remarkable for its absence of national characteristics as for the diversity of its civilization, in which the culture of Byzantium was mingled and confounded with that of Islam. Above this hybrid mixture of peoples, the Norman sovereigns had established a constitution which was feudal in its forms but absolutist in reality, and which had adopted the methods of the Byzantine administration. Despite their devotion to the Papacy, these Norman princes, in their political lucidity of thought, allowed both their Musulman and their Orthodox subjects to practise their respective religions. Their financial system was admirable. The culture of rice and cotton, which the Musulmans had introduced into Sicily, and the Oriental industries carried on in the great cities of Palermo, Messina and Syracuse, furnished the Treasury with revenues more abundant than those of any other State, and collected in the most scientific manner. Having always been accustomed to the most improved methods of administration, whether those of Byzantium or of Islam, the population allowed itself to be governed with docility; the Norman nobles constituted the only element to be feared. While they had quickly lost their pristine vigour, and were softened by the luxuries of their semi-Oriental life, they were none the less greedy and seditious.

The acquisition of such a kingdom placed Henry VI in possession of resources which, compared with the miserable revenues that Germany still furnished for the monarchy, might well seem inexhaustible. He hastened to get himself crowned by the Pope, after which he broke with the pontiff, cast off the bonds of suzerainty which tethered Sicily to the Holy See, and revived the claims of Frederick to the city of Rome and the States of St. Peter. But his plans were far from ending here. They envisaged nothing less than the reconstitution of the Roman Empire; but this time in the Mediterranean basin, formerly conquered by Rome, and now shared between Byzantium and Islam. Byzantium, especially at this particular juncture, was in a state of anarchy, what with dynastic intrigues, palace revolutions, and military revolts, and in this condition it seems to have appealed to the Emperor's ambition. Even before his time, it had excited the covetousness of the Norman princes. Had not King Roger II taken advantage of the Second Crusade to ravage Dalmatia, Epirus, and Greece, and to seize the islands of Zante and Corfu? As enterprising and as chimerical as his father, Henry had entered into relations with the Crusader States in Syria and the Musulman princes of the African coast, and was preparing a great expedition against Constantinople when his unexpected death (November 27th, 1198) made an end of all these fine plans, and also spared him the embarrassment of an inevitable war with the Papacy, which, even if he had lived, would have rendered the execution of these plans impossible.

Thanks to his Sicilian riches, he had succeeded in obtaining the election, by the German princes, of his son Frederick II as King of the Romans. The child was then two years of age. The princes immediately forgot his existence and set about choosing another king. But they were no longer able to agree. The two parties into which they were divided, the Guelfs and the Ghibellines, were simply two feudal factions, one as little concerned as the other with the interests of the monarchy, and seeking merely to place in power a sovereign who would allow his electors to enrich themselves at the expense of their adversaries, and of the State itself. Foreign money, which in the time to come would so often determine the issue of the royal elections in Germany, now openly intervened for the first time. The pounds sterling of Richard Cœur-de-Lion were lavished in favour of his candidate, Duke Otto of Brunswick, the son of Henry the Lion, reared in England, and having little of the German in his composition apart from his hatred of the Hohenstaufens. In opposition to him, the partisans of the Hohenstaufens supported the brother of Henry VI, Philip the Swabian, who purchased the alliance of Philip Augustus by the cession of Imperial Flanders. He also gave the royal crown to the Duke of Bohemia in order to attach him to his fortunes. And civil war broke out from the Alps to the North Sea and from the Elbe to the Rhine, all the princes falling upon one another on the pretext of defending the legitimate monarch (1198).

This war was just what the Pope wanted. Basing his action on the old claim that the election of the King of the Romans must be approved by the Holy See, he intervened between the rivals. Philip could not renounce the traditions of his house and sacrifice the rights of the Empire. Weak as he was, he regarded himself as the successor of the Caesars, so that he actually called himself Philip II, having remembered that in the 2nd century Philip the Arabian had governed the Roman Empire. As for Otto IV, he promised all that was required of him: abstention from the episcopal elections, renunciation of all claims to sovereignty over Rome, and the surrender of the Kingdom of Sicily. Innocent pronounced in his favour; however, his decision, and the excommunication pronounced against Philip and his supporters, did not weaken their cause to the point of compelling them to lay down their arms (1201). The struggle continued until Philip's assassination in 1208. Once rid of his rival, Otto set out for Rome, and the following year he received the Imperial crown. A few months later he was excommunicated. Hardly was he crowned, indeed, when the Guelf turned Ghibelline, and proceeded to claim, just as the Hohenstaufens had done, all the powers and pretensions which he had renounced a few years earlier.

The weapon destined to lay him low was already in the hands of the Pope. The son of Henry VI, Prince Frederick, whose mother, dying a few months after her husband, had confided him to the guardianship of Innocent III, while acknowledging that Sicily was a fief of the Holy See, had just attained his 14th year, and had taken over the government of the Kingdom of Sicily. What more ingenious policy could be conceived than to send him to Germany, to see that he was acknowledged as king there, and in his interests to incite the Ghibellines—who this time would be acting on behalf of the Holy See—to fall upon the Guelfs? But in order to carry out so bold a plan the Pope must have an ally. The question of his identity was solved by the war which had just broken out between France and England: Philip Augustus was the man. Philip, indeed, knew that Otto had promised his support to John Lackland, and nothing could have suited him better than a rising in Germany against his enemy's auxiliaries. Just as the English treasury had formerly bought Otto's electors, so the French treasury now purchased the electors of Frederick II. Almost as soon as the young prince had shown himself in Swabia a number of the princes declared for him (1212). Two years later the crushing blow of Bouvines defeated, in the person of Otto, the last representative of the Imperial policy as conceived by all the German emperors since Barbarossa. On November 19th, 1212, Frederick concluded with France a treaty against Otto and England. On July 12th, 1213, at Eger, he recognized all the possessions of the Pope in Italy, and renounced the right of supervising the episcopal elections, in conformity with the Concordat of Worms. The war was decided, simultaneously, between him and Otto, between the Empire and the Church, and between France and England.

This was the final end of the chimera which these Emperors had pursued as they dreamed of the revival of the Roman Empire. The Pope was triumphant: he could not suspect, in 1214, that his ward would presently become the most persistent of the enemies of the Holy See. But the struggle which was about to begin between the Emperor and the Pope inaugurated an entirely new phase in the relations of Papacy and Empire. In this conflict, however, Germany was to play no part; since Frederick left Germany for Italy, and the former country, left to herself, finished by falling into a state of political decomposition; before foundering in the anarchy of the great interregnum.

*Book Seven*

# THE HEGEMONY OF THE PAPACY AND OF FRANCE IN THE THIRTEENTH CENTURY

CHAPTER I

# THE PAPACY AND THE CHURCH

## 1. *The Situation of the Papacy in the 13th Century*

Between the battle of Bouvines at the beginning of the century and the conflict between Philip the Fair and Boniface VIII at its close, the 13th century stands out as an epoch characterized by the double hegemony of the Papacy and of France. Whether separately or by common agreement, they determined the course of policy, while both exerted a profound influence over intellectual, moral and social life: the one through the Church which it directed, and the other through the superiority of her civilization. Fatal as the triumph of the Papacy over the Empire was to Germany, it was equally favourable to France, whom circumstances had associated with it.

It must be repeated that the motive which for two and a half centuries had determined the hostility of the Emperors to the Papacy was by no means their eagerness to defend the temporal power against the encroachments of the Church. To envisage the question thus is to transport into the heart of the Middle Ages ideas and problems which belong only to our modern times. Neither the humiliation of Henry IV at Canossa, nor that of Frederick Barbarossa at Venice, nor that of Otto IV at Bouvines, was the humiliation of the civil power before priestly arrogance. In reality, the conflict was not a conflict between State and Church: it was an intestine struggle within the Church itself. What the Emperors wanted was to compel the Popes to recognize them as governing the universal Church, a right which they claimed was theirs from the time of the Carolingian Empire, as the Ottos and Henrys had done, or from the time of the Roman Empire, as the Hohenstaufens had done. Their pretensions thus imperilled, in every country, that temporal independence of which, by the strangest of confusions, they had been regarded as the defenders. The cause of the Pope was the cause of the nation, and with the liberty of the Church was bound up the liberty of the European States; to such an extent that the victory of Philip Augustus at Bouvines was the triumph of both causes.

But the collapse of Otto IV did not mean the end of the Empire. It continued to exist until the threshold of our modern age. Napoleon I, who shattered so many things in Europe, abolished this venerable relic in 1806 by the creation of the confederation of the Rhine (July 1806). Yet we may say that from the beginning of the 13th century the historic rôle of the Empire was finished. It ceased to exist as a universal power, as a European authority. While the Emperors continued to entitle themselves "ever-august Roman Emperors," while they retained the terrestrial globe among their emblems, and while, down to Charles V, they continued to go to Rome for their coronation, they were actually merely the sovereigns, or to speak more exactly, the suzerains, of the medley of principalities and municipal republics constituted by the Germany of the late Middle Ages and the modern epoch, and which from the 14th century onwards was known as the "Holy Roman Empire of the Germanic nations."

After the fall of the Empire only one universal power was left in Europe: that of the Pope, and its isolation made it seem greater than ever. The whole government of the Church depended on the Pope: this government was a monarchy, a truly universal monarchy, and it was steadily becoming more completely centralized. All the bishops now swore fealty to the Pope; no religious order could be founded without his authorization; the Court of Rome heard appeals from all Christendom, and in every country his legates watched over the execution of his orders and the maintenance of discipline. To govern such a body, and to direct its activities, two things were indispensable: a code of law, and finances. The canon law, whose most ancient monument, the Decree of Gratianus, was proclaimed in Rome in 1150, was rapidly enlarged under those great jurists, Innocent III and Innocent IV. By the end of the 13th century it was complete, and suffered hardly any subsequent modifications. As for the pontifical finances, which must be carefully distinguished from the finances of the Pope as sovereign of Rome, they were furnished by "St. Peter's Pence," levied upon England and Aragon, and by the more and more numerous taxes imposed upon the dignitaries of the Church: annates, reservations, dues of the Pallium, of indult, etc. It was these taxes that constituted the treasury of the Holy See, and enabled it to play the universal rôle which was allotted to it: to subsidize the Crusades, to maintain the missions, and to add to its spiritual influence the purely worldly influence of gold. It is impossible to realize the immense ascendancy of such a pontiff as Innocent III if we fail to regard him as a financial power. On the other hand, it must be noted that this financial power, which was nourished and maintained by the Catholic hierarchy in every part of Europe, was made possible only by the economic progress due to the revival of trade. So long as the West had remained in the stage of agricultural civilization the Pope had not and could not have had other resources than those of the domains of St. Peter's patrimony. Hence the Pope's efforts to increase his power in Italy, and secure the possessions of the Countess Matilda in Tuscany, and his original resistance to the expansion of the Norman State. But when the circulation of money was an accomplished fact, when it was replacing, more and more completely, the system of revenues in kind, the fiscal system of the pontiff was free to develop within the extreme limits of the pontifical authority. It was then that this innovation appeared: the pontifical taxes. Before this they would have been impossible. In the history of ecclesiastical organization they are the consequence of the economic transformation which was at the same time beginning to render possible a regular system of taxation in the various States. And it is interesting to see how the Pope took advantage, as regards their collection, of the capitalist organization which was beginning to evolve in the great Italian communes. The men whom he entrusted with the collection and transmission of his revenues were merchants, the bankers of Siena, and afterwards those of

Florence. The Popes, even earlier than the lay sovereigns, were in intimate relations with the financiers, and the fact that the latter had to collect their revenues in all parts of Europe, convert them by exchange into Italian or international money, and place them at the Pope's disposal, without the necessity of transporting them, at the cost of great expense and danger, across the mountains, contributed in no small degree to the origin of the first banking operations and the first letters of credit, the remote ancestors of our bills of exchange. Compared with their predecessors of the 11th century—a Gregory VII, an Innocent II, and even with the contemporaries of St. Bernard—the great Popes of the 13th century undoubtedly seem more worldly characters. One might say that they had dragged God and the heavens down into the Church. They gave the Church an incomparable power and majesty, but on considering this power and majesty one is too conscious of the human effort. It was an admirable attempt to constitute a perfect society on earth. One is put in mind of a Gothic cathedral; it shoots up into the heavens, yet it does not contain them, however lofty its vaulted roofs, nor does it contain all humanity, however numerous its sculptures, where men and kings are represented beside God and the saints and demons. Like ecclesiastical law, theology was essentially an achievement of the 13th century. The scholastic philosophy of the previous centuries finds its climax in the *Summa* of St. Thomas (1274), in which Christian morality and the Christian dogmas are expounded in accordance with the Aristotelian method.

The point of departure, of course, was revelation. Faith provided the unshakable foundation of a rational theological construction which comprised the whole of society and the whole of life. Its aim, of course, remained what it had always been: eternal salvation. But men no longer sought to attain salvation through mysticism, through immediate contact with God. Everywhere the Church interposed. A St. Bernard would have been inconceivable in the 13th century, as the counsellor of Popes who regarded St. Francis of Assisi with suspicion. What men were now seeking to achieve was the government of their souls by the Church, itself governed by the Vicar of Jesus Christ. And these souls were accepted in the bodies which they animated; which is to say, that society was accepted; heroism was not required of it, nor were men expected to desert the world. They had only to obey the Church, and allow it to lead them to salvation. Every human being, every profession was subject to the Church, and therefore to the Roman pontiff. There were political sins (unjust wars) and commercial sins (under-cutting) which ecclesiastical law defined and punished. Thus the whole of life was placed under the perpetual control of the Church, the secular life no less than the religious. The ecclesiastical tribunals, in their *forum mixtum*, were the ordinary instance, not only for churchmen, but for a host of purely secular questions: testaments, civil status, marriages, usury. All those who had received baptism belonged to the Church, and had to bow to its teaching, under penalty of penitence, or excommunication, or, in case of need, of taking part in a Crusade. Here was a majestic unity, a complete doctrine, which imposed itself upon a world of believers, all of whom accepted it; a doctrine so complete that it gave rise to the one truly universal poem in European literature: the Divine Comedy of Dante, completely steeped in the spirit of St. Thomas. In the same way, of course, the whole of intellectual life was subjected to the authority of the Church. All the scholars of the period were theologians or jurists. Philosophy, *ancilla theologiae*, and the universities, all modelled on that of Paris, were placed under the direct authority of the Pope. All their teachers were clergy from the monasteries and the cathedral schools; it was there that learning was now to be found. And learning was completely impregnated with the dialectical spirit that inspired the new knowledge. It broke the last ties that bound it to antiquity, if we make an exception of Aristotle, and what had been learned of Plato through the Jews and the Arabs. A new Latin was in course of formation, the true Latin of the Middle Ages, which was to survive until the Renaissance: lucid and analytical, everywhere the same, the language of the jurists and theologians. The *belles lettres* of the Latin language disappeared. The new tongue was what one might describe as Gothic Latin, for although, like Gothic architecture, it had its origin in antiquity, it had become as independent of the literature of antiquity as Gothic architecture had become of its art.

At the moment when the Church, having vanquished the Empire, had arrived at this summit of power, which gave it the hegemony of the Occidental world, a new adversary rose up against it: heresy. Since the Arian heresy, which the Goths had brought from the East in the 4th century, the Latin Catholic world, for many centuries, had unanimously professed the same faith, and acknowledged the same dogmas, presenting a notable contrast, in the permanence of its orthodoxy, to the religious disputes which, down to the 10th century, had never ceased to trouble the Greek Church. This tranquillity may be readily explained. In the West, as contrasted with the Byzantine Empire, there was no philosophical tradition, no learning outside the ranks of the clergy; there were no contacts with civilizations professing different religions, no social conditions liable to direct men's minds toward dangerous innovations. How could faith have been disputed, in a society living in isolation, accustomed by its purely agricultural civilization to respect tradition and authority, and in which the Church, the only literate body in the midst of universal ignorance, knew no other literature than the Latin—that is, a completely orthodox literature? The 11th century, which saw the revival of commerce, the development of navigation, and the rise of the first cities, was also to see the first symptoms of restlessness appear in religious life. By unknown ways, but probably by the trade routes, the Manichaean doctrines were trickling in from the East—into Lombardy, and from Lombardy into France and Rhenish Germany. Few at first, their adepts became more numerous in the course of the 12th century, and for reasons of which we know little they were concentrated more especially in the County of Toulouse and the region of Albi, whence their name of Albigenses. Even more mystical and ascetic than their orthodox contemporaries, they went so far as to reject in the name of the Spirit, the sole principle of life and truth, not only society, but the Church itself, corrupted as it was by wealth and power. In order to attain to Christ, whose only disciples they declared themselves to be, a man must divest himself of his whole terrestrial nature, arriving at a state of perfect purity. Hence their name of Cathars (καθαροί), as greatly dreaded and abhorred in the 12th century as the name of Anabaptist was in the 16th, and from which is derived the word that denotes the heretic in the Germanic languages (*Ketzer*, *Ketter*). Like the Anabaptists, moreover, these visionaries menaced both the social and the religious order. They preached both the community of goods and the annihilation of the Church, and we cannot be surprised that the French barons responded with enthusiasm to the appeal of Innocent III when he preached the crusade against the Cathars. Between 1208 and 1235 they were hunted down and exterminated in every part of Languedoc, amidst such circumstances of horror as were not to be seen again until the outbreak of the religious wars of the 16th century. However, the Catholics did not succeed in slaying them all; and as always, persecution, though it killed the body, did not destroy the spirit, and in this respect their doctrine was justified. Until the appearance of Wycliffe nearly all the heretical sects—Apostolics, Brothers of the Free Spirit, Begards, etc.—the Waldenses alone excepted—seem to have had some fundamental relation with the Cathar mysticism. And for this very reason none of them was really very dangerous. The radicalism of their aspirations could never be realized in practice, and everywhere it excited the hostility of the social authorities. It was among the proletariat of the cities that they recruited most of their adherents; and this explains both the naïvety of their communistic dreams and—except for certain moments of crisis—their somewhat restricted diffusion. Save in a few of the great industrial cities, the proletarian workers constituted only a very small minority of the bourgeoisie. The great majority of the bourgeois consisted of small employers, master craftsmen, etc.; in short, that middle class which is as hostile to capitalism as it is to communism.

Moreover, from the end of the 12th century the Church employed every means of persecuting and opposing heresy. It tolerated the Jews because they were outside the Church; but it could not tolerate the heretics, in whom it saw, so to speak, traitors guilty of spiritual lèse-majesté. If they refused to abjure their doctrines it cut them off from its communion; then, having passed its capital sentence on the soul, it delivered them to the secular power, which undertook to destroy the body. This division of labour corresponded perfectly to the conception that allied the Church to the State, while reserving to each its own domain—the souls to the former, the bodies to the latter. Before the 12th century we find, here and there, in the upper ranks of the clergy, the expression of doubts as to the legitimacy of inflicting the sentence of death on heretics. But no such doubts recurred after Innocent III had ascended the Papal throne, and the Church had achieved its majestic and powerful unity. Here again we see a manifestation of the juridical and governmental spirit with which the ecclesiastical constitution was impregnated. Orthodoxy, having become a body of doctrine which was imposed on all men and on all their activities, could no longer tolerate dissidence, and every individual opinion, every deviation from the norm, became a crime. The Order of the Dominicans, founded in 1215, devoted itself especially to the examination and prosecution of heretics. Side by side with the ancient episcopal Inquisition there now appeared the pontifical Inquisition created by Gregory IX in 1233, a kind of universal police whose function it was to watch over the safety of dogma. And the secular authority eagerly collaborated with it. In accordance with the principle of the State religion, anyone who placed himself outside the Church was regarded as a criminal. Did not the kings hold their power from God, and were they not the protectors of the Church? In the cities, perhaps, the civic sentiment may unconsciously have disapproved, not of the faith, but of the consequences involved by its abandonment. There, and there only, we see feeble manifestations of the first symptoms of the independence of secular society in respect of religious society.

## 2. *The Papal Policy*

It is often said that the 13th century was a theocracy. But we must define the term. If by theocracy we mean a state of affairs in which the Church enjoys an incomparable prestige and in which no one can escape from its moral ascendancy, the 13th century was undoubtedly a theocracy. But it was not a theocracy if theocracy consists in confiding to the Church itself the guidance and government of political interests.[1]

It was only when a sovereign was the open enemy of the pontiff—as Frederick II had been—that the Pope deprived him of the sovereign power. But this case must be regarded merely as an ultimate consequence of the relations between the Papacy and the Empire, and the vassal status of Sicily. Elsewhere, although the kings were obedient sons of the Church, they took good care to prevent it from intervening in their private affairs. Of course, there were few political events between the end of the 12th century and the beginning of the 14th in which the Popes did not intervene. But they did not intervene as masters; whether as allies or opponents, they acted as an individual power, in so far as intervention forwarded their own policies. They had, it is true, a terrible weapon: excommunication, but it was blunted by abuse.

For the Popes had their own policy, both as the heads of the Catholic world and as Italian sovereigns. The two policies were often confounded; but they were really quite separate.

The true Papal policy was the policy of the Church, as derived from the universal mission of the Church. It was summed up in a two-fold activity: the Crusade, and union with the Greek Church; the two motives being so often confounded that it is not always easy to separate them. Even Urban II had hoped to put an end to the schism by means of the First Crusade. Actually, however, the Crusade merely rendered the schism more tenacious, owing to the antipathy which it excited between the Latins and the Greeks. Moreover, the position of the Latins in the East was so precarious that a Second Crusade was necessary in 1143. This, preached by St. Bernard, provoked a wave of mysticism comparable to that which had inspired the First. However, although it had been inspired by the Pope, it was not so completely subject to his guidance as the wholly feudal expedition of 1098. The King of France,

[1] Theoretically the Popes aimed at theocracy, although they never actually achieved it, but it was acknowledged that they possessed—and in any case they claimed for themselves—a rudimentary power of supreme arbitration, which, however, often excited opposition, though not open conflict.

Louis VII, and the King of Germany, Conrad III, both took part in it, and although their collaboration had no important results, it showed that Rome would henceforth have to reckon with the political powers of the West. For the rest, the object of the Crusade was not achieved. The settlements of the Crusaders in Syria were not saved from the perils that threatened them. A few years later Saladin captured Jerusalem, and once more the West had to be summoned to deliver the tomb of Christ. The Third Crusade brought the rulers of three States upon the scene: Frederick Barbarossa, Philip Augustus, and Richard Cœur-de-Lion. Frederick died without having succeeded, as he had hoped, in restoring the prestige of the Empire; Philip and Richard thwarted each other and parted full of rancour, without achieving anything. The experience was conclusive. It was evident that thenceforth the Holy Land would not be reconquered, and that worldly ambitions were playing a greater and greater and always more disastrous part in the "Holy War." Henry VI, during his short reign in Sicily, had conceived the notion of what one may call a purely temporal crusade, from which he expected nothing but the extension of his power in the Mediterranean. Innocent III, however, still inspired by Christian idealism, made preparations for a new expedition with the intention of attacking Egypt, the base of the Fatimid power. This time, however, the kings had had their fill of crusading. Their affairs kept them at home. The princes of the Low Countries, Champagne, and Blois, set out on the Crusade; but the Venetians, the owners of the fleet, who had not been paid in full for their services (these expeditions were becoming more costly, and the nobles were ruined), persuaded the Crusaders to attack Zara, a Christian city which incommoded their trade in the Adriatic. The Pope excommunicated them, but in vain. At Zara, Alexius Angelus, the brother-in-law of Philip of Swabia, an enemy of the Pope, and the son of Isaac Angelus, who had just been blinded and dethroned by his brother Alexius III, implored them to attack Constantinople, promising them, as reward, the union of the Greek with the Roman Church. The Pope was opposed to this change of plan, for he could not trust a kinsman of the Hohenstaufens.

However, his opposition was ignored: they were no longer to be ruled by Rome. On the June 23rd, 1203, the fleet appeared before Constantinople, and Isaac was restored to the throne. But the hatred of the Greeks for the Crusaders who had restored the Emperor to the throne provoked a revolt. The people chose the valiant Alexius Ducas Murtzuphlos as their Emperor. He broke with the Latins, who thereupon seized the city (April 12th, 1204). On May 16th Baldwin, who had the largest number of soldiers, was elected Emperor and crowned by a Papal legate. Innocent III had suddenly reversed his policy. His confidential agent, the Venetian Tomaso Morosini, was created Patriarch of Constantinople. However, it was not really the Church that profited by this expedition, but mainly Venice, who founded a magnificent colonial empire in the ancient Byzantine provinces.

As for the Latin Empire, an improvised creation, born of the commercial ambitions of Venice, the dynastic quarrels of the Byzantines, and the impetuosity of the Western knights, to what future could it look forward? When we think of the consequences, then, and even now, of the capture of Constantinople by the Turks two hundred and fifty years later, one can but conjecture the prospects of a Latin Constantinople at the beginning of the 13th century. But in history nothing is improvised, and here once more we can see how untrue it is that little causes lead to great results. Here the events were on a small scale, and so were their results. The Westerners could enter Constantinople by assault, but they could not keep it. To retain and govern such a city, against the will of its people, would have called for such resources in men and money as were not then to be found in Europe. It would have been necessary to occupy and hold Thrace and Asia Minor. What State was capable of such an effort? It would have needed standing armies, and a constant influx of reinforcements. Constantinople could be taken and kept only by a warlike and barbarous people like the Turks, still in the phase of the invasions, or by a civilization which from the military and administrative point of view was the equal of the great States of our own age. As it was, the capture of Constantinople in 1204 was no more than a skirmish. We have only to read Villehardouin to realize that the conquerors had no suspicion of the stupendous consequences that might have followed from the capture of Constantinople. They did what they could: they created an Emperor, and on the sea-coast they constituted fiefs, principalities, and colonies—and that was all. In 1205 Baldwin fell into the hands of the Bulgars. His brother Henry (1206–1216) had, on the whole, a glorious reign, despite enormous difficulties: it is true that just then the Greeks of Nicaea were having much trouble with the Seldjuks and various Greek rivals. After this the condition of the Latin Empire was pitiable: Pierre de Courtenay (1217–1219) sold his possessions in France in order to maintain himself in power. Robert, his son, failing to repulse the Greeks, was reduced to the possession of the city. Baldwin II went to Europe to beg for money, sold the Crown of Thorns to St. Louis, and pawned his County of Namur. It was useless; the Greek State of Nicaea was now confident of victory. In 1261 Michael Palaeologus, with the help of the Genoese, who were jealous of the Venetians, recaptured Constantinople and restored the Empire. Of the union of the Greek and Roman Churches not a trace was left. The only result had been to increase the colonial empire of Venice at the expense of Byzantium, unable to recapture the islands or the settlements in Greece. The Empire was weaker than it had been, less capable of resisting the Turks. This was the practical result of the Crusade!

Yet the Papacy still had its illusions. Urban IV and Clement IV negotiated with Michael Palaeologus for the union of the Churches, and in 1274 the Council of Lyons proclaimed that union. But it soon had to admit the reality, which was that Michael, in negotiating for the union of the Churches, was merely sounding the possibility of obtaining military assistance. Martin IV proclaimed the rupture of the union and favoured Charles of Anjou's designs upon Constantinople.

The Crusades were rapidly degenerating. The Fifth (1218–1221), enthusiastically supported by Honorius III, was merely an expedition led by the titular king of Jerusalem, Jean de Brienne, against Damietta, with troops recruited from Hungary, the North of Europe, France, and Europe. It failed, because, in defiance of common sense, it was directed by the Papal legate, and because Frederick II, who had promised his assistance at the time of his coronation in 1220, did not keep his word.

The last three Crusades, of which more will be said later, had little of the Crusade about them but the name.

What was the reason of this *decrescendo* in the achievements of the Crusades, which had been so pompously inaugurated? It is readily explained. The Crusade in itself, as the Pope had originally intended it, was quite unrelated to any temporal aim, and in this lay both its greatness and its weakness. Europe had no need of Syria and Jerusalem. She took them in a fit of enthusiasm and had not the strength to retain them. Their retention would have involved a permanent crusade, and the transformation of all Europe into a military Order. This was impossible. Moreover, the agricultural civilization which had made the levy *en masse* possible was gradually disappearing, so that each successive Crusade was recruited with greater difficulty. The urban populations, and the rural populations who maintained them, could no longer be uprooted. The knights were ruining themselves, and they had to be paid. But it was long before the crusading spirit was quite extinct among them. In the maritime cities, on the other hand, which had profited only too well by the Crusades ever since the sea route had been followed, it very soon disappeared. And lastly, there were political reasons for its decline. There was the policy of the kings of Northern Europe, who could no longer fling themselves into such purposeless adventures, and there was the Sicilian policy of Frederick II and Charles of Anjou, which had conquests in view. Faith had not declined, but the Crusades were no longer possible. The Pope alone remained faithful to the old ideal. It was his constant preoccupation. It outlasted everything: the transplantation of the Teutonic Knights to Prussia and the punishment of the Templars. The Knights of St. John of Jerusalem were at last the only reminder of the original spirit. In the Christian sense of the word, in the sense understood and intended by the Popes, the Crusade had failed, and with it, the pontifical policy. It was shattered against the realities of a Europe whose conditions of political and social life had evolved while the Papacy had remained faithful to its ideals. It was wrecked because it sought the impossible. Taking it all in all, the universal policy had been as unsuccessful in the spiritual sphere, with the Popes, as with the Emperors in the temporal sphere.[1]

[1] Nevertheless, the spirit of the Crusade continued to survive in Spain, because there it was associated with the necessity of self-preservation. Elsewhere, contact with Islam resulted in a greater commercial activity; in Spain it continued to give rise to war.

CHAPTER II

# THE PAPACY, ITALY, AND GERMANY

## 1. *Italy*

Compared with the rest of Occidental Europe, Italy, from the 11th century, was notable as the land of cities. In no other part of the Continent were these so numerous and so active, and nowhere else did they play so preponderant a part. To the north of the Alps, even in the regions where they were most fully developed, as in Flanders and the Low Countries, they were far from governing the entire social life of the country: the nobility and the rural classes existed independently beside them, and had different interests. In Italy everything was subject to their influence, or contributed to it. The rural population was subject only to the cities, and laboured only for them; and in the cities the nobles had their crenellated "palaces" and towers, as different in their aspect from the castles of the Northern barons, which were scattered about the countryside, as was the life of their inmates from that of the Northern chivalry. This social concentration upon the cities must doubtless be attributed to the persistence of the ancient tradition. The municipal organization of the Roman Empire had impressed itself upon Italy so profoundly, and had packed the population so densely around the cities, that when the latter woke to life again under the stimulus of commerce it was inevitable that they should reassume their dominant situation. Municipal life became as preponderant in Lombardy and Tuscany as it had been in antiquity, but while its material conditions were almost unchanged, its spirit was different. The Roman municipality had enjoyed only a local autonomy, subordinated to the formidable power of the State. The Italian city of the Middle

Ages—at least, in the north and the centre of the peninsula—was a republic.[1]

From the 11th century onwards the mercantile and industrial class which was in process of formation took advantage, as we have seen, of the conflict between the Pope and the Emperor to rebel against the bishops, and to wrest from them the administration of the cities. The first Italian communes were sworn by the "Patarenes"[2] in the midst of the turmoil of the War of Investitures: a time of mystical exaltation. Their origin was purely revolutionary, and from the time of their birth they contracted a habit of violence that was to characterize them to the end. By force or by agreement, the commune imposed itself, in each city, on the mass of the population, and its elective consuls, like the aldermen of the Belgian cities, exercised both the judical and the administrative power. But as the bourgeoisie developed the social contrasts in its ranks were accentuated, and parties were formed in support of various conflicting interests. The names by which they were known are sufficiently eloquent of their nature. The party of the *grandi* was composed of the urban nobility, with whom were associated a good many enriched merchants; the party of the *piccoli* comprised the corporations or guilds of artisans of every kind, whose numbers multiplied as prosperity increased. The absence of a princely power, above the parties and capable of moderating their quarrels, gave the conflicts between the two groups, arising from questions of taxation and the organization of municipal power, a bitterness and severity unequalled elsewhere. From the middle of the 12th century civil war became a chronic epidemic. The *grandi* had the best of it; the *piccoli* were pitilessly massacred; if they surrendered they were driven out of the city; their houses or palaces were destroyed, and while waiting for the moment when they could avenge themselves they lived on the adjacent countryside, pillaging and harassing their compatriots.

As a general thing these exiles found protection and allies in a neighbouring city. For while there was permanent warfare in the

[1] Except in the Kingdom of Sicily, of which more later.

[2] The name of Patarius seems to be a mere corruption of Catharus.

heart of the bourgeoisies, the mutual relations of the cities were also generally warlike. Constituting as they did so many independent economic centres, each of them thought only of itself, doing its utmost to force the peasants and population of the surrounding countryside to furnish its food supply, striving to compel the traffic of the surrounding region to centre upon it, to exclude its rivals from its market, and, if possible, to deprive them of their trade outlets. Thus the clash of interests was as violent outside the city as within it. Trade and industry were developed by means of battles. In all these little closed and immured worlds, watching one another from the height of their towers, human energy was expended with equal vigour in production and in destruction. Each city imagined that its prosperity depended on the ruin of its rivals. The progress of urban economy was accompanied by an ever narrower and more ferocious policy of municipal particularism. There was no truce to mutual hatred save under the pressure of a common peril. It took the threats and brutalities of Frederick Barbarossa to unite the Lombard League against him and to bring about the victory of Legnano.

Although the Hohenstaufens did not succeed in imposing their Caesarism on the Italian bourgeoisies, it did furnish them with a new element of discord. Having ceased to be dangerous after Legnano, the Emperor was able to act as auxiliary in the civil conflicts if one of the parties appealed to him for assistance. Those who did so appeal were usually the *grandi*. The names of Guelf and Ghibelline found their way from Germany into Italy, and became so well acclimatized there that they remained in use until the end of the 15th century, the name of Guelf being given to the adversaries and that of Ghibelline to the allies of the Imperial intervention, even when the Emperor was no longer a member of the house of Hohenstaufen. Neither of the two parties flying at each other's throats had any notion of the origin of the names which they had adopted, and which, transported into the midst of these urban quarrels, no longer had any correspondence with their primitive application. The Guelfs and the Ghibellines were both republican; the only difference between them was that the

Ghibellines looked to the Emperor to help them against their adversaries, while the Guelfs, in order to maintain themselves in power, naturally endeavoured to ally themselves with the enemies of the Emperor.

The ferocity with which the parties sought to destroy each other did not prevent them from devising means of strengthening the municipal government. From the second half of the 12th century attempts were made to render it independent of civil conflicts by confiding it to a podestà. The podestà was, so to speak, a temporary prince elected by the commune, and in order to guarantee his impartiality and his independence of the parties it usually chose him from an alien commune. However, the institution did not yield the results which had been expected of it. Almost always the podestàs were obliged, in order to make their power respected, to rely on the support of one of the hostile factions. In certain cities they succeeded, as early as the 13th century, in possessing themselves, either by cunning or by violence, and thanks to the general lassitude, of the supreme authority, and in founding the first of those tyrannies which were to play so considerable a part during the epoch of the Renaissance. I need only mention the Scaligers of Verona and the Visconti of Milan.

The political and social ferment of the Italian cities naturally influenced their religious life. There were simultaneous outbreaks of mysticism and heresy, which provided fresh aliment for the fever that consumed them. St. Francis of Assisi was the son of a merchant, and the Order of Franciscans found its true field of action in the bourgeoisies. Moreover, there were swarms of Cathars, Brothers of the Free Spirit, and Waldenses. In 1245 the Dominicans provoked a revolt against the podestà of Florence, whom they accused of favouring the heretics. The atrocious laws against heretics promulgated by Frederick II prove that their numbers must have been considerable—at all events, in the larger cities—but it is unfortunately impossible to determine with any exactitude the importance of their activities.

It can hardly be doubted that they would have recruited the majority of their adherents among the workers engaged in production for export. As in Flanders, this trade was already highly developed in the Italy of the 13th century, and as in Flanders, it resulted in the formation of a veritable working-class proletariat. The weavers of Florence, the great cloth-producing centre of Southern Europe, differed as widely as the weavers of Gand, Ypres or Douai from the usual type of urban artisan. Far from working on their own account, they were mere wage-earners, employed by the merchants. The nascent capitalism of the age subjected them to its influence, and its power, like its influence, increased in proportion as the merchants developed the export trade. By the first half of the 13th century the Florentine cloths were exported to all parts of the Orient, and the merchants of the city were importing their wool from England. Such an active manufacture naturally presupposes a considerable degree of capitalistic development. The fortunes accumulated by the trade in merchandise were still further increased by financial transactions. In the course of the 13th century the money-changers (bankers) of Siena and Florence found their way into all parts of Western Europe, where they were known as Lombards, and in England, to this day, the words "Lombard Street" are a synonym for the money-market. We have already seen what services they rendered to the Papacy as financial agents. But in England, the Low Countries, and France they advanced larger and larger sums to the cities, princes, and kings, and were employed as collectors, treasurers, and guardians of money. Under Philip the Fair the Sienese Mouche (Musciatto) and Biche (Albizo) Guidi played the twofold part of bankers and financial ministers to the Crown, and were also employed by the Pope and the King of Sicily, while they were interested in the affairs of various commercial companies, like that of the Peruzzi. The Sienese company of the Bonsignori was still more important. A document relating to its bankruptcy in 1298 informs us that it was the most celebrated company in the world, which had rendered services innumerable to popes, emperors, kings, cities and merchants. That very year it had already paid two hundred thousand golden florins to its creditors, and it was given time to pay the rest, part of its capital being engaged in loans made in various parts of the world, which could not be realized immediately. On the disappearance of this company Florence became the chief money-market and banking centre of Europe, and so remained until the 15th century. The relations between the city and the Orient must at an early date have drawn the attention of its men of affairs to the trade in metals. The low prices of gold in the Levant enabled them readily to acquire great quantities of the precious metal, of which they disposed at considerable profit. We know that it was in the form of Florentine florins, minted from 1252 onwards,[1] and presently imitated by Venice (ducats), and then in France, that gold coins, abandoned since the Merovingian epoch, once more made their appearance in international trade, providing the instrument of exchange which had become indispensable to its progress. The cessation of commerce had given Europe its silver money; its revival gave it its golden coinage.

The social position of the Italian bankers and merchants brought them so closely into touch with the nobility that they were often confounded with it. This process took place all the more rapidly, inasmuch as the Italian nobility, instead of residing in the country, like the nobility of Northern Europe, had its dwelling-houses in the city. By the end of the 12th century the nobles were already beginning to interest themselves in commercial operations, while the merchants, on the other hand, were often ennobled. In short, under the influence of capital the line of demarcation between the juridical classes, which elsewhere remained so clearly drawn, in Italy grew fainter, almost to the point of disappearance, during the course of the 13th century. An aristocracy was formed for which social position was of greater importance than blood, while individual worth overcame the prejudice of birth. Social life was more varied, political life more individual; the ambitious man saw no limit to his prospects; there were fewer conventions, fewer castes, more humanity; there was also more passion. Here again Florence took precedence of all the other cities. Florence, to the undying honour of her people, produced and shaped the genius to whom

[1] Frederick II, in 1231, had already caused golden Augustales to be struck in Sicily, but their circulation seems to have been somewhat restricted.

the world owes what was, with the Gothic cathedrals of France, the greatest achievement of the Middle Ages: the Divine Comedy.

Neither in their wealth, nor in their political, social or intellectual activity could the Papal States bear comparison with Lombardy or Tuscany. They presented, from the beginning, and retained until the end, the artificial character of a purely political creation, intended to assure Rome of the independence of the Holy See. Spreading across Italy between the Kingdom of Sicily and Tuscany, cut in two by the Apennines, and without good ports, either on the Mediterranean or the Adriatic, their situation could hardly have been more unfavourable. Moreover, the Pope's government was never able to make itself respected. The families of the great nobles, even when they had ceased to fight for the tiara, still retained considerable power, both in Rome and in the surrounding countryside, and their private wars were unending. To this must be added the state of insecurity to which the country was condemned by the Imperial claims, and the difficulty, in Rome itself, of governing a vain, arrogant and idle people, always ready to follow the tribunes who flattered them by recalling their ancient greatness. It is a characteristic fact that the greatest of the Popes—those who, like Innocent III or Innocent IV, had the power to depose or excommunicate kings—were never at peace in their capital, and were exposed without defence to the insurrections of the mob. Although the Roman people lived, so to speak, by the Papacy, it might almost be said that the Papacy was encamped in its midst. Rome was the centre of the universal Church, the headquarters of ecclesiastical policy, but the life of the Church was not centred within its walls. It contained no great educational establishment, and none of the learned doctors of the period, no Albertus Magnus, no Thomas Aquinas, ever lived there. The artistic life of the city was as insignificant as its intellectual life. No new religious movement ever had its source in Rome. St. Francis came from Assisi, St. Dominic from Spain. One might say that in the climate in which the government of the Church had evolved, neither art nor faith nor science was able to prosper.

The Kingdom of Sicily, in the south of the peninsula, was another world. While it was as wealthy as Northern Italy, and while its life was feverish and exuberant, it was politically apathetic. The Byzantine and Arab administrations had trained the people to accept the discipline of the State. It knew nothing of autonomy; it had no communes; its great cities were governed by the administration; the people were trained to pay their taxes and obey the authorities; these authorities were salaried and permanent officials, and the sovereign was all powerful: this was the spectacle presented by the country whose agricultural development was far in advance of all the rest of Europe. It was more densely populated than any other part of Europe. In the 13th century (1275) it was estimated that the inhabitants numbered 1,200,000, a population greater than that of England. Henry VI, and after him Frederick II, had developed the administration in the direction of a pure despotism. There was an administration of the State domains, monopolies, and magazines, a fiscal organization which knew nothing of privilege, and which was not unlike a sort of proto-mercantilism, while the creation of the University of Naples and the toleration extended to the Musulmans are suggestive of an enlightened despotism. There is more than one point of similarity between the Frederick II of the 13th century and the Frederick II of the 18th century, and this is easily explained, if we reflect that they could both do anything they liked with the peoples whom they governed. The constitutions promulgated by Frederick II in 1231 completed the Norman institutions, in the sense that they equipped them with what might be called a bureaucracy. In the Europe of the 13th century the Kingdom of Sicily was something unique, with its expert and despotic constitution, borrowed from the Byzantine and Musulman worlds which had shared the country between them until the Normans made their appearance. Not until the modern era did the European States achieve so complete an administrative system. But here we have the proof that a constitution which does not originate with the people is unable to influence its civilization, and that organization is not everything. In point of government, this Prussianized Sicily was greatly superior to all the rest of Europe. But it did not produce a Dante, nor a Gothic art, and it played no part, later on, in the flowering of the Renaissance.

## 2. *Frederick II*

The destiny of the Hohenstaufens had made it increasingly necessary that they should make Italy their political base. From Conrad III to Frederick Barbarossa, and from Frederick to Henry VI, they became less and less German in character, and with Frederick II their evolution was completed. Born of a Sicilian mother and reared in Sicily, he was himself a pure Sicilian. His fair hair, like the fair hair of that pure Spaniard Philip II, if we insist upon always regarding it as a sign of Germanic "race," merely proves that race is without influence upon moral tendencies and mental characteristics.

Gregory IX and Innocent IV accused Frederick not only of heresy, but of blasphemy, and his enemies declared that he was the author of a celebrated pamphlet in which Moses, Jesus and Mohammed were alike treated as impostors. He did not believe in God (*fidem Dei non habuit*), according to Salimbeni, who knew him personally, and by this, of course, we must understand that he did not believe in the Church. His more than semi-Oriental morals, his harem of Moslem women, and the incredulity of his son-in-law Ezzelino da Romano, who refused the sacraments when dying (1259), justify us in believing that he was actually a "libertine" in the matter of faith. However, he always denied the imputation. What is more, he promulgated, against heretics, laws whose cruelty was never equalled until the reign of Charles V. He did so because he thought his policy would benefit, and because for him, as for the Italian tyrants of the 15th century, to whom he bore a striking resemblance, all means were good that achieved their end. Lying, cruelty and perjury were his favourite weapons; in a later age they were to be the favourite weapons of a Sforza or a Visconti, and to make the analogy more complete, he had their love of art and their respect for learning. He has been called the first modern man to ascend the throne, but this is not true unless we understand by a modern man "the pure despot who will stop for nothing in the search for power."

This Frederick, whom the Popes were later to describe as the Beast of the Apocalypse, the servant of Satan, the prophet of the Antichrist, began his career under the auspices of Innocent III, and as an instrument of the Church. We have seen already how Rome incited him to oppose Otto of Brunswick, and ho the battle of Bouvines won him the throne of Germany. It now only remained to make sure of the Imperial crown, and in order to obtain this from the Pope he lavished his promises with a liberality that was all the greater inasmuch as he was resolved to honour none of them. He renounced all control over the episcopal elections and all claim to the territories of the Holy See, acknowledged the Kingdom of Sicily to be a fief of the Papacy, pledged himself never to unite it with the Empire, and took an oath to set out on a Crusade in the following year. How could the pacific Honorius III, who had just succeeded Innocent III, hold out against so much goodwill? Frederick was crowned in Rome on November 22nd, 1220.

Thenceforth his long reign was passed almost entirely in Italy. Of Germany he asked only one thing: that it would not give him any trouble. In 1232, by the famous statute *in favorem principum* he renounced the shadow of power that the monarchy had still retained in Germany, granting the princes complete independence under the nominal rule of his sons—Henry, followed by Conrad. This realistic policy shows that he was very well aware that this was the only means of solving the problem. The truth was that Germany had become ungovernable. Any attempt to restore the royal prestige in that country would have meant to condemn himself to an interminable and sterile war against the princes, to revive the conflict of the Guelfs and the Ghibellines, to provoke fresh intervention on the part of France and England, and once more to become subject to the arbitrage of the Pope. The simplest course was to make an end once and for all of an impossible situation, and to throw to the princes the remnants of a power which actually was not worth the trouble of defending it. For that matter, what did Germany mean to Frederick? He did not even know the German language. For him it was merely the path which he must follow in order to obtain the Empire. The basis of his strength was in Sicily. There, thanks to absolutism, he had the financial and military resources necessary for the accomplishment of his designs.

It is always difficult to determine exactly the aims of a policy which has failed. Frederick's first intention would seem to have been to subject the whole of Italy to the despotic administration of Sicily; then, this end having been attained, to seek in his turn, as his father and his grandfather had sought, to restore the Roman Empire. However, as he could not accomplish even the first part of this programme, he barely made a beginning with the second part. His policy was exclusively Italian; it was hardly in any sense Imperial.

Yet it was destined, even more than the policy of his predecessors, to bring him into conflict with the Papacy. The Papacy regarded him as its most constant and most dangerous enemy, and there are historians who see in the conflict between Frederick and Gregory IX and Innocent IV a clash of principles, which won him the honour of having, for the first time, upheld the independence of the temporal power against the pretensions of the Church. But the question is not so simple as it appears at first sight. Personally, if you will, Frederick was a freethinker, but he was the opposite of an anti-clerical. He had no political theories but those of his contemporaries. With them he acknowledged, at all events in words, the divinity of the ecclesiastical institution, the duty of princes to defend it and to persecute heretics, and the obligation which was incumbent upon them of professing the Catholic dogmas. His treatment of the Church was inspired, not by a principle, but solely by his personal interests. Provided the Church did not hinder the realization of his policy he was ready to make it every concession. But this policy was directly contrary to that of the Holy See. In reality, the Popes made war against him for temporal rather than religious reasons. The quarrel between Frederick and the Popes reveals itself, in its essentials, as a quarrel between two Italian powers. It was only towards the end that it became something more comprehensive, impelling Frederick, excommunicated and deposed by Innocent IV, to represent himself as the champion of the cause of the kings as against the pretensions of the Church.

But from the very beginning his position in respect of the Church was extremely unfortunate. In order to justify his claims upon Italy he had to become Emperor, and in order to become Emperor he had to tie his own hands. The promises which he made at his coronation gave the Papacy an advantage over him. By acknowledging that Sicily was a fief of the Holy See he had placed himself in the falsest position. The suzerainty of the Pope over the kingdom of Sicily was incompatible with the absolute power which he himself exercised in that kingdom. He therefore made up his mind that he would simply ignore his engagements. The patience of Honorius III prevented the immediate outbreak of the conflict. But Gregory IX had hardly ascended the throne of St. Peter (1227) when Frederick was called upon to fulfil his obligations, and, first and foremost, to set out on a Crusade. He tried to gain time; he embarked, and then returned. He was immediately excommunicated. He tried to put matters right by complying with the Papal requirements. In July 1228 he set sail for the Holy Land, and concluded a treaty with the Sultan which enabled him to enter Jerusalem without striking a blow, and to stipulate that Christians should be free to visit the tomb of Christ. The Pope remained inexorable. The Papal interdict was placed on all the towns through which he passed, and the prayer which he offered up at the Holy Sepulchre was made to seem a profanation. Not a priest could be found who would consent to crown him King of Jerusalem, and he was reduced to placing the crown on his own head.

However, Gregory IX renewed the alliance between the Papacy and the Lombard cities, and invaded Sicily. Frederick returned to Italy to fight him. Peace was at last concluded on August 28th, 1230. Once more the Emperor accepted the conditions dictated by the Papacy, and guaranteed the completest liberty of the Sicilian Church, which he had subjected to taxation and to the jurisdiction of the State, and at this price he was absolved from the excommunication which had been pronounced upon him three years earlier.

Reconciled with Rome, he directed all his efforts against the

Lombards. The struggle was long and violent. Not until 1238 did fortune at last smile upon Frederick; and he then thought the moment had come to extend the Sicilian administration to Northern Italy, stifling by his despotism the autonomy and the republican spirit of its cities. Puffed up by his success, he believed himself henceforth the master of Italy; he appointed his "vicars" and "captains" throughout the country, made the heiress of Sardinia marry his bastard Enzio, and gave the latter the title of king. Of his promises to the Papacy nothing remained. He had forgotten that Sardinia, like Sicily, was a fief of Rome, and the Sicilian Church was subjected more completely than ever to the secular power. Moreover, as the States of St. Peter were henceforth enclosed between the Imperial possessions in the North and the South, there was a danger that they would become dependent upon the latter. This time Gregory IX acted both as a sovereign and as the head of the Church. Once more excommunication was launched against Frederick (1239), and at the same time his subjects were absolved from their duty of obedience to him. A furious war of pamphlets broke out, the Emperor reproaching the Pope with his perfidy and ingratitude, the Pope accusing the Emperor of perjury and heresy. Frederick appealed to the judgement of the Council, and when the Pope took him at his word and summoned the bishops to Rome, Frederick sent out vassals to attack the ships which were carrying them Romewards, seized them, and kept the prelates in captivity. Death prevented Gregory IX (1241) from taking his revenge, and the long vacancy of the Holy See gave Frederick some respite. But Innocent IV, almost immediately after his election (1243), assembled the Council at Lyons, and having subjected the Emperor's case for examination before the Assembly, he solemnly deposed him and excommunicated his followers.

Of old, the Emperors excommunicated by the Popes used to have the Pope deposed by a German Synod and replaced by an Antipope. But those days were gone and would not return. Now the entire Church was obedient to Rome. Already, in Germany, the Archbishops of Mayence and Cologne had proclaimed the Landgrave of Thuringia king (May 1246). This king, Henry

Raspe, who died a few months later, was succeeded by a second anti-king, who, like him, was a mere instrument of Innocent IV: Count William of Holland (October 1247). All that Frederick could do was to endeavour to persuade the other kings that their cause was one with his. He did his best; while resuming the struggle against the Lombard cities, which had again risen against him, he exhorted the sovereigns to support him, and to refuse, in their own interest, to allow the Pope to dispose at will of the temporal power. His protests aroused no echo; and they could not have been echoed. Whatever he might say, there was nothing in common between his cause and that of the national and hereditary monarchs who were reigning in France and England. These were well aware that the Pope had no hold upon their crowns, and that their dynastic right was not in any way involved in the Hohenstaufen's quarrel. Frederick forgot that the Pope had a twofold advantage over him. As King of Sicily, was he not the vassal of the Holy See? as Emperor, had he not received the crown from the Holy See? It was idle to compare the ceremony of the coronation with that of the anointing of the kings; no one could accept the comparison. For the ceremony of anointing did not make the king, while his coronation did create the Emperor. In short, this Empire, which had fought so long against the Papacy, revealed itself, at the decisive moment, in all its weakness, and incapable of defending the independence of the temporal power whose champion it professed to be. Its religious origin condemned it to remain attached to the Papacy. In claiming autonomy it gave the lie to history and deprived itself of its foundation. The problem could only be solved by a king upon whose crown the Pope could formulate no sort of claim. The man who was destined to solve the problem was not the Emperor but the King of France, and where Frederick II failed, Philip the Fair, fifty years later, succeeded.

The reign of Frederick was a sort of epilogue to the tragedy which began with Gregory VII and ended at Bouvines. Since the reign of Otto of Brunswick the Empire had existed only in name. Frederick's attempt to restore it by means of his Sicilian kingdom could only end in catastrophe. He wore himself out, fighting against all hope, waging war against Lombardy and wasting his troops and finances on a lost cause. On December 13th, 1250, he died, shortly after suffering a bloody defeat by the forces of Parma. His death made no impression in Germany, but it caused a tremendous sensation in Italy. Prophecies relating to the coming of the Antichrist were accepted as referring to Frederick, and more than once it was rumoured that he had returned to earth. It was the echo of these Italian rumours that gave birth, in Germany, to the legend of the Emperor who was sleeping in the mountain of Kyffhäuser, a legend which the popular imagination, deceived by the similarity of the names, was presently to accept as relating to Frederick Barbarossa.

As for the Kingdom of Sicily, the Pope hastened to retrieve it for ever from that "generation of vipers," the Hohenstaufens. He decided to give it to France.

### 3. *Germany*

The Empire was not only fatal to Germany because it imposed upon its kings a universal policy, forcing them to sacrifice the nation to the Church, and finally compelling them to leave their quarry and chase its shadow; it had the further result of allowing the Pope to intervene directly in German affairs. Since the King of Germany, or to speak more exactly, the King of the Romans, was the Emperor designate, Rome, directly she was strong enough to do so, claimed that her approval was indispensable to his election. The Hohenstaufens had clearly recognized this danger, and in order to guard against it they had endeavoured to make their dynasty hereditary. But heredity, the indispensable condition of all monarchical power, of all power based upon the State, since in the Middle Ages the monarchy was the only possible form of the State—heredity, which constituted the strength of the King of England or the King of France, had become impossible in Germany from the beginning of the 12th century. The country was merely an agglomeration of ecclesiastical and secular principalities, incapable of common action, and still more incapable of enduring the government of a central authority. To explain this situation by the accepted fable of Germanic individualism is futile. For there were no territorial principalities among the Scandinavians, nor among the Anglo-Saxons, though these were both Germanic peoples, but they did exist among the French, a Latin people. To the right as to the left of the Rhine, they had their origin in the dissolution of the Carolingian Empire at a time when its economic system was dominated by the great estates; they resulted from the seizure of the royal prerogatives by officials who had become autonomous, thanks to their domainal power. But in France the king also possessed his own domain; like his great vassals, he was rooted in the soil, and from the 10th century onwards he patiently awaited the moment when he should be able to claim from them the prerogatives which were his by virtue of the crown. This moment came in the 12th century, which made him the natural head of the resistance to England, brought him the support of the bourgeoisies, and led him to choose the "capital" city as his residence. And toward this city gravitated the whole activity of the nation, excited and increased by the great economic and social transformation inaugurated by the revival of trade and the ever-increasing circulation of men and of goods. In Germany, on the other hand, the kings were nowhere at home. They remained faithful to the Carolingian custom of wandering about the country. They had their palaces, but no fixed residence. There was nothing in Germany like the Île de France; still less was there anything resembling Paris. And yet, until the end of the 11th century, the personal power of the kings was very great. The gradualness with which the feudal system had developed on the right bank of the Rhine enabled them to dispose of a quantity of estates and counties which in France would have been appropriated long before by the seigneurs. But the economic system did not allow them—why, we have already seen[1]—to retain these reserves and appropriate the profits to their own use. It was still too early to dream of an administrative organization of the monarchy. On the whole, they adopted the best solution possible, by transferring the rights and the domains at their disposal to bishops appointed by them and attached to their service. Hence-

[1] See p. 174 et seq.

forth their power was of necessity bound up with the maintenance of this Imperial Church; and after the War of the Investitures, when this support was withdrawn, their power collapsed. It was then too late to re-establish it on a new basis. The Hohenstaufens have been blamed for not relying on the support of the cities. But those who blame them forget that except along the Rhine the German cities were then only beginning to develop.[1] This is why the cities, in order to escape from the control of the princes, constituted themselves, as in Italy, free republics. Nominally they were dependent on the Emperor; in reality they were so far independent of him that he could not draw upon their resources. He had to choose between them and the princes, and Frederick Barbarossa, like his successor, could not hesitate to choose the princes. Thus, at the moment when in France the king was beginning to impose his power upon his great vassals, in Germany he was becoming subordinate to them. In order to maintain himself on the throne he had to constitute a party among the princes. But as he had to pay for their services by means of all sorts of privileges and concessions, he could keep in power only by exhausting his resources, and even in Barbarossa's time the king was reduced to what was really a policy of expedients. The war between Philip of Swabia and Otto IV finally demolished, if not the authority of the royal power, at least what prestige remained to it. Frederick II, in 1231, merely recognized in law what already existed in fact, in ceding to the princes the last nominal prerogatives of the Crown, by recognizing them officially as the lords of their estates (*domini terrae*), and by renouncing the right to build fortresses on their domains or to appoint judges, or to mint money, or to regulate trade and circulation. Henceforth Germany was merely a federation of individual sovereigns whom the Emperor left to their own devices. It is true that he had left in his place his son Henry, a child who was elected King of the Romans in 1222, and who, having grown up under the tutelage of Archbishop Engelbert of Cologne, rebelled against his father, who left him to die in prison; and after him his other son, Conrad IV, who was nine years of age when

[1] I do not include the cities of the Baltic, which hardly belonged to them.

in 1237 the princes accorded him the royal title! But neither the Emperor nor the princes could or did believe that such regents could exert any real influence. Moreover, after the excommunication and deposition of Frederick, Innocent IV, resolved to make a clean sweep of the Hohenstaufen dynasty, ordered a new election. No one, apart from a few cities in Swabia, supported Conrad's interests, and the crown, as we have already seen, was given first to Henry Raspon, Landgrave of Thuringia, and then to Count William of Holland. As a matter of fact, the princes took little interest in these elections, which were essentially the work of the Archbishops of Cologne. Henry and William merely served to confirm the victory of the Pope. Henry died a few months after his election: William, as a Dutchman almost a foreigner to the Germans, hardly showed himself except in the valley of the Rhine. His County of Holland meant more to him than his kingdom, and almost the only profit that he derived from his title, which he owed to the protection of Rome, was to assert, to the detriment of the Counts of Flanders, the claim of his house to Zeeland. It was again his Dutch policy that induced him to undertake an expedition against the Frisians, in the course of which he was killed, on January 28th, 1258, in the battle of Hoogwoude. When he was dead, Alfonso X, King of Castile, whose mother Beatrice was the daughter of Philip of Swabia, made this Hohenstaufen connection a pretext for claiming the crown of Germany, through which he hoped to obtain that of Sicily. But Sicily excited the covetousness of the King of England also, the old ally of the Guelfs, who had hopes of obtaining the crown for his son Edmund. In order to obtain support for him, he incited his brother, Richard Earl of Cornwall, to obtain the succession to Count William of Holland. In order to obtain it, the two rivals relied only on their treasury, and like Charles V and Francis I three hundred years later, they bid against each other for the dignity of the King of the Romans. The national ideal was so completely alien to the German princes, and the monarchy seemed to them of such secondary importance, that their one thought was to sell it on the most favourable terms. Some allowed themselves to be bought by Alfonso of Castile, others by Richard of Cornwall, and in 1257 both princes received the crown, as though it had been a parcel of merchandise. Seven princes had taken part in this double election. This was the origin of the College of Electors, which henceforth exercised the right of electing the king of the Romans!

The bargain concluded by Alfonso and Richard could not hold good unless the Pope interested himself in the matter. But it was enough for Rome that she had extirpated the Hohenstaufens; she allowed the two rivals to overwhelm her with their solicitations without intervening on either side. Under these conditions, it seemed to Alfonso that he might as well stay where he was, and Germany never saw him. Richard spent some time on the banks of the Rhine, had himself crowned at Aix-la-Chapelle, signed a few State documents, and was then recalled to England by the disturbances which occurred during the reign of Henry III; he never went back to Germany, and in 1272 he died. The electors were in no hurry to replace him. For that matter, Alfonso was still living. But the Pope would not hear of his claim, as he had no wish to quarrel with the new King of Sicily, Charles of Anjou.[1] On the other hand, he made haste to dispose of Charles's intervention in favour of the candidature of his nephew, the King of France, Philip the Bold, whose nomination would have reconstituted the Empire of Charlemagne for the benefit of the Capetian dynasty. He gave the electors to understand that they had better make haste if they did not wish him to create a new king himself. They complied, and in 1273 they gave the crown to Rudolf of Habsburg, whose talents, as mediocre as his fortune, were not such as to cause them any disquietude. The period of the "great interregnum" which had begun with the nomination of Henry Raspe was at last ended.

Engrossed in their duel with England, the kings of France did not attempt to take advantage of the increasing weakness of Germany in order to reopen the Lotharingian question which had so preoccupied their Carolingian predecessors in the 10th century. Philip Augustus, Louis VIII, and St. Louis actually maintained the

[1] See p. 341 et. seq.

most cordial relations with the Hohenstaufens, who naturally inclined, in consequence of the Guelf alliance with England, to take the side of France. However, it was impossible that the decline of the German monarchy should leave the question of the western frontier unaffected. Drawn by the Treaty of Verdun, in an age of purely agricultural civilization, it had divided the territories affected as one divides a domain, the chief object of the division being to assure each of the sons of Louis the Pious of an equal share, without any regard for the populations or the geographical situation. In the Europe of the 13th century, awakened to new life by the circulation of trade and the new social relations which were the consequence of that trade, the old frontier was merely an archaism, which the respect for the status quo could not preserve indefinitely. The cities which had sprung up in the basins of the Meuse and the Scheldt were naturally looking westwards, attracted by those two great economic centres, the fairs of Champagne and the ports of Flanders. Under their influence, those populations whose language was Romanic—the populations of Lorraine, Luxembourg, Liége and Hainaut, as well as the Germanic populations of Holland and Brabant—were insensibly detaching themselves from Germany, which, being more and more subdivided, did nothing and could do nothing to retain them. The feudal tie which bound the princes of the frontier to the Empire was growing weaker and weaker. Towards the end of the 13th century the Dukes of Lorraine and Brabant, and the Counts of Luxembourg, Hainaut, and Holland, had become almost completely alienated from the Empire. Even under Frederick Barbarossa, the Hohenstaufens' agent in the Low Countries, Count Baldwin V of Hainaut, had regarded himself as independent, and considered that he had acquitted himself of his duty to the Emperor by declaring himself neutral in respect of France and Germany. The kingdom of Burgundy, acquired by Conrad II, in 1033, detached itself still more rapidly from the Imperial bloc. Stretched out along the Saône and the Rhone, and inhabited by a people who spoke a Romanic language, everything attracted it toward the Mediterranean, or toward France. The kings of Germany, to whom its last possessor had bequeathed it at a period when it was regarded merely as so much territory, had never been other than foreigners in Burgundy, and had never made any attempt to strike root there. Marseilles and Lyons had never felt that they belonged to the Empire, nor did the Counts of Provence, Dauphiné and Franche Comté ever trouble their heads about the nominal suzerainty which it exercised over them. Thus, the old frontier, drawn on the map at a period of economic stagnation, was erased, so to speak, by the friction of a more intensive civilization and more complex interests. No one attempted to rectify it, people were content simply to ignore it, and as the Imperial power declined the outlines of the Empire became more vague and undefined.

The kings of France could not and did not fail to take advantage of a situation which they had not created, but which increasingly demanded their attention. As the princes of the frontier forgot the Emperor they turned toward the kings of France, seeking to obtain their support or appealing to their arbitrage. Many of them received fiefs or pensions from the Crown. In the Low Countries, where the territorial constitutions were robust, and the principalities compact, the influence of France was purely political. But it was otherwise along the border of Lorraine and in the valley of the Rhone. Here the dovetailing of territories, the confusion of rights and prerogatives, and the great number of seigneurs who possessed land both in France and in the Empire, gave rise to incessant disputes, of which the kings took advantage by extending the influence of their bailiffs on the other side of the frontier. With the consent of the interested parties they thus increased their own influence, by successive advances, by gradual and amost imperceptible efforts, over this intermediate zone, so that presently their power had actually replaced that of the Emperor.

While in the West Germany was gradually crumbling under the influence of a civilization superior to her own, in the East she was expanding largely at the cost of the Barbarians. The conquest of the Slav regions on the banks of the Elbe, which had been begun by Otto I, but was abandoned after his death, was resumed, and had made rapid strides since the middle of the 12th century. It seems at first sight strange that German colonization should have made such progress, advancing further and further as the power of the Emperors declined in the interior of the country. The fact is that this great effort of expansion, which was afterwards to exert so essential an influence over the destinies of the German people, owed nothing to the Emperors. It was accomplished without their participation, and without the manifestation of the slightest interest on their part. While Frederick Barbarossa was uselessly wasting his strength in Italy, the princes on the banks of the Lower Elbe, and above all Henry the Lion, and the Margrave of Brandenburg, Albert the Bear (1170), energetically furthered the Germanization of the Wendish lands along the Baltic shore. There was no question here of a purely political conquest, but rather of a veritable work of colonization, thanks to which, by a refluent movement, the Germans took the place of the Slavs in the countries which they had abandoned at the time of the great invasions of the 4th century. Its success would have been impossible without the economic transformations which we have already indicated: the increase of the population in the course of the 12th century, the abandonment of the domainal system, the appearance of a class of free peasants, and lastly, the formation of the bourgeoisies. Thanks to these changes the physical and moral conditions indispensable to the peopling of the new country were both present: a surplus population and the spirit of enterprise. As the raids of the Duke of Saxony's and the Margrave of Brandenburg's knights drove back the Slavs and massacred them, the colonists, under the direction of contractors (*locatores*), took possession of the regions thus cleared. They came from Franconia, Thuringia, Saxony, the banks of the Rhine, and even Flanders and Holland, the Dutch being especially useful on account of their skill and experience in the operations of draining and embanking. Each colonist received, on the payment of a modest quit-rent, sufficient land for a single holding (*Hufe*), and he could easily recruit the necessary workers from among the Slavs who had escaped massacre. Cistercian monks founded their monasteries among the new villages and furnished the clergy for the parish churches. Before the end of the 12th century the wave of colonization had already reached the banks of the Oder. Along the rivers the cities were founded which furnished the peasants with the necessary supplies and served as markets for the surrounding countryside: Brandenburg, Stendal, Spandau, Tangermunde, Berlin, and Frankfort-on-the-Oder.

The Slav States to the east and the south—Poland and Bohemia—sought before long to attract these Germans, who brought from beyond the Elbe the methods of Western agriculture and the knowledge of various urban trades. The Polish dukes of Silesia (Piastes) did their utmost to induce the Germans to settle in and around Breslau. The King of Bohemia, Wenceslas I (1230–1253), and his successor Ottocar II offered these pioneers still more favourable conditions. German villages were scattered amidst the Czech villages, and German towns—Kuttenberg, Deutchbrod, Iglau—were called into being by the mining or weaving industries: burgesses and peasants retaining intact their language, their customs, and their law, in the midst of the native population, thereby bequeathing formidable problems to the future. The Germanic colonists even made their way into Hungary, where they settled in Transylvania under the protection of the king, who in 1224 conferred important privileges on them.

This expansion makes one think involuntarily of the invasions of the Roman Empire in the 5th century. In each case there was the same surging forward of a people seeking fresh means of subsistence outside their own country. But while the Germans of the 5th century were rapidly absorbed by the Romanic population, whose customs and language they adopted, those of the 12th century imposed their own nationality by violence on the Slavs, or retained it where they settled in their midst. To explain this contrast, it is not enough to invoke the inferiority of the Germanic civilization in the 5th century as compared with the Romanic civilization, and its superiority in the 12th century as compared with the Slav civilization. The Normans who invaded England in the 11th century were far more civilized than the Anglo-Saxons, yet in the long run they became intimately mingled with them, and the mixture constituted a new people. It was the same with the Swedes who in the 9th century seized the government of Russia. Nothing of the sort was observed beyond the Elbe. Even to this day the difference between the descendants of the emigrants of the 12th century and the Slav populations in whose lands they settled is as great and as clearly marked as it was at the time of the invasion. It would be puerile to suggest that this phenomenon is explained by "race," since it is a matter of everyday experience that the Germans very readily become denationalized in an alien environment. The explanation of their persistence in Bohemia, Poland, and Hungary must be sought, first of all, in the fact that they settled in compact groups, unlike the Normans in England, who were dispersed amidst the Anglo-Saxon population; but undoubtedly the principal explanation is the fact that among the Slavs they were the initiators, and for long centuries *par excellence* the representatives of the urban life. The Germans introduced the bourgeoisie into the midst of these agricultural populations, and the contrast between them was, perhaps, from the very first, that of social classes rather than national groups. Thanks to the Germanic peasants of the surrounding districts, the German towns were always able to recruit their populations by an influx of compatriots, while the influence which they brought to bear upon these peasants prevented their absorption by the Slav population.

While the Germanic expansion in Slav countries was explained, in the first place, by economic factors, it was not long before religious motives played their part in this expansion, and very notably accelerated its progress. The paganism which had disappeared before the advance of the German colonists between the Elbe and the Oder still persisted throughout the plain that extends from the shores of the Baltic between the Elbe and the Niemen. Its inhabitants, the Prussians, a people of Slavic origin, resisted the attempts at their conversion made at the end of the 10th century by St. Adalbert, Bishop of Prague, and later by the Cistercian monks of Poland. At the beginning of the 13th century the Polish Duke of Mazovia summoned the knights of the Teutonic Order to undertake the conversion of these obstinate heathen. Founded at Saint-Jean d'Acre in 1198 among the Friars Hospitallers of German nationality, this order had been invited, twenty years earlier, by King Andrew II of Hungary, to fight the hordes of pagan Kumans who were invading his eastern frontiers. But before long disputes arose between the Hungarians and the knights, and the appeal of the Polish Duke of Mazovia offered them an opportunity of displaying their zeal for the faith in a more favourable field of action. The poor Prussians, with their bows and their wicker shields, could not resist the heavily-armed knights who came to conquer with the sword a new land for Catholicism, but not a new people. For there was no question of converting the Prussians. They were treated as the enemies of Christ and the Pope, though they knew nothing of either. Since the Crusades evangelization had been replaced by the Holy War. And this Holy War was a war of extermination. It ended only in 1283, when there were no more pagans to massacre. As the Teutonic knights advanced they organized the country. Fortresses, of which a curious specimen may be seen at Marienburg, not far from Danzig, marked the stages of the conquest. German colonists come to occupy the surrounding country, and there too, as between the Elbe and the Oder, Germanization was the consequence of war. Nothing was left of the Prussians but the name, which was now borne by the invaders. The knights retained the lordship of the country, which they received as a fief from Pope Gregory IX in 1234.

While the Germans were thus colonizing the great plain to the south of the Baltic, they were also swarming along the shores of this sea, which had hitherto been navigated only by the Scandinavians. Here the movement started from Lübeck, a Slav village destroyed by Henry the Lion, and then repeopled by emigrants from the adjacent German districts. The new settlement was admirably situated. The proximity of Hamburg destined it to become the intermediary between the trade of the North Sea and that of the Baltic, and its development was surprisingly rapid. From 1163 Visby, on the island of Gothland, became a sort of factory, in constant communication with Lubeck, and from this point the German ships very soon began to sail for the eastern shores of the Baltic. The mouth of the Duna, which offered an excellent means of communication with the Russian regions of the interior, was constantly frequented by the German ships. And here trade cleared the way for Christianity. In 1201 a bishopric was established at Riga, and there Bishop Albert of Bienne created the Order of the Brothers of the Sword, whose mission was to fight the pagans of Livonia and Esthonia. A few years later the German merchants were trading with Novgorod. However, in the north Dorpat, captured from the Russians by the Brothers of the Sword, became, like Riga, the seat of a bishopric.

The German preponderance in the Baltic was first menaced by the kings of Denmark. The War of Investitures had enabled the latter to shake off the yoke to which they had been subjected since the reign of Otto I. In 1104 the Pope had detached their country from the diocese of Bremen, and Lund had been created the religious metropolis of the Northern kingdoms. When war broke out between the Hohenstaufens and the Guelfs the Danes naturally sided with the latter. Waldemar, under whose reign a beginning was made with the development of the port of Copenhagen, was the ally of Henry the Lion, whose daughter married his son Canute VI (1182–1202). He took part in Henry's expeditions against the Wends, and conquered the island of Rügen. Canute refused to swear the oath of fealty to Frederick Barbarossa, and imposed his rule upon Pomerania, Mecklenburg, and even Lübeck and Hamburg. Waldemar II (1202–1241) increased his brother's conquests by the addition of Schwerin, and subjected Norway to tribute. Presently his fleet appeared in the Eastern Baltic. In 1219 he landed in Esthonia, and after a great victory over the Esthonians (the victory mentioned in the legend of the Danebrog), he founded the city of Reval. About the same time he seized the island of Oesel (1221) and threatened Riga. But this expansion was purely political, and it included territories which were already largely colonized by the Germans. When Waldemar fell unexpectedly into the hands of the Count of Schwerin (1223), a general revolt broke out against him. Four years later he made a vain attempt to recover his position. The defeat which he suffered at Bornhöved (July 22nd, 1227) decided the future, and made the Germans for a long time the masters of the Baltic.

The trade of the Baltic, a sea surrounded by new and sparsely populated countries, could be developed only by the export of corn from the North of Germany and Russian furs to the Western countries, in return for wines, spices, and costly fabrics. Bruges, which was the terminus of the great trade route between Flanders and Italy, had long been the objective of the German navigators of the North Sea. The navigators of the Baltic made for the same destination, and the community of their interests resulted in an immediate rapprochement. These economic relations were the origin of the Hansa: that is to say, the confederation not of the merchants alone, but of the cities of which they were burgesses, from Riga to Cologne. In the end it even included a few inland cities, such as Breslau and Münster. Lübeck, in the middle of the long stretch of coast extending from the Scheldt to the Duna, became the headquarters of the Hansa as early as the middle of the 13th century. The commercial interest of all the members of the League were sufficiently homogeneous to ensure the maintenance of a good understanding between them, apart from local and ephemeral differences. Thanks to the Hansa, German navigation retained its preponderance in the two northern seas until the middle of the 15th century.

The gist of these last few pages may be expressed by saying that since the close of the 12th century Germany had been playing a more and more insignificant part in European politics, and had been occupying a larger and larger area on the map of Europe. Assisted by a number of enterprises aiming at conquest and religious propaganda, the Germanic colonization extended from the Lower Elbe to the Niemen, and interposed itself between the sea and the Slav States of the interior, Poland and Russia, thus preparing the way for the conflicts and the wars which, from the 14th century onwards, did not cease periodically to disturb the peace of Eastern Europe. The absence of natural frontiers in these regions, where only the difference of language divided people from people, predestined them to become the theatre of a struggle which was bound of necessity to assume the character of a national conflict, in the most brutal—that is to say, the ethnograpical—sense of the word. Where the contours of the soil divide the States into distinct areas, and where Nature herself, so to speak, has traced the frontiers of the different countries, wars are purely political, and conquest does not involve the enslavement of the vanquished. The various foreign governments to which the Italian people was subjected from the 10th to the 19th century did not in any way change its essential nature. But it was otherwise in these vaguely delimited plains where there was nothing to protect a people against the aggression of its neighbours. In these regions, consequently, war assumed the character of a war of extermination. The conqueror did not feel that he was safe until he had dismembered the enemy State, extirpated its institutions, and destroyed its language and religion, in order to replace them by his own. Such was the treatment which the German colonists of the 12th century meted out to the Slavs of Pomerania and Prussia; it was thus that the Hohenzollerns treated Poland at a later date, and Russia the Germans of the Baltic provinces. Under such conditions of life men became hard and callous; energy and the spirit of discipline and of organization were predominant because they were indispensable; might appeared the supreme right and the only basis of the law. And such conditions existed from the first in the new Germany which extended eastward from the Elbe. In respect of intellectual culture these colonial regions were far in arrears of the Germany of the West and the South. It is hardly possible to cite the name of a single scholar or poet or artist previous to the 18th century. They have no energy to spare for anything but work and warfare. In the Margraves of Brandenburg and the Teutonic Knights of the 13th century, in the petty nobles who employed the knights and fought for them, were emerging the first characteristics of what was one day to be known as the Prussian spirit.

## CHAPTER III

# FRANCE

### 1. *France and European Politics*

By defeating at Bouvines the coalition which had been formed against it the French monarchy had given proof of its military strength, and with that it won its place at the head of the European powers. From Germany, where its victory had given the crown to Frederick II, it had nothing more to fear. It profited by the situation and proceeded to attack England. The circumstances could not have been more favourable. The English barons, in rebellion against John Lackland, called upon the son of Philip Augustus to defend the Great Charter and offered him the crown. For a moment the future King of France was King of England. But the death of John (1216), which, fortunately for his son, Henry III, aroused the sentiment of nationalism and the spirit of feudal loyalty, disposed of the possibility of a dynastic union which certainly could not have lasted. Louis returned to France, and seven years later, in 1223, he succeeded his father as Louis VIII.

Philip Augustus, on ascending the throne, was still the immediate ruler only of the ancient royal domain, a little enlarged by Louis VI and Louis VII, but still without outlets to the sea, and threatened on the west and the north by the alliance of the Count of Flanders and the King of England. On his death he left his son in possession of Brittany, Poitou, and Normandy, and assured of the obedience of the Count of Flanders, who was reduced to the rôle of a protégé of the Crown. There was no longer any prince in the kingdom who was in a position to oppose him successfully. However, the Midi was still independent of the monarchical power. In respect of the County of Toulouse, Louis VIII was in almost the same situation as Clovis had been, eight hundred years earlier, in respect of the kingdom of the Visigoths. As with Clovis, it was a religious motive that furnished him with the opportunity of intervening. Clovis in the 5th century attacked the Visigoths on the pretext that they were Arians; Louis VIII was impelled to annexe the County of Toulouse on account of the heresy of the Albigenses. In both cases the religious motive merely served to hasten what was inevitable. In the interests of the geographical unity of France its political unity was indispensable. The North and the South were not opposed to each other; on the contrary, each was merged into the other. Add to this the attraction of the Mediterranean, the highway *par excellence* of maritime trade, the sea-road to the East. It had been this under Clovis; and had become it again at the beginning of the 13th century. From Paris, the kings of France were bound to make for it, as the kings of the Franks had done. Moreover, their suzerainty extended to the Pyrenees. At the beginning of the 13th century there was perhaps no region in Europe so radiant with life as Languedoc. Thanks to the Mediterranean trade, its cities were numerous and prosperous. Like Genoa and Pisa, Marseilles and Montpellier despatched their vessels to the ports of Egypt and Syria. Like Siena and Florence, Cahors was engaged in the silver trade, and the fame of her bankers extended even to the Low Countries. The importance of Toulouse, in the plain of the Garonne, was analogous to that of Milan in Lombardy. However, the French cities of the Midi, unlike the Italian, were not autonomous republics. As in the North, they acknowledged the overlordship of the territorial principalities which had been constituted since the dismemberment of the Carolingian Empire, the most important of which was the County of Toulouse. The situation of the Counts of Toulouse, in the south of the kingdom, was very like that of the Counts of Flanders at the opposite extremity. Rich and powerful like the latter, they took advantage, like them, of their excentric position, behaving, as far as the king was concerned, with almost absolute independence. Lastly, just as a certain proportion of the subjects of the Counts of Flanders spoke "Thiois," the subjects of the Counts of Toulouse spoke Provencal, and this linguistic individuality helped to emphasize the political individuality which distinguished the County of Toulouse from the rest of France; the more so as the Provençal literature of the 12th century was greatly superior to that of the north of France. Its songs of love and war (*sirventes*) were greatly appreciated by the nobles of the Midi, and they made their way into Italy, and even into the north of France, thanks to an infatuation analogous to that which in the 16th and 17th centuries set all the *beaux esprits* reading the Italian, and then the Spanish writers. Richard Cœur de Lion, Frederick II, and Henry II, Duke of Brabant, composed poems in the Provençal language, whose literary development was in advance of that of all the other Romanic languages. This alone is enough to show that the intellectual activity of the Midi was in no way inferior to its economic activity. Indeed, this intellectual activity was so potent that while it inspired the poets it also provoked a formidable religious crisis.

At the end of the 12th century Languedoc was swarming with those mystics who aspired to lead the Church and the age back to apostolic simplicity, condemning both the religious hierarchy and the social order[1] as manifestations of the love of evil—that is, of the flesh—for which they wished to substitute the reign of the spirit. These "Cathars" were especially numerous in the County of Albi, dependent on that of Toulouse, whence their name of Albigenses. Their propaganda had won them adherents not only among the people of the cities, but also among the wealthy merchants, and even in the ranks of the nobility. Despite the objurgations of the clergy and the remonstrances of the Pope, Raymond VI, Count of Toulouse, who was the great-grandson of the hero of the First Crusade, treated the heretics with a tolerance that drew suspicion upon himself. In 1208 Innocent III had him excommunicated by a legate, Pierre de Castelnau, when a knight in the Count's service, beside himself with fury, felled the prelate with a blow of his lance. This was too much for the Pope; he banished from the communion of the faithful a prince and a country guilty of outraging the majesty of Rome and the Catholic faith. From the

[1] See p. 296 et seq.

north of France, under the leadership of Simon de Montfort, companies of knights hastened southwards, equally inspired by their hatred of the heretics and their hope of booty. The war was merciless and atrocious. Béziers and Carcassonne were sacked. King Pedro II of Aragon, having come to the aid of Raymond VI, his kinsman, fell in battle, as did Simon de Montfort in 1218. Simon bequeathed to his son Amaury the territory which he had conquered from the Count of Toulouse. However, Raymond VI was succeeded by his son Raymond VII, and Amaury appealed for assistance to the King of France. Louis VIII, who as prince royal had taken part in the crusade against the Albigenses, now appeared in Languedoc as sovereign arbiter, at the head of an army. Amaury ceded his rights to him; Raymond VII did not dare to resist. The Midi in its turn submitted to the Crown. However, Louis VIII had no time to complete the process of absorption: on November 8th, 1226, in the course of the campaign, death unexpectedly closed his career.

A child of eleven succeeded to the throne. A long regency was in prospect. The deceased king had appointed as regent Queen Blanche of Castile, who thus assumed a rôle that no Queen of France would play again before the advent of Catherine de Medicis.

It was natural that the great vassals should take advantage of this opportunity and seek to recover the ground which they had lost since the advent of Philip Augustus. But nothing is more eloquent of the consolidation of the monarchical power than the suppression of their rebellion, despite the support of the King of England, Henry III. The social order had been transformed. At the time of the dissolution of the Carolingian Empire, when the civilization was still agricultural, and the revival of trade was a thing of the future, it had favoured the princes, and had procured for them the acquiescence of the population, since the princes alone were capable of preserving the public order, which the kings could no longer maintain. To-day, in a society liberated from the domainal system, traversed by the merchants, and transformed by the novel needs of the bourgeoisies, the small local parties naturally tended to group themselves under the powerful tutelage of the Crown, and to detach themselves from the princes, whose pretensions no longer corresponded with the needs of the age. However, the opposition of the princes was neither general nor very vigorous. Like that of all the reactionary parties, it was lacking in enthusiasm and confidence, because it was inspired only by personal interests. It quieted down as soon as the princes realized that success was impossible. Raymond of Toulouse, who naturally took part in the revolt, lost the half of his territory that still remained to him, and was obliged to betroth his heiress to the brother of the king, Alphonse de Poitiers, who in 1249, on the death of his father-in-law, inherited the county.

The reign of St. Louis (Louis IX, 1226–1270) began, like that of Louis XIV, amidst the turmoil of a tumultuous regency. It also resembled the latter reign in respect of the glory that it won for France—but in no other particular. For the rest, the contrast between the two policies was as striking as that between the characters of the two princes, each of whom has remained, for posterity, the very incarnation of his epoch. The absolute State of the 17th century found its classic representative in Louis XIV, just as the Christian State of the Middle Ages found its representative in St. Louis. Religious minds will always prefer this gentle figure, so simple and pious that he almost makes one think of a crowned St. Francis of Assisi—and yet he was a great king—to the great and domineering Popes of his time. The Christian ideal of peace, justice and charity was far more completely realized during the reign of St. Louis than during the pontificate of Innocent III or Innocent IV. But we must realize that this flower of mediaeval royalty could not have unfolded its full beauty save for a fortunate conjunction of circumstances. It was a piece of good fortune for St. Louis that he did not ascend the throne until after the Crusade of the Albigenses, so that he never had to soil his hands with the massacres of this bloody enterprise, into which the ardour of his faith would doubtless have drawn him. It was another and even greater piece of good fortune that he had inherited from his father and his grandfather a kingdom which was both powerful and respected. Imagine if he had been born in the 12th century, and had been obliged to fight his vassals, and to wage a difficult war on the frontier of Normandy against the King of England! History might have remembered him as a Louis the Pious, but nothing more, for he was neither a great politician nor a great warrior. He was merely a good man, and the virtues which he could not have displayed if he had been forced to fight for power were able to unfold themselves at ease, thanks to his possession of the power which made possible the accomplishment of his ideal. He had the good fortune to reign over a kingdom which contained no heretics and no enemies, and it was reserved for him to ennoble and consolidate and complete in peace what his predecessors had achieved with the sword.

In the interior of the country the royal authority made itself felt without difficulty, and there were no obstacles to its growth, because each step in advance was accompanied by a benefit to the country. Hitherto the monarchical administration had served, more than anything else, to safeguard the rights of the Crown, to favour its jurisdiction, and to develop and systematize its finances. Under the new reign it was employed to safeguard public order and to improve the condition of the people. The practical Christianity which inspires the ordinances of St. Louis reminds us of the capitularies of Charlemagne. Even the institution of the *missi dominici* had its counterpart in that of the royal commissioners whose duty it was to check the activities of the bailiffs and to see that they did not oppress the persons under their jurisdiction. Charlemagne, as we have seen, could realize his intentions only very imperfectly, as the executive means were lacking. St. Louis, on the contrary, possessed in the Parlement and the functionaries created by Philip Augustus the necessary personnel for the accomplishment of his designs. Private wars were abolished, personal serfdom was suppressed on the royal domains, the judicial system was completed by the organization of an instance of appeal, and taxation was rendered more equitable. The Parlement exercised its control over the provincial courts of law, and its activities contributed to the unification of the law and the suppression of such superannuated usages as trial by battle and the ordeal. A Chamber of Accounts, by systematizing the finances, helped to make things easier for the taxpayers. For the first time the people felt that the government was not merely a machine designed to oppress them, an instrument of exaction; for the first time the official seemed not a master but a protector; for the first time the people realized that the power of the Crown was allied with justice, that the king watched over them from afar and had compassion on their misfortunes. The monarchy was becoming popular; it was striking root in the provinces, rallying public opinion, and showing itself to be necessary, indispensable, because beneficent. It really seems that the form of national sentiment which finds expression in the cult of the monarchy dates, in France, from St. Louis. The kingdom became a mother-country, whose inhabitants were bound together by their common love of the king. This love was to find its incomparable expression, two hundred years later, in Joan of Arc. But it was St. Louis who first inspired this love in the French, an affection so indelible that it was transferred to all his successors.

The peace and justice that he wished to prevail among his subjects were also the constant criteria of his foreign policy. He might have attempted, with the greatest possibility of success, to wrest from the King of England the last remnant of his continental possessions, or he could have deprived the King of Aragon of the fiefs which he held in Languedoc. Despite the advice of his counsellors, he offered to make friendly arrangements with both princes. By the Treaty of Abbeville (1259) he agreed to acknowledge Henry III's rights in Perigord and Limousin, provided he abandoned his claim to Normandy, Anjou, Touraine, Maine and Poitou, which had been added to the Crown by Philip Augustus. By the Treaty of Corbeil he obtained from Jaime II of Aragon his Languedocien territories in return for the cession of the French suzerainty over Catalonia (1258).[1] During the furious conflict between the Pope and Frederick II he never departed from his attitude of neutrality, and this, in so obedient a son of the Church, may be taken as a discreet condemnation of the violence of Innocent IV. The confidence inspired by his equitable behaviour won for him, in the outer world, a political prestige which was all the more substantial

[1] On the north of the Pyrenees, Aragon retained only the County of Roussillon and Montpellier.

in that he had not sought it. In the Low Countries the d'Avesnes and the Dampierres appealed to him as arbiter in their long quarrel, while in England Henry III and the rebellious barons submitted their differences to him.

But for him, as for the great scholastic philosophers of his time, while a war between Christians was always a misfortune and often a crime, war against the infidel was an obligation. His faith was so ardent and his sincerity so complete that he was bound to regard the reconquest of the Holy Sepulchre as the foremost of his duties. The calculating and interested spirit which was withdrawing more and more of his contemporaries from the Crusade had no meaning for this idealist. For him, as for the Popes, the Crusade still constituted the honour and the essential business of Christendom. In vain did those about him remind him of the dangers of the enterprise, its cost, its uselessness, and its almost certain failure; their arguments were powerless to convince a king who valued his crown mainly because of the obligations toward God—that is, toward the Church—which it imposed upon him. The more prosperous and peaceful his kingdom, the more ardently he longed to depart. The enthusiasm of the first Crusaders was born again in this prince, who wrote the final chapter of the history of the Crusades. But were the two expeditions which he undertook against Islam—the first in 1248, the second in 1270—really Crusades? Yes, if we consider their aim, but not if we consider their composition. Christendom as a whole paid absolutely no attention to them. They were both purely French undertakings, in which the chivalry of France followed the king rather in a spirit of personal devotion and loyalty and love of adventure than in a spirit of religious enthusiasm. Both expeditions were complete failures. It was only after six years of effort (1248–1254), after a long and persistent siege of Damietta, after falling into the hands of the Turks, after seeing his best beloved companions die, and sorrowfully enduring the reproaches of the others, that the king at last resigned himself to returning to France. He would doubtless have shown the same constancy in the second expedition (1270), but he had hardly disembarked at Tunis when sickness procured for him the death of which he had always dreamed: he died, as he had wished, while battling for the Faith. His death put an end to an undertaking upon which no one but himself had entered in sincerity of spirit. It was for the sake of his brother, the new King of Sicily, Charles of Anjou, who laid claim to the suzerainty of Tunis, that St. Louis had made for this city before setting sail for Egypt. Without suspecting it, the pious monarch had been a tool of the realistic and predatory policy which his reign had for a time interrupted.

The problem of Sicily, which was at the bottom of the war between the Pope and Frederick II, had not been solved by the death of the Emperor. After the premature death of his son Conrad IV his bastard Manfred, instead of administering the country in the name of Conrad's heir (known to history by the name of Conradino, which the Italians gave him), seized the crown for himself (1258). Alexander IV, who had just succeeded to Innocent IV, had first of all acceded to the proposals of the King of England, and had bestowed the Kingdom of Sicily upon the king's son, Edmund, a child who could and did accomplish nothing. It was necessary to solve the problem once and for all, and to choose some powerful prince, upon whom Rome could rely, to restore Sicily once and for all to her proper place under the suzerainty of the Holy See. France alone could provide such a prince. St. Louis having refused the crown on behalf of his younger son, Urban IV entered into negotiations with the king's youngest brother, Charles of Anjou, whose marriage in 1246 had made him Count of Provence. Charles, who was ambitious, had long paid close attention to Italian affairs, and the Guelfs of Italy regarded him as their protector and their future leader. In 1266 he received the crown of Sicily, in Rome, from the hands of Clement IV, and set out to take possession of his kingdom, at the head of a numerous and brilliant retinue of knights, excited by the lure of Sicilian wealth. The French arms brilliantly justified the reputation which they had acquired since the battle of Bouvines. The battle of Benevento (February 1266) destroyed Manfred's army, and Manfred himself was slain. Thirty months later (August 1268) the army which

Conradino had brought from Germany was likewise destroyed at Tagliacozzo. The young prince contrived to escape, was recaptured, delivered to the conqueror, sentenced to death for the crime of lèse-majesté, and executed. The Hohenstaufen dynasty, that "generation of vipers," as Innocent IV had called it, was annihilated. The Pope would not allow Conradino, whom he had excommunicated, to be buried in consecrated ground. Some time later the Archbishop of Cosenza had the body of Manfred removed from the tomb which the French knights had raised above it in homage to his courage, and ordered that it should be buried by the banks of the Verde. His wife died in prison. This rancour on the part of the victorious Curia is enough to explain poor Conradino's fate. The romantics of the 19th century deplored his death, regarding him as a victim of France, the hereditary enemy of Germany, and their indignation was naturally utilized for the purpose of nourishing the national hatred which the adroit politician so skilfully exploits. Nothing could be more completely misleading than these retrospective hatreds. The Franco-German hostility which has been so carefully cherished in our own time is of quite recent date, and it would be impossible to discover any trace of it in the 13th century. Conradino was sacrificed merely for reasons of State, and the person responsible for his death, after the Pope and Charles of Anjou, was Frederick II himself. For Frederick II was the first to pursue to its final consequences and to apply without mercy to his adversaries the principle that no law can be superior to the interests of the prince. Did not Roman law justify this theory, which harmonized so admirably with his own unscrupulous nature? Conradino's judges were merely his disciples; there would be others later—the Italian tyrants.

Charles of Anjou's policy might be defined by describing it as that of the last Hohenstaufen's, with the difference that the Papacy supported instead of opposing it. Like Henry VI and Frederick II, Charles maintained and even increased the absolutism of the Crown in Sicily; like them, he endeavoured to subject the whole of Italy to his control; and like them, he dreamed of extending his power to the Orient. Rome became alarmed by the progress of this ally in whom she had hoped to find a tool, and who was now imposing his will upon her and involving her in his policies. But in order to escape his control she would have to find a rival to oppose him, who would of necessity obtain support from the Ghibellines and the malcontents of Sicily, who were recruited from among the partisans of the hateful Hohenstaufens. Moreover, troublesome though he might be, Charles was a zealous son of the Church; he had restored the privileges of the Sicilian clergy, and his designs upon Constantinople, now that the Latin Empire had at last disappeared (1261) and the Palaeologi had restored the schism, might serve to re-establish the union and the obedience which were among the essential objectives of the Papal policy. The Emperor Michael was not unaware of the dangers that threatened him. He secretly fomented in Sicily the unrest which the high-handed behaviour and arrogance of the Frenchmen who had followed the new king thither were aggravating day by day. His intrigues were actively supported by Pedro III of Aragon, who had married one of Manfred's daughters, and cherished the ambition of becoming his father-in-law's successor.

Spain, in which country the advance of the Christian kingdoms against the Musulman States had made constant progress since the beginning of the 13th century, while Barcelona was beginning to play an active part in the trade of the Mediterranean, now appears for the first time on the political stage of Europe. Her geographical situation being what it was, she was bound, as soon as she was strong enough, to pursue a maritime policy, and to play her part with the rest on the waters of the inland sea whose western extremity was closed by her own shores. Pedro of Aragon went to work both cleverly and vigorously. The revolt which broke out at Messina in 1282, and to which posterity has given the name of "the Sicilian Vespers," was largely due to his instigation. It rapidly spread over the whole island. Charles despatched to Sicily the fleet which he had been preparing for the attack upon Constantinople. It was destroyed by the Aragonese admiral, Andrea Loria, off Trapani, in the battle which made a glorious beginning for the history of the Spanish navy. Charles died shortly afterwards, in

1285, before he could succeed in suppressing the insurrection. His son Charles II followed him, and despite his efforts, and the support of the Pope, he was at last obliged to abandon the island of Sicily to the Spaniards. There were thenceforth two Kingdoms of Sicily, one, beyond the Strait of Messina, belonging to the house of Aragon, while the other still acknowledged the Angevin dynasty, which established itself in Naples.[1]

While Charles of Anjou's intervention in Italy testified to the increasing prestige of France, it could not be regarded as part of the French policy. St. Louis left his brother's hands free; but did nothing to support him, as he considered that Sicilian affairs were alien to the kingdom. The case was altered under his successor Philip the Bold (1270–1285). Before his time the conduct of the kings of France had been shaped exclusively by their anxiety to consolidate the kingdom, to preserve it from foreign influences, and to group the various parties under their control. Their great enemy, indeed their only enemy, had been England, and if they had sought allies in the outer world, it was only in order that they might triumph over England more completely in their own country. They had succeeded in their task, and France had become a great power. St. Louis had employed his forces only to safeguard peace; Philip the Bold entered upon a policy of expansion which certainly owed something to the ambitious and restless spirit of his uncle, Charles of Anjou. In 1272, on the death of Richard of Cornwall, he allowed Charles to persuade him to become a candidate—or rather to allow his candidature to be discussed—for the crown of the King of the Romans. If his candidature had been successful it would have involved France—to the advantage of the King of Sicily—in the inextricable entanglement of Germany's quarrels. Fortunately, the election of Rudolph of Habsburg prevented the realization of this plan. One result of this election was to inspire in Rudolph a condescending attitude with regard to the house of France. Charles took advantage of this to make him renounce all his claims to Sicily, and Philip to obtain from him in 1281 the

[1] A definitive peace between Frederick of Aragon and Robert of Anjou was signed in 1302.

protectorate of the Bishopric of Toul. Naturally, so much benevolence merely encouraged the king to extend his power still further beyond the frontier of the Empire. Already, in 1272, he had obtained an oath of fealty from the Archbishop of Lyons. In the Low Countries he supported the Count of Flanders, Guillaume de Dampierre, in his conflict with the house of Avesnes, helped him to obtain the County of Namur, and used his interest to procure the bishopric of Liége for one of his sons, thereby making the influence of France felt wherever the Flemish interest had penetrated. The Count of Hainaut, Jean d'Avesnes, sought in vain to interest Rudolph in his cause, and implored him in virulent terms to fall upon the Low Countries, where his enemy the Count of Flanders was insolently deriding the blunted sword of the Empire. As a matter of fact, the German suzerainty over these wealthy countries was already a thing of the past, and it seemed that it would soon be replaced by that of France.

This expansion of the Capetian power toward the north and the east, into territories which their geographical situation, their customs, and, to some extent, their language naturally oriented toward France, was the inevitable consequence of Germany's weakness. It was so natural that it was bound to follow from the moment when France no longer encountered, behind the artificial frontier which she had crossed, the resistance of a State superior to her in strength, and determined to keep what the old Carolingian treaties had attributed to her in the 9th century. In order to succeed in his designs, Philip the Bold had only to take advantage of the circumstances, and of time, both of which were working for him. But conditions were very different in the south of the kingdom. Here the Pyrenees had set a barrier between the countries and the peoples on either side which political ambitions and conquerors had always, in the end, to recognize. Clovis had never crossed the Pyrenees, and although the Arabs had done so later, they were soon driven back again. The Spanish March which Charlemagne had constituted beyond the mountains had before long detached itself from France. All that remained of it was the ill-defined rights of suzerainty of the kings of France over Catalonia and of the kings of Aragon over Languedoc. St. Louis, for the sake of peace, had replaced this confusion by clarity. Since the conclusion of the Treaty of Corbeil the Pyrenees had delimited political rights as definitely as they divided the adjacent countries. One may ask why Philip the Bold should have resolved once more to unsettle so satisfactory an arrangement and to meddle in Spanish affairs. No danger threatened him from beyond the mountains, and there was no question of claiming any rights or protecting any interests. The dynastic problems which had occasioned his intervention in Navarre and Castile since 1275 were merely pretexts. He made use of these pretexts because he wanted to make war: the sort of war that in the days of Louis XIV was described as a war of magnificence, and which we should call a war of hegemony. Having the power, he made use of it to enforce his will, with no other object in view than the glory of his crown. This, I believe, was the first war of pure political ambition to be recorded by the history of Europe. However, it may be that we should attribute his unwarrantable interference in Spain to his desire to support the Sicilian designs of Charles of Anjou, to whom the House of Castile was hardly less hostile than that of Aragon. At all events, this holds good of the Aragonese campaign of 1283. After the Sicilian Vespers the Pope, having excommunicated the King of Aragon, offered his kingdom, which was a fief of the Church, to the King of France, for one of his sons. Philip's choice fell on Charles de Valois, and he crossed the Pyrenees in order to win for him the throne of Pedro II. He did not succeed in winning it, for he died during the campaign.

What St. Louis had achieved was completely ruined. His son, at his death, left France involved in the affairs of Italy and Spain, while England, having emerged from the troubles of Henry III's reign, was on the point of once more taking up arms against her, at the solicitation of her new enemies. Yet if the position of France was not so stable as it had been twenty years earlier, it was more brilliant. She had considerably enlarged her frontiers at the cost of the Empire, and had crossed the Pyrenees; despite the Sicilian Vespers, with the accession of Charles II of Anjou a French dynasty was finally installed in Naples, and shortly afterwards one of its branches was established on the throne of Hungary.[1] In the Europe of the 13th century France had no rival. Nowhere else was there a kingdom so extensive, so well situated, thanks to its outlets upon the North Sea and the Mediterranean, and as populous; and with the exception of England, there was no other country with so robust a political constitution.

## 2. *The French Civilization*

Intellectual hegemony is not always accompanied by political hegemony. Germany had exercised the latter in the 11th century, without possessing the former, since a people can impose itself upon another by force without at the same time imposing its civilization. Countries whose power was really insignificant, like the Italy of the 15th century, may propagate their manners, their ideas, and their art in the outer world by the mere manifestation of their superiority. France, in the 13th century, had the good fortune to be superior to the rest of Europe both as a State and as a society. Her strength merely rendered more rapid and more irresistible a moral ascendancy which was of much earlier date, and which had nothing in common with the military and political achievements of the monarchy.

If we observe the general state of European civilization after the Carolingian period, we see that nearly all its essential characteristics made their appearance in France earlier than elsewhere, and also that it was in France that they achieved their most perfect expression. This applies to religious as well as to secular life. The Order of Cluny, the Order of the Cistercians, and the Order of the Premonstrants had their birth in France; the Order of Chivalry was a French creation, and it was from France that the Crusades obtained their most numerous and most enthusiastic recruits. It was in France, too, at the beginning of the 12th century, that Gothic art suddenly rose as from the soil and imposed its supremacy on the world, and in France the first *chansons de geste* made their appearance. All these coincidences were not merely fortuitous. That so

[1] See p. 482.

many eminent personalities should have existed in one country, that the basin of the Seine, from the 10th century onwards, should have been the scene of so many achievements and so many innovations, means that there must have existed there, as in Greece, in the Attica of the 5th century, an environment which was peculiarly favourable to the manifestations of human energy. And it is a fact that the two great social forces which operated, on the ruins of the Carolingian Empire, to constitute a new Europe—the monastic and the feudal system—were nowhere so active and so predominant as in Northern France. Of course, there were monks everywhere, and vassals everywhere, but only in Northern France had the old order of things disappeared so completely as to give them full scope and perfect freedom of action. Hence the monastic orders and the knightly caste, which Europe naturally borrowed from France as the evolution which had produced them gradually made its way into other countries. Hence the extraordinary enthusiasm of the Frenchmen of the North for the Crusades: that is, for the completest imaginable manifestation of a society which was dominated at once by the religious and the military spirit. And hence, again, evoked by the same ideas and the same feelings, the simultaneous birth of Gothic art, which transformed religious architecture, and of the feudal epopee, which was the beginning—at first in France, and then, through imitation of France, in the rest of Europe—of literature in the vulgar tongue.

Thus the ascendancy of French civilization long antedated the ascendancy of the French monarchy. It began at a time when the Capetians were still living in the shadow of their great vassals. It would be perfectly accurate to say that both civilization and politics had a feudal character when they first made their appearance in France. We must not forget that the monastery of Cluny was built by the Duke of Aquitaine, and that the Counts of Flanders and the Counts of Champagne were among the most ardent patrons of the Clunisian movement, and also of the Cistercian and Premonstrant Orders. Moreover, the heroes whose deeds were celebrated by the *chansons de geste* were the ancestors, actual or mythical, of the princes who built the monasteries. These heroes were feudal barons, and the virtues which the *chansons* extolled were courage, fidelity and piety. Their finest type of hero, Roland, was the ideal knight as imagined by the sons of those who had fought in the First Crusade. During the course of the 12th century this feudal civilization embellished and purified itself. The life of the court, with its refined and conventional manners, which the Middle Ages very exactly describe as "courteous manners," was first developed, not in the entourage of the king, who long continued faithful to the Carolingian tradition, but in the princely residences. It was there that the rules and the ceremonial of chivalry were established; there the sentiment of honour had its birth; there the worship of womanhood first made its appearance; and there a literature de-deloped to which Rome and Brittany contributed motives, to its great enrichment, while the various lyric forms of the *langue d'oc* made their way into the *langue d'œil*. And already this blossoming of the feudal life was not restricted to France alone. At the close of the 11th century it made its appearance in England, with the companions of the Conqueror, and it appeared in the East wherever the Christians had established themselves. French was the language spoken in Jerusalem, Antioch, and Saint-Jean d'Acre. From that time until our own days French has been the international language of Europeans in the basin of the Eastern Mediterranean.

In Europe itself its progress, from the beginning of the 13th century, was extraordinary, and here the political power acquired by the monarchy very greatly increased the power of expansion which it derived from its social prestige. As in the 17th and 18th centuries, it became in every country, for the upper ranks of the aristocracy, a sort of second mother-tongue. In the regions where "Thiois" was spoken French tutors were employed to teach the French language to the sons of the nobility, as the indispensable complement of good breeding and "courtesy." Even in Italy, Brunetto Latini gave French the precedence over all other languages.

And even earlier than the French language, the literature of France made its way into all parts of Europe. From the Low Countries, about the middle of the 12th century, it spread into Germany, and from Germany into the Scandinavian countries. It was translated into or imitated in all the Germanic and Latin tongues. Every fresh example of French literature attracted attention and found readers; indeed, it is only through Norwegian translations that we have learned of the existence of certain French branches of the "cycle" of Charlemagne. The greatest German poets of the 13th century—Hartmann of Strasbourg and Wolfram von Eschenbach—are full of reminiscences and paraphrases of French poems. To find a parallel to such prestige in the previous history of Europe we must go back, despite the fundamental difference of the times and societies in question, to the diffusion of the Greek language and literature in the Roman Empire from the beginning of the 2nd century before Christ.

The comparison is all the more exact inasmuch as, in the case of France as in that of Greece, it applies to art as well as to manners and literature. We have only to consider the conquest of Europe by Gothic architecture, for this epithet of "Gothic," which it owes to the disdain of the Italian humanists, was applied, as we know, to an essentially French creation. The invention of the pointed arch, at the beginning of the 12th century, somewhere on the confines of Normandy and the Île de France, had the effect, in a few years, thanks to the genius of French builders, of completely transforming the fundamental structure and the style of architectural monuments. Until then the methods of the builder's art had remained, in their essentials, what they were in antiquity. But now there was a sudden change. The conditions of equilibrium, the relations of buttresses and the pitch of roofs, of horizontal and vertical elements, of full and empty spaces, were revolutionized, and from this transformation was born the one great school of architecture which the history of art can place on an equality with Greek architecture. Notre-Dame of Paris was begun in 1163; the Cathedral of Reims in 1212; the nave of Amiens dates from 1220; the façade of Chartres from 1194. The admiration which such monuments evoked may be readily understood, and it was attested by the fact that the French architects were soon in demand everywhere. A French architect built the choir of Magdeburg Cathedral; another built the Cathedral of Lund, in Sweden. Villard de Honnecourt, whose sketch-book has happily been preserved for us, drew plans for buildings to be erected in all parts of Europe. Of course, the former pupils of the French architects did not confine themselves to mechanical reproduction. They adapted the new art to the materials at their disposal, modified it in accordance with their own genius, and to some extent harmonized it with the traditions of their own country. There is an English Gothic and a German Gothic, just as there is a Spanish Gothic and an Italian Gothic. But they are all the immediate offspring of the French Gothic, and none of them has attained the supremacy of its parent. The cathedrals of France may be inferior to those of other countries in respect of size, imaginative decoration, and luxuriance or resplendent materials, but in their harmony and their majesty they are incomparable: they are the Parthenons of Gothic.

The hegemony of France in the domain of literature and art in the 12th and 13th centuries is quite simply explained by the superiority of the French civilization. We cannot say quite the same of its intellectual hegemony, which made a much greater impression on the contemporary world. Here it was not the national but the clerical life of France that was in question. All the knowledge of the Middle Ages, if we make some exception in the case of law and medicine, was ecclesiastical, and its exclusive medium of expression was the Latin language. It was essentially universal and international. And yet its central point, its focus, was in France; or to be exact, in Paris. The two cardinal sciences of the epoch, those which dominated all the others—theology and philosophy—seem to have chosen, from the 12th century onwards, to make their home on the banks of the Seine. It was there that the scholastic method was evolved, which until the Renaissance dominated human thought as completely as the Gothic style had dominated art. It was there that the necessities of education created a new sort of Latin, which borrowed its syntax from the French: a dry and impersonal language, but incomparably lucid and precise; so that even the derision of the humanists could not deprive it of the glory of having been for three centuries not only the written, but also the spoken language of learned men in all parts of Europe. From

Abelard to Gerson there was not a single thinker of any mark who did not either teach or study in Paris. The University, which had been created in the reign of Philip Augustus by the amalgamation of the masters and scholars of the various schools of Paris, exercised its irresistible and unexampled power of attraction to the very limits of the Catholic world. Johann of Osnabrück, at the close of the 13th century, awarded to France the monopoly of science; the Flemish poet Van Mearlant celebrated France as the land *par excellence* of the clergy; and we know that the University of Paris was the model by which Charles IV was inspired when he founded the University of Prague (1348), the prototype of the German Universities. And the universal ascendancy exercised by Paris was matched, if one may say so, by the cosmopolitanism of the masters who taught in the University. They came not only from France, but from Germany (Albertus Magnus), the Low Countries (Siger of Brabant), Scotland (Duns Scotus), and Italy (Thomas Aquinas). In short, just as Rome was the headquarters of the government of the Church, Paris was the seat of its theological and philosophical activities. It was the keystone of its scholastic system.

What was the reason of this extraordinary destiny? Why had Catholic science made its home in this northern city, although no literary or religious tradition seemed to justify the mission which had devolved upon it? No other explanation offers itself, beyond the peculiar character which had resulted in the choice of Paris as the residence of the royal court. The Carolingian traditions of the monarchy naturally predisposed it to interest itself in the ecclesiastical schools, and to accord them its protection. While the great feudal magnates had favoured the mystical foundations of the Church, the kings extended their patronage to its scholastic foundations. It is therefore not surprising that the schools of Paris should at a very early date have enjoyed a privileged situation. The progress of the monarchy, which from the beginning of the 13th century had enhanced the importance and the attractions of the capital, is sufficient explanation of the further developments. The national centre of France became the focus of the scientific life of

Europe. It was not the French alone who broadcast through the world that proverbial saying of the 13th century, which was doubtless due to some student's play upon words: "*Paris absque pare*, Paris without peer."

The influence of French civilization in the 12th and 13th centuries was not everywhere felt with equal intensity. It attained its maximum in those countries to which it was carried by the Frenchmen who had settled there: in England and the Crusader communities in the East. Elsewhere it was introduced as a borrowed thing; it was imitated, became the fashion, and spread by contagion and example. But everywhere this influence was communicated only to the upper classes of society; to the nobles, in lay circles, and to the students and scholars among the clergy. In this respect it may be compared with the influence of the Renaissance in the 15th century; like the latter, it affected only the social aristocracy, or the aristocracy of intellect and learning. It is not difficult to understand why this was so. The France of the Middle Ages had not so far developed her economic life that she was able to propagate her influence by means of commerce and industry. In this domain she was far behind Italy and Flanders. Nevertheless, in Flanders, owing to the close proximity of the two countries, their political relations, and their commercial interests, the influence of French civilization affected even the bourgeoisie. The patricians of the great Flemish cities of the 12th century were more than half French; even employing French as their administrative language, and in business. The bilingual character which Flemish Belgium has preserved to this day dates from this period. It was not in any degree the result —as was the bilingual character of Bohemia, for example—of a foreign occupation; it was a natural and peaceful consequence of the fact that France was Belgium's next-door neighbour, and the best evidence of the power of attraction exercised by her civilization.

## CHAPTER IV

# PHILIP THE FAIR AND BONIFACE VIII

### 1. *The Causes of the Crisis*

The death and the catastrophic failure of Frederick II (1250) ended the secular conflict of the Papacy and the Empire. Once that was ended, the Pope had no enemies. The universal power which he exercised over the Church was contested by no one. He was able to devote himself to the realization of the important aims of the pontifical policy: union with the Greek Church and the Crusade. For a moment it seemed as though the union of the Churches was on the point of being realized. The Emperor of Byzantium, Michael Palaeologus, hoping to obtain the support of the West against the Turks, declared that he was ready to recognize the primacy of Rome, and Gregory X, at the Council of Lyons, in 1274, was able to proclaim the end of the schism which for three hundred years had divided Christendom. But this was the triumph and the dream of a moment only. The Greek Church was too deeply rooted in the religious sentiment and the national tradition of the Eastern Christians to bow itself under the Latin yoke. It repudiated the Emperor's overtures. In 1281 Martin IV, abandoning hope, had once more to pronounce his anathema upon the schismatics. The end which had seemed to be achieved was as far from attainment as ever. The Crusade, which was solemnly announced in the Council simultaneously with the reconciliation with the Greeks, met with no greater success. Louis IX was the last Crusader. It is true that Charles of Anjou, inspired by political ambition rather than by religion, made preparations for an expedition which, if it had ever sailed for the East, would probably have been as unsuccessful as his brother's attempts. But the Sicilian Vespers compelled him to employ his fleet against Messina, and to apply himself to the defence of his threatened kingdom.

Thus the Papacy had arrived at its apogee only to witness the failure of its grandiose plans of once more receiving the Greeks into the bosom of the Catholic Church, and recovering the Holy Sepulchre from Islam. And even in the West its power was undermined. The hour of its victory was at the same time the hour that marked the beginning of its decline.

Of this there are various explanations. To begin with, now that the conflict with the Emperor was ended, the Papal cause, in Italy, was no longer confounded with that of the Guelfs, and above all, with that of the Lombard cities, which the Emperor had threatened equally with the Papacy. The Pope was henceforth merely an Italian sovereign, and his temporal power was reduced to the measure of his territorial interest. And this temporal power of the Popes was so inconsiderable that it could not successfully resist Charles de Valois, whose preponderance soon made itself felt throughout the peninsula; even in the States of the Church, even in Rome itself, where his title of senator made him the protector—which meant the master—of the people. But as though this was not enough, his power made itself felt even in the heart of the Curia. Formerly, in the days when the Popes were elected by the clergy and the people, the Roman barons had sought to rally the mob to their own candidate by means of violence or corruption. The creation of the College of Cardinals by Nicholas II (1059) had put an end to such practices, assuring liberty of election by removing it from the influence of popular riot. In 1179, as a further safeguard, Alexander III had decreed that in default of unanimity at least two-thirds of the cardinals must agree upon the choice of a candidate. It goes without saying that as the ascendancy of the Papacy in European affairs increased, the voting was swayed by political as well as religious considerations. However, since the cardinals were nearly all Italian, it was long since foreign interests had played any but a very secondary part in their deliberations. But the case was altered since the advent of Charles of Anjou. It was his constant preoccupation to assure himself of the support of a party in the Sacred College, and he did his utmost to secure the introduction of Neapolitan, Provençal and French cardinals on whom he could rely. His efforts were crowned with success. Clement IV, a Provençal by origin, and entirely devoted to Charles, furthered his designs by promoting the formation of an Angevin faction among the cardinals. Clement's death (1268) was the signal for the outbreak of a desperate conflict between these "Angevins" and their adversaries. It was only after three years of struggle and intrigue that they resigned themselves to the election of Gregory X (1271). It was not surprising that Gregory should wish to make an end of a state of affairs so damaging to the good government of the Church. It was he who was responsible for the institution of the Conclave, almost as it exists to-day. He decreed that on the death of the Pope the cardinals should assemble in a closed chamber, where they would have no communication with the outside world, being forbidden, under penalty of excommunication, to leave the Conclave before they had elected a Pope. However, these precautions did not prevent Charles de Valois, in 1280, from compelling the Conclave to elect the Frenchman, Martin IV, who eagerly seconded all his plans. After Charles's death the Angevin party, though less powerful, was no less active. The Conclave became a mere formality; Nicholas IV was elected only after a year's negotiations between the cardinals (1288), and when he died, in 1292, the quarrels broke out again with renewed force, so that after two years of fruitless agitation the cardinals finally decided, since no party was strong enough to force its candidate upon the others, to elect an aged hermit, ignorant of the world, whom the people regarded as a saint: the innocent sport of intrigues which would have disgusted him if he had understood them. The new Pope, Celestine V, knew hardly any Latin, and when he had exchanged the solitude of his mountains for the Lateran Palace, where he was abashed and bewildered, he did not realize that he was merely the tool of the king of Naples, Charles II of Anjou, who, the better to make use of him, installed him in his own capital. Before long his one thought was to abdicate. The cardinals asked nothing better than to take him at his word. He had given them time to come to an agreement. On December 12th, 1294, they elected, in the place of the poor old man, a Roman noble, Benedetto Gaetani, who took the name of Boniface VIII.

In his person the last Pope of the line of Innocent III and Innocent IV ascended the throne of St. Peter. His manifest aim was to restore to the Holy See the splendour, the prestige, the moral authority, and the universal political dominion which it had enjoyed in their time. The pomp with which he surrounded himself on the occasion of public ceremonies, the two swords which he had carried before him, the crown with which he adorned the pontifical tiara, were so many means of affirming the primacy in the Church of the successor of St. Peter, and of reminding the world that the temporal power was subordinate to the Church, since, as part of the Church, it could make no pretension to shake off the authority of the head of the Church. There was nothing new in this, nothing that had not already been pointed out by Nicholas I and Gregory VII, clearly formulated by Innocent III, and logically demonstrated by the Scholastics. The famous Bulls addressed to Philip the Fair contained nothing more than the doctrine concerning the relations between the two powers as accepted by all the theologians. Boniface had merely summarized and repeated the principles of his great predecessors, without adding anything to them.

Why, then, did they excite such a storm of indignation, and result in catastrophe? Simply on account of their immutability. They were not in accordance with political realities; times were changed, and what the Pope, in comformity with tradition, promulgated as the essential truth, now excited the opposition of the most advanced nations in Europe, since both kings and peoples were agreed in regarding them as an insupportable encroachment on their most legitimate rights and interests.

One thing, indeed, must be understood: it was not only with France that Boniface VIII found himself in conflict. He found Edward I no more tractable than Philip the Fair, and the English Parliament repudiated his claims no less vigorously than the States General in Paris. While current events so aggravated the conflict with France that it amounted to a complete rupture, it is none the less true that the pontifical policy aroused, at the same time, and for the same reasons, the opposition of the two countries which, from the end of the 13th century, possessed a veritable constitution.

Until then the Pope had had to contend against a single enemy only: the Empire, or rather the Emperor; and we must once more repeat that the question at issue between them was not comprehended within the limits of a single nation: it involved the whole of Christendom. Of course, in undermining the Imperial power the Pope was also undermining the power of the King of Germany. But German opinion, far from being incensed against him, regarded the impairment of the monarchical power with satisfaction, and the princes who represented this opinion, instead of opposing the enterprises of Rome, supported the Pope, and facilitated their success. Under Frederick II, it is true, the circumstances were somewhat different. The issue of conflict was the Kingdom of Sicily rather than the Empire, and the Kingdom of Sicily was a State; but it must be observed, in the first place, that this State was not independent, since it was a fief of the Holy See; and above all, it was not a national State. Its heterogeneous population, bandied about for centuries from one foreign conqueror to another, did no more than endure the despotic government which they inflicted upon it, and we cannot perceive that it ever displayed the slightest tendency to make common cause with them. The Sicilians had paid their taxes to Frederick II and had provided him with soldiers, but he was perfectly well aware that they cared nothing for his quarrel. He never for a moment thought of appealing to them for their opinion as to the legitimacy of his rights. He contented himself with the theoretical defence of these rights by legal experts.

How great was the difference between this absolute despot, this Hohenstaufen to whom a politic marriage had given Sicily, and the kings of England and France! In England, since the death of John Lackland, the liberties consecrated by Magna Carta had been consolidated. Under the long reign of Henry III (1216–1272) the barons and the burgesses, under the leadership of Simon de Montfort, had imposed on the Crown the control of a Council of State.

Representatives of the cities sat beside those of the nobles in the national assembly, which the king pledged himself to convoke three times a year, and which in 1258 adopted, officially, for the first time, the name of Parliament, a name so glorious in the history of modern Europe. Its attributions were clearly defined under Edward I, and its essential prerogative, the basis of the first free constitution that the world had ever known—the prerogative of granting taxation—was formally acknowledged in 1297. Henceforth the nation and the sovereign were associated in the government of the country. Although the personal power of the prince was subjected to definite limitations, and although, alone among his European peers, he had to renounce the possibility of waging wars inspired by mere dynastic ambition, and apply himself solely to enterprises approved and subsidized by his people, yet, on the other hand, what strength he derived from this compliance! From the end of the 13th century the English policy was truly, in the full acceptation of the term, a national policy. It was national both at home and abroad. Hence the striking contrast which it presented through the centuries, the contrast between unrest and intestine conflict at home, and a foreign policy which revealed a continuity of purpose, and a persistence and pertinacity in the execution of that purpose, peculiar to this country, where the enterprises of the Crown were necessarily those of the nation.[1]

This extraordinary strength, which gave such a modern character to the England of the late Middle Ages, was something unknown to France. France had another kind of strength, less deeply rooted, but for the moment equally effective, in the incomparable prestige of her king. For what France had become she owed exclusively to the monarchy. It was the monarchy that had liberated her from the particularism of the feudal system, had defended her against external enemies, had protected her nascent cities, and had endowed her with financial and administrative institutions which safeguarded the people against violence and exaction. Against the oppression

[1] It should be noted that at the same time Simon de Montfort and the barons compelled the king to sanction the English liberties and to abandon his designs upon Sicily.

exercised by an all-powerful dynasty England had created the guarantee of Parliament; against the abuses resulting from the feudal supremacy, France obtained protection from her king. Thus in France the king enjoyed the same popularity which in England was enjoyed by the Parliament. In either country the national sentiment was in harmony with the political constitution, and the two developed simultaneously. In England the distinguishing feature of this national sentiment was pride, a pious respect for the monarchy. It gave each of these two peoples its individual character, its collective temperament, so to speak; the product of its historic evolution, which we shall strangely misconceive if we seek to explain it by that mysterious factor of race which can be made to justify anything because it explains nothing.

Philip (IV) the Fair, who succeeded to his father, Philip the Bold, in 1285, made a new addition to the kingdom on ascending the throne. His wife was the heiress of the Kingdom of Navarre, and, what was more important, of the County of Champagne, which was united to the royal domain. With the exception of Guyenne, in the possession of the King of England, Brittany, which had always maintained an independence which was not particularly embarrassing, on account of the outlying position of the country, and Flanders, all the great fiefs had now returned under the direct power of the Crown. Philip the Bold had allowed himself to be dragged by Charles of Anjou into a war of prestige against Aragon. His son made haste to end the war, and took great care not to waste his strength in furthering the Sicilian ambitions of the King of Naples. He kept it intact for more useful and practical ends. To complete the kingdom internally by annexing Flanders and Guyenne, and to continue a vigorous policy of expanion in the east and the north, to the detriment of the Empire, seems really to have been the twofold aim of his policy. In this Philip the Fair continued the tradition of his predecessors. What distinguished him from them was the method which he employed. Before his reign the king had governed in the midst of his court, and all the members of his usual entourage were well acquainted with his affairs. This was no longer the case under Philip the Fair.

With him the old familiar methods of the palace were replaced by secret intrigues; he hid himself, so to speak, behind the ministers whom he employed, dissimulating his influence to such a degree that people asked, with a certain ingenuousness, whether his policy was not simply the policy of his agents, and whether he did not simply allow them to do as they thought fit. This question might be asked in respect of all modern sovereigns who have not been men of genius, and the fact that it has preoccupied the historians of Philip's reign is the best evidence of the innovations which were introduced during this reign in respect of the exercise of the monarchical power. The king was henceforth so strong, so certain of being obeyed, that he could safely confide the most important affairs to men of obscure birth, who had emerged from the bourgeoisie or the *petite noblesse*, but who were recommended by their juridical or practical knowledge, while the mediocrity of their fortune, and their hope of increasing it in the service of the prince, were sufficient guarantee of their devotion. It is true that before Philip's reign a certain number of these new men had already made their way into the councils of the Crown. Under Philip the Bold Pierre de la Brosse, at first the king's physician and then his intimate counsellor, had given great offence, and had ended on the scaffold a career which was too brilliant to please the court. But what had been merely an exception now became the rule. All the men employed in the business of the government, entrusted by Philip the Fair with diplomatic missions, or the manipulation of the finances, were mere "clercs de loi," like Pierre Flote, Enguerrand de Marigny, and Guillaume de Nogaret, or Sienese bankers like the two brothers Guidi (Guy). With them a political personnel made its appearance, entirely distinct from the court, deliberating only with the king in private, and its members were the only persons who were in his confidence and were initiated in his designs. They were mere instruments in the hands of their master, who could break them whenever he chose. They knew that they were surrounded by ferocious hatred and that if they fell it might well be to mount the scaffold. Consequently, they contended zealously for the royal favour, and spared no one. Without class prejudices, and hostile to the privileges of the great nobles who despised them, they worked with a will for the establishment of absolutism, and here their conviction was in harmony with their passion for their interest, for the study of Roman law had taught them to perceive the political truth in absolutism. They were dry, abrupt, ironical, pitiless. It was not the king who spoke through them, but the anonymous monarchy, superior to all, subduing all to its power, and they served it with triumphant joy, proud to find the greatest seigneurs eager to solicit their protection and to pass in public for their creatures. It is not astonishing that Philip the Fair's policy, in the hands of such men, should have been characterized by frigid violence and a complete absence of scruples. St. Louis' ideal of justice and charity was replaced by exclusive consideration for the interests of the Crown. As its strength constantly increased, the monarchical power eventually refused to tolerate obstacles, and began to justify the means which it employed by the ends which it elected to pursue.

This at once becomes evident if we briefly consider the intervention of the Crown in the affairs of the Low Countries. Hitherto it had always supported the house of Dampierre against the rival dynasty of Avesnes, and had helped it to extend its influence over Namur, Liége, Guelders and Luxembourg. In this way it set up the power of one of its vassals in those portions of the ancient Lotharingia which were dependent on Germany, and its support of the Count of Flanders against the Count of Hainaut was part of its skilful policy of encroachment at the expense of the Empire. Jean d'Avesnes had vainly attempted to interest Rudolph of Habsburg in his cause. He could obtain nothing from him beyond some futile proclamations against Guy de Dampierre. It was daily becoming more obvious to the princes of the Low Countries that their traditional suzerain could no longer do anything for them, and that in their own interests they would have to seek the friendship of the King of France, by which the Count of Flanders had profited so greatly. Jean d'Avesnes, making a complete *volte face*, ventured to sound the French court. He found it quite prepared to welcome his advances. In 1293, breaking with his past, he definitely took his place among the protégés of the Capet dynasty. In this way Philip the Fair became the ally of the mortal enemy of the House of Flanders, whose suzerain he was, and to whom, according to feudal law, he owed comfort and assistance! But the feudal law was no longer invoked by the Crown except when it furnished the latter with pretexts for its pretensions; it repudiated, in the name of sovereignty, the obligations which this law imposed upon it. It had obtained from the Count of Flanders all the services which he could render it. Now that the vassal princes of the Empire were seeking its alliance, it was useless and even dangerous to increase the count's power in Lotharingia. The moment had come to show him that he was nothing without the support of the king, and to reduce him to the rôle of a mere instrument of the Crown.

The social unrest which was manifested in the Flemish cities from the middle of the 13th century offered the royal policy a fresh occasion to intervene, which it did immediately with extraordinary success. In the great industrial centres of Gand, Bruges, Ypres, Lille and Douai, the masses of the workers—weavers, fullers, clothworkers, etc.—were inspired by a veritable class hatred of the patricians who constituted the municipal government. They accused the aldermen of administering the affairs of the municipalities to the sole advantage of the wealthy bourgeoisie, of sacrificing the workers to the interests of the rich wool and cloth merchants, and of reducing them to starvation wages. Strikes (*takehans*) had broken out, conspiracies had been discovered, and the exasperation of the people increased as the measures of precaution or defence taken against them were multiplied. In 1280 a general revolt broke out simultaneously in all the Flemish and Walloon cities, leading to veritable street battles in several of them. Guy de Dampierre had taken this opportunity of intervening. Incapable, unassisted, of dealing with the patrician municipalities, which for some time past had openly defied his authority, he adopted an attitude of great benevolence to the people, in order to induce them to defend his princely prerogatives. Threatened by the alliance between the count and the "vulgar," the patricians immediately sought a protector in the suzerain of their prince, the King of France. Already, in 1275, under the reign of Philip the Bold, the Thirty Nine of Gand,[1] dismissed by Guy de Dampierre, had appealed to the Parlement of Paris. The Parlement had pronounced an equitable judgement. Convinced of the reality of the abuses of which they were accused, it nonsuited them, without giving its approval to the new organization which the count had set up in the city. But the legists of Philip the Fair had before long to replace the impartiality of the law by the *parti pris* of politics. Since they were guided only by the interest of the Crown, their object was not to try the issue between the count and the patricians, but systematically to support the patricians against the count. Everything possible was done to convince them that they could count absolutely on the king, and the protection accorded them was all the more effective inasmuch as the means to which it resorted were most humiliating to the count. Mere "sergeants" were despatched to the Flemish cities as "guardians," in the name of the Crown; the fleur-de-lys banner was flown from the city belfries, conferring upon them an immunity which enabled them to confront their seigneur and his bailiffs with flat defiance. The arrogant plutocracy which dominated the cities had nothing to fear now that it could take shelter beneath this formidable emblem of the royal power. Henceforth it could laugh at the efforts of the count and the "vulgar." It gloried in the name of *leliaerts* (lily-men) which the people conferred upon it as a term of abuse. To the novel methods of the pitiless policy now directed against him, Guy de Dampierre, threatened from without by the alliance of Philip the Fair with Jean d'Avesnes, and from within by the king's protectorate over his great cities, could have devised no means of resistance, had not the war which had just broken out again between France and England inspired him with the hope of opposing force to force.

Since the beginning of the 13th century the English monarchy, engrossed in the civil commotions from which the national constitution was one day to emerge, had found itself unable to continue the policy of expansion inaugurated by Henry II. Amidst the

[1] Aldermen, representatives of the patriciate who governed the commune.

mountains of the West the principality of Wales still maintained its independence, and in the North the kings of Scotland paid no heed to the vassalage which had been imposed upon them by the great Plantagenet. Such a state of affairs could not long continue. The geographical unity of an island makes the introduction of political unity a natural tendency. Moreover, the English found the Welsh and the Scots highly dangerous and inconvenient neighbours, and when Edward I resolved to subjugate them he had the enthusiastic support of the nation. Wales was united to the kingdom in 1284, though it retained an autonomy of which the title of Prince of Wales, borne by the heir to the crown, was thenceforth the symbol. The war against the Scots was a more difficult matter. Despite their diverse origin and their different idioms—Anglo-Saxon in the Lowlands and Gaelic in the mountains of the North and West—the Scots were inspired by a common love of independence. When their king John Baliol acknowledged the suzerainty of England and took the oath of fealty to Edward (1292) their indignation was such that Baliol was forced to break his oath and to take up arms against the English. He might perhaps have hesitated if he had not been encouraged in his attitude by Philip the Fair. It had seemed to Philip that he ought to take advantage of the moment when Edward was embroiled with Scotland in order to strip England of her last continental possessions. He gave orders for the occupation of Guyenne, and at the same time concluded a treaty with Baliol, thus inaugurating that policy of alliance between France and Scotland which through all the fluctuations of European history made itself felt at intervals, century after century, uniting the two countries against the common enemy. However, the first results of this policy were unsuccessful. Edward, content with assuming the defensive in Guyenne, concentrated all his forces against Baliol, whom he took prisoner after defeating him at Dunbar (1296), and thereupon the stone on which the kings of Scotland were crowned was removed to Westminster Abbey, where it is to-day. For the time being the kingdom of Scotland had ceased to exist, and was merely an English province.

Edward was now able to deal with France. But an attack delivered by the English forces alone was hardly likely to be successful. He endeavoured to form a coalition against France: such as John Lackland, eighty years earlier, had formed against Philip Augustus. Greatly as the power of the monarchy had declined in Germany, Edward entered into negotiations with Adolphus of Nassau, or, to speak more exactly, hired his services, and induced him to declare war on the pretext that France had recently annexed certain territories of the Empire. But he based his hopes more especially on the princes of the Low Countries; for his plan was to attack France from the north—that is, on the only side which was not protected by natural frontiers. He was especially anxious to obtain the assistance of the Count of Flanders, and here the ground was already prepared for his advance by the harsh measures of Philip the Fair. On January 9th, 1297, Guy de Dampierre sent his challenge of defiance to his suzerain. The war began in June. Adolph of Nassau, who had merely wanted to make sure of the good pounds sterling of England, did not put in an appearance. Edward disembarked in Flanders, but almost as soon as he had landed a general rebellion broke out in Scotland. From that moment his only anxiety was to withdraw from an expedition from which it was impossible to expect a favourable result. On October 9th he concluded a truce with the King of France, and made haste to grapple with the northern enemy. The threatened clash between the two great Western States was postponed. Guy de Dampierre, abandoned by Edward, who in 1299 signed a definitive peace in which he was not included, was left to confront the French army unaided. It did not take the French long to conquer his county, for its powers of resistance were disorganized by the Leliaerts (May 1300). The old count was treated as a traitorous vassal, and imprisoned, with his sons. Flanders was confiscated, and placed under a royal governor. It seemed that its annexation must soon be followed by that of all the Low Countries. The Count of Hainaut, Jean d'Avesnes, who had become the trusted ally of Philip the Fair, inherited the counties of Holland and Zeeland and inflicted a sorry defeat on the new King of Germany, Albert of Austria, who had advanced as far as Nimeguen in order to occupy the two counties. Already the French were beginning to regard the Rhine as the natural frontier of the kingdom. The power of the Capets had attained its apogee.

## 2. *The Crisis*

The events which have just been related were the occasion of a crisis which was to strike a deadly blow at the somewhat ill-defined arbitral power over the princes and the peoples which was claimed by the Pope simply because the princes and peoples belonged to the Catholic Church.

Having been on the point of waging war against each other, Philip the Fair and Edward I had vied with each other in the matter of military preparations, and the consequent expenditure. They had both imposed heavy taxes on the estates of the Church, as though they had been making preparations for a Crusade. There was naturally no lack of protests. Rome had been warned of what was happening, and Boniface VIII felt that he must take this opportunity of solemnly reminding the princes of the limits which theology assigns to the temporal powers. The Bull *Clericis laïcos* (February 25th, 1296) strictly prohibited laymen from imposing taxes on the clergy without the consent of the Pope, annulled all dispensations which might have been accorded in this connection, and threatened all transgressors with excommunication. The document was addressed to Christendom in general; neither the King of France nor the King of England was mentioned in the text, but no one could doubt that it was directed against them. As a matter of fact, it contained nothing that departed in any way from the principles constantly proclaimed by the religious authorities. Since the end of the Roman Empire the financial immunities of the clergy had been constantly extended, and for centuries had been considered as natural as its judicial immunities.

In the conflict which was now beginning it was not the Pope but the kings who violated tradition. The rôles allotted were exactly the converse of what they had been during the War of the Investitures. Then Henry IV, in conflict with Gregory VII, had played a conservative part, defending his acquired prerogatives against claims that he considered revolutionary. Now it was

Boniface VIII who was defending his acquired prerogatives, while the revolutionary claims were made by Philip and Edward. But in the dispute between Henry IV and Gregory VII the issue was debated on religious grounds, and for that very reason public opinion had supported the Pope. The issue between Boniface and the two kings, on the contrary, was debated on political grounds; the sovereign powers of the monarchy, the very existence of the State, and the most obvious interests of the nation were in question, so that this time public opinion, instead of supporting Rome, was bound to turn against the Papacy.

It was evident that the Pope had not expected that his claims would arouse such opposition. His whole course of behaviour goes to show that he was not aware that anything had changed in Europe since the days of Innocent IV and Frederick II, or that France and England, in 1296, were no longer what they had been a hundred years earlier. He had not realized that the prerogatives of the Crown were based on the consent of the peoples, and that the solidarity of the nation was so great, not only among the laymen, but also in the ranks of the clergy, that it was quite capable of defeating any attempt to intervene in the king's affairs, to paralyse his government, and imperil his finances or his military strength, in the name of the privileges of the Church. If Philip and Edward had been abandoned by their subjects, as the result of religious scruples, or of mere indifference, they could have done nothing but humbly make their submission. What enabled them to triumph was the consciousness that they were supported by the assent of their peoples; that is, they had moral strength on their side, the only thing that could give them the victory in a conflict of this nature.

Neither king saw fit to discuss the matter. Edward regarded the Bull as null and void, and continued to levy the prohibited taxes. Philip took measures calculated to show the Pope how dangerous it was to meddle in his affairs: since his financial resources were threatened, he himself threatened the finances of the Pope. He prohibited the export, beyond the frontiers of the kingdom, of monies or letters of credit. Immediately all the revenues which the Papacy drew from France, and all those that were conveyed through

France by the medium of the Pope's Italian bankers, were interrupted. The greater the Pope's need of money, the more highly developed his fiscal organization, the more overwhelming was such a blow. A century earlier such a counter-stroke would have been impossible, for the means of delivering it were lacking. But the arm of the French monarchy was now so long, and its administration so complete and well-disciplined, that the order was punctually obeyed. The State, being attacked, defended itself with its own weapons, and Europe witnessed the novel spectacle of a sovereign resisting the orders of Rome and opposing them by simple administrative measure. The thing was so unexpected that Boniface VIII did not know where to turn. His intervention in the Sicilian war, and the revolt of the Colonna in his own States, meant that he was in pressing need of money. Above all, France must open her frontiers. Before she would consent to do so he had to resign himself to making advances to the king which must have been very painful to a man of his arrogant nature. Without retracting the Bull he modified it to such an extent that it had no practical importance, and the canonization of St. Louis, pronounced in 1297, might be accepted as an act of homage to the House of France. The incident was hardly closed when another dilemma arose. Like his predecessors, Boniface VIII cherished the hope of uniting Europe in a new Crusade. Since the war between France and England, the two most powerful States of the West, rendered such an enterprise unrealisable, he offered his services as mediator to the belligerents. Out of respect for their susceptibilities it was understood that this was a purely private proceeding on his part. However, since peace was solemnly promulgated in a Bull, Philip regarded the latter as an encroachment upon his sovereign prerogatives and an affirmation of the temporal supremacy of the Papacy over his crown. He immediately gave expression to his resentment by openly giving his support to the Colonna.

Just as the situation was becoming intolerably strained, preparations were made for the great jubilee of the year 1300. This was the first solemnity of the kind that Europe had ever seen, and it was an incomparable triumph for the Pope. From all parts of

Christendom the faithful flocked to Rome in their thousands and hundreds of thousands (it was said that they numbered two hundred thousand), to obtain the indulgences accorded to those who visited the tomb of the Apostles. The homage and veneration and affection which these enthusiastic masses lavished on Boniface VIII intoxicated him with pride. He forgot the misadventures of the last few years; and the spectacle of so many pilgrims prostrate at his feet deluded him into the belief that the kings and the peoples were equally ready to obey his orders. He was soon forced to realize that the sincerity of their religious fervour and their devotion to the Church were not so great as to induce them to sacrifice their independence and their dignity.

Edward I, taking advantage of his peace with Philip, had once more marched against the Scots. The Scots having appealed to Rome, Boniface VIII intervened, accusing Edward of violence and injustice, and claiming the right to judge between the two parties. He had addressed himself only to the king; the king decided to address himself to the nation, and in January 1301 Parliament was convoked and required to pronounce upon the Papal claims. Thus, this famous question of the temporal sovereignty and its limits, which had hitherto been discussed only by hermits, theologians, and legists, was now to be considered by the mandatories of a whole people. Their response was a categorical affirmation of the sovereign rights of the Crown. Prelates, barons, knights and burgesses were equally indignant with the Pope's interference in a war which was thoroughly popular, and which had been gloriously terminated by the battle of Falkirk (July 22nd, 1298). "Never," they replied, "shall we suffer that our king should submit to such unheard-of demands!"

Boniface ignored these words. At the moment when they were reported to him his relations with France had assumed such a serious character that he could not run the risk of complicating them by a quarrel with England. At the request of the Archbishop of Narbonne, who complained of the confiscation of certain fiefs which he claimed were held from his Church, the Pope had sent to Paris, as legate, the Bishop of Pamiers, Bernard Saisset. The arrogant language of the legate had offended the king. He concealed his indignation, and allowed the bishop to report on the result of his mission in Rome; and then, shortly after he had returned to his diocese, the king had him arrested, and accused, by Pierre Flote, his Chancellor, of lèse-majesté, rebellion, heresy, blasphemy and simony. An assembly of prelates and doctors having found him guilty, the Pope was requested to deprive him of his episcopal functions.

The Pope's reply to these proceedings was to demand the immediate liberation of Saisset, and to revive the prohibition which forbade the taxation of Church property, while he convoked an assembly of the French clergy in Rome, to deliberate with him upon the means of rebuking the king. At the same time he personally addressed the king in the Bull *Ausculta fili*, in which he reminded him that God had placed the successor of St. Peter over the heads of princes and States. "For this reason," said the Pope, "give no credit to those who would persuade thee that thou hast no superior. Who thinks thus deceives himself, and he who persists in this error is an infidel." Innocent III would not have spoken otherwise, and St. Thomas Aquinas, some fifty years earlier, had expounded at length the theory by which these words were inspired. But this time they evoked the most passionate contradiction in the ranks of the jurists and doctors. Pierre Dubois and Jean de Paris, the author of the *Dialogue entre un clerc et un chevalier*, repudiated with indignation the Pope's claim to intervene in temporal questions. According to them, his competence extended only to purely religious matters. They even went so far as to debate the legitimacy of his Roman sovereignty, and one of them (Jean de Paris) attributed the decadence of the Church to the Donation of Constantine! Frederick II and Pierre de la Vigne had already said almost the same thing. These discussions, however, interested only the learned, and the crisis would not have been very serious if it had been restricted to a battle of pamphlets. But Philip, like Edward a year earlier, and doubtless inspired by his example, resolved that his quarrel should be the quarrel of his people. France had no parliament. Never yet had the delegates of the whole nation been convoked to advise the Crown. This great debate, in which the very principle of the king's sovereignty was at stake, was the occasion of the first assembly of the States-General: the first, and a worthy, example of those assemblies of which the last, five hundred years later, was to proclaim the Rights of Man and inaugurate the Revolution.

The delegates of the clergy, the noblesse and the bourgeoisie assembled at Notre-Dame de Paris on April 10th, 1302. Opinion had been adroitly manipulated by manœuvres which clearly revealed the spirit of the government to which all means were lawful if they were successful. False Bulls, insulting the king, and a false reply, insulting the Pope, had been widely distributed: crude methods, but characteristic of the period when policy was beginning to feel the need of appealing to the support of public opinion. Pierre Flote expounded the point in dispute before the States. All the delegates, clergy and laymen alike, enthusiastically declared their approval of the king's attitude. The clergy couched their reply to the Pope in the Latin tongue; the other two orders replied to the cardinal in French.

From this moment the Pope's was a lost cause. The States-General decided the question of sovereignty in favour of the Crown—that is, in favour of the State—and their verdict was delivered with much greater emphasis than that of the English Parliament of the preceding year. It was enough that a national assembly had spoken its mind; the result was attained for which the Emperors had striven through two centuries of exhausting campaigns, which had drenched Germany and Italy in blood. To the brutal force of the Germanic Caesars Rome, of old, had victoriously opposed her moral force; her resistance to their attempts to secure universal dominion had rallied the nations to her cause, and Italy, by joining her in her resistance to the Hohenstaufens, had at the same time fought for her own liberty. Today the ancient allies of Rome were deserting her because she in her turn was threatening their liberty and independence. In Germany there was no solidarity between the people and the policy of the Emperors, but the whole of the French people was behind the policy of its king. What was to be done with this declaration of war on the part of a whole people? To whom could the Pope appeal? To England? But in this particular France's quarrel was also that of England. What was more, it was that of all the nations. For unlike the Emperors, France did not propose to offer violence to the Papacy or to oppress it to her own advantage; she merely demanded that the Papacy should not arrogate to itself the right of intervention in her government; she was threatening no one; she laid claim to nothing but her own temporal autonomy, and every State, in its own interests, was bound to hope for her success. Boniface VIII consequently found himself isolated. By the irony of history, not knowing where to turn, he appealed to the King of Germany, Albert of Austria, whose election he had hitherto refused to recognize; and now, in his necessity, extolling that Imperial majesty which his predecessors had so sorely humiliated, he reminded Albert that the Empire enjoyed primacy over all kingdoms, "and that the French lied in saying that they had no superior, since they were in law subordinate to the Emperor." The Bull *Unam sanctam*, which he published on November 18th, 1302, was Rome's last solemn affirmation of her primacy over the temporal power. It contains a long exposition of the traditional theory of the two swords, and the subordination of all princes to the successor of St. Peter, *ratione peccati*.

Thus the contradictory claims of Church and State were in absolute conflict. And there matters might have rested. For the declaration of principles contained in the Bull was henceforth merely a harmless manifestation. But Philip the Fair had determined to overthrow his adversary. It was in his power to employ a terrible weapon against him. And it was not his policy to spare the enemy.

The Pope's personal situation in respect of the king was indeed most unfavourable. The king's orthodoxy was so complete and so evident that it was impossible to launch against him the formidable accusation of heresy which had been brought against Frederick II. On religious grounds his position was unshakable, and the Pope's was not. The election of Boniface, which had taken place during the lifetime of his predecessor, and thanks to the abdication of the latter, had been so singular that his enemies had not failed to invoke it, long ago, as a reason for regarding it as null and void. The Colonna kept on repeating that the Pope was merely an intruder, and it was so much in Philip's interest that he should be an intruder that the king was quite willing to believe, or to pretend that he believed, that the Colonna were right. In June 1303 a fresh assembly of the States-General approved of his intention to submit the question to a general Council. This was a good beginning, and the partisans of the Crown were careful not to let the matter drop. The University of Paris, and many of the monasteries and cities, vied with one another in demanding the Council, while the government canvassed the foreign States in favour of this project.

However, Nogaret was sent to Italy in order to get into touch with the Colonna, seize the person of the Pope, and if possible force him to abdicate. On August 15th he took him by surprise at Anagni. Violence had no effect on the old man. Threatened with death by the Colonna, he remained immovable, confronting his furious captors with proud majesty, and remaining worthy of himself even in calamity. But this last blow had shattered him. Liberated by a popular rising, he returned to Rome only to die there, on October 12th, 1303.

The problem was not solved by his death. The king's appeal to the Council was felt as a threat by his successor. Benedict XI (1303–1304) did not live long enough to solve this distressing problem. Clement V (1305–1314) avoided it only by involving the Papacy in a crisis which finally destroyed the incomparable prestige which it had enjoyed in the 13th century.

His election, to which the cardinals resigned themselves only after eleven months of deliberation, was in itself a signal defiance of Boniface's contention. For the new Pope was a Frenchman, and in electing him the Conclave had submitted to the will of Philip. It very soon realized that it had placed on the throne of St. Peter a pontiff who was incapable of forgetting that he was born a subject of the King of France. Clement V was not content with filling the Sacred College with the relatives and protégés of his sovereign;

impressed with the pre-eminence which his country had acquired in Europe, he was insensible to the majesty of Rome, and to the tradition of twelve hundred years which had made the city of the Emperors the city of the Popes. For this Frenchman *aurea Roma* was merely a city like other cities, with an unhealthy climate and a dangerous and fickle population; no doubt he thought it greatly inferior to Paris. Was not the Papacy wherever the Pope might be? What did it matter whether he lived in the Lateran and pontificated in St. Peter's? Clement V took up his residence in Avignon, and there his successors remained until 1378. In 1345 it passed into the possession of the Church. But surrounded as it was by the domain of the King of France it was actually in France, and the outer world was not deluded. In deserting the banks of the Tiber for those of the Rhone, the Popes derogated from the position which they had occupied for the past century, between God and the kings, and degraded themselves, if not always in fact, yet at least in appearance, to the rank of protégés and instruments of the French Crown. This was the final consequence of the policy of Boniface VIII! What mattered henceforth the attacks made upon his memory? For some years Philip continued to intimidate the Pope. Having forced him, in 1312, to pronounce sentence against the Templars, whose wealth he coveted, he spoke no more of the matter. What remained henceforth of the arrogant declarations of the Bull *Unam sanctam*, and what likelihood was there that the Popes, when in future they addressed the kings of France, should ever again adopt such a tone? It is true that the propositions contained in the Bull still held good. In theory the claims of the Papacy had never been refuted. In reality they were merely harmless declamations; at all events, as far as France was concerned. And this was all that Philip required. In politics the practical result is all that need be considered, and this had been more decisive, and, above all, more rapidly achieved than anyone would have ventured to hope. In the clash between the Church and the National State the latter had shown itself the stronger. The Papacy was tottering, in its turn, on the ruins of the Imperial power which it had overthrown. It was almost as though in leaving Rome for Avignon it had endeavoured to conceal its humiliation by seeking a less conspicuous stage.

Thus the 13th century saw both the apogee of the Papal power and its decline. At the very moment when, triumphing over the Empire, it believed itself in a position to assume control over Europe, to unite the Continent against Islam, and to impose its tutelage on all the peoples, the economic and political transformations which had taken place, almost unnoticed by Rome, rendered the realization of the Papal designs impossible. The lofty ideal which the Papacy had conceived in a period of agricultural and feudal civilization no longer responded to the social realities. Faith was no less ardent and no less general than of old, while the discipline of the Church was enforced more completely than ever before. But the Crusade was now regarded merely as an impossible chimera, while the progress of trade and of urban life had profoundly modified men's habits and their way of life. At the same time, the constitution, in France and England, of national States, which could not subsist without an autonomous administration and an independent policy, was bound to end in the conflict which was so disastrous to Boniface VIII. And yet, during the brief reign of St. Louis, it had been possible to realize the Christian policy. This was the greatest moment of the 13th century, a moment of calm in the continual tempest into which the tumultuous forces of life were sweeping humanity.

*Book Eight*

# THE EUROPEAN CRISIS

## (1300–1450)

The Avignon Papacy, the Great Schism, and the Hundred Years' War

## CHAPTER I

# GENERAL CHARACTERISTICS OF THE PERIOD

### 1. *Social and Economic Tendencies*

Nothing more involved and bewildering and more full of contrasts can be imagined than the period extending from the beginning of the 14th to about the middle of the 15th century. The whole of European society, from the depths to the surface, was as though in a state of fermentation. While the Church, harassed to begin with by its exile in Avignon, and then by the Great Schism, and finally by the quarrels of the Popes and the Council, was shaken by convulsive movements, of which the heresies of Wycliffe and Huss were the most formidable manifestations—while France and England were at war—while the Empire was finally disintegrating amidst the quarrels of the rival houses contending for the crown of Germany—while in Italy, more dismembered than ever, every type of State and every imaginable policy might be observed—while the Slav States were reacting to the German advance, and repulsing it—while the Turks, profiting by the intestine quarrels of the West, were invading the Balkan peninsula, and were soon to seize Constantinople, the peoples were perturbed by social insurrections, excited by the hasty quarrels of the parties, or the prey of a general unrest which sometimes found expression in tentative reforms, and sometimes by the oppression of the weaker classes by the more powerful. A spirit of restlessness was abroad, affecting men's minds as well as their policies; even religion was not immune; it was a restlessness that almost amounted to mental confusion. The world was suffering and struggling, but it was hardly advancing. For the only thing of which it was clearly conscious was the fact that all was not well with it. It longed to escape from its ills, but it did not know how it could do so. No one had anything to offer in the place of the tradition that weighed upon it and from which it could not liberate itself. Though they were badly shaken, the old ideals still survived; one finds them everywhere, modified, no doubt, or impaired, but still unchanged in any essential. In their fundamental characteristics the Church, the State, and the social and economic constitution remained, throughout these hundred and fifty years, what they had been at the close of the 13th century. The same may be said of art and science. Gothic architecture and the Scholastic philosophy still had enough vitality to produce interesting work, but the period of their masterpieces was past. Everywhere the world was in labour, but it produced only abortive births. There was a definite feeling abroad that it was waiting for a spiritual renewal. But the dawn was slow in coming, though here and there a gleam was visible. The men of this period were restless, nervous, melancholy. Not one of them achieved true greatness. Compare John XXII or Clement VII with Innocent III or Boniface VIII; Charles V with St. Louis, Charles IV with Frederick II! These, no doubt, were singular or attractive personalities, but personalities of the second class, not one of whom could be regarded as the embodiment of his age, for the thing most conspicuously lacking in this period of instability was a really specific character, an ideal which might inspire it and which it might strive to attain.

What is really new about this period, what strikes one immediately upon a general survey, is its revolutionary tendencies. They were nowhere triumphant, but they were felt in every department of life. The State and the Church were no more secure against them than was society. All the traditional authorities were criticized and assailed: the popes and kings no less than the landowners and the capitalists. The great masses of the people, who had hitherto endured or supported the power of the State, were now rebelling against it. No previous epoch had ever furnished so many names of tribunes, demagogues, agitators, and reformers. But there was no coherence in all this unrest, and no continuity. There were numerous and violent crises, but they were dispersed and of brief duration; the symptoms of a social unrest which was felt more acutely in some regions than in others, and which, according to the region, expressed itself in different ways. If we wish to realize the progress and the extent of this unrest, we must look for it, first of all, in the simplest and most general phenomena of social life—that is, in phenomena of an economic order.

But here we shall discover no essential novelty, nothing to be compared with the effect of the revival of trade and the rise of the cities.

The frontiers of Europe had not been extended since the foundation of the Italian settlements in the East, and of the German cities on the Baltic; and there had been no further increase of population since the end of the 13th century and the first part of the 14th.

Venice in the South and Bruges in the North remained the two busiest commercial centres: Venice as the point of contact between East and West, and Bruges the connecting link between the trade of the North and that of Italy. The Germans of the South had their "fondaco" in Venice, just as the Germanic Hansa had its factory in Bruges.

In Italy a true system of capitalism was evolving, though it was hampered by the more and more restricted economic demands of the cities.

The towns engaged in the Flemish weaving industry in the North, and Florence in the South, were still, as in the 13th century, the two great centres of industry and the export trade. Cotton was only beginning to make its appearance. No technical progress was manifested. Machinery and methods were still very much what they were in the days of ancient Egypt. The curing of herrings first introduced in Holland, during the 14th century, seems to, have been the only novelty of any importance to be recorded.

It is true that the circulation of men and goods had undergone some development. While the roads were still generally defective navigation was increasing in importance: larger ships were built, and they made longer voyages. From the beginning of the 14th century the galleys of Venice and Genoa made their way to Bruges and to London. On the Atlantic coast the Basques and the Bretons maintained an active coastal trade. The cogs of the Hansa cities sailed to all parts of the North Sea and the Baltic. Holland and England were so far interested only in local navigation.

The circulation of money was even more noticeable than that of manufactured and other products. This explains why, from the end of the 14th century, gold coins were regularly struck in France, Flanders, Poland and Hungary. Under the influence of the Italian merchants, who had already brought it to a high pitch of perfection in the 13th century, the minting of money was undergoing still further improvement.

The bill of exchange with acceptance made its appearance in the first half of the 14th century. Pegolotti wrote the *Practica della Mercatura*. Book-keeping by double entry seems to date back to 1394. But however notable these improvements may have been, they were not enough to constitute the point of departure of a new era of economic history. They undoubtedly betray a tendency toward the development of capitalism and the improvement of trade and commerce, yet if we consider the period as a whole we shall readily perceive that one of its most obvious characteristics was its hostility to capitalism, except in Italy.

The explanation of this must be sought in the evolution of the bourgeoisie; that is to say, of the class responsible for the entire commercial and industrial activity of Europe. Apart from very rare exceptions, of which the most conspicuous was Venice, from the end of the 13th century, the preponderance of the patricians in the cities was replaced, more or less completely, by that of the handicrafts, trades and professions.

Even if the artisans could not obtain political control of the local government, they could at least influence the organization of the municipal economy. This means that from being under the control of the great merchants it came under that of the small producers, and that henceforth the spirit which inspired it underwent a corresponding change.

In the beginning, the guilds or trade fraternities were free associations of artisans following the same calling, who combined for the defence of their common interests. As far as their aims were concerned, they could quite accurately be compared with the voluntary syndicates or trade unions of our own days; their most important function was to regulate competition. Every newcomer, under penalty of ostracism, had to affiliate himself to a guild. It will be understood that in the beginning such a situation must have given rise to disputes and conflicts between the syndicated confraternities and those recalcitrant workers who refused to sacrifice their liberty. The municipal authorities were as much concerned as the artisans themselves to make an end to such disturbances. In order to do so, they only had to give the trade organizations a legal status: or in other words, to transform them from voluntary into obligatory syndicates recognized by the communal authority. The oldest examples of this transformation date back to the 12th century; by the beginning of the 14th century it was general, and as the same causes everywhere produced the same result it took place all over Europe. Henceforth, in every city, each trade was the monopoly of a privileged group of masters. Only those could exercise it who had been officially admitted as members of the group. In its main features the organization was everywhere identical. Between the French *corps de métier*, the Flemish *ambacht*, the English "craft," the Italian *arte* and the German *Zunft* there were only superficial differences, due to the differences of national customs, or the degrees of autonomy which the corporation enjoyed in respect of the urban power. Among the Germanic as among the Latin peoples its nature was the same. Here again, as in all the fundamental phenomena of European life, the national element was expressed only in externals; the essential phenomenon was the consequence of necessities to which, under the same circumstances, human nature is everywhere subject.

Everywhere the trade corporation had its chiefs (deans, syndics, *vinders*, etc.), who were clothed with official authority; everywhere it drew up professional regulations and saw to it that they were observed; everywhere it enjoyed the right of assembly; everywhere it constituted a moral personality, having a treasury and common premises, and everywhere the hierarchy of its members was the same. The craftsman entered the guild or corporation as apprentice, was promoted to the rank of journeyman, and finally became a master.

Generally speaking, we must envisage the master as the head and proprietor of a workshop, in which were employed, under his orders, one or two journeymen, and an apprentice. In him we have the most perfect type of the artisan—that is to say, the small producer working in his own home. The raw material which he elaborated was his own property, and he sold the finished product at his own exclusive profit. The consumers on whom his livelihood depended were the burgesses of the city and the peasants of the surrounding countryside. The petty character of his industry and the small amount of capital involved were thus in proportion to the restricted nature of his market. If he was to live at all he had to be protected against competition; not only the external competition of the foreigner, but also the local competition of his fellow-craftsmen. To prevent such competition was the first object of the corporation. In order to assure the independence of the masters it restricted their liberty, subjecting it to curious regulations. The economic subordination of each member guaranteed the security of all; hence the circumstantial prescriptions by which the artisan was encompassed. He was forbidden to sell his wares at a price below the tariff fixed by the regulations; he was forbidden to work by artificial light; he must not use tools of unusual form, or modify the traditional technique, or employ more journeymen or apprentices than his neighbours, or allow his wife to work, or such children as were not of age; and lastly—and this prohibition was absolute—he must not advertise his wares or praise them to the detriment of those produced by others. Thus each worker was given his place in the sun, but it was a place very strictly delimited, and it was quite impossible for him to emerge from it.[1] But no one ever dreamed of doing so. For when a man's livelihood is secure his desires are moderate. The corporations provided the *petite bourgeoisie* with a framework admirably adapted to its character. With-

[1] Capitalism s not in itself opposed to the tendencies of human nature, but its restriction is. Economic liberty is spontaneous. The trade corporation suppresses liberty because it threatens the majority. It presupposes, of course, that this majority exercises political power.

out a doubt, it had never been so happy and contented as under their régime. For this class, but for this class alone, they had solved the social problem. By safeguarding it against competition they also protected it against the intervention of capitalism. Until the French Revolution the craftsmen and petty manufacturers were obstinately faithful to the corporations that so well safeguarded their interests. Few economic institutions have been so tenacious.

The first half of the 14th century was the period when the handicrafts attained their apogee. But as they evolved, the two essential features of their constitution—monopoly and privilege—naturally became more and more prominent. Each group of artisans racked its brains to increase, and to go on increasing, the protectionism that surrounded it like the walls of a fortress. The admission of new members was made more difficult; apprenticeship became more protracted and more exacting; promotion to the rank of master became more costly, so that the poor journeyman could hardly hope to achieve it. A sort of industrial Malthusianism began to make its appearance, which surrendered the local market to a small number of masters, and the absence of competition among them simply meant that the consumer was exploited. The sudden check in the increase of the urban population which was a general phenomenon about the year 1350 was undoubtedly due to this corporative exclusivism, which was gradually making it impossible for people to leave the country and establish themselves in the cities. But in the cities themselves, in the ranks of the bourgeoisie, what complaints and protests were heard! What indignant reproaches were bandied about between the different trades, each condemning in the others the excesses of the monopoly which it felt to be justifiable in its own case alone! At the same time, the original spirit of fraternity was replaced, among the craftsmen, by an increasing opposition of interests between the masters and the journeymen, who were more and more reduced to the status of mere wage-earners. Riots broke out; there were strikes; and in many regions "compagnonnages" of journeymen were formed, mutual associations of workers organized to defend their interests against the employers. In short, from the beginning of the 15th century the abuses of the system were so evident that there were those who demanded the abolition of the corporations and the liberty of the handicrafts.

The situation was much more serious in those cities which were the centres of the textile industry, such as Florence in the South and the Flemish and Brabançon cities in the North, which carried on a regular export industry. The kind of trade organization which was suitable for craftsmen whose livelihood depended on the local markets was obviously unable to satisfy the needs of workers engaged in mass production for an unrestricted market. It could not possibly afford protection against the influence of capital to the weavers, fullers and clothworkers, masters or journeymen, who crowded the lanes and alleys of Gand, Bruges, and Ypres, or the *vicoli* on the banks of the Arno. Here the artisan was necessarily subordinated to the rich merchant who provided him with wool, and to whom the manufactured product was delivered after the various manipulations which it had to undergo. As to its external form, the cloth trade presented the same aspect as the other trades; here, as elsewhere, the home industry was predominant. But in this case the employer himself was merely a wage-earner employing other wage-earners. Further, the workers in the cloth trade, instead of numbering only a few dozen or a few score, as in the trades which provided the bourgeoisie with the necessities of life, numbered hundreds and even thousands. But the great industry which employed all these workers was subject to crises. If a war broke out, if the export of English wool was forbidden, unemployment supervened, with all its miseries. Even in normal times there were incessant disputes as to wages, whether between the merchant-manufacturers and the heads of weaving-sheds or workshops, or between the latter and their journeymen. Thus, the condition of the workers in the cloth industry in those cities where the industry provided the basis of a considerable export trade was very like that of the modern proletariat. And they were an organized proletariat. For, like the artisans properly so called, they were grouped together in corporations; and although the incredible demands of wholesale trade prevented them from ruling the market and regulating prices and wages, these corporations did at least enable them to oppose too excessive exploitation and to provide for mutual aid in times of crisis.

The political result of these corporative organizations was naturally to wrest the government of the cities from the patrician oligarchies who were in power in the 13th century. It was no longer possible for a few "lineages" of landowners and merchants, sitting in the city council, to do precisely what they chose in the matter of regulating trade and commerce, and assessing taxes and personal contributions, etc. They did not surrender their position without resistance. Their government had been, in the full force of the term, a class government, and they obstinately clung to their privileged position. The whole of the 14th century was filled with the conflict of the *grandi* and the *piccoli* for the possession of municipal power. It is natural to compare these conflicts with those which were provoked in the 19th century by the question of the parliamentary franchise. In each case the masses, refused the right to manage their own affairs, persisted in their demands. The fundamental cause of the two crises was the same. However different men's manners, sentiments and ideas may have been, what the patricians were defending against the claims of the handicrafts was the same preponderance which the property-owners' Parliaments of our own time defended so long and so obstinately against the demand for universal suffrage. The whole of the 14th century, like the whole of the 19th, was shaken by the struggles of democracy. The democracy of our days, however, takes the form of a régime which safeguards the political rights of every citizen. In those petty States, the cities of the Middle Ages, the conception of democracy was proportionately restricted; it was as narrow as the limits of the city, and it could not have been otherwise. Society was too subdivided, subject to too many clashes, too localized to permit of the emergence of the concept of general liberty. The city was a little enclosed world, living for itself, indifferent to the feelings and the interests of classes which were alien to it. The artisan was as strictly bourgeois as the patrician, and quite as exclusive in his feelings toward all who did not inhabit his commune. He knew nothing of the levelling spirit of proselytism, as indifferent to local groups as it is to juridical classes, which the spectacle of the modern democracies has accustomed us to regard as inherent in any popular régime. Fundamentally, democracy as he conceived it was merely a democracy of privileged individuals, since the bourgeoisie itself, as compared with the inhabitants of the countryside, was a privileged class.

However, the pure democratic régime was triumphant in only a few cities. In most cases some sort of compromise was arrived at. The patriciate, voluntarily, or under pressure from the mob, made way for the corporations, and constitutions came into force of which we may say, despite innumerable differences of detail, that they organized a sort of representation of interests. Once the opposing interests had achieved equilibrium, these constitutions, as a general thing, became congealed into fixity. It is certainly a fact that urban legislation was much more active and more fertile of innovation in the 13th than in the 14th century. These democracies of privileged *petits bourgeois* were characterized by egoism and protectionism. Urban politics became even more exclusive than before where, as in France and in England, it was not compelled to reckon with the State. Its aim was the achievement of complete political liberty, of the free city, as it already existed in Germany. Economic progress was naturally affected by such a programme. Capital, encompassed by suspicious and fumbling legislation, could develop only beyond its control, in the domain of inter-urban trade. Here men still made their fortunes, though less frequently than in the previous century. The local patriciate no longer played a part in the development of capitalism, and became a class of *rentiers*. By the side of the patriciate new men were making their appearance, who taxed their ingenuity to evade the regulations of protectionism; but it will be time to consider their activities in our survey of the following period.

However, all the cities were not of the same type, nor were they inspired by the same spirit. They were not all controlled by the *petite bourgeoisie*, and where the export industry produced a proletariat they offered a very different spectacle. In Italy, the upheavals of the Florentine democracy afford a striking example of this difference. In Florence the system of trade corporations could not establish itself as readily as elsewhere. The workers in the woollen industry and other manufactures for export were too numerous; and special provision had to be made for them. As a matter of fact, from 1282 onwards the *nobili* were excluded from the government of Florence by the constitution, which confided the power of government to six *priori delle arte*, chosen from among the twelve great corporations, one for each of the six wards of the city; and they were changed every two months. This was a government of merchants and manufacturers, a government of the *popolo grasso*. But the *popolo minuto* was socially oppressed. In 1341 it supported Gauthier de Brienne, who overthrew the ruling plutocrats and set himself up as tyrant. Two years later he was overthrown in his turn. The *popolo grasso* then returned to power, but was violently expelled in 1378 by the democratic revolt of the *Ciompi*,[1] led by the guilds of the wool-carders, but it once more returned to power in 1382.

The same sort of thing happened in the Flemish cities. From the beginning of the 13th century the weavers and the fullers had been complaining of the oppressive government of the patriciate. The patriciate looked to France for support, and the battle of Courtrai was in reality a social victory for the artisans. But the new régime, which depended on the support of the wool-carders, was unable to hold its own; inevitably the merchants came to the top again. And so, during the whole of the 14th century, there was a series of convulsions and upheavals. The workers had vague dreams of an impossible communism. There were Flemish workers among the followers of Wat Tyler, as there were later among the Hussites, and in the sect of the Adamites. Gand, above all, where the weavers were in greater strength than anywhere else, was distingiushed by its sullen violence. Under Louis de Maele their audacity reached its height. For six years, despite amazing vicissitudes, they held their own against the prince, the nobles, and all "good folk who had anything to lose." From all parts of Europe the suffering proletarians fixed their gaze upon Gand. There were cries of "Vive

[1] The name given to the inferior guilds in Florence.

Gand" in Paris and Rouen. It was felt that they were threatening the entire social order, and at Roosebeke (1382) the King of France inflicted upon them a terrible defeat. The weavers of Gand were certainly the most ardent protagonists of democracy to make their appearance in the 14th century. But all their energy could achieve nothing. It was impossible for them to escape from the capitalism under which they suffered. The factors which gave rise to that capitalism were beyond their reach. Constantly rebelling, they were constantly defeated. The other trades turned against them. The fullers, who were even poorer, and whom they oppressed, made common cause with their enemies. The result of their efforts was to make the merchants and business men look to the princes for support, and to take steps to remove the industry from the cities to the countryside.

While these internal commotions or transformations were occurring within the cities, they were acquiring a political importance in the outer world which they had never before possessed, and which, as a matter of fact, they had never sought. The increasing expenditure which war imposed upon the State or the princes compelled the latter to find some new means of replenishing their treasuries; for now that bands of mercenaries and fleets were playing a greater part in warfare, it was becoming more costly than ever. The old sources of revenue were insufficient. It was possible to borrow from the Italian bankers. And the princes did raise money from them, but this involved them in onerous obligations. It was possible to debase the currency, but this again was a dangerous expedient. To decree a fresh impost was not possible; at the most, fresh *tonlieux* could be imposed. There was no financial absolutism about the juridical State of the Middle Ages. Consequently, the only thing to be done was to apply to the Third Estate—that is, to the cities—and to ask them to open their purses. They were willing enough to do so, but they demanded guarantees. The State knew only how to spend; it did not yet understand how to create resources for itself. It was completely dependent on taxation, and a taxation that was a drain on its wealth. From the beginning of the 14th century the necessity of taxation dominated the prince's policy, and compelled him to accede to the demands of the cities and the Estates, which wrested privileges from him, and would presently even claim the right to participate in his power; in the Duchy of Brabant the Charter of Cortenberg, the Walloon Charter, and finally the Joyous Entry; in the Pays de Liége, the Peace of Fexhe, and in the County of Flanders, the Constitution of the Members of Flanders, all originated in this way; and in France the same predicament provoked the disturbances of the epoch of Étienne Marcel. The States-General of 1355 attempted to restrict the rights of the Crown; in 1413 the Ordonnance Cabochienne was forced upon the king by the trade corporations of Paris; and in England the parliamentary influence of the cities was constantly increasing. The 15th century was the epoch in which the bourgeoisie began to play a political as well as a class rôle. It took its place beside the clergy and the *noblesse*.[1] In Aragon too, under Pedro IV (1336–1387), the cities began to impose their will on the Crown. That taxation came from the cities was evident in Spain, where, under Alphonso XI of Castile (1312–1358), the war against the Moors compelled Burgos to introduce the *alcalaba*, which was then extended to cover the whole kingdom.

The financial needs of the princes made the 14th century a century of parliamentarianism, or shall we say, a century of Estates. In Belgium there were annual assemblies of the Estates in all the provinces. In France they insisted on meeting despite the opposition of the Crown. And every assembly of Estates was always to the advantage of the Third Estate. It was the Third Estate alone which supported the institution and profited by it, because it disposed of the finances. And it was the Third Estate alone which made conditions and demanded guarantees.

But the Third Estate was itself merely a class of privileged persons, and beneath it was the majority of the nation, the Fourth Estate, which was never mentioned, though it bore the burden. Undoubtedly its condition was much less tolerable after the 14th century than it had been for two hundred years. We have seen

[1] It was in the 14th century that the financiers began to acquire political importance.

how the rise of the cities, by unsettling the economic status of the countryside, shattered the domainal system, releasing great expanses of territory and great numbers of the rural inhabitants. At that time the rural classes gave evidence of unusual energy. They cleared uncultivated ground, they emigrated, and yet the population was rapidly increasing. But there was an end to all this during the first half of the century. Emigration no longer offered an outlet; the available land was occupied (in Eastern Germany), and the cities were closing their gates. Meanwhile taxation was heavier than ever and was still increasing. Moreover, there was a surplus of workers, so that the situation of the peasants was most unfavourable. The nobles took advantage of this, endeavouring to re-establish their old feudal rights, and, in a general manner, to exploit the peasants, for the old patriarchal relations of the domainal epoch no longer existed. In maritime Flanders a terrible rebellion broke out, which lasted from 1324 to 1328. The peasants hunted the chevaliers, and refused to pay their tithes. A true social hatred finds expression in the *Kerelslied*. This terrible rising ended in the massacre of Cassel, and in wholesale confiscations. In France, the so-called revolt of the Jacques in 1357—which, I admit, may have been partly the result of the sufferings caused by the war—gave evidence of a profound hostility between the rural masses and the noblesse, which must have had causes of a more general kind. The English rebellion of 1381, which is that concerning which we are best informed, was due to attempts on the part of the nobles to re-establish the old corvées, in order to avoid paying the higher wages which were one of the consequences of the Black Death. In Germany we shall find no popular movement of this kind until the beginning of the 16th century. However, since the end of the 14th century the condition of the peasants had been growing visibly worse; especially, it seems, in the South. The nobles took advantage of their need of land in order to oppress them.[1]

[1] The victory of the men of Schwis, Uri and Unterwalden over Duke Leopold of Austria in 1315 cannot be regarded at a social insurrection. These were free peasants fighting to preserve their independence. The rising was more nearly analogous to the struggle of the Frisians against the Counts of Holland, which ended in the battle of Stavoren (1345).

Generally speaking, people began to despise the peasant as a helot who stood outside society. There were no more charters of rural franchises in the 14th century, except in a few new countries, such as Northern Holland. The cities too oppressed the rural districts, taking care that no industries should be practised there. All through the 14th century Gand was organizing expeditions which destroyed the looms and the fullers' vats in the villages and country towns. And the monasteries no longer extended the old social protection over the "villeins," but added to their wretchedness by their exaction of the tithe.

As for the nobles, they too were passing through a serious crisis. They had retained the ancient forms of chivalry, but the spirit was no longer present. It had vanished with the end of the Crusades. I cannot find that anything remained of the old idealism, apart from certain outward gallantry. Fidelity to the seigneur was now merely a word. The chief preoccupation of the chevalier was now his fief. Homage (that noble word) now meant little more to him than registration. What did survive was the military character of the noble class. But this often assumed the aspect of mercenary military service. The knights of the Rhine valley, Austria, and Hesbaye, began to hire themselves to the King of France. Knights-errant began to make their appearance, fighting on all fronts and for all causes; Froissart has given us the portraits of many such. These were professional soldiers, who were not very far removed from the *condottiere*—leaders of bands, experienced captains to whom war was a lucrative calling. Du Guesclin, one of the most typical of these knights, was a pure soldier. The literature of the *chansons de geste* came to an end or was rewritten. What men of this class read was narratives of campaigns, fought for no matter what or whom, but yielding handsome profits, and there must be feasting and women, as described by Froissart. At heart these knights were adventurers: very valiant men, but also violent and greedy. They were fond of sport: we see them engaging in tournaments, and in Lithuania, in the winter, in man-hunts, and even in expeditions like that of Nicopoli, where they were defeated by the Turks (1396). Some also went to break a lance in Granada.

In countries where manners were still more brutal than elsewhere, as in Germany, matters were even worse. Here the *Raubritter* made his appearance, a sort of bravo who made use of the pretext of *Fehden* (private wars) to hold the adjacent countryside to ransom; a brutal bandit, robbing the merchants; a village tyrant, oppressing the peasants who lived beneath his castle walls; who fled before the Hussites or the Swiss peasants.

For it was no longer by this military noblesse that battles were won. Artillery, which was first heard at Crecy, still played only a secondary part in any campaign, but the infantry was gradually recovering the position which it had lost since the Carolingian epoch. At Courtrai it destroyed the French chivalry; the Swiss infantry had been winning battles since 1315; the foot-soldiers were the backbone of the English army, where they were formed into companies of archers; and the tactics of Johann Ziska, leader of the Hussites, was based on the infantry. Thus, despite appearances, the part played by the noble and the knight was constantly diminishing. It is very significant that the purest military figure of the time, Joan of Arc, was a peasant. And while, from the military point of view, the nobles were in retreat, they were not distinguishing themselves in other respects. They played no part in the government, and they were not becoming more cultivated. Obviously the services which they rendered were not commensurate with the position which they occupied. And this is all the more striking inasmuch as their position was more advantageous than ever. The upper ranks of the clergy, and the chapters, became the monopoly of the younger sons of noble families. The democratic character of the Church was disappearing. Consider the type of canon represented by Jean Le Bel and Froissart; think of bishops like Adolphe de la Marck! In the upper ranks of the ecclesiastical hierarchy there was a stupendous moral and intellectual decadence; in accordance with the tastes of society, the clergy were becoming worldly.

If we examine them closely, shall we not see among the nobles, considering them as a whole, a tendency analogous to that which we may observe in the patriciate of the bourgeoisie? Neither class was undergoing any further development; they were digging themselves in, so to speak, in the position which they had acquired. Their only care was to preserve their privileges and their property. They were no longer capable of idealism, and hardly of disinterestedness. Consider the great examples of devotion in the 14th century: the "Bourgeois of Calais," Étienne Marcel, van Artevelde: there was not a nobleman among them. There were no such figures in the 14th century as Simon de Montfort, Villehardouin, or Joinville. Manners were embellished by a veneer of elegance, but under that they were brutal. We have only to read Froissart to see that these nobles loved money above all things. On the whole, they were brutal sensualists. Not one of them was distinguished for his piety or his beneficence. And here I am speaking of those who played some part in the life of the world. The others hunted, looked after their estates, and oppressed the peasants. It is surprising to discover how completely sterile were the nobles of the 14th and the beginning of the 15th century, despite their numerical strength.

However, a new social stratum was beginning to spread over the old basis of the feudal chivalry. In the 14th century we see the first traces of what may be called the *noblesse de cour*. In the 13th century it hardly existed. Then, of course, as always, the king's entourage consisted of nobles. But their position was independent of the court. They frequented the court as the king's companions. They did not constitute his household. There was a royal household in the Frankish epoch, a somewhat heterogeneous mixture of dignitaries and servitors, whose names have been preserved in those of the great officers of the Crown. But as soon as the monarchy became powerful they disappeared, or were transformed into functionaries, or merely ornamental personages. The hereditary nature of their duties, which bound them to the king, was abolished. They began as members of the king's domestic staff, who were not freemen; in the feudal period they became metamorphosed into great hereditary officers, only to disappear upon the reconstitution of the monarchical power. But the powerful monarchy which had demolished the ancient court since the 12th century had to create a new court for itself.

It would seem that the nucleus of this court consisted not of nobles, but of commoners: councillors, servants in charge of the king's plate and his wardrobe, etc., with a few clerks. But was the king to be surrounded by plebeians? The court is a resort of the nobility. Consequently the king proceeded to ennoble his officers and his functionaries. This was a new nobility, entirely different from the old military chivalry. It was now conferred for civil services, and intelligence or learning, rather than for military service and valour. And this new nobility was entirely dependent on the sovereigns. In the beginning any knight could "arm" another. It was no longer so in the 14th century. The king alone was the source of nobility, and so he remained until the end of the *ancien régime*. From the end of the 13th century, anyone who was ennobled was ennobled by the king alone. The nobles of the robe—such as the Chancellor Rolin, Jacques Cœur, and many another—took their place beside the nobles of the sword.

Here was a novel factor of very great social importance. To my thinking, it saved the noblesse, which was decaying as a military caste, and could not enrich itself, because it constituted a juridical caste, which was becoming more and more a closed social category. In the person of these newcomers it received fresh recruits, and they were commonly very wealthy recruits, thanks to their participation in the government. It despised them, but it was they who saved it.

Here again we note the influence of tradition. In point of formation, and in respect of its occupation, the *noblesse de robe* was a kind of lay clergy. It had nothing in common with the old nobility in whose ranks it now installed itself. Why then did the new nobility enter the old? Because there was no other place for it in the society of those days. It could not, on coming to court, remain in the ranks of the bourgeoisie, which would have continued to influence it and to detach it from the prince. Could it enter the ranks of the clergy? A few of the new men did so, and were rewarded with bishoprics and cardinals' hats. But for the rest there was no society available but that of the nobility, for the plebeian class consisted only of peasants. Thus, by a process which was necessary though it was not natural, the high government officials became a sort of annexe of a social class whose origin was purely military. The social habits and interests of the new class merged themselves in those of the old. And with this the nobility acquired a more comprehensive status. Henceforth it included the entire élite of the nation. To be an *homme convenable* a man must be a member of the noblesse. The consequences of this fact were hardly perceptible in the 14th century and the beginning of the 15th. They were to be incalculable later, and even to this day there are many States which have not yet shaken them off. The Renaissance was powerless to dissolve this social bloc. This was reserved for the modern democracies. However profound the influence of the bourgeoisie might be in the State, the noblesse, during the whole of the *ancien régime*, retained its primacy of social rank, and every man who emerged from the bourgeoisie endeavoured to enter it.

## 2. *The Religious Movement*

The 13th century saw the Catholic Church attain its apogee. It presented the grandiose spectacle of a government endowed with all its organs, so powerful that not only could it victoriously resist the attacks made upon it, but every victory left it still more powerful. In form this government was a monarchy, which was strongly reminiscent of the Roman Empire in whose midst it was born, and it had retained the capital, the language, and, with necessary modifications, the law and the administrative traditions of the Empire. And again, as in the Roman Empire, its head, the Pope, was uplifted above the rest of mankind, a sacred personage, whose commands were laws, and who was amenable to no man's judgements. However, it was not this that gave the Papacy its extraordinary vitality. This it derived from the religious society whose enthusiastic support it enjoyed, which lived in close communion with it through its faith, and from whose ranks it was continually receiving an afflux of fresh recruits, a perpetual source of rejuvenation. Piety was continually inspiring the masses to establish new monastic orders, adapted to the needs of the period, which, subject to its guidance, furnished it with the spiritual army which it needed to discipline or defend the Church: Clunisians in the 11th century, Cistercians and Premonstrants in the 12th, Franciscans and Dominicans in the 13th. To enable him to deal with heresy the Pope had his police, the Inquisition. And he had only to appeal to the peoples for help, and immediately thousands of champions of orthodoxy leapt forward to massacre the infidel. Lastly, all education was under his control; the learning of the Universities was no less obedient to his influence than the zeal of the religious.

But it is evident that about the middle of the 13th century the Church had attained the maximum of its power. It had ceased to grow, and presently began to decline. The principal cause of this decline must be attributed, as we have already seen, to the attitude which lay society had adopted in respect of the Church. On the one hand, the national States, in their need of independence, shook off the tutelage of the Papacy; on the other hand, the more active and laborious peoples, mainly concerned with their economic interests, and becoming inaccessible to the naïve idealism of the Crusades, were also beginning to escape from the exclusive control of religion. Evidently the Church was ceasing to be the sole mistress of the faithful, or rather, its influence upon men's souls was no longer without a rival. Its authority was no longer all-powerful because it no longer imposed itself spontaneously on every aspect of political and social life. Without intention, without being really conscious of what they were doing, men were gradually turning away from the influence of the Church. And the Church was not aware of this desertion. Although its moral strength and its political influence were diminishing, it surrendered none of its pretensions, none of its hopes. Even after the disaster suffered by Boniface VIII, even after the exodus of the Pope to Avignon, even during the conflict of the Popes with the Council, it remained obstinately faithful to the ideal of the Crusade, and continued to claim supremacy over the peoples and their kings. It even revived the old quarrel with the Empire, and John XXII excommunicated Louis of Bavaria (1324) as Innocent IV had excommunicated Frederick II —but what a difference between this performance and the grandiose drama of the 13th century! However loud the accusations of the two parties, the rest of Europe remained indifferent. The monks, jurists, and theologians were involved in the quarrel, but the States stood aside. The Minorite Friars, whose doctrine of evangelical poverty had been condemned by the Pope, went over to Louis of Bavaria, who found it impossible to refuse these strange auxiliaries, and, tormented by scruples, allowed them to involve him in the accusations of heresy which they hurled against John XXII. However, in the midst of the battle of pamphlets the omnipotence of the pontiff, which was violently debated, provoked certain words which should not be forgotten. The *Defensor Pacis* of Marsilius of Padua, which was presently translated into French and Italian, expounded ideas of which we may note the first traces in the entourage of Frederick II and Philip the Fair. But only now were they fully developed, and they amazed the world by their boldness. For Marsilius the pretensions of the Papacy were merely an intolerable usurpation, as incompatible with the interpretation of the Holy Scriptures and the usages of the primitive Church as they were disastrous to the peace of the world. The Pope was merely a bishop like any other. His entire mission consisted in preaching the faith and administering the sacraments. All interference in the temporal domain, all jurisdiction over laymen should be refused him. And expatiating on this question, Marsilius defined the Church: the community of all those who believe in Jesus Christ. Before Wycliffe and before Huss, he declared that the layman belonged to the Church no less than the priest, and he categorically insisted that the "clerks" should be subject to the secular power in all temporal relations. Of course, we must not exaggerate the influence of these declarations. It is not apparent that they produced any practical effect. They had, as yet, only the importance of a symptom, and in religious as in social questions, contemporaries do not usually notice the symptoms which precede a crisis.

How far can Marsilius of Padua have been influenced by the religious tendencies of his age? There is, at all events, between the mysticism of his day, and his conception of a Church which should comprise both the laity and the clergy, a concordance which must doubtless be attributed to that mysterious harmony which may be observed, at this time, between the various manifestations of the intellect. In its profoundest and most spontaneous features the piety of the 14th century was essentially mystical. In its efforts to attain to God the Church no longer sufficed it. Without hesitation, it took flight towards Him; it sought to contemplate Him face to face in the intimacy of the consciousness, without the intermediary of the priest. Moreover—and this is a peculiarly characteristic innovation —it no longer expressed itself in the tongue of the Church. Nearly all the mystics—Eckhardt († 1327), Tauler († 1365), Ruysbroek († 1381)—wrote in the language of the people, thus for the first time giving religious thought a secular form, and so undermining the prestige of the clergy, who had hitherto enjoyed the sole monopoly of religious ideas.[1] At all events, it is certain that the clergy, whether regular or secular, no longer had the same influence over the faithful as of old. It is true that the ascetic ideal of monasticism was still attracting many novices to the convents, but monasticism was no longer regarded by all as the highest and most perfect form of Christian life. Mysticism took alarm at the fact that a conventual rule necessarily imposes constraint upon spiritual liberty. It preferred solitary contemplation, as a voluntary practice, or such congregations as were exempt from perpetual vows, like the *béguinages*, or the community of the Brothers of the Common Life, founded by Goert Groot († 1384). Here piety could still expand beyond the boundaries which the Church had created to confine it. For neither the Béguines nor the Bégards nor the Brothers of the Common Life were religious Orders. They did not consider that the secular life was incompatible with devotion, or that it was necessary to flee the world in order to enter into relations with God. Thus the most original and most active manifestations of piety in the 14th century were to be found outside monasticism. As for the latter, it made no further progress. It founded no new Orders, unless we give this name to a few communities which were so closely related to the Franciscans that it is very difficult to

[1] Cf. Bridget, Catherine of Siena, Gerson, Vincent-Ferrier, Pierre de Luxembourg.

distinguish them from the latter, and in any case they played only a very secondary part.[1]

This spread of mysticism in the lay community was doubly perilous for the Church. To begin with, it represented a danger to orthodoxy. Without the curb of a rule and the permanent control of authority, the contemplative life might easily cross the frontiers of the Roman dogma. The danger was all the greater inasmuch as these naïve zealots were without theological training, since most of them came from the ranks of the people or the *petite bourgeoisie*. As a matter of fact, during the whole of the 14th century they constantly attracted the attention of the Inquisitors, and sailed very close to the perilous reefs of heresy. The Pope even went so far as to condemn the religion of the Béguines as suspect. During the Black Death of 1347–1348 bands of penitents, urged onward by a sort of ecstatic delirium, went from city to city, exciting the people, like Oriental fakirs, by their singing, their dancing, or their public flagellations. In Italy, France and Germany obscure sects appeared which seemed to have preserved something of the doctrines and the dreams of the Albigenses; they were known as "Spirituals, Apostolics, Friends of God." All these mystics—and this was the second danger to the Church—aspired to lead the world back to evangelical poverty. This question of poverty troubled the whole of the 14th century. Among the workers in the manufacturing cities, and the English rebels in 1381, it gave rise to communistic aspirations, which the secular power proceeded to stifle. But even more widespread, and even more difficult to contend with, was the criticism of the religious authorities, beginning with the highest of all, the Papacy. For the more completely the Church had adopted the monarchical form, the more zealously it surrounded its head with pomp and luxury. In respect of the artists which it attracted and employed, the majesty of its ceremonies, the number of its servants, the expert hierarchy of its bureaucrats, and the abundance of its revenues, the court of Avignon was so far in advance of the royal courts, even those of France and England, that the very comparison was impossible. And the cardinals who

[1] For example, the Carthusians.

were gathered about the Pope vied with one another in point of magnificence and luxury. The fiscal system of the Papacy, which even in the 13th century was so highly developed, was still further extended, and strove to find new resources which would meet the increased expenditure. From the pontificate of John XXII it subjected the ecclesiastical hierarchy to a system of expedient taxes and dues, though it was difficult to persuade the pious that this was not tainted with simony. By the creation of *Reservationes* and *Provisiones* the Pope now had at his disposal, in all parts of Christendom, a quantity of benefices, which he could confer at will in return for payment. The natural consequence was that the Curia was besieged with applications, and the system was further extended by which ecclesiastical dignities were obtained by favour or in return for payment. Little attention was paid to the merit of the candidates, nor was it asked whether they possessed the requisite qualities for the post which they coveted. We have only to take a random glance at the episcopal catalogues of the 14th and 15th centuries in order to make some singular discoveries. Firstly, we observe the great preponderance of Italians and Frenchmen; then we shall note how short a time they commonly continued to officiate; and lastly, we shall see that nearly all belonged to the *haute noblesse*. Here we perceive the inevitable results of the system. Not only did it award the highest positions in the hierarchy to the younger sons of great families—not only did it introduce into many dioceses prelates who were unfamiliar with the manners and language of the faithful—but it also had the result of multiplying the translations from one see to another, each such transfer being, for the Curia, a source of taxes in proportion to the revenue of the vacant see (annates). It is not surprising that St. Bridget implored Gregory XI (†1378) to destroy the "lupanar" which the Holy Church had become.

To the offence which such practices gave to all pious souls, may be added the discontent of all those whose interests they injured, or who felt them as an affront to their national self-respect. The higher clergy and the princes of Germany were filled with indignation when they saw that the Curia was systematically favouring the Italians and the French, and that the heavy taxes imposed upon their dioceses mostly went into the pockets of foreigners. But Germany, dismembered and divided as she was, had no effective power, and her complaints merely attested to her impotence. It was otherwise in England. From the close of the reign of Edward III Parliament entered upon a vigorous campaign against the Curia's self-arrogated right of taxing the national Church and refusing to reserve all dignities and benefices for subjects of the king. The hostility to France excited by the war was extended to the Pope, whose partiality for that power was only too visible since he had left Rome for Avignon. In 1376 the "Good Parliament" demanded the suppression of the *Reservationes* and *Provisiones*, the expulsion of the pontifical collectors, and a law forbidding the exportation of money. Already voices were heard in the Commons demanding the secularization of the properties of the English Church.

It was in the midst of this political agitation that Wycliffe began his activities. It was almost inevitable that this agitation should have directly influenced his religious ideas. In him we see for the first time that concordance, or rather, that unconscious alliance of speculation and practice, of a tendency to universality and anxiety for the welfare of the nation, which was afterwards to characterize the genius of so many English thinkers, and which may doubtless be explained by the strong national solidarity with which the English people had been endowed by circumstances, long before any other European people.

Wycliffe was the first to tread the path which was to lead to the Reformation. He had nothing in common with the heretics who had troubled the Church before his time, and whose doctrines had their essential foundation, like that of the Albigenses, in the dualism of flesh and spirit. Wycliffe, who was utterly unlike them, brought nothing to Christianity that was not already there. He did not rebel against Christian dogma nor against Christian morality, but simply against the Church, and even more than against the Church, against the Papacy. The only head of the Church, he taught, was Christ. His word, recorded in the Bible, sufficed for the salvation of those who had faith. Now the Bible knew nothing of that powerful and religious hierarchy which the Church had become. Its ideal was poverty; it made no difference between the priest and the layman, from which one most conclude that the priests, like the rest of the faithful, were amenable to the secular laws and could not claim any privilege. England was absolutely independent of the Pope, for the temporal power of her king, like the spiritual power of the Church, was derived directly from God. As for the Pope, far from being the representative of Christ on the earth, he was actually the Antichrist. Before the people could practise the true religion it must go back to the Bible, with which it was no longer familiar; so, in order that the people might know the Bible, the reformer undertook to translate it into the vulgar tongue, inaugurating, by this great achievement, the history of English prose.

Hitherto England had been so orthodox that by great good fortune there had been no need to introduce the Inquisition. No people had been more docile to the teachings of the Church than the English, although, since the reign of Edward I, it had plainly manifested its intention of preventing the Church from exerting any influence in the political domain. By uniting, in his campaign against the Papacy, the religious and the political aspect of the matter, Wycliffe could not fail to interest in the religious question all those who were deeply interested in the political question. Within a few years he had enthusiastic supporters among both the nobles and the burgesses, while many members of the lower clergy accepted his doctrines, and as "simple priests" spread them among the people, surprising and attracting their hearers by the evangelical simplicity of their manners and the strength of their convictions. And in proportion as his influence increased, the reformer became bolder and more radical. He even went so far, in the name of the Bible, to as deny the Transubstantiation of Christ in the Communion. The Chancellor of the University of Oxford, and the Archbiship of Canterbury, might vainly accuse him of heresy, and his enemies might hold him responsible for the great agrarian rising of 1381, but the attitude of Parliament was so obviously favourable to Wycliffe that no one dared to persecute him, and in 1384 he died peacefully in his own parish of Lutterworth. It was only after the advent of Henry of Lancaster (Henry IV), that the king, desiring to obtain the support of the Pope for his new dynasty, turned against Wycliffism, or, to use the term employed by the adversaries of the reformers, against the sect of the Lollards.[1] At the very beginning of his reign—1401—he introduced the first law which ever condemned heretics to be burned at the stake in England, and which forbade the translation of the Bible into the national tongue, and sent Lord Cobham, the protector of the Lollards in the House of Lords, to the stake (1417). These violent measures hampered the movement without suppressing it. Until Protestantism made its appearance, the disciples of Wycliffe never ceased to influence the religious thought of England and to prepare it for the great transformation of the 16th century. Moreover, just as they were subjected to persecution in their own country, enthusiastic emulators, at the other end of Europe, took up the passionate defence of their doctrine. Transplanted into Bohemia by John Huss, this doctrine, becoming associated with the outburst of nationalistic passions and democratic instincts, was to shake the very foundations of the Church and of Germany.

At the very moment when it seemed that the Papacy should have concentrated all its forces to resist its enemies, it flung itself into the famous crisis which is known as the Great Schism, and which for forty years was to rend Western Christendom in twain (1373–1417). This catastrophe was due to no religious cause. The double election which was its point of departure would doubtless have remained an incident of no particular significance, but for the fact that the European States, actuated by political interest, arrayed themselves in two hostile groups, one subject to French and the other to English influence, both envenoming the schism and seeking to derive advantage from it. But it should be clearly understood that although secular policy drove the States to take sides in the schism, and although it exploited the schism and delayed the possibility of agreement, it was incapable of originating it. The old Carolingian conception, which by associating the Pope and the Emperor in the government of the Church, had formerly enabled

[1] "Lollium" means a noxious weed.

the Emperor to appoint Antipopes, had lost its last representative by the death of Frederick Barbarossa. The Church had triumphed so completely over the Empire, had so completely shaken off any temporal intervention in its government, had encompassed the pontifical elections with so many guarantees of independence, and was so profoundly venerated by the faithful, as an authority divine in its essence, that the very idea of forcing a Pope upon it by violence, and in opposition to the traditional rules of the Conclave, would have been inconceivable. In France and England at least, at the end of the 13th century, the State had been able to repudiate the interference of the Church in its own affairs, but it could not and did not dream of subjecting the Church to its own intervention. All that the State desired was to secure the neutrality or benevolence of the Church, and to prevent the Church from acting, with all the enormous strength of its hierarchy, in opposition to its designs or interests; and even, if it were possible, to find in the Church an ally against its external enemies. The kings of France had skilfully profited by the sojourn of the Papacy at Avignon to secure these advantages. Their attitude to the Papacy had been completely different from that of the Emperors, in the days when the Empire still stood for something. Unlike the Emperors, they did not claim to possess the least right to share in the government of the universal Church, and their relations with the Church were purely external, as those of one power with another. The line of demarcation between the spiritual and the temporal power had always been a cause of contention between the Pope and the Emperor, because both the Pope and the Emperor were inside the Empire. For the King of France, who was outside the Empire, the line of demarcation was very clear. It was drawn by the independence of the king in his kingdom. And the Pope derived too many advantages from the king's protection to dream of spoiling the good relations between the monarchy and the Papacy by reviving old quarrels. Though he maintained all his claims in respect of the kings of Germany, he no longer mentioned them to Paris. He surrounded himself more and more with French cardinals, and, as we have already seen, a good proportion of the benefices of which he disposed so generously was reserved for Frenchmen. And so harmony reigned between the Church and the State, each avoiding any cause of conflict. There was actually a concordat between them, unwritten, but none the less real. The relations between the king and the Pope were still further facilitated by the fact that in France the question of the temporal power of the Papacy did not arise. Avignon and the County of Venaissin were of so little importance that the king did not dream of contesting the Pope's possession of them. It seems to me that this has been too little remarked; I think it is evident that the *modus vivendi* of the Pope and the King of France during the sojourn at Avignon (1314–1377) was in many respects an anticipation of the modern age, and a mutual accommodation of Church and State.

But this situation was profitable only to France. This fact was very evident to the outer world, which spoke of this period as that of the "Babylonian captivity." The idea that the Pope should no longer dwell beside the tomb of the Apostles was intolerable to pious souls. The non-French States were infuriated by this long succession of French Popes: Clement V (Bertrand de Goth), John XXII (Jacques d'Eux de Cahors, 1316–1334), Benedict XII (Jacob Fournier de Saverdun, 1334–1342), Clement VI (Pierre Roger, 1342–1352), Innocent VI (Jean Birel, 1352–1362), Urban V (Abbé de St. Victor de Marseille, 1362–1370), Gregory XI (of the Roger family, 1370–1378).[1]

Avignon, of course, was merely a temporary home, in which the Papacy seemed inclined to linger. But it could not remain there permanently. John XXII was elected in 1316 only after he had promised to restore the Holy See to Rome. But there were very serious troubles in Italy, by which the Papacy was not unaffected. King Robert of Naples (1309–1343), who had succeeded to Charles II, had received his crown at the hands of the Pope in Avignon, and had defeated the expedition led by the Emperor Henry VII. But before long Rome was in a state of anarchy. In 1347 Cola di Rienzo was appointed tribune, and during the few

[1] These were all Provençaux, doubtless owing to the influence of the Angevins of Naples.

months of his dictatorship he dreamed once more of restoring the Roman Empire. The territory of the Church was in a state of decomposition. Innocent VI sent Cardinal Albornoz to Italy as Vicar-General (1353), to reconstitute the Papal State. Cola joined him, but was killed by the people. At Naples, after Robert's reign, a war had broken out between his daughter Joanna and King Louis of Hungary, who laid claim to the crown as a member of the House of Anjou; and hostilities continued until 1350.

Urban V (1362–1370), the best of the Avignon Popes, who reacted against the luxury and abuses of the Papal court, was anxious to return to Rome, as he actually did in 1367. The city was half depopulated, and many of the ancient monuments had fallen into ruin. The "Great Companies" of disbanded mercenaries were ravaging the country. The Emperor Charles IV came to Rome and remained in Italy until 1369, without doing anything more than fill his purse by punishing a few cities. In the midst of this anarchy the Emperor of Constantinople, John Palaeologus, came to implore the support of the Pope against the Turks. The situation was so lamentable that in 1370 the Pope returned to Avignon, where he died in the following year.

His successor Gregory XI (1370–1378) was also to take the road for the Eternal City. The voices of St. Bridget and St. Catherine of Siena were raised so loudly, and carried so far, that the Pope could not pretend that he did not hear their objurgations. But his return was demanded even more imperatively by the political situation. Bologna had just been taken. The Florentines, hitherto the most faithful allies of Rome in Italy, combined with the other Tuscan cities against the government of the "legates." The Pope left Avignon in 1376. He died in March 1378, without having brought order out of anarchy. For the first time since the election of Boniface VIII, seventy-five years earlier, a Pope was about to be elected in Rome. It was impossible that the people should not demand a Roman Pope. The cardinals, assembled in Conclave, deliberated amidst the clamour of the mob, with which mingled the tocsin of St. Peter's. The Vatican was surrounded by armed bands. It was a revolutionary "day." It ended in the election of

Cardinal Bartolomeo Prignano, Archbishop of Bari, who on his coronation took the name of Urban VI, 1378–1379. But the French cardinals who had collaborated in the election had acted only under the influence of terror. Some of them protested; the rest soon quarrelled with the Pope, who announced that he wished to reform the Sacred College, and make an end of the financial abuses which were the origin of its wealth. On the top of this came the urgent entreaties of the King of France, Charles V, and the downfall of Naples. No more was needed to make them declare the election of Urban null and void. On September 20th they assembled at Fondi and gave their suffrages to Robert of Geneva, Bishop of Thérouanne. The name of Urban, adopted by his competitor, spoke of Rome; he chose a name which spoke of Avignon, styling himself Clement VII (1378–1394).

Of old, whenever two Popes had disputed the right to wear the tiara, the question of legitimacy had been capable of a plain answer. One of the two Popes, forced upon the Church by the Emperor, was obviously a mere intruder, from whom Christendom resolutely turned away. But how, on this occasion, was the true successor of Peter to be discerned? Who were in the right—the cardinals who acknowledged Urban, or those who had voted for Clement? The theologians of the Universities debated the matter; and pious souls, with equal conviction, addressed their prayers to heaven on behalf of the Roman Pope (as did Catherine of Siena), or on behalf of the Avignon Pope (and among these were Vincent Ferrier and Pierre de Luxembourg). But as in all problems of law which are really political problems, the solution was furnished by political interest. France, and all the States which gravitated around her—Naples, Scotland, Castile, Aragon—pronounced for Clement. This was enough to make England support Urban. He was also acknowledged by the Emperor Charles IV, in virtue of the traditional connection between the Empire and Rome. The States of the North, Bohemia and Poland, followed suit, without taking much interest in the question. The King of Hungary, being the enemy of the Queen of Naples, who was for Clement, gave his support to the opposite party. Thus, in a dispute which involved such serious consequences for the Church, Christendom refused to be guided by other than considerations of temporal expediency. The Papacy, so triumphant only a century earlier, suffered the humiliation of perceiving that the obedience of the faithful was subordinated to the interests of the various governments concerned. And not only did it accept this situation, but it consecrated it, so to speak, by its attitude. In order to retain his political supporters, each of the Popes manifested a singular condescension where they were concerned. The arrogant declarations by which their predecessors had claimed to dispose of kingdoms were things of the past. Now the question was which of the two contending pontiffs could show himself the more accommodating in his treatment of his adherents. As for the peoples, they passively imitated the attitude of their princes unless they were at war with them, when they gave their support, in a spirit of opposition, to the Pope of the opposing party.

In the midst of all this confusion, the abuses from which the Church had been suffering, more and more visibly, since the beginning of the 14th century were bound to undergo aggravation. The court of Rome, like that of Avignon, subjected the Church to an exploitation which was all the more intensive inasmuch as half Christendom had now to provide each of these courts with as much revenue as had formerly been furnished by the whole Christian world. The system of *provisiones*, *annates*, and *reservationes* was applied in the extremest manner, while simony, nepotism and favouritism became deplorably prevalent. The hierarchy was more and more at the mercy of money.

Such a situation was indefensible. Had it been prolonged it must undoubtedly have ended in the ruin of the Church. The success of Wycliffe in England was significant. And in Bohemia, John Huss, inspired by Wycliffe, was beginning to rouse the people (1403). But in opposition to these revolutionary reformers, the ancient university of Paris, that home of conservative theology, was ardently seeking a solution compatible with orthodoxy. On the one side were Pierre d'Ailly, Gerson and Clémangis; on the other, Wycliffe and Huss. This was the great religious conflict of the beginning of the 15th century. One might be tempted here, in accordance with a convenient formula, to invoke the racial element: the Latins being on the side of the Church, and the Germans opposing them. In this case, the Germans and the Slavs. But the attitudes of the different parties are very readily explained. In England, as we have seen, the increasing difficulty of that country's relations with the Pope naturally tended to make her accept the Wycliffian theology, and Huss merely borrowed Wycliffe's theses, while basing them on Czech nationalism. In France, on the contrary, since the Papacy had been resident in Avignon, the State could but support it. It had no motive for breaking with the Papacy; and the people were in no sense hostile to it. It was quite possible to correct abuses, re-establish discipline, and restore piety without overturning everything, without denying the whole past and suddenly going back to the Bible and primitive Christianity. An oecumenical council could deal with the question, and at the same time put an end to the schism, and give the Church the reforms of which it stood in need. Unfortunately, neither of the two Popes would give way to the other. The States were unable to come to an agreement under which they would proclaim, to one Pope or the other, a general "subtraction of obedience," which would compel them to yield. France did her very utmost to end the schism, but she was hampered by her intestine quarrels. The assassination of the Duke of Orleans, when the country came under the influence of the Duke of Burgundy, Jean Sans Peur, forced her to adopt a more definite attitude. For Jean, since the Flemings over whom he reigned were in favour of Rome, was greatly embarrassed by the quarrel, and did his very utmost to force a solution. The cardinals of the two parties, feeling that they were supported, grew bolder. In 1409 they at last convoked a General Council, which opened its proceedings at Pisa on March 25th.

It was an unheard-of innovation in the Church that a Council should assemble in obedience to a summons from the cardinals. The revolutionary spirit which was abroad in lay society had evidently spread to the religious community. The two Popes, Gregory XII (Rome) and Benedict XIII, protested equally, and did their utmost to wreck the proceedings of the Council. But the Council had resolved to proceed to extreme measures. On June 5th it solemnly declared that Pietro de Luna (Benedict XIII) and Angelo Corrario (Gregory XII) were notorious schismatics and heretics, deposed them both, and declared the Holy See to be vacant. Ten days later the cardinals gave the tiara to Alexander V (1409–1410). They then dispersed, leaving the reformation of the Church to a future Council. The outlook appeared more gloomy than ever, for neither Gregory nor Benedict acknowledged the validity of the sentence which had been pronounced against them. There were thenceforth three Popes contending for the government of Christendom. And as though it was not enough that the government of the Church should be undermined, it was at the same time torn by heresy, thus recalling the spectacle of the Carolingian decadence, when the sons of Louis the Pious were contending for the crown while the rising feudality was undermining the political constitution of the Empire.

Wycliffism had found in John Huss an apostle who was even more ardent than the founder of the doctrine, and whom circumstances were to render much more dangerous. Just as the success of Wycliffe in England was explained, as we have seen, by the political discontent which the Papacy had provoked in that country, the success of Huss was due to the increasing hostility of the Czechs of Bohemia to Germany since the middle of the 14th century.[1] The national sentiment was in favour of each of these reformers, but it favoured them in a very different manner, which is naturally explained by the composition of the two peoples. In England, where the population was homogeneous, Wycliffe had the support of all those who resented, in the Papacy, the unwarrantable interference of a foreign power. In Bohemia, where the Czechs lived side by side with the immigrants whom Germany had been pouring into the country since the 12th century, Huss was supported by the entire Slav portion of the nation, which greeted in him the reformer who had liberated it from a Church which it regarded, above all, as the Church of the Germans. From the very first, Huss

[1] As to this hostility and its origins, see p. 413 et seq., and p. 471 et seq.

relied on the sole support of his Czech-speaking compatriots. The religious zeal with which he inspired them by his eloquence and his conviction was intensified by the full force of the nationalistic passions of the people, so that we have the singular spectacle of a theologian who had become so completely the apostle of his people that no authority would have dared to think of resisting him. The excommunication launched against him, and the interdict placed on the city of Prague (1412), did nothing to check his propaganda, which was already beginning to recruit supporters in Poland, Hungary and Croatia.

It seemed that the only thing that could save Christianity was the task of ecclesiastical reform which the Council of Pisa had adjourned to a later Council. John XXIII (1410–1415), who had just succeeded Alexander V, convoked a new Council in Rome (April 1412), but this was soon compelled to disperse, owing to the invasion of the city by the King of Naples, Ladislas. At the proposal of the King of Germany, Sigismond, who was happy to assume an importance which would not have been his had not France and England been absorbed in their quarrel, Constance was selected as the site of a new assembly, which opened its sessions on November 5th, 1414. After three years of deliberations and negotiations it succeeded in putting an end to the schism. John XXIII was deposed, Gregory XII was induced to renounce the tiara, and Benedict XIII, who refused to, was condemned as a heretic and schismatic. On November 11th, 1417, Martin V was elected, not by the Conclave, but by a commission of cardinals and delegates of the nations represented in the Council. The unity of the Catholic government was at last re-established. As for the reformation of the Church "in her head and in her members," of which the best minds of the day were so desirous, it was hardly begun. Little more was done beyond mitigating in some degree the power which the Curia had arrogated to itself in respect of the distribution of benefices. On the other hand, the Council felt that it had crushed the Bohemian heresy by condemning John Huss to be burned at the stake. Provided with a safe-conduct by Sigismond, he had gone to Constance in the hope of converting the fathers to his doctrine (July 6th, 1415). His disciple, Jerome of Prague, was also condemned and put to death a few months later. Both died as martyrs, and their sufferings had no other result than to serve the cause which had cost them their lives. They fanned the religious and national enthusiasm of the Czechs to a paroxysm. Their hatred of the Church and their hatred of Germany increased simultaneously. Was not Huss the victim at once of the Council and of Sigismond? How could they regard the safe-conduct which he had received from the king as other than a proof of the monarch's abominable perfidy?

Hitherto the followers of Huss had confined themselves, like their master, to professing the ideas of Wycliffe. A certain number of them remained faithful to these ideas: these were the Utraquists, so called because they communicated "in the two elements." But the mass of the people, under the spur of religious passion, suddenly pushed the doctrine to its extreme consequences. Since the Bible proclaimed the Word of God, it must be obeyed in everything, not only in such matters as regarded the soul, but also in all that related to the body. Hence the ecclesiastical organization, no less than the civil organization, ought simply to disappear. The Kingdom of God must be established in this world, by reconstituting the whole of humanity in accordance with the Holy Scriptures. Such was the enthusiastic dream of a young people, a people full of illusions, and history shows no pendant to their behaviour save that of the Russian Bolsheviks of 1917. They set to work immediately, under the conviction that the Czech nation was the Chosen of the Lord. The Catholic clergy was dispersed, its property confiscated, and the churches and monasteries were destroyed. A patriarchal constitution, on the lines of the Old Testament, was given to the people, and on the site of the castle of Kozihradek, where Huss had passed his last years, the Holy City of Tabor was built, from which the New Hebrews received their name of Taborites. The sudden death of the King of Bohemia, Wenceslas (August 16th, 1419), left them a free field, the more so as his successor was the hateful Sigismond, who had played the Judas to the martyr of Constance. The revolution was thus in full control of the country. The Germans of Bohemia, who had remained faithful to the Church, bowed their heads to the storm. However, from all parts of the world exalted mystics, members of the associations of Bogards, or of the proletariat of the industrial cities, hastened toward this country in which the Kingdom of God had been proclaimed, and their communistic aspirations, or their paradisiacal visions, gave rise to some singular sects amidst the Biblical rigorism of the Taborites. The sect of the Adamites, founded by a Belgian weaver, affords a curious example of the exaltation of their adepts. The disciples of the new Adam, who settled on an island in the river Nezarka, professed to live there, in a state of the completest communism, the life of the Garden of Eden. Like the first of our race, they wore no clothes, and their morals were as primitive as their costume. They soon caused such a scandal that John Ziska, in 1421, had them massacred.

The faith of the Hussites was too ardent to allow them to neglect the duty of propagating it. As early as 1419 Bohemia had become a centre of fervent propaganda, from which a revolutionary religion poured forth ints fiery doctrines like a stream of lava. The adjacent Slav regions, Poland, Moravia and Silesia, where the language of its apostles was readily understood, and where the masses of the people were living wretchedly under the oppression of the nobles, immediately provided it with thousands of adepts. It even made some progress among the poorer inhabitants in the German regions of Austria. And its prestige appeared more dazzling than ever in the light of its triumphs. The victories of John Ziska and Procopius over the German chivalry sent against them by the Pope and Sigismond inevitably reminded the faithful of the victories of David or of Gideon over the Amalekites.[1]

The Hussite peril was invoked by all those members of the Church who were calling for the assembly of a new Council. Martin V succeeded in temporizing; his successor Eugenius IV (1431–1437), yielding to circumstances, and to the general opinion, convoked the Council, which opened its sessions at Basle in July 1431. It had to deal with two important problems: the Bohemian

[1] See p. 472.

heresy, and the reform of the Church. Events enabled it to solve the first of these problems.

The religious and social radicalism of the Taborites ended by provoking a definitive rupture between them and the Utraquists. Almost the whole of the nobility had gone over to the side of the Utraquists, and at Lipan, on March 30th, 1434, they won a bloody victory for their cause. Bohemia, exhausted by the war, asked for nothing more than peace, and the negotiations which were opened between the Council and the Utraquists ended at last in a somewhat obscure solution, with which the two parties decided to content themselves (1436). The difficulties were evaded rather than solved. All the efforts, all the enthusiasm, all the bloodshed, profited, in the end, only the Czech nobles, who divided the property of the convents among themselves. At the cost of the spoliation of the Church, the nobles were reconciled with it. They thereby acquired such power that little danger was to be feared henceforth from the discouraged sectators among the people. Their further discomfiture was left to time.

As for the reformation of the Church, there was at first some reason for believing that this time it would really be accomplished, in accordance with the programme which had formerly been expounded at Constance by men like Pierre d'Ailly and Gerson. The majority of the fathers were apparently resolved to replace the monarchical constitution of Catholicism by a conciliary constitution. Even more emphatically than at Constance, they proclaimed the superiority of the Council over the Pope, and vigorously thwarted the efforts of Eugenius IV to dissolve the assembly. Not content with suppressing the financial abuses of the Curia, correcting the morals of the clergy, requiring ecclesiastical dignitaries to reside in their sees, attacking simony, and forbidding plurality of benefices, they manifested, in respect of the Pope, so revolutionary a spirit of defiance and criticism that dissension finally crept into their ranks. This dissension was skilfully exploited by Eugenius. The Emperor John VII Palaeologus and the Patriarch of Constantinople had just arrived in Italy, once more seeking to obtain the aid of the Occident against the Turks, and once more promising in return the union of the Greek Church. The Pope immediately convoked the Council in Ferrara, and then in Florence, to deliberate on this proposal; the last expedient of despair, which men could pretend or persuade themselves to take seriously. A certain number of the fathers answered his summons, and the proclamation of the union on July 5th, 1439, was regarded as a brilliant success—but the Eastern Church repudiated it four years later. The opposition, which had remained in Basle, was henceforth discredited. It sought to mask its weakness by violence. On June 5th, 1439, it deposed Eugenius IV and appointed in his place Felix V, whom no one in Europe took seriously, and who was the last of the Antipopes. Persisting in its hopeless opposition, the Council dragged out its obscure existence for ten years longer, finally dissolving on April 25th, 1439. Felix V abdicated and resumed his rank among the cardinals. The great crisis through which the Papacy had been passing was terminated, and by its victory. Of the work of the Council nothing survived. The Church had preserved its monarchical form; after so much effort, so many hopes, everything was as it had been in the beginning.

And yet something remained as the result of all this agitation, and for a moment it had seemed that this new factor would give Catholicism a new form. It was something that no one in the Church had ever desired: the increasing independence of the States in ecclesiastical affairs. The quarrels between the Popes and the Council had enabled the princes, whom both parties were equally concerned to humour, to restrict the intervention of Rome within their frontiers, and to acquire a certain amount of influence in the recruiting and disciplining of the national clergy. The Pragmatic Sanction proclaimed by Charles VII in 1438, and in which we may see the germ of the famous Gallican franchises of the Church of France, was the most noteworthy result of these conjunctures. The Papacy remained supreme within the Church. But the Church was no longer what it had been in the Middle Ages. It no longer extended its authority over the temporal as over the spiritual domain. To a certain extent it turned inward upon itself, and, so to speak, decided to specialize in its religious rôle. Following the

Emperor, the Pope in his turn disappeared from the stage of the world as a universal power. From the middle of the 15th century there were to be no more Antipopes. However, after the deposition of the King of Bohemia, George Podiebrad, by Paul II, the quarrels of the kings would no longer be submitted to Papal arbitration.

## CHAPTER II

# THE HUNDRED YEARS' WAR

### 1. *To the Death of Edward III* (1377)

Since the close of the 13th century France had no longer exercised the uncontested hegemony which she had enjoyed from the time of Philip Augustus to that of Philip the Fair. She could not have retained this mastery over Europe unless her civilization had continued to progress, while her political power remained undiminished. But the progress of her civilization came to a standstill, and her political power began to decline. Neither her art, nor her literature, nor her science, whatever interest they might still possess, produced anything essentially new. As for the strength and prosperity of the nation, they were both compromised by the formidable crisis of the Hundred Years' War.

As a matter of fact, this great conflict spread far beyond the frontiers of Western Europe. The two States immediately concerned were so powerful that it was impossible that their quarrel should involve only themselves. As a matter of fact, all the princes were dragged into it, and by virtue of the alliances which it provoked among them, or the extent to which it influenced their conduct, it assumed a European importance. In a Europe whose equilibrium had been upset by the political preponderance of the Papacy it was, for good or for ill, a centre of attraction, or at any rate, the cardinal event, which impressed a few common motives and tendencies on the restless confusion of the period which it dominated. A war so long and so bitterly contested was possible only between France and England. They alone had governments disposing of sufficient resources, and peoples endowed with a sufficient national unity, to endure such an ordeal without perishing. But it is appalling to compare the vast expenditure of effort with the futility of the results obtained. Fundamentally, this conflict between France and England was like that of the Popes and the Councils: it was essentially abortive. After all the shedding of blood, after all the misery and devastation, the two adversaries found themselves still more or less at the point of departure, so that the Hundred Years' War had been merely a futile and terrible calamity. It is only too easy to say, after the event, that it could not have been anything else. It is perfectly obvious that the kings of England could not possibly have conquered the Crown of France. And yet this was precisely the end which they had proposed to themselves. Apart from this, they had no urgent motive for going to war. Above all, the English people had no motive for going to war. For France was not threatening or even incommoding England. Neither England nor France had as yet become a maritime nation. Nowhere did their merchants come into contact as rivals, as they were to do later, or as the merchants of Genoa or Venice had done, in the ports of the Levant, since the 13th century. Guyenne, still the Continental possession of the kings of England, meant no more to the English people than the Kingdom of Hanover was to mean in the 18th century. It is quite comprehensible that France might have attacked England in order to recover this province, the last remnant of the Angevin possessions, which was still an obstacle to the unity of the kingdom —but it was not France, it was England that provoked the war. One issue in the war was Edward III's claim to the crown of the Capets. But one cannot see that this interested England as a nation; indeed, it was against the national interest. The alliance between France and Scotland affords no better explanation of the origin of the conflict. It is, in fact, only too clear that by complicating the conquest of Scotland with a war in France, this conquest was rendered infinitely more difficult, and even impossible. In short, from whatever point of view we regard it, the Hundred Years' War is seen to have been a useless war, a needless war, in the sense that it was not provoked by any vital necessity. As a matter of fact, it must be regarded merely as a war of prestige. And this, precisely, explains the passion with which the English people followed its kings into this war.

The Parliamentary constitution had become further consolidated under Edward I (1272–1307). In 1297 the king formally acknowledged the right of Parliament to vote on questions of taxation. The reversion of his successor, Edward II (1307–1327), to the exercise of personal government provoked, as under Henry III, a popular rebellion, led by the barons. The king's ill-success in Scotland, where he was confronted by Robert Bruce, who had taken up arms again, and who defeated him at Bannockburn (June 24th, 1314), made him hateful to the people. In 1326 the malcontents gathered about the queen and the heir to the throne. Parliament proclaimed the deposition of the king (January 7th, 1327). Thus the reign of Edward III (1327–1377) began, like that of Edward I, with a fresh victory of the nation over the Crown. But by admitting the accomplished fact, as his grandfather had done, and by frankly co-operating with the Parliament, Edward III turned this national victory to the advantage of the Crown. The more he allowed Parliament to intervene in his policy, the more popular this policy became. The approval of the Lords and the Commons (it was only during Edward's reign that they were divided into two chambers) made them conscious of their solidarity with the king's undertakings. Whatever they might cost, the honour of the nation was henceforth engaged in them, and was one with the honour of the king. Parliament, of course, did nothing to encourage the king to make war upon France. Indeed, Edward seems to have been so uncertain of its attitude at first that he began by borrowing the money necessitated by his preparations from the Florentine bankers. But his bankruptcy in 1339 compelled him to address himself, henceforth and until the end, to his faithful Parliament. His quarrel had thus become the quarrel of his people. England felt that her honour was engaged in her king's war, and she continued the war in a sentiment of national pride, the most powerful of all incentives. No one, of course, from the beginning of this war could have imagined what it would lead to. Certainly the English had not expected to find in France a self-esteem and a national passion like their own. Having begun a war which would admit of no compromise, because it aimed at nothing less than giving their king the crown of France, they were obliged to go on to the bitter end, and to lay down their arms only when forced to do so by sheer exhaustion.

But how can we explain the fact that France was not able to repel Edward's aggression immediately and decisively? It would seem that all the advantages were on her side. Not only had she the great advantage of defending herself on her own soil, but her population was certainly two or three times greater than that of England, and she was very much wealthier. Moreover, the defeats which she had suffered at Crecy, Poitiers, and Agincourt were not in any way decisive. Serious though they may have been, they did not annihilate her forces, nor did they prevent her from continuing the campaign. The causes of her weakness must be sought elsewhere. They must be sought in the disorders to which she was a prey from the middle of the 14th century; which were explained, at least to a great extent, by the nature of the French State as it was constituted from the reign of Philip Augustus to the reign of Philip the Fair.

This State, as we have already seen, was essentially monarchical. There was no independent political power beside the king; there were only functionaries or councils, and none of these were derived, like the English Parliament, from a source which was distinct from the Crown. The royal authority, which from reign to reign had extended itself farther and farther, and had amalgamated the portions detached by the feudal princes, manifested itself essentially in affording protection and administering justice. The king was the attorney of his kingdom, the first justiciary in the land, the guardian of his subjects. It was from this that he derived his social function, and this was the foundation of his popularity. The State over which he presided was essentially based upon the idea of law. Its principal functionaries were the bailiffs, officers of justice: its most important central organ, the Parlement of Paris, was a court of justice. And the popular sentiment that cherished the picture of St. Louis dispensing justice under the oaks of Vincennes was in complete accordance with the reality. Philip the Fair had always upheld this conception of the monarchy, and his conflict with the Pope was fundamentally a dispute concerning the juridical sovereignty of the king.

But the State, in order to maintain itself, had greater and greater need of financial resources. Now all that was left of the ancient Roman fiscality, the old taxes transmuted into fines, had passed, since the 10th century, into the hands of the great vassals. The court had nothing to depend on apart from its domains and their revenues. To this may be added the revenue from the coinage, which had been to a great extent withdrawn from the great vassals since the reign of Philip Augustus.[1] The court also had recourse to borrowing. But this was not enough. It would evidently be necessary to resort also to taxation. But there was no tax which the court could collect. Hence the expedient of monetary depreciation under Philip the Fair, the taxation of the clergy, which made the Pope go to war, the suppression of the Templars, which was a scandal, and dealings with the Italians which went far to drain the Treasury. The idea that the State could impose a tax upon its subjects did not occur to it, for this was not a legal notion. The notion that the State could extend its competence so far as to draw upon the private fortune of those whom it protected had not yet arisen. From the financial point of view the evolution of the State was backward as compared with its development from the juridical point of view. Indeed, at the close of the 13th century the State had not really progressed beyond the conception which confused the public finances with the revenues of the king. This was naturally the cause of extreme embarrassment on the outbreak of the Hundred Years' War. In order to pay the armies, to hire mercenaries, and to subsidize allies, the King had to contract debts, and the disorder of his finances was soon so great that he had to appeal for assistance to the subjects whom he dared not tax, convoke the States-General, and ask them for money. The result was a terrible crisis. It meant the outbreak, when the country was at war, of a sort of revolution, which reminds one of the rebellion in England at the time of the Great Charter. But in France the situation was much more serious; for in that

[1] The *taille* (tallage) was not properly a tax, but a permanent due.

country the national cohesion which the Norman conquest had given England did not exist. The monarchy, which had reunited the *membra disjecta* of the country, caused a general commotion by addressing itself to the people.

It was a terrible muddle. The Orders of the States-General could not come to a mutual understanding. The Third Estate, which had money and was supported by the cities, wished to introduce reforms which the monarchy would not accept. The princes profited by this contingency to recover the influence which they had lost. The conflicts of the parties excited the political ambitions of the seigneurs of royal blood. Étienne Marcel mobilized the Burgundians and the Armagnacs. If we except the restorative reign of Charles V, we may say that from the States-General of 1355 to the reign of Louis XI France was the victim of a double intestine war: that of the Third Estate against the king, and that of the princes against the Crown, both being really due to the fiscal crisis which was rendered necessary by the constitution of the kingdom: a crisis of confidence, so to speak, which was necessary in order to replace the Capetian conception of the State by a more complete conception: a crisis in which it seemed as though the State was on the point of foundering amidst the disasters of the war.

During the years which preceded the great war there was nothing to indicate the approach of such a crisis. The three sons of Philip the Fair, who, lacking male heirs, succeeded in turns to their father, Louis X (1314–1316), Philip V (1316–1322), Charles IV (1322–1328), profited by the position which he had bequeathed to them, but did nothing to improve it. No new problems arose. The Papacy, established at Avignon, was henceforth full of consideration for the Crown; France was at peace with England, whose king, Edward II, in conformity with the stipulations of the Treaty of Montreuil, married Isabelle, the sister of the three kings. The only war was a war with Flanders, which dragged on for a few years, to be concluded, under Philip V, by the Treaty of Paris (1320), which ceded to the kingdom the Castellanies of Lille, Douai and Orchies, while the heir of the county, Louis de Nevers, married a member of the royal family.

On the death of Charles IV, therefore, the kingdom was in a state of profound tranquillity. Even the extinction of the Capetian dynasty did not give rise to any difficulty. On the death of Louis X his daughter's claim to the crown had been waived, so that on ascending the throne Philip of Valois was merely profiting by a principle which had been proclaimed twelve years earlier, in conformity with the ancient Frankish law, accepted without dispute by the whole nation, and so manifestly unassailable that Edward III, the grandson, through his mother, of Philip the Fair, made no protest at the decisive moment. Moreover, his rights, even in the female line, were second to those of Jeanne, the daughter of Louis X, and wife of Philippe d'Evreux, to whom the new king, as a measure of prudence, ceded the kingdom of Navarre, to which the so-called "Salic law" did not apply so clearly as it did to France.

His reign opened under favourable auspices. When the Count of Flanders appealed for his assistance against the great insurrection of the bourgeois weavers and peasants of maritime Flanders, who since 1325 had been fighting, respectively, against the nobles and the patricians, Philip won a victory at Cassel, on August 23rd, 1328, which put an end to the revolt. The following year, Edward III took the oath of vassalage, in respect of Guyenne. War seemed so improbable that the king, with the concurrence of the Pope, made preparations for a Crusade, or rather, the French expedition to the East, which was to sail in 1332.

In England the reign of Edward III had begun less favourably. The further military successes of the Scots forced him to recognize (1328) the independence of their country, so that their king, Robert Bruce, broke the bond of vassalage to which Edward I had subjected these tenacious adversaries. Fortunately for King Edward, Baliol's revolt against David Bruce, the successor of Robert Bruce (1331), enabled him to restore the broken bond. He declared for Baliol, defeated the troops of the legitimate king at Halidon Hill (1333), and forced him to take refuge in France, where Philip VI welcomed him as Louis XIV was one day to welcome James Stuart. Baliol made haste to safeguard his situation by ceding Berwick to the conqueror, and acknowledging the suzerainty of

England over the kingdom which the English had won for him (February 1334).

The sympathy with which David Bruce was received by the French court was felt as an insult by Edward III. He retorted by lavishing proofs of confidence upon Robert d'Artois, the mortal enemy of Philip VI, receiving him in London with great display. His claims to the crown of France, whether he believed or not in their validity, presently made him incline to the idea of resuming the war which his grandfather had been obliged to terminate so suddenly in 1297. Young and active, and popular since his victory over Scotland, he allowed himself to be carried away by ambition. But like all very ambitious persons, he was prudent, and he would risk nothing until he had every chance of success. Following the example of Edward I, he first of all set about securing the alliance of the princes of the Low Countries. The most important of these, the Count of Flanders, Louis de Nevers, proved to be as faithful to Philip VI, who had saved him from a popular insurrection, as Guy de Dampierre, in 1297, was ready to break with Philip the Fair, who had helped the patricians in their conflict with him. But on the other side of the Scheldt, in the ancient Lotharingia, now divided into flourishing principalities, which since the great interregnum had enjoyed complete independence under the nominal suzerainty of the Empire, it would be easy to recruit supporters, provided they were well paid. Thanks to the Florentine bankers, who allowed him the most generous credit, Edward could spend without counting the cost. He gave *carte blanche* to Count William II of Hainaut and Holland, whose daughter Philippine, the patroness of Froissart, he had married in 1328, and it did not take him long to make arrangements, in return for cash payment, with the Duke of Brabant and others of less importance—the Counts of Guelders, Clèves and Juliers. Just as in 1297 Edward I had bought the support of the King of Germany, Adolphus of Nassau, Edward III thought it best to hire the services of the Emperor, Louis of Bavaria. He hoped, no doubt, that this unfortunate man, recently excommunicated by John XXII, would find in his rancour against the Avignon Papacy a motive for avenging himself on France.

To the English coalition Philip VI opposed, in the Low Countries, an old ally of France, the Bishop of Liége, and John, the blind King of Bohemia, with whom he was connected by marriage, but who brought with him only a few knights from his County of Luxembourg. In Scotland he supported the partisans of David Bruce, who took up arms again.

Hostilities began in 1337. The French made surprise attacks on Guernsey and on Portsmouth, which they burned; and the English attacked a body of Flemish troops on the island of Cadzant. In the following year, July 22nd, 1338, Edward III disembarked at Antwerp, with the intention of doing great things. But his allies were completely lacking in enthusiasm. Louis of Bavaria did not move; he contented himself with bestowing upon Edward the title of Vicar of the Empire. The Duke of Brabant and Guillaume III, Count of Hainaut-Holland, who had just succeeded his father, were plainly trying to wriggle out of their engagements. In order to drag such auxiliaries into a conflict which for them was merely an opportunity of exacting subsidies it was necessary to pay through the nose, and Edward, overburdened with debts, went bankrupt, ruining his Florentine creditors. Fortunately, in order to compel the Count of Flanders to come over to his side, he had repeated the tactics which had already proved effective in dealing with the count: he prohibited the export of wool, which was indispensable to the cloth trade of Gand, Bruges, and Ypres. Despite the crisis provoked by this measure, Louis de Nevers had remained unshakable in his loyalty to France. But the trade corporations and the merchants of the cities had no intention of allowing themselves to be ruined or starved, and since their prince preferred the cause of his suzerain to theirs, they undertook to work out their own salvation. Gand, where the corporations of the cloth trade had for some years been in power, took over the government of the county, under the direction of a wealthy burgess, Jan van Artevelde. Artevelde got into touch with Edward; the embargo on wool was raised, and in order to dispel the scruples which might have deterred the burgesses from abandoning Philip VI, their suzerain, Edward went to Gand, where he was solemnly acknowledged, in the market-place, as King of France. Thus the solidarity of their interests brought about an alliance between Edward's monarchical and dynastic policy and the bourgeois and economic policy of the Flemish cities, an alliance to which Flanders was to show herself unshakably faithful. In this essentially industrial country, where the bourgeoisie was predominant, politics, sooner than anywhere else in the North of Europe, were subordinated to economic considerations.

The entry of Flanders into the English alliance assured Edward of a solid base in the north. Hitherto the war had consisted of operations along the French frontier: skirmishes and the burning of villages. Meanwhile the cardinal envoys from Avignon sought vainly to negotiate a peace, which Edward discussed only in order to gain time. Operations of the magnitude of which Edward had dreamed were about to become possible. He hastened to England to demand from Parliament the subsidies which his bankruptcy had rendered indispensable, and which were granted him, in view of the existing situation. On June 23rd, 1340, his fleet won a brilliant victory over the French fleet off Sluys; then, accompanied by the Flemish militia, and with the aid of the princes, encouraged by this splendid victory, he proceeded to besiege Tournai (July 22nd–September), but the siege was unsuccessful, and ended in the Truce of Esplechin, which was several times renewed during the following years.

Thus, despite the assistance of Flanders, the plan of attack from the north had failed. Van Artevelde was killed in 1345, during a rising fomented against him by the weavers of Gand. The coalition of the princes was dissolved. Louis of Bavaria, without returning the money which had been paid to him, actually went over to Philip VI, but he was no more effective as his ally than he had been as Edward's. As regards the situation of the two belligerents, that of France appeared to be more favourable. She had profited by the truce to extend her eastern frontier. In 1343 she bought, for cash payment, the Dauphiné from the Dauphin Humbert II, whose title was thenceforward borne by the heir to the crown.

The truce did not prevent Edward III from going to Brittany, to the help of the Countess of Montfort, who was disputing the

Duchy with Charles of Blois, supported by France, or from sending the Earl of Derby to make war upon Gascony. In 1346 he suddenly landed in Normandy. This was the beginning of a complete change of policy. A new system of tactics, based on the rôle of the archers on the battlefield, gave the English a series of brilliant victories. Moreover, the purely natural composition of Edward's army must have given him the same advantage, over an adversary whose troops were largely foreign mercenaries, as the Spanish armies enjoyed in the 16th century. The battle of Crecy (August 26th) proved the quality of his army. Despite the advantage of numbers, the French suffered a defeat *moulte grande et moult horrible* (Froissart). The King of Bohemia, the Count of Flanders and a number of other great seigneurs were among the dead. The victor profited by this unhoped-for success to besiege Calais, which was taken after a siege of eleven months, and was not restored to France until 1558. A few weeks after the battle of Crecy, David Bruce, driven across the Scottish border, was defeated and taken prisoner at Nevil's Cross (October 17th). The English were triumphant everywhere. But both sides were equally in need of a breathing-space. On the Pope's intervention a truce was concluded in September 1347. This, owing to the appearance of the Black Death, was prolonged into the following year, and being repeatedly renewed was terminated only in 1355.

Both sides had profited by this period of repose, and had made preparations for a decisive action. Thanks to the subsidies granted by Parliament, the English had mustered three armies: one in Guyenne, another in Brittany, and a third in Normandy. The new King of France, Jean II the Good[1] (1350–1364), had decided to convoke the States-General, which had furnished him with the means of equipping 30,000 men. These he led against the Black Prince, who was ravaging Guyenne. The battle of Maupertuis, near Poitiers, on September 19th, 1356, ended in a catastrophe even more overwhelming than that of Crecy. Jean himself was taken prisoner and sent to England as a captive.

[1] Jean I was the posthumous son of Louis X, who lived only a few days, and was succeeded by Philip V.

In France this disaster immediately provoked the first of the crises with which the monarchy was repeatedly confronted until the middle of the 15th century. The States-General of 1355, in which the influence of the bourgeoisie was predominant, led by the Provost of the merchants of Paris, Étienne Marcel, had demanded, in return for voting the taxes required by the king, a considerable voice in the government. They had stipulated that they themselves must levy and administer the new taxes, and they demanded guarantees in respect of their right to assemble in the future, and the introduction of administrative reforms. A great victory would doubtless have enabled the king to stifle an opposition which his misfortunes rendered irresistible. This opposition was all the bolder inasmuch as it was encouraged by the King of Navarre, Charles the Bad, an ambitious and unscrupulous prince, who was all the more inclined to embroil the situation inasmuch as only a state of turmoil would enable him to advance his pretended claim, as the son of Jeanne D'Evreux, to the crown of France. Thus the French monarchy found itself, in the middle of the 14th century, suddenly obliged to reckon with the bourgeoisie which had formerly helped it to fight against the feudal seigneurs and establish the unity of the kingdom. Unassailed and undisputed for a century past, the monarchy was asked to share its power with the nation. France, after the battle of Poitiers, was in the position which had been occupied by England a hundred and fifty years earlier after the battle of Bouvines. In both cases financial disorder and defeat provoked a revolution. It is not surprising that this revolution should have occurred much later in France than in England. The political and national unity which is a necessary condition of a revolution had been suddenly forced upon England, at the end of the 11th century, in the days of the Norman conquest, while in France it was not achieved until the reign of Philip the Fair, after long-continued efforts. But the difference presented in this particular by the history of the two countries was not a mere chronological difference. In England the resistance to John Lackland was organized by the barons: that is, by the military class, behind which the rest of the nation was gathered, complaining of the same grievances and demanding the same rights. There was nothing of the kind in France under Jean the Good. There the bourgeoisie—that is to say, the commercial and industrial class—headed the movement. Now between this bourgeoisie and the nobles no understanding was possible. The privileges of the one class were opposed to those of the other, giving rise to a mutual hostility, which the disasters of Crecy and Poitiers, for which the bourgeoisie held the chivalry responsible, increased to a maximum. It was too late, in the middle of the 14th century, for another Simon de Montfort to emerge from the ranks of the French feudality. If a few *grands seigneurs* supported the efforts of the Third Estate, this was only by reason of personal interest, resentment or ambition, and on the first opportunity they abandoned the allies whom they despised. The same may be said of the clergy. Its representatives were concerned only to defend their prerogatives and immunities. In short, between the English Parliament and the States-General of France the contrast could not be greater. The English Parliament confronted the king with the united representatives of the various classes of the nation, who deliberated together, and by mutual agreement gave expression to their will; the States-General, composed of three orders which debated and voted separately, constituted in reality three distinct assemblies of privileged persons, incapable of agreement, so that their disagreements and their conflicts offered the Crown only too easy a means of evading their intervention. Moreover, in the course of the 13th century the competence and the attributions of Parliament were in all essentials determined by custom, so that it became an indispensable organ of the government. The States-General, on the contrary, were merely an institution adapted to the circumstances, an *ultima ratio* to which recourse was had only at a time of financial distress. Every one of their convocations corresponded with a crisis of the Treasury: they were assembled only that they might be asked for money. And it was precisely this fact that gave the bourgeoisie the preponderant rôle in the States. For since it did not enjoy the financial immunities of the nobles or the clergy, it was the bourgeoisie above all that was called upon to make payment, and it was natural that in return for the taxes which it voted it should stipulate for certain guarantees. As far as can be judged from the sixty-seven articles submitted to the Dauphin by Étienne Marcel, its ideal was to inspire the administration of the kingdom with the same spirit of control and legality which prevailed in the urban administration. The agents of the king, above all the financial agents, must no longer be irresponsible in respect of the taxpayers. The government must accept the permanent collaboration of the States-General and associate them in its activities. But when Marcel spoke of the States-General he was thinking before all of the bourgeoisie, and especially of the Parisian bourgeoisie. From the time of this first encounter between the King of France and the nation, Paris actually assumed the leadership of the movement, and no one dreamt of disputing its position. The importance of Paris as the capital, which it owed to the Crown, was now exploited by the people of Paris against the Crown. The royal city was so truly without peer, it so far surpassed all the other cities of the kingdom, by its population, its wealth, and its activity—and also by its turbulence—and it was already so truly the centre of the country, the focus of universal attention, that from the middle of the 14th century its tumults shook all France, the voice of its tribunes was heard by the whole nation, and its riots were "historic days" (*journées*). The Dauphin understood this so fully that he introduced a tactical expedient which was often employed afterwards, down to the 19th century: he decided to remove the States-General from this turbulent centre and to assemble them at Compiègne (1358). This merely exasperated the Parisian opposition. Civil war seemed on the point of breaking out. Marcel negotiated with the King of Navarre and the King of England, and he was exhorting Gand and the Flemish cities to unite their efforts to his in opposing "wicked and foolish enterprises, in such a manner that we may all live in full liberty," when the explosion of the Jacquerie led to the dénouement of the crisis.

The burden of the new taxes, accompanied by the excesses of the troops of mercenaries disbanded after Poitiers, who were dispersing in all directions and living on the country, had driven the peasants of Champagne, Picardy, and Beauvaisis to extremities. The defeat of the nobles at Crecy and Poitiers had dispelled the dread with which the peasants had regarded them. They attributed their distress to the cowardice of the nobles. They felt, confusedly, that the privileges of the nobles could be justified only by their military rôle, and this they had just shown themselves incapable of fulfilling. Suddenly they envisaged the gentleman as the enemy of the people. Bands of peasants armed with iron-bound cudgels proceeded to scour the country and to attack the châteaux. Their first successes emboldened them. Before long there was a general rising among the peasants. Yet there was no general plan of revolt. There were no recognized leaders, and no precise claims were advanced. It was a reaction of despair, an explosion of rage. The startled bourgeoisie, in the shelter of its walls, watched the movement without taking part in it, doubtless intending to profit thereby if it should succeed. But how could it have succeeded? The heavily-armed knights whom the English archers had defeated could not fail to overcome these "villeins, black and stunted and poorly armed" (Froissart, v, 105), who were killing their children, violating their wives, and burning their manors. Their superiority was like that of regular troops over a mob of strikers. After the first moment of confusion the nobles took the field, and the result was a massacre. The decimated "Jacques" returned to their villages, convinced of their impotence. There were no further rural insurrections in France until the French Revolution.

This insurrection brought the nobles over to the side of the Dauphin, snapping the very feeble bonds which here and there united some of the party of the nobles to the party of the bourgeois reformers. Marcel's enemies grew bolder. A conspiracy was hatched against him, and on July 31st, 1358, he was assassinated, just as Jan van Artevelde, between whose policy and his own there was a striking resemblance, had been assassinated fifteen years earlier. His death did not put an end to the assembly of the States-General. The Dauphin could not dispense with their assistance in the exhausted condition of the country. Edward III, in 1359–1360, besieged the city of Reims and advanced as far as Burgundy without encountering any resistance. It was imperative that peace should be concluded.

It was signed at Bretigny (near Chartres) on May 9th, 1360. Edward received Gascony, Guyenne, Poitou, Calais and the County of Guines in full sovereignty, plus three millions of gold, in return for which he renounced his claim to the rest of France. England thus once more became a Continental power, to the detriment of France. The situation was strangely like that which obtained in the time of the first Plantagenets. The area of the kingdom had been diminished until it was almost what it had been at the beginning of the reign of Philip Augustus.

This fact alone is enough to show that the results of the Peace of Bretigny were indefensible. A French State was not like the territorial possessions of the houses of Bavaria, Luxembourg and Austria, a mere juxtaposition of countries and peoples which the dynasties could amalgamate as easily as they could dismember them. It was as definitely based on geographical unity as it was on national unity and solidarity of interests. Rescued by the kings from its state of feudal subdivision as soon as the agrarian economy on which this subdivision was based had disappeared, it had crystallized round them through successive reigns, and the only reason why the action of the monarchy had been so prompt and so fruitful was that it was in correspondence with the nature of things. The annexations which had of necessity been conceded to Edward III were obviously only a temporary sacrifice. It was as impossible that England should be able to retain her new French provinces as it would have been for France to take and retain possession of Kent. The Peace of Bretigny was plainly no more than a truce. What hope could there be that France would accept as lasting a situation which was not only humiliating to her, but which constituted a permanent menace? And how could England retain, against the will of the population, conquests as extensive as her own territory?

Charles V (1364–1380), who succeeded his father Jean II in 1364, could not hope to break the peace which had barely been concluded. The kingdom was exhausted by taxation, and more than ever victimized by the companies of mercenaries who were living on the inhabitants. The king very skilfully succeeded in relieving his subjects of the nuisance of these mercenaries by employing them against England. Henri de Transtamarre, who was fighting Pedro the Cruel, an ally of Edward III, in Castile, had appealed to France for help. Du Guesclin received orders to march to his assistance at the head of the companies. Pedro the Cruel was defeated (1369), and a treaty of alliance was concluded between Charles V and Henri de Transtamarre, so that an enemy threatened the flank of the English possessions in Aquitaine. At the same time the king's diplomacy won another success in the north. The Count of Flanders, Louis de Maele, the son of Louis de Nevers who was slain at Crecy, had abandoned his father's policy and adopted an ambiguous neutrality, which, as it compelled both France and England to treat with him, had procured for him a situation which was all the more advantageous, in that having no male descendant, he was able to keep the two belligerents in suspense by negotiating with both for the marriage of his daughter Marguerite. In this conflict between the two bidders, Charles V was victorious. In return for the restitution to Flanders of Lille, Douai and Orchies, ceded in 1320, Louis consented to the marriage of his daughter (June 29th, 1369) with the King's brother, Philip the Bold, who in 1361 had received the Duchy of Burgundy as his appanage. It seemed that the "Flemish question" which had so greatly preoccupied the Crown since the reign of Philip Augustus was on the point of being solved, since the succession of the powerful County was assured to a royal prince.

Charles V now felt himself strong enough for a frontal attack upon England. A revolt against the Black Prince in Guyenne served him as a pretext for denouncing the Peace of Bretigny. The States-General hastened to grant the necessary subsidies, and the war, energetically waged by Du Guesclin, resulted in an uninterrupted series of successes. In 1372 the fleet of Castile defeated the English fleet off La Rochelle. On land the English had retained hardly anything more than Calais, Bordeaux and Bayonne when Edward III died, in 1377, two years after the Black Prince, bequeathing the crown to the Black Prince's son, Richard II, a child of nine; and three years later another child, Charles VI, inherited the crown of France on the death of Charles V.

## 2. *The Burgundian Period* (1432)

The two regencies, which began almost simultaneously in France and England, were equally stormy. Though the actual happenings on either side of the Channel were of a very different nature, they were influenced by the same motives: the discontent of the people, due to the heavy burden of war taxation, and the ambition of the royal princes invested with the regency.

The reign of Richard II is memorable on account of the great rural insurrection of 1381. The fundamental cause of this rising, like that of the Jacquerie, was the poverty of the rural population, whose sufferings were as little regarded by Parliament as they had been by the States-General. How should the political assemblies concern themselves with the troubles of the people, since they consisted only of the representatives of the privileged classes? Parliament regarded the people much as the governments of landowners, at the beginning of the 19th century, regarded the industrial proletariat: as the unprivileged multitude, on which the social edifice rested, and which received attention only when its commotions shook the society which was based upon it.

In England, as everywhere, the situation of the peasants was much improved in the 13th century. But during the first half of the 14th century progress was arrested by the action of the general causes which have already been indicated. The greater cost of living and the increased wages which were a consequence of the ravages of the Black Death led the nobles, in 1351, to insist that Parliament should pass a law reducing the wages of agricultural labourers to the tariff obtaining in 1347 (Statute of Labourers). Emboldened by their success, they thereupon endeavoured to re-establish their old domainal rights, to revive the system of corvées, which had fallen into desuetude, and once more to degrade the peasants to the status of serfs attached to the soil. If we consider that all these wrongs were aggravated by the increasing burden of taxation we can understand what a ferment of hatred must have filled the minds of the people. The religious movement provoked by Wycliffe led to the final catastrophe, just as in the 16th century the Lutheran propaganda led to the outbreak in Germany of the Peasant War. Of course, neither Wycliffe nor Luther urged the masses to rebel, but both reformers, by undermining the people's respect for religious authority, taught them to revolt against the social order which was the cause of their sufferings, and which the traditional Church had taught them to respect. It was in this particular that the English rebels of 1381 differed from the Jacques of France in 1357. The Jacques were driven to revolt only by their poverty; the English rebels were all the more formidable in that they were spurred onward not merely by poverty, but also by the feeling that they were the victims of a Church and a society both of which were corrupted by the love of riches. They had at their head not only journeymen like Wat Tyler, but also poor priests like John Ball, whose Lollardist preaching had inspired so many poor folk with passionate hopes of a naïve communism.

But the peasants could not hold their own against the nobles, those steel-clad policemen. Like the Jacquerie, their rising ended in a massacre, and like the Jacquerie it was not repeated.

However, the war with France resulted in a series of defeats. The English allowed the men of Gand to be crushed in the battle of Roosebeke, and in the following year the English expedition against Ypres, under the command of the Bishop of Norwich (1383), was a pitiable failure. In 1388 the English had to resign themselves to accepting a truce, which was renewed for twenty years in 1396. These reverses increased the dissatisfaction with the king's government. Richard had hardly emerged from the tutelage of the regency when he attempted to undermine the increasing authority assumed by Parliament during the reign of Edward III. The only result of his efforts was that in 1388 he had the humiliation of seeing his counsellors condemned to death. The opposition had been led by his uncle, Thomas of Gloucester. The king joined forces against him with his other uncle, John of Lancaster, with the result that Gloucester was accused of high treason; he also succeeded in obtaining from Parliament a permanent tax, which he found highly advantageous, as henceforth he was able to abstain from convoking that formidable assembly. This new attempt to restore the personal power of the Crown in England, which followed the unsuccessful attempts of Henry III and Edward II, was no more successful than the latter. How could the king have got the better of Parliament, the organ of the triple strength of the nobles, the clergy and the burgesses? He seems to have had some vague notion of seeking support from the Lollards, and from the mass of the people, who were still seething with rebellion. However, when Henry of Lancaster, after the death of his father, summoned the nobles to take up arms against the king, no one raised a hand to defend the monarch. In 1399 Parliament, making use for the second time of the right which it had arrogated to itself under Edward II, deprived him of the crown, which it gave to Henry of Lancaster (1399–1413), although he was not the next heir.

The new king found himself in the situation which in 1689 was that of William of Orange on succeeding to James II. Parliament, to which he owed the throne, expected guarantees, which he hastened to give. In order to conciliate the spiritual lords he made a clean break with the Lollards, introduced the methods of the Inquisition into England, and forbade the translation of the Bible into the vulgar tongue.

War with Scotland and a rebellious Wales made it impossible for him to satisfy the bellicose aspirations of the nobles and to break the truce which had been concluded with France. It was reserved for his son Henry V to reopen this fruitless struggle, and to win fresh victories, as brilliant and as ephemeral in their results as those of Crecy and Poitiers had been.

While Richard II, Henry IV and Henry V succeeded one another on the throne of England, the long regency to which the youth of Charles VI (1380–1422), and presently his insanity, condemned France during his reign resulted in a return of the commotions and the rivalries which Charles V had interrupted, though he had not removed their cause. The king's uncles, entrusted with the government during his minority, were chiefly concerned to exploit their position to their personal advantage. Louis of Anjou, whom Queen Joanna of Naples had recently appointed her heir, busied himself with making preparations for an expedition into Italy, while Philip of Burgundy turned an anxious gaze upon Flanders, his future heritage.

Since the Black Death the increasing cost of living had not been balanced by an increase of wages, so that the industrial populations of the cities were in a state of the most dangerous unrest. The weavers, who were the most numerous, the best organized and the boldest of the cloth-workers, were everywhere assuming a threatening attitude, and were posing as the champions of the poor against the rich. Year after year the social antagonism increased, still further excited by the communistic mysticism which had so many adherents in the ranks of the proletariat. In 1379 the weavers of Gand succeeded in seizing the power of government, and were immediately imitated by their comrades of Bruges and Ypres. In this region of Flanders, where the wealthy employers had so long been predominant in the cities, and had reduced the majority of the workers to the condition of wage-earners, the latent economic conflict between employers and employed broke out into a veritable class warfare. The rebels were by no means content with demanding political rights. What did they actually want? They themselves could not have explained very clearly what they wanted, for what they wanted was that indefinable State which was at once the objective of the grossest appetites and the purest love of justice, an ideal which alternately consoled or exasperated the unfortunate. The immediate effect of their victory in the three great cities was to assemble against them, and to gather about the Count, all those "who had something to lose": merchants, employers, courtiers, wealthy artisans—the defenders of the order which protected their property against the revolution which was threatening them. The weavers of Bruges and Ypres were unable to resist the coalition of their enemies. But the weavers of Gand remained indomitable. Their city, blockaded by the chivalry of Louis de Maele, who dared not make a direct attack, attracted the impassioned interest of all who suffered under the rule of the rich and powerful. The trade corporations of Liége sent provisions to Gand; the men of Malines followed its example and revolted, while in France the people of Paris and Rouen rose to the cry of "Vive Gand." A veritable social contagion was spreading from the heroic city. It was starving, but it had no thought of surrender. Philip van Artevelde, whom Gand chose for its leader, encouraged the rebels to make a supreme effort. Under the walls of Bruges they offered battle to the army of Louis de Maele, and, against all expectations, cut it to pieces. Once more Gand was the mistress of Flanders, and everywhere the weavers once more laid down the law in the Flemish cities.

Philip the Bold, by invoking the necessity of dealing drastically with the centre of so contagious a rebellion, had no difficulty in persuading the court to despatch an expedition which would assure him of his heritage. The men of Gand and their adherents were defeated at Roosebeke, and Louis de Maele resumed possession of his County. He had just inherited from his mother Artois and the Franche Comté of Burgundy, so that on his death in 1384 Philip became the possessor of these territories, as well as Flanders. Combined with his Duchy of Burgundy, they gave him a power which no vassal of the Crown had ever before possessed. However, his dazzling position was regarded merely as a victory won by the policy of the Crown. The result at which Charles V had aimed was achieved. Flanders was now ruled by a prince of the blood. Did not this mean the definite rupture of the English alliance, and was it not the prelude to a closer union in the future?

Philip did not fail to profit by the conjuncture which identified his own interest with that of the kingdom. From the beginning of the 13th century it had been the policy of the Crown to endeavour to subject to its influence all the princes of the Low Countries. Nominally vassals of the Empire, they had really been quite independent of it since the great interregnum, and were entirely indifferent to its quarrels. Just as the whole economic life of their territories was oriented upon the Flemish coast, so their policy was wholly Occidental. Turning their backs on the Empire, their sympathies were given now to Paris, now to London, according to their interests of the moment. The advanced civilization of these regions, the general diffusion of French manners, the similarity of the institutions which analogous economic needs and the general preponderance of the bourgeoisie had bestowed upon the various principalities, had saved them, despite the fact that in the north the population was Flemish and in the south Walloon, from the racial conflicts which in Eastern Europe had broken out, with all the brutality of instinctive hostility, between the Slavs and the Germans. Thus the dynastic amalgamations of various originally independent territories effected during the 13th century were of a durable nature. Since 1286 the union of the Duchies of Brabant and Limburg, and since 1250 that of the Counties of Hainaut, Holland and Zeeland, had constituted, as it were, the prodrome of a movement of unification which was to undergo still further development. At the very moment when Philip the Bold took possession of Flanders the extinction of the petty local dynasties had given these territories to two of the houses which were struggling for preponderance in Germany. The House of Bavaria had inherited the Counties of Hainaut, Holland and Zeeland in 1345, and in 1355 the marriage of Jeanne, the heiress of Brabant and Limburg, to Wenceslas, the brother of the Emperor Charles IV, enabled the House of Luxemburg to anticipate the future possession of these two fair provinces. But engrossed as they were in their German quarrels, neither of these two houses was capable of giving effective support to their representatives in the Low Countries. Philip the Bold, on the other hand, who, under his nephew Charles VI, was able to make use of the resources and the troops of the government, quickly prevailed over both houses. In 1385 he contrived a double marriage: his son Jean married Marguerite of Bavaria, and William of Bavaria, Count of Hainaut, married his daughter, while in order still further to safeguard the alliance, which was in reality a protectorate, he made the king, Charles VI, marry Isabella of Bavaria, the daughter of the Duke of Hainaut-Holland. Three years later, the Duchess of Brabant being at war with the Duke of Guelders, he persuaded Charles VI to lead the French army against this ally of England. The only result of the expedition was to give the Duchy to Philip. Wenceslas of Luxemburg having died some little time before this, the Duchess of Brabant tore up the convention by which she acknowledged the Luxemburgers as her heirs and secured the succession to Philip, who ceded it to his second son Antoine, in order not to offend the Brabançon sentiment of autonomy. Thus, when he died in 1404 the influence of his dynasty was enormously increased in the Low Countries. But these regions were so wealthy, and their political situation was so advantageous, that before long the dynasty took root there, when, forgetting its French origin, and actuated by an ambition which naturally identified itself with the interests of its northern subjects, it became naturalized among them. Charles V, by assuring his brother's possession of Flanders, had hoped to recover it for the Crown. But by the irony of history the marriage of 1369 was the beginning of that Burgundian power which was presently to become the cruellest enemy of France.

Already, under Jean the Fearless (1404–1419), the successor of Philip the Bold, we see the beginning of the evolution which was to make him, the son of a pure-blooded Valois, above all things a Burgundian prince. There can be no doubt that the interest of his northern possessions, and above all of Flanders, determined his political principles. In the interests of Flemish industry he was obliged to humour England, and he began to conciliate that country from the very beginning of his reign, and as the Flemings acknowledged the Pope of Rome he did all that was in his power to bring about the end of the schism. At the same time he set to work to improve the position of his house in the Low Countries. He brought about a marriage between his nephew Jean of Brabant and Jacqueline of Bavaria, the future heiress of Hainaut-Holland. In 1408 he extended his influence as far as the Meuse by aiding the Bishop of Liége, John of Bavaria, against the Liégeois rebels, whom he cut to pieces at Othée.

This increase of the Burgundian power in the north constituted such a direct threat to France that she could not look on unmoved. The king being insane and incapable, his brother, the Duke of Orleans, forced the government to adopt an attitude which was entirely hostile to Jean the Fearless. On November 23rd, 1407, his rival had him assassinated. This was the signal for the outbreak of a civil war which had only awaited some such occasion.

The defeat of the men of Gand at Roosebeke in 1382 had decided the fate of the Parisian insurrection. Returning to his capital victorious, the king made it clear that he was the master. He abolished the franchises of the city and put an end to that era of reforms and convocations of the States-General which had begun with Etienne Marcel. The opposition was defeated, but it was more exasperated than ever. It only awaited a leader to take up arms again. Jean the Fearless, seeing that the partisans of the Duke of Orleans were making ready to oppose him, under the leadership of the Count of Armagnac, immediately allied his cause with that of the urban democracy. He posed as the champion of the people against the exploitation of the nobles and the court, and affected demagogic manners, so that the cry of "Vive Bourgogne" replaced the cry of "Vive Gand" which had resounded through the streets of Paris twenty-five years earlier. Thus the dynastic policy which in the Low Countries had made the Duke the enemy of the Liége artisans placed him in France at the head of the Parisian artisans, and led him to support all their claims and to work hand in hand with the butcher Caboche, allowing his slaughterers to massacre the Armagnacs. When the States-General, which had not assembled for thirty years, were convoked in 1413, he supported all the reforms demanded by the "Cabochiens," being anxious above all to remain popular with the masses. As for the interests of the kingdom, we find no trace of them in his policy. In the following year, when Henry V took up arms against France, he preserved a neutrality so benevolent that it came near to being an alliance.

The state of disorganization into which France had fallen rendered her incapable of vigorous resistance. The king being insane, and the bourgeoisie hostile, while the Duke of Burgundy pursued his own ends, the burden of the war rested on the Armagnac party, as though the war with England had been merely an episode of the civil war. The disaster of Agincourt (October 25th, 1415) gave Normandy to the English. The French wished to negotiate. The claims of the victor were so exorbitant that Jean the Fearless, who had merely wished to see France and England neutralize each other, made approaches to the Dauphin, round whom the Armagnacs had rallied. But men's passions were too unbridled to subordinate themselves to the national interest. On September 20th, 1419, on the occasion of their meeting at Montereau, a blow from an axe avenged the murder of the Duke of Orleans.

At the very moment when the House of Burgundy was becoming reconciled to France, this crime led it to conclude an immediate alliance with the English. For sixteen years the son of Jean the Fearless, Philip the Good (1419–1467), strove to overthrow the kingdom, with an energy inspired by the spirit of vengeance and directed by political interest. For although he placed his troops at the disposal of England, it was on condition that England should give him a free hand in the north, and help him to conquer the Low Countries as he was helping England to conquer France. The popularity which his father had enjoyed among the bourgeois facilitated his task. The States-General did not fail to recognize Henry V as the successor of Charles VI. The Dauphin, without energy, or military talent, or popularity, and whose troops were both insufficient and lacking in confidence, was soon obliged to fall back along the Loire. The death of Henry V, and that of Charles VI, which occurred a few months later in 1422, enabled the English and the Burgundians to proclaim Henry VI, a child only a few months old, King of France and England, the proclamation being made in Paris. After seventy years of war the end pursued by Edward III and bequeathed by him to the ambition of his successors was at last attained. The Duke of Bedford was invested with the regency and entrusted with the final conquest of the kingdom. The future of the Dauphin, who had withdrawn to Bourges, and who on the death of Charles VI had immediately assumed the royal title of Charles VII, appeared extremely precarious.

However, it was far less precarious in reality than it seemed. The advance of the English in the north had been favoured by the Burgundian alliance. But Philip the Good evidently could not allow his troops to operate too far from the Low Countries, where he was pursuing an increasingly active policy. On the other hand, Bedford and his brother Gloucester, the Regent of England, found it hard to agree, with the result that there was an immediate decrease of vigour in the conduct of the campaign. Lastly, and above all, the national feeling of the French had to be reckoned with. The proclamation of Henry VI as King of France had not aroused any popular indignation. The people either ignored it, or regarded it as null and void. For the French there were not two kings in France: there was only one legitimate and possible monarch, only one appointed by God and by tradition: the heir of the late king, Charles VII. Neither the miseries of the war, nor the burden of taxation, nor dissatisfaction with the government, nor the insanity of the last king, and the scandals provoked by the flagrant misconduct of the queen, had undermined the people's feeling for the dynasty. This feeling was as universal and as deeply rooted as their religious sentiments, and even in the remotest parts of the country, even among the descendants of the poor Jacques who were massacred in 1358, a veneration was felt for the king almost like that which was paid to the saints. This monarchical piety does not explain Joan of Arc—the superhuman cannot be explained—but it was, so to speak, her point of departure, the indispensable condition of her career, just as faith is the indispensable condition of martyrdom. Without it the heroic and visionary soul of the Domrémy shepherdess would never have heard the voices that determined her destiny. Those voices would never have spoken had she been born in the ranks of the nobility or the bourgeoisie, where the idea of the monarch was allied with too many considerations of interest or of politics. The exalted, simple, pure and ingenuous conception of the king entertained by Joan was possible only in a child of the people. Joan of Arc was no more than the sublime expression of the national sentiment of the French peasants, a sentiment which was blended with their religious faith, and which their memories of the good king Saint Louis had indissolubly associated with the monarchy.

By its very unlikeness to that of the Armagnacs of the court, her popular royalism must have contributed greatly to the extraordinary influence which she exercised over the best of Charles's soldiers—over La Hire and Dunois. As for the nation, discouraged and disillusioned, the deliverance of Orléans (1429) gave it the sudden stimulus that restored its confidence and energy. The Pucelle dispelled the last remnants of party quarrels. Men began to hope again, and they recalled the old prophecies which announced that a virgin would save the kingdom. It needed no more than this pure apparition: France was herself again, and ready to confront the English and the Burgundians. The brief career of the "Bonne Lorraine" restored the latent energies of the people. Her capture at Compiègne in 1430, and her execution at Rouen in 1431, did not check the work which she had begun. Though the king showed little enough energy, though he took little advantage of the circumstances, he could now be certain that his cause would be victorious. Moreover, Bedford, paralysed by Gloucester, was not conducting the campaign with any vigour. And when in 1435 Philip the Good at last concluded a peace with Charles VII, so that henceforth France had to deal only with the English, the final result was only a question of time. In 1435 Paris opened her gates to the royal troops, and the "King of Bourges" at last took possession of his capital. Then, when the war, interrupted by a truce, was resumed in 1445, it was one series of victories. In 1449 Rouen was recaptured. In 1450 the victory of Formigny gave the French the whole of Normandy; Bordeaux and Bayonne were theirs in 1451, and finally, in 1453, after the battle of Chatillon, the enemy evacuated the last positions which he still occupied in the south of the kingdom. Of all the English conquests, Calais alone was left, and the empty title of King of France, which figured on the English currency even in the 19th century. The only lasting result of the Hundred Years' War was the creation, on the northern frontier of the kingdom, of a powerful Burgundian State. Philip the Good, in assisting the English, was really working for himself. He took effective advantage of Charles VII's weakness, reaping the results of the policy initiated by his grandfather and his father, and united under his power the various territories of the Low Countries. He purchased the County of Namur in 1421. In 1428 he was acknowledged by Jacqueline of Bavaria as the heir to Hainaut, Holland and Zeeland; in 1430 he succeeded his cousin Jean IV as Duke of Brabant and of Limburg; and when he concluded the Peace of Arras it was only in return for the cession by the King of Artois and the towns of the Somme. The following years brought him the possession of Luxemburg, and the protectorate over the ecclesiastical principalities of Liége and Utrecht.

But this State must not be regarded as one of those mere collections of territories such as the Houses of Luxemburg and Habsburg were at this time assembling in Germany, and which, being held together merely by the fragile tie of dynastic union, fell to pieces as rapidly as they were made. Although its populations were heterogeneous, their general civilization and the interests were the same. If the peoples themselves had not tended to unite, nothing would have been easier than to prevent their union, for the rights invoked by Philip in respect of his succession to Hainaut, Holland and Brabant were, to say the least of them, doubtful. The Emperor Sigismond protested furiously against this annexation of Imperial fiefs to the Burgundian power, and urged the States to resist it. They did not listen to him, because the dynastic ambition of the prince was in accordance with their own desire, so that in the unification of the Low Countries the nation itself supported the plans of the dynasty.

In respect of its admirable geographical situation, the length of its sea-coast, the number of its cities, and the industry and wealth of its inhabitants, the Burgundian State had no equal in Europe, save Italy. But for France its creation was a check to the plan which she had pursued, from reign to reign, since the beginning of the 13th century, of subjecting to her influence these wealthy countries that lay upon her northern frontiers. It was only to be expected that once France had recovered from the terrible crisis by which Philip the Good had profited so greatly, she would never cease endeavouring to recover the preponderance which she had lost in the basins of the Meuse and the Scheldt. Her enemies just as obstinately disputed this preponderance, so that the creation of the Burgundian State created also that problem of the Low Countries which, until the 19th century, when it was finally solved, was to give rise to so many European crises that it served, so to speak, as a pressure-gauge in the international relations of the great powers.

## CHAPTER III

# THE EMPIRE. THE SLAV STATES AND HUNGARY

### 1. *The Empire*

Germany, during the great interregnum, had assumed the political form which she was to retain down to modern times. It is not very easy to define her constitution, in which were comprised, without any real coherence, a monarchy which possessed none of the attributes of sovereignty, a multitude of ecclesiastical or lay princes, urban republics (Free Cities), and "immediate" (unmediated) nobles, enjoying complete independence, with a Diet (*Reichstag*) whose attributions were as ill-defined as its composition was bizarre. An anarchy in monarchical form: that perhaps is the best description of this extraordinary political entity, which had neither common laws, common finances, nor a common body of functionaries. It is strictly correct to say of it that it was a totality composed of parts which did not constitute a whole. Compared with France and England, it seemed amorphous, illogical, almost monstrous. The fact is that the mainspring of this strange mechanism, subjected too soon to an excessive tension, was broken. By the end of the War of Investitures it was evident that the monarchy, which everywhere else gave its form to the State, had no longer the strength to fulfil its task. Its Imperial ambitions had drawn it into adventures from which it had emerged half shattered, and while under the Hohenstaufens it gathered up what strength remained to it and endeavoured to take its revenge, this attempted recovery ended in a decisive catastrophe. After the election of Rudolph of Habsburg (1273) it was so completely devoid of prestige and authority that one may wonder why the electors still took the trouble to appoint a king.

Perhaps it was really the Imperial ideal, the cause of its fall, which preserved its existence. The necessity of an Emperor, who no longer corresponded to any existing reality, was imposed by tradition. And since the King of Germany was the Emperor-designate, to suppress him would have been to abolish the Empire. He therefore continued to exist, and by the most paradoxical of destinies he retained his illusory monarchical power only in order to secure an Imperial power which had become even more illusory.

For since the death of Frederick II nothing remained of the Empire but the empty forms. The attitude adopted by the Papacy since Innocent III, and the formation of national States in France and England, finally deprived it of any further possibility of compelling Europe to acknowledge its temporal primacy. If this primacy was still acknowledged anywhere, it was in the schools, where the professors of Roman law continued to regard the Emperor, in theory, as the master of the world. It might also be invoked, from time to time, against a political adversary, as Boniface VIII invoked it in his conflict with Philip the Fair. Or some idealist might see in it, as Dante saw, a beautiful dream to which reality gave the lie. As a matter of fact it was a dead ideal, a relic of the past, and it would have been a majestic relic, if the weakness of the Emperors had not only too often contrasted too sharply with the memories which they evoked. The Emperor's precedence over other sovereigns was still recognized, as was his right to create nobles and to institute notaries in all countries. And this was almost all that was left of his old universal power. And he still derived some prestige from his relations with the Pope, with whom he was necessarily allied. In the 14th century these relations gave rise to an epilogue to the great conflicts of the past, and in the 15th century they enabled Sigismond to play what we may call—with a lack of reverence in some degree justified by his pretentious demeanour—the part of impresario to the Council of Constance.

Rudolph of Habsburg never found time, during his long reign (1273–1291), to go to Rome in order to receive the Imperial crown. Germany provided him with sufficient occupation. He did not need to be a great politician to realize that a restoration of the monarchical power in that country was impossible. The first condition of such a restoration would have been the hereditary nature of the Crown. It was useless to think of such a thing. Neither the Pope, nor the electors, nor the princes would have consented to it. The idea of rallying the cities to the cause of the monarchy was even more chimerical. It would have been possible only if they had felt the need of a protector, and they were not conscious of any such need. The princes were not powerful enough to imperil their position, and in the event of danger the regional leagues which they had concluded were a sufficient guarantee of their independence. Was there at least some hope of rallying the nation against a foreign power—of profiting by the encroachments of France on the western frontier in order to take his place at the head of the nation and make it accept him as his defender? To make that possible, Germany must have been inspired by the nationalist ideal, and the country was quite devoid of any national feeling. Each thought only of himself, and the only frontier that gave him any anxiety was that of his own domain. In the midst of this universal egoism, Rudolf had no intention of devoting himself to the cause of the monarchy, which interested no one. Needy and burdened with a large family, he contented himself with profiting by the position which had been conferred upon him to attend to his own affairs, or rather, those of his house. Totally devoid of idealism, he felt that it would be a mockery to sacrifice himself and to leave the Crown as poor as when he had received it. The circumstances favoured his designs. The victory which he won over the King of Bohemia, Ottocar II, at the beginning of his reign, with the assistance of the King of Hungary (1278), left vacant the Duchies of Austria and Styria. He hastened to bestow them as fiefs on his son Albert. Thus a lucky chance had suddenly endowed the petty House of Habsburg with the wealthy Danubian duchies. This was the sole result of Rudolph's policy. Though he reigned without governing, at least he left his family well established, and provided with an example of the art of profiting by contingencies which it was to follow only too often in the future.

The electors had appointed Rudolph simply because he was weak and poor. Although he had disappointed them, they replaced him by a king who was still weaker and poorer, and gave the crown to Adolphus of Nassau (1291–1298). However, it was inevitable that the good fortune of his predecessor would induce him to proceed upon the same lines. But he was not, like Rudolph, favoured by chance. For the want of any better policy, he decided, in 1294, to sell to Edward I his services as ally against Philip the Fair. The encroachments of France on the German frontier sufficed to provide an honourable pretext for this bargain. But he was really as indifferent to these encroachments as he was to Edward's quarrel. What he really had in mind was to seize Thuringia, and the pounds sterling which he had received were employed merely in defraying the cost of a war by which he hoped to enrich his house. The electors were not disposed to countenance a second *parvenu.* They deposed him, replacing him by Albert, the son of Rudolph of Habsburg (1298–1308). In accordance with the tradition which was a legacy from his father, Albert was cherishing hopes of uniting the Kingdom of Bohemia with Austria, when his assassination, in 1308, led to the failure of a plan which was never again forgotten by the tenacious memory of his heirs.

For the third time a petty prince from whom it seemed that there was nothing to fear was called to the throne. Appointed through the influence of his brother, the Archbishop-Elector of Treves, Count Henry of Luxemburg (1308–1313) belonged to the Low Countries, which, although they were comprised within the frontiers of the Empire, were now only nominally dependent on Germany. Like his neighbours of Liége, Hainaut, Brabant and Flanders, he was steeped in the civilization and the manners of France, and was also of Walloon origin, so that once he had crossed the Rhine he seemed a complete foreigner. Nevertheless, it was this foreigner, this "Welche," who restored the Imperial tradition, which his three predecessors had neglected in order to attend to their own affairs. His initiative was sufficiently explained by his origin. Since by virtue of this origin he was indifferent to German affairs he was bound to turn his attention to the affairs of the Empire. He dreamed of the glory of donning in Rome the crown which had never been worn since the reign of Frederick II, and, by reconciling the Empire with the Papacy, of winning for it by peaceful means a new and beneficent majesty.

The news of his arrival sent a thrill of hope through Italy. The annihilation of the Hohenstaufens had not restored tranquillity to the fiery cities of Lombardy and Tuscany. Under the old name of Guelfs and Ghibellines the factions still continued to wage war upon each other with a ferocity which was enhanced by the divergence of economic interests, the conflicts of the artisans and the patricians, and the mutual hatreds of the nobles. Pisa had recently surrendered to the Genoese forces, and Florence profited by her defeat, subjecting Tuscany to her democratic government. In Lombardy the majority of the cities, exhausted by their quarrels, accepted the *signoria* of a successful soldier or a podestà, and resigned themselves to tyranny for the sake of peace. The Della Torre ruled in Milan, the Della Scala in Verona, and the Este in Ferrara. In Rome, which had been abandoned by the Popes, the Colonna and the Orsini were in desperate conflict. Venice alone, under her powerful aristocracy, preserved a state of tranquillity which enabled her to devote herself with all the greater energy to the naval war which she was waging against Genoa.

Henry VII made his appearance in this world of unbridled passions and appetites as the restorer of order and peace. He had been sincerely anxious to reconcile the parties and to rally them to himself by the justness of his policy. But how could he impose justice without the aid of force? He had brought with him only three or four thousand knights, and the hope which had greeted his arrival was followed almost immediately by disappointment. Despite his intentions, he found himself obliged, if he was to obtain any support, to choose between the adversaries whom he had dreamed of pacifying. King Robert of Naples, who felt uneasy at seeing Henry's influence replacing his own in the peninsula, assumed a threatening attitude. When Henry arrived in Rome the troops of his enemies were in occupation of the greater part of the city. He could not reach St. Peter's, and had to content himself with receiving almost secretly, in the Lateran, from the hands of the cardinals appointed by the Pope, the Imperial crown, which it would perhaps have been better not to receive at all rather than receive it thus (June 1312). Of his plan for restoring the majesty of the Empire nothing was left. Without finances, and almost without an army, he was reduced to subordinating his policy to that of the Neapolitans, and soliciting the support of the King of Sicily against them. In Tuscany Florence closed her gates against him. In order to fight Florence he had to depend on Pisan support. The descent was too great after such brief and exalted illusions. Worn out by chagrin, Henry died at Buonconvento in August 1313. He was buried at Pisa; his sarcophagus is still there, under the gallery where the terrible frescoes of Orcagna represent so cruelly the vanity of human ambitions.

But he had reopened the road that led from Italy to Germany, and Louis of Bavaria, his successor, followed in his footsteps (1314–1347). He had hardly conquered Frederick of Habsburg, whom some of the electors had opposed to him, and taken him prisoner, when he took it into his head to cross the Alps. He was immediately confronted by the most desperate opposition from the Pope. The Holy See, forced by France and England to abate its claims, could not capitulate before the kings of Germany. By reviving the question of the Empire, which had been so long forgotten, they were reviving also the hateful memory of the Hohenstaufens, and there was reason to fear that they might rally around them in Italy all the enemies of the Papacy, and of the Kings of Naples, its auxiliaries. War was all the more certain in view of the fact that their political power was so disproportionate to their ambitions that the Papacy, when it attacked them, was almost sure to be victorious. Already the rupture between Henry VII and Robert of Naples had embroiled Henry with Clement V, and only his premature death had prevented the outbreak of war. John XXII was resolved to surrender none of the supremacy which his great predecessors of the 12th century had won over the Empire. On ascending the pontifical throne he had solemnly declared that the Pope held from St. Peter both the spiritual and the temporal empire, and that it was his duty to watch over the latter in the absence of the Emperor. Immediately putting this theory into practice, he appointed Robert of Naples Vicar Imperial in Italy.

Encouraged by the adversaries of the Neapolitans, Louis of Bavaria believed that he was strong enough to accept battle. His excommunication and deposition, pronounced by John XXII (1324), brought over to his camp the spiritual Minorite friars, who, like him, had just been excommunicated, while Marsilius of Padua took advantage of his quarrel to launch against the Pope the *Defensor Pacis*. Bewildered, and carried away by this political and theological opposition, for which he was less the centre of gravity than the pretext, and unable to perceive that it was merely trying to use him under colour of serving him, he allowed himself to be dragged into an adventure which was to be his ruin. His coronation, in 1327, in the Capitol, by two excommunicated bishops, and four syndics of the city, who represented the people, was a sorry parody, in which reminiscences of the anarchy of the 10th century and the mystical republicanism of Arnold of Brescia were curiously blended. Having thus accepted the crown, Louis could refuse nothing, whether to the Roman people, now the victims of one of those crises of pride which made them believe themselves the masters of the world, or to the enemies of John XXII, blinded by their hatred and their dreams or illusions. He allowed a popular assembly to pronounce the deposition of the Pope, who was accused of heresy and lèse-majesté, while a commission of ecclesiastics and laymen appointed in his place a mendicant monk who took the name of Nicholas V. The poor man then perceived that he had been merely an actor in a revolutionary comedy. Horrified by what he had done, he sadly returned to Germany. Less than two years later the Romans were begging the Pope to grant them absolution, and Nicholas V, a rope round his neck, knelt at his feet in Avignon and implored his forgiveness.

The death of John XXII (1334) a few days after he had pronounced, in a solemn Bull, the separation of Italy from the Empire of Germany, did not in any way change the attitude of the Curia toward Louis of Bavaria. Benedict XII and Clement VI remained pitiless; they seem to have taken the harmless insult to the majesty of the Holy See more seriously than it deserved. As for Louis, who had completely lost his bearings, he wore himself out with attempts at reconciliation, which were disdainfully rejected. At one moment he seems to have cherished hopes of compelling Avignon to make peace by allying himself with Edward III against France. This was yet another illusion, and he was soon cured of it. Completely incapable of making war, he not only did not support Edward, but he presently allied himself with Philip of Valois. If Germany had been a State, this would have been the moment for acting as France and England had done under Boniface VIII, and making an end of the humiliations which the Papacy was inflicting on her king. The Electors, supported by the Diet, confined themselves to protesting against the right which the Pope had arrogated to himself of ratifying their nomination of the king; and that was all. They had seen no more in the quarrel than an opportunity of confirming the unjustified privilege which enabled them to dispose of the crown. In short, Louis of Bavaria was left to his own devices. His quarrel with the House of Luxemburg was disastrous. Forgetting their declarations of independence, the Electors, being required by Clement VI to appoint a new king, sold their votes to Charles, Margrave of Moravia, the son of the blind King John of Bohemia, and the grandson of Henry VII, who took the name of Charles IV (1346).

By a fortunate chance Henry VII was able, at the beginning of his reign, to marry his son John (the Blind) to the heiress of the Kingdom of Bohemia. The House of Luxemburg was thus transplanted from the Roman to the Slav frontier of the Empire. And there it maintained itself for more than a century. John having fallen at Crecy soon after the election of his son, Charles IV was able to unite the crowns of Germany and Bohemia. In 1355 he added to these the Imperial crown, going to Rome, in order to receive it, with a small retinue, and taking every possible precaution to remain on good terms with the Pope. It is not surprising that he was concerned before all else to augment the position of his house. To Bohemia and Moravia he added Silesia and Lusatia, and in 1372 the Mark of Brandenburg. In this way a compact power was constituted in the east of Germany, but it was not a German power. Its centre was Bohemia, where Charles introduced an administration which was modelled upon that of France.

The Golden Bull by which Charles IV had finally confirmed, in 1356, the attributions and the composition of the College of Electors, as they were to continue until the end of the 18th century,[1] had reconciled him with these king-makers. Without paying too dearly for the honour, he induced them to appoint his son Wenceslas, during his lifetime, to the dignity of King of the Romans (1376). This was the first time since the reign of Frederick II that a son had succeeded to his father on the throne of Germany.

The reign of Wenceslas (1370–1400) was really an interregnum for Germany. Exclusively occupied with Bohemia, the king took no interest in the rest of the Empire. He neither cared to take the Imperial crown nor to intervene in the incessant quarrels of the German cities and the German princes. In 1400 the four Electors of the Rhine arrogated to themselves the right to depose him, and in this case we may perhaps regard their action as a sort of protest against a king who showed only too plainly that he was a foreigner. If it was their intention, on giving the crown to the Count Palatine Rupert, to set up a truly national sovereign in opposition to their Bohemian sovereign, the experiment was a lamentable failure. The new king was hardly acknowledged by anyone apart from those who had given him the crown. He thought he was striking a masterly blow when he risked an expedition to Italy. The Imperial crown would have given him some prestige, and he counted on seizing Milan on his way south, for the Duke of Milan, Gian Galeazzo Visconti, was on the best of terms with the House of Luxemburg. The naïvety of this plan tells us what the policy of such a king and such electors was worth. Having no money, he calculated that as soon as he had crossed the Alps the Florentines, as the enemies of the Milanese, would kindly place their troops at his disposal. But the Florentines despised him as heartily as did the

[1] The College comprised three ecclesiastical Electors: the prelates of Mayence, Trèves, and Cologne, and four lay electors: the King of Bohemia, the Count Palatine of the Rhine, the Duke of Saxony, and the Margrave of Brandenburg.

Milanese. Having reached Brescia with a few knights, he found it impossible to proceed any further. He was forced to return, covered with shame, to hide himself in the Palatinate, where he died in 1410. His death reminded the world that he had worn the crown. The Electors, who had learned something from experience, reverted to the House of Luxemburg. Wenceslas had two brothers, the Margrave John of Moravia, and Sigismond, King of Hungary. The Electors appointed both, since they had not all contrived to sell their votes to the same candidate. Thus Germany had three kings, for Wenceslas calmly continued to bear the title. Fortunately the death of John in 1416 reduced the number to two, and when Wenceslas followed him in 1419, Sigismond alone was left.

The activity of this last Luxemburger (1410–1437) offers a strange contrast to the apathy of Wenceslas. His interest in his Kingdom of Hungary, which from year to year was more seriously threatened by the Turks, inspired him with the hope of finding salvation in a Crusade against the infidels. And as a Crusade was impossible so long as the schism continued, he did his very utmost, though his zeal was a little indiscreet, to bring about the convocation of the Council of Constance and to ensure the success of its deliberations. The heir, since the death of his brother, to the Kingdom of Bohemia, the revolt of the Hussites, which prevented him from taking possession of his kingdom, was yet another motive for urging the reformation of the Church. His title of King of the Romans was an excellent pretext for meddling in the affairs of the Papacy while attending to his own. The expeditions ordered by the Popes, and the Councils convoked for the purpose of dealing with the Hussites, were one and all unsuccessful, to the confusion of the German chivalry. At last, in 1434, after the war against the Taborites and the Utraquists, the *modus vivendi* of the Compactates having been accepted, Sigismond was able to make his entry into Prague. He died three years later, on December 9th, 1437, and his Kingdoms of Bohemia and Hungary passed to his son-in-law, Albert of Austria. Thus the vast territories of the House of Luxemburg were added to the Duchies of Austria and Styria. The aim envisaged by the House of Habsburg since its establishment in the valley of the Danube was achieved.

A great dynastic power, a hybrid mixture of German, Slav and Magyar countries, was constituted on the east of Germany. All the efforts of so many kings to establish the power of their families had the final result of promoting the Habsburgs to the rank of the most powerful sovereigns in Europe. Chance, of course, played its part in the fortunes of their house, as it plays its part in the destinies of every rich heritage. A miscarriage, a childless marriage, the premature death of a child would have compromised everything. Yet we must not exaggerate the influence of the unforeseen and the unexpected. Do we not find it in military operations just as often as in matrimonial arrangements? It must be acknowledged that if fortune favoured the Habsburgs, it was because they helped it to do so. From the end of the 14th century their whole policy consisted in establishing, by means of politic marriages, their claims to the crowns of Bohemia, Hungary, and even Poland. They counted on the generative power of their race, as others counted on their sword, and they had not miscalculated. If their policy had been applied to countries whose civilization was more ancient, and whose national consciousness was more highly developed, the result might of course have been different. In this connection we have only to recall the measures taken by France at the beginning of the 14th century to prevent the Kings of England from claiming the crown. But neither in Hungary nor in Bohemia was the monarchy as yet so intimately wedded to the nation as to make the latter refuse to yield the crown to a foreigner. It was enough to come to an understanding with the great nobles, however much they might really hate the Germans, and to make them certain concessions, in order to be accepted. What would not have been possible in the West of Europe was possible in the East. None of the conditions that gave rise to the Hundred Years' War existed in the basin of the Danube. The extraordinary luck of the Habsburgs was therefore far less the result of chance than one might suppose. Their matrimonial policy alone does not suffice to explain it. The indispensable and primordial condition was the absence of any political spirit in the peoples who were the instruments or the victims of that policy.

Germany also, if we consider her as a whole, seems to have been just as completely devoid of this political spirit. The rapid survey of the reigns of her kings contained in the last few pages affords an irrefutable proof of this statement. If we compare the history of Germany with that of France and England during the same period, we shall see that in the latter countries the three privileged classes, clergy, nobility and bourgeoisie, were associated, either through taxation or by military service, with the actions of the king, and also that they intervened immediately in the government of the country, while the crises which were provoked by their claims or their quarrels were merely the tumultuous manifestations of an incontestable public life. Germany, on the contrary, had neither a system of taxation nor anything resembling a parliamentary organization. The Diet (*Reichstag*) was merely an assembly of prelates, princes, nobles, and representatives of the cities, whose competence was restricted to paralysing the activities of the sovereign, but which did not replace him in the government of the country, and merely weakened this government by complicating it. The Crown possessed no administration and no finances. The archaic majesty of its language and its emblems was in almost comical contrast with its actual strength. Sigismond, who for the sake of greater majesty gave the eagle of the Empire a second head, was obliged to pawn his crown, and was pursued from city to city by a flock of creditors. If Germany had been a State, the Hundred Years' War would have provided that State with an excellent opportunity of consolidating itself. Since France and England had cancelled each other out, such a State could have imposed its will upon Europe. But Germany was incapable of doing anything of the kind. In Italy she had lost her last actual outposts. The alliances of Adolphus of Nassau and Louis of Bavaria with Edward III merely added to the troubles of these two needy princes, who, having been paid for their services in advance, never rendered any. Consequently France continued to expand upon her eastern frontier without even eliciting a protest from the Emperors. The Dauphiné was acquired by France in 1349. If Charles IV, in 1365, had himself crowned at Arles in order to maintain his right to the ancient Kingdom of Burgundy, this was doubtless only in order that he might sell it at a better price. For almost immediately he appointed the Dauphin Vicar of the Empire at Arles. The Franche Comté became the possession of Philip the Bold. In 1388 a French army waged war upon the Duke of Guelders, and no one protested. We have seen how the House of Burgundy extended its power in the Low Countries, absorbing Hainaut, Holland, Zeeland, Namur and Brabant, establishing its protectorate over Liége and Utrecht, and in the end actually annexing Luxemburg, the cradle of one of the Imperial houses. Philip the Good defied Sigismond. Placed by him under the ban of the Empire in 1433, he responded by addressing an insolent manifesto to the princes and cities of Germany. From every side he received the assurance of the neutrality on which he had counted. When at last, in 1437, the Emperor, driven to extremities, endeavoured to take action, he was reduced to sending Ludwig of Hesse with four hundred lances into Brabant in support of his pretended rights. The peasants of Limburg were able, unaided, to drive the Imperial agent back into Aix-la-Chapelle.

The episode is characteristic. It throws a vivid light on the true nature of the Empire: an agglomeration of princes and cities caring nothing for the sovereign unless his policy favoured their interests. Germany was not a State; it was an aggregate of local sovereignties, lay or ecclesiastical princ. alities, and free cities (about seventy). Moreover, the free cities hardly counted. Only a few of them—Cologne, Nuremberg, Augsburg—were strong enough to defend themselves unaided; not one of them was strong enough to pursue, as did the Italian cities, an influential policy. Their politics were little more than parochial. It is true that the German bourgeoisie had greatly developed in the course of the 14th century. But its progress profited no one save itself. The princes tried to restrict its activities, and the king did not support them. It therefore did not play in Germany the very considerable part which it played in the general development of France and England. An exception must be made in the case of the Hansa. Although there was no very effective alliance between them, the common interests of the Hansa cities united them against their enemies, who, fortunately for them, were very weak. Denmark was the most dangerous. King Valdemar was aefeated in 1369, and the Baltic remained, until the beginning of the 15th century, a German lake.

In the interior of the country there was continual conflict between the princes and the cities, which, since there was no central power in the country, resulted in a state of insecurity, by which the petty nobles joyfully profited, the pillage of the merchants being one of their normal means of livelihood. Here the *Raubritter*, who elsewhere would have been a soldier or a functionary, became a professionl robber.

As for the principalities, apart from Bavaria and the territories of the Houses of Luxemburg and Habsburg, none of them were very large. And they were much less stable than those of Italy, for example. They were continually being divided between the children of the princes. In the interior of the country the administration was rudimentary. If there were assemblies of the Estates, the bourgeoisie was nowhere powerful enough to counterbalance the nobility, which had the say in everything and enforced its will upon the country. A large proportion of the nobles were not the descendants of freemen. They were still numerous in the 14th century. The prince surrounded himself with them, and recruited from their ranks his confidential agents and advisers. Brute force enjoyed a predominance quite unknown elsewhere. The peasants, who from the middle of the 14th century were entirely at the mercy of the nobles, were beginning to relapse into serfdom,[1] for emigration was no longer possible, and there was not, as elsewhere, a king who might intervene for them. One of the most striking features of German life was this regression of the people into servitude under nobles of whom many were themselves of servile origin. Here and there the peasants resisted the nobles. The origin of the Swiss Confederation may be referred to such resistance: the three original cantons, Schwiz, Uri and Unterwalden, defeated Leopold of Austria at Morgahten in 1315. This was the beginning of a federation which was joined by Lucerne (1332), Zürich (1351), and Berne (1353), and which was further consolidated by the battle

[1] In Flanders serfdom disappeared in the 13th century. In France it was largely abolished in the 14th century.

of Sempach, which was fought against Leopold III of Austria in 1386.

This centrifugal tendency of Germany cannot be explained merely by the weakness of the monarchy. We must allow also for the fact that the economic life of the country, down to the middle of the 15th century, was very poorly developed. There was no unity about it. On the sea-coast the Hansa ports exported the corn of Northern Germany to Flanders, and brought back the products of the Orient. The Rhine gravitated towards the Low Countries, but its importance was diminishing now that there was direct navigation between Flanders and Italy. In the South the cities maintained commercial relations with Venice, for the Danube was not a trade route below Vienna. Moreover, there was hardly any export industry apart from the metals of Bohemia and the Tyrol.

In the centre of the country there were no important cities. On the whole, the greater part of the country was still rural. It had need of the outer world, but the outer world had no need of it. The Low Countries looked westward.

As for the seaport cities of the North, they played hardly any part in the life of the interior. Until the middle of the 14th century the Rhine and the South were the true Germany. But with the advent of Rudolph of Habsburg there was for a moment—as there had been, sporadically, before his time—a tendency toward an eastward orientation. This was very obvious in the case of Luxemburg. The Slav countries lent themselves to political absorption. There was no longer any colonization in these countries, but there was a dynastic orientation toward the East, which, at the same time, produced in the Slav peoples a corresponding orientation towards Germany.

## 2. *The Slav States and Hungary*

At the moment when the Slav peoples made their appearance in history they occupied the region extending from the Upper Vistula and the Carpathians to the Dnieper. In the course of the 5th century, following upon the general movement of the Germans, their western neighbours, in the direction of the Roman Empire, they advanced in their turn and occupied the territories which the Germans had vacated. The Poles installed themselves in the basin of the Vistula; the Wends spread from the Elbe to the Baltic Sea; while the Czechs took possession of Bohemia and Moravia. Others, moving toward the south-west, colonized the valley of the Danube and penetrated far into Thrace, at the expense of the Greek Empire: these were the Bulgars, the Serbs, the Croats, and the Slovenes. As for those Slavs who had remained in the East, and who, thanks to their position on the Dnieper, lay across the trade route connecting Byzantium with the regions of the North, in the 9th century, as we have already seen, they fell under the domination of the Scandinavian Vikings—half merchants, half warriors—from whom they acquired their name of Russians. Kiev, where the eldest son of Rurik's dynasty established himself under the name of the Great Prince, became the centre of a political group of secondary principalities which extended from Novgorod to the shores of the Black Sea.

The economic organization of this country presented a character which was not to be found elsewhere in the territory of any other Barbarian people. It was essentially commercial. The Vikings, who were gathered round their princes in the fortified enclosures (*Gorod*) established along the Dnieper and its affluents, subjected the Slav population to the payment of tribute, consisting mainly of honey, wax and furs, which the hunters and bee-keepers of this forest region were able to furnish in abundance. In the spring of each year their boats assembled at Kiev and carried this merchandise to Constantinople, together with a considerable number of slaves, bringing back in return wine, textiles, and manufactured objects. When at the beginning of the 11th century the Scandinavians became Slavized, these commercial practices, together with the political exploitation of the rural population, did not disappear, but the aristocracy of *boyars*, at once military, mercantile and urban, dominated the rest of the nation. Such was the salient character of the Russian State at this period.

Being in constant touch with Byzantium, the Russians were bound before long to become Christianized. As early as the first half of the 10th century Christianity was beginning to make its way, following the course of trade, among the inhabitants of Kiev. The Princess Olga professed it openly about 955–957. However, Paganism maintained itself as the dominant religion as late as the reign of her grandson Vladimir, who still encouraged the sacrifice of human beings, and to whom ecclesiastical tradition attributed, no doubt a little generously, as many as eight hundred concubines, whom it compared with those of Solomon. But after his marriage with a Greek princess the inevitable conversion took place (983), and the conversion of the prince was immediately followed by that of the *boyars*. As for the people, they were evangelized by methods whose simplicity recalls those which Charlemagne employed in converting the Saxons. The inhabitants of Kiev were baptized *en masse* in the waters of the Dnieper. The idols were overthrown, and the prince commanded that churches should be built on the sites of the pagan temples. In order to furnish recruits for the clergy, he seized the children of the leading families and entrusted their education to the Greek and Bulgar priests who had been sent from Byzantium to guide the first steps of the young Russian Church.

If external causes had not supervened to hinder it, the historical development of Russia would have brought about a progressive orientation toward Constantinople. For Russia this great city was not merely, as was Rome for the Christians of the West, the religious centre *par excellence*: it was also the great commercial market, and for both these reasons its influence was bound, in the long run, to make itself felt in all the domains of social life. We know that even in our days the ecclesiastical architecture of Russia retains the Byzantine forms which were then imposed upon it, and the *Ruskaja Pravda*, the most ancient compilation of Russian laws, is completely imbued with the spirit of Byzantine law.

But the situation of Russia exposed her to the repercussions of all the tumultuous movements of those Asiatic peoples whose territory extended, across the Great Plain, toward the mountains and the inland seas of the true Europe. The steppes on the shores of the Black Sea and in the basin of the Don and the Volga were the domain of nomadic hordes of Turki or Mongol origin, against whom the Russian principalities were perpetually forced to fight.

The victory of the Great Prince Jaroslav over the most powerful of these peoples, the Petchenegs, in 1036, dispelled the danger for some time. It recurred in a more dreadful form with the advent of the Kumans. In 1096 their Khan advanced to the very walls of Kiev; and from that time onwards the attacks of these ferocious Barbarians never ceased. By the middle of the 12th century it was becoming impossible to resist them. The region of Kiev, hitherto so flourishing, was becoming impoverished and depopulated. When the Barbarians occupied the mouths of the Dnieper there was an end of the trade with Constantinople. Gradually the country was deserted, some of the inhabitants migrating to Galicia and Volhynia, and others, more numerous, moving off in a north-easterly direction toward the upper reaches of the Volga (Sousdal).

This migration from south to north determined the future of the Russian people. Not only did it impose upon it a new manner of life, but it even modified its national character. The Slav colonists of Sousdalia mingled with the Finns, who had hitherto been the sole inhabitants of its immense forests, and from this mingling of the peoples modern Russia (Great Russia) emerged. At the same time a purely agricultural life replaced the old commercial activity. Henceforth deprived of all communication with the sea, the Russians were restricted for long centuries to a purely rural economy, which had no outlets. The neighbourhood of Constantinople had caused them to practise commerce at a time when it was still unknown in Western Europe, and the fatality of circumstance made them abandon it just when it was beginning to develop in the West. Kiev had been a great international emporium, but the towns of central Russia—like the castles of the West in the early Middle Ages—were merely the residences of the princes, their *boyars*, and the servants necessary for their maintenance. Moscow, founded in 1147, acquired more importance than its neighbours only through purely political causes, and in so far as its prince was more powerful than the other princes. Novgorod alone, which was assiduously frequented, from the beginning of the 13th century, by the merchants of the Hansa, was a centre of commercial importance, and this importance it owed entirely to the foreigner. It was a German factory in Russia rather than a Russian economic centre.

Novgorod was the only point from which the civilization of the West might have been diffused throughout Russia. Unfortunately, the rude and rapacious merchants of the Hansa were incapable of revealing any but the least attractive features of that civilization; and their contact with the inhabitants had little result beyond provoking a mutual hatred and contempt. Religious differences still further envenomed the relations whose beginnings were so unfortunate. The Greek Orthodoxy which the Russians brought from the banks of the Dnieper kept them isolated from Europe, while the civilizing influence of Byzantium, since they were now too removed from the metropolis, could no longer remedy the disastrous result of this isolation.

As a crowning misfortune, this isolation was rendered still more complete by the great Mongolian invasion of the 13th century. In 1223 Juji, the son of Jenghiz Khan, conquered the whole region occupied by the Kumans between the Don and the Volga. His son Batu, pushing further west, captured Moscow in 1234 and Kiev in 1240, and extended his power over the whole of Russia, now terrorized and half depopulated. However, the Mongols did not establish themselves beyond the Don. Their Khan contented himself with imposing his overlordship upon the Russian princes and subjecting them to tribute. Nevertheless, as long as the Empire of the "Golden Horde" retained its power, they were nothing more than the humble vassals of an Asiatic despot, and even though this did not make them become Asiatic, it was at least enough to prevent them from becoming Europeanized. The decadence of the Golden Horde after the death of Usbek (1313–1341) left them a liberty of action of which the princes of Moscow took advantage by annexing the neighbouring principalities. With Ivan III (1462–1505) this work of unification was completed. Ivan, allied with the Khan of the Crimea, made an end of what was still left of the Mongol domination. With his reign a new era of Russian history began.

As in the case of the Russians, it was the invasion of an Asiatic people, the Hungarians, which determined the destiny of the Slavs of the South and West. Before the arrival of these barbarians the Slav peoples were in immediate touch with one another, from Thrace to the shores of the Baltic Sea. If this state of things had continued it is evident that the Greek Church, which had converted the Bulgars and the Serbs as early as the 9th century, would have continued its apostolate, favoured by the community of manners and of language, amongst their brothers of Bohemia and Poland, and would have absorbed them as it absorbed the Russians in the 10th century. But the sudden and unexpected arrival of the Hungarians altered the course of history. Making their way into the valley of the Danube, they interposed themselves between the Slav peoples, dividing them into two groups, which henceforth had nothing in common. Cut off from Byzantium, and at the same time separated from the Serbs and the Bulgars, the Czechs and the Poles, like the Hungarians themselves, naturally went over to the Roman Church.

Their conversion was wholly agreeable to the religious zeal and the political interests of the German sovereign. Otto I did not fail to attach the young Slav bishoprics to the Germanic metropolis of Mayence, while he subjected the princes of Bohemia and Poland to a rather vague protectorate. His successors—embarrassed by their expeditions to Italy, and then engrossed in the War of Investitures—far from continuing his efforts, could not even safeguard their results. Prague in Bohemia, and Gnesen in Poland, became independent archbishoprics, while the dioceses established among the Wends on the right bank of the Elbe disappeared, leaving paganism a free field.

We have seen further back how the great economic revolution of the 12th century had the unexpected consequence of provoking a decline of the Slav nationality to the advantage of the Germans. The surplus rural population of Germany overflowed into the country on the right bank of the Elbe, where the Saxon knights, as they advanced, massacred the pagan natives. Under the pretext of evangelization the Teutonic Order continued this policy of massacre and repopulation into the 13th century. Prussia was Germanized by them, as Mecklenburg and the Mark of Brandenburg had been. The shores of the Baltic, which had hitherto been Slav, now became German. The Poles, who were endeavouring to reach to the Baltic across Pomerania, were cut off from the sea.

Hitherto the political constitution of Bohemia and Poland had exhibited the natural development of those tribal institutions which we find in almost identical forms among all agricultural peoples when they adopt a sedentary life. This is readily explained by the absence of that direct contact with the Roman civilization which had lifted the Germans out of barbarism. The progress of a society is all the more rapid in proportion as it is more completely subjected to external influences. In consequence of the remoteness of the Western Slavs it was long before they emerged from the narrowness and poverty of their isolated existence. Despite their local importance, we need not here dwell on manners and institutions which did not exert any influence over Europe. Princes of whom each had his entourage of noble retainers, on whom they depended more than the nobles depended on them, until one of these princes, gradually raising himself above his rivals, seized their lands and rallied their followers to himself—this, in a few words, is the essential character of the first few centuries of history both in Bohemia and in Poland. The introduction of Christianity, which was not brought into these countries by foreign conquest, did not in any way change their political condition. The religious character which it gave to the princely power did not alter the fact that this power had to reckon with a landed aristocracy from which it could not possibly liberate itself, because, if united, this was definitely the stronger. But there was nothing in these Slav States to correspond with the feudality of Western Europe. And this may be readily understood. The great vassals of the West were merely the descendants of royal officers who had profited by the king's inability to administer the State and had usurped the powers which they ought to have exercised in his name. But neither in Bohemia nor in Poland do we find, from the very beginning, any trace of that administrative character which the Roman tradition had impressed upon the West. There the prince was merely a military leader, surrounded by noble companions who assisted him in time of peace, and represented him, as *starosts* or châtelaines, in various parts of the country. They were not his servants, but his natural auxiliaries. The government was exercised by them and by the prince in common, and none of them could appropriate to himself the power which was temporarily delegated to him in his circumscription. The very insignificance of the political attributions of the prince, and the permanent control exercised over these attributions by the aristocracy, rendered impossible the formation in the Slav States of such territorial principalities as had been constituted, ever since the 10th century, in all parts of France and Germany. The power of the great landed nobility, both in Bohemia and in Poland, was exercised from the beginning by the participation of each of its members in the government of the whole country. This did not lead to the subdivision of the country, for its political and national unity were preserved by the very weakness of a central authority which was dependent on the aristocracy. It should be added that these peoples, being cut off from the sea, had no bourgeoisie until a very late stage in their history.

The immediate neighbourhood of Germany, and the rights which Germany claimed over Bohemia, naturally involved the latter country in her quarrels. The Bohemian princes took advantage of the disorders which followed the death of Frederick Barbarossa to increase their independence. Being at war with Otto IV, Philip of Swabia, in order to secure the support of Duke Ottocar I, conferred upon him, in 1198, the title of king. The intervention of the Kings of Bohemia in German affairs was henceforth of sufficient importance to enable these Slavs to enter the College of Electors. It might well have seemed, after the accession of Wenceslas II (1230–1253), that the kingdom was destined to become Germanized. Wenceslas did everything in his power to encourage German immigration into the country, which was still wholly agricultural. Above all, he encouraged the immigration of artisans and traders, who established themselves *en masse*, during the whole of the 13th century, in the "burgs" of Bohemia, where they retained their own law and their own language. For a long while the bourgeoisie was, in the literal sense of the word, a foreign population in the midst of the Czechs. But this fact made it only the more conscious of its dependence on the monarchy, and its loyalty greatly augmented the resources, the prestige, and the strength of the dynasty. The progress of this dynasty was made strikingly apparent under Ottocar II (1235–1238). The nobles of the Duchy of Austria, whose duke had fallen in battle against the Hungarians, appealed to him for aid, and acknowledged him as their seigneur. He added the Duchy of Styria to Austria, expelling the Hungarians, and forcing the Duke of Carinthia to acknowledge him as his heir. From the Riesengebirge his power henceforth extended to the shores of the Adratic. It seemed as though the crown of Bohemia was on the point of annexing the whole of Danubian Germany. Encouraged by success, Ottocar, on the death of Richard of Cornwall, offered himself as a candidate for the title of King of the Romans. The title was conferred upon Rudolph of Habsburg, and henceforth war between the two rivals was inevitable. If Rudolph had been forced to rely on his own resources he could not have coped with his adversary. But now the Hungarians, for the first time, played the part which they were so often to play afterwards, assisting the Germans against the Czechs. Ottocar was defeated and killed in 1278, at the battle of Marchfeld. The Danubian duchies became the property of the Habsburgs, who henceforth never ceased to covet Bohemia. Ottocar's successors no longer attempted to expand in the direction of Germany; but they cast their eyes on Hungary and Poland. Wenceslas II (1278–1305) contrived to procure the crown of Hungary, for a time, for his son Ladislas, and in 1300 he obtained the crown of Poland for himself. With his son Wenceslas III, assassinated in 1306, the ancient Slav dynasty of the Przemislides became extinct. The throne being vacant, the King of the Romans. Albert of Austria, hastened to secure it for his son Rudolph. But this first attempt to absorb the country for the benefit of the House of Habsburg was unsuccessful. Rudolph lived only a few months, and the Bohemian aristocracy elected as their king the husband of the eldest daughter of Wenceslas III, Duke Henry of Carinthia. This second German king reigned hardly longer than his predecessor. Profiting by the discontent which he had excited, Elizabeth, the younger daughter of Wenceslas IV, proposed to take as her husband John the Blind, the son of Henry of Luxemburg, who had succeeded Albert of Austria as King of the Romans. The marriage was concluded in 1310. It gave Bohemia a Walloon dynasty, only a few years after a French dynasty had established itself in Hungary by the accession of Robert of Anjou.

Hitherto the German influence in Bohemia had continually increased. Its progress was checked by the advent of the House of Luxemburg. Although John the Blind passed the greater part of his reign travelling about Europe, occupied with political intrigues or military enterprises, which ended in his meeting his death, at the age of fifty, on the field of Crecy, he did not forget to introduce into his kingdom a very large number of men from the Low Countries, who, as advisers or functionaries, taught the Bohemians the improved methods of the French administration. His son Charles IV, who from 1333 was entrusted with the government of the country, continued and perfected the improvements introduced by his father. A Frenchman by education and in his tastes, and speaking the French language, this King of Bohemia, who was at the same time King of the Romans and Emperor, was nevertheless regarded by his Czech subjects as a national prince. It was probably enough that he should have shaken off the German influence without systematically opposing it. Bohemia being the centre of his power, he applied himself to making it capable of independent development. In 1348 he founded in Prague the first university of Central Europe, modelled upon that of Paris, and he delighted in adorning the city with monuments that gave it the aspect of a capital, so that its like did not exist in the whole Empire. His beneficent and intelligent administration, by encouraging the economic development of the country, resulted in the formation of a native bourgeoisie side by side with the German bourgeoisie. All this explains the popularity of his government, and the fact that his reign saw the awakening of a national sentiment which was soon to provoke a reaction against the Germanic elements which had been introduced into Bohemia by the colonization of the 13th century. This reaction found violent expression under his son Wenceslas (1378–1419), on the occasion of the Hussite explosion. John Huss has remained for the Czechs what Luther is to the Germans, a national hero. In a certain sense he is even more truly a national hero than Luther, for not all the Germans followed Luther, whereas all the Czechs followed Huss. The religious conflict which he inaugurated in Bohemia was complicated by a conflict of nationalities. The Germans represented Catholicism, and the Czechs the new heresy, and in proportion as this heresy had spread among them they persecuted the foreigners, as much because they regarded them as intruders as because they considered them infidels. The war which they had to fight in order to defend their religion diffused their hatred of Germany throughout the country. For it was from Germany that those armies of knights came which John Ziska, and then Procopius, so often cut to pieces. One can hardly avoid comparing the mentality of the Hussites with that of the French revolutionists at the end of the 18th century. Both peoples were fighting against the foreigner in defence of their ideal, and in each case the national sentiment was sublimated by the conviction that supported and inspired it.

The comparison is all the more inevitable inasmuch as Hussitism soon assumed a revolutionary form. The Taborites, as we have seen, aspired to the complete renovation, not only of the Church, but of society. Abandoned by the Utraquists, and then conquered by them, they were obliged to surrender. The "Compactat" (1434) negotiated with the Council of Basle was a somewhat ambiguous compromise, which, while it reconciled Bohemia with the Church, left her in the enjoyment of a religious autonomy which no one thought it prudent to define. However, a good proportion of the nobility, alarmed by the violence of the Taborites, had returned to Catholicism. The nobles took advantage of the circumstances to increase their domains by the addition of the confiscated ecclesiastical estates, and to impose serfdom on the rural masses.

Sigismond, the brother of Wenceslas, and his successor, was at last able to take possession of his kingdom. He was childless, and on his death in 1437 his son-in-law Albert of Austria succeeded him, both in Bohemia and in Hungary. However, he was acknowledged only by the Catholics and the Utraquists. What was left of the Taborites gave the crown to Casimir of Poland. The moment for the final union of Bohemia with the domains of the Habsburgs had not yet arrived. Albert was killed in 1439 while campaigning against the Turks, and a Czech noble, George Podiebrad, who at first governed the country in the name of Ladislas, the posthumous son of the king, received the crown on the death of Ladislas in 1457. Bohemia thus became a national and independent kingdom. But this was to be only a brief interlude in its tragic history. About the same time, while German influence was declining in Bohemia, it was doing the same in Poland, but in consequence of events of a totally different character. While Bohemia was clearly outlined by the mountains that enclosed her, Poland, stretching from the Oder to the Vistula across the vast plain by which Russia is prolonged into the north of Europe, was exposed on every side except on the south, where she was protected by the Carpathians, to the aggression of her neighbours. No other people had such fluctuating frontiers. Like a garment they followed the movements of the nation; they expanded or contracted according as the nation was strong or weak, sometimes extending themselves until they enclosed all sorts of heterogeneous nationalities, sometimes shrinking until they were no longer wide enough to enclose the whole nation.

Boleslas Chrobry (the Valiant), who had taken the title of king in the 10th century, extended his influence to the Russian principalities of the Dnieper, leaving his successors only an artificial power, for it was based upon nothing but the energy of the man who had created it. Of these successors, none was able to retain it. The royal title itself disappeared at the end of the 11th century, and the dukes divided the Polish territories among themselves, amidst intestine conflicts which have no interest for the general historian, except that they explain why the Teutonic Order, in the 13th century, was able to take possession of Prussia and cut off Poland from the Baltic Sea, without encountering any resistance. However, the settlement of the Teutonic Knights was only an episode in the mighty movement of German expansion, which, at this same period, was spreading through Poland as it had spread through Bohemia. These immigrants were all the more warmly welcomed inasmuch as the country had just been ravaged by the Mongol invasion, which, overflowing from Russia, had reached Silesia, where it made a protracted halt, and began to flow backwards on receiving the news of the death of the great Khan Ogotai (1241). The Germans did not settle in great numbers except in Silesia, which from that time forward began to show signs of Germanization. Those who penetrated into the interior introduced urban life there and constituted a bourgeoisie, which, protected by privileges and provided with Magdeburg law, retained its nationality for centuries. It found itself in juxtaposition with the Jews, whom the persecution of the era of the Crusades had swept out of Germany and Hungary into Poland in the 11th and 12th centuries,

The introduction of the Bohemian dynasty of Poland under Wenceslas II and Wenceslas III (1300–1305) was followed by the restoration of the royal title. On the death of Wenceslas III the great nobles called Duke Wladislas I to the throne. His son Casimir (the Great) was to Poland much what his contemporary, Charles IV (1333–1370), was to Bohemia, and he was incontestably inspired by Charles's policy. He wished to make of Cracow what Charles had made of Prague, and following the latter's example he established a university there (1364). He endeavoured to organize a royal administration by the institution of a central court of justice, a treasurer and a chancellor, and to model his government on the Western type adopted by Bohemia. But a strong monarchy can impose itself upon a country only by trusting to the services which it renders to the people, thereby interesting the latter in its maintenance. In the 12th century the kings of France had counterbalanced the power of their great vassals by allying themselves with the bourgeoisie, but the scattered German bourgeoisies of Poland could not serve as auxiliaries of the Crown. In this purely agricultural country the nobles, in the middle of the 14th century, by reason of their power and their ascendancy, were as incompatible with monarchical government as those of the Frankish Empire had been three centuries earlier. They were not so very different from the

Frankish nobles. The predominant characteristic of the nobility of the Occident was their social function, while that of the Polish nobility was their juridical character. In consequence of a much simpler historical evolution, the nobles were directly related to the freemen of the Barbaric epoch; they retained the pride of the freemen, and claimed for themselves that they alone constituted the nation. Apart from the nobles, there were only the servile peasants whom they exploited and despised. Above them there was only the king, whose authority they acknowledged on the condition of his reigning only for them and with them. The spirit which inspired the nobility, and which never ceased to inspire it, was a spirit of liberty, but a liberty of caste which was to give the Polish State, more and more definitely, until its final collapse, the paradoxical character of an aristocratic democracy.

Thus the task of which Casimir had dreamed was incapable of execution. His attempts to introduce a monarchical centralization were bound, whatever his intention, to diminish the nobility. It was so perfectly aware of this fact that it gave him the nickname of "King of the Peasants," while the wretched agrarian plebs which it dominated even to our own day has piously cherished, through the centuries, the memory of this prince, who enabled it for a moment to hope that its miseries would be ended.

With Casimir, in 1370, the dynasty of the Piastes became extinct. His successor, King Louis of Hungary, hastened to come to terms with the nobles. The concessions which he granted them constituted the first of those *Pacta Conventa* which from that time forward they so often imposed upon the Crown, and by which they gained increasing control of the destinies of the nation. However, the first use they made of these prerogatives resulted in an extraordinary increase of the Polish power.

Casimir had conquered Galicia and Volhynia, and by these conquests had extended the frontiers of the kingdom to Lithuanian territory. Since the beginning of the 14th century the Lithuanians of the Baltic shore, driven back from the sea by the Teutonic Order, had turned southwards; they had extended their power over the principalities of Western Russia, and had reached the shores of the

Black Sea. They had remained pagans, but on being brought into contact with their Orthodox subjects they began to adopt their religion, and their future adhesion to the Greek Church appeared to be certain. Now, on the death of Louis of Hungary (1382), the Polish nobility, in order to escape the rule of his brother Sigismond, offered Prince Jagellon of Lithuania the hand of the king's younger daughter, Elisabeth, on condition that he accepted baptism and professed the Catholic Faith. The bargain was accepted. Jagellon became King of Poland under the name of Wladislas II, and at the same time his people adopted the religion which he had just accepted. With this the Lithuanian principality was united with the kingdom, although it retained a formal independence (1386).[1]

Since their establishment in Prussia the Teutonic Knights, on the pretext that the Lithuanians were pagans, had waged against them a war of extermination. It was now evident, however, that these Barbarians were not obstinately attached to their cult. But it was more profitable and, extraordinary though the use of such a word may seem, more enjoyable to hunt them, for the Order organized veritable man-hunts in its persecution of this people. The fame of these hunts had spread throughout the Empire, and the princes and seigneurs of the West assembled, as people now assemble at the Olympic Games, to take part in these expeditions, which were organized every winter, when the ice had rendered the marshes of the country practicable. Such a degradation of the religious spirit, and such brutality of manners, shows how completely the Order, in the course of time, had lost the spirit of Christian proselytism and heroic mysticism of an earlier day. The military monasticism created to fight Islam could preserve its traditions only by remaining faithful to its original mission, as did the Knights of St. John of Rhodes, or the Knights of Alcantara or Calatrava in Spain. The Teutonic Knights, on the contrary, like the Templars, having turned away from the East, were now distinguished only by the energy which they applied to the pursuit of purely temporal objects. Their rule, rebelling, so to speak, against the sentiments which had originally inspired it, now employed the strength which it gave

[1] The perpetual union of Poland and Lithuania was proclaimed in 1499.

them only in the search of wealth and power. Just as the Templars, since the middle of the 13th century, had become a formidable financial power, so the Teutonic Knights, having destroyed the pagans of Prussia, now exploited the country as "consummate economists." One may say, indeed, that they were the first "Agrarians" of Prussia. Their vast domains, administered by *Gros-schäffer*, provided grain for a considerable export trade, for which Bruges was the market. The money derived from this trade was invested to advantage or lent at interest. But the Order had become merely an oligarchy of knights; and their pride and egoism finally exasperated the population of which they considered themselves the masters. The cities, from the end of the 14th century, and the rural nobility, endured their yoke with impatience.

The new King of Poland did not fail to profit by these circumstances. As a Lithuanian he was passionately hostile to the Germans. His accession rendered a war with the Teutonic Knights inevitable. It broke out in 1409. In the following year the Polish army inflicted on the Order a terrible defeat at Tannenberg (July 15th, 1410). For the Knights this was the beginning of the débâcle. The cities and the nobles were not slow to rise against them. In 1454 they placed themselves under the Polish suzerainty. At last, in 1466, the Grand Master resigned himself to surrendering East Prussia, with Danzig, Thorn, Marienbourg and Elbing, to Casimir III. The rest of Prussia retained its political autonomy, but henceforth made part of the Polish State. No one in Germany felt any concern for this decline of Germanic influence. The population of the country, with the exception of the sea-board cities, became rapidly Polonized, and the Slav nationality resumed possession of the regions from which it had been expelled in the 13th century. Poland henceforth possessed a wide frontier in the shape of the Baltic coast. In the South it extended to the Black Sea. It might have had a brilliant future but for the fact that at this same period the Turkish advance had put an end to the trade between the Christian countries and Asia. Moreover, no one was concerned with the economic development of the country. For the nobles the accession of Jagellon had been merely an opportunity for finally consolidating their position. The new king had promised them, amongst other privileges, immunity from taxation. Under the sceptre of its kings the Polish State was definitely becoming an aristocratic republic.

The Slavs of the South—the Croats, Slovenes, Serbs and Bulgars —presented a very different spectacle from that of the Poles and Bohemians. In consequence of their weakness, the Croats and the Slovenes soon fell under the domination of Hungary, who took care to deny them the least measure of political autonomy. The Serbs and the Bulgars, on the other hand, established to the south of the Danube on the territory of the Greek Empire, and faithful to the Greek Church, profited by the weakness of the Empire, after the reign of Justinian, to penetrate deeply into Macedonia, and even into Greece. While in the long run they became Hellenized, the Slavs of Macedonia preserved their language and their customs, as did the Germans who had occupied the north of the Empire. In the 10th century, under the Emperor Romanus Lacapenus (920–944), the Bulgars threatened Constantinople, which was forced to pay them tribute. Nicephorus Phokas (963–969), followed by John Tzimiskes and Basil II Bulgaroktonos (976–1075), reduced them to a state of dependency on the Empire. But they revolted on the eve of the Fourth Crusade, and from this revolt emerged the new Bulgar Empire, that of the Asen dynasty. Baldwin made war upon them, and perished.

As for the Serbs, under Stephen Nemanja they shook off the Byzantine domination. His son Stephen I, in 1221, assumed the title of king. His successors increased their territory to the detriment of the Empire and the Bulgars, and Stephen III Ourosch destroyed the Bulgarian power. His son Stephen IV Duschan conquered the whole of Macedonia and Albania, and even advanced to the north of the Save. He took the title of Tsar, and had himself crowned "Emperor of the Serbs and Romans" (1346). The Empire, of course, since the Latin conquest, could not continue to fight, and sought only to preserve the coasts, allowing a Serb empire to establish itself on its frontier; and this empire would probably have installed itself on the Bosphorus if the arrival of the Turks had not caused a general upheaval in the Balkans.

Driven like a wedge into the Slav mass, the Hungarians or Magyars, after long terrorizing Germany, and even Northern Italy and Eastern France by their terrible raids of horsemen, had at last settled down, owing to the victories of Henry I and Otto, in the plain of the Danube. The Church of their conquerors eventually became their own. Under Sylvester II they went over to Rome, and the erection of the archbishopric of Gran gave them a religious metropolis.

If one wished to invoke an example in order to prove the unimportance of race in historical development, such an example is certainly provided by the Hungarians.[1] By their origin, and by virtue of their language, these Finns, who were related to the Turks and the Mongols, were completely alien to the ethnographical group of the Indo-European peoples. However, they had hardly taken their place in the midst of these peoples and adopted Christianity, when, despite the nature of the blood that flows in their veins, their cephalic index, and the linguistic characteristics of their idiom, their social life became so similar to that of their neighbours that it would be quite impossible, if one did not know the facts beforehand, to recognize them as intruders. The fact is that the physical individuality of a people is entirely subordinated to its moral existence. Still Barbarians, and without any civilization of their own, the Hungarians could have preserved their Finnish peculiarities only by retaining their religion. Having become Christians, they were bound to enter the European community, and so prove that they too possessed that pretended "faculty of assimilation" which a certain school of ethnologists claims as peculiar to the "Germanic race," though it is really a characteristic of all Barbarians. Having entered the plain of the Danube as conquerors, they subdued the Slav population of the country and reduced it to servitude. There is nothing in this procedure that can be attributed to their race. The Lombards had done exactly the same thing, in the 7th century, in Cisalpine Gaul. But being less

[1] It is amusing to note that at the beginning of 1917 the Finnish Republic sent a deputation to Hungary to notify its birth to the Hungarian people, related to the people of Finland by virtue of their Finnish origin.

civilized than the people they had conquered, the Lombards were rapidly Latinized by them, while the Hungarians, in contact with a subject people no more advanced than themselves, had no difficulty in preserving their nationality and remaining the dominant people. As in all agricultural nations, a nobility of magnates was quickly created. But the feudal system did not make its way into Hungary, for the same reasons that prevented its naturalization in Bohemia and Poland. When Stephen I (997–1038) had succeeded in getting rid of the princes who had hitherto shared the country between them, and had assumed, with the crown which Pope Sylvester sent him, the title of king, these magnates were necessarily associated with the king in the exercise of the monarchical power. In 1222 they exacted from King Andreas II a Golden Bull, which consecrated their political status and acknowledged their right to assemble each year at Stuhlweissenburg, together with the bishops, and also the right of rebellion in case their privileges were violated. This Golden Bull was almost contemporaneous with the Magna Charta of England. The contrast between the two texts is extremely instructive. In England the clergy and the burgesses stood behind the nobles, and the law which the Crown was compelled to accept was a truly national law. In Hungary, on the contrary, a single caste made a covenant in respect of its own interests, and in so far as it succeeded in safeguarding these interests the rest of the people was sacrificed to them.

Things would doubtless have been otherwise if Hungary had possessed a bourgeoisie. But like those other late-comers, Bohemia and Poland, Hungary was a backward country, her economy being purely agricultural. Just as in Bohemia and Poland, so the only bourgeois in Hungary, from the 12th century onwards, were the German immigrants, who remained aliens in the heart of the Hungarian nation, and were further divided from the nation by the privileges which the kings conferred upon them. It is possible that the conquest of Dalmatia, which was effected at the beginning of the 12th century, and which gave Hungary an outlet on the Adriatic, might in the long run, thanks to Spalato and Zara, have given rise to commercial activities in the interior which would have resulted in the creation of an urban population. However, this could have happened only if Hungary had lived in peace; but the fact that the country was in contact with so many peoples upon its various frontiers—Bohemia, Poland, Germany, the Southern Slavs, and the Byzantine Empire, to say nothing of Venice, jealous of retaining her control of the Adriatic—meant that it was always at war, now on one frontier, now on another. The eastern frontier of Hungary gave upon the indeterminate domain of Asiatic Barbarism, and the Hungarians had either to repulse, or submit to, the Petcheneg hordes, and later the Kumans, who came down from Southern Russia. They had, moreover, to defend themselves against a people which consisted of Slavs and Finns, intermingled with the descendants of the ancient Roman colonists of Dacia, whose Roman dialect they finally adopted, and who were one day to be known as the Roumanians. This much-tried people was in danger of being destroyed by the Mongol invasion. Nowhere, unless in Russia, were the ravages of the Mongols so terrible as in the plain of the Danube. When they had at last retired the country had almost to be colonized afresh. King Bela IV (1235–1270) did his best in this direction, inviting the Italians to settle in the country and sending for more Germans, to augment the number of those who had already settled in Transylvania, where they have remained to this day. Buda was founded in 1245. The Italians introduced the culture of the vine. The Roumanians made their way into all parts of the Hungarian plain as agricultural labourers. Thirty years later Hungary had become strong enough to support Rudolph of Habsburg against Ottocar of Bohemia, and to curb, on behalf of Germany, the menace of Czech expansion. It was soon evident to Hungary that the Habsburgs, now her neighbours, had included her in their dynastic projects. When Ladislas IV died without children Rudolph of Habsburg, disposing of the country as a fief of the Empire, gave it to his son Albert. But since Pope Sylvester II had sent the crown to Stephen the Popes regarded Hungary as a fief of the Holy See, and this fief was immediately claimed by Nicholas IV on behalf of Charles Martel, the son of Charles II of Naples, and the brother-in-law of Ladislas. In order to get rid of these foreigners the magnates gave the crown to Andrew III, a scion of the national dynasty; but on his death in 1301 they acknowledged the son of Charles Martel, Charles Robert, as their king (1308–1342). Thus the French dynasty of Anjou, which the Papacy had established in Naples in opposition to the Hohenstaufens, was now established in Hungary in opposition to the Habsburgs. There it held its own until 1382, contributing largely to the "Westernization" of the country. The greatest king of this dynasty was Louis (1342–1382), who occupied Moldavia, abandoned by the Mongols, subdued Croatia, and forced the Venetians to surrender the coast and the islands of the Adriatic as far as Durazzo.

His policy reveals the resource and ambition of a great king, but it was almost megalomaniac. His brother Andrew, the husband of Queen Joanna of Naples, having been assassinated, he undertook two expeditions against this kingdom. Besides this Italian policy, he also pursued a northern policy, for as we have seen, he was King of Poland, so that his influence extended from the Vistula to the Adriatic and the Black Sea.

The contemporary of Charles IV and Casimir of Poland, it is interesting to note that he pursued the same policy. He founded a university at Fünfkirchen. The polished manners of the court began to diffuse themselves among the magnates. The middle of the 14th century was an interesting period in Bohemia, Poland, and Hungary, owing to the influence, Occidental rather than specifically French, which had replaced the German influence of the 13th century.

But the position which Louis had made for himself had no lasting consequences. Since he had no son, the enormous structure which he had created was fragile in the extreme. Poland passed under the sceptre of Jagellon. An Angevin kinsman, Charles of Durazzo, was assassinated in 1387, and Sigismond of Luxemburg, who had married Maria, Louis' daughter, was finally acknowledged as king.

His was not a distinguished reign. The Turks were beginning to appear on the frontier. An Adriatic policy was henceforth impossible. The titles of King of the Romans and Emperor bestowed upon the King of Hungary were powerless to save the country. On the contrary, they involved it in the Hussite war. As we have seen, the plans of the Council were explained by the Turkish peril, but they were ineffective. On the death of Sigismond in 1437, Albert of Austria, who had married his daughter Elizabeth, inherited the crown of Hungary. He died prematurely in 1439, having had no time to assure the Habsburg rule over Hungary. And now, for a long while to come, the history of the country was to be substantially the history of the Turkish peril.

The total impression produced by the history of the Slavs and the Hungarians up to the middle of the 15th century may be summed up by saying that although they had entered into the Christian community, they had remained almost entirely outside the European community. They had never experienced that initiation into the Romanic civilization which the Germans had received from the Carolingian Empire. They had never lived, like the Germans, under that theocratic régime whose intimate alliance of the spiritual with the temporal power enabled it to propagate all that the Church had preserved of the Roman administration, law, learning and literature. The Empire of Otto, prematurely and too exclusively oriented toward Italy, had abandoned the attempt to subject the Hungarians to its influence, and the process of Westernization was effected only through the medium of their bishops and monks. But since the latter had to rely exclusively on their own resources, had no political power, and were far removed from the centres of religious life, their influence was inevitably quite superficial and was confined to the domain of religious worship and discipline. These peoples knew nothing of the domainal organization, nor of the feudal system; they played no part in the War of Investitures, nor in the Crusades. For them the only consequence of the great *épopée* was the advent of the Jews who sought refuge in their territories, having been driven across the Elbe by the followers of Christ. And when the economic life of the Occident was revived by the influence of commerce, and the bourgeoisie made its appearance everywhere between the Mediterranean and the North Sea, they were made aware of this great movement only by the sudden afflux of German colonization. Placed at a disadvantage by their old agricultural institutions, they yielded to the German pressure; retreating along the Elbe before the invaders, they allowed the latter to establish themselves among them, and to found cities which were like foreign islands in the midst of the national population. With the arrival of these newcomers, who looked down upon them but were a necessity for them, there began a period of superficial Germanization which continued until the middle of the 14th century. Then a reaction began to make itself felt, of which, almost simultaneously, Charles IV in Bohemia, Casimir I in Poland, and Louis I in Hungary were the instruments. The German penetration ceased, and in all three countries there was a sudden awakening of national energy. This was manifested, under very different forms, by the explosive outbreak of Hussitism in Bohemia, the conquest of Prussia by Poland, and Hungary's advance toward the Adriatic. It seemed as though the moment had come for the Western Slavs and the Hungarians to play an active part in European civilization. But the Turks were advancing across the Balkan peninsula, and the Slavs and Hungarians had to meet the thrust, turning back to the East in order to defend the civilization of the West instead of beginning to collaborate with it.

## CHAPTER IV

# SPAIN. PORTUGAL. THE TURKS

### 1. *Spain and Portugal*

The Crusades had attacked Islam at its centre. The Mohammedan world surrounded Palestine on every side, and in order to maintain its position and to counterbalance the pressure of Islam on this narrow strip of coast without being driven into the sea, the West would have had to develop a vigorous offensive, which at this distance from its base, and with the resources at its disposal, was beyond its power. Once it had lost the positions which had been captured by the enthusiasm of the First Crusade it struggled in vain to reconquer them. After the reign of Saint Louis, the Levant, ceasing to be a base of military operations, became and remained, until the discovery of the New World, the half-way house for trade between Europe and the East.

In Spain the respective situation of the Musulmans and the Christians was very different. There the two adversaries were far less unequally matched. They met face to face on a well-defined battlefield, and both adversaries, in the event of a reverse, could fall back and repair their losses before taking the field again. Under these conditions, that side would finally be victorious which was capable of the most long-continued aggression; that is, the poorest adversary would be victorious; in other words, the Spaniards. For it was not their faith alone that impelled them to make war. The fierce desire to possess the noble cities and the beautiful champaigns which, thanks to Musulman industry and agriculture, offered such an insolent contrast to their own rugged mountains, fanned their hatred of the infidel to a white heat. Their attack upon Islam was almost like an invasion of Barbarians, at all events in the beginning.

But these Barbarians were Christians, which prevented them from merging themselves in the conquered population, as the Germans had formerly merged themselves in the Latin population of the Empire. Race had nothing to do with the matter. The Turks, in the 10th and 11th centuries, became thoroughly assimilated, despite their Mongol origin, with the Semitic civilization of the Arabs of Baghdad. There is no reason to suppose that had the Spaniards been pagans, like the Turks, at the time of their first contact with Islam, they would not, like the Turks, have been converted. The material superiority of the superior civilizations was the most potent means of religious propaganda among the pagans. But when these civilizations came into contact with the adepts of an alien and exclusive faith, their very wealth and brilliance exasperated religious hostility until it became hatred, because that wealth and brilliance seemed an impiety, an offence against the true God. And then, pillage and devastation being justified in advance, the most brutal instincts could give themselves free vent without troubling men's consciences. Duty, sentiment, and interest all combined to rally the Christians of Spain to the Holy War. It was a Holy War in the full meaning of the term, for its aim was not the conversion but the massacre or expulsion of the infidels. In the Spaniards there was no trace of that tolerance which allowed the Catholic subjects of the Musulmans, the Mozarabs, to practise their religion unmolested. Their religious exclusivism was so complete that it was not softened by offers of abjuration, and they regarded the Moriscos (baptized Musulmans) with insurmountable suspicion. It was not enough to be a Christian; a man must be an "old Christian," which really meant that he must be "of old Spanish stock"; so that nationality became the proof of orthodoxy, and national feeling, becoming confounded with faith, was imbued with its uncompromising spirit and its fervour.

We have already seen that the Moors, who after the middle of the 11th century were no longer capable of resisting the victorious Christian armies, appealed for aid to the Almoravides of Morocco. The battle of Sabacca (1086) checked the advance of the Spaniards, but did not shatter it. While for the next hundred years the war was not distinguished by any more great military actions, it was waged with untiring tenacity. The exploits of national heroes provided matter for the "romances" which, about the time when the feudal *épopée* of France found expression in the *chansons de Roland*, extolled the glory of the Cid Campeador, who met his death in 1099, the year Jerusalem was captured. While Roland became a great figure in European literature, the Cid remained a local hero. The fact is that the attention of contemporaries, attracted by the more impressive spectacle of the Crusade, overlooked the Spanish war of the 12th century, just as in 1812 it overlooked the Spanish war for the Russian campaign. Nevertheless, it was in Spain that the decline of Napoleon had its beginnings, and it was Spain that furnished the Catholicism of the Middle Ages with its only lasting victories over Islam. These victories would have been more quickly won and more decisive if the Christians had combined their efforts against the common enemy. Unfortunately the Kings of Castile and Aragon, constantly at war with each other, or obliged to defend themselves against the encroachments of the nobles, made it only too easy for the enemy to recover from their blows and to avenge themselves. In 1195 the Emir Iacub Almansor won such a signal victory over Alfonso VIII of Castile at Alarcos that for a moment there seemed a danger of a general catastrophe. But the Papacy, though engrossed in the Holy War, had never lost sight of the fact that Spain constituted the right wing of Christendom in that war. Innocent III immediately intervened. He urged the faithful to take the Cross, sent money to Spain, and extended his protection to the kings of the peninsula. Pedro II of Aragon went to Rome to be crowned by the Pope, and acknowledged that his kingdom was a fief of the Holy See. For once, thanks to the exhortations of Rome, Aragon, Castile, Leon and Portugal combined their forces. In 1212 the battle of Navos de Tolosa avenged the disaster of Alarcos and shattered the Musulman resistance.

Henceforth the advance of the Christians was irresistible and definitive. Jayme II of Aragon (1213–1276) obtained a foothold in the Balearics, and in 1238 captured Valencia. Ferdinand III of Castile captured Cordova in 1236 and Seville in 1248. Meanwhile

Alfonso III of Portugal annexed the Algarves and gave the kingdom the expanse which it has retained to this day. Of all its possessions in Spain, Islam retained only the territory of Granada, and even this was subject in vassalage to Castile.

As they enlarged themselves by extending southwards at the expense of the Moors, the Spanish States, so numerous in the beginning, became more compact by a process of agglomeration. The States of Asturias, Galicia and Leon (1230) were united to Castile, and Catalonia was combined with Aragon. Navarre, now ruled by a French dynasty, and too confined within her mountains to compete with her more fortunate neighbours, was restricted to a local existence. Portugal, inevitably oriented toward the West by her long seaboard and the course of her rivers, the Douro and the Tagus, turned her back upon the peninsula, which was divided between Castile and Aragon. Of these two kingdoms Castile was much the larger, but Aragon was more favourably situated, and for this reason was brought into contact with the outer world much earlier than Castile. I am not thinking here of the considerable fiefs on the north of the Pyrenees which had long been in the possession of the Aragonese dynasty. They would only have involved the kings of Aragon in wars with the kings of France, in which they would inevitably have been the losers, and Jayme II had the good sense to cede them to St. Louis in return for the French king's renunciation of his suzerainty over Catalonia (1258). What drew Aragon toward Europe and gave it, from the 14th century, a character less narrowly Spanish than that of Castile, was its situation on the shores of the Mediterranean. Owing to this situation it was encouraged to take part in that Levantine trade which was, *par excellence*, the important trade of the Middle Ages. Barcelona was not slow to follow in the track of Venice, Pisa, and Genoa, and in the 12th century the Catalan sailors mingled with the Italians and the Provençaux in the ports of Syria and Egypt. It was this maritime activity, rather than the relationship of Pedro III (1276–1285) to Manfred, that involved Aragon in the affairs of Sicily, and in 1285 gave Spain a foothold in this kingdom, one of the sensitive points of European politics, from which she was afterwards to expand over the rest of Italy. Under Pedro's successors the Mediterranean expansion of the kingdom continued. Alfonso III (1285–1291) conquered the whole of the Balearic archipelago, which, after existing for some time as a vassal kingdom, was annexed to the Crown under Pedro IV (1336–1387). Alfonso IV (1327–1336) made war upon Genoa for the possession of Corsica and Sardinia. Under Alfonso V, in 1443, the conquest of the Kingdom of Naples was effected. Aragon was thus a Mediterranean power. It was Aragon that opened up for Spain, cut off from Europe by the Pyrenees, the only possible means of communication, the highway of the Mediterranean. Think what the reign of Charles V would have been if Sicily had not been included in his heritage!

However, not Aragon but Castile was the true Spain. It was Castile that played the greatest and the most glorious part in the war against the Moors, and Castile could lay claim to the most popular of heroes, the Cid in the 11th, and Perez de Castro in the 13th century, and the "romances" which sing their exploits are also Castilian. In Castile the nobles were more numerous and more influential than elsewhere in Spain. It was in Castile that the national character and the national language were formed. Of course, the country was not entirely cut off from the outer world. The ports on the Gulf of Gascony maintained a fairly active coasting trade with Flanders, and in 1280 the Castilian merchants obtained a Charter of Privileges from Bruges. But neither the trade nor the fleet of Castile would bear comparison with those of Barcelona. We should not therefore be surprised that the kings of Castile were not drawn, like the kings of Aragon, into the orbit of European politics. We have already seen that when a somewhat singular ambition had induced him to buy the title of King of the Romans, Alfonso X (1252–1284) was unable to derive any advantage from it. The dynastic quarrels which marked the reign of Sancho IV (1284–1295), who was attacked by the sons of Fernando de la Cerda, provoked the intervention—which was, however, unsuccessful—of the King of France; and later Pedro the Cruel (1350–1369) allied himself with the Black Prince in order to cope with his rival, Henry of Trastamara, who was supported by Du Guesclin. And here we have almost the whole story of the foreign relations of Castile until Spain, having suddenly become a great power, began to overrun the world. Until the close of the 15th century the influence of Castile was rigidly circumscribed by the frontiers of the peninsula.

The activities of Castile were not confined to making war upon the Moors. In contact with Portugal on the west and Aragon on the east, the kingdom was constantly involved in conflicts with its neighbours, for which the relationship between the royal families furnished only too many occasions, perhaps in respect of the regency of an infant prince, or the legitimacy of the heir to the throne. It was these continual quarrels between the Christian States that enabled the Kingdom of Granada to survive despite its weakness. There were even occasions when it participated in, and so prolonged, the quarrels which it found so useful.

In spite of their dynastic wars, there was a striking resemblance between Castile, Aragon and Portugal, a sort of family likeness, which is very easily explained by the similarity of their histories. Except in Catalonia, to which the preponderance of Barcelona gave a special character, which impresses the observer even to this day, the same institutions and the same social groups were to be found everywhere. The nobles, who were essentially military, long preserved a haughty and arrogant attitude in respect of the monarchy, and of this attitude the right of the grandees of Spain to remain covered in the presence of the sovereign survived, under the absolute monarchy, as a harmless but significant relic. In order to resist this nobility of *ricos hombres* and *hidalgos*, the kings, from the beginning of the 13th century, depended on the support of the bourgeoisie. In this connection their conduct was dictated by political interests, as was that of the kings of France after Louis VII. But the alliance of the cities and the Crown was far more intimate and of far longer duration in Spain than in France. Why was this? Perhaps it was on account of the greater arrogance of the nobles. What the bourgeois expected of the king was peace and security on the highways. In order to obtain these, they themselves formed leagues (*hermandades*), like the German cities, and the leagues also reinforced the judicial power of the king, for the judicial function played a very important part in the activities of these kings. Under Alfonso X the *Codigo de las siete pardidas* was compiled for Castile, and Jayme II of Aragon won fame as a legislator. King Denis of Portugal (1279–1325) was known as *el Justo*. Pedro I (1357–1367) was praised for his pitiless severity. Consequently the bourgeoisie did its utmost to support the king, as against the military nobles, in his rôle of guardian of the law and the public peace. The *hermandades* may therefore be said to have provided him with a voluntary police, which dealt with bandits and malefactors. It goes without saying that the cities, being so intimately associated with the exercise of the royal power, obtained representation in the Cortes at a very early date. From the 13th century their deputies sat beside those of the nobles and the clergy. The dynastic quarrels which troubled Spain in the 14th century afforded the Cortes an excellent opportunity of increasing their intervention in the government, and more than once they prescribed to the kings, above all in Aragon, where the cities were more influential than elsewhere, concessions not unlike those which were obtained from the princes of the Low Countries in the same period. Here, however, their influence ceased. Spain, like the other continental States, did not evolve beyond the system of political dualism, in which the prince on one hand, and the privileged orders on the other, met together and agreed upon compromises. Neither here nor elsewhere had the parliamentary system made its appearance, the collaboration of the two elements of the nation in the English manner. As elsewhere, questions of taxation played their part in the constitutional struggles of the 14th century. That essentially Castilian tax, the *alcalaba*—a tax on sales and purchases—was granted for the first time to Alfonso XI (1312–1350) by Burgos, on the occasion of an expedition against Algeciras. Subsequently it was gradually introduced throughout the country.

Dynastic quarrels and political disputes kept the Spanish kingdoms so fully occupied that during the 14th century and the greater part of the 15th they did little in the way of resuming the war against the Moors of Granada. On the other hand they developed their commerce and added to their wealth. Sheep began to cover the countryside, and in the trade with the North of Europe Spanish began to compete with English wool. The exports of wool to the Low Countries were considerably increased, and sheep-farming began to give Castile its characteristic aspect and to enrich the nobility. There was also an increasing trade with the North in iron from Bilbao, olive oil, oranges and pomegranates. Bruges was the central market for this trade; and in the first half of the 15th century the Spanish nation was almost as strongly represented in that city as the Hansa. This economic orientation toward the North must not be overlooked; indeed, we can hardly avoid regarding it as a preparation for the dynastic alliance which in 1494 was to bind the Low Countries to Castile.

But at the same time, on the Atlantic coast of Portugal another kind of expansion was beginning, and this was to change the future of the world. Opposite the Algarves lay the coast of Morocco, and religious zeal inspired the Portuguese to make war upon Islam. Henry the Navigator (1394–1460), the son of King John I, in whom curiosity was blended with the spirit of Christian propaganda, devoted his life to equipping maritime expeditions which inaugurated the great era of discovery. In 1415 he took part in his father's expedition against Ceuta and in the capture of that city. What lay beyond? What unknown world was in hiding beyond Cape Bojador, past which no ship had ever sailed? Navigation was now sufficiently advanced to venture upon the high seas. In 1420 a ship despatched by Henry discovered the Madeira Islands, and another, in 1431, the Azores. In 1434 Cape Bojador was passed. Before his death in 1460 Henry was able to receive tidings of the discovery of the Cape Verde Islands and the coast of Senegambia. The path to the southern world lay open. This Atlantic Ocean, which had hitherto seemed the end of the world, was about to become the highway leading to a new world.

Thus, in the middle of the 15th century, even before the marriage of Ferdinand and Isabella, which was to affect the permanent union of Castile and Aragon, Spain had won a position in the world whose future possibilities no one could as yet foresee, but which prepared her for the part which she was about to play. Through Barcelona and Sicily she was involved in the affairs of the Mediterranean; she was in contact with the North of Europe through the trade of the seaports of Gascony; and she had just ventured forth across the Atlantic. Her power, still divided, was not yet very considerable, but no other State, not even Venice, had undergone such expansion. And if we reflect that the Spanish people had been tempered by the wars against Islam, that it had the profoundest confidence in itself, and that it was both a military and a sea-going people, we shall have no difficulty in realizing the strength of this new factor which was about to play its part in the life of Europe.

## 2. *The Turks*

The only result of the foundation of the Latin Empire improvised in Constantinople by the Fourth Crusade was to hasten the decomposition of the Byzantine State. Venetian and Genoese factories had been established on most of the islands of the Ionian Sea, and upon the coast, while Greece was divided into feudal principalities—the Duchy of Athens, the Duchy of Achaia. The Bulgars and the Serbs had occupied Thrace and Macedonia. Hardly anything was left of the European possessions of the Empire, apart from Constantinople, Salonica, Andrinople and Philippopoli, when Michael VII Palaeologus, in 1261, re-established the Greek rule. On the other side of the Bosphorus, however, in Asia Minor, which the Latins had not yet penetrated, the Empire still possessed Western Anatolia with Broussa, Nicaea, and Nicomedia.

This Empire was obviously destined to fall asunder. Exploited by Venice and Genoa, it had lost all economic viability and was no longer capable of providing for the enormous expenditure necessitated by its defence. Trade and industry, as they declined, had made way for the preponderance of the great landowners, a preponderance not unlike that which they had enjoyed in the West after the fall of the Empire. As matters stood in the reign of Michael VIII (1261–1282) it seemed inevitable that the Empire would shortly be subjected to a triple dismemberment. In Sicily Charles of Anjou coveted Greece, and was evidently making preparations for its conquest; the Serbs, who were increasing their possessions in the north, made no secret of their ambition to capture Constantinople; and lastly, there were the Turks in Asia Minor. The catastrophe of the Sicilian Vespers, for which the intrigues of Michael VIII were to some extent responsible, put the Angevins out of the running. They were obliged to turn back from the East in order to face their Aragonese rivals. From the European standpoint this was a great misfortune. The formation in the south of Italy of a State powerful enough to subject Greece to its influence would have been the best of safeguards against the Turkish advance. For it was obvious that the Slavs of the Balkans could not hold the Turks in check unaided. Since in any case the Greek Empire was no longer capable of defending itself, the essential thing was to ensure that it should not be forcibly detached from the European and Christian communities. But the policy of a State is rarely concerned with anything beyond its immediate and actual interests. Michael VIII regarded the disaster which had befallen Charles of Anjou as a triumph for Byzantium.

From the 10th century the Turks, Barbarians of Finnish origin, had been for the Caliphate of Baghdad very much what the Germans, six hundred years earlier, had been for the Roman Empire. They had invaded it, and naturally were immediately converted to its religion. The brilliant civilization of Islam was too fragile to endure contact with these rude neophytes. The Turks derived nothing from this civilization beyond a few purely external characteristics. They remained, in its midst, essentially peasants and soldiers, but the less polished they were the more eagerly they received the new faith, and the zeal which inspired them against the infidels necessarily helped to nourish their military spirit. The great Mongol invasion of the 13th century, which so brutally devastated Hither Asia, drove them into the mountains of Armenia. But they soon descended from the mountains, under the leadership of Omman, and moved westwards into Asia Minor, which was easily wrested from the feeble grasp of the successors of Michael Palaeologus. Broussa (1326), Nicomedia, and Nicaea (1330) fell into the hands of the invader. Nothing was left of the Empire's Asiatic possessions, and its impotence still further aggravated the political intrigues amidst which it was floundering. After the death of Andronicus III (1341) the Grand Domestic Cantacuzene, taking advantage of the minority of John V, assumed the purple, and in order to hold his own against the Bulgars and Venetians whom the court had called to its assistance he negotiated with the Turks, allowing them to cross the Bosphorus. The conquest of Europe followed immediately upon the conquest of Asia. Murad I captured Andrinople in 1352 and Philoppopoli in 1363, defeated the Serbs in 1371, drove them back into Macedonia, and entered Sofia in 1381. Imprisoned within the walls of Constantinople, the Greeks left the defence of Thrace to the Slavs. In 1387 the Serbs were victorious in Bosnia, but two years later they were defeated in the bloody battle of Kossovo (June 15th, 1389), in which both their prince, Lazar, and the victorious Sultan were slain. The Slav resistance appeared to be shattered. Bajazet (1389–1403), the son of Murad, subdued Bosnia, Wallachia, Bulgaria, Macedonia, and Thessaly. The whole Balkan peninsula, as far as the Danube, was now merely an annexe of the Musulman world. The Cross was no longer seen save on the domes of Constantinople and Salonica, and in the mountains of Albania. The frontiers of Hungary, and with them those of the Latin Church, were threatened. The desperate appeals of the Palaeologi were heard at last. Boniface IX preached the Crusade. Sigismond of Luxemburg called the Hungarians and the Germans to arms. In France the Duke of Burgundy, Philip the Bold, doubtless as much to enhance the prestige of his house as in any spirit of Christian enthusiasm, sent his son Jean (the Fearless) at the head of a brilliant army of knights to fight the infidel. All these efforts were defeated at Nicopolis by the impetuosity and the unfamiliar tactics of the Turks (September 12th, 1396). It seemed as though Constantinople's hour had nearly come. It was delayed for fifty years by the unexpected incidence of a fresh Mongol invasion.

Once again, and happily for the last time, following in the trail of Attila and Jenghis Khan, a Barbarian of genius, Tamerlane, had just released a torrent of yellow hordes. His conquests had been as overwhelming as those of the terrible destroyers to whom he was a worthy successor. He had pushed westward as far as the Volga, had subdued Persia and Armenia by terrorism, and had finally conquered that cradle of so many successive civilizations, Mesopotamia, which has never since recovered from the devastation that he wreaked upon it. The Turkish Empire was menaced. Bajazet had just laid siege to Constantinople; he raised the siege in order to hasten to the defence of Asia Minor. The two Barbarians met in 1402 at Angora, and the man whom the Europeans had been powerless to check was vanquished by the Mongols (July 20th, 1402). But Tamerlane's career was as brief as his rise had been sudden. After his death (1405) the peoples bowed under the Mongol yoke raised their heads amidst the ruins of their civilization. Sulieman, the son of Bajazet (1402–1410), succeeded in reorganizing the débris of Turkey-in-Asia. This would have been the moment for the Christians to take the offensive. But the Emperor Manuel contented himself with a treaty which gave him Salonica and a few of the islands, and arranged a marriage between one of his nieces and the Sultan. The tribute demanded from the Greeks and the Serbs was abolished. The world was pleased to think that the peril was averted, as though a defeat could ever subdue a barbarian peo plefor longer than the time needed to replace the warriors who had fallen on the field of battle. There was only one possible means of stopping the Turks, and that was to absorb them into Western civilization; but since they professed Islam, this was simply unthinkable. Consequently the catastrophe which had been averted for the moment was soon more imminent than ever. Murad II (1421–1451) reappeared before the walls of Constantinople and recaptured Salonica; and despite the heroism of George Castriotis (Scanderberg) in Albania, and Hunyadi Janos on the Hungarian frontiers, the Turkish domination, after the battle of Varna (1444), was re-established throughout the Balkan peninsula.

This time the fate of Constantinople was inevitable. What help could be anticipated from Europe, where France and England were exhausted by the Hundred Years' War, Germany was troubled by Hussitism, and the Church was a prey to the disputes of the Pope and the Council? The union of the Greek and Latin Churches, which the Emperor Manuel had allowed Eugenius VI to proclaim in 1439, had attracted little attention in the West, and its only result was to exasperate the Byzantine populace and the Orthodox clergy, who were ready to turn Turk rather than Papist. In the Low Countries, it was true, Duke Philip the Good spoke of organizing a Crusade, but he made no move, and even if he had set out for the East! . . . No mere military expedition, however powerful, could have saved Constantinople. In dealing with an enemy like the Turk, who was always able to bring up fresh reserves from Asia, and to carry on the war without excessive expenditure, thanks to the robust energies of a whole nation of warriors, what was really needed was a powerful and permanent military base on the shores of the Bosphorus, in the islands, and on the Danube. What State, under the political and economic conditions of the time, could have organized such a base, and borne the expense of it, and provided for its upkeep? Uncivilized though they were, the Turks were at least the equals of the Westerners in the military arts. They had warships, artillery and an incomparable cavalry, and theirs was the brute impetuosity and heroic fanaticism of a primitive people. Moreover, the States which should have been readiest to oppose them, whether or not they would have proved more powerful, either would not or could not move against them. The Venetians thought only of safeguarding their factories. Dismembered Germany was incapable of any effort. She left the Hungarians to their own devices, and what could they do beyond defending their own frontiers? As for the Serbs and the Bulgars, they were exhausted. When in 1452 Mahomet II laid siege to Constantinople, no one came to the help of the city. Its fall was inevitable. And we must not blame Europe for its failure to intervene. The necessary effort would have been too great. And this Europe realized. From the moment when the Byzantine Empire had failed to defend Asia Minor against the Turks Constantinople was lost. It is therefore not surprising that the West turned a deaf ear to Aeneas Sylvius (Pius II) and Nicholas V. For the West realized that it must resign itself to the inevitable. Honour at least was saved. Constantine XI was a worthy last representative of the long series of Emperors who derived directly from the Roman Emperors whose title they continued to bear. On the day of the final assault, May 29th, 1453, he fell fighting against the enemy. On the morrow, amidst scenes of pillage and massacre, the victor entered the Basilica of St. Sophia, and transformed it into a mosque; a Barbarian's unconscious act of homage to the superior civilization over which he had triumphed.

*Book Nine*

# THE RENAISSANCE AND THE REFORMATION

## INTRODUCTION

The period extending from the beginning of the 14th century to the middle of the 15th offers the spectacle of a disturbed and tormented society, struggling against the tradition which oppressed it, and which it could not contrive to shake off. The barrier which the past opposed to the thrust of the future held firm; it appeared to be still intact, and yet, undermined by invisible flaws, it suddenly gave way, and the energies which it had contained poured through the breach and gave the historic landscape an entirely new aspect.

Before the Renaissance, the intellectual history of Europe was merely a chapter of the history of the Church. There was so little secular thought that even those who contended against the Church were entirely dominated by it, and thought only of transforming it. They were not freethinkers but heretics. With the Renaissance the supremacy of the Church in the domain of thought was questioned. The cleric no longer had the monopoly of learning. Spiritual life, in its turn, became secularized; philosophy ceased to be the servant of theology, and art, like literature, emancipated itself from the tutelage which had been imposed upon it ever since the 8th century. The ascetic ideal was replaced by a purely human ideal, and of this ideal the highest expression was to be found in antiquity. The humanist replaced the cleric, as virtue (*virtus*) replaced piety. Of course, although we can say, truthfully enough, that the Renaissance replaced the Christian by the man, it was not anti-religious. Were there not many Popes amongst its most enthusiastic promoters? But it is perfectly true to say that it was anticlerical. Not only for the Italian humanists, but also for Christians as convinced as Erasmus or Thomas More, the claim of the theologian to domineer over learning and letters, and even morality, was as ridiculous as it was harmful. They dreamed of reconciling religion with the world. They were tolerant, not unduly dogmatic, and extremely hostile to the secular studies which Scholasticism had superimposed upon the Bible. They were interested above all in moral questions. Their programme, which we find in *Enchiridion militis Christiani* and the *Utopia*, is that of a broad, rational Christianity, entirely devoid of mysticism, which would make the Church, not the Bride of Christ and the source of salvation, but an institution for moralization and education in the highest sense of the word. They felt very strongly that if the Church was to be this it must be reformed. But they were optimists, and they hoped that it would be possible to induce it, by gentle pressure, to enter upon the new path.

We may say, then, that the Renaissance stated the religious problem in its own way. But it went no further than sketching the moderate, prudent and aristocratic solution which it proposed. The Reformation, on the other hand, attacked the problem with passion, violence and intolerance, but also with profound faith, and the passionate longing to attain to God and to salvation which was destined to conquer and subjugate men's souls. There was nothing in common between it and the Renaissance. It was properly speaking the antithesis of the Renaissance. It replaced the human being by the Christian; it derided and humiliated the power of reason, even when it condemned and repudiated dogmatism. Luther was much more akin to the Middle Ages than to the humanists, his contemporaries. Indeed, he horrified the majority of the humanists. Erasmus and More very soon turned aside from this revolutionary, whose brutality and radicalism were as disturbing to their intelligent opportunism as they were repugnant to their good taste and moderation. They divined the tragedy which was about to commence, and they shuddered at it, understanding that it meant the end of their hopes of reconciliation.

Yet it was not Lutheranism that provoked the catastrophe of the wars of religion. After a first popular effervescence, marked by the rising of the German peasants and the insurrection of the Anabaptists, it submitted with docility to the control of the princes. It abandoned the Church to the secular power so completely that when Charles V decided to take action against it he had to fight the princes, and the conflict that followed was far more political than religious. As for Rome, surprised by the success of a movement in which she had seen, at first, no more than a monkish dispute; wholly engrossed in temporal interests, and having allowed the Catholic masses to become lukewarm in their faith, she could do nothing more effective, at first, to stem the rising flood of heresy than to launch her impotent anathemata. The kingdoms of the North adopted the new confession. Henry VIII, in England, founded a State Church which was half schismatic and half heretical, but above all, the National Church to which the followers of Wycliffe had already aspired. All this was effected without any great disturbance; there were a few sentences of banishment, and a certain amount of torture was inflicted, but there was no civil war; less blood was shed, incomparably less, than by the war of the Albigenses or the Inquisition.

But then Calvin made his appearance, and with him the hitherto comparatively peaceful course which the Reformation had followed under the control of the State was suddenly modified. An austere, exclusive, intolerant religion claimed the right to impose itself upon the government, and to force it, even by rebellion, to obey the Word of God. Calvinism was no longer satisfied with the national existence which had hitherto contented Protestantism. The Calvinist propaganda aspired to conquer the world. The faith which it inspired in its "elect" urged them to political action, and this action was the beginning of the tragic epoch of the wars of religion.

The indispensable condition of the success of the Renaissance, and also that of the Reformation, was the decline of the Catholic Church, which, as we have seen, had been constantly accelerated since the beginning of the 14th century. This alone had rendered possible the enfranchisement of thought and the renewal of faith. European society was too vigorous to remain tied by the fetters that bound it to the past. And it was not only in the domain of faith and of thought that a movement of renewal had been manifested since the middle of the 15th century. It had been perceptible everywhere. While the thinkers were shaking off the yoke of Scholasticism, and while the artists were freeing themselves from the restrictions of the Gothic style, the industrialists, capitalists and politicians were protesting and rebelling in their turn against the restrictive system of the trade corporations, against the economic limitations, the traditions and prejudices that impeded the free expansion of their activities. Everything was undergoing transformation, the economic world no less than the intellectual; the birth of modern capitalism was almost contemporaneous with the appearance of the first scientific works, and it collaborated with science in the discovery of the East Indies and America. The constitutions of the States felt the influence of the ideas, necessities, appetites and ambitions which were affecting the community as a whole. Indeed, we should do wrong to restrict the application of the word "Renaissance" to the new orientation of thought and art; it should be extended to the whole field of human activity, as revealed in its manifold aspects from the middle of the 15th century. If at the same time we reflect that this exuberant life was poured into the veins of a Europe in which a new State, Burgundy, had just been created, while Spain had lately acquired the rank of a "great power," and the arrival of the Turks had resulted in a formidable Eastern problem, we shall appreciate the enormous magnitude and the absorbing interest of the spectacle of European history at the moment when, about 1450, it suddenly quickened its pace, affording a conspicuous contrast, in its vigorous decisiveness and its lucid enthusiasm, to the painful and groping confusion of the preceding period.

## CHAPTER I

# THE TRANSFORMATION OF SOCIAL LIFE FROM THE MIDDLE OF THE FIFTEENTH CENTURY

### 1. *Italy and Italian Influence*

The Renaissance, in the more general sense of the term, does not appear to have been a more specifically Italian phenomenon than the expansion of urban life had been at the close of the 11th century. Neither the Renaissance nor the new form of urban life could have become so rapidly diffused had not the conditions favourable to its success existed to the north of the Alps. But it is true that these conditions, in each case, were of earlier occurrence in Italy, and more favourable than anywhere else. Just as Florence took precedence of all the cities of the Middle Ages, so the Italian Renaissance manifested a variety and originality and vigour unknown elsewhere, and to which it owed its astonishing influence.

The fact is that the traditional authorities which dominated both social and intellectual life declined or disappeared far earlier in Italy than in the rest of Europe. And this was largely a consequence of the extraordinary development of urban life. Just at first the nobles inhabiting the cities were involved in incessant conflicts with the bourgeoisie, but gradually, insensibly, they began to engage in commerce, so that the very clear line of demarcation which elsewhere divided the noble from the non-noble was slowly effaced, the descendants of knights and the offspring of enriched merchants intermingling in a community of manners and interests, independently of birth. The social status became more important than the juridical status; moreover, in the course of the 14th century the Italian nobility abandoned the profession of arms, thereby losing the *raison d'être* of its constitution as a distinct and privileged class. War became a profession which was left to specialists, the *condottieri*, men of the most various origins, the majority being successful *parvenus*; men in whom there was no trace of the old feudal loyalty. And while the noble was divesting himself of his specific class characteristics a similar transformation was proceeding in the ranks of the wealthy bourgeoisie. The progress of economic organization, the development of commercial society, and the improvement of instruments of credit had the consequence, from the very first, of requiring in the banker or the man of affairs an intellectual ability and culture which were not found in the same degree among the merchants of the North, and far less than the latter was he "subdued to what he worked in." While giving due attention to his business, he allowed himself some hours of leisure, so that he was able to distract himself by intellectual interests, embellish his house with works of art, and acquire a refinement which made him singularly unlike the "patricians" of Germany, Flanders or France. And so, recruited at once from the nobility and the bourgeoisie, a sort of mundane aristocracy came into existence, comprising all those who lived the same kind of life, enjoyed the same degree of education, had the same tastes, and indulged in the same pleasures; and this kind of aristocracy had not its like in any other country. The old society was disintegrating. New groups were in process of formation, no longer determined by convention and prejudice, but coming into existence freely, by virtue of affinities; and in these groups one may say that the spirit of class was replaced by the spirit of humanity.

The development of capitalism involved still further consequences.[1] We should note, as a quite extraordinary phenomenon, the effective principality of the Medici in Florence, which had no other origin than their wealth.

Florence presented every possible kind of political and social problem, every imaginable contrast of fortune, and was ready to

[1] Here I should need my books and my notes before I could say anything definite.

test every possible device of the political spirit to which she had given birth. Florence is the only European city that could be compared with Athens; and like Athens, Florence was in every sense of the word a State which had to deal with as many foreign as domestic problems. It is not surprising that the first political theorists worthy of the name, Machiavelli (1469–1527) and Guiccardini (1483–1540), should have been born upon this fertile soil. Their political judgement was no longer subject to any doctrinal influence. They were as independent of theological conceptions as of the juridical constructions which had hitherto influenced political ideas. Urban life was overflowing the narrow frontiers of the Middle Ages and becoming civic life.[1]

The spectacle of the other Italian cities exhibits with the same completeness the breaking away from political traditions. There, as the result of intestine rivalries, they finally placed themselves in the hands of tyrants, all *parvenus*, who exercised, without any legitimate title, relying only on force, a government against which there was hardly any other recourse but assassination. Aeneas Sylvius (Pope Pius II) says: "In our Italy, amorous of change, where nothing endures, and where no ancient lordship exists, varlets may readily aspire to become kings." These tyrants, who got the Emperors to give them titles which had no legitimate basis, like the Visconti of Milan, established a monarchical power which had nothing in common with that of the kings, or even of the ultramontane princes. One could not imagine a Joan of Arc in Italy! In her place, the sovereigns made use of people of whom they could never be sure, so that it was best to contrive their disappearance as soon as they became powerful. Their principle was the *raison d'État*. They stood outside all traditions, and they were bound by nothing; neither by suzerainty, nor sworn charters, nor customs, nor privileges of any kind; still less by any religious or juridical ideals. Like the old Roman Emperors, they could permit themselves everything. There were among them monsters like

[1] Cf. on the contrary, the passage in which Commines describes the bourgeois of the Flemish cities: "Ce n'estoient que bestes et gens de villes, la plupart." Cf. also the Gantois, who, under Charles V, could find nothing better to do but return to their constitution of the 14th century.

Giovanni Maria Visconti (1412), who fed his dogs on human flesh, or Gian Galeazzo Sforza, whom Commines describes: "the builder of the Certosa of Pavia, a great and evil tyrant, but honourable." (Book VII, Chap. VII.) The absence of any political unity in Italy, which Machiaevelli regretted so bitterly, was doubtless the condition of her breaking with the past. Never having been squeezed into a single State, Italy was then able to become, in respect of the rest of Europe, something of what ancient Greece was for Rome. If the policy of Frederick II had succeeded in unifying Italy, Florence would have been impossible.[1]

The overthrow of social and political traditions was accompanied by the decadence of manners and morals. Completely dominated by the Church, the morality of the Middle Ages had been essentially ascetic. This morality saw human perfection in renunciation. It regarded the secular life as something secondary and inferior; its ideal was the monk, and the laymen themselves accepted this ideal. Hence the extraordinary number of pious foundations—monasteries, convents and hospitals—which princes, nobles and bourgeois vied with one another in establishing. Those who did not live within the cloister sought to atone for their inferiority by founding cloisters, and to assure their salvation by acquiring some portion of their merits. Hence the veneration paid, not to the secular priests, but to the monastic clergy; so that princes gave orders that they should be buried in the robe of the Minorite friar, while merchants and bankers required their executors to make restitution of property wrongly obtained. How often the conscience of such men must have been tormented in the hour of death! For actually, in accordance with the strict theological precept, all commercial profit, all successful speculation, all bargaining was to be condemned as proceeding from the sin of avarice; the doctrine of the just price restricted profit to the minimum necessary for the maintenance of the vendor and his family. One must read compilations like those of Caesar von Heisterbach (1180–1240) or

[1] We must also remember that although the Italian States—such as Milan or Florence—were small, their influence was none the less universal, thanks to their political situation.

Thomas de Cantimpré (1201–1263) to obtain an exact idea of the mentality of the 13th century with regard to commerce. It could hardly imagine the merchant's strongbox without picturing the devil squatting on the lid. From first to last, the Church never ceased to enlarge upon this text of St. Jerome: *Homo mercator vix aut nunquam potest Deo placere.*

Asceticism was so intimately allied with the pessimistic conception of life which lay at the root of mediaeval Christianity that the two cannot be separated. Under the shock of a powerful moral stimulus the ascetic ideal would sometimes resume its empire, a fact which explains the prodigious success of Savonarola in the wealthy, luxurious and libertine Florence of the end of the 15th century, and the *autos da fé* of jewels, ornaments, musical instruments, books, and works of art—miserable mundane vanities—which were provoked by his sermons. But this was only a momentary blaze, fanned from the dying embers. Life was henceforth too exacting, too absorbing, too intensely interesting for even the noblest minds to feel at ease within a conception of things that condemned them. As for the others, they let life have its way with them, and they did so all the more readily inasmuch as the majority of the clergy set them the example. For the clergy allowed itself to be carried away with the tide. The pontifical court indulged in the most dazzling luxury, and nothing could have been less edifying than the conduct of the secular priests. The monks themselves, in the shaken and tormented Church of the 15th century, and perhaps the monks above all, contributed to the decline of faith. Not that their morals justified the attacks, the sarcasm, and the disdain which the literature of the period lavished upon them. The cloister was still the asylum of many pure and noble souls. But on the whole, the monasteries no longer fulfilled their mission, because they were no longer adapted to the needs and requirements of the moment. The scholastic and mystical education of the monks rendered them so ignorant of the ideas prevailing in the world that they were powerless to influence them. The lettered aristocracy regarded them as the representatives of a bygone period; they pitied them, and it is but a short step from pity to contempt. The monks themselves

were conscious of this, and resigned themselves to exercising only a popular apostolate, which degraded them, because they had not wished to undertake it. Moreover, they were now recruited only from the ranks of the people and the lower middle class, and of their new confrères many entered the cloister merely in order to live in security under the protection of the monastic rule. Thus, the prestige so long enjoyed by the Franciscans and the Dominicans was a thing of the past. Educated laymen spoke of them now only in a jesting tone, and the pious tales which were formerly told of them were replaced by ribald anecdotes. Before the monks could recover their influence in the world a new order had to make its appearance, that of the Jesuits, in which asceticism mastered the new intellectual culture in order to combat its effects. But it must not be supposed that the men of the 15th century had lost their respect for sanctity. They were very far from having done so; and in proof of this, it is enough to cite their veneration for the Carthusians. Did not a tyrant like Gian Galeazzo Sforza surround the Cortosa of Pavia with the most magnificent architectural setting, as a venerated relic might be encrusted with jewels? But the Carthusians were purely contemplative monks, who took no part in the life of the world, leaving to its own devices the society which admired them, and which they could not hope to influence otherwise than by prayer.

While the Renaissance had liberated itself from the ascetic morality of the Middle Ages, it did not replace this by any other morality. The strongest and noblest souls imposed upon themselves an ideal of virtue and honour; for others glory was the dominant motive; but the majority seem to have obeyed no other rules than those of personal interest, or they allowed themselves to be led by their tastes and their passions. The loosening of the conjugal tie, and the frequency of assassinations, poisonings, and crimes of every kind and in every class of society, are incontestable evidence of a moral crisis. And yet, in the midst of this disorder, we see the beginnings of a sense of individual liberty, of human dignity, of the beauty of energy, and of the responsibility of the private man before his own conscience. Shall we go too far if we credit the Renaissance with having realized, more or less definitely, that morality should not consist of a mere code of precepts, and that it cannot be complete without the free adhesion of the personality? This, no doubt, is an aristocratic conception; in the sense, at least, that it is given to few to attain to it. But was not the whole achievement of the Renaissance aristocratic? Was it not characterized above all by the formation of an intellectual élite?—in which it was completely opposed to the Middle Ages, when a priestly caste possessed the monopoly of learning and knowledge. And was it not to this intellectual élite that it owed its most striking feature, which—above all in Italy—gave it its final and proper physiognomy—the return to antiquity?

We know that in its first acceptation the very word "Renaissance" means simply the re-birth of antiquity. And yet if we employ it only in this sense we shall strangely restrict its scope. The change in the ideas, the manners and the morals of the 15th century was not, as we have seen, a consequence of the study of the classic authors. It proceeded naturally from the social life of Italy. If the literature of antiquity had had the power of provoking it, the Renaissance would have occurred as early as the reign of Charlemagne. For after all, the majority of the Latin authors were known and studied then; they were constantly copied and re-copied until nearly the end of the 12th century, and their influence can readily be detected in the style of many of the chroniclers. Virgil above all was held in the greatest honour by the clerks of the Middle Ages, and so great was the respect which he enjoyed that he was regarded as a precursor of Christianity. Dante was accompanied by him in the other world, and the homage which he pays him in the "Divine Comedy"—*tu duca, tu signore e tu maestro*—is more enthusiastic, more sincere and eloquent than all the panegyrics of the humanist in honour of the Mantuan poet. Nevertheless, between the Aeneid and the "Divine Comedy" there is a gulf. Dante did not understand Virgil, and could not have understood him; he was too profound, too exalted a Christian and a mystic. What the Middle Ages was able to feel and appreciate in the thought of antiquity was neither the form nor the spirit, but a few sentences, a few anecdotes, a few "moralities," understood in a symbolic sense. And what is true of literature is even truer of the art of antiquity. The unknown masters who built the Romanic and Gothic Cathedrals had before their eyes a great number of ancient monuments, and they lived in their midst without seeing them. Their conception of beauty was exclusive, as is that of all sincere and vital schools. Their incomprehension of classic art is comparable only to the incomprehension of the art of the Middle Ages itself after the triumph of the Renaissance. As a matter of fact, the influence exercised by antiquity over the Renaissance may be compared with the influence exercised by the Middle Ages over Romanticism. Without a preliminary orientation of thought and feeling, neither the Renaissance, at the close of the 14th century, nor Romanticism, at the beginning of the 19th century, would have found so many and such fervent adepts. For a long time men had observed the works of art of these periods without really seeing them; had read the books, without understanding them. For neither these works of art nor these books had impressed themselves on men's minds by virtue of their intrinsic qualities. People came to them, admired them, and understood them, or thought to understand them, when the bandage fell from their eyes, when the authority which had governed their minds had ceased to impress them. Just as unless the classical, rationalistic and cosmopolitan ideals of the 16th century had been abandoned, the Romantics would not have been filled with enthusiasm for the Middle Ages, so, unless the men of the Renaissance had been enfranchised from theological and ecclesiastical tradition, they would not have found in antiquity a new source of knowledge and beauty.

However, it must be admitted without question that the influence of antiquity was incomparably more profound and more fruitful in the epoch of the Renaissance than the influence of the Middle Ages in the epoch of Romanticism. The Middle Ages, in fact, gave the Romantics only their picturesqueness and their local colour. Antiquity, on the other hand, offered secular thought, at the moment of its awakening, a treasury of science and the humanities, embellished with all the prestige of form. At the very moment when the

Church was ceasing to satisfy the needs of the intellect, it happened, by an extraordinary piece of good fortune, that an incomparable art and literature became available, which did satisfy them. Men deserted the cathedral to find themselves before the open doors of the temple of antiquity.

It is not surprising that the cult of antiquity had its beginnings in Italy. It had never quite died out there. Rome was still a living memory. Consider, for example, Arnold of Brescia. Petrarch regarded all other peoples as Barbarians. As soon as men's eyes were opened and able to see the beauty of antiquity, they felt that they had found something that was akin to them. They began to describe the art of the Middle Ages as *gotico*. The art of Greece had come to them from Byzantium.

It is impossible here to give even a rapid sketch of the Italian humanism of the 15th century. In spite of its exuberance and its overweening presumption, it has none the less exerted a most enduring influence on modern thought. To begin with, it made Latin—not the scholastic Latin of the universities and the jurists, but a classic Latin, correct and elegant—the international language of all educated people, down to our own day. It thus created, for the benefit of laymen, a uniform culture, externally very like that of which the clergy had hitherto retained the monopoly. In so doing it completed the constitution of that intellectual aristocracy which social evolution had created in the heart of the nation. But it did more than this: at the same time it imposed an aristocratic influence on the development of all modern literatures. Writers whose taste was formed by the study of the classics transferred to their national languages the ideal of beauty which they discovered in the classics. Writing became an art which, although it was inspired by antiquity, was not enslaved to it, but preserved a liberty of its own, just as the sculpture and architecture of the Renaissance treated their Greek and Roman models with a peculiar freedom. Men assimilated the forms and the ideas of antiquity, but did not allow themselves to be dominated by them. Their minds were sufficiently enfranchised to retain their independence; they did not abdicate their individuality, their originality. When they wrote in Latin they wrote imitations, or, if you will, *pastiches* of the ancients. But as soon as they began to write in their national tongue they sought to rival the ancients, and imitation gave way to emulation. Their admiration of antiquity, and its lessons, served to stimulate and refine their creative genius rather than to stifle it. This is as true of Donatello, Andrea del Sarto, Bramante and Raphael as it was of Ariosto, Tasso, Guiccardini or Machiavelli.

These last two names remind us that while the literature in the national tongue acquired a greater beauty, it also became more intellectually comprehensive and profound. For a long while, of course, Latin still remained the language of science. But it no longer had the monopoly of science. The modern languages were now sufficiently rich and flexible to lend themselves to the expression of the most abstruse ideas, and those who made use of them were sure of finding readers among that intellectual aristocracy who had become aware of the need of thought. A universal curiosity was abroad. Hardly anything was known of the philosophy of the ancients, apart from Aristotle, and he was discredited by the portrait which the Scholastics had drawn of him. Platonism was therefore welcomed with all the greater enthusiasm. The Greek literature which Byzantine refugees had revealed to Italy, even before the Turkish capture of Constantinople, opened up new intellectual horizons. Already a few pioneers dreamed of going even further, and ventured into the domain of Hebraic studies and Oriental philology. Lastly, the exact sciences began their glorious careers. Physics, astronomy and mathematics flourished in that springtime of modern thought which gave the Italy of the 15th century its incomparable charm. It must not be forgotten that Copernicus studied at Padua and Bologna, and that the scientific labours of Toscanelli and Luca Paccioli contributed largely to the discovery of the New World.

### 2. *The Renaissance in the Rest of Europe*

The Renaissance of the North was very far from being a mere imitation of that of Italy. If it had been no more than this, it would have been a somewhat superficial and comparatively restricted phenomenon. No: the essential fact is that at the moment when the North gave welcome to the Italian Renaissance it was passing, quite independently of Italy, through a crisis of social and economic transformation. For the North the middle of the 15th century was the beginning of a period of renewal, a time of profound travail, which, though it did not alter its intimate constitution as violently as the revival of commerce had done in the 12th century, and as the discovery of steam power was to do in the 19th century, nevertheless shook the whole fabric of that constitution and gave it the form which it was to retain more or less until the end of the *ancien régime*. And we must thoroughly realize the obscure travail that was stirring from 1450 to about 1550 if we are to understand the Renaissance and the Reformation. Not by any means because this travail was the cause of the Renaissance and the Reformation, but because it explains the manner in which they acted, and the force which they set in motion, both for resistance and for attack.

The great novelty which appeared at this time was capitalism. It would not be true to say that it was making its first appearance. It had already undergone considerable development in the 12th and 13th centuries, and the urban patricians were the heirs of the enriched merchants of that epoch. Two causes had checked this first expansion. In the first place, the irresistible competition of Italian capital, which, from the end of the 12th century, had everywhere monopolized the traffic in money. And secondly, the organization of the trade corporations favoured the *petite bourgeoisie*. The free economic expansion of the earlier period was followed—as we shall have occasion to show in a later chapter—by a period of rigid regulation.

From that time, capitalism, to the north of the Alps, although it had not entirely disappeared, was hindered, supervised, restricted. It could operate only by evading the regulations, and it had little vitality, being crushed by Italian competition. The ecclesiastical and civil laws with regard to lending money at interest were also not without effect. In short, the patricians were transformed into a class of *rentiers* who no longer engaged in business. It has even been said that the great merchant by profession did not exist in the Middle Ages. This is false if the statement is accepted in a general sense; but it is true enough if we restrict it to the 14th century. The only persons who still engaged in affairs of any magnitude were those who had interests in the Italian companies, and the brokers. There was no such thing as a great commercial house or a great bank to the north of the Alps. Even in Flanders the capital which fed the cloth industry and furnished it with wool was almost exclusively Italian.

But this situation began to undergo transformation as early as the first half of the 15th century. A new class of capitalists began to make its appearance almost everywhere in Flanders, France, and England, and in those cities of Southern Germany which maintained commercial relations with Venice. It consisted of new men; it was not in any sense the continuation of the old patriciate. It was a group of adventurers, of *parvenus*, like all those groups that made their appearance during each economic transformation. They did not work with old, accumulated capital. This they acquired only at a later stage. Like the *mercatores* of the 12th century, and the inventors and industrialists of the late 18th and the 19th century, these pioneers bought, as their sole investment, their energy and their intelligence or cunning.

Their device, the device of the conquistadors of wealth, was: liberty. It was liberty that their predecessors of the 12th century had demanded—enfranchisement from the shackles of the agricultural and feudal system, which prevented the expansion of commerce. The liberty that the new men demanded was that which would enfranchise them from the urban regulation of the monopolies enjoyed by the trade corporations, the restrictions imposed upon sale and purchase, the control of the markets, the fixing of wages by the law, the official apprenticeship, and the privileges which, in every city, reserved commerce for the burgesses and reduced the stranger to the status of a pariah. What they claimed was the common right to engage in industry and commerce, which must be rescued from municipal exclusivism, and disencumbered of those privileges which were doubtless indispensable when industry and commerce were in their infancy, but which were now preventing their development. What they wanted was "natural liberty," liberty without qualifications, not a restrictive liberty as understood by the bourgeois, which was as incompatible with the "general liberty" as the "liberty" of the nobles had been with that of the villeins. They wanted the cities to be accessible to all, so that all could share in their commerce; so that they would no longer exist merely for their own burgesses. But they also wanted the power to industrialize the countryside, to draw upon that great reservoir of labour, to employ hands that were accustomed to guide the plough, and by their aid, thanks to the low tariff of wages, to compete with the trade guilds of the cities: and all the more victoriously, inasmuch as, not being subject to their regulations, they could manufacture, at their own pace, as much as they wished, employ such methods as were convenient or useful, follow the changes of the fashion, market their products where they chose, and conclude such contracts as suited them.

These adventurers—for they were just as truly adventurers as the *mercatores* of the 12th century—were favoured by the political changes no less than by the inability of the cities to maintain their privileges in the midst of a progressive civilization. The princes, who required more and more money as the cost of wars increased, had need of them. It was more convenient to make use of these men of business than to parley with the States-General for taxes. Hitherto the men of affairs at the courts of Philip the Fair and Edward III had been Italians. But now the native man of affairs was beginning to replace the Italian. In Austria the Fuggers obtained the right to exploit the silver mines of the Tyrol, Bohemia and Hungary, thereby laying the foundations of their fortune outside the cities. In France, the story of Jacques Cœur (1466) is particularly interesting. Beginning with nothing, he joined a consortium, one of whose members was a bankrupt merchant, which leased the privilege of minting money from Charles VII. This was a profitable business. All the master-minters were robbers who considered that the profits which they made in minting money were as legitimate as the profits which our modern bankers make by the issue of Government loans. In 1432, having learned the ins and outs of the trade in metals, Cœur began to export silver to the East and import gold, which he disposed of in France at an enormous profit. From this time forward we see him constantly increasing his business interests. He leased the Crown mines in Lyonnais and Beaujolais, in which he employed German miners. He became "argentier," which made him purveyor to the court, to which he advanced considerable sums of money at from 12 to 50 per cent interest. Nevertheless, he continued to increase his business interests, acting either on his own account or in association with other capitalists. It was estimated that he had no less than three hundred factories, extending from Famagusta to Bruges, and into England. He was accused of ruining "honest merchants," presumably by speculation and forestalling. His career had nothing in common with that of these "honest merchants," who were faithful to the traditions of the Middle Ages. He built himself a palace at Bourges, and houses in Paris, Tours, and Montpellier. He was ennobled, and became a councillor to the king. At a rough estimate, his fortune, at the moment of his fall in 1451, was equivalent to more than twenty-two millions of our francs.

These new capitalists did not appear in consequence of an extension of the market, since the outlets for goods had not multiplied, nor had the population increased, but in consequence of the unaccustomed necessities which arose in the course of the formation of new States.

If Jacques Cœur was a kind of 15th-century Rothschild, he was not the only one. He was merely the most illustrious specimen of a group of new men who were beginning to replace Italians like the Rapondi, who fulfilled the same function at the court of Philip the Good. In the Low Countries, a little later, the Laurins also enriched themselves in the service of the princes. The hôtel of Jean Laurin, seigneur of Watervliet at Malines, was so luxurious that the Governess, Margaret of Austria, bought it in 1507. In 1506 Jerome Laurin built the town of Philippine in his Philippus Polder. He too, owing to his office as treasurer, rose from "very great poverty, not possessing the value of a denier, to the possession of an income of 10,000 marks." Just as intelligence, three hundred years earlier, amidst the lethargy of the agricultural and feudal system, had created the first accumulations of capital in the hands of the burgesses, so now, in a society of ampler structure, it served as the instrument of the *parvenus*, who, discovering new outlets, and profiting by the favour of the prince, escaped the net with which the cities thought to have enmeshed commerce and industry to their own advantage. The cities could not contend on equal terms against these newcomers, who had their agents everywhere, forestalling and monopolizing, and supporting the new political powers. By means of their capital new industries were established in the countryside. We have already mentioned the mining industry. And a "new" textile industry had been established in Flanders, at Hondschoot and Armentières, despite the opposition of the cities, which vainly insisted on their privileges. The same thing happened in England, where new manufacturing centres were established. For example, the making of tapestries became a rural industry. And a rural industry was a capitalist industry. A completely novel mode of production made its appearance. The supervision which the trade guilds imposed upon the workers and the market was replaced by liberty. The peasant turned weaver contracted with a "master," but his wage and his labour were not subject to regulation. The masters themselves worked in conjunction with a contractor or wholesaler, from whom they received the raw material, and who disposed of their products. The small workshop survived, but it became degraded, so to speak; it lost its independence by subordinating itself to a new system—the system of manufacture. The urban industry, encompassed by its privileges, like a rampart raised against capital, managed to survive by producing for the local market. Its guilds and corporations continued to exist until the end of the *ancien régime*. Elsewhere, apart from a few special and artistic industries, it was compelled to abandon the struggle. The whole of the new industrial development, from the 15th century onwards, was opposed to it and outside it. The urban cloth industry of Flanders, the great export industry of the Middle Ages, lapsed into decadence after the middle of the 14th century. Owing to its excessive prices and its conservatism, it could not cope with the competition of the new English cloth trade and the rural weaving industry. The linen industry which replaced it until the age of factories was entirely rural.

Naturally, the organization of commerce, like that of industry, was stimulated by the pressure of capitalism, and by liberty. All the restrictions with which it had been surrounded—markets, brokers, the obligation to transact business only through the medium of the burgesses—were for commerce merely so many obstacles that hindered its progress. The example of Bruges is characteristic. As early as the middle of the 15th century its cosmopolitan customers were beginning to desert it for the young port of Antwerp. Here business was not burdened by tradition; commerce was able to organize itself from the very outset in accordance with the new spirit. This was a city which was adapted to future needs; for economic history shows us clearly how new needs were accompanied by a displacement of social classes and business centres. In England the "merchant adventurers" made their appearance, while the Dutch merchant fleet began to replace that of the Hansa. At the moment when this development had already made considerable progress an unlimited field of enterprise was opened by the discovery of the New World. This so completely transformed the surface of the globe that it seemed almost like a planetary catastrophe. The only thing that we can compare with it, as having had analogous results, although much less in degree, was the expansion of Islam. This too transformed the surface of the globe, changed populations and languages, and acclimatized new civilizations under alien skies; it also, in some degree, orientalized the Occident. But this was a small thing in comparison with the stupendous transformation which made the Atlantic an inland sea; the discovery of the Pacific, the propagation of Christianity beyond the Equator, the diffusion of Spanish and Portuguese, and presently of French and English, throughout America, the transformation of so many peoples, the hybridization of some, the annihilation of others, and the appearance of so many new products, which modified the conditions of life: tea, coffee, and tobacco, which conquered the markets of Europe, the introduction of cotton, and of our domestic animals, in America; and lastly, the gigantic achievements which were to open new highways for world traffic—Suez, Panama. Of course, all this did not happen all at once, and the immortal mariners who "saw new stars emerging from the waves" neither desired nor could have divined the future that they were opening up for Europe. The economic motive had very little to do with their designs. The Europe of the 15th century was not over-populated; it had no need of colonies, and Portugal in particular, who inaugurated the new discoveries, was not conscious of the least need of extending her commerce. There was nothing of the mercantile prince about Henry the Navigator. He was actuated by scientific curiosity and the desire to propagate the Faith. They were purely spiritual aspirations that gave rise to the discovery of the lands of gold and spices. These expeditions are in no way comparable with those of the ancient Phoenicians. But it must be admitted that without the development attained by Mediterranean navigation at the beginning of the 15th century these discoveries would have been impossible. It was the Mediterranean that furnished the ships and their captains. As in the case of the Crusades, moreover, there were exciting factors: the old tales of the Indies, memories of the journeys of De Plano Carpini and Marco Polo, and all the rumours of the Levantine port .

This is not the place to retell this wonderful story. It will suffice to recall the principal dates: the Madeira Islands were discovered in 1419 and the Azores in 1431, and the Cape Verde Islands and the coast of Senegambia some little time before the death of Henry the Navigator (1460), who lived long enough to hear of their discovery. After these first groping ventures progress was accelerated. In 1482 Diego Cam sailed as far as the mouths of the Congo; in 1486 Bartolomeo Diaz reached the Cape of Good Hope, and saw the Indian Ocean lie open before him. In 1497 Vasco da Gama ventured upon that ocean, reaching Calicut in 1498. The Cape had justified the name which King John II had given it. At last the marvellous Indies had been attained; the Western caravels, after a protracted voyage upon desert seas and along wild coasts, came into contact with the dhows of the Arabs, and reached at last the source of that stream of wealth of which Europe had hitherto known only the Levantine outfall.

The Portuguese were the first pioneers to sail the unknown seas. They proceeded slowly, keeping at first within sight of the coast, and then, making enquiries as they advanced, they rounded the Cape, touched at Zanzibar, and set sail for the East; in short, their plan consisted in rounding the Cape, and circumnavigating Africa, so as to get to the further side of Syria and Egypt, for they knew that beyond these they would find the Indies. Thanks to their patience and energy, the thing was done. They had sufficient indications to guide them. Relying on a mass of empirical data, they felt that each fresh advance brought them nearer to their goal. All that the Portuguese needed, in order to succeed, was certain technical improvements; that is to say, vessels large and seaworthy and handy enough to keep the sea for some months at a time.

The voyages of Christopher Columbus, on the other hand, would have been inconceivable without the science of the Renaissance. Had he reposed a less heroic confidence in the works of Toscanelli and the Italian geographers of the 15th century, how could he ever have brought himself to sail straight across the Atlantic, hoping to arrive at the Indies by encircling the globe? His plans were too audacious for the Portuguese court, but the Spaniards allowed themselves to be persuaded. On August 3rd, 1492, the caravels disappeared below the horizon; on October 12th they reached the Antilles. There was still more than half the circumference of the earth between them and the Indies! The world was much larger than Toscanelli had supposed; all his calculations were erroneous, but, as so often happens, the very errors of science were fruitful, and in this case they led to the discovery of America. The subsequent voyages of Columbus (1492–1502) and the voyage of his compatriot Sebastian Cabot, who had entered the service of Henry VII of England, revealed the stupendous nature of the discovery, by reaching the American mainland: Columbus discovering the Orinoco and the Isthmus of Panama, and Cabot the coast of Labrador. In 1500 Cabral, blown out of his course, touched another point of the immense coast-line, in Brazil. It was not until 1513 that the Pacific Ocean was seen from the heights of the Isthmus of Panama. In 1520 Magellan doubled Cabo Deseado, set out across the wilderness of this vast new ocean, and discovered the Philippines. His companions returned to Spain by way of the Moluccas and the Indian Ocean. The voyage round the world had been accomplished for the first time.

From the first years of the 16th century the consequence of these marvellous discoveries were manifested in the economic life of Europe. The first of these consequences was that the headquarters of the Oriental trade was removed from the Italian ports of the Mediterranean to the shores of the Atlantic Ocean. The spices which the caravans brought to the ports of the Levant, whence they were carried by the trading vessels of Genoa and Venice, could not long compete, either in quantity or in price, with those which the Portuguese and Spanish ships brought direct from the Equatorial countries in which they were produced. Italy, which had hitherto been the intermediary between Europe and the long mysterious Indies, found that the springs of her prosperity were drying up, and the drought was a prolonged one. Until the day when the piercing of the Suez Canal (1869) made it the highway to the Indian Ocean, the Mediterranean lost the great commercial importance which it had enjoyed without interruption since the dawn of civilization. But neither Spain nor Portugal took its place; neither Cadiz nor Lisbon was the heir of Venice and Genoa. The commercial hegemony which these ports had hitherto enjoyed fell to the lot of Antwerp.

There were two obvious reasons for this. To begin with, the international importance of a seaport depends on both its import and its export trade. It is not enough that ships should bring merchandise to the port; they must also be able to obtain wares in exchange. Venice and Genoa in the south, like Bruges in the north, had fulfilled these conditions during the Middle Ages; Venice and Genoa thanks to the industries of the Italian cities, and Bruges thanks to those of the cities of the Low Countries. Moreover, by reason of their geographical situation they were in touch with the interior of Europe, whose roads were centred upon them, providing ready access for the products of the hinterland. The situation of the Iberian ports was not so favourable from either point of view. Their position, on the shores of an outlying peninsula, and the undeveloped state of the national industries, made it impossible for them to attract a considerable import trade. Lastly, the manner in which the trade in spices and precious metals was carried on in Portugal and Spain prevented the establishment of powerful commercial houses. The Crown, as the possessor of the overseas factories and colonies, excluded foreigners from them, and reserved for itself, as a monopoly, the greater part of the import trade. Its agents were entrusted with the sale of the imported products, and in order that they might sell them more promptly and more readily the Crown took good care not to exclude those very foreigners who were forbidden access to the country where the merchandise was produced. Accordingly, from the beginning of the 16th century the capitalist merchants of Antwerp maintained at Cadiz, and above all in Lisbon, factors who were entrusted with the purchase of the precious wares. Consequently the seaport on the Scheldt became the great international emporium for spices. Only there did they become the objects of commercial transactions and enter into circulation. As we have already seen, the economic importance of Antwerp antedated the period of discoveries. But the afflux of the wealth of the Indies and the New World was the beginning of a period of extraordinary prosperity, which soon exceeded that of Venice in the days of her greatest splendour. Never has any other port, at any period, enjoyed such world-wide importance, because none has ever been so open to all comers, and, in the full sense of the word, so cosmopolitan. Antwerp remained faithful to the liberty which had made her fairs so successful in the 15th century. She attracted and welcomed capitalists from all parts of Europe, and as their numbers increased so did their opportunities of making their fortune. Germans, Englishmen, Frenchmen, Portuguese, Spaniards and Italians, all hurried thither. And there was not a single great bank or commercial house without its representatives in Antwerp. The greatest financial power of the 16th century, the Fuggers, had their headquarters at Augsburg, but it was their Antwerp branch that made the most enormous profits. This rendezvous of contractors, merchants, sailors and adventurers became the centre of the commercial world. One can hardly imagine a more striking and more complete contrast with the economic organization of the Middle Ages. In Venice the foreigners could buy only from Venetians; in Bruges they had to employ a broker who was a burgess of the city. But no such restrictions were in force in Antwerp. There was no supervision, no control: foreigners did business with other foreigners as freely as with the burgesses and the natives of the country at their daily meetings. Buyers and sellers sought one another and came to terms without intermediaries. Prices were fixed, and credits were opened by the commercial companies, and speculation claimed its first victims. From the year 1531 all this commercial activity was concentrated under the galleries of a special building constructed at the expense of the city, the Bourse, the forerunner and model of the future Exchanges of London and Amsterdam.

The great wars of the beginning of the 16th century gave a fresh impetus to the spirit of capitalism. Charles V especially, whose immense States provided him with resources which were singularly inadequate in proportion to his power, was an extraordinary client for the financiers. Without the development of capitalism it may be said that his reign, which set so many armies on the march and launched so many fleets, would have been impossible. However, the profits of the bankers were fully comparable to the services which they rendered him. The prosperity of the Low Countries was largely responsible for maintaining the Emperor's credit, enabling him to reimburse his creditors, despite the fact that he had to pay from 12 to 50 per cent interest. The Fuggers owed a great part of their fortune to the advances which they made to him. However, the readiness with which princes were able to borrow, and the tempting profits within reach of the bankers, soon resulted in their exceeding the limits of prudence. The bankruptcies of Philip II in 1575 and 1596 put an end to the alliance of private capitalism and monarchical policy.

At this moment, however, another source of gain offered itself to the insatiable financiers. About 1550 the silver mines of Peru and Mexico began to furnish Spain with ingots which presently found their way all over Europe in the form of silver coins. This inundation of precious metals reduced the purchasing power of the currency, the result being a general rise of prices. Trade, and especially industry, received a powerful stimulus, and had yet one more motive for enfranchising themselves from the insupportable control of the guilds and corporations. Manufacture—that is, the form of production in which the artisan worked under his own roof, and was paid and given orders by a contractor—became, from the middle of the 16th century, the typical form of industrial organization; and so it remained until the appearance of the modern factory, of which, however, some precocious examples might already be found here and there.

Remarkable as the development of capitalism may have been, we must not exaggerate its scope. It was superimposed on the old economic organization of the privileged cities, but it did not abolish this organization. The *petite bourgeoisie* continued to live in the shelter of the trade corporations and to supply the local market. Bakers, butchers, cabinetmakers, shoemakers, etc., remained faithful, until the end of the *ancien régime*, to the protectionism which reserved for them the exploitation of their municipal clientèle. In no case did the governments think it wise or prudent to make them amenable to the common law. They were well aware of the faults of the system, which became increasingly apparent as time went on: routine methods, high prices, and the increasing restriction of each trade to a small number of masters; but their fear of democracy persuaded them to tolerate these defects as the best means of keeping the "compagnons" in a docile mood. They contented themselves with gradually suppressing the obstacles which the municipal regulations offered to the development of trade and the circulation of wealth: markets, commissions, etc. Above all they began to abolish the political privileges of the guilds, and to keep a tight hand, or at least a close watch, over the urban administrations, and despite the resistance which was offered in France during the disorders of the League, and again, to some extent, in the 18th century, they were everywhere successful. The cities could have retained their political and economic autonomy intact only by retaining their military strength. But what could their guilds and corporations do against regular armies, and what could their ancient walls avail against artillery? Only where the State was powerless, as in Germany, did they hold their own. Elsewhere they submitted. The few attempts at resistance, such as that of the Liégois against the Dukes of Burgundy, the people of Gand against Charles V and the people of La Rochelle against Francis I, showed that their claims were inspired only by a past which was indeed the past. The democratic policy which the *petite bourgeoisie* had so ardently supported in the 14th century was henceforth a lost cause. Just as capitalism was supreme in the domain of wholesale trade, so the State was supreme in the domain of politics.

Under the influence of the new conditions which were transforming social life the conception of the bourgeoisie was transformed in its turn. The political and juridical characteristics which had given it its special position in the society of the Middle Ages, beside the clergy and the *noblesse*, were gradually becoming less marked. From the beginning of the 16th century the bourgeoisie had become essentially a class of men living by exploitation or by the revenues of their wealth. The mere manual worker, according to current ideas, had ceased to belong to the bourgeoisie. It now rejected the artisans in whom its strength had formerly resided. It began to affect definitely plutocratic manners, which distinguished it from the *petite bourgeoisie* and brought it nearer to the noblesse. In each country, of course, it developed its special features, and it is impossible to frame a description of the bourgeoisie which would be equally applicable to the Low Countries, to France, and to England. It is enough to say that henceforth wealth was everywhere the sign *par excellence* of the bourgeoisie. The bourgeois of the Middle Ages was privileged by law; the modern bourgeois is privileged by virtue of his economic situation. But there is yet another difference between the two. In the Middle Ages the bourgeois depended on his city for his livelihood, and existed for his city; the commune of which he was a member was the indispensable guarantee of his person and his interests; his mode of life and his ideas alike were dominated by the municipal group to which he belonged. But after the Middle Ages these conditions disappeared. For the modern bourgeois the city is merely a place of residence and a business centre; it is no longer the centre of his affections, his ideas and his interests. The sources of his wealth are widely dispersed, no longer contained within the municipal boundaries. If he is a manufacturer his factories may be in the country; if he is a merchant his correspondents and his merchandise are distributed over distant ports and markets; if he lives on his dividends his money may be invested in distant countries, in loans, or in commercial or industrial enterprises of every kind. His livelihood is now dependent upon a multiplicity of conjunctures; it is implicated in the existence of the nation as a whole, and its relations to foreign nations. He has to know what is happening in all parts of the world. Hence the development of the post, and presently, of the Press, whose object, in the beginning, was merely to bring within reach of all the news which until then had been translated only by private correspondence.

Economic liberty, indissolubly bound up with the development of capitalism, immediately imposed its consequences upon the world of workers. While the corporative legislation of the Middle Ages did not prevent the master artisan from lording it over the countryside, it did set a limit to his exploitation of the latter. The regulations of the guilds determined the worker's rights, safeguarded his wages, and guaranteed him against too glaring abuses; they often granted him aid in case of sickness or old age, and sometimes they even allowed him a certain degree of intervention in the nomination or control of the heads of the trade corporation. Moreover, the *compagnonnages* or trade unions which had been constituted since the 15th century, comprising the journeyman of a particular trade, not only of one city, but of a whole group of cities, or even a whole country, created a system of mutual aid which might be regarded as a rudimentary labour organization. But there was no trace of all this in the new system of manufacture. Here, in conformity with the "common law," the employer and the employee entered into contracts directly, without the interposition of any authority or association. The one sold his labour, the other bought it, and the price depended only on their "free will." This means that it was actually imposed upon the weaker by the stronger. Completely unorganized, whether in the city or the country, the workers of the new industries had to submit to the law of the capitalist. Since the workers elaborated the raw material supplied by the capitalists under their own roof, they were particularly liable to exploitation, thanks to the regulations of all kinds which the capitalist was able to impose upon them. And in fact, from the beginning of the 16th century there is abundant evidence of the wretchedness of their conditions, and of their discontent. The rise of prices in the middle of the century exasperated them still further, and contributed largely to the success of the semi-social, semi-religious propaganda of the Anabaptists. As for the government, it did nothing for them, ignoring them as long as they did not trouble the public peace. While a pioneer like Thomas More had dreamed, in his *Utopia* (1516), of labour legislation of a communistic type, the State and the public authorities, whether then or for centuries after, did not envisage what we to-day should call the labour question except as a matter concerning the police. Hence their intervention, after the end of the 15th century, against the abuses of mendicity, and, a little later, their reforms in the domain of charity.

Here again we have striking evidence of the degree in which social changes had weakened the influence of the Church. The magnificent impulse of Christian charity which the Church had inspired in the Middle Ages no longer corresponded with the needs or the spirit of the age. The numberless charitable foundations which the Church had encouraged and inspired confined themselves, in accordance with its mystical ideal, to succouring the poor; to maintaining them in that state of life without seeking to help them to emerge from it. The poor man had his definite place in society, and very pious souls even regarded him with a certain veneration, which is sufficiently explained by the ascetic spirit of the period. But as this ascetic spirit declined, the halo of sanctity which surrounded the mendicant faded. People began to regard him as a vagabond, dangerous to the public peace, a professional loafer. On the other hand, the increasingly rigid regulations of the urban guilds, which condemned great numbers of men to unemployment, and the demobilization of bands of mercenaries, which left these old soldiers without a profession, so multiplied the numbers of wandering men who had no other resources than alms, that towards the beginning of the 15th century they had become a veritable social plague. The authorities therefore began to persecute them mercilessly, in the hope of compelling at least the able-bodied among them to work. The first administrative regulations directed against mendicity authorized it only in the case of children, the aged, and the infirm, and sought to prevent others from begging by the threat of corporal punishment. This, of course, was only a palliative. It was well understood, from the beginning of the 16th century, that it would be necessary to attack the root of the evil and abolish mendicity by removing its cause. Hence, for example, the reforms introduced at Ypres in 1525, under the influence of Vivès, which, by concentrating the resources of all the charitable establishments of the city, appointing visitors to the poor, and sending children in receipt of charity to school, or apprenticing them to a trade, sought to abolish pauperism by enabling the poor man to earn his living. From this time forward attempts of the same kind were made in all parts of Europe. It is interesting to note that they were especially numerous and effective where the development of capitalism and manufactures enabled the charitable societies to find situations for their charges. The example of Holland, and above all of England, is particularly significant in this respect. The English laws of 1551 and 1562 relating to the employment of the poor were the precursors of the famous *Act for the relief of the poor* of 1601, which was so admirably adapted to the needs of modern industry that in its essential features it has survived to this day.

The contribution of the new society to the problem of social legislation was, however, confined to the organization of charity. Society contented itself with compelling the poor man to work;

it did not attempt, as the cities of the Middle Ages would have done, to regulate the work itself. Until the 19th century it subjected labour to no restrictions, and this fact is eloquent of the capitalistic character which was henceforth the essential feature of the economic world.

It is therefore not surprising that from the second half of the 15th century, contemporaneously with free industry, and increasing with its expansion, a proletariat made its appearance whose history has yet to be written. It is true that there existed, in the Middle Ages, in the workers engaged in the cloth industry of Flanders and Florence, a class of wage-earners whose condition was very nearly that of the proletariat. It differed from the latter, however, in respect of the organization imposed upon it by the corporative system. Once he was excluded from this system, the modern proletarian was completely at the mercy of his employer. He had no redress against the employer; the public authorities gave him no assistance, since they abstained from intervention, and he had not even the help which spontaneous association might have furnished, for the workers were forbidden to form associations. Moreover, they were too wretched and too uneducated to organize themselves, and the authorities which refused to intervene on their behalf protected the employer, and were very ready to intervene in his interests if the workers, driven to extremities, declared a strike. Moreover, it must not be forgotten that the home industry, the general form of industrial organization until the end of the 18th century, was as favourable to the exploitation of the workers as it was unfavourable to any mutual co-operation and understanding. However, we must not exaggerate the importance of the proletariat, or that of unrestricted industry, during the three centuries that began about 1450. Despite its definitely capitalistic form and its continual progress, manufacture, even in those countries in which it was most advanced, still played only a limited part in the activities of the nation. The urban industry of the guilds and corporations, which, side by side with free manufacture, continued to supply the majority of the cities, very greatly hindered its progress. It was far less important than commerce, and above all, than agriculture, which everywhere remained the essential branch of production.

But in the domain of agriculture itself, what a revolution! Here too the advance of capitalism was profoundly felt. In some countries it had the effect of enfranchizing the peasant, while in others it forced him back into a state of servitude far completer, and above all, much harsher than that of the Middle Ages. The explanation of these contradictory consequences is not far to seek. In those countries which were economically the most advanced, like Italy and the Low Countries, the landowners, like the manufacturers (and for the same reasons), were inclined systematically to favour free labour.

Just as the trade corporations hampered the expansion of industrial capitalism, so the old hereditary ties which bound the peasant to the soil, and gave him rights over it, hampered the capitalism of the landowner. In the 14th century the seigneurs had hoped to increase their revenues by accentuating their rights over the villeins. They now saw that they had been following the wrong course. However strictly they were demanded and collected, the rights of *corvée*, *champart* (field rent paid in kind), *formariage* (dues payable when serfs married who belonged to different lords), etc. etc., never furnished more than an inconsiderable revenue, quite out of proportion to the value of the soil, which was increasing, thanks to the progress of commerce and the greater circulation of produce. The true means of benefiting by this plus value was by free farming, or the direct exploitation of the soil by means of free labourers, working for a wage. Thus, as early as the beginning of the 15th century we see that in Italy what was left of the ancient servitude was replaced by personal liberty. As early as 1415 a Florentine statute decreed the obligatory suppression of serfdom, of personal services in lieu of quit-rent, of the attachment of the man to the glebe, of all kinds of corvées, of all juridical conditions incompatible with personal liberty, and of all feudal or judicial subordination of the individual to the profit of another. In the Low Countries, from 1515 onwards, the prince issued a number of edicts whose purpose was to enfranchise both the man and the soil. In 1531 seigneurs were forbidden to demand of their tenants "gratuitous gifts, services, days of labour," etc., under penalty of twofold repayment and arbitrary punishment. In 1520 the establishment of new tithes was prohibited, and all seigneurial rights which had existed for less than forty years were abolished. Everywhere free farming was substituted for the ancient feudal and hereditary tenures. The enfranchisement of the peasants was in reality the enfranchisement of the landowner, who, having henceforth to deal with free men who were not attached to his land, could dispose of the latter by means of simple revocable contracts, whose brief duration enabled him to modify them in accordance with the increasing rent of the land. Here again, of course, we must not exaggerate the consequences of this innovation. Capitalism did not cause the disappearance of personal servitude in the rural districts, any more than it suppressed the trade corporations in the cities. Not until the French Revolution were both abolished by proclamation. But just as the trade corporations ceased to develop, and merely vegetated, after the 16th century, so what was left of serfdom was merely an archaism, a survival, a relic of a bygone epoch, which still obtained on the estates of a few abbeys or in the depths of the provinces. Wherever the new mode of life had penetrated it disappeared, being swept away as an inconvenient obstacle to progress.

Further, as serfdom disappeared, and in the same degree, the technical methods of agriculture were improved and modernized. In the 15th century the cultivation of rice was introduced in the Lombard plain; the rearing of silkworms became general in the Midi in the reign of Louis XI. In Flanders the method of triennial rotation of crops was abandoned. Fallow land was sown with clover, so that it no longer lay idle. Moreover, the general development of commerce impelled the landowners to specialize in production. Spain and England sacrificed the cultivation of cereals to sheep-farming, with a view to exporting the wool. It was the flocks of sheep that gradually made Castile the stony, treeless desert which it has become, and it was owing to sheep-farming that pastures began to cover a larger and larger area of the English soil, where the sheep replaced the peasant and his plough. From the reign of Henry VI onwards Parliament was continually passing Enclosure Acts, which authorized the conversion of arable soil into pasturage, driving the evicted tenants into the ranks of the proletariat, from which the manufacturers recruited their workers.

While in Western Europe the evolution of capitalism tended to make the peasant a farmer or a worker for wages, in Germany it created a new form of serfdom. The essential cause of this phenomenon, which is at first sight so surprising, must be sought in the omnipotence and brutality of the nobles, whom the territorial princes did not dare to oppose. As soon as the colonization of the Slav territories beyond the Elbe had ceased, which was towards the end of the 13th century, the nobles took advantage of the distress caused by the excess of population in order to oppress the rural class. If agriculture had been further advanced, or if industry had been more extensively developed, the peasant might have discovered new resources on the spot. But the feeble economic development of Germany delivered him, defenceless, into the hands of his seigneurs. And since then the situation had grown worse and worse. To the west of the Elbe the change had no particular consequences beyond a recrudescence of corvées, prestations, and arbitrary measures of every kind. But beyond the river, in Brandenburg, Prussia, Silesia, Austria, Bohemia, and Hungary, the most merciless advantage was taken of it. The descendants of the free colonists of the 13th century were systematically deprived of their land and reduced to the condition of personal serfs (*Leibeigene*). The wholesale exploitation of estates absorbed their holdings and reduced them to a servile condition which so closely approximated to that of slavery that it was permissible to sell the person of the serf independently of the soil. From the middle of the 16th century the whole of the region to the east of the Elbe and the Sudeten mountains became covered with *Rittergüter* exploited by *Junkers*, who may be compared, as regards the degree of humanity displayed in their treatment of their white slaves, with the planters of the West Indies. The negro in the New World, and the German peasant in the Old World, were the most typical victims of modern capitalism, and they both had to wait until the 19th century for their enfranchisement. This is a fact which must never be forgotten when considering the modern history of Germany and Austria. The enslavement of the peasant to his noble master explains many things.

The expansion of capitalism and the development of commerce and industry were followed by a general increase of population, analogous to that which characterized the 12th and 13th centuries. This must be attributed to the new fields which industry had opened to labour, and to the progress of trade, which put an end to those alimentary crises that had caused such cruel suffering as late as the 14th century. There were still periods of dearth, but there were no more famines. It is unfortunately impossible to estimate with any exactness the population of Europe in the 15th century. It would seem, however, that there may have been something like forty inhabitants per square kilometre in the two regions that were then most densely populated: Italy and the Low Countries. France, about 1550, seems to have had a population of something like 18,000,000. At the same date the commercial metropolis of the West, Antwerp, which had then reached its apogee, did not contain more than 100,000 inhabitants.

In respect of its social composition this population exhibited contrasts which were far more accentuated than those of the Middle Ages. The total amount of wealth had increased, but this increase was distributed in a very unequal manner. Practically no one profited by it excepting the great landowners, the nobles, the Church, the wholesale merchants, and the manufacturers. That middle class which was composed of small independent producers, which was so widely distributed in the 13th century, and whose turbulence gave the 14th century its tumultuous character, was visibly declining. In the cities a superannuated protectionist legislation enabled it to hold its own without progressing; in the rural districts it was ousted by the wholesale exploitation of the soil, free farming, or serfdom. On the other hand, the juridical demarcation of the classes was less rigid than of old. If the *noblesse* of the modern era seems in many respects to have been even prouder and more arrogant that that of the Middle Ages, that is because it felt the need of maintaining the social distinction, in respect of the "nouveaux riches," wchih the similarity of fortune, education, and interests might easily have led the latter to overlook. However, nothing could have been easier than for the new men to obtain letters patent which would enable them to enter into the ranks of the noblesse, and share in the prestige which it owed to tradition, but which was maintained by its wealth. Aristocracy and plutocracy—these, in the last resort, are perhaps the two words which best characterize the social transformation which was accomplished at the time of the Renaissance.

### 3. *Ideas and Manners*

There was, it seems, a rather striking difference between the intellectual evolution of Italy during the Renaissance and that of the countries lying to the north of the Alps. In Italy the new orientation of ideas, manners, and artistic feeling began at the very moment when the economic development of the nation had reached its apogee. It was not contemporary with this development, but subsequent to it, and while the intellectual movement continued to progress the economic development was already beginning to decline. This intellectual development was the fine flower of the entire civilization that preceded it; the product of thought and beauty succeeding to the product of force. This development was not unlike that of ancient Greece in the days of Pericles: Athens in the 4th century, and Florence in the middle of the 15th century, shone with a glory which was no longer commensurate with their real strength; the dazzling radiance which they shed upon the world, before they made way for more vigorous successors, had the splendour but also the ephemeral quality of a sunset. At the very moment when the genius of Machiavelli, Guiccardini, Raphael and Leonardo da Vinci was in flower, the discovery of the New World was diverting the current of European life from the Mediterranean.

The case was very different to the north of the Alps. Here the Renaissance was not a sunset but a sunrise. It meant the beginning, in every sense, and in every domain of social activity, of a new life, of which the economic phenomena that we have just been considering reveal only one aspect, and of which we have now to consider the moral physiognomy. The historian, unfortunately, is obliged to exhibit piecemeal matters that were parts of a concerted whole. But it must not be believed that capitalism provoked the renaissance of thought which was contemporaneous with it. The one and the other were different symptoms of the same crisis of growth. And it is curious to note that in each case the crisis was divided into two corresponding periods. What the discovery of the New World was for capitalism, the Italian Renaissance was for the intellectual movement. In its beginnings this intellectual movement was independent of the Renaissance, but the rapidity of its advance and the extent of its influence were explained by its submission to the guidance of the Renaissance.

To be sure, the symptoms of a new orientation of men's minds in the countries to the north of the Alps, about the middle of the 15th century, were not as yet very numerous nor very striking. Scholasticism in science, Gothic style in the arts, and the traditional forms in the literature of the vulgar tongue, were still incontestably predominant. The mysticism of the 14th century still survived, and in the *Imitation* it found its most complete expression. The great Flemish or Walloon painters of the Low Countries, Van Eyck, De la Pasture, Memling, etc., merely continued, by their genius, a long-established school. When the stupendous invention of printing made its appearance, about 1450, no one foresaw its future. Gutenberg himself had no idea of the future importance of the Press. All he had in view was to provide the clergy and students with cheaper manuscripts. His standpoint was that of the mere industrialist, and the humanists of Italy were at first disdainful of a discovery which in their opinion detracted from the charm and majesty of intellectual masterpieces by the cheapness and mechanical character of its products. Thus, even in the most lasting and most remarkable achievements of the period, in its most beautiful and most influential innovations, we do not find that it was opposed to the past. And yet, although it is very evident that it was largely a continuation of the past, it is none the less true that it did in some degree diverge from it. As in Italy, and before the influence of Italy had made itself felt, life was beginning to escape from the custody of tradition; here, as in Italy, the ascetic morality of the Middle Ages was beginning to lose its authority. The relaxation of morals in the 15th century, and the predominance of temporal interests, were no less striking in Northern Europe than in Italy. And they were most perceptible in countries whose civilization was most advanced. The Low Countries, under the Dukes of Burgundy, between France and England, the one exhausted by war and the other a prey to civil discord, were enjoying a period of peace and prosperity, and they afforded a spectacle which presented curious analogies with that of Italy. One might have observed, at the court, in the society of the great nobles, and among the government officials and the capitalists, whether landowners or merchants, a kind of life whose principal features were precisely those which are commonly attributed to the early Renaissance in Tuscany and Lombardy: a general relaxation of morality, a love of luxury and social festivities, a demand for elegance and comfort in private dwellings, a pronounced taste for fine clothing, and for the nobler pleasures of art, and the general diffusion of education and good breeding. Here, very obviously, we see that the aristocracy of birth, like the aristocracy of wealth, was living a social life of a kind that no longer had anything in common with the conventional *cortesia* of the Middle Ages. Philip the Good and Charles the Bold patronized artists, surrounded themselves with painters and musicians, and founded a library whose splendour is attested by the remnants which have survived to this day. In 1465 the Sieur de la Grunthuse built in Bruges a spacious hotel, the handsome, roomy and comfortable habitation of a *grand seigneur* who was at the same time a passionate lover of books, and the patron of Colard Mansion, who had just introduced the art of printing to Bruges. The chancellor Rolin and the treasurer Bladelin commissioned pictures by Van Eyck and De la Pasture. And it is enough to recall the adorable landscapes which assuredly contributed to the success of the Belgian school of painting in the 15th century in order to realize that the discovery of Nature at this period was by no means a purely Italian discovery. The same may be said of the discovery of the individual. The individual portrait was painted as truthfully and conscientiously by the brush of Van Eyck and De la Pasture as by the pen of Chastellain and Commines. And in the work of these last two, I believe, we may see the begininngs of the modern Press; already seeking, in the case of the former, to embellish itself, though clumsily enough as yet, with the prestige of style, and nourished, by the latter, with thought so vigorous that almost the only pendant to his *Mémoires* is *The Prince* of Machiavelli.

This worldliness of manners and of thought in and about the court of Burgundy was also to be observed, though in a less degree, in France and England. Is it not a striking fact that the first mistress of the King of France whose name has been recorded by history was Agnes Sorel? It must not be supposed, of course, that the kings of the Middle Ages had no mistresses. Edward I gave a fief for the purpose of *custodiendi Domino Regi sex damisellas scil. meretrices ad usum Domini Regis*. But in the case of Agnes the king's favourite showed herself in public, and had become something more than a *meretrix*. I admit that this was hardly a symptom of an improvement in morals, but it is a proof that their relaxation was accompanied by their refinement. In England the Duke of Gloucester (the husband of Jacqueline) caused a scandal by the gallantry of his manners, but he also earned the admiration of scholars for the library which he bequeathed to Oxford. We see here the beginning of a kind of "gallantry" which was the very antithesis of the "courtesy" of the Middle Ages; but we must not forget the court's increasing taste for luxury, which to some extent explained the accumulations of such fortunes as that of Jacques Cœur. We should note, moreover, that the private hotels—the Hotel Grunthuse at Bruges, the Hotel Cœur at Bourges, the Hotel Bourgtheroulde at Rouen—were all of the 15th century, and there had been no such buildings previously. No doubt the love of luxury contributed to the spread of that venality which was so strikingly apparent in the political life of the day, as we may learn from Commines. But this luxury, as we may judge from the paintings of the time, was not purely material. It valued art and literature. I believe the 15th century may be regarded as the period when laymen began to read. It is interesting to ask what they read. What was the nature of the literature in the vulgar tongue? What were the first books to be printed? When Caxton established his printing-press in London, his customers, who consisted for the most part of noblemen, but included also a city haberdasher, asked him to produce translations from the French and Latin. He himself translated the Aeneid. His principal purpose was to provide reading for noblemen. Naturally, antiquity furnished only part of the reading-matter of that time. People read everything, eagerly, and without exercising much choice. The old heroic literature was metamorphosed into simple romances. People read, wholesale, moralities, the *Golden Legend*, *The Dictes of the philosophres*, *The Fayttes of Chyualrye*, etc. The printing-press did not create the taste for reading, for that already existed, but it hastened its diffusion. Would it be too much to say that the aristocracy had begun to read again for the first time since the age of Charlemagne? But the great difference between the 15th century and the age of Charlemagne and the Middle Ages was that the culture which the men of the 15th century acquired by reading was purely secular. The Church had no part in it. Very visibly, the world was beginning to take an interest in the things of the intellect. Edward IV was interested in Caxton's translation of Cicero, and the translation of the *Ordre de Chevalerie* was dedicated to Richard III. In France, Louis XI accorded his patronage to the first printer. The Dukes of Burgundy, Margaret of York, Earl Rivers, Margaret Duchess of Somerset, and many others, were munificent patrons.

We cannot doubt that in all these people there was an insatiable thirst for learning: an awakening—unconscious, I believe, but none the less an awakening—of curiosity, eager to see beyond the two narrow frontiers within which the traditions of caste and religion had hitherto imprisoned it. In the 14th century Maerlant thought it proper that laymen should be given only works by the clergy. And now people were turning away from such works. All this secular literature was produced outside the Church. It was, however, fertile rather than elegant. Only the rhetoricians were concerned with the art of writing.

I think we must say that the essential feature of this period was the fact that a public was coming into being for literature as well as for art. The artists who worked for this public were great artists. The writers, on the other hand, were nearly all third-rate. And this, I think, can be explained, as far as literary mysteries can ever be explained. The fact is that all the traditional types of literature were dead. There was only a desiccated literature, as at the close of the 15th century; the literature which was a survival. Could it have renewed itself without help? Who can say? In any case, the impulse came from without; potent and irresistible, it came from Italy. It was an overwhelming influence, and even art bowed to the fashion and proceeded to become Italianate. It was a phenomenon like that of Romanticism at the beginning of the 19th century.

The Renaissance began to make itself felt at the end of the 15th century; in all the arts at first, excepting music; and in the arts its influence was essentially Italian, and not classic; just as the invasion of Gothic art in Europe had been essentially French. But here we should note a symptomatic effect. Gothic art was propagated outside France by the Church. The Italian art of the Renaissance, on the contrary, was propagated through the profane arts, and the Church was the last stronghold that it penetrated. Those who patronized it were the kings and the great nobles. Francis I sent for Leonardo da Vinci to come to his court. Guillaume de Clèves and Margaret of Austria made it the fashion in the Low Countries. Were not the first buildings of the new style in France the châteaux of the Loire? In short, the new orientation of taste was wholly profane and worldly in its origin.

It was otherwise with the intellectual influence of the Renaissance, which could make itself felt only through the medium of Latin, and which, unlike the artistic influence, was classical rather than Italian. The "New Learning," as the English called it, was a direct return to antiquity, provoked, of course, by the example of the humanists, but not subordinated to them. It is true that there had been humanists in the North, and especially poets, like Pierre Gilles and the author of the *Basia*, Jean Second, while the *Certamen poeticum Haftianum* of Amsterdam was in the direct line of descent.

Longolius of Malines belonged to the same school. But not so the great writers: neither Roechlin in Germany, nor Colet and More in England, nor the greatest of all, Erasmus. The literature of antiquity influenced them less by its form than by enfranchising their thought. It enfranchised it from the scholastic tradition, not only by means of the classic tongue, which they immediately adopted, but by the new standpoint which it gave them. The *Miles Christianus* of Erasmus might be described as their programme. And what do we find in it? The secular spirit! By no means the anti-religious spirit; on the contrary. But religion is envisaged as an exhortation to morality, addressed to the honest man. The ideal is no longer asceticism, but the life of the citizen, with all its duties. This had been considered as something accessory, to be regarded almost with tolerance; now it became the essential thing. Hence the aggressive sarcasms of Erasmus, the insults addressed by Ulrich von Hutten to the monks and *magistri nostri* (*Epistolae obscurorum virorum*, 1515). But hence, also, a whole plan of reforms, with a view to the future, and especially pedagogic reforms, which would replace the schools of the clergy by new schools, in which children should be educated in the cult of *belles lettres*, and in which "politesse" would have its place in a training which was to prepare the pupil not for the cloister, but for life. The *Adagia* of Erasmus, which appeared in 1500, exercised a pedagogical influence comparable only to that of Rousseau's *Émile*. For the first time, in the Renaissance, it was seen that the function of the school was to impart intellectual culture. One may say that the whole organization of education to this day is based on the conception of education evolved by these northern humanists. For them, the object of education was the free development of the personality. Hence, of course, the attacks upon the methods and the asceticism of the Church, which had their logical and final consequence in the "fais ce que vouldras" of the Abbey of Thélème. More, like Erasmus, was opposed to monasticism, asceticism, the celibacy of priests, and the worship of relics; and both, if the truth be told, tended to transform Christianity into a *philosophia evangelica*. But they went further: they wished to change not only the ecclesiastical tradition, but the entire social tradition, and if we can compare the *Adagia* to *Émile*,we can also compare the *Moriae encomium* (The Praise of Folly) and the *Utopia* to the *Contrat social*. It is true that in the North the spirit of the Renaissance was revolutionary, but it was purely theoretical, and it contented itself with verbal onslaughts, of which the *Gargantua* of Rabelais may be regarded as the synthesis. It made war upon the Church. It spared the State, hoping that the progress of enlightenment would win acceptation for its opinions.

In return, all the social authorities made much of the humanist, just as they made much of the philosophers before the French Revolution. No doubt they saw nothing more dangerous than a *jeu d'esprit* in the *Utopia*, in which More showed them a society founded on religious toleration, with universal education, community of goods, and compulsory labour. Perhaps they were chiefly impressed by the attacks upon the monks and the Scholastics. It was these attacks that were responsible for the prodigious success of the *Moriae encomium* (1509), the most widely read book of its time. And this is not surprising. Did not More, like Erasmus, proclaim the superiority of the secular life over that of the cloister? In their optimism they believed that the world might be changed. Vivès wanted the *Utopia* to be placed in the hands of schoolboys, together with the *Colloquia*. If governments, and even popes and kings, applauded these books, as did all the high officials also, it was because they were careful to avoid political discussion. Their attitude was precisely that of Voltaire. In order that enlightenment should triumph, they had need of a strong government, an authority superior to the parties, more powerful than the Church. Like all intellectuals, they were, though they did not confess it, in favour of the "intelligent despot." The revolution of which they dreamed was to be carried out from above, because they expected that it would be the work essentially of science and reason. No doubt they wanted to extend its benefits to all men, but it must begin at the top, and as for the means by which it was to be brought about, they relied on the social aristocracy, hoping for the final constitution of an intellectual aristocracy. In 1517 Jerome Busleyden, acting on the advice of Erasmus, founded at Louvain the "College of the Three Tongues," whose purpose was to apply, through the knowledge of the three current languages (Latin, Greek and Hebrew), the philological method to the Holy Scriptures, independently of all positive theology. A little later Francis I installed and endowed the Collège de France in Paris. Wolsey, with the same object, founded the "Cardinal College"—later Christ Church—at Oxford. Henry VIII was as great a patron of the Hellenists and the innovators as was Francis I in France. When in 1514 the quarrel broke out between Roechlin and the University of Cologne, in respect of the opinion expressed by Rome concerning the sacred books of the Jews, the Emperor, the Cardinal-Bishop of Gurk, the Elector of Saxony, the Duke of Bavaria, and the Margrave of Baden all supported Roechlin, and the Pope, when he bade Cologne be silent, made no secret of his own sympathies. In vain did the Dominicans protest and raise outcries of heresy; they were merely treated with disdain. It seemed as though the immense fabric of Scholasticism was on the point of being overthrown, as so many Gothic castles had been overthrown, and rebuilt in a contemporary style. Only in Spain was it holding its own; the Renaissance affected only its form, but left the Catholic spirit untouched.

Everywhere else, during the twenty years which elapsed between the end of the 15th century and the appearance of Protestantism,[1] it seemed as though a new world was on the point of birth. All that was strong and youthful and vigorous revolted against the past. Never, perhaps, have the social authorities so unanimously supported an intellectual movement. It seemed as though there were no conservatives left among them. All were moving and straining in the same direction: authority, society, fashion, the politicians, the women, the artists, the humanists. There was a boundless confidence abroad, a feverish joy. The mind was liberated from authority, was free to wander under the heavens; the monopoly of knowledge was abolished, and it was now the possession of the whole community. And the knowledge that was derived from antiquity was all the more seductive, inasmuch as it went

[1] Luther exposed his theses in 1517.

hand in hand with beauty, and was, so to speak, almost identical with beauty.

This species of Roman patriotism, which did something to contribute to the success of the Renaissance in Italy, did not exist in the North. There antiquity was regarded more objectively, valued for its own sake, as the source of beauty and wisdom. Possibly, if it inspired less affection, it was regarded with all the more respect. And men were more conscious of its liberating force, for Scholasticism had never enjoyed the same predominance in Italy as beyond the Alps. In France, England and Germany it was far more aggressive than in Italy. In adopting the Latin of the classics as their language, the humanists of the South were bent merely on continuing the work of the ancients; those of the North were eager to indicate, by its adoption, their break with *magistri nostri*. The barbarous style for which they quite wrongly reproached the Latin of the universities and the Scholastics—forgetting that it was an artificial and scientific language, perfectly adapted to its purpose—seemed to them eloquent of the barbarity, crudity, and absurdity of the ideas which it expressed. However, they did not undertake to attack the philosophy of the Middle Ages; they were content to despise it. For them, everything had to be reconstructed. Theology must be reconstructed, beginning with the study of the sacred texts. The great achievement of Erasmus was a Greek edition of the New Testament with Latin translation and paraphrase. As for morality, based on a Christian foundation, it must be remodelled and adapted to the necessities of secular life.

When we speak of the rationalism of the Renaissance, we must realize that it did not proceed beyond the limits of common sense. The liberty of thought which it claimed for man stopped short of the great religious and philosophical problems. Its standpoint was purely human and terrestrial. It did not attack the problems of destiny and the origin of the world; in this connection it accepted the Christian ideas. Its philosophy did not venture beyond the domain of practical morality and politics, and the commonplaces of the ancients on these subjects were accepted as the final utterance of wisdom. It was quite ready to admit the existence of mysterious and demoniacal powers beyond the limits of the visible world. It is interesting to note that this rationalism coincided with a recrudescence of magical practices, and it uttered no protests against the increasing frequency of the abominable trials for witchcraft, which must never be forgotten if we are to form an accurate notion of the mentality of the new era.

What this rationalism brought with it, then, was not free thought in the actual sense of the word, but what might be described as an intellectual and moral liberalism. Now liberalism is synonymous with individualism, and assuredly one of the most definite consequences of the Renaissance was that it substituted for the social conception of the Middle Ages, according to which the world was a hierarchy of perfectly distinct classes, each having its own function and rights and duties, the idea that worth and esteem are purely personal things, appertaining to every man, by virtue not of his rank, but of his merit. It is interesting to observe that in this connection the Renaissance placed on earth what the Church had reserved for heaven. For while the Church admitted and approved of inequality, the result of mundane relations, it made salvation depend only on personal merit, so that the individual, whatever rank he might have occupied here below, would assume, in the face of Divine justice, and in the eternal life, the rank of which he was worthy. This difference is perhaps deserving of remark, for is it not a striking proof of the essentially secular and mundane inspiration that animated the Renaissance?

But let us at once admit that the liberalism of the Renaissance was an aristocratic liberalism. By no means did it proclaim the rights of man, but only, in the words of Rabelais, the rights of men who were "free, well born, well educated, and conversant with honest company." In short, its ideal was the *vir bonus dicendi peritus* of antiquity; that is, the "honnête homme," the "gentleman" of the modern era. It regarded the privileges of birth as absurd, but it insisted, all the more vigorously, on the privileges of intellectual culture. In this its point of view approximated pretty closely to that of antiquity. Regarded in this sense, Rousseau's declaration that the arts and letters were destructive of equality is a protest against society as envisaged by the Renaissance. The opposition between the freeman and the slave was replaced by the opposition between the literate and the illiterate. The Renaissance felt nothing but disdain for "mechanic trades," and the prejudice in favour of the liberal professions, which survives to this day, dates from the Renaissance. This prejudice was doubtless largely responsible for the indifference to the lot of the lower classes which characterizes the modern era. Moral ideas have surely played as much part in this as the economic interests of landowners and capitalists.

Taking a bird's-eye view, it is obvious that society, as it evolved, after the beginning of the 16th century, under the influence of the Renaissance, presents a less imposing spectacle than the society of the Middle Ages, governed, instructed, and inspired by the Church, with its hierarchy of classes, sharing between them the work of society, subordinating the individual to the community of which he was a member, and inspiring one and all with the same religious faith and the same Christian ideal. But what had happened? The incessant wear and tear of life had undermined the foundations of the majestic edifice; since the end of the 14th century it had been foundering on every side, and the Renaissance merely accelerated the inevitable ruin. The organic unity which was lacking in the modern world would, however, be compensated for by the prodigious animation provoked and maintained by the enfranchisement of thought and action. In order to arrive at a just appreciation of the Renaissance, we must remember that for three hundred years the art and literature of every people have been evolving in the direction which it struck out for itself. If we work back against the current of evolution we come at last to the Renaissance. One might liken our civilization to a river which became navigable only from the point where the affluent of antiquity mingled its waters with the stream. Of course, the river has its source at a much remoter point, but its upper reaches are accessible only with difficulty; to explore them, to become familiar with their aspect, so that we can understand them, requires a considerable effort. Barely a century has elapsed since the Middle Ages ceased to be regarded with disdain. But in spite of the reaction which has occurred in their favour, they are so remote from us that we cannot blend them with our own life in a really intimate fashion. More often than not, Neo-Gothicism[1] is merely the form affected by ideas and tendencies which are in reality extremely modern. The Renaissance, on the contrary, still surrounds us on every hand. It was only yesterday that Renaissance furniture began to disappear from our houses. Despite the admirable vigour of contemporary art, our governments continue to maintain their "Écoles de Rome," their "travelling scholarships," while our Athenaeums, Lyceums and Gymnasiums are merely the continuation of the Latin schools of the 16th century. From the Renaissance, too, dates the development of the sciences; for a long while they exerted no influence upon human history, accumulating the new knowledge in silence, until, at the end of the 18th century, the spate of discoveries, increasing our knowledge of Nature, led to a second renaissance of thought, and thanks to the progress of technique, multiplied a hundredfold the output of human effort.

Nevertheless, the influence of the Renaissance upon civilization was by no means so efficacious as its early years might have led man to expect. Another force, even more powerful—the religious Reformation—began to clash with it at the very moment when it was beginning to trace the direction of intellectual progress, and it was their twofold action, sometimes combined, but more often opposed, that determined the destinies of the modern world.

[1] The allusion here is to the "neo-Gothic" architecture which flourished, especially in Belgium, before the war.

## CHAPTER II

# THE REFORMATION

### 1. *Lutheranism*

The victory of the Pope over the Councils had enabled the Church to retain its monarchical constitution, but it could not and it did not restore to the Holy See the European hegemony which it had lost since the pontificate of Boniface VIII. In vain did Pius II solemnly remind the Catholic princes (1460) of their subordination to the sovereign pontiff; the princes were so well aware of the emptiness of this pretension that they did not even think it worth while to protest against it. Though Pius obtained from Louis XI the withdrawal of the Pragmatic Sanction, this merely gratified his vanity. The monarch, whose complaisance was rewarded with the title of "Most Christian King," was happy to be rid of the guarantees with which the Pragmatic Sanction encompassed the episcopal elections, and hastened to profit by their disappearance by exercising a stricter control over the clergy of France. In England, Spain, and the Burgundian States—in short, wherever the monarchy was powerful—Rome was unable to prevent it from disposing as it pleased of the highest ecclesiastical dignities, and contented herself with the marks of deference which the monarchy lavished upon her on the condition that it was allowed to do as it chose. The prestige of Rome was so definitely on the down grade that her exhortations to arm against the Turks were almost disregarded. No doubt the deplorable impotence which Europe displayed in the face of these Barbarians was explained mainlv by the rivalries, jealousies, and divergent interests of the States; nevertheless, we are bound to regard it as in some degree the result of their indifference toward the head of the Church. At the summons of Urban II Christendom had risen with enthusiasm against the Musulmans of Syria, who were not threatening it; to the appeal of Pius II, despite the imminence of the danger, it remained indifferent; unmoved, it saw the successor of Peter reduced to "taking the Cross" himself, and dying of grief and fatigue at Ancona on embarking for the Holy War (1463). The Venetian fleet, with which he was to have sailed, hastened to turn back when the news of his death became known.

Henceforth, the Papacy was a political power only in Italy, and even there it was greatly inferior to Venice, the King of Naples, the Medici, and the Sforza. In order to maintain itself at all it was obliged to divert, to the profit of its temporal power, a good part of the resources which it derived from Christendom; so that its spiritual primacy over the Catholic world seemed often to be subordinated to its territorial interests. The prince often seemed to take precedence of the Pope in the person of the sovereign pontiff, the more so as the tiara was now conferred only upon Italians: Adrian VI (1521–1523) was to be the last of the ultramontane Popes. By thus Italianizing itself the Papacy escaped in some degree from the interference of the great powers, but it also became more alien to them, since it was imbued with a national character which assorted ill with its oecumenical mission. It is not surprising that under such circumstances nepotism should have made the most alarming progress in the bosom of the Curia. Each Pope profited by his elevation to assure the future of his family, and of his policy, by introducing, without regard for their capacity or their morals, the greatest possible number of his kinsmen into the Sacred College. Already the cardinals of Avignon had caused distress to the many pious souls. But what can we say of those of the 15th century! Even in the world of the Renaissance, accustomed to the extreme licence of court life, their appointment was regarded as a scandal. We have to go back to the 10th century, to the days of Theodore, Marosia, and John XII, to find a spectacle of moral anarchy comparable with that which was offered by Rome under the pontificate of Alexander VI (1492–1503), and even by the pontificates of Julius II and Leo X. Again, the brutality of the feudal system afforded some excuse for the 10th century which could not be adduced in favour of the end of the 15th century. Imagine what an impression a believer must have carried away from the capital of the Christian world at a time (1490) when there were 6,800 courtesans in Rome, when the Popes and cardinals consorted publicly with their mistresses, acknowledged their bastards, and enriched them at the cost of the Church! It was really too much that a Borgia should have been able to sit on the throne of St. Peter. There is an only too painful contrast between what the Papacy should have been and what it actually was; and one would have liked to find more religious sincerity in the patrons of Bramante, Raphael, and Michelangelo. Wonderful though the achievements of the Renaissance may have been in Rome, there was something repulsive about it; the splendour which it conferred upon the metropolis of the Catholic world made it too sadly unlike the Rome of the great mediaeval Popes. The successors of Innocent III and Boniface VIII were so steeped in the new spirit that they no longer respected the tradition to which they owed what ascendancy they still retained over the world. It almost seems as though for them the Church was no more than a means of asserting their personal eminence, and that it was to their greater glory, rather than to that of Christ, that so many monuments were erected, so many works of art produced.

The Church fulfilled its religious mission hardly better than the Papacy. Discontented or discouraged by the defeat of the Councils, it fell into a state of apathy, tolerant of abuses, and of the laxity which their persistence seemed to justify. The higher clergy, almost entirely recruited from among the protégés of the Curia or the courts of the princes, were complete worldlings. Many bishops received the order of priesthood, if they received it at all, only when they took possession of their sees, and it was evidently a mere formality; as regards the majority, their morals made it plain that it caused them little inconvenience. Some, in accordance with the tastes of the day, took pleasure in posing as humanists, and gained a reputation as patrons of the arts. Others, interested in politics, spent more time at court than in their dioceses. Nearly all lived a full and joyous life, hunting, drinking and otherwise diverting themselves. Naturally, the Chapters were no better. As a general thing their prebends were reserved for the younger sons of influential families, many of whom did not take orders, did not wear clerical costume, hardly ever officiated, and publicly kept concubines. The incumbents of parishes generally contented themselves with collecting the revenues of their cure, which was administered by an assistant, who was paid a salary that barely enabled him to live. Despised by his parishioners on account of his poverty, he was obliged to make money in any way he could, overcharging for his services in respect of births, marriages and deaths. As for the monasteries, their decadence was all the more deplorable, inasmuch as more zeal, austerity and learning might have been expected of them. It may fairly be said that at the beginning of the 16th century they were all vegetating in routine and mechanical obedience to their rule. Those truly pious souls who still sought refuge in the monasteries found themselves ill at ease in the midst of companions who were completely without ideals, and asked of the cloister nothing but a quiet, comfortable and secure existence. Only the Dominicans still displayed a certain activity. But since Scholasticism had done its work, there was nothing left for them but their inquisitorial duties, and for lack of heresies to cope with they devoted themselves to the study of demonology. In 1487 two of them published, at Strasbourg, the *Malleus Maleficarum*, an abominable treatise on the crimes of witches.

Such a clergy was bound to shock public opinion. The contrast was too striking between its conduct and the consideration which it demanded, the privileges which it enjoyed, and the revenues at its disposal. The aristocracy despised it for its vulgarity and ignorance, while the bourgeoisie was scandalized by its financial or judicial immunities. The governments were already beginning to take measures against the multiplication of estates subject to mortmain, and the intervention of ecclesiastical tribunals in civil causes.

However, the faith was still intact. Since the 12th century, it would really seem that there had never been so few heretics as during the fifty years that preceded the outbreak of Protestantism.

Wycliffism in England and Hussitism in Bohemia were almost extinct. And this in itself is a proof of the religious lukewarmness of the age. No one deserted the Church, or dreamed of doing so; but religion had become little more than a habit, a rule of life for those who observed the letter rather than the spirit. Hence the success of the indulgences, of which the Papacy, always short of money, was continually authorizing new emissions on all sorts of pretexts. Those who bought them forgot, of course, that contrition was indispensable to their efficacy, and believed that they were simply taking out an insurance against the risks of the future life. Naturally, this did not apply to all. There were still ardent and religious souls for whom faith was a vital necessity. But they, more often than not, sought satisfaction outside the Church, in some form of individual mysticism.

And yet at the beginning of the 16th century mysticism was far less widespread than in the middle of the previous century. The general tendency of thought was too completely opposed to it. As the influence of the Renaissance became more widely diffused, the choicer spirits envisaged religion less as an introduction to the future life than as a moral doctrine. The ideal of humanity conceived by Erasmus, More, and Vivès was completely pervaded by Christianity, but by a Christianity which was adapted, so to speak, to the necessities of earthly existence. Hence their antipathy to asceticism and the traditional theology. They had very little regard for dogma, and virtue seemed to them the supreme form of piety. For the rest, though they vigorously attacked the monks and did not conceal their disdain for the Scholastic morality, they were careful not to attack the Church. They were Catholics of a rather troublesome character, but they were Catholics; the higher clergy, the European courts, and the Pope himself did not conceal their sympathy for them. They hoped, without sensationalism, without a crisis, merely by the influence of intellectual progress, common sense, and learning, and thanks to the support of the social authorities, to bring about a religious reformation full of moderation, breadth, and tolerance.

This pleasing dream lasted only for a moment. It was, as a matter of fact, impossible of realization, for the anti-ascetic Christianity of the humanist had nothing in common with that of the Church, and there would inevitably have been a rupture between the two if time had permitted. The theologians who made common cause against Erasmus saw this plainly enough, and if the Pope compelled them to keep silence it was because the Church was so infatuated with the Renaissance that it could not immediately perceive the danger. The higher clergy paid court to the Erasmians much as the French nobility paid court to the "philosophers" at the end of the 18th century. The former no more expected a religious revolution than the latter anticipated a political revolution. There was nothing, indeed, that could have enabled anyone to foresee the sudden explosion of Lutheranism. Of course, since the lamentable end of the Council of Basle, Germany had been seething with a sullen dissatisfaction with the Papacy. This had been accused of disposing, as of sovereign right, of the highest ecclesiastical dignities, and its accusers never reflected that this was a direct consequence, not of any ill-will to the German nation, but of the anarchical constitution of the Empire, which excluded any possibility of subjecting the Church, as in France, England or Spain, to the power of the State. The humanists, for their part, aggravated this bad feeling. It infuriated them that the Italians should speak of the Northern peoples as barbarians, and in their vanity they boasted, in classical Latin, of their descent from those Germans who had once victoriously called a halt to the ambition of Rome. In their writings, and above all in those of Ulrich von Hutten, we find for the first time, expressed with some naïvete, an opposition of Germanism and Romanism at which we should be tempted to smile if the political passions of the 19th century had not exploited it, with such blind fury, to the detriment of civilization. These declamations did not go beyond a small clan of scholars, but they none the less contributed in their way to the maintenance of an anti-Roman mentality. Moreover, had not the Emperors of the Middle Ages found in the Popes their constant adversaries? Whether in its pagan or in its Catholic form, Rome was thus regarded as the perpetual enemy of the German people.

To these complaints of wounded vanity the bourgeoisie added more concrete grievances. As everywhere, it was impatient of the immunities of the clergy, and showed itself rather brutally anti-clerical when any incident provided it with a pretext. But nowhere was there any manifestation of the need of religious reform. Men were accustomed to tradition, and they accepted it. It would be incorrect to suppose that Germany was devoured by a spiritual thirst which the Church was no longer able to assuage—that it felt itself cabined and confined in Catholicism, and was seeking to unite itself more intimately with God. It is only too easy to point to a religious opposition between the Germanic and the Latin soul. Reality shows us nothing of the kind. Although Protestantism was born in Germany, and while the form which it first assumed, and its early progress, can only be explained by the German environment in which it was born, this is no proof whatever of its alleged Germanic character. It would be only too easy to oppose the Frenchman, Calvin, to the German Luther. The Reformation was a religious phenomenon; it was not a national phenomenon, and although it is true that it was most widely diffused among those peoples that spoke the Germanic tongues, this was not because it found in these countries minds which were specially qualified to understand it, but because it was there favoured by political and social conditions which it did not encounter elsewhere.

Luther belonged to the number of those who, in all countries and in all ages, are troubled in the most secret places of their hearts by religious problems which are more readily felt than defined. Born in 1483, the son of a miner of Eisleben (in Saxony), he, like so many other sons of the people, after distinguishing himself at school, was destined by his father for the jurist's career. He had been studying in the University of Erfurt since 1501, when in 1505, terrified by the idea of death, which had nearly taken him during a thunderstorm, he renounced his career and assumed the robe of a monk in an Augustinian monastery. Like so many others, he failed to find spiritual peace in the ascetic life, and in 1508 he was relieved at being chosen by the general of the order to fill a chair in the faculty of theology in the University of Wittenberg. There, in 1517, his famous thesis against the sale of indulgences made him suddenly emerge from his obscurity, and inaugurated the Reformation.

Had Luther already decided to break with the Church? It is difficult to say. But his fiery and obstinate temper, excited by contradiction, soon drove him to extremes. Moreover, he was encouraged by public opinion. The protests of the Diet of Augsburg in 1518 against the exactions of the pontifical fiscality must have fortified his resolution. He had confidence in himself, he was by nature a fighter, and he was supported, in the contest, by the fire of the orator and the pen of the pamphleteer. Like Wycliffe and Huss, he wanted to address the nation, and it was in the national tongue that he wrote. Nothing could have been better calculated to rouse and win his fellow-countrymen than his humorous, passionate, angry style. Moreover, the printing-press of his little University of Wittenberg sent his mighty words all over Germany. Almost as soon as the quarrel began the sound of it filled the country. For the first time a religious question was debated in the hearing of the people, was brought within its competence and submitted to its judgement. The *Letter to the German Nobles*, and the little treatises entitled *The Babylonian Captivity of the Church* and *The Liberty of the Christian*, all published in 1520, were, so to speak, propagandist pamphlets, and their success was prodigious. Until then, the doctrine of the adversaries of the Church had been spread by preaching and apostleship. Lutheranism was propagated by means of letterpress, and in the rapidity of its diffusion we see the first manifestation of the power of the Press.

As Luther fought his battle his thought became more definite and bolder. The debate concerning indulgences transformed itself almost immediately into an attack upon the Papacy, and then an attack upon the whole traditional organization of the Church. In 1518 the question was merely whether an appeal should be made from the Pope to the Council. But no later than the following year the Papacy was proclaimed an institution of purely human origin; the Council itself was said to be capable of error, and Scripture alone was infallible. In 1520 the decisive step was taken:

the Christian was justified by his faith, not by his works; faith in Christ made every Christian a priest; the Mass, and all the sacraments excepting Baptism, the Eucharist, and Penitence, were rejected; the clergy had no privileges that were not possessed by lay society; both were subject to the power of the secular sword, whose authority was extended to the Church as well as to the State.

Luther was merely advancing still further upon the path which had been trodden before his time by Wycliffe and John Huss. His theology was a continuation of the dissident theology of the Middle Ages; his ancestors were the great heretics of the 14th century; he was absolutely untouched by the spirit of the Renaissance. His doctrine of justification by faith was related to the doctrines of the mystics, and although, like the humanists, though for very different motives, he condemned celibacy and the ascetic life, he was in absolute opposition to them in his complete sacrifice of free-will and reason to faith.

However, the humanists did not fail to applaud his sensational début. They applauded him discreetly, it is true, like people who were anxious not to compromise themselves. They were a little disquieted by so much violence, but delighted with the smashing blows rained upon the monks and the Scholastics; after all this uproar men would listen more willingly to their moderation and their wisdom. Wherever the spirit of humanism prevailed Lutheranism, in its beginnings, was regarded with sympathy: in the Low Countries, at the court of Margaret of Austria, and in France, at the court of Francis I. And as for Germany, there the new movement was received not only with sympathy but with enthusiasm. The bourgeoisie of the free cities of the South especially, more turbulent and more active than those of the North, gave their immediate support to the new movement. But to tell the truth, the religious ideas of the reformer were understood only by a very small number of genuinely pious souls. The enthusiasm of the masses was excited mainly by the attacks upon the clergy and upon Rome. The doctrine of justification by faith was beyond their comprehension, and so far no one was thinking of a dogmatic rupture with the Church, but the masses were profoundly moved by the fiery attacks upon the traffic in holy things, and in the sacraments, upon the abuses of the monastic life, and finally, upon the arrogance of the priests who proclaimed that they were the Church, whereas the Church belonged to all Christians. Already numbers of monks were deserting the cloisters; and priests, preaching from the pulpit, proclaimed their adhesion to the movement. People were beginning to read and interpret the Bible. They were filled with naïve indignation against the clergy who had so long deceived them by concealing from them the true religion contained in the Holy Book. Among the nobles there was a party which was inspired with no less ardour. The knights who gathered about Ulrich von Hutten and Franz von Sickingen were moved alike by German patriotism and by hatred of Rome, and they hoped vaguely for a regeneration of the Empire, both political and religious. Meanwhile, the princes were pondering the situation. What seductive prospects were offered by the hope of secularizing the ecclesiastical estates! How much more attractive was the Word of God, how much more seductive the task of helping the cause of the Gospel to triumph, if the good work was going to facilitate the most profitable of business transactions! To tell the truth, among the very great majority of its first adherents Lutheranism was far more a revolt against the Papacy than a genuine religious awakening.

Its progress was greatly facilitated by the fact that the Church had no defenders. Neither the people nor the princes came to its aid. For its own part, it displayed an amazing apathy. It is true that a few theologians conducted polemics against Luther, but the Church made no attempt to influence the masses who, after so long obeying it, had suddenly turned against it. It was as though it doubted its own strength, and its impotence, in the midst of such a conflict, naturally increased the audacity of its adversaries. Luther had no hesitation in burning the Bull that condemned him in the Wittenberg market-place (December 10th, 1520).

The Emperor Maximilian died on January 12th, 1519, at the very moment when the crisis was about to assume its gravest aspect. But this did not in any way influence the decision of the Electors. In choosing between Francis I and Charles V it was not the religious question, but simply the question of money that made them vote for the latter.

There was no doubt as to what the new Emperor's attitude would be in respect of the Reformation. Even if he had felt any sympathy for it, his policy would have prevented him from showing it. His power was founded above all upon Spain, and was it likely that the King of Spain would compound with heresy? Moreover, how could Charles have dreamed of embroiling himself with the Papacy at the very moment when its support was indispensable if he was to hold his own against the French invasion of Italy? His most obvious interests, and his personal convictions, combined to make him the defender of the Church. It was not that he was wilfully blind to the abuses of the Church; he called most urgently for a general Council, and he most vigorously opposed the temporal pretensions of the Papacy. But being as true a Catholic as he was a conservative, he held the traditional belief that the Church was the condition and the very foundation of social order, and that its maintenance was as indispensable to the salvation of men's souls as it was to the existence of all terrestrial authority.

If Germany had been a State, the destinies of the Reformation would have been singularly compromised under the government of a prince who held such opinions. In France, or in England, it must immediately have surrendered to the Crown, or have fought it. The Protestant historians have mistakenly deplored the lack of political unity in Germany at the beginning of the 16th century; it was the weakness of the monarchical power, and the backward and particularistic character of its institutions that saved Lutheranism, or at all events assured it of its rapid and easy diffusion, compared with the formidable conflicts in which Calvinism, in more advanced and powerful States, was involved from its very beginnings.

Almost immediately after his election as Emperor, Charles hastened to submit the religious problem to the Diet convoked at Worms in the month of April 1521. Luther, summoned before the assembly, a great part of which was favourable to him, and to whose doors he advanced amidst the acclamations of the crowd, had no reason to fear the fate of John Huss at the Council of Constance. He refused to retract, and he was allowed to leave the city unmolested (April 17th, 1521). A few weeks later (May 8th) an Imperial edict pronounced the ban of the Empire upon him and his adherents. But no one was under any illusion as to the actual importance of this measure. The Empire had no means of enforcing it, and as a matter of fact, it was nowhere executed. It did not hinder the diffusion of the ideas which it condemned any more than it imperilled the security of those who continued to spread them.

Charles had to resign himself to this defeat. Being at war with Francis I, he could not possibly have provoked, in Germany, a religious conflict which would have doubled the chances of his adversary. But what he could not do in the Empire he could do in the Low Countries, and there he hastened to organize the repression of heresy with pitiless severity. As early as 1520 he had promulgated a first "bill" against heresy, and in the following year he ordained that the Edict of Worms should be strictly observed. This was only the prelude to what he had in mind. What he had wished to do was to introduce the Spanish Inquisition into his Burgundian provinces, and although he abandoned this project, in submission to the unanimous opposition of his councillors, he nevertheless organized in those provinces a system of repression as exactly modelled upon the Spanish Holy Office as was possible without rousing public opinion. In 1522 he entrusted a member of the Council of Brabant with the prosecution of heretics. The protests of the Pope against this lay inquisition, which was instituted merely by the State, led him to abandon it in the following year. In 1524 apostolic institutors—who, however, were appointed by the government—functioned in its place. And further, until the end of his reign, a series of more and more violent and merciless "bills" were promulgated, which even went to the length of compelling the lay courts to prosecute and sentence to death persons who, not being theologians, had discussed questions of faith, or who, being acquainted with heretics, did not denounce them.

The effect of this religious persecution was similar to that of all its predecessors. It aroused a truly heroic spirit in the noblest and sincerest souls. It was reserved for the Low Countries to furnish the Reformation with its first martyrs. On July 1st, 1523, two Augustinians of Antwerp, Henri Voes and Jan van Essen, were burned alive in the great market-place of Brussels. Luther celebrated them in one of his most beautiful canticles, and in the following year Erasmus declared "that their death had made many Lutherans."

One may ask oneself what would have become of Lutheranism in Germany if men had been able to profess it only at the peril of their lives. We may be sure, at all events, that its propagation would have been very greatly delayed, and that the rapidity of its diffusion is explained more than anything by the very few risks which the innovators incurred. Nothing could have been less heroic than its history, and it is reasonable to believe that the compliance which the Lutheran Church was to manifest subsequently in its dealings with temporal authority would not have been so pronounced if it had been compelled, in the beginning, to sacrifice the blood of its faithful to its faith. As a matter of fact, before very long, far from having to resist the princes, it was to place itself under their protection.

For centuries the Church had been so completely interblended with society that whenever the former had been attacked the foundations of the latter had been shaken. The heresy of the Albigenses in the 12th century had given rise to communistic aspirations. Wycliffe, without intending it, had contributed to the Agrarian rebellion of 1381, and we know that Hussitism was closely implicated with all sorts of social claims. The Lutheran propaganda was to prove no exception to the rule. Of course, from the temporal standpoint, no one could have been more conservative than Luther. Very different from the humanists, and much less modern, he accepted the traditionally established order of things; he was a revolutionary only in religious matters, and his furious attacks upon the authority of Rome were in strange contrast with his docility in respect of the secular authorities. But when it reached the heart of the masses his propaganda was bound, before long, to awaken the confused emotions born of extreme poverty; a formidable force, which, once unleashed, escapes all guidance, obeying only itself.

It will be remembered that since the end of the 14th century the condition of the German peasants had been continually deteriorating. The capitalistic tendencies of the following century had still further favoured the exploitation to which the brutal and merciless nobles subjected them. In the German art and literature of the 16th century the *Bauer* was treated with extraordinary disdain. He was apparently regarded merely as a disgusting or ridiculous brute; where he was concerned, anything was permissible. And as a matter of fact, the nobles did really behave as though anything were permissible in dealing with these unhappy creatures: the re-establishment of serfdom, the multiplication of corvées, the confiscation of communal property, the diminution of holdings, the increase of all sorts of prestations in kind, the arrogation of the right of dispensing justice, and demands for services of every nature. Against the feudal *Burg* which oppressed them the poor people of each seigneurie were quite defenceless. They had accepted their fate, and had resigned themselves, when the religious agitation which was troubling the cities began to make itself felt among them. Religion was the most ancient and the most sacred of habits, the necessary form, the very foundation of existence, and they saw it attacked with impunity, derided and defied. Their dread of and respect for the clergy disappeared. How then should they continue to dread and respect their lords? The abuses of which the Church was accused were much less obvious to them than the injustice which they had to suffer at the hands of the nobles. And in proportion as this agitation spread among them they drew closer together in their common anger. Their weakness had been the consequence of their isolation. Moved by the same passions, they became conscious of their strength, and in 1524 the first riots suddenly revealed the magnitude of a peril which no one had foreseen because it had been so utterly disdained.

The movement rapidly spread through the whole of Southern Germany, from Luxemburg to the mountains of Bohemia. And here and there the rebels were actually joined by the people of the cities. Their demands, which were advanced in the "Twelve Articles of the Peasants," were far more social than religious. They called for a return to the Gospel, but above all they demanded liberty, liberty as they understood it, which meant the liberty to enjoy the free use of forest and field, and to rid themselves of the illegal corvées and the arbitrary tyranny of the landlords. Their bands broke loose in all directions, and the terror which they excited paralysed all resistance. To the brutality under which they had so long suffered they responded by brutality. Castles and monasteries were given to the flames. The terror was so general, the outbreak so sudden, that counts, princes, and Electors humbled themselves to the extent of negotiating with the insurgent masses and agreeing to the "Twelve Articles." But already these seemed insufficient to hopes excited and passions fired by success. Once more the old dreams of a mystical communism, which had lingered amongst the people ever since the Middle Ages, had taken possession of their minds. Thomas Münzer, in Thuringia, excited the fanaticism of the peasants by the promise of a world of love and justice, in conformity with the Divine will, whose realization demanded the massacre of the unrighteous. The effect of such preaching upon simple and violent souls was to transform the agrarian revolt into a sort of mystical Terror. Its excesses hastened the organization of a resistance which had at first been delayed by the suddenness of its initial successes, but which was, of course, inevitable. The nobles united their forces against those of the peasants. The peasants accepted battle, and on May 15th, 1526, they were cut to pieces at Frankenhausen. The conquerors were pitiless in proportion to the terror they had suffered. Their hatred took a long revenge upon the people who had dared to defy them. The yoke imposed upon the peasants was heavier than ever, and henceforth they were to bear it with docile resignation, until the beginning of the 19th century.

The crisis of Anabaptism was even greater proof of the religious confusion into which the too sudden disappearance of ecclesiastical authority had plunged the soul of the people. Accepting Luther's preaching literally, the first Anabaptists, who before 1525 had made their appearance in Switzerland, claimed that not only their faith, but society itself must be reformed in accordance with Holy Scripture. Since the Bible contained the Word of God they must conform to it strictly in all things. What need was there of Church or State? Obedience to the Word of God should suffice to save men's souls as well as to regulate their mutual relations. Inevitably, the old heresies of the Middle Ages contributed their doctrines to the interpretation of the Scriptures. The popular form of Manichaeism, based on the opposition of flesh and spirit, had never completely disappeared since the days of the Albigenses. Now it was revived, mingled with the apocalyptic visions and the mystical tendencies which had become so widespread since the 14th century. The righteous believed that they were called upon to create a new world, in which all things would be fraternally held in common, wives as well as property. This notion found very ready acceptance in the lower classes of the urban populations, among the journeymen of the guilds and the wage-earning workers in the nascent capitalistic industries. Spreading by contagion among the manual workers, it soon reached the Low Countries, where industry, more intensive than elsewhere, had prepared a most fertile soil for such a movement. It is not surprising that its adepts were savagely prosecuted by the public authorities. Catholics and Lutherans vied with one another in their ferocious suppression of this revolutionary heresy. However, persecution merely aggravated the peril. Utopian though it had been in the beginning, Anabaptism now became a doctrine of hatred and conflict. The poor looked to it not only for deliverance, but for vengeance. Many of them seem to have been actually hallucinated, and as ready to die for their faith as they were to sacrifice, without mercy, the rest of their world. About 1530 a sort of mystico-social delirium seems to have seized upon Holland. Nearly all the lower classes of the cities became a prey to it. In some of the cities it is estimated that two-thirds of the inhabitants were infected, and the massacre, the summary condemnation, the drownings, and the outlawry of all those who adhered to the sect were powerless to arrest its progress. It was from Amsterdam and its suburbs that those prophets came, in

1534, who, taking advantage of the fact that the city of Munster had rebelled against its bishop, went thither to establish the "Kingdom of God." At no other moment of history, perhaps, has there been a more striking example of the lengths to which the masses may be driven by passion, religious illusion, and the hope of realizing social justice. For twelve months, blockaded by the troops of the neighbouring princes, Protestants and Catholics, the Anabaptists of Munster organized, in a sort of insanity, their "New Jerusalem." Polygamy and communism were instituted and practised by the whole population. For a moment a mystical and socialistic Utopia became a reality. The city was taken by storm on June 24th, 1535, and this access of collective madness was quenched in blood. Not until our own days were the iron cages brought down from the tower of the cathedral in which the charred bones of the prophet John of Leyden and the Burgomaster Knipperdalling had so long swung in the wind. The capture of Munster put an end to the violent crisis of Anabaptism, but it did not abolish it. Until almost the close of the 16th century its revolutionary ferment continued to work in the hearts of the people, as did the ferment of Catharism after the great persecution of the 13th century. But among the majority of its adherents it reverted to the evangelical simplicity of its beginnings, and it is in this form that it has been perpetuated down to our own days in the heart of the Protestant world of Europe and America.

The Peasant War, and the tragedy of Anabaptism, resulted in turning the humanists and the Erasmians away from Luther; horrified by so much violence, they moved in the direction of the Church. Luther was no less dismayed. He violently attacked the rebels and pitilessly applauded their defeat. This was the end of the popular tendencies which he had revealed in the beginning. It seemed to him that the only means of saving the Reformation was to place it under the protection and control of the princes. Knowing them as he did, he was aware that they were generally lukewarm in their religion. With the exception of the Dukes of Bavaria, who were as firmly Catholic as the Habsburgs, they were inclined to make their faith conform to their interests. We do not find in any one of them the least trace of idealism, the slightest evidence of any sincere and disinterested conviction. Doubtless they were dissatisfied with the Church, but doubtless also they would not have broken with it if this rupture had not afforded them the opportunity of secularizing its property and confiscating its revenues; and by proclaiming themselves, in their own principalities, the heads of their territorial Churches, they acquired a twofold authority and influence over their subjects. Such were the wholly mundane considerations which determined the conduct of these defenders of the new faith. Of all religious confessions, Lutheranism is the only one which, instead of exhorting its protectors to sacrifice their life and their fortune to it, offered itself to them as a profitable business transaction.

The Elector of Saxony and the Landgrave of Hesse first trod the path which others were soon to follow. In 1525 the Grand Master of the Teutonic Knights, Albert of Brandenberg, supported the Reformation so that he might secularize the Order and transform it, to his own advantage, into a lay principality. The Dukes of Anhalt, Luneburg, and Friesland, and the Margraves of Brandenberg and Bayreuth, also declared for the Gospel. After its beginnings in the heart of the bourgeoisie in the South of Germany, Lutheranism thus became, through the adhesion of the princes, the religion of the North. For the confession of the princes determined that of their subjects, just as formerly, during the Great Schism, it had determined their obedience to the Pope of Rome or the Pope of Avignon. The question of conscience was therefore treated as a question of discipline. One would hardly have expected this of a religion that proclaimed justification by faith and saw a priest in every Christian. There is surely a contradiction here, which can only be explained by the necessity, of which Luther was becoming more and more conscious, of safeguarding the future of his followers by the protection of the temporal power. As for the people, they allowed their religion to be imposed upon them by the temporal authority with a docility which sufficiently proves the truth of the old literary cliché concerning Germanic individualism. The most sacred convictions of the individual were at stake, yet there was no rebellion, no resistance. The German Catholics seem to have adopted Lutheranism in obedience to the commands of their princes as readily as the Franks of the 5th century renounced their gods when Clovis was baptized. We must conclude, no doubt, that their faith was not very fervent, but another reason for their attitude may be found in the complete stagnation of political life in Germany. No one dreamed of contesting the rights of the princes. The people were accustomed to obeying their commands; and nowhere in Germany were their prerogatives restricted by privileges, as in the Low Countries or in Spain. They were therefore allowed, without protest, to put themselves in the place of the bishops, appoint superintendents of the clergy, suppress the ecclesiastical foundations, close the monasteries, secularize their properties, and organize the schools: in short each of them, in his own principality, replaced the universal Church, subject to the Pope, by a territorial Church (*Landeskirche*) subject to the secular power.

Yet the Edict of Worms was not abrogated: Luther and his adherents were still under the ban of the Empire, and in the Low Countries Charles V was promulgating more and more sanguinary "bills" against them. But his war against Francis I kept him out of Germany and compelled him to bide his time. His brother Ferdinand, to whom he had ceded the hereditary domains of the House of Habsburg, and who represented him in his absence, was himself too occupied by the attacks of the Turks in the valley of the Danube, and the difficulty of getting the Hungarians to recognize him as the successor of their king Louis, who had perished in the battle of Mohacz (1526), to think of impeding the progress of the Reformation. It was therefore the French and the Turks who gave the ideal of the Reformation the time it needed to consolidate its position. In 1526 the Diet of Spire decreed that pending the arrival of the Emperor all could claim freedom of action in the matters judged by the Edict of Worms. When three years later Charles attempted to make it revoke this decision, five princes and certain of the cities immediately formulated a protest, and from that time onwards the partisans of the new faith were known by the name of Protestants.

It was not until 1530, at the Diet which Charles had convoked at Augsburg after his coronation, that the inevitable break occurred. The theological debate, in the course of which Melanchthon read aloud the "Augsburg confession," could only have the result of confirming each party in its own belief. It was too late to hope for a reconciliation which might have been possible ten years earlier. The Protestant princes quitted the assembly, of which the majority, encouraged by the Emperor, solemnly ratified the Edict of Worms, condemned all religious innovations, and ordained a general return to the Church.

Thereupon the Protestant princes made their preparations for a conflict which they judged inevitable. In 1531 they formed a confederation at Smalkalde, in association with a certain number of the cities. They were not unaware that the Emperor, still involved in the war with France, would give way if their attitude were sufficiently firm. In the following year, indeed, he proclaimed the Nuremburg Peace of Religion, forbidding any religious war until a Council, or the impending Diet, had assembled. This confession of impotence naturally increased the confidence of the Protestants. Philip of Hesse, the most turbulent among them, profited by the situation to do his utmost to undermine the power of the House of Habsburg. Supported by the subsidies of the King of France, he restored the Duke of Wurttemberg to the possession of his Duchy, which Ferdinand had united with Austria, and Protestantism was immediately introduced into the Duchy (1534). A little later the last lay prince in Northern Germany who had remained faithful to Catholicism was expelled from his domains (1542). Already the Archbishop of Cologne had expressed his intention of going over to the Reformation. The archbishoprics of Magdeburg and Halberstadt were secularized.

At last, having concluded peace with France at Crespy (1544), Charles V was able to attend to affairs in Germany. The Pope had decided to assemble a General Council, and thus to absolve himself from his Nuremberg engagements. The moment had come to attack the League of Smalkalde.

If in the case of the Protestant princes the interests of the faith had taken precedence over their personal interests, all would now have united in order to meet the attack upon them. But it proved that nothing was easier than to secure the neutrality or even the co-operation of many of them against their co-religionists by promises of aggrandisement. The Lutheran Maurice of Saxony won particular distinction as the ally of the Catholic sovereign in this war upon the Lutherans. The Spanish bands of the Duke of Alva did the rest. The battle of Muhlberg annihilated the League of Smalkalde (April 24th, 1547). The Electorate of Johann Friedrich of Saxony was given to Maurice. Philip of Hesse made his submission. In the same year Charles made the Diet of Augsburg accept an interim, which, pending the decision of the Council, established the religious position of the reformed estates.

It was not the triumph of Catholicism, it was the triumph of the Emperor that terrified the vanquished. They were much more afraid of falling under the yoke of Charles, and losing their princely autonomy, than of once more submitting to the jurisdiction of Rome. Maurice of Saxony, who was no more anxious than they were to see the Habsburgs supreme in the Empire, went over to their side. They were even more deficient in national than in religious idealism. Germans and Lutherans though they were, they did not hesitate to buy the aid of the Catholic King of France, Henri II, by surrendering to him a part of that which anywhere else than in the Empire would have been called the Fatherland, or at least, the State. By the Treaty of Chambord (1552) they recognized his right to annex the three Western bishoprics of Metz, Toul and Verdun. Pretending to fear that Charles would impose "the Spanish servitude" upon them, they saluted Henri with the name of "the Protector of German liberty." As a matter of fact, of course, they regarded him only as the protector of their political particularism, which was so conveniently accentuated by their religious particularism.

Once again, then, Lutheranism was saved by France. Charles, obliged to hasten to the Lorraine frontier, left it in possession of the field, and never, until his abdication, had he an opportunity of returning to the attack. As Catholic as himself, his brother and successor Ferdinand, still menaced by the Turks in Hungary, hastened to pacify Germany. The Peace of Religion concluded by the Diet of Augsburg on September 25th, 1555, settled the problem. It acknowledged the *jus reformandi* of the princes—that is to say, their right to embrace the Reformation—whether they had already done so, or whether they wished to do so in the future. Subjects were required to profess the religion of their princes, except that they were allowed to emigrate after selling their possessions. An exception was established in favour of the ecclesiastical principalities, which were in any case to remain Catholic. There the prince's change of confession could only result in his abdication.

Thus conceived, the Peace of Augsburg appeared to be much less a peace of religion than a mere political compromise. It would have been impossible to show more absolute disrespect for liberty of conscience. By it the religion of the people was left to the arbitrary decision of the prince, as though it had been a mere matter of internal administration. The privilege of a free profession of belief was admitted only in the case of crowned heads; the masses had no privilege but that of obedience. This, of course, must be regarded as a consequence of the principle of the State religion, which, hitherto applied to the advantage of the Church alone, was now extended to Lutheranism. Intolerance was just as great on either side, and the new religion was no more inclined than the old to suffer dissidence in its midst. However, the Peace of Augsburg introduced no innovations. The state of affairs which it ratified was that which already existed in fact, as we have seen, in all the Reformed principalities.

But with the Peace, *de facto* became *de jure*; Protestantism obtained its place in the sun, and its future was assured. The majestic unity of Christendom was officially shattered. The Church, because it had not reformed itself with sufficient promptitude, had to watch the erection of a rival Church. Hitherto it had mercilessly crushed heresy, and henceforth it would be forced to suffer its presence. The fact was that the secular power, ceasing to fight for the Church, had itself gone over to the heretics. Not only did it recognize heresy as the religious truth, but it even profited by the heretics' need of its protection in order to impose upon it an ecclesiastical organization of which it was the master. With Lutheranism, in fact, it was a State Church that made its appearance, rather than a State religion. The State which appointed, trained and supervised the clergy was henceforth to benefit by the tremendous power which they exercised over men's souls. Through the clergy it would obtain that control over education which had hitherto evaded it. From the 17th century onwards it would make education compulsory, and its functions would be extended—we can divine with what benefit to itself—to the formation and control of ideas.

Obedience to the prince was inculcated as effectively by the pastors as obedience to the Pope by the Jesuits. The civil power benefited by the progress of the new faith in proportion as it gained empire over men's minds. Discipline, respect for authority, and belief in power were among the characteristics which were finally transmitted to modern Germany. In the last resort, it was the new faith that rendered possible such a State as Prussia: that is, a State in which the virtues of the subject, the official, and the soldier coincide, but where we shall look in vain for the virtues of the citizen.

## 2. *The Spread of the Reformation. Calvinism*

It would perhaps be impossible to find an example better calculated to enable us to appreciate at its exact value the rôle of the historic "hero" than that of Luther. However great a part he played in assuring the success of the Reformation, that success was chiefly due to the moral and political situation of Germany at the beginning of the 16th century. It was because the times had changed that the dispute with regard to indulgences almost immediately assumed the form of a religious revolution. Fifty years earlier the same man, with the same conviction, the same fire, the same eloquence, would have interested, at the very most, a few theologians in his own province, and history would have passed over him in silence, as it must have passed over so many of his precursors. And further, it may readily be shown that the fundamental ideas of Lutheranism itself were not really individual to Luther. In the Low Countries

Wessel Gansfort, who died ignored in 1489, and whose works were not published until 1522, had already formulated the majority of these ideas; and we find them again in France among the members of the little circle that gathered, about 1515, round Lefèvre of Étaples. They were waiting, so to speak, on the threshold of the Church for the right moment to invade it. Luther brought his ideas into the foreground and then directed their development. He was a great moral "leader," but we know that leaders, though they are indispensable to revolutions, are not their authors.

Moreover, it is in the nature of revolutions to be contagious, and this was to prove no exception to the rule. However, the form which was so early assumed by Lutheranism in Germany, owing to its intimate alliance with the princes, was to prevent it, once it had inaugurated the Reformation, from directing the destiny of the latter, and retaining control over it. Wittenberg, which had seemed for a moment as though it would become the common centre of the followers of the Gospel, very soon disappointed their hopes. Closely subjected to the secular power, the *Landeskirchen* lacked the liberty of procedure and the independence which would have been necessary for an effective external propaganda. They were too completely adapted to the political environment of Germany to possess the power of adapting themselves to other environments. Their nationalism, so to speak, made it impossible beforehand that they should exercise a universal influence. The only conquest of Lutheranism was that of the Scandinavian countries, and it was victorious there because the kings declared for it. In Sweden Gustavus Vasa, by agreement with the nobles, who coveted the ecclesiastical estates, imposed it on the people in 1527. The Catholic insurrections, which were fairly numerous until 1543, were severely repressed, and their only result was to consolidate the royal power, and to give the country a strong monarchical constitution which before long enabled it to intervene in the affairs of Europe. In Denmark Christian II (1503–1523) favoured the Reformation in order to enhance his authority by imposing it on the Church. The nobles and the bourgeois of Copenhagen rallied to it, the former out of interest, and the latter because they were hostile to the clergy.

Under Christian III, in 1536, the reformed faith was proclaimed the State religion. Norway and Iceland, then dependencies of Denmark, had hitherto preserved their autonomy. The king took advantage of the resistance which they offered to the Danish Church in order to deprive them of this autonomy. Lutheranism was imposed upon them by force. The Icelandic bishop Jan Areson died on the scaffold.

Lutheranism, then, was triumphant only where the princes or the kings supported it. Religious conviction had little to do with its propagation. In the beginning its really sincere and disinterested adepts appear to have been very few. Promulgated by authority and accepted in obedience, it progressed, if one may say so, by annexation. Conversion came afterwards, and slowly, just as a conquered people is slowly assimilated to the conquering nation.

The harmony between the monarchical government and Lutheranism was so complete that the Reformation, even among the German-speaking peoples, turned away from Lutheranism when it was not supported by the government. It is interesting to note that the democratic cantons of Switzerland, under the influence of Zwingli, gave themselves an independent religious constitution to which, in the beginning, a number of the free cities of Southern Germany adhered.

It is only too evident that in those countries whose princes remained faithful to Rome the Church had nothing to fear from the Lutherans. Respecting the sovereign power, they never for a moment thought of resisting it, nor even of disobeying it. They observed the stipulations of the "bills" promulgated against them, and abstained from preaching the faith in public; the only propaganda which they permitted themselves was that of martyrdom. It was soon realized that they were not very dangerous, and even in the Low Countries the Inquisition of Charles V, so ferocious in its treatment of the Anabaptists, prosecuted the Lutherans with a certain laxity.

It appears certain, however, that the religious disturbances in Germany were not without influence in respect of England's break with the Papacy. But this influence was only indirect, acting, if one may say so, as an encouragement to measures which in themselves had no relation to Lutheranism. Henry VIII, who prided himself on his theology, regarded Luther as a mere heretic, and attacked him in his *Assertio septem sacramentorum*, which earned him the title of "Defender of the Faith," conferred upon him by Leo X. He persecuted Tyndale, and placed an interdict on his translation of the Bible. The motives of his opposition to Rome, and of the constitution of the Anglican Church, were entirely external to the domain of faith. Neither Henry nor—above all—the English people felt the least inclination to reject the traditional beliefs of Catholicism. To attribute Henry's behaviour simply to his passion for Anne Boleyn is to confuse the occasion of events with their cause. The Pope's opposition to the King's divorce from Catherine of Aragon certainly induced him to have himself proclaimed by the assembly of the clergy "the chief protector of the church and clergy of England" (1531), in order that he might obtain the dissolution of his marriage (1533). But there matters might have stopped, and if they had done so England's situation, in respect of Rome, would certainly not have been irremediably compromised. The elevation of Thomas More to the post of Chancellor, after the condemnation of Cardinal Wolsey (1530), proves that the government had no thought of turning away from Catholicism. Parliament, which supported the King's cause with all its might, wished to profit by the situation and establish a national Church. But no one was dreaming of a schism, much less of a heresy. On accepting the post of Chancellor, More no doubt intended to lead the English Church, without commotion or violence, toward those moderate reforms of which the humanists had dreamed. Like Erasmus, he wished to preserve the traditional faith while purifying it. If he looked to the government to help him in this task, it was on the sole condition that it should act from motives as purely religious and disinterested as his own. But the government was then in the hands of a man who was devoting all his energies and his genius to making England an absolute monarchy. Formed in the school of the Italian politicians, Thomas Cromwell's only conception of the State was one in which the Crown was omnipotent. For him, as for Machiavelli, the Church was merely a factor of politics, but a factor whose importance was proportionate to its influence over men's minds. To place it at the service of the prince was therefore to invest him with a power and ascendancy which he derived from its sacred character. In 1534, profiting by the obedience of Parliament and its hostility to the court of Rome, he caused it to pass the "Act of Supremacy," acknowledging the king as the sole and supreme earthly head of the Church of England, with all the honours, jurisdictions, authorities, immunities, profits and advantages pertaining to this dignity, and with full power to examine, redress, repress, reform and amend all errors, heresies, abuses, disorders and enormities which might be or were capable of being legally reformed by any spiritual authority or jurisdiction. In the following year the king appointed Cromwell his vicar-general in ecclesiastical affairs. The English Church was thus laid prostrate at the foot of the throne, and henceforth the sovereign who sat upon this throne occupied, for that Church, the place which had been filled by the Pope. This was schism, but it was not yet heresy; yet it was not long before the schism gave rise to heresy.

It had not taken Cromwell long to make the Church a mere instrument of the monarchy. The Chapters were required to raise to the episcopate only persons indicated by the King. What is more, preachers were even required to obtain a royal licence. At the same time, all the monasteries were subjected to a "visit," the result of which was a foregone conclusion. The all-powerful minister had resolved to confiscate their property, partly for the benefit of the Crown, and partly for that of the nobles, in order that the lords and gentlemen of the country might henceforth be unanimous in favour of maintaining the new ecclesiastical constitution, just as the purchasers of national properties in the France of the Revolution were in favour of the maintenance of the Revolutionary régime. Since the nobles were predominant in Parliament, it was not difficult to secure the passage of the Acts which from 1536 to 1545 decreed the suppression of all the monastic communities in the country. The "Articles of Religion" which the assembly of the clergy accepted without protest in 1536 cut the last tie which, by community of faith, still bound the English Church to the Catholic Church. As the bases of dogma they accepted only the Bible and the three first Oecumenical Councils ("the Bible and the Three Creeds"), retaining as sacraments only Baptism, Penitence and the Eucharist. No modification was introduced either in the ritual or in the organization of the hierarchy. A position was adopted which was half-way between Protestantism and Catholicism, and apparently very like that toward which the humanists had wished insensibly to lead the Papacy.

Yet the best and most celebrated of these humanists, Thomas More, had resigned his position as Chancellor as early as 1532, and two years later his head had fallen on the scaffold. The most pious and enlightened spirits among those who aspired to reform the Church were revolted by the violence which was imposed upon it. The government appeared to them, and actually was, a moral despotism imposed by terror. Cromwell's police carried on a veritable inquisition, and victims, chosen for the sake of example among the most illustrious men in the country, were pitilessly sacrificed to the end envisaged by the terrible minister. In vain did the nobles of the North rebel in the name of Catholicism and liberty; their efforts resulted merely in the sacrifice of fresh victims.

The severity displayed against the Catholics was in singular contrast to the fluctuations of the king in questions of dogma. After 1536, alarmed by the manifestations of a not very numerous group of Protestants, he obviously sought to return to tradition, and the six Articles which were submitted for the approval of the clergy in 1539 marked a fairly definite revulsion in the direction of the Catholic faith. The sensational fall and death of Cromwell in 1540 were explained in part by his attempts to draw England into an alliance with the Lutherans of Germany. At one moment it seems that Henry VIII actually had thoughts of reconciliation with Rome, or at all events that he was in favour of the idea of reforming the Church by means of a General Council. However, the attitude of the Council of Trent made him abandon such notions. At the time of his death in 1547 he was thinking of concluding a "Christian

League" with the German princes, and of replacing the Mass by a simple Communion service.

After him there was chaos. The minority of Edward VI (1547–1553) enabled the "Protector"—the Duke of Somerset, followed by the Earl of Warwick—openly to favour Protestantism. The Mass was suppressed, images were removed from the churches, the celibacy of the priests was abolished, and a Prayer Book was adopted, together with new articles of religion, constituting the doctrine to which the Anglican Church has remained faithful to this day. All these things were imposed by violence, in the midst of a veritable religious anarchy. While the exasperated Catholics were inciting to revolt on every side, a new party had lately made its appearance, which demanded a radical reform of the faith and of the Church. Calvinism had entered upon the scene.

A generation separated the birth of Calvin (1509) from that of Luther. The religious crisis which no one could have foreseen at the moment when the German reformer began his career was the object of general concern when the French reformer entered the arena. Luther, like all his contemporaries, had been born into the world of scholastic theology. Calvin grew up in an environment which was passionately concerned with the questions of the authority of the Scriptures, grace, justification by faith, the validity of the Sacraments, the celibacy of the priesthood, and the primacy of the See of Rome. Luther was impelled by his conscience and by events to leave the Church in which he had vainly sought spiritual peace. Calvin, as a matter of fact, had never belonged to this Church. It cost him no effort to break with it; from the very first he had regarded it as a monument of error and imposture. He was spared the intimate tragedies of the conscience. He had no need to seek for God. He was positive that he had God's Word in the Bible, and that it was to be found only in the Bible. He was to devote his life to arriving at an understanding of the Bible, and imposing upon other men the teachings which he discovered in it. His heart and his emotions played no part in his religion. In him there was no trace of the Lutheran mysticism. Reflection, reasoning, logic—these were his means of conviction.

No doubt this was largely to be explained by his personality. Yet we should consider that what the Reformation needed, after its first outbreak, was a definite, rigid and coherent doctrine; a body of dogma, so to speak, to oppose to the old dogma, and a Church to contend against the old Church. And it had all the more need of this inasmuch as Catholicism was healing its wounds, was drawing new energies from the Council of Trent, and was preparing a powerful counter-attack, which the Reformation could certainly never have resisted without the aid of Calvinism.

There was no trace in Calvin of the pugnacious and impulsive character of Luther. It was by intellectual labour that he satisfied his religious cravings, and it is almost certain that without the events that determined his destiny he would have influenced the world only by his pen. He had arrived at adult years when the French monarchy was induced to assume a definite attitude in respect of the Reformation.

Just at first it had apparently felt the same sympathy for the Reformation as for the Renaissance; indeed, it seems to have confused the two. Francis I felt for Erasmus, to whom he offered a chair in the Collège de France, an esteem which disquieted and exasperated the theologians of the Sorbonne. Louis de Berquin, one of the disciples of Lefèvre of Étaples, preached at his court. His sister, Marguerite, professed a very liberal Christianity, marked by Platonic tendencies, and an evangelical mysticism which was closely akin to Protestantism. She openly protected the innovators, and it was in her little Kingdom of Navarre that Lefévre peacefully spent the last years of his career. Diane de Poitiers herself was said to have a tenderness for the Lutheran doctrines. And it is certain that the king continued for some time to restrain the University and the Parlements from manifesting their zeal against heresy. But it is equally certain that he never dreamed and never could have dreamed of embroiling himself with the Papacy. The Concordat concluded with Leo X in 1516 assured him of an influence over the French Church (since it acknowledged his right to appoint bishops and abbots of monasteries, and imposed restrictions in respect of appeals to the court of Rome) which was so advantageous that he could not have been tempted to renounce it. Since the reign of Philip the Fair the Curia, in a spirit of prudence or of gratitude, had always abstained from restricting the exercise of the prerogatives which the Crown had arrogated to itself in respect of the clergy. The government had no reason to complain of the existing situation. None of the motives which impelled the German princes, or Henry VIII, to break with Rome, and replace the Roman Church by national Churches, had any application to France. The political interests which elsewhere did so much to favour the cause of the Reformation here impelled the government to resist it. It was therefore bound to happen, and it did happen, that the king was unable to prolong his toleration for a movement to which Rome was becoming more and more openly hostile, without incurring, in the eyes of the nation, the reproach of being its accomplice. From 1530 or thereabouts he ceased to resist the demands of those who wished to persecute the heretics, and although he did not go to the length of establishing a State Inquisition on the model of that of Spain, he allowed the religious and civil authorities to deal with heresy as they thought fit, the result being a ferocious persecution.

Calvin was twenty-five years of age when this persecution, in 1534, drove him into exile. The Low Countries, which had already been, and were so often to be in the future, a place of refuge for French exiles, were then inaccessible, owing to the laws of Charles V against heresy, so that he turned to Romansh Switzerland. For some years Geneva had been in a state of political and religious ferment. In order to resist their hereditary enemy, the Duke of Savoy, the burgesses had solicited and obtained the aid of Berne. In 1526 the Eiguenots (*Eidgenossen*) had driven the partisans of the Duke out of the city, but Berne was Protestant, and the alliance concluded with Berne quickly familiarized the Genevese with the Reformation. A French refugee, Guillaume Farel, conducted an impassioned propaganda in favour of the Reformation. As elsewhere, the bewildered Church offered little resistance, or none, and the new faith, favoured by the love of autonomy and the hatred of Savoy, whose partisans were blockading the city (1534–1535), was quickly triumphant. On August 10th, 1535, the Mass was discontinued by order of the Council; the people began to break the religious images, and the greater part of the clergy took to flight. The victory won over Savoy in the following year made Geneva an independent Republic. Thus a new political régime was introduced simultaneously with a new religious faith, and thenceforth the two were to remain indissolubly united.

It was while these things were happening that Calvin, on passing through Geneva, was detained by Farel. He was already a man who knew his mind; he had just published, in 1536, his *Institution Chrétienne*. Here was an opportunity to apply its principles in this young republic, still thrilled by its victory. Covered in the rear by the Swiss cantons, protected by the policy of France against the repetition of the Savoyard offensive, Geneva had no reason to fear for its independence, and could safely institute within its walls the theocratic government which was to be the most intensive, or perhaps one should say the only, application of pure Calvinism, and which was to contribute so powerfully to the diffusion of the latter in the outer world. For Calvinism Geneva was the "Holy City" which the Anabaptists ten years earlier, in their mystical dreams, had hoped for a moment to establish in Munster.

Everyone knows that the cardinal dogma of Calvinism is that of predestination. Salvation depends solely upon the Divine will, and by that Divine will the elect are chosen from all eternity. The Church consists in the union of these elect. But as it is impossible to know if one has been elected by grace, it is each man's duty, so to speak, to prove it to himself by devoting himself with all his energies to the service of God. The Calvinist predestination, instead of leading to quietism, accordingly incites to activity. It does this all the more so inasmuch as God is not conceived as a father but as a master, whose word, revealed by Scripture, is the supreme law. One's whole life must be subject to this law, and the State is legitimate only in so far as it respects the law. While Luther confined religion to the domain of the conscience, and left the temporal power to organize the Church and follow its political interests after its own fashion, Calvin submitted all human actions to theology.

He was as universal, as absolute as the Catholic Church. I would even say that he was more universal and absolute. For, after all, the Church acknowledged that the "temporal sword" had its own mission, above and beyond the mission which had devolved upon the "spiritual sword." The one governed men's bodies, the other their souls, and the first was subordinated to the second only in questions of faith. For Calvin, on the contrary, the State, being willed by God, had to be transformed into an instrument of the Divine will. It was not subordinated to the clergy, in the sense that it existed independently of the clergy, and did not derive its power from them, but it acted in conformity with the end for which it was created only by associating itself intimately with the clergy, in order that the mandates of the Most High should triumph here on earth, and in order to combat all that opposed these mandates or insulted His majesty: vice, heresy, idolatry, and more especially the Roman idolatry, the most abominable of all. Such a system of ideas, if it is fully applied, inevitably leads to theocracy, and under the inspiration of Calvin the government of Geneva did actually constitute a theocracy.

The Consistory, an assembly of pastors and laymen, exercised, so to speak, the moral superintendence of the Republic. It did not govern, but it supervised and controlled the councillors of the Commune, and kept them in the strait way. The "ecclesiastical ordinances" were applied by the civil authorities. The death-penalty, torture, banishment and imprisonment were imposed, according to the gravity of the offence, but always with exemplary severity, upon contraventions of the ecclesiastical or moral regulations. Attendance at the temple was obligatory; adultery was a capital crime; the singing of a profane song was punished by the imposition of public penitence. Each person's conduct was subjected to a permanent inquisition which pursued him even into his dwelling, and extended to the most trivial actions of his private life. Heresy was mercilessly repressed; it is enough to recall the martyrdom of Michael Servetus in 1553.

And while it became the pattern of the Christian State, Geneva also became an ardent centre of religious propaganda. The French refugees who flocked thither during the persecutions of the reign of Henri II provided Calvin with the first disciples who were truly inspired with his spirit. The most celebrated of them, Théodore de Bèze, was for him what Melanchthon was for Luther, the organizer of that education without which no Church was possible. In 1559 the Academy of Geneva was founded, whose essential purpose was the training of "ministers," or, one might almost say, of Calvinistic missionaries. For the training which they received there prepared them above all for the propagation of the doctrine. For Calvin the Apostolate, which Luther completely neglected, was the indispensable condition of the propagation of the faith. He would not have rejected the collaboration of the princes, but he came too late to be able to count on them. They had already taken up their positions. In Germany only the Elector Palatine adopted Calvinism, and therefore imposed it upon his subjects. Outside Germany the Continental monarchs had everywhere declared for Rome, and the King of England had recently imposed a national Church upon his subjects. Therefore, in order to ensure that the Word of God should triumph, it was necessary to prepare for battle. Everywhere the State was hostile to the new faith. More: the Roman Church, bewildered for a moment by the sudden attack, which had taken it by surprise, had recovered its wits, and was showing itself ready not only to defend itself but to reconquer the positions which it had lost. Paul III in 1542 revived the Inquisition, and in 1545 he convoked the Council of Trent. Already the young Society of Jesus was beginning to wage war upon heresy, to rouse men's souls from their lethargy, to stimulate Catholic piety, and to found the first Jesuit colleges. The situation was therefore infinitely more difficult for Calvin than it had been for Luther, who had been able to take the enemy by surprise; Calvin found him everywhere on the alert and fully armed. In order to undertake a successful offensive against such an enemy, he would have to employ all the resources of organization and to proceed with unfailing energy.

For that matter, although the Catholic defence was in a very much better position about the middle of the 16th century than it had been in 1517, the Protestant offensive was also more powerful.

The religious problem now appeared everywhere with formidable clarity. The convulsions of the Peasant War and the Anabaptist risings, which had first tended to obscure it by their social demands, had ceased. On the other hand, it was no longer possible to hope for a reconciliation with the Church. It was therefore necessary to make the choice between the old faith and the new. Both were laying claim to men's souls, both were appealing to the conscience, and by that very fact were compelling men to undertake an examination of the conscience which in many persons led to what some called an apostasy and others a conversion. The religion of habit which had enabled so many to drowse through the 15th century was a thing of the past. Now it was necessary to take sides in a debate in which the question of eternal salvation was at stake, and every man, according to his decision, had to enter one of the two opposing camps and prepare for battle. Personal conviction, as we have seen, played a very secondary part in the authoritarian diffusion of Lutheranism; it played an enormous part in the diffusion of Calvinism, which could hope to conquer only through the loyalty of its adherents.

It was greatly helped by the social constitution of the 16th century. Capitalism, which was hampered by the restrictions imposed by the Church upon trafficking in money and speculation, must surely have benefited it by procuring the unconscious adhesion of great numbers of commercial adventurers and men of business. It must not be forgotten that Calvin acknowledged the lawfulness of lending money at interest, which Luther, faithful in this respect, as in so many others, to the traditional theology, had still condemned. The first resources placed at the disposal of the new Church to cover its costs of propaganda, if we may employ a very modern expression, which corresponds perfectly with the nature of the case, were advanced by the successful merchants. In Antwerp, about 1550, there were already a considerable number of new converts among the frequenters of the Bourse. The Catholics complained that they took advantage of their power over their workers to compel them, at least in appearance, to adhere to their faith. The nobles also, from the very first, provided a numerous contingent of adepts. This is readily understood if we reflect that they were now, for the most part, men of some education, and that under the influence of the humanists the foundations of the ancient faith had been undermined, while that influence had given rise to a taste for discussion and a love of innovations. Moreover, the French-speaking nobles had read the *Institution Chrétienne* as eagerly as the German nobles had read Luther's pamphlet. And we can imagine the impression which the impassioned logic of this little book must have produced upon minds which were only too ready, thanks to the perusal of Rabelais, whose work had appeared almost at the same time, to deride the Church, and to regard it as an obsolete institution. Lastly, the industrial proletariat, cherishing a rancorous memory of the persecution which had not wholly stifled the Anabaptist faith, furnished predestined recruits to the new faith, though in the beginning, at all events, these recruits were more remarkable for their turbulence than for their sincerity.

The democratic and authoritarian constitution which Calvin had given his Church was an astonishing aid to its progress. In effect, it summoned the faithful to collaborate directly in the organization of each religious community. While the minister was the spiritual head of the community, the consistory, which functioned at his side, was recruited among the laymen. The devotion of each believer was constantly kept on the alert in this little group of the elect, surrounded by enemies and able to rely only upon its own resources. The zeal, conviction and courage, and even the fanaticism of the ministers, assured them, wherever they went, of a contagious ascendancy. And their numbers, no less than their energy, attested to the vigour of the young Church. In the 1540's they were already to be met with in all parts of France, in the Low Countries, and in England. Trained at first at Geneva, but presently at Lausanne, Strasbourg and Heidelberg, they displayed all the characteristics of a regular clergy, but a clergy as active and as learned as the Catholic clergy was generally ignorant and apathetic. Educated, acting in concert, and keeping in touch with one another, they devoted themselves body and soul to their task. They made their way into the cities in disguise or under borrowed names, preaching the

Gospel in the evenings behind closed doors in a hostelry, or a courtyard, or some remote corner of the suburb. Sometimes they exercised their mission at a meal or banquet in a friendly house, seeking to convert the guests by their edifying conversation, and distributing books and canticles to them. If they were surprised, they could expect no mercy, and they knew it. But their voices, which rose even amidst the flames and the smoke of the pyre, propagated to the last the faith for which they died. Before long the dismayed executioners gagged their victims before they led them out to die. We must go back to the origins of Christianity to find such constancy and such courage. And just as in those early days, the last moments of these martyrs were piously related in popular narratives, which, diffused through the printing-press, immediately became the most efficacious means of propaganda. On the other hand, by hunting down the faithful the Catholic persecution spread far and wide the flame which it was seeking to extinguish. In France, in the Low Countries, the refugees carried the faith from province to province. Others emigrated to England and Scotland. In the East of Europe, Poland and Hungary were visited by the ministers, and before long reformed communities were established in nearly all the cities.

Thus Calvinism was distinguished by the international character of its diffusion. The diversity of languages, manners, and political régimes was no obstacle to its progress. The ecclesiastical organization at its disposal gave it a penetrative force and an independence of conduct which were far to seek in Lutheranism. Instead of submitting, like the latter, to the tutelage of princes, it relied only upon itself. It did not ask for protection, nor did it avoid conflict. Wherever it appeared it loudly affirmed its dogmas and boldly took the offensive, and its radicalism tolerated no compromise. Between it and the sectators of the "Roman idolatry," the followers of the "Whore of Babylon," no reconciliation was possible. It was necessary to be for the new faith or against it. To the Catholic intolerance it responded by an equal intolerance. To persecution it presently replied by rebellion, and the violence of its conduct, the audacity of its provocations, and the extreme and bitter quality of its polemics angered and wounded even those who in their religious lukewarmness would not have opposed it. The quarrel which it provoked assumed a personal character for every protagonist; it fomented hatred in men's hearts, and was finally to end in civil war.

CHAPTER III

# THE EUROPEAN STATES FROM THE MIDDLE OF THE FIFTEENTH TO THE MIDDLE OF THE SIXTEENTH CENTURY

## 1. *International Politics*

The great social transformations, the great crises of thought, do not of necessity coincide with the modifications of international politics. The Renaissance, the Reformation, and Capitalism undoubtedly exerted a profound influence over the life of the various States; but they did not in any way influence the wholly novel condition which, since the middle of the 15th century, had determined the mutual situation of these States. It was in consequence of the hazard and interaction of events that Europe, just when it was passing through so many intellectual, religious and economic changes, was also disturbed by a radical transformation of the system of forces which had been in mutual opposition since the beginning of the 13th century. The fifty years which had elapsed since the end of the Hundred Years' War had sufficed to revolutionize the traditional order of politics. The conclusion of the great struggle between France and England merely confronted the European community with unexpected problems. While in the West new powers had made their appearance—the Burgundian State on the shores of the North Sea, and to the south of the Pyrenees the Spanish State, henceforth including Castile and Aragon in a single monarchical bloc—in the East the Turkish Empire was threatening the Christian world with a new Islamic invasion. Thus hazard, that mysterious force which continually delights in frustrating the calculations of men, ordained that just as a critical period of the internal history of the Continent was beginning Europe was compelled to stem the external danger.

The Turkish invasion was undoubtedly the greatest misfortune to afflict Europe since the end of the Roman Empire. Wherever the invaders advanced they brought with them economic ruin and moral decadence. All those peoples which were subjected to the Turkish yoke—Bulgars, Serbs, Rumanians, Albanians, and Greeks—relapsed into a state verging upon barbarism, from which they never emerged until the beginning of the 19th century. The Germans, who had invaded the West in the 5th century, were no less brutal than the Turks. But they became assimilated to the superior civilization of the West; converted to Christianity, they were presently absorbed by the conquered population. Between the Islamism of the Turks, on the contrary, and the Christianity of their subjects no reconciliation was possible. The difference between the two religions rendered them mutually impenetrable and perpetuated the abominable system of a State founded only on force, supporting itself only by exploitation and existing only at the price of maintaining, in the hearts of the conquerors, contempt for the vanquished, and in the hearts of the vanquished hatred of the conqueror. With the exception of a portion of the Albanian people, not one of the nations subjected to the Sultan was converted to Islam, and for that matter the Turks made no effort to convert them. From the religious standpoint it glorified Allah sufficiently that His faithful should reign over the *giaours*; from the political standpoint all that was necessary in order to maintain the State, which never rose above the primitive conception of a pure military régime, was to reduce the Christians to the status of taxpayers. Thus their religion, by depriving them of all rights of whatever kind, helped to ensure their servitude. From the reign of Selim I (1512–1520) even their flesh and blood was subjected to taxation. Periodically the most beautiful children were torn from their parents, the girls to serve men's pleasure, and the boys to be enrolled in the corps of janissaries, having first been initiated into Islam.

Europe, which had been powerless to prevent the capture of Constantinople, was equally powerless to check the advance of the

Turkish power across the Continent and along the shores of the Mediterranean. The Popes endeavoured in vain to revive the spirit of the Crusades. Their propaganda—of which the monk Campistan was the most remarkable agent—certainly succeeded in raising bands of volunteers, half enthusiasts, half adventurers, but what was needed was the co-operation of the various States in the common defence, and such co-operation was impossible. Historians who attribute this lack of co-operation to the alleged national egoism of the modern State forget that the States of the Middle Ages never put up a common defence against the Musulmans. The universal character of the Crusades was due to the participation of the peoples, not of the governments. Their failure, against adversaries far less formidable than the Turks, proves that nothing could really have been expected of them, even had not the moral and social conditions which favoured them disappeared for ever. The only means of successfully resisting the Turkish offensive would have been a general European league combining the financial and military resources of the Continent for a period of several years. The coalitions of the 17th century against Louis XIV, of the 19th century against Napoleon, and of 1914 against Germany, give one a notion of the kind of effort that might have succeeded. But the States of the 15th century were materially incapable of such an effort. Moreover, to the most powerful of these States the peril appeared merely as a menace too remote to call for their intervention. They left the burden of the conflict to those who were directly involved.

Unfortunately, the immediate neighbours of the Turks were in no condition to hold their own against them. Nothing could be more lamentable than the incapacity which they exhibited, and which rendered useless so many instances of heroic devotion. By uniting their forces, the Republic of Venice, the Habsburgs of Austria, and the kings of Bohemia, Hungary, and Poland could have opposed an effective barrier to the enemy. But instead of doing this, each State allowed itself to be guided by its ambitions or its interests; they never acted with one common accord. Venice resigned herself to making desultory attempts, prosecuted without vigour, which ended in the disastrous peace treaties of 1479 and 1502, which of all her magnificent domain of the Levantine ports and islands left her only Candia. As for the Habsburgs, who with a little magnanimity might have become the saviours or at least the champions of Europe, they never contrived to raise themselves above the level of a greedy and hesitating policy. Frederick III (1440–1493) and Maximilian (1493–1519) prudently remained far from the line of battle, envisaging events whose importance they were capable of understanding solely from the dynastic standpoint, watching for an opportunity of appropriating the crowns of Bohemia and Hungary, the supreme end of the equivocal intrigues of their ancestors.

After the death of Albert of Austria in 1439 his widow, supported by Frederick III, had endeavoured to preserve Bohemia and Hungary for her son Ladislas, a posthumous child whose long minority promised to be as disastrous to the peoples as it was advantageous to the plans of the Habsburgs. The Hungarian nobles thwarted this machination by offering the crown to the King of Poland, Vladislav III, while the Czechs acknowledged George Podiebrad as their regent. Vladislav perished in 1444, sword in hand, at the battle of Varna, fighting against the Turks. Ladislas was then five years of age. The Hungarian magnates requested Frederick III to surrender him to them, but he refused, whereupon they entrusted the government and the defence of the country to the most valiant among them, Hunyadi Janos. Hunyadi died in 1456 after saving Belgrade, and Ladislas himself died in the following year, whereupon Frederick III hastened to claim the crowns of Bohemia and Hungary for his house. However, being as cowardly as he was greedy, he did not venture to take active steps, and the Czechs, ignoring his pretensions, elected George Podiebrad king, while the Hungarians chose Matthias Corvinus, the son of Hunyadi (1458). This son of a hero was a politician. Instead of taking up arms against the Turks—who seized Serbia in 1458, overcame the resistance of Albania (1479) after the death of George Castriotes (Scanderbeg, 1468), took possession of Bosnia and Herzegovina, and compelled the principalities of Moldavia and Wallachia to pay them tribute—he preferred to work for his own aggrandisement, to the detriment of his Christian neighbours. When the Pope excommunicated George

Podiebrad, who was supported by the Czech Utraquists, and pronounced his deposition, Matthias took this opportunity of attacking him and having himself proclaimed King of Bohemia (1469) by the Catholics. He then turned against Frederick III, who was cunningly seeking to undermine his power, marched against him, and expelled him from Vienna in 1485. He died five years later; Hungary owed to him a brief period of glory and some barren successes. He left no heir, and the Habsburgs, always on the alert, immediately claimed the succession. It escaped them again, but their patience was unwearied. The Hungarians acknowledged as their king the Polish Prince Vladislas, to whom the Czech Utraquists had already given the crown during the lifetime of Matthias Corvinus. Maximilian of Austria concluded with him one of those matrimonial treaties which the House of Austria excelled in devising. A double marriage united Louis, the son of Vladislas, to Maria of Austria, the granddaughter of Maximilian, and Ferdinand, his grandson, to Anne of Hungary. After the death of his father (1516) young Louis II had to march against Soliman II, who, having completed the conquest of the Balkan peninsula, was now turning towards Hungary, and had just entered Belgrade (1521). He was defeated and killed at Mohacz in 1526. This battle was a magnificent triumph for Austria, for it gave her the long-coveted crowns of Bohemia and Hungary, at last assured to her by the victory of the Turks. For the rest, Ferdinand contented himself with inheriting the rights of his brother-in-law. This would have been the moment to summon Germany to the defence of her menaced frontiers. But Germany, in the throes of the crisis of the Reformation, was more incapable than ever of any collective effort. The Protestant princes regarded the Turks as providential allies; and the Catholic princes had no intention, by fighting against them, of assuring the Habsburgs of an augmentation of their power, which already filled them with jealousy. Soliman therefore advanced without difficulty as far as Pest, and in 1529 he reached the walls of Vienna, which the inclement weather and sickness in his army prevented him from capturing. However, he retained all Hungary as far as the Enns, and Ferdinand, who was compelled to conclude a peace with him in 1547, undertook to pay him tribute. Hungary was divided into *sandjaks*, with the exception of a narrow strip of territory in the north and the west and some portions of Croatia and Slavonia which remained in the possession of the Habsburgs. Transylvania and the eastern portion of the country formed separate principalities under vassalage to the Porte. Soliman himself transformed the principal church of Pest into a mosque.

Under his reign (1520–1556) the Turkish Empire covered the largest area which it was ever to attain. The shores of the Black Sea had already been occupied under Selim I (1512–1520), and the Tartars of the Crimea were subjected to tribute. Rhodes, in the Aegean, was conquered in 1522, and the Knights of St. John, who had heroically defended it, removed to Malta, whither Charles V had summoned them, and which they were to retain until the French Revolution.[1] Mesopotamia, Syria, and Egypt were annexed (1512–1520). Algiers and Tunis, conquered by the renegade corsair Barbarossa, became the outposts of the Grand Seigneur in the eastern Mediterranean. Thus, in the middle of the 16th century the situation of Islam in Europe was far more formidable than it had ever been in the period of its great expansion. But this second advance was to share the fate of the first. The moment of its apogee was also the moment of its decline. But the Turks did not, like the Musulmans in the 10th and 11th centuries, atone by their civilization for their subsequent loss of martial vigour. Barbarians they were and Barbarians they remained. In my opinion, however, their barbarism had nothing to do with their race. Whether in Asia or in Europe, the Turks came into contact only with the decadent civilizations of the Caliphate of Baghdad and the Byzantine Empire, which were too feeble to impose themselves upon their conquerors. On the other hand, the purely military organization of the State prevented any social progress. But as such a State is unproductive, it can maintain itself only by conquest. It becomes exhausted as soon as war ceases to provide it with the resources which it is incapable of producing for itself. It must be for ever enlarging itself, for ever subduing fresh tributaries in order to provide for its

[1] Malta was captured by Napoleon in 1798, when he was on his way to Egypt.

upkeep. Financial disorder and fiscal oppression, with all their political, economic, and moral consequences, made their appearance in Turkey directly her expansion was checked. It is true that she still exhibited momentary outbursts of energy. But regarded as a whole, the history of Turkey after the death of Soliman II was that of an incurable decline. She would have disappeared long ago as a State if the European powers had not safeguarded her existence, because they could not agree upon the partition of the spoils. The admirable situation which she occupied on the Straits gave her an international importance which saved her from the fate of Poland. Europe tolerated the crime committed against a Christian people; she has not yet succeeded in expelling the Musulman invaders, whose presence upon European soil is a misfortune and a disgrace to civilization. It is astonishing to think that the industrious and inoffensive Moors of the Kingdom of Granada were driven back into Africa at the end of the 15th century and that the Turks are still in Constantinople in 1918. Being unable to expel them, we have gradually become accustomed to their presence, and without ceasing to regard them as intruders we have ended by giving them a place in the European community. More, we have even sought to involve them in our quarrels. Did not Francis I seek the help of Soliman II against Charles V?

This alliance, so monstrous at first sight, was only one of the consequences of the political disorder of Christianity since the middle of the 15th century.

The conclusion of the Hundred Years' War had left France and England in very different situations. In England the war between the Houses of York and Lancaster broke out almost immediately. While the nobles were slaughtering one another on the battlefield, and while, by means of abominable crimes and treacheries and murders, Henry VI, Edward IV, Edward V, and Richard III ascended the throne or were hurled from it, the country had to renounce all active intervention in the affairs of the Continent, until peace was restored with the advent of the first Tudor, Henry VII, in 1485. France, on the contrary, enjoyed a restorative period of tranquillity under Charles VII. One might have concluded that she was exhausted by the terrible crisis from which she had emerged. But in a few years all traces of the crisis had disappeared. For the first time the nation gave proof of the resilience and the nervous energy which it has always displayed after the great catastrophes of its history. When Louis XI succeeded to his father in 1461 France was incontestably once more the greatest power in the West. But the international position in which she found herself was entirely novel, and it was radically to modify the direction of her foreign policy.

One may say that since the end of the 12th century her foreign policy had always been determined by the vital necessity of expelling England from the soil of France. Her interventions in the Low Countries, like her relations with the Empire, or with the Iberian peninsula, were referable, almost without exception, to this great struggle. England was not only the essential enemy: she was the only enemy of France. She had no enemies on the Continent, or only such as were incited against her by England: Otto IV in Germany, and the Counts of Flanders in the 13th and 14th centuries. Apart from this, she had no enemies in the rear, and could devote all her energies to confronting the enemy in the West. Now, directly the Hundred Years' War came to an end this state of affairs ceased for good. There was an end of the ancient Continental security of the kingdom. Henceforth she would have to fight upon her land frontiers, and by a complete reversal of tradition England would never attack her in future except by entering into a coalition with the European enemies of France.

The formation of the Burgundian State marked the beginning of this new orientation of political history. We have seen already how Philip the Fair took advantage of his participation in the Hundred Years' War in order to group under his power, in addition to Flanders and Artois, the greater number of those territorial principalities which were nominally dependencies of the Empire, and which extended from the Ardennes to the Zuyder Zee: the Duchies of Luxemburg and Brabant, with the Counties of Hainaut, Namur, Holland, and Zeeland.

To this amalgam of possessions Charles VII, on concluding the

Peace of Arras with the Duke (1435), annexed the cities of the Somme. The Duchy and the Franche Comté of Burgundy were added to this magnificent domain, from which they were divided only by Lorraine and Alsace, which they were threatening to absorb. Thus, in a few years there was constituted on the north and the east of the kingdom a new power which occupied approximately the place formerly occupied, in the 9th and 10th centuries, by the ephemeral Kingdom of Lotharingia. The Low Countries emerged from their feudal subdivision to unite themselves, under a single dynasty, in a single State, the common ancestor of Belgium and modern Holland. A fertile soil; an incomparable geographical situation on the shores of the North Sea; deep rivers and excellent harbours; a laborious population, denser than in any other part of Europe to the north of the Alps; flourishing cities, famed throughout the world for their cloth industry or their commerce, one of which, Bruges, had been for three centuries the great international port of the Occident, while another, Antwerp, was entering upon an even more astonishing period of prosperity, since the enterprising navigation of Holland and Zeeland was beginning to replace that of the declining Hansa; and lastly, in the agricultural regions of the Walloon country a robust and warlike people—all these things seemed to be united as by a miracle to make the young State a "promised land," and to confer upon its sovereigns the extraordinary prestige which surrounded Philip the Good and his son Charles the Bold. But the wealthier and more powerful this new neighbour became, the more dangerous was it to France. Whether it would or not, it was a permanent menace. From Amiens its troops, in two days' march, could appear under the walls of Paris; and above all, owing to its situation it imposed itself upon England as a natural ally. There was reason to fear that in the first war it would play once more the part which the Counts of Flanders had so often played in the Middle Ages, but this time with tenfold effect. In short, it seemed as though France had expelled the English from her soil only to find herself exposed on her northern frontier, which was everywhere open and without natural defences, to the aggression of Burgundy.

The conflict, already latent between Charles VII and Philip the Good, was destined to break out under their successors, Louis XI and Charles the Bold. The crisis was violent but brief. The civil disorders in England prevented her from intervening at the opportune moment. In the beginning Charles was able to count only on the Duc de Berry, the King's brother, the Duke of Brittany, the last great vassal of the Crown, and a few seigneurs who were leagued with him on behalf of the "public welfare" of the kingdom. But the allies did not agree among themselves. After his defeat at Montléry the King at once entered into negotiations, and had no trouble in detaching them from one another. He now faced the Burgundian only, and was able to devote himself entirely to his destruction. He excited the Liégeois against him, to disown them in the moment of danger, and intrigued in Germany, England, Switzerland, Savoy, Milan, and Venice subtly and imperceptibly, gradually entangling his impetuous adversary in the meshes of the most cunning diplomacy. Charles and Louis XI have often been described as the last representative of the feudal system grappling with the first modern sovereign. Nothing could be more inaccurate. Apart from the difference of their personal genius, the King being as prudent and as skilful as the Duke was rash and adventurous, the difference of their policies arose from the very difference of their States. The State of the French sovereign held him fast to a secular tradition, so that he followed the same ends of national unity and defence which had been followed, since the 12th century, with more or less success and ability by all the predecessors whose crown he inherited. The Burgundian power, on the contrary, was too recent, had been constructed too rapidly, was still too imperfectly consolidated, too loosely knit, to be able to impose precise and constant views upon its ruler. Created by conquest, it urged him to proceed to further conquests, inasmuch as the resources with which it furnished him were very considerable, and easily deceived him as to his actual strength. The conduct of Charles justifies the saying of Machiavelli, that a State is maintained by the same forces that have created it. It must be realized, moreover, that many of his undertakings presented themselves to him as the completion of the work of Philip the Good. The annexation of Guelders and Liége completed in the north the bloc of the Low Countries, and his attempts to appropriate Alsace and Lorraine are explained by the necessity of uniting the Franche Comté and the Duchy of Burgundy. But it is difficult for a conqueror to stop. Dazzled by success and the love of glory, Charles soon lost all sense of the possible and actual, and forgot the interests of his peoples. He dreamt of having himself crowned King of the Romans, and of forcing old René of Anjou to cede his claims to the Kingdom of Naples. His expedition against Neuss (1474–1475), in which he persisted out of a morbid longing to humiliate the Emperor and the Empire, caused him to miss the moment for joining forces with Edward IV of England, who had just disembarked at Calais in order to march against Louis XI, and who, on seeing himself abandoned by his ally, hastened to conclude peace with the King. In the following year the occupation of Lorraine involved the Duke in a war with the Swiss. Defeated first at Granson, then at Morat (1476), his prestige as a soldier, which had still imposed upon Europe, was destroyed. Louis XI made ready to take the offensive. René of Lorraine re-entered Nancy. Charles's final overthrow was certain. It was more rapid, more tragic, and more complete than his enemies could have hoped. Attacked by the Swiss while he was besieging Nancy, with an army reduced to a few thousand by the treachery of his Italian mercenaries, he flung himself desperately into the mêlée. Two days later (January 7th, 1477) his body was found on the surface of a frozen pond, half devoured by wolves and pierced with three mortal wounds.

If it had only depended on Louis XI, the Burgundian State would have disappeared with Charles. While he was seizing the cities of the Somme and invading Artois and Burgundy, the King devised a plan for partitioning the Low Countries which, by reserving a part for himself and giving the rest to French seigneurs or German princes, would have reduced them again to a condition of subdivision and impotence. The particularist reaction provoked by the death of the Duke in all the provinces exasperated by this despotism admirably seconded his project. He was too subtle a diplomatist to fail to impose his will on the ingenuous bourgeois ambassadors, deputies elected by the States-General hurriedly assembled at Gand, and blinded by their desire for peace and the restoration of urban privileges and franchises. But a genealogical hazard, one of those mysterious factors on which the destinies of States depended above all in the days of monarchical politics, was about to confront him with a danger much more serious for France than the Burgundian peril which he flattered himself he had destroyed. Charles the Bold had left only a daughter, Marie of Burgundy, whose marriage would decide the fate of his domains. Naturally, the Habsburgs had not failed betimes to cast their eyes upon so wealthy an heiress. Seven times betrothed in accordance with the enterprises and alliances of her father, she had finally been promised to Maximilian of Austria. Doubtless this promise would have been worth no more than the others if the Duke had lived. For Marie of Burgundy it became the sole hope of salvation in her distress. In order to escape from the attempts of Louis XI, she offered her hand to the Austrian. The opportunity was too good to miss. Maximilian hastened to her side, and the marriage was concluded at Bruges on August 28th, 1477. This was an expedient hastily devised under the pressure of necessity; yet never has a political marriage exercised such an influence over the future of Europe. By bringing the young Burgundian State into the hybrid complex of the Habsburg domain, not only did it condemn it to suffer henceforth the repercussions of the various schemes of the most ambitious and greedy of dynasties, but at the same time it opened between France and the House of Habsburg the long conflict which came to an end only in the 19th century. Austria, a power which everything had seemed to orientate upon the Danubian countries, suddenly obtained a footing on the shores of the North Sea between the two great monarchies of the West. Nothing but territorial greed had called her thither. She had no mission to fulfil there, no interest to defend, save that of her princes. From the very first her purely dynastic policy was in conflict with the needs and the aspirations of the peoples. If it had been her aim to re-establish over the Low Countries the obsolete suzerainty of the Empire! But on the contrary, her only purpose was to keep them for herself, and it was always her endeavour to separate them from Germany. Her position in the Low Countries, regarded from the standpoint of the European community, seems therefore as absurd as it was artificial. And it was this anomaly that was responsible for the catastrophes which she was to bring upon the country. For the interests of the princes and those of the peoples to be completely divergent has always, in any period of history, been disastrous. Of this the history of the House of Habsburg is the most striking proof. By its acquisition of the Low Countries it found itself drawn into that career of universal domination, that policy of aggrandisement for the sake of aggrandisement, in which nations were reckoned only as heritages and countries as domains, and which was to make the Habsburgs, down to our own days, the sworn enemies of all national aspirations and all public liberties.

We must not be astonished that the Low Countries allowed an action so fatal to themselves to be accomplished in silence. Their fusion into a single State was still too recent to have provoked the sentiment of national independence. Moreover, in the heat of the particularist revolution each province was thinking only of itself, and the burgesses of Gand, the leaders of the movement, were concerned only to re-establish the old municipal privileges and did not look beyond the narrow circle of their local policy. When they found themselves confronted with the accomplished fact it was too late for action. The marriage of their "natural princess" had made them the subjects of the House of Austria while they were debating upon their franchises.

Under Louis XI, as under Charles VIII, there was no lack of French intrigues to excite and to nourish the general discontent in the Low Countries; to rouse the men of Liége and encourage Guelders to revolt, and thus to paralyse the forces of Maximilian. After the death of Marie of Burgundy (1482) the majority of the cities and of the nobles regarded him merely as an intruder, and attempted to claim the tutelage of his son, Philip the Handsome. The people of Liége, subjected by Charles the Bold, recovered their independence, and Guelders did the same. Maximilian, treated with complete indifference by the Empire, struggled impotently in the midst of this chaos. In 1488 he even had to suffer the humiliation of being detained for several weeks as the prisoner of the people ot Bruges. Despite his alliance with the King of England and the Duke of Brittany, his intermittent war with France could not lead to any definite conclusion. It was provisionally interrupted in 1493 by the Peace of Senlis.

The changes introduced into international policy by the birth of the Burgundian State were presently followed by complete confusion, in consequence of the unification of Spain, which resulted from the marriage of Isabella of Castile and Ferdinand of Aragon (1469). Until then the Spanish kingdoms had been too weak to intervene actively in the destinies of Europe. The war against the Moors had absorbed all their energies until the middle of the 13th century. Then, just as the task was on the point of accomplishment, dynastic rivalries, the quarrels between the kings and the nobles, and between the nobles and the cities, had interrupted the war, safeguarding the precarious existence of the Musulman Kingdom of Granada. Favoured by its maritime situation, Aragon had been busy beyond its frontiers, expelling Anjou from Sicily on behalf of a collateral line of its dynasty, conquering the Balearics and obtaining a foothold in Corsica and Sardinia. But this vigorous expansion was checked in the middle of the 14th century, as the result of conflicts with Castile, dissensions in the royal family, and revolts in Barcelona and Catalonia. Castile was even more disturbed and enfeebled by the insubordination and the claims of the nobles. Force had been powerless to subdue this vigorous but anarchical society; but the doubly national union of Ferdinand and Isabella, while it put an end to the long mutual conflict which was exhausting their kingdoms, enabled them also first to rally and then to subordinate the peoples to their power. So completely did they subject them to their guidance in every domain that assuredly, in no country and at no period of history, have sovereigns exercised so profound an influence. In the Spanish State, as established by them, Catholic and political sentiment were associated so completely that it was impossible to dissever them. The monarchy summoned to its aid the old religious fanaticism of its subjects, and in their eyes its cause was identified with that of the Faith. Its zeal for orthodoxy had rendered it profoundly national, and now, surrounded by the most intolerant of peoples, its intolerance was the instrument of its success. From 1480 onwards the Inquisition, entrusted with the task of watching over the converted Jews (*maranos*), became, without losing its ecclesiastical character, a State institution, since the State appointed the Grand Inquisitor and there was no appeal to Rome against the sentences which he pronounced. The figure of Torquemada is inseparable from the figures of Ferdinand and Isabella. All three were sincere in their hatred of heresy, and while the Crown confiscated for its own benefit the property of the victims who died at the stake, enriching itself by their agonies, it employed this wealth only in fresh enterprises, which were as profitable to itself as they were to the Church. The Holy War, long interrupted, was resumed against the Moors, so that the final constitution of the national territory seemed like the result of a Crusade. But it was not enough to fight the Musulmans; the Jews, no less than they, were the enemies of Christ. In 1492, the very year of the conquest of Granada, they were expelled from the State. This conquest and this expulsion swelled the treasury to overflowing, and provided the necessary resources for further political and religious expansion. While Christopher Columbus set forth to discover a new world to subject and convert, the expeditions against the coasts of Morocco, Algeria, and Tunis seemed to announce that all the forces of Spain were about to league themselves against Islam. Nothing appeared to be more consonant with her character, her historic rôle, and even her interests as a Mediterranean people. And in any case nothing could have won her greater glory and greater ascendancy than to constitute herself, in the face of the Turk, the champion of the Church and of Europe. And lastly, nothing could have more completely justified the title of "Catholic Kings" which Ferdinand and Isabella had just received from Alexander VI. But having arrived at this decisive moment of her history, Spain turned aside. She turned aside from the Holy War and allowed herself to be involved in the dynastic ambitions of her princes. Without understanding that she was renouncing her mission, she proceeded to concentrate all the energies which she had acquired in her secular conflicts with the Crescent in order to subject the Christian Continent to her princes; only in the end to collapse, ruined and exhausted by two hundred years of effort, almost as barren as the neighbouring shores of that Morocco whose certain and profitable conquest she had sacrificed to her sovereigns' dreams of universal dominion.

To find the point of departure of so remarkable a development, we must go back to the intervention of Aragon in the affairs of Sicily. Since then the Anjou dynasty, in possession of the Kingdom of Naples on the mainland, and the Aragonese princes reigning in the island, had been in continual conflict. The death of Queen Joanna of Naples (1435), who, after acknowledging Alphonso of Aragon as her successor, had afterwards bequeathed her crown to René of Anjou, would certainly have resulted in the outbreak of a war if the weak and indolent René had been capable of the effort. But on his death-bed (1480) he bequeathed his claims to the House of France. Charles VIII, the heir of Louis XI, was eager to assert them. Having provisionally safeguarded the northern frontier from the encroachments of the House of Habsburg by the Peace of Senlis (1493), he crossed the Alps (1494), and to the astonishment of Italy marched southwards to assume the crown of Naples. This was destined to be no more than the brief adventure of a young prince in love with glory. In the following year the Pope united Milan and Venice against the invader. Ferdinand and Isabella, supporting their Sicilian relatives, joined the coalition. Charles had only just time to beat a retreat and return to France, where he died in 1498. His successor, Louis XII, unfortunately followed in his footsteps. In addition to Naples, he claimed the crown of Milan as a descendant of Valentino Visconti, and in 1499 he took possession of the city without striking a blow. A treaty with Ferdinand of Aragon, which stipulated the partition of the Kingdom of Naples, enabled him without further difficulty to take possession of that part of the kingdom which the treaty granted him. But Ferdinand very soon broke the pact. War broke out, the French were defeated, and Louis XII in 1505 renounced all his claims to Naples, which was to remain, down to modern times, a mere Spanish possession. He did not retain Milan very much longer. Pope Julius II in 1511 united against him Venice, Ferdinand, and not long afterwards Maximilian and Henry VIII of England. Louis had to leave Italy and hasten northwards in order to confront the English, who, after defeating him at Guinegat, re-embarked, dissatisfied with Maximilian, and concluded peace.

Regarded against the entire background of French history, the Italian expeditions of Charles VIII and Louis XII had the appearance of mere excursions. They were not related to any national necessity. Inspired purely and simply by dynastic ambition, they were "wars of magnificence"; which is to say, useless wars. No doubt they helped to accelerate in France the diffusion of a passionate interest in the Renaissance. But the policy which they inaugurated, and which was not definitely abandoned until the reign of Henri II (Peace of Cateau Cambrésis), had no other consequence than a futile waste of men and money. Their only lasting result was that they orientated Spain toward Italy, and so, as an inevitable consequence, produced a *rapprochement* with the House of Habsburg.

It was evident, in fact, that between Maximilian, fighting against France in the Low Countries, and the Catholic kings, fighting against France in the Kingdom of Naples, a political alliance and its inevitable consequence, a dynastic alliance, was imminent. In 1496 the double marriage of Don Juan, the heir of Ferdinand and Isabella, with Margaret, the daughter of Maximilian, and of Philip, the son of Maximilian, with the Infanta Juana bound the two families closely together. At the moment there was nothing that could enable it to be foreseen that their several heritages would ever be united. But once more Nature favoured the Habsburgs. Death cleared the way for them. The successive deaths of Don Juan (1497), of his elder sister Isabella (1498), and of Isabella's son, Don Miguel (1500), resulted in the inheritance by Philip and Juana of the succession to the Spanish kingdoms. Six years later Philip was unexpectedly carried off by inflammation of the lungs, bequeathing his rights to his son Charles, then barely seven years of age.

Ferdinand lived long enough to save his weakly brother from the danger of succeeding to him before he had emerged from childhood. When the old king died in 1516 his grandson had just been declared of age.

Charles V was one of those very rare characters of modern history whose name was to become universally known. He became very nearly as famous as Charlemagne or Napoleon. Yet it was not to his genius but to his heritage that he owed his eminence. With no more than mediocre abilities, he was raised by circumstances to such a position that only Charlemagne before him, and Napoleon after him, exercised such an influence over Europe. He was the meeting-point of three dynasties and three histories: those of Austria, Burgundy, and Spain. The grandson of Maximilian of Habsburg and Marie of Burgundy, and also of Ferdinand of Aragon and Isabella of Castile, he found himself in possession of so many portions of Europe that it seemed as though his power would finally extend over the whole Continent. In Germany he possessed the Austrian Duchies; on the shores of the North Sea, the Low Countries; on the Atlantic coast, Spain; and in the Mediterranean, the Kingdom of Sicily. And with these heritages went the claims attaching to them: the claims of Austria to the Empire, to Bohemia and Hungary; the claims of the Low Countries to Burgundy; and the claims of Spain to Italy and the coasts of Barbary. And to all this must be added the new world which the conquistadors had laid at his feet. Fernando Cortez made himself master of Mexico between 1519 and 1527, and Pizarro of Peru between 1531 and 1541. The astonishing conquest of South America was completed before Charles died. During his reign, however, it was still too recent to augment his power or influence his policies. Its consequences became manifest only under his son. For him all his projects, like his resources, were still determined by Europe. His title of "Ruler of the Isles of the Ocean" and his motto, *Plus oultre*, were merely prophecies of the future which he could do no more than foresee.

At the moment when Spain fell into his hands through the death of Ferdinand (January 23rd, 1516), and Austria through the death of Maximilian (January 12th, 1519), he knew no more of the one country than of the other. Educated in the Low Countries by Belgian seigneurs, who, regarding him merely as "their natural prince," did not even think to have him taught German—and he never did learn it—nor Spanish, he so shocked the Castilians when he appeared among them in 1517, speaking only French and surrounded by Flemish and Walloon favourites, that they welcomed him by the revolt of the Comuneros. But it did not take him long to adopt the distant, cold, and impersonal attitude which seemed necessary in a prince destined to reign over such a variety of countries and peoples. If he retained all his life some preference for the Belgians, among whom his youth was passed, he did not really belong to any of the peoples whose crowns he inherited, and he found it easy to treat them all with an impartiality which arose from his indifference. Insensible to all national feeling, he thought of nothing but the greatness of his house. He reigned over the countries which chance had brought under his sceptre without taking an interest in any of them; or perhaps one should say he was interested in them only in so far as they facilitated his designs. There was a striking contrast between him and his contemporaries, Francis I and Henry VIII, who seemed the very incarnation of France and England. Compared with them he was merely a sovereign, without a character of his own because he was without a country, and a sovereign who was nowhere popular.

Ferdinand and Isabella, by their Italian policy, had already begun to divert Spain from the war against Islam, and to involve her in the quarrels of Europe. Charles V definitely and finally embroiled her in these quarrels. It is true that he did not absolutely abandon the attempt to conquer the coasts of Barbary. His expeditions against Tunis in 1535, and Algiers in 1541, were still in accordance with tradition. But these were only brief interludes, ventures without a sequel. Charles had to make his choice between war in Africa and war in Europe, and how could he have abandoned war in Europe without at the same time renouncing his inheritance? His policy was not and could not be that of a King of Spain; it was and it had to be the policy of a Habsburg, and Spain, under his guidance, devoted her energies to the realization of schemes that were not only alien but opposed to her true interests.

As for these schemes, France was bound of necessity to resist them with all her might. The long duel between Charles V and Francis I is not explained by the opposition of their characters or their ambitions. Its fundamental cause was the incompatibility of the dynastic policy of Charles with the national policy of Francis. One might describe this duel by saying that it was a conflict of a dynasty, a House of Habsburg, with a nation, the French nation. Hemmed in on every side by the domains of Charles, in the south by Spain and Italy, on the west by Burgundy, in the north by the Low Countries, France found herself in danger of being stifled by an adversary who, once he had triumphed over her, would exercise universal dominion over Europe. It was not only the prestige of France but her security that was threatened by a veritable encirclement. And to this must be added the danger involved by her expansion into Italy, where Francis I had reconquered the State of Milan on the field of Marignan (September 1515).

The death of Maximilian in 1519 rendered the situation still more formidable. Charles could not fail to put himself forward as a candidate for the Empire, which, since the reign of Albert of Austria, had always been held by the House of Habsburg. Francis did his very utmost to turn the Electors against this too powerful rival, and to induce them to give their votes either to himself, or at the worst to Frederick of Saxony. But the Medici could not provide him with as much money as the Fuggers advanced to Charles. The Electors, being in the market, sold themselves to the highest bidder. On June 28th, 1519, the German bank having purchased all their suffrages, they concluded the bargain, and delivered the crown of Germany to the King of Spain.

Henceforth war was certain. It broke out in 1521, on the frontiers of the Low Countries at first, where the forces of Henry VIII joined those of Charles, and was then transferred to Italy, being interrupted only by the signal defeat of the King of France at Pavia (February 25th, 1525). Having fallen into the hands of his enemy, Francis finally consented to the Peace of Madrid (January 14th, 1526). But he had fully made up his mind to disregard the peace and to take up arms again. His defeat had improved his position. Charles's victory had startled the whole world, and France now appeared as the champion of European liberty. Pope Clement VII, in order to free Italy from the Spanish yoke, made approaches to France, and after the sack of Rome by the German troops of the Emperor he formally entered into an alliance with that country. Henry VIII did the same, perceiving when it was too late that in the recent campaign he had been merely an instrument of the Habsburg hegemony. Finally, the outbreak of Protestantism in Germany, and the invasion of Hungary by the Turks, ensured the neutrality of the Empire. Equilibrium was re-established. In 1529 the Peace of Cambrai restored Burgundy to France, who on her side renounced her lapsed suzerainty over Flanders and Artois, as well as her claims in Italy. However, the two adversaries were merely awaiting a fresh opportunity for resuming the struggle. The attitude of the Lutheran princes encouraged the King of France to do so, and he even went so far as to conclude a treaty of peace, in 1546, with Soliman II. Thus, in order to wage war upon the Catholic king who had recently sacked Rome, the Most Christian king allied himself with heretics and Musulmans! The Peace of Crespy, concluded after indecisive campaigns (1544), left matters in statu quo. The peace at all events enabled the Emperor at last to turn against the Protestant princes of Europe. His victory over them at Muhlberg had the effect of flinging them, terrified, into the arms of France. In order to obtain the assistance of the successor to Francis I—Henri II, who in his own country was cruelly persecuting the heretics—they offered him the three bishoprics, Metz, Toul, and Verdun (1552). This finally directed French policy to one of the aims which it had envisaged in the patient campaign which it had been conducting ever since the 13th century with a view to restoring the frontier traced in 843 by the Treaty of Verdun. Charles was immediately compelled to face towards the west and turn his back upon the Protestants. All his efforts failed before Metz, which was obstinately defended by the Duke of Guise. Before abdicating he concluded with his adversary the Truce of Vaucelles (1556).

He left Europe in a condition that was full of menace and pregnant with inevitable wars. The succession which he transmitted to his son Philip II comprised, in addition to Spain, the Kingdom of Naples, the Milanese State, the Franche Comté of Burgundy, and the Low Countries, without speaking of his immense possessions in the New World. Italy, subjugated in the north and the south, bade farewell to the dreams of liberation which had inspired men of such diverse genius as Guiccardini, Machiavelli, Julius II, and Clement VII. Italy, until the modern era, was to be no more than a geographical expression, and the heavy-handed dominion of Spain was finally to crush what still survived of the civilization of the Renaissance. The States of the Pope, and those of the Venetian Republic, alone preserved their independence, that of the first being guaranteed by Catholic tradition, while that of the second was due to their maritime situation. As for the Low Countries, enlarged by the final annexation of the Duchy of Guelders and the Frisian provinces, they were henceforth to constitute in the north of Europe the "citadel of steel" of the Spanish kings. By the Pragmatic Sanction (1549) Charles had been careful to regulate the right of succession in such a manner that they could not escape his descendants, and by including them, by the Convention of Augsburg (1548), in the sphere of Burgundy he had so conditioned their relations with the Empire that the latter really had no other right over them than that of defending them. The Imperial dignity had served him only to assure the future of his house. He had not only taken the Low Countries from Germany; he had even obtained for his brother Ferdinand, in 1521, the crown of the King of the Romans, and had ceded to him the patrimonial duchies of Austria, which, together with the crowns of Bohemia and Hungary that fell to Ferdinand in 1526, finally safeguarded the Habsburg power in Central Europe. Divided into two branches, the family none the less remained united by its dynastic interests. Through Italy, Spain communicated with Austria; through the Low Countries, Austria was more readily able to dominate Germany; and thanks to the services which she was able to render her, she was assured beforehand of that nation's docility.

Thus the Continent was crushed by the Habsburg colossus, established in Austria and Spain. Beside it France and England appeared weak indeed, and seriously menaced. But this was a case of David and Goliath. They had something that was lacking to the monstrous dynastic power which confronted them. Instead of being, like that power, a juxtaposition of peoples and countries agglomerated by the hazard of inheritance, with no mutual bond save the rights of their sovereign proprietor, they possessed that collective conscience that resulted from the community of their destinies, the constancy of their efforts, and the harmony between the policies of their kings and their national tendencies. It was from this that their strength was derived, and it was this that enabled them not only to escape the danger but to triumph over it, after vicissitudes to which the religious problem posed by the Reformation was to give the poignant interest of the wars of religion.

## 2. *Internal Politics*

What strikes us first of all, if we take a general survey of the constitution of the European States between 1450 and 1550, is the increase of monarchical power. With Louis XI in France, with Henry VII in England, and with Ferdinand and Isabella in Spain, it attained a strength and a prestige which it had never before possessed, and which were to attain still further development under their successors. In Hungary, under Matthias Corvinus, and in Sweden, under Gustavus Vasa, it made such progress that the whole political organization was transformed by it. It imposed itself upon the young Burgundian State under Philip the Good and Charles the Bold. Germany was the only country that did not feel the increase. For there, while the Kings of the Romans and the Emperors continued to exert only a nominal authority, the individual princes, in their territories, assumed more and more the character of local sovereigns; while on Austria, Bavaria, Saxony, and Brandenburg institutions were imposed which were in fact monarchical.

A phenomenon so general presupposes causes as general as itself. Naturally the personality of the princes, tradition, and circumstances gave the monarchy an individual character in each country. But however great the local differences, the similarity of certain essential features shows that this development corresponded everywhere with irresistible social tendencies. Here we have a movement analogous to that which in the 10th century produced the feudal system, and in the 12th century the urban régime. And as in the case of these latter, it is permissible, without paying attention to the details and the subtler differences, to sketch the main outlines of a movement which manifested itself throughout the whole of Western Europe.[1]

The monarchical power was too closely related to the social constitution to escape the influence of the great economic and intellectual transformation to which the latter was subjected from the middle of the 15th century. Capitalism, the Renaissance, and Lutheranism could not fail to affect it, and it is easy to see that they all played their part in endowing it with new vigour. Each of these great forces, in conflict with the past, had of necessity to seek and obtain the alliance of the monarchical authority. Their hostility to the ancient privileges and institutions and ideas which restricted this authority assured them of its co-operation. It assumed the same attitude toward them which it had assumed in France and Spain in respect of the bourgeoisies when the latter had solicited its aid against the feudal nobles. Now, as then, its own development depended on the general development of society. By acting for the benefit of society it was acting for itself. It was most obviously to its advantage that it should be modern, that it should combat the conservative tendencies which opposed its own progress as well as that of society. Was it not acting in its own interests when it helped capitalism to defeat the particularism of the cities, when it favoured the propaganda of the humanists against moral and political prejudices, and when it protected the Lutherans who offered it the direction and the properties of the Church? All the privileges that were opposed to the power of the Crown were based on tradition.

[1] In Russia also the expansion of the principality of Moscow began at the end of the 15th century, and the power of its princes began to increase at the same time. But these movements were due to the collapse of the Tartar domination, and had nothing in common with European developments. Poland also remained outside the European movement.

It was only necessary that it should approve in good faith of all the criticisms of this tradition, and that it should conceive it to be its mission to enfranchise from this same tradition both its subjects and itself.

The facts illustrate the issue with perfect clarity. In all those countries in which capitalism was developing we see that the princes lavished upon it the proofs of their benevolence. In the Low Countries they constantly pronounced in its favour and against the reactionary policy of the urban guilds; and they did their utmost to encourage the development of Antwerp, the stronghold of commercial liberty. In England, from the reign of Henry VII onwards, the Crown supported the enterprises of the merchant adventurers and interested itself in all schemes of maritime expansion. In Spain it was the intervention of the Crown that rendered possible the discovery of the New World; in France Louis XI acclimatized the silk-worm in the Midi, caused the mines to be exploited, and encouraged economic initiative in every possible way; while Francis I tried to introduce some of the Italian industries. Protected by the sovereigns, capital in return placed its resources and its credit at their disposal. Thanks to it, they were able to avoid resorting to the Estates in order to procure the sinews of war. The bankers liberated them from the embarrassing control of their subjects. The long duel between Charles V and Francis I would have been unthinkable without the co-operation of the financiers. During the whole of the Emperor's reign the Fuggers, and a number of other business houses in Antwerp, continued to advance him the colossal sums which he required.

The princes favoured intellectual liberty no less definitely than economic liberty. With the exception of the kings of Spain, all manifested their sympathy for the ideas which were propagated by the men of the Renaissance, without regarding the protests of the theologians. Erasmus was protected by Charles V and Francis I. Thomas More was made Chancellor of England by Henry VIII. Gattinara and Granvelle, the two chief ministers of the Emperor, were convinced adherents of the new orientation of the intellect. It was only too evident, as a matter of fact, that this new orientation was entirely to the advantage of the State, for since the humanists could obtain the reform which they desired only from the princes, the government of the princes appeared to them, for this very reason, the essential instrument of progress. Their disdain of the past made them expect everything of the monarchy, and they brought it the support of that intellectual aristocracy which in every nation was henceforth to enjoy the monopoly of representing public opinion.

The Reformation, in fact, at all events in its beginnings, shared no less than the Renaissance in this conspiracy of all the great social forces on behalf of the sovereign power. Whether the princes protected it or fought against it, they none the less profited by it.

# INDEX